Analysis and Design of Integrated Electronic Circuits

Analysis and Design of Integrated Electronic Circuits
Volume 3 Analog Electronics

PAUL M. CHIRLIAN

Stevens Institute of Technology

Harper & Row, Publishers
London

Cambridge
Hagerstown
Philadelphia
New York

San Francisco
Mexico City
Sao Paulo
Sydney

Analysis and Design of Integrated Electronic Circuits

Harper & Row Ltd.
28 Tavistock Street
LONDON WC2

British Library Cataloguing in Publication Data

Chirlian, Paul M.
Analysis and design of integrated circuits–
Vol. 3: Analog electronics
1. Integrated circuits
I. Title
621.381′73 TK7874

ISBN 0-06-318214-9

Printed and bound by The Pitman Press, Bath

To the memory of my father Gustave Chirlian,
with very much love.

Contents

Volume 2 Digital Electronics

Chapter 13 Operational Amplifier Applications 622

Chapter 14 Operational Amplifier Circuitry—The Practical Operational Amplifier 674

Chapter 15 Untuned Power Amplifiers 749

Chapter 16 Feedback Amplifiers 799

Chapter 17 Bandpass Amplifiers 860

Preface

The United Kingdom edition of this book is divided for convenience into three separate volumes. Volume 1, 'Semiconductor Devices', contains Chapters 1 to 7 of the original single-volume text, plus a completely new Appendix dealing in detail with the cathode ray tube.

Volume 2, 'Digital Electronics', comprises Chapters 8 to 11 and Volume 3, 'Analog Electronics', contains Chapters 12 to 21. Pages are numbered consecutively throughout the three volumes, and the general index for the whole book is reprinted in each volume, as is the List of Contents.

To preserve the integrity of the original text and the numbering system the pages containing the new material presented in the Appendix to Volume 1 are numbered using Roman numerals.

This is an undergraduate textbook that covers the core topics in electronics that all electrical engineers should know. It is intended to provide students at the junior and senior levels with a thorough understanding of most electronic circuits and the procedures used to analyze and design them. Integrated circuits and their applications are stressed. However, the use of discrete devices such as junction transistors and FETs is also considered. Many numerical examples of both analysis and design are incorporated throughout the book. It is hoped that, from these, the student will develop a general design philosophy that can be used with all electronic circuit designs.

This is an electronic circuits text and, therefore, there will be no detailed discussion of semiconductor physics. However, the first four chapters of the book do present enough information in order that a basic understanding of semiconductor electronic devices can be obtained.

In Chapters 1 through 3, the physics and basic principles of semiconductors, *p-n* junction diodes, and transistors are discussed. The discussion of physics is brief. It is sufficiently detailed, however, so that the reader will understand the basics. Such things as junction capacitance, switching speed, characteristics, and ratings are discussed in detail.

The fabrication of integrated circuits is discussed in Chapter 4. The problems encountered are considered, and all types of fabrications are discussed. In Chapter 5 the graphical analysis techniques are presented. Because of the wide use of direct coupled circuits, their graphical analysis is considered in detail.

Modeling is discussed in Chapters 6 and 7. Chapter 6 concerns itself with linear models. Since the hybrid-pi model for the transistor is used throughout the book, this model is stressed. However, the h-parameter model is also thoroughly developed and related to the hybrid-pi model. The linear high-frequency model for the FET is also developed, and some basic amplifier circuits are also studied here. Pulse and large-signal models are the topics of Chapter 7. The Ebers and Moll model for the transistor and low-speed models for the FET are developed. Next, high-speed models are obtained. The use of approximate models is discussed.

Chapters 8 through 11 are concerned with the basic ideas and circuits of digital systems. In Chapter 8, fundamental ideas such as number systems and gates are considered, and switching functions and Karnaugh maps are studied. All the commonly used logic families are discussed in Chapter 9. The electrical analysis of the various families is discussed there in great detail. Sequential circuits are the topic of Chapter 10. The design of both synchronous and asynchronous circuits is discussed in considerable detail. Various devices such as registers and counters are considered from both a design and an applications viewpoint. Memories are presented in Chapter 11. All of the semiconductor memories are thoroughly considered. There is also a discussion of CCD and magnetic bubble memories.

Broadband amplifiers are discussed in Chapter 12. This chapter starts with a general discussion of amplification. Next, single-stage amplifiers are studied, and finally, the design of multistage amplifiers is discussed. Transient and steady state response are considered. The chapter concludes with a discussion of noise. Operational amplifier applications are presented in great detail in Chapter 13. Many analog and digital circuits are discussed here to provide the reader with a thorough understanding of how operational amplifier circuits perform and how such circuits can be designed.

The actual circuitry within the operational amplifier chip is discussed in Chapter 14. Techniques for analyzing these circuits are presented. Small-signal and bias analyses are presented in a thorough analysis of the operational amplifier. Power amplifiers are discussed in Chapter 15. Transformerless push-pull amplifiers are stressed here and graphical analysis and design techniques are developed.

Feedback amplifiers are thoroughly discussed in Chapter 16. A rigorous, accurate discussion is given here. Although the mathematics level is kept suitable for a junior or senior level course, sufficient material is included, so the student understands what he or she is doing. The design of feedback systems using the Nyquist criterion and frequency compensation is discussed in great detail. Bandpass amplifiers are the topic of Chapter 17. Active filters and conventional tuned amplifiers are studied, Butterworth and Chebyshev frequency responses are developed, and the superhetrodyne receiver is discussed.

Both sinusoidal and nonsinusoidal oscillators are studied in Chapter 18. Topics such as linear and nonlinear operation and frequency stabilization are also presented.

In Chapter 19, amplitude, frequency, and phase modulation are studied from both a mathematical and a circuits point of view. Design of detectors using the phase locked loop is discussed in detail. Pulse modulation techniques are considered and delta modulation is discussed. Power supplies are considered in Chapter 20. Rectifiers, filters, and voltage regulators are studied. The design of switching regulators is considered in detail.

There are numerical examples amply distributed throughout the book. In addition, a large selection of homework problems is included at the end of each chapter. The instructor need not, of course, follow the order of these chapters exactly.

The author would like to express his thanks to his colleagues Professors Alfred C. Gilmore, Jr., Stanley Smith, Edward Peskin, and Yusuf Z. Efe for the many helpful discussions during the writing of this book.

The author would also like to thank the reviewers Professors J. D. Bargainer, A. J. Broderson, R. E. Lee, and J. H. Mulligan, Jr., for their many helpful comments.

Loving gratitude and many heartfelt thanks are again due my wife Barbara, who encouraged me during the writing of this book and contributed substantially to it by correcting the copy and typing and retyping the manuscript.

PAUL M. CHIRLIAN

Chapter 12

Small-Signal Untuned Amplifiers—Broadband Amplifiers

In this chapter we shall discuss linear amplifiers. That is, we shall assume that the signal levels are small enough so that the analysis procedures developed in Chapter 6 can be applied to them. Such amplifiers are assumed to be free of nonlinear distortion (see Sec. 5-13). In Chapter 15, we shall discuss the design of large-signal amplifiers where nonlinear distortion considerations are important.

The amplifiers that we shall consider here are untuned, that is, they are *not* designed to amplify only a single range of frequencies and to *reject* signals at all other frequencies but are designed to amplify a broad range of frequencies. Typical untuned amplifiers are *audio* amplifiers which are designed to amplify signals at those frequencies that fall within the audible spectrum (20–20,000 Hz). Similarly, *video* amplifiers, which amplify the picture information in television receivers, are also untuned amplifiers.

If an untuned amplifier is designed to amplify a very wide range of frequencies, it is called a *broadband* amplifier. We shall consider the design of these amplifiers in detail.

An important class of untuned amplifiers is the *operational* amplifier which is incorporated in a single integrated circuit chip. In the next chapter, we shall discuss these amplifiers in great detail.

We shall start this chapter with several sections where we discuss some general ideas. Then, we shall discuss the analysis and design of specific amplifiers.

12-1. FREQUENCY DISTORTION

The output signal of an ideal amplifier is an exact reproduction of the input signal except that it is multiplied by a constant. Any departure from this is called *distortion.* In Sec. 5-13 we discussed a type of distortion which results because of the nonlinearity of the amplifier characteristics. Another type of distortion can occur even if the amplifier is linear. If the amplification varies with frequency, then the output signal will not be a faithful reproduction of the input and *frequency* distortion is said to have occurred.

Let us illustrate frequency distortion with a simple example. Suppose that the square wave of Fig. 12-1 is to be amplified. A Fourier analysis of this signal yields

$$v_1(t) = \frac{4}{\pi}[\cos t - \tfrac{1}{3}\cos 3t + \tfrac{1}{5}\cos 5t - \cdots] \tag{12-1}$$

If this were the input to an ideal amplifier, then the output would be of the form

$$v_2(t) = \frac{4}{\pi}A[\cos t - \tfrac{1}{3}\cos 3t + \tfrac{1}{5}\cos 5t - \cdots] \tag{12-2}$$

where A is a real constant. In an actual amplifier, A will not be a constant but will vary with frequency. Not only will the magnitude of the amplification vary with frequency, but, in addition, the phase shift will also vary with frequency. In general, in response to a square wave input, the output will be of the form

$$v_2(t) = \frac{4}{\pi}\left[A_1\cos(t - \theta_1) - \frac{A_3}{3}\cos(3t - \theta_3) + \frac{A_5}{5}\cos(5t - \theta_5) - \cdots\right] \tag{12-3}$$

where $A_1, A_3, A_5, \ldots$ are not equal. In such a case, the output will not be a faithful reproduction of the input and frequency distortion has resulted. The phase shifts $\theta_1, \theta_3, \theta_5, \ldots$ will also lead to frequency distortion. We shall discuss this subsequently. Figures 12-1b and 12-1c illustrate two typical effects of frequency distortion when the input is a square wave.

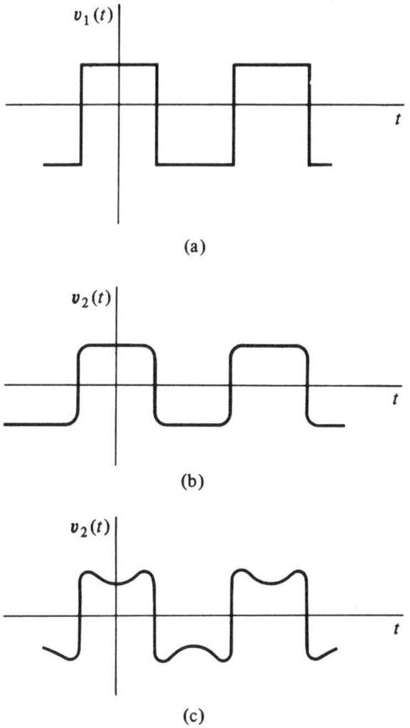

Figure 12-1. (a) A square wave voltage. (b) and (c) Typical effects of frequency distortion.

If there is to be no frequency distortion, then stringent requirements must be placed upon both the magnitude and phase of the amplifier as a function of frequency. The magnitude of the amplification must remain constant over all frequencies of interest. Then, for the case of the square wave input, we must have (see Eq. 12-3)

$$A_1 = A_3 = A_5 = \cdots \tag{12-4}$$

Let us now consider the phase shift as a function of frequency. There will be no distortion if the phase shift is 0 or $n\pi$ rad where n is an integer. The latter case corresponds to multiplying the signal by ± 1.

There is another condition of phase shift which is often considered to be distortionless. This occurs when we allow the output signal to be a faithful reproduction of the input signal except that the output is delayed. That is, we allow

$$v_2(t) = AV_1(t - T) \tag{12-5}$$

Let us consider the implication of this in terms of the phase response. Substituting Eq. 12-1 into Eq. 12-5, we obtain

$$v_2(t) = \frac{4A}{\pi}\left[\cos(t - T) - \tfrac{1}{3}\cos 3(t - T) + \tfrac{1}{5}\cos 5(t - T) - \cdots\right]$$

Manipulation yields

$$v_2(t) = \frac{4A}{\pi}\left[\cos(t - T) - \tfrac{1}{3}\cos(3t - 3T) + \tfrac{1}{5}\cos(5t - 5T) - \cdots\right] \tag{12-6}$$

Comparing this with Eq. 12-3 we see that the phase shift in this distortionless case varies *linearly with frequency.*

We have considered the case of a square wave here. Actually, the results that we have obtained apply to all signals. In general, if we are to have an amplifier that is free of frequency distortion

1. The magnitude of the amplification must be constant over all ranges of input frequencies.
2. The phase shift of the amplification must be 0 or $\pm n\pi$ where n is an integer, or it must vary linearly with frequency as $-k\omega$ where k is a positive constant.

Both conditions must be met if there is to be no frequency distortion. If condition 1 is not met, then this is termed *amplitude distortion,* while if condition 2 is not met, it is called *phase distortion.* In most cases, these two types of distortion are related and it is possible to calculate one from the other.

Several procedures are used to rate an amplifier's frequency distortion. Such ratings not only allow us to compare amplifiers, but they also aid in the design process. One rating procedure is to compare the input and output waveforms, such as the square waveform of Fig. 12-1, and note how much they differ. Such rating is based upon the *transient response* of the amplifier and will be discussed in Sec. 12-17.

Another means of rating the amplifier's frequency distortion is to study the amplification as a function of frequency. This is called the *frequency response.* In such cases, plots are made of both the amplitude and phase as a function of frequency. A typical plot is shown in Fig. 12-2. Note that the frequency axis is plotted on a log scale. This is

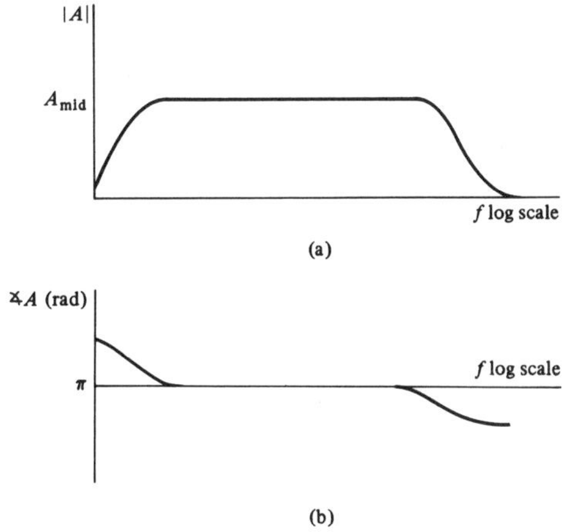

Figure 12-2. Typical amplifier frequency response plots. (a) Amplitude. (b) Phase.

done so that all pertinent frequency ranges can be exhibited. For instance, $|A|$ falls off at the low frequencies over a range of frequencies which typically varies from 0 to 40 Hz, while the high-frequency falloff might occur over the range above 100,000 Hz. If a linear scale were used, then both of these ranges could not be simultaneously displayed in a useful way.

Very often, as is illustrated in Fig. 12-2, these plots have regions wherein both $|A|$ and $\measuredangle A$ remain constant and $\measuredangle A$ is some integral multiple of π rad. If the frequency components of the input signal lies in this range, then there will be no frequency distortion. This "flat" region is called the midfrequency range. The magnitude of the amplification there is called $|A_{\text{mid}}|$. This number is the nominal amplification of the amplifier. Those frequencies that lie above the midfrequency range are termed high frequencies while those that lie below the midfrequency range are termed low frequencies. In many amplifiers, the response does not fall off at low frequencies. In such cases, the midfrequency range extends down to zero frequency and there is no low-frequency region.

When we consider a plot of $|A|$ we are often concerned with the departure of A from its midband value. In such cases, it is convenient to plot $|A|/|A_{\text{mid}}|$. In this case, we are said to have normalized the response with respect to $|A_{\text{mid}}|$. Note that no information concerning frequency distortion is lost by doing this. Such a normalized plot is shown in Fig. 12-3.

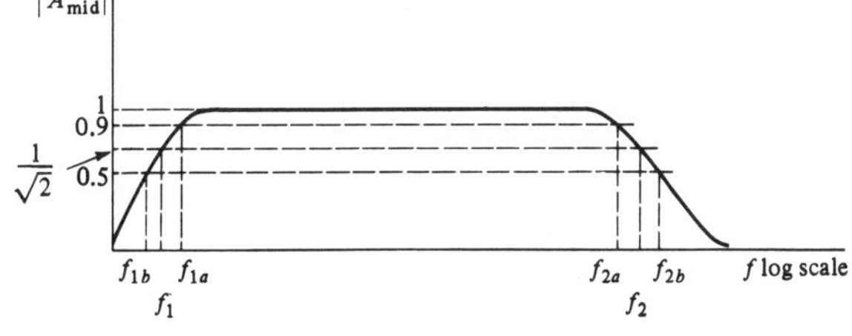

Figure 12-3. A normalized amplitude response.

The *bandwidth* of an amplifier is defined as the useful range of frequencies amplified by the amplifier. (Actually, we are attempting to characterize a curve by a single number and this is not always totally satisfactory.) The bandwidth depends upon the application for which the amplifier is intended. For instance, suppose that we want to use the amplifier as part of an accurate voltmeter. The bandwidth could be defined as that range of frequency where

$$0.9 \leqq \left| \frac{A}{A_{\text{mid}}} \right| \leqq 1$$

Then, the bandwidth $B_{0.9}$ will be given by

$$B_{0.9} = f_{2a} - f_{1a} \tag{12-7a}$$

(see Fig. 12-3). On the other hand, for less stringent conditions, we might define the bandwidth as that range of frequencies where

$$0.5 \leqq \left| \frac{A}{A_{\text{mid}}} \right| \leqq 1$$

Then (see Fig. 12-3), the bandwidth would be given by

$$B_{0.5} = f_{2b} - f_{1b} \tag{12-7b}$$

When specific information is not given, the bandwidth is usually considered to lie between those frequencies where

$$0.707 = \frac{1}{\sqrt{2}} \leqq \left| \frac{A}{A_{\text{mid}}} \right| \leqq 1 \tag{12-8}$$

Then,

$$B = f_2 - f_1 \tag{12-9}$$

This is called the *half-power bandwidth* since, when a voltage or current falls off by a factor of $1/\sqrt{2}$, the power has halved. f_1 and f_2 are called the *lower* and *upper half-power frequencies*, respectively. Again, it should be stressed that the criteria used to determine the bandwidth depends upon the application for which the amplifier is to be used.

12-2. DECIBEL NOTATION

It is often convenient to work with ratios of output quantities (e.g., voltages) to input quantities in *logarithmic* form. This is especially true in the case of audio devices since the ear functions approximately logarithmically. We shall see that such logarithmic ratios are often convenient to use even if we are working with amplifiers that are not audio amplifiers.

Consider the amplifier represented in Fig. 12-4. If P_1 is its input power and P_2 is the power delivered to the load, then the number of bels of power gain is a logarithmic ratio defined as

$$\text{number of bels} = \log_{10} \frac{P_1}{P_1} \tag{12-10}$$

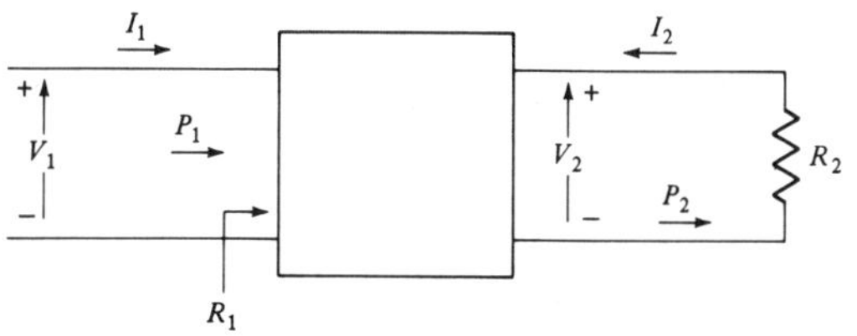

Figure 12-4. A representation of an amplifier.

The bel is a large unit and the *decibel*, which is one tenth of a bel, is usually used. The number of decibels is given by

$$\text{number of dB} = 10 \log_{10} \frac{P_2}{P_1} \tag{12-11}$$

If the input impedance of the amplifier is purely resistive and equal to R_1, and the load impedance is purely resistive and equal to R_2, then we can write

$$\text{number of dB} = 10 \log_{10} \frac{|V_2|^2/R_2}{|V_1|^2/R_1} = 10 \log_{10} \frac{|I_2|^2 R_2}{|I_1|^2 R_1} \tag{12-12}$$

If $R_1 = R_2$, then we have

$$\text{number of dB} = 20 \log_{10} \left| \frac{V_2}{V_1} \right| = 20 \log_{10} \left| \frac{I_2}{I_1} \right| \tag{12-13}$$

If we consider that Eq. 12-11 is the definition of the decibel, then the only time that Eq. 12-13 can be used is when $R_1 = R_2$. However, Eq. 12-13 is *widely used even when this is not true.* It is permissible to use decibels in this way as long as you realize that *only* a voltage ratio or *only* a current ratio is expressed. That is, the voltage, current, and power ratios in decibels for the *same* device will no longer be equal. The voltage, current, and power gains of an amplifier can be expressed in decibels using the following relations

$$A_{v\,\mathrm{dB}} = 20 \log_{10} |A_v| \tag{12-14}$$

$$A_{i\,\mathrm{dB}} = 20 \log_{10} |A_i| \tag{12-15}$$

$$A_{P\,\mathrm{dB}} = 10 \log_{10} A_P \tag{12-16}$$

Note that $A_{v\,\mathrm{dB}}$, $A_{i\,\mathrm{dB}}$, and $A_{P\,\mathrm{dB}}$ will not, in general, be equal (neither will $|A_v|$, $|A_i|$, and A_P). When amplifiers are cascaded, the overall gain is found by multiplying the gain of the individual stages. When the gains are expressed in decibels, the overall gain in decibels is found by *adding* the individual stages' gains in decibels.

Although decibel notation is usually used to express a logarithmic ratio, it is sometimes used to express an absolute level. In such cases, a standard reference level is chosen. For instance, the dBm expresses power in terms of its ratio to 10^{-3} W (1 m). The dBm is given by

$$\text{number of dBm} = 10 \log_{10} \frac{P}{10^3} = 10 \log_{10} 10^3 P \tag{12-17}$$

where P is the power level in watts.

Decibel Frequency Response Plots

In the last section we discussed the plotting of amplification versus frequency. Often, when the magnitude of the amplification is plotted it is plotted in decibels. In audio amplifiers, such a plot is meaningful since the ear is a logarithmic device. We shall discuss, subsequently, that such a plot can be very easily obtained and can be used to quickly ascertain the frequency response of amplifiers.

A typical normalized response in decibels is plotted in Fig. 12-5. Note that, in the midband region, the normalized response is 0 dB, since $\log_{10} 1 = 0$. In the last section we discussed that the half-power frequencies are used, at times, as a criterion for bandwidth. Let us consider the level in decibel which corresponds to half-power $10 \log_{10} \frac{1}{2} = -10(0.30103) = -3$ dB. The half-power bandwidth is thus spoken of as the 3 dB bandwidth. The upper and lower half-power frequencies, or, equivalently, the upper and lower 3-dB frequencies, are shown in Fig. 12-5.

Let us demonstrate how the decibel frequency response curves can be easily obtained. In general, an amplifier's response can be factored and written in a form such as

$$\frac{A}{A_{\text{mid}}} = \frac{1 + jf/f_a}{(1 + jf/f_b)(1 + jf/f_c)^2} \tag{12-18}$$

The magnitude of this expression is given by

$$\left|\frac{A}{A_{\text{mid}}}\right| = \sqrt{\frac{1 + (f/f_a)^2}{[1 + (f/f_b)^2][1 + (f/f_b)^2]^2}} \tag{12-19}$$

Writing this in decibel notation, we have

$$\left|\frac{A}{A_{\text{mid}}}\right|_{\text{dB}} = 10 \log_{10}\left[1 + \left(\frac{f}{f_a}\right)^2\right] - 10 \log_{10}\left[1 + \left(\frac{f}{f_b}\right)^2\right] - 20 \log_{10}\left[1 + \left(\frac{f}{f_c}\right)^2\right] \tag{12-20}$$

We want to plot this expression. It consists of an algebraic sum of three similar terms. Let us start by plotting one of them. Let

$$x = 10 \log_{10}\left[1 + \left(\frac{f}{f_a}\right)^2\right] \tag{12-21}$$

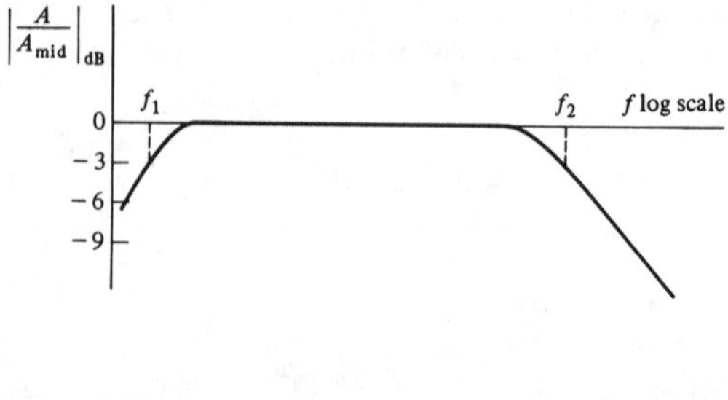

Figure 12-5. A normalized amplitude response plotted on a decibel basis.

We shall see that these curves can easily be sketched once the asymptotes have been drawn. Let us start by considering the asymptotic response of this curve. If

$$0 < \frac{f}{f_a} \ll 1 \tag{12-22}$$

then

$$x \simeq 10 \log_{10} 1 = 0 \text{ dB} \tag{12-23}$$

If

$$\frac{f}{f_a} \gg 1 \tag{12-24}$$

then

$$x \simeq 20 \log_{10}\left(\frac{f}{f_a}\right) \text{dB} \tag{12-25}$$

Now let us consider a plot of x and its asymptotes (see Fig. 12-6). Equation 12-23 plots as a horizontal straight line. Now consider Eq. 12-25. The abscissa of the graph is log f so the plot of $20 \log_{10}(f/f_a)$ is also a straight line which intersects the 0 dB abscissa at $f = f_a$. Let us determine the slope of this asymptote. If f doubles (log 2 = 0.30102) then x increases by 6 dB (actually 6.02 dB). Thus, the slope is 6 dB/octave (1 octave corresponds to a doubling of frequency). Similarly, if f increases by a factor of 10, then the asymptote increases by 20 dB. Thus, the slope of the asymptote of Eq. 12-25 can also be stated as 20 dB/decade. The two asymptotes intersect at $f = f_a$ which is called the *break point* or *break frequency*.

Let us consider the departure of the actual curve from its asymptotes. At $f = f_a$

$$x = 10 \log_{10} 2 \approx 3 \text{ dB} \tag{12-26}$$

Thus, the actual curve is 3 dB from the asymptotes when $f = f_a$. This is illustrated in Fig. 12-6

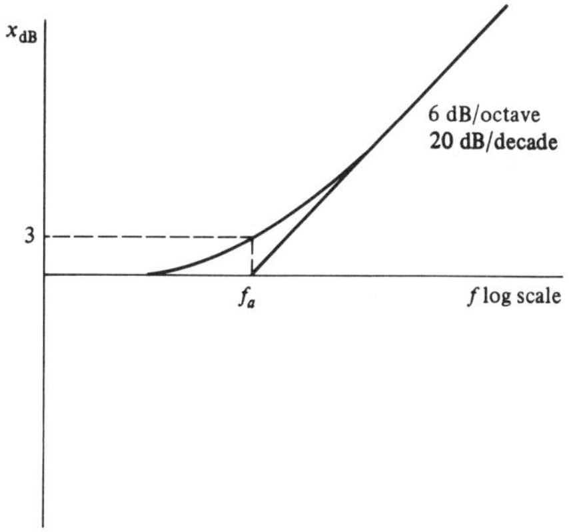

Figure 12-6. The plot of Eq. 12-25 showing asymptotes.

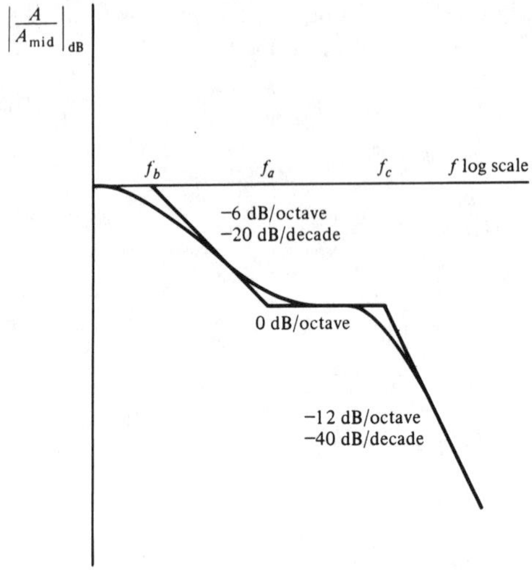

Figure 12-7. The plot of Eq. 12-19 on a decibel basis where $f_b < f_a < f_c$.

An expression such as Eq. 12-20 can easily be sketched using the asymptotic response. Let us consider this. We assume here that

$$0 < f_b < f_a < f_c \tag{12-27}$$

The asymptotes are drawn first. The asymptotes of the curve for the complete function are drawn by adding (or subtracting) the asymptotes of its individual terms. The first break frequency is f_b. Since there is a minus sign before this term, the asymptote for $f > f_b$ *falls off* at 6 dB/octave (see Fig. 12-7). The next break frequency occurs at $f = f_a$. Since there is a positive sign before the term in question, its asymptote rises at 6 dB/octave. When this asymptote is added to the 6 dB/octave falloff previously encountered, the net result is the horizontal "asymptote." This is shown between f_a and f_c. The last break point occurs at $f = f_c$. The corresponding term in Eq. 12-18 is squared. Thus, the slope of the asymptote for $f > f_c$ is doubled to yield −12 dB/octave. When this is added to the 0 dB/octave slope, the curve of Fig. 12-7 results. Once all the asymptotes have been drawn, the curve can be sketched as shown.

The asymptotes can easily be drawn from an inspection of Eq. 12-18. Therefore, decibel plots provide a means of quickly and easily sketching frequency response curves.

12-3. FREQUENCY RESPONSE OF ONE STAGE IN A FET COMMON-SOURCE AMPLIFIER CASCADE

Most amplifiers consist of several stages. That is, a single amplifier stage usually does not supply sufficient gain, so a cascade is formed wherein the overall gain is the product of the gains of the individual stages. We shall discuss such cascaded stages in a subsequent section. As preparation for this, in this section, we shall consider the gain of a single stage in the cascade.

Junction transistors and FET's are used in amplifiers, the junction transistor being most commonly used. We shall start our discussion with the FET since it has a simpler model and, thus, the analysis is simpler.

In Sec. 5-4, we discussed two forms of coupling that are used, RC (resistor-capacitor) and DC (direct coupled). Cascades using these types of coupling are illustrated in Figs. 12-8a, 12-8b, and 12-8c respectively. We shall analyze each of these amplifiers. The model that we shall use for the FET was developed in Sec. 6-9. It is shown in Fig. 6-32b.

We shall start our discussion with the circuit of Fig. 12-8a. The analysis of Fig. 12-8b will proceed similarly and we shall consider it subsequently. Only one stage in the cascade will be analyzed. That is, we shall compute the voltage gain

$$\mathbf{A}_v = \frac{\mathbf{V}_2}{\mathbf{V}_1}$$

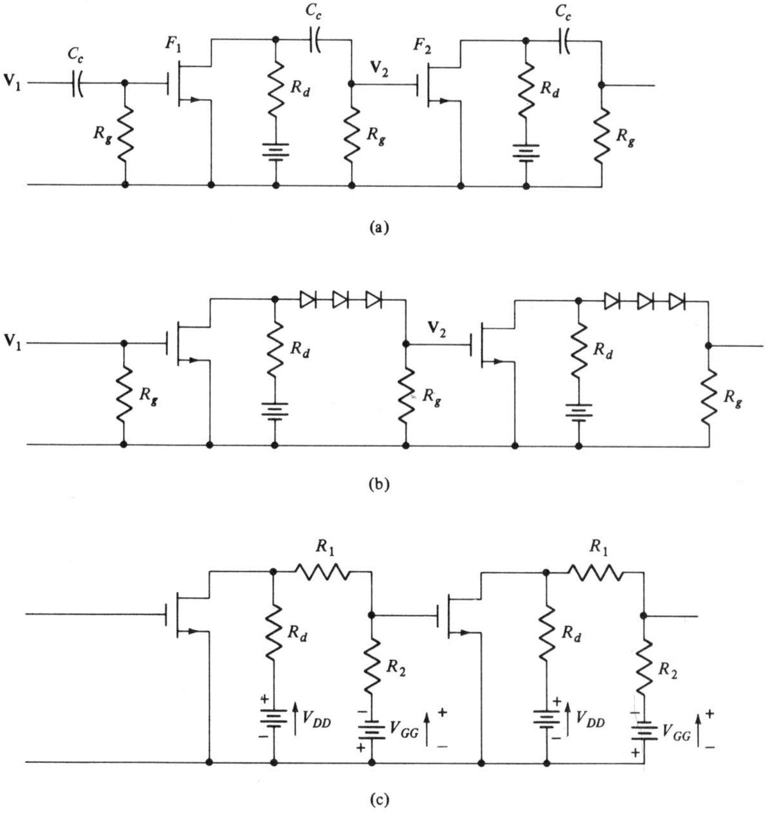

Figure 12-8. Cascaded depletion MOSFET amplifier stage. (a) *RC* coupled. (b) Direct coupled using diode level shifting. (c) Direct coupled using series resistance and two power supplies.

In order to obtain the high-frequency response, the parasitic capacitance of the FET must be included in the model. We must also consider the input capacitance of the next stage. The Miller effect will cause this to be substantial (see Sec. 6-10). Let us assume that the capacitance is known and call it C_1. Actually, this is an approximation since the Miller effect results in an input admittance which is not purely capacitive (see Sec. 6-10). If, however, we assume in this analysis that the input admittance is a pure capacitance calculated on the basis of midband gain, sufficiently accurate results are obtained.

A model for one stage of the amplifier of Fig. 12-8a is shown in Fig. 12-9. Noting that $\mathbf{V}_{gs} = \mathbf{V}_1$, we have the following nodal equations.

$$(-g_m + j\omega C_{gd})\mathbf{V}_1 = \left[\frac{1}{r_d} + \frac{1}{R_d} + j\omega(C_c + C_{gd} + C_{ds})\right]\mathbf{V}_d - j\omega C_c \mathbf{V}_2 \quad (12\text{-}28a)$$

$$0 = -j\omega C_c \mathbf{V}_d + \left[\frac{1}{R_g} + j\omega(C_c + C_i)\right]\mathbf{V}_2 \quad (12\text{-}28b)$$

Solving for the voltage gain $\mathbf{A}_v = \mathbf{V}_2/\mathbf{V}_1$, we have

$$\mathbf{A}_v = \frac{j\omega C_c(-g_m + j\omega C_{gd})}{\left[\frac{1}{r_d} + \frac{1}{R_d} + j\omega(C_c + C_{gd} + C_{ds})\right]\left[\frac{1}{R_g} + j\omega(C_c + C_i)\right] + \omega^2 C_c^2} \quad (12\text{-}29)$$

This equation can be simplified somewhat. Let us consider this. In general, $g_m \gg \omega C_{gd}$ for most frequencies of interest. Actually, we can consider that $\mathbf{A}_v$ can be broken up into two components, one multiplied by g_m and the other by $j\omega C_{gd}$. The component multiplied by g_m represents the amplification of the signal while the component multiplied by $j\omega C_{gd}$ represents the *direct transmission* of the signal through C_{gd}. That is, it just represents the transmission of the signal through passive components. Actually, this is an attenuation. That is, the signal is reduced by this process. Thus, over all frequencies of interest

$$g_m \gg \omega C_{gd}$$

Hence, Eq. 12-29 can be approximated by

$$\mathbf{A}_v = \frac{-j\omega C_c g_m}{\left[\frac{1}{r_d} + \frac{1}{R_d} + j\omega(C_c + C_{gd} + C_{ds})\right]\left[\frac{1}{R_g} + j\omega(C_c + C_i)\right] + \omega^2 C_c^2} \quad (12\text{-}30)$$

If typical element values are used, a plot which is of the form of Fig. 12-2 results when Eq. 12-30 is graphed. Let us consider the physical reasons for this. At low frequencies, the

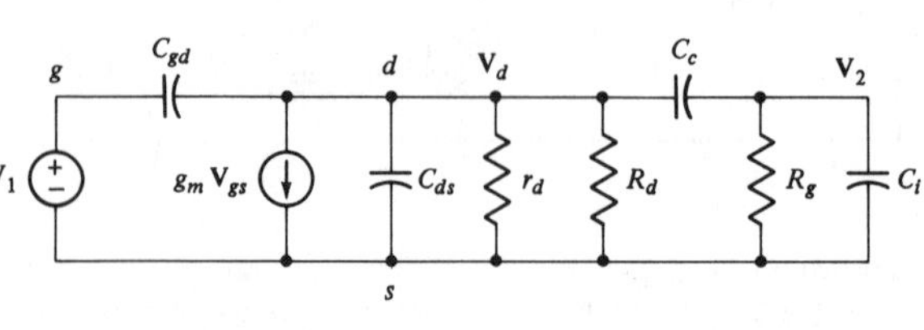

Figure 12-9. A model for one stage of the amplifier of Fig. 12-8a.

gain falls off, approaching 0 at $\omega = 0$ while the phase shift approaches 270°. This is because, at low frequencies, C_c acts as a very high impedance. The coupling capacitor is, in effect, the series arm of a voltage divider. Therefore, it causes the gain to fall off as the frequency decreases.

As the frequency increases, the gain increases to $\mathbf{A}_{\text{mid}}$ and the phase shift becomes equal to π rad (180°). This is because, at these higher frequencies, the impedance of C_c has decreased to the point where it can be considered to be a short circuit.

If the frequency is increased still further, the gain falls off again, approaching 0 as ω approaches infinity and the phase shift approaches 90°. This is because the parasitic capacitances that are in parallel with the current generator and the load effectively short-circuit them as the frequency become sufficiently high.

The capacitance C_c is an actual capacitance which is added to the circuit (not a parasitic capacitance). Typically, its value is in the order of microfarads (1 μF = 10^{-6} F). The other capacitances are due to stray capacitance and they are in the order of picofarads (1 pF = 10^{-12} F). Thus, C_c is very much larger than the other capacitances. Usually, the circuit behaves in the following way. In the midfrequency region, the impedance of the series C_c is small enough so that it can be ignored while the impedances of the shunting parasitic capacitances are so large that they too can be ignored.

Suppose that the frequency is reduced. The parallel parasitic capacitances act as larger impedances and do not affect the gain. However, when the impedance of C_c increases, it now reduces the gain of the circuit. Conversely, at high frequencies, C_c does not affect the gain, but the shunting parasitic capacitances cause it to fall off.

The previous discussion indicates that, if we are analyzing the circuit, C_c need only be considered in the low-frequency region (see Sec. 12-1) while the shunting capacitances, C_{gd}, C_{gs}, and C_i, need only be considered in the high-frequency region. Actually, this need not be the case. For instance, if C_c were made very small, then the low- and high-frequency regions might "overlap." In general, if there is a well-defined midband region, then we can use the above discussed approximation. In most practical amplifiers of this type, there will be such a well-defined midband region so that signals can be amplified without frequency distortion (see Sec. 12-1).

We shall now analyze the amplifier by analyzing the low-, mid- and high-frequency regions separately. This will allow us to eliminate components from the model. The resulting simplification in the results will allow us to gain insight into the operation of this circuit.

Midfrequency Region

In the midfrequency region, the reactance of the shunting capacitances is so high that they can be ignored. Similarly, the reactance of the series coupling capacitor is so small that it can be ignored. Thus, the midfrequency approximation to Fig. 12-9 has the form shown in Fig. 12-10a.

Let us define R_{sh} as the parallel combination of r_d, R_d, and R_g. Thus,

$$\frac{1}{R_{\text{sh}}} = \frac{1}{r_d} + \frac{1}{R_d} + \frac{1}{R_g} \tag{12-31}$$

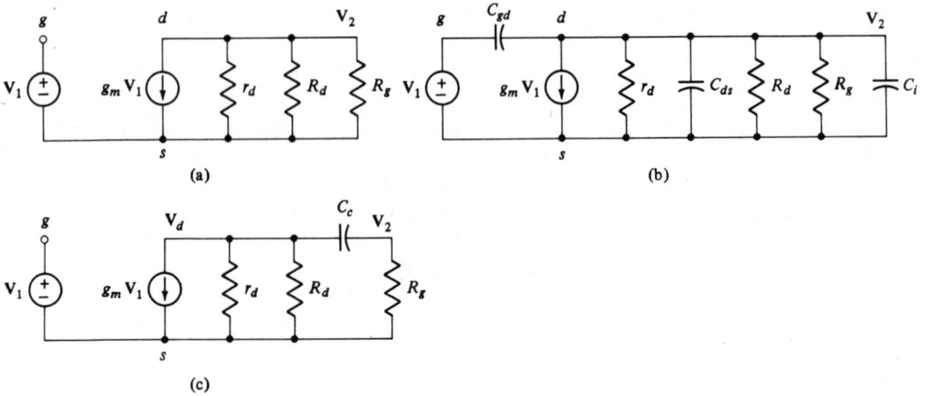

Figure 12-10. (a) The midfrequency model for the amplifier of Fig. 12-8a. (b) The high-frequency model. (c) The low-frequency model.

Then,

$$\mathbf{A}_{v\,\text{mid}} = \frac{\mathbf{V}_2}{\mathbf{V}_1} = -g_m R_{\text{sh}} \tag{12-32}$$

We shall consider the significance of this relation subsequently.

High-Frequency Region

In the high-frequency region, the model of Fig. 12-10b is valid. Applying nodal analysis to this circuit, we have

$$(-g_m + j\omega C_{gd})\mathbf{V}_1 = \left[\frac{1}{R_{\text{sh}}} + j\omega(C_{ds} + C_i + C_{gd})\right]\mathbf{V}_2$$

Let us define

$$C_{\text{sh}} = C_{ds} + C_i + C_{gd} \tag{12-33}$$

That is, C_{sh} is the total shunting capacitance. Note that, in some circuits, there is appreciable stray wiring capacitance which should be added to C_{sh}. The high-frequency gain is given by

$$\mathbf{A}_{v\,\text{high}} = \frac{-g_m R_{\text{sh}} + j\omega C_{gd} R_{\text{sh}}}{1 + j\omega C_{\text{sh}} R_{\text{sh}}} \tag{12-34}$$

In general, (see Eqs. 12-29 and 12-30),

$$g_m > \omega C_{gd} \tag{12-35}$$

over all frequencies of interest, so that we have

$$\mathbf{A}_{v\,\text{high}} = \frac{-g_m R_{\text{sh}}}{1 + j\omega C_{\text{sh}} R_{\text{sh}}} \tag{12-36}$$

Let us normalize this with respect to the midband gain. Thus,

$$\frac{\mathbf{A}_{v\,\text{high}}}{\mathbf{A}_{v\,\text{mid}}} = \frac{1}{1 + j\omega C_{\text{sh}} R_{\text{sh}}} = \frac{1}{\sqrt{1 + \omega^2 C_{\text{sh}}^2 R_{\text{sh}}^2}} e^{-j\omega \tan^{-1} \omega C_{\text{sh}} R_{\text{sh}}} \tag{12-37}$$

The upper half-power frequency occurs when

$$\left| \frac{\mathbf{A}_{v\,\text{high}}}{\mathbf{A}_{v\,\text{mid}}} \right| = \frac{1}{\sqrt{2}}$$

Let us call this f_2 and call the corresponding angular frequency ω_2. Therefore,

$$\omega_2 = \frac{1}{C_{\text{sh}} R_{\text{sh}}} \tag{12-38a}$$

or

$$f_2 = \frac{1}{2\pi C_{\text{sh}} R_{\text{sh}}} \tag{12-38b}$$

It is convenient to replace R_{sh} and C_{sh} in Eq. 12-37 by the half-power frequency. In this way we obtain a more general relation, which does not explicitly contain the amplifier components. Thus,

$$\frac{\mathbf{A}_{v\,\text{high}}}{\mathbf{A}_{v\,\text{mid}}} = \frac{1}{1 + jf/f_2} = \frac{1}{\sqrt{1 + (f/f_2)^2}} e^{-j \tan^{-1} f/f_2} \tag{12-39}$$

We shall consider the significance of this expression after we discuss the low-frequency response.

Low-Frequency Region

The low-frequency model is shown in Fig. 12-10c. Analyzing this circuit we have

$$\mathbf{A}_{v\,\text{low}} = \frac{-g_m r_d R_d R_g/(r_d + R_d)}{[r_d R_d/(r_d + R_d)] + R_g - j/\omega C_c} \tag{12-40}$$

Let us define

$$R_{\text{low}} = R_g + \frac{r_d R_d}{r_d + R_d} \tag{12-41}$$

Note that R_{low} represents the R_g in series with the parallel combination of r_d and R_d. Also note that

$$\frac{r_d R_d R_g/(r_d + R_d)}{R_{\text{low}}} = \frac{r_d R_d R_g/(r_d + R_d)}{[r_d R_d/(r_d + R_d)] + R_g} = R_{\text{sh}}$$

Hence,

$$\mathbf{A}_{v\,\text{low}} = \frac{-g_m R_{\text{sh}}}{1 - j/\omega C_c R_{\text{low}}} \tag{12-42}$$

Normalizing with response to $A_{v\,\text{mid}}$, we have

$$\frac{\mathbf{A}_{v\,\text{low}}}{\mathbf{A}_{v\,\text{mid}}} = \frac{1}{1 - j/(\omega C_c R_{\text{low}})} = \frac{1}{\sqrt{1 + (1/\omega C_c R_{\text{low}})^2}} e^{j \tan^{-1}(1/\omega C_c R_{\text{low}})} \tag{12-43}$$

The low half-power frequency is

$$\omega_1 = 1/C_c R_{\text{low}} \tag{12-44a}$$

or

$$f_1 = 1/2\pi C_c R_{\text{low}} \tag{12-44b}$$

Then, we have

$$\frac{\mathbf{A}_{v\,\text{low}}}{\mathbf{A}_{v\,\text{mid}}} = \frac{1}{1 - jf_1/f} = \frac{1}{\sqrt{1 + (f_1/f)^2}} e^{j \tan^{-1} f_1/f} \tag{12-45}$$

Let us consider plots of the various normalized responses. These are shown in Fig. 12-11. Let us start by considering the plot of $\mathbf{A}_{v\,\text{high}}/\mathbf{A}_{v\,\text{mid}}$. The amplitude response is shown in Fig. 12-11a. As the frequency increases, the normalized response falls off from unity. At $f = f_2$ it is equal to 0.707. The phase angle of $\mathbf{A}_{v\,\text{high}}/\mathbf{A}_{v\,\text{mid}}$ is plotted in Fig. 12-11b. In the midfrequency region, this angle is 0. As the frequency increases, the phase angle asymptotically approaches $-90°$. When $f = f_2$, the phase angle is equal to 45°. Remember that the phase angle of $\mathbf{A}_{v\,\text{mid}}$, which has been removed from these plots by the normalization, is 180°.

The plots for the low-frequency response are similar to those for the high-frequency response except that the response falls off and the phase shift increases as the frequency is decreased.

Now let us plot the amplitude response on a decibel basis. Proceeding as in Sec. 12-2, we obtain the graph of Fig. 12-12. Note that the asymptote falls off in the high-frequency region at 6 dB/octave.

The low-frequency response is plotted in a manner similar to that of the high-frequency response. The asymptotes are given by

$$\left|\frac{\mathbf{A}_{v\,\text{low}}}{\mathbf{A}_{v\,\text{mid}}}\right|_{\text{dB}} = 0 \tag{12-46a}$$

for $f > f_1$, and

$$\left|\frac{\mathbf{A}_{v\,\text{low}}}{\mathbf{A}_{v\,\text{mid}}}\right|_{\text{dB}} = -20 \log_{10} \frac{f_1}{f} = 20 \log_{10} \frac{f}{f_1} \tag{12-46b}$$

for $f < f_1$.

In the midband and high-frequency regions, $\mathbf{A}_{v\,\text{low}}/\mathbf{A}_{v\,\text{mid}} \simeq 1$, while, in the mid- and low-frequency regions, $\mathbf{A}_{v\,\text{high}}/\mathbf{A}_{v\,\text{mid}} \simeq 1$. Thus, an approximate expression for gain that is valid at all frequencies is

$$\frac{\mathbf{A}_v}{\mathbf{A}_{v\,\text{mid}}} = \frac{1}{(1 + jf_1/f)(1 + jf/f_2)} \tag{12-47}$$

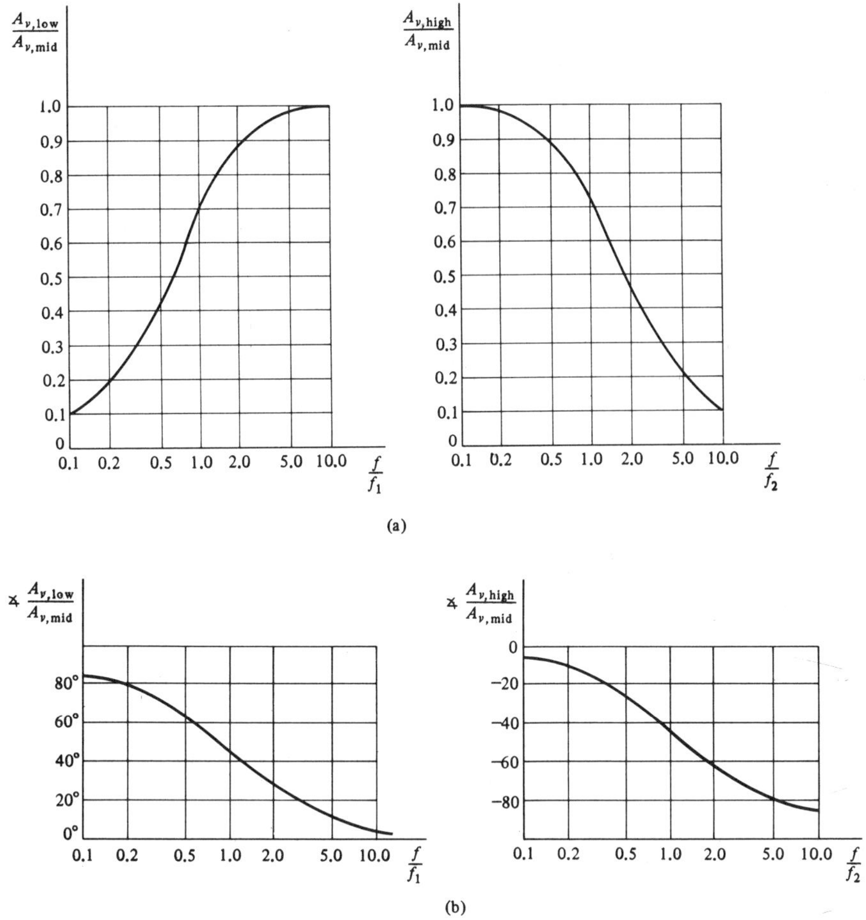

Figure 12-11. Frequency for *RC* coupled FET amplifier. (a) Amplitude response. (b) Phase response.

The accuracy of the approximate analysis that we have performed depends upon the existence of a well-defined midband region which requires that $f_2 \gg f_1$. If the approximate responses given by Eqs. 12-39 and 12-45 or Eq. 12-47 are compared with the actual responses, it is found[1] that the error in the amplitude response will be less than 0.5% if $f_2 > 100f_1$. If $f_2 > 25f_1$, then the error in the amplitude will be less than 2%. If f_2 is not greater than $10f_1$, then the approximations should not be used. Even for most poor

[1] T. S. Grey *Applied Electronics*, 2nd ed. (New York: Wiley, 1954), pp. 520–521.

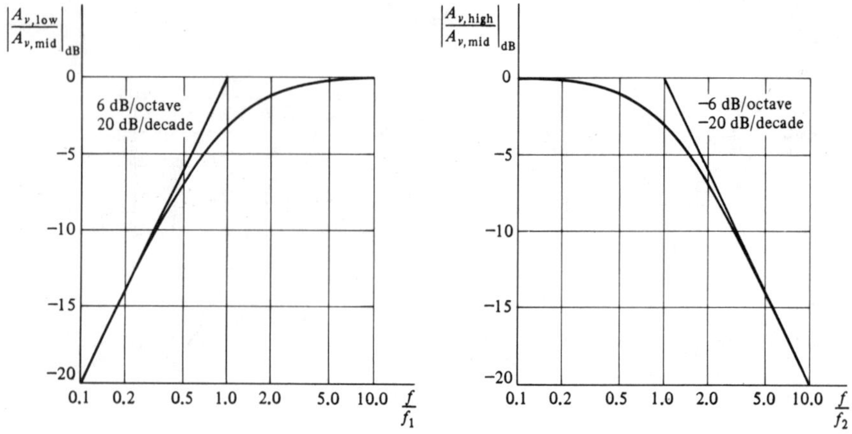

Figure 12-12. The normalized amplitude response for a *RC* coupled FET amplifier. The asymptotes are shown.

audio amplifiers, $f_2 > 100f_1$. Usually, $f_2 \gg 100f_1$. Thus, the approximations are very accurate.

Response of the Direct Coupled Amplifier of Fig. 12-8b

The diodes in the amplifier of Fig. 12-8b have an essentially constant voltage drop across them so they act as short circuits for signal frequencies. However, the direct voltage drop reduces the value of v_{GSQ} to acceptable values. The mid- and high-frequency response of this amplifier are then exactly the same as that of the amplifier of Fig. 12-8a. There is no low-frequency falloff. That is, the midband extends down to zero frequency. The diodes represent a simple form of direct voltage level shifting. In Chapter 14, we shall consider other forms.

Response of the Direct Coupled Amplifier of Fig. 12-8c

The direct coupled amplifier of Fig. 12-8c will have poorer mid- and high-frequency response than that of Fig. 12-8b. The inclusion of the resistor R_1 and the second power supply allows the bias to be adjusted very precisely. However, the signal voltage drop across R_1 causes the gain and high-frequency response to deteriorate. In general, this amplifier is *not* used in integrated circuit amplifiers but is used for some special purpose direct coupled amplifiers that use discrete components.

The amplifier of Fig. 12-8c can be analyzed in essentially the same way as was that of Fig. 12-8a. That is, we can, in general, break the analysis into two regions, one for mid- and the other for high frequencies. Note that there is no low-frequency falloff since the amplifier is direct coupled. Let us consider each region in turn.

Midfrequency Region

The model that is valid in the midfrequency region is shown in Fig. 12-13a. An analysis of this circuit yields

$$\mathbf{A}_{v\,\mathrm{mid}} = -g_m \frac{R_g}{R_1 + R_g} R'_{\mathrm{sh}} \tag{12-48}$$

where

$$\frac{1}{R'_{\mathrm{sh}}} = \frac{1}{r_d} + \frac{1}{R_d} + \frac{1}{R_1 + R_g} \tag{12-49}$$

In general, the gain of the amplifier of Fig. 12-8a will be greater than that of Fig. 12-8c, because the resistors R_1 and R_g form a voltage divider which attenuates the output signal.

High-Frequency Region

The model that is valid in the high-frequency region is shown in Fig. 12-13b. Applying nodal analysis, we have

$$(-g_m + j\omega C_{gd})\mathbf{V}_1 = \left[\frac{1}{r_d} + \frac{1}{R_d} + \frac{1}{R_1} + j\omega(C_{gd} + C_{ds}\right]\mathbf{V}_d - \frac{1}{R_1}\mathbf{V}_2 \tag{12-50a}$$

$$0 = -\frac{1}{R_1}\mathbf{V}_d + \left(\frac{1}{R_1} + \frac{1}{R_g} + j\omega C_i\right)\mathbf{V}_2 \tag{12-50b}$$

Solving for V_2 and manipulating, we obtain

$$\mathbf{A}_{v\,\mathrm{high}} = \frac{(-g_m + j\omega C_{gd})\dfrac{1}{R_1}}{\dfrac{1}{R_1}\left(\dfrac{1}{r_d} + \dfrac{1}{R_d}\right) + \dfrac{1}{R_g}\left(\dfrac{1}{r_d} + \dfrac{1}{R_d} + \dfrac{1}{R_1}\right) - \omega^2 C_i(C_{gd} + C_{ds}) + j\omega\left[(C_{gd} + C_{ds})\left(\dfrac{1}{R_1} + \dfrac{1}{R_g}\right) + C_i\left(\dfrac{1}{r_d} + \dfrac{1}{R_d} + \dfrac{1}{R_1}\right)\right]} \tag{12-51}$$

In general, for frequencies of interest

$$g_m \gg \omega C_{gd} \tag{12-52a}$$

$$\frac{1}{R_1}\left(\frac{1}{r_d} + \frac{1}{R_d}\right) + \frac{1}{R_g}\left(\frac{1}{r_d} + \frac{1}{R_d} + \frac{1}{R_1}\right) \gg \omega^2 C_i(C_{gd} + C_{ds}) \tag{12-52b}$$

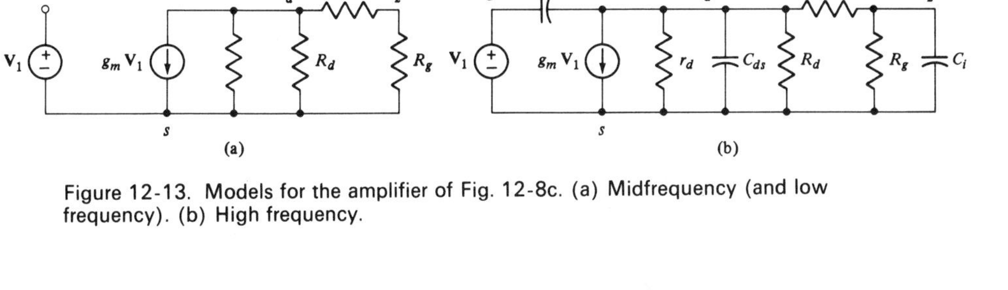

Figure 12-13. Models for the amplifier of Fig. 12-8c. (a) Midfrequency (and low frequency). (b) High frequency.

Thus, after some manipulating, we can write

$$\mathbf{A}_{v\,\text{high}} = \frac{-g_m \dfrac{1}{R_1} \Big/ \left[\dfrac{1}{R_1}\left(\dfrac{1}{r_d} + \dfrac{1}{R_d}\right) + \dfrac{1}{R_g}\left(\dfrac{1}{r_d} + \dfrac{1}{R_d} + \dfrac{1}{R_1}\right)\right]}{1 + j\omega \dfrac{\left[(C_{gd} + C_{ds})\left(\dfrac{1}{R_1} + \dfrac{1}{R_g}\right) + C_i\left(\dfrac{1}{r_d} + \dfrac{1}{R_d} + \dfrac{1}{R_1}\right)\right]}{\dfrac{1}{R_1}\left(\dfrac{1}{r_d} + \dfrac{1}{R_d}\right) + \dfrac{1}{R_g}\left(\dfrac{1}{r_d} + \dfrac{1}{R_d} + \dfrac{1}{R_1}\right)}}$$

Manipulating, we obtain

$$\frac{1}{R_1} \Big/ \left[\frac{1}{R_1}\left(\frac{1}{r_d} + \frac{1}{R_d}\right) + \frac{1}{R_g}\left(\frac{1}{r_d} + \frac{1}{R_d} + \frac{1}{R_1}\right)\right] = \frac{R_g}{R_1 + R_g} R'_{\text{sh}} \tag{12-53}$$

Then, using Eqs. 12-48 and 12-49 and manipulating, we have

$$\frac{\mathbf{A}_{v\,\text{high}}}{\mathbf{A}_{v\,\text{mid}}} = \left\{1 + j\omega R'_{\text{sh}} \frac{R_g}{R_1 + R_g}\left[(C_{gd} + C_{ds})\left(1 + \frac{R_1}{R_g}\right) + C_i\left(1 + \frac{R_1}{r_d} + \frac{R_1}{R_d}\right)\right]\right\}^{-1} \tag{12-54}$$

Let us define

$$R''_{\text{sh}} = R'_{\text{sh}} \frac{R_g}{R_1 + R_g} \tag{12-55}$$

and

$$C''_{\text{sh}} = (C_{gd} + C_{ds})\left(1 + \frac{R_1}{R_g}\right) + C_i\left(1 + \frac{R_1}{r_d} + \frac{R_1}{R_d}\right) \tag{12-56}$$

Then, Eqs. 12-48 and 12-54 become

$$\mathbf{A}_{v\,\text{mid}} = -g_m R''_{\text{sh}} \tag{12-57}$$

and

$$\frac{\mathbf{A}_{v\,\text{high}}}{\mathbf{A}_{v\,\text{mid}}} = \frac{1}{1 + j\omega R''_{\text{sh}} C''_{\text{sh}}} \tag{12-58}$$

The upper half-power frequency is given by

$$f_2 = \frac{1}{2\pi R''_{\text{sh}} C''_{\text{sh}}} \tag{12-59}$$

Thus, Eq. 12-58 can be written as

$$\frac{\mathbf{A}_{v\,\text{high}}}{\mathbf{A}_{v\,\text{mid}}} = \frac{1}{1 + j\omega f/f_2} = \frac{1}{\sqrt{1 + (f/f_2)^2}} e^{-j\tan^{-1} f/f_2} \tag{12-60}$$

This expression is the same as that of Eq. 12-39. Therefore, the shape of the high-frequency response curve of the amplifier of Fig. 12-8c is the same as that of Fig. 12-8a, subject to the approximations that we have made. Of course, the upper half-power frequency for each of these amplifiers will, in general, be different. In fact, because of the voltage drop across R_1 the value of f_2 for the amplifier of Fig. 12-8c will usually be considerably less than f_2 for either of the amplifiers of Figs. 12-8a or 12-8b. For this reason the amplifier of Fig. 12-8c is usually *not* used when high-frequency response is important.

Let us consider an example which will illustrate the results of this section.

Example

The FET used in the amplifier of Fig. 12-8a has the following parameter values.

$$g_m = 10{,}000\ \mu\text{mho}$$
$$r_d = 500{,}000\ \text{ohms}$$
$$C_{gd} = 0.25\ \text{pF}$$
$$C_{gs} = 3\ \text{pF}$$
$$C_{ds} = 1.5\ \text{pF}$$

The elements of the circuit are

$$R_d = 10{,}000\ \text{ohms}$$
$$R_g = 10^6\ \text{ohms}$$
$$C_c = 0.01\ \mu\text{F}$$

Find the values of $\mathbf{A}_{\text{mid}}, f_1$, and f_2.

Using Eqs. 12-31 and 12-32, we obtain

$$\frac{1}{R_{\text{sh}}} = \frac{1}{500{,}000} + \frac{1}{10{,}000} + \frac{1}{10^6}$$
$$R_{\text{sh}} = 9708.7\ \text{ohms}$$
$$\mathbf{A}_{v\,\text{mid}} = -g_m R_{\text{sh}} = -10{,}000 \times 10^{-6} \times 9708.7 = 97.08$$

Using Eq. 12-38, we have

$$f_2 = 1/2\pi C_{\text{sh}} R_{\text{sh}}$$

We must determine C_{sh}. From Eq. 12-33 we have

$$C_{\text{sh}} = C_{ds} + C_{gd} + C_i$$

Let us compute C_i. We assume that the next stage is identical to this one. Hence, (see Eq. 6-111)

$$C_i = C_{gs} + C_{gd}(1 - \mathbf{A}_{v\,\text{mid}}) = 3 + 0.25(1 + 97.08) = 27.5\ \text{pF}$$

Then,

$$C_{\text{sh}} = 1.5 + 0.25 + 27.5 = 29.3\ \text{pF}$$

Hence,

$$f_2 = \frac{1}{2\pi \times 29.3 \times 10^{-12} + 9708.7} = 559{,}488 \text{ Hz}$$

In the next section we shall discuss procedures for increasing f_2. In Sec. 12-13 we shall consider the design of broadband amplifiers.

Before proceeding, let us check the approximation of Eq. 12-35. At $10f_2$, $|\mathbf{A}_{v\,\text{high}}/\mathbf{A}_{v\,\text{mid}}| = 0.01$. This is so small that any higher frequencies are probably of no interest. Then, let us verify that inequality 12-35 is true for $f = 10f_2$.

$$g_m \overset{?}{\gg} \omega C_{gd}$$

$$10{,}000 \times 10^{-6} \overset{?}{\gg} 2\pi \times 5.59 \times 10^{6} \times 0.25 \times 10^{-12}$$

$$10^{-2} \overset{?}{\gg} 8.78 \times 10^{-6}$$

This is certainly true. Hence, the approximation is valid.

Now let us compute the lower half-power frequency. From Eq. 12-44 we have

$$f_1 = 1/2\pi C_c R_{\text{low}}$$

where

$$R_{\text{low}} = R_g + \frac{r_d R_d}{r_d + R_d}$$

Then,

$$R_{\text{low}} = 10^6 + \frac{500{,}000 \times 10{,}000}{500{,}000 + 10{,}000} = 1.01 \times 10^6$$

and

$$f_1 = (2\pi \times 0.01 \times 10^{-6} \times 1.01 \times 10^6)^{-1} = 15.8 \text{ Hz}$$

Note that $f_2 = 35410 f_1$. Hence, the assumption that we can use low, mid- and high-frequency models is valid.

12-4. FACTORS AFFECTING THE FREQUENCY RESPONSE OF THE ONE-STAGE COMMON-SOURCE FET AMPLIFIER

Let us now consider the significance of the results derived in the last section. In general, we shall see that the midfrequency gain and the upper half-power frequency are related such that if one is increased, the other is decreased. The low-frequency response is essentially unrelated to these gains, as we shall see. Of course, in the direct coupled amplifier, the low-frequency response is not a consideration since the amplification is flat down to 0 Hz.

Let us first consider the low-frequency response of the amplifier of Fig. 12-8a and then consider the more important mid- and high-frequency responses. We shall use half-power frequencies in our discussion, since any other bandwidth (90%, etc.) varies linearly with them. The lower half-power frequency of the amplifier of Fig. 12-8a is given by (see Eq. 12-44),

$$f_1 = \frac{1}{2\pi C_c R_{\text{low}}} \tag{12-61}$$

where

$$R_{\text{low}} = \frac{r_d R_d}{r_d + R_d} + R_g \tag{12-62}$$

If we want to increase the low-frequency bandwidth, that is, reduce f_1, then C_c and/or R_{low} must be increased in size. In general, R_d is limited in size since the quiescent drain current must pass through it, producing a voltage drop. If R_d were too large, then the power supply voltage would become excessive. In general, $R_g \gg R_d$ so that

$$R_{\text{low}} \simeq R_g \tag{12-63}$$

The size of R_g is limited since any coupling capacitor C_c will not really have infinite leakage resistance R_{leak}. (The typical leakage resistance of a high-quality capacitor may be 10^9 ohms, i.e., 1000 megohms.) Let us consider this. If V_{DSQ} is the quiescent drain to source voltage of F_1 (see Fig. 12-8a) the resulting direct voltage between the gate of F_2 and ground will be

$$V_{G1} = \frac{V_{DSQ} R_g}{R_{\text{leak}} + R_g} \tag{12-64}$$

If R_g is too large, then an appreciable dc component of voltage will be applied to F_2, which is undesirable. Note that R_{leak} is not known since it will vary from capacitor to capacitor, with dirt on the surface of the capacitor, and so forth. Thus, R_s must be kept small enough so that V_{G1} is very small for all reasonable values of R_{leak}. In practice, the maximum value of R_g is about 10^7 ohms.

The size of C_c is limited by practical considerations. If it becomes too large, then its volume becomes excessive. The increased physical size not only increases the size of the amplifier, but it also increases the value of C_{sh} because the stray capacitance to ground of the coupling capacitor acts as though C_{ds} were increased. Typical maximum values of C_c are 0.5 to 1.0 μF, with values of C_c considerably less than this being more desirable. Note that even when considerably smaller values of capacitance are used these capacitances cannot be fabricated within an integrated circuit chip. Thus, these *RC* coupled amplifiers are usually only used with discrete components. In Sec. 14-7 we shall see that sometimes it is not desirable to have the amplifier response flat down to 0 Hz. At times, an amplifier is composed of many direct coupled stages which are located on several chips. In such cases, *RC* coupling can be used between the chips so that the overall amplifier's response falls off as the frequency is decreased.

Now let us consider the mid- and high-frequency response of the amplifiers of Figs. 12-8a and 12-8b The midband gain and upper half-power frequency are given by (see Eqs. 12-32 and 12-38)

$$\mathbf{A}_{v\,\text{mid}} = -g_m R_{\text{sh}} \tag{12-65}$$

$$f_2 = \frac{1}{2\pi R_{\text{sh}} C_{\text{sh}}} \tag{12-66}$$

where

$$\frac{1}{R_{\text{sh}}} = \frac{1}{r_d} + \frac{1}{R_d} + \frac{1}{R_g} \tag{12-67}$$

and

$$C_{\text{sh}} = C_{gd} + C_{ds} + C_i \tag{12-68}$$

$|\mathbf{A}_{v\,\text{mid}}|$ represents the nominal gain of the amplifier, that is, it is the gain for most frequencies of interest. Suppose that we want to increase f_2 (i.e., the high-frequency bandwidth). Then, either C_{sh} or R_{sh} must be reduced. The effects of stray shunting capacitance are represented by C_{sh} which is then made as small as possible. However, it cannot be reduced to zero since in theory, some capacitance must exist between all conductors. The fabrication of small discrete or integrated circuit components tends to minimize this capacitance. Let us assume that C_{sh} has been reduced as much as is possible. If we want to further increase f_2, then R_{sh} must be reduced but this will also reduce $\mathbf{A}_{v\,\text{mid}}$. Let us take the product of $|\mathbf{A}_{v\,\text{mid}}|$ and f_2. This is called the *midband-gain, high-frequency bandwidth product* or, more simply, the *gain-bandwidth product*. Using Eqs. 12-65 and 12-66, we obtain

$$|\mathbf{A}_{v\,\text{mid}}|\, f_2 = g_m/2\pi C_{\text{sh}} \tag{12-69}$$

The product of the midband gain and f_2 is a constant which is a *figure of merit* for the amplifier. That is, if we want both high gain and broadband response, then the FET's to choose are the ones where the g_m/C_{sh} ratio is high. It is not sufficient to only have high g_m or only have low C_{sh}.

Note that the Miller effect (see Eq. 6-111) complicates the discussion. Suppose that we reduce $\mathbf{A}_{v\,\text{mid}}$. This will not only increase f_2 for the stage in question, but it will also increase it for the preceding stage since the reduction in $\mathbf{A}_{v\,\text{mid}}$ will reduce C_i. In Sec. 12-13 we shall consider the design of such cascaded stages.

In general, the gain and high-frequency bandwidth are varied by varying R_{sh}. In most circuits, r_d and R_g are much greater than R_d. Hence,

$$R_{\text{sh}} \simeq R_d \tag{12-70}$$

Variations in R_{sh} are, in general, obtained by varying R_d.

Now let us consider the midband gain and high-frequency response of the amplifier of Fig. 12-8c. These are given by (see Eqs. 12-57 and 12-59)

$$\mathbf{A}_{v\,\text{mid}} = -g_m R''_{\text{sh}} \tag{12-71}$$

$$f_2 = 1/2\pi R''_{\text{sh}} C''_{\text{sh}} \tag{12-72}$$

where

$$R''_{sh} = R'_{sh} \frac{R_g}{R_1 + R_g} \tag{12-73a}$$

and

$$\frac{1}{R'_{sh}} = \frac{1}{r_d} + \frac{1}{R_d} + \frac{1}{R_1 + R_g} \tag{12-73b}$$

and

$$C''_{sh} = (C_{gd} + C_{ds})\left(1 + \frac{R_1}{R_g}\right) + C_i\left(1 + \frac{R_1}{r_d} + \frac{R_1}{R_d}\right) \tag{12-74}$$

Now let us take the gain bandwidth product.

$$|\mathbf{A}_{v\,\mathrm{mid}}|\, f_2 = g_m/2\pi C''_{sh} \tag{12-75}$$

This appears to be the same as Eq. 12-69 which was the gain bandwidth product for the amplifier of Fig. 12-8a. However, Eq. 12-75 will result in a lower gain bandwidth product since

$$C''_{sh} > C_{sh} \tag{12-76}$$

This can be seen by comparing Eqs. 12-74 and 12-68. This reflects the voltage divider action that occurs because of the presence of R_1 in the circuit. If we reduce R_1, then C''_{sh} will be reduced. If $R_1 = 0$, then $C''_{sh} = C_{sh}$. The reason that R_1 is included is to properly adjust the gate to source bias of F_2 (see Sec. 5-4). In that section we demonstrated that

$$V_{GSQ} = \frac{V_{DSQ} R_g}{R_g + R_1} + \frac{V_{GG} R_1}{R_g + R_1} \tag{12-77}$$

where V_{GSQ} is the quiescent gate to source voltage of F_2 and V_{DSQ} is the quiescent drain to source voltage of F_1. If we assume that $V_{GSQ} = 0$, then

$$V_{GG} = -\frac{R_g}{R_1} V_{DSQ} \tag{12-78}$$

If R_1 is made too small, then the magnitude of the negative power supply V_{GG} may become excessive. Thus, we cannot reduce R_1 at will and some compromise is necessary. The amplifiers of Figs. 12-8a or 12-8b are used, rather than the amplifier of Fig. 12-8c, when large gain and high-frequency bandwidth are desired.

12-5. FREQUENCY RESPONSE OF ONE STAGE IN A JUNCTION TRANSISTOR COMMON-EMITTER AMPLIFIER CASCADE

In this section we shall consider the frequency response of one stage in a cascade of identical common-emitter amplifiers. In a subsequent section, we shall consider the design of the overall amplifier. At times, as we shall discover, a cascade of identical stages may not be the most desirable form. Nevertheless, the results that we shall derive here are basic to the design of all cascaded transistor amplifiers.

A cascade of RC coupled common-emitter amplifier stages is shown in Fig. 12-14a. A cascade of direct coupled amplifiers is shown in Fig. 12-14b. Let us start by analyzing the RC coupled amplifier. Then, we shall turn our attention to the direct coupled amplifier.

A model for the amplifier of Fig. 12-14a is shown in Fig. 12-15. The impedance $\mathbf{Z}_i$ represents the input impedance of the next stage. The resistance R_B represents the parallel combination of R_{B1} and R_{B2}.

$$\frac{1}{R_B} = \frac{1}{R_{B1}} + \frac{1}{R_{B2}} \tag{12-79}$$

If we compute the voltage gain of the amplifier using typical parameter values, we find that the amplification versus frequency is characterized by curves similar to those of Fig. 12-2. That is, there is a well-defined midband region where the response is flat. It falls off at the low and high frequencies. Then, just as in the case of the RC coupled FET amplifier (see Sec. 12-3) we can simplify the results by analyzing low-, mid- and high-frequency ranges separately. In the midfrequency region, the reactance of the coupling capacitor C_c is low enough so that C_c can be assumed to be a short circuit. In addition, the reactances of the parasitic capacitances $C_{b'e}$ and $C_{b'c}$ are high enough so that they can be considered to be open circuits. In the high-frequency region, the parasitic capacitances now must be considered, but C_c can still be assumed to be a short circuit. Conversely, in the low-frequency region, the parasitic capacitances can be considered to open circuits but the effect of the coupling capacitor must now be considered. Let us determine the gain in each of these regions.

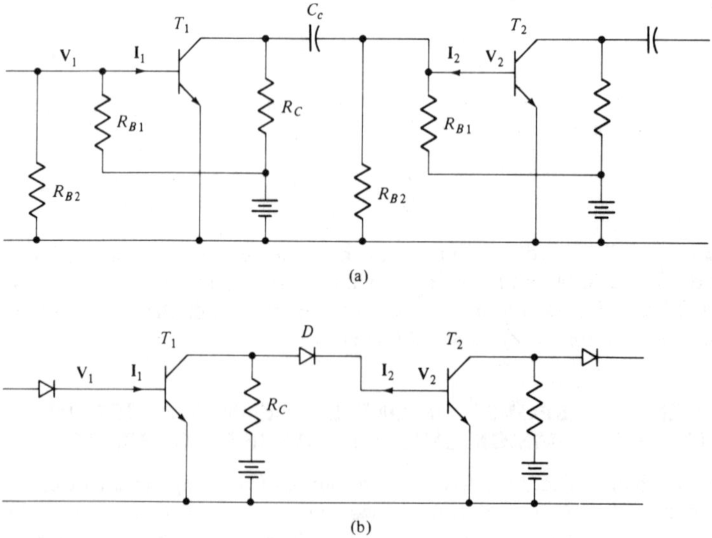

Figure 12-14. Single stages in a cascade of common-emitter transistor amplifiers. (a) RC coupled. (b) Direct coupled.

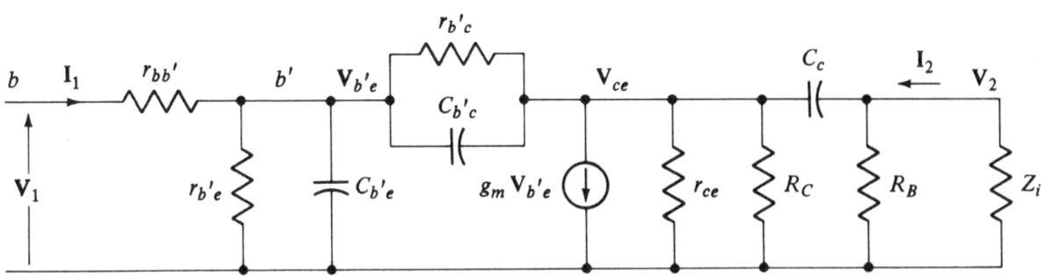

Figure 12-15. Model for the amplifier of Fig. 12-14a.

Midfrequency Region

A midfrequency model is shown in Fig. 12-16a. In general, in the midfrequency region, the input impedance of the next stage is purely resistive. We have called this input impedance R_i.

Applying nodal analysis to the circuit of Fig. 12-16a, we have

$$\frac{V_1}{r_{bb'}} = \left(\frac{1}{r_{bb'}} + \frac{1}{r_{b'e}} + \frac{1}{r_{b'c}}\right)V_{b'e} - \frac{1}{r_{b'c}} V_2 \tag{12-80a}$$

$$0 = \left(g_m - \frac{1}{r_{b'c}}\right)V_{b'e} + \left(\frac{1}{r_{b'c}} + \frac{1}{r_{ce}} + \frac{1}{R_C} + \frac{1}{R_B} + \frac{1}{R_i}\right)V_2 \tag{12-80b}$$

Manipulating, we obtain the voltage gain

$$\mathbf{A}_{v\,\text{mid}} = \frac{V_2}{V_1} = \frac{-\dfrac{1}{r_{bb'}}\left(g_m - \dfrac{1}{r_{b'c}}\right)}{\left(\dfrac{1}{r_{ce}} + \dfrac{1}{R_C} + \dfrac{1}{R_B} + \dfrac{1}{R_i}\right)\left(\dfrac{1}{r_{bb'}} + \dfrac{1}{r_{b'e}} + \dfrac{1}{r_{b'c}}\right) + \dfrac{1}{r_{b'c}}\left(g_m + \dfrac{1}{r_{bb'}} + \dfrac{1}{r_{b'e}}\right)} \tag{12-81}$$

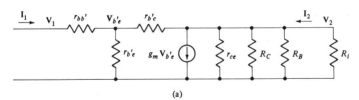

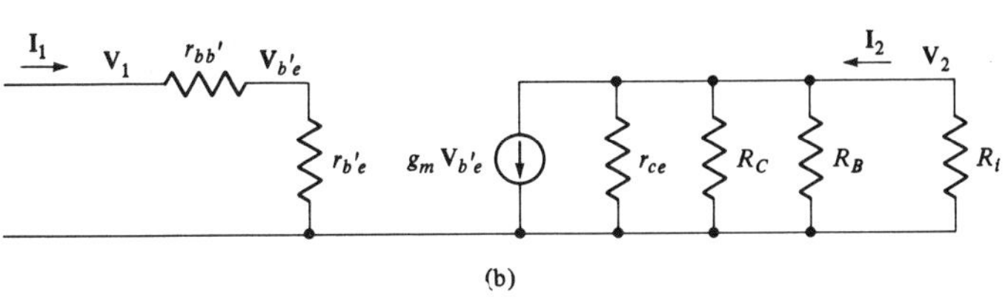

Figure 12-16. (a) Midfrequency model for the amplifier of Fig. 12-14. (b) An accurate approximation to this model.

We can make some simplifying approximations here. In general,

$$g_m \gg \frac{1}{r_{b'c}} \tag{12-82}$$

If we ignore $1/r_{b'c}$ here, it is equivalent to ignoring the direct transmission component (see Sec. 12-3). Also, the following approximations are valid.

$$\frac{1}{r_{bb'}} + \frac{1}{r_{b'e}} \gg \frac{1}{r_{b'c}} \tag{12-83a}$$

$$\left(\frac{1}{r_{ce}} + \frac{1}{R_C} + \frac{1}{R_B} + \frac{1}{R_i}\right)\left(\frac{1}{r_{bb'}} + \frac{1}{r_{b'e}}\right) \gg \frac{1}{r_{b'c}}\left(g_m + \frac{1}{r_{bb'}} + \frac{1}{r_{b'e}}\right) \tag{12-83b}$$

Use of these inequalities and manipulation yields

$$\mathbf{A}_{v\,\text{mid}} = -\,g_m \Bigg/ \left(\frac{1}{r_{ce}} + \frac{1}{R_C} + \frac{1}{R_B} + \frac{1}{R_i}\right)\left(1 + \frac{r_{bb'}}{r_{b'e}}\right)$$

Let us define

$$\frac{1}{R_{\text{sh}}} = \frac{1}{r_{ce}} + \frac{1}{R_C} + \frac{1}{R_B} + \frac{1}{R_i} \tag{12-84}$$

Note that R_{sh} represents the parallel combination of resistances shunting the current generator. Thus, it plays the same role as it does in Sec. 12-3. Hence, we have

$$\mathbf{A}_{v\,\text{mid}} = \frac{-g_m R_{\text{sh}}}{1 + (r_{bb'}/r_{b'e})} = -g_m R_{\text{sh}} \frac{r_{b'e}}{r_{bb'} + r_{b'e}} \tag{12-85}$$

In deriving these expressions, we essentially consider that $r_{b'c}$ was infinite so, in essence, we have used the model of Fig. 12-16b. If we consider Eq. 12-85, then we can interpret the equation in the following way. $g_m R_{\text{sh}}$ represents the voltage produced across the dependent current generator, while $r_{b'e}/(r_{bb'} + r_{b'e})$ is a voltage divider ratio, which indicates that the dependent generator is not a function of V_i but of $V_{b'e}$.

High-Frequency Region

The high-frequency model for the amplifier of Fig. 12-14 is given in Fig. 12-17a. As we have just discussed, $r_{b'c}$ has been replaced by an open circuit. Applying nodal analysis to the amplifier, we obtain

$$\frac{\mathbf{V}_1}{r_{bb'}} = \left[\frac{1}{r_{bb'}} + \frac{1}{r_{b'e}} + j\omega(C_{b'e} + C_{b'c})\right]\mathbf{V}_{b'e} - j\omega C_{b'c}\mathbf{V}_2 \tag{12-86a}$$

$$0 = (g_m - j\omega C_{b'c})\mathbf{V}_{b'e} + \left(\frac{1}{R_{\text{sh}}} + j\omega C_{b'c}\right)\mathbf{V}_2 \tag{12-86b}$$

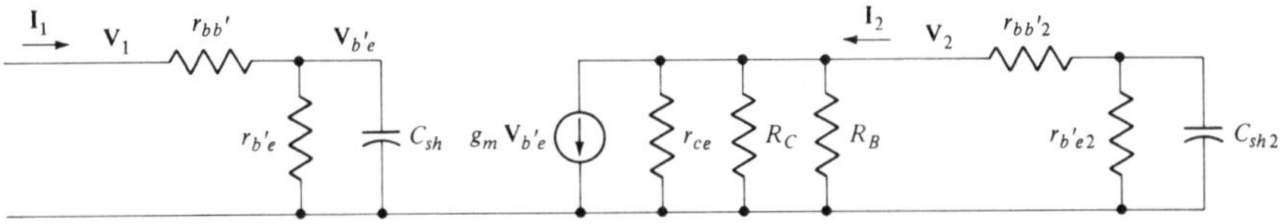

Figure 12-19. A high-frequency model for the amplifier of Fig. 12-14a which used the model of Fig. 12-16b and takes the input admittance of the next stage into account.

and

$$\frac{\mathbf{V}_2}{\mathbf{V}_{b'e}} = \frac{-g_m R_{sh}(1 + j\omega C_{sh2} R_{p2})}{1 + j\omega C_{sh2} \dfrac{r_{b'e2}(r_{bb'2} + R)}{r_{b'e2} + r_{bb'2} + R}} \tag{12-95b}$$

where

$$\frac{1}{R_{p2}} = \frac{1}{r_{bb'2}} + \frac{1}{r_{b'e2}} \tag{12-95c}$$

and

$$\frac{1}{R} = \frac{1}{r_{ce}} + \frac{1}{R_C} + \frac{1}{R_B} \tag{12-95d}$$

Let

$$R'_{sh} = \frac{r_{b'e2}(r_{bb'2} + R)}{r_{b'e2} + r_{bb'2} + R} \tag{12-95e}$$

Note that R'_{sh} is equal to the parallel combination of $r_{b'e2}$ with $r_{bb'2}$ and R in series.

Then, considering Eqs. 12-95, we have

$$\frac{\mathbf{A}_{v\,high}}{\mathbf{A}_{v\,mid}} = \frac{1 + j\omega C_{sh2} R_{p2}}{(1 + j\omega C_{sh} R_p)(1 + j\omega C_{sh2} R'_{sh})} \tag{12-96}$$

If the two stages are identical, then this result can be simplified somewhat.

$$C_{sh2} = C_{b'e2} + C_{b'c2}(1 - \mathbf{A}'_v) = C_{b'e2} + C_{b'c2}(1 + g_{m2} R_{sh2}) \tag{12-97}$$

Compare this with Eq. 12-91. Let us assume that

$$1 + g_m R_{sh} \gg \frac{R_{sh}}{R_p} \tag{12-98}$$

This inequality may not always be strongly satisfied. However, if it is, then

$$C_{sh2} \simeq C_{sh} \tag{12-99}$$

(Even if relation 12-98 is not strongly satisfied, C_{sh2} will not differ widely from C_{sh}. For a cascade of identical stages (Eq. 12-96), the gain of a single stage reduces to

$$\frac{\mathbf{A}_{v\,high}}{\mathbf{A}_{v\,mid}} = \frac{1}{1 + j\omega C_{sh} R'_{sh}} \tag{12-100}$$

since $R_p = R_{p2}$. The upper half-power frequency for this amplifier stage is characterized by

$$\omega_2 = 1/C_{sh}R'_{sh} \tag{12-101a}$$

$$f_2 = 1/2\pi C_{sh}R'_{sh} \tag{12-101b}$$

We shall consider the significance of these relations in the next section.

Low-Frequency Region

The low-frequency model for the amplifier of Fig. 12-14a is shown in Fig. 12-20. We have used the simplified model of Fig. 12-16b here. Analyzing this circuit, we obtain

$$\frac{\mathbf{A}_{v\,\text{low}}}{\mathbf{A}_{v\,\text{mid}}} = \frac{1}{1 - j/\omega C_c R_{\text{low}}} \tag{12-102}$$

where

$$R_{\text{low}} = \frac{r_{ce}R_C}{r_{ce} + R_C} + \frac{R_B R_i}{R_B + R_i} \tag{12-103}$$

Note that R_{low} represents r_{ce} in parallel with R_C plus that combination in series with the parallel combination of R_B and R_i.

The low half-power frequency is characterized by

$$\omega_1 = 1/C_c R_{\text{low}} \tag{12-104a}$$

and

$$f_1 = 1/2\pi C_c R_{\text{low}} \tag{12-104b}$$

Hence, we have

$$\frac{\mathbf{A}_{v\,\text{low}}}{\mathbf{A}_{v\text{mid}}} = \frac{1}{1 - jf_1/f} = \frac{1}{\sqrt{1 + (f_1/f)^2}}\, e^{j\tan^{-1} f_1/f} \tag{12-105}$$

This equation has the same form as Eq. 12-45 so the normalized low-frequency response is given by Figs. 12-11 and 12-12. We shall discuss the significance of these results in the next section.

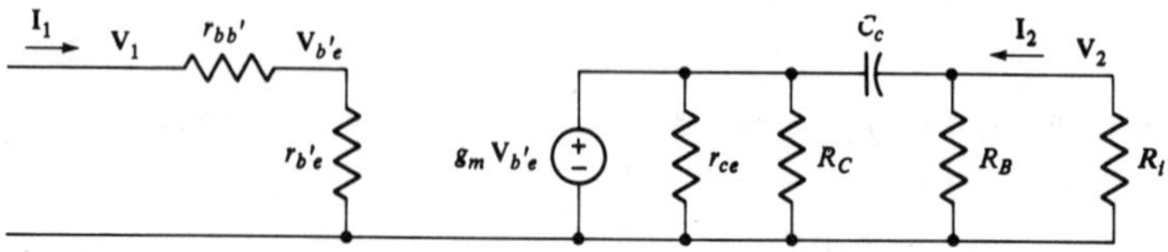

Figure 12-20. A low-frequency model for the amplifier of Fig. 12-14a.

The Direct Coupled Amplifier of Fig. 12-14b

Let us now turn our attention to the direct coupled amplifier of Fig. 12-14b. This amplifier was analyzed on a quiescent basis in Sec. 5-9. Here we shall discuss its small signal behavior. The diode can be modeled as a small resistance in series with a fixed direct voltage. Since such fixed voltages do not enter into the small signal model, the diode can be modeled as a small resistor. Thus, the model for the circuit is shown in Fig. 12-21a. This is the high-frequency model. The midfrequency model can be obtained from this one by removing C_{sh} and C_{sh2}. Note that there is no separate low-frequency model since the response is flat down to 0 Hz. In general, the resistance of the forward biased diode is very small, much smaller than $r_{bb'2}$. Hence, very accurate results can be obtained if we consider that r_D is zero. Consequently, the simplified model of Fig. 12-20b can be used in almost all instances. This model is essentially the same as the one used to analyze the amplifier of Fig. 12-14a in the mid- and high-frequency regions (i.e., Figs. 12-16b, 12-17b, and 12-19). The only difference is that R_B has been replaced by an open circuit. Thus, we can use all the previously developed mid- and high-frequency results with the proviso that $R_B \to \infty$.

Response in Terms of Current Gain

Most amplifier applications call for voltage gain, that is, the specifications are given in terms of the ratio of output voltage to input voltage. Thus, most designs are done in terms of the voltage gain. However, the transistor is a current operated device so it is also of interest to consider the current gain of the common-emitter circuit. Let us obtain the current gain of the amplifier of Fig. 12-14a. We can, in general, use the mid-, high-, and low-frequency models developed for the previous analysis.

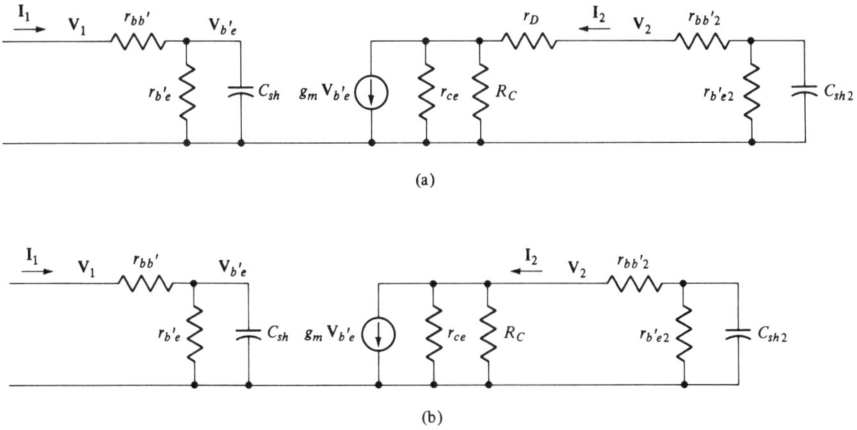

Figure 12-21. (a) A model for the amplifier of Fig. 12-14b. (b) Model obtained assuming that r_D is zero.

Midfrequency Region

We shall use the model of Fig. 12-16b to perform the midfrequency analysis. Thus, we have

$$\mathbf{V}_{b'e} = \mathbf{I}_1 r_{b'e} \tag{12-106a}$$

$$\mathbf{V}_2 = -g_m \mathbf{V}_{b'e} R_{\text{sh}} \tag{12-106b}$$

$$\mathbf{I}_2 = -\frac{\mathbf{V}_2}{R_i} = \frac{g_m \mathbf{V}_{b'e} R_{\text{sh}}}{R_i} \tag{12-106c}$$

Manipulating, we obtain

$$\mathbf{A}_{i\,\text{mid}} = \frac{\mathbf{I}_2}{\mathbf{I}_1} = \frac{g_m R_{\text{sh}} r_{b'e}}{R_i} \tag{12-107}$$

Note that $g_m r_{b'e} = \beta_0$ (see Eq. 6-131b). If R_i represents the input resistance of a second transistor stage, then

$$R_i = r_{bb'2} + r_{b'e2} \tag{12-108}$$

If the second stage is identical to the first one, then

$$\mathbf{A}_{i\,\text{mid}} = \frac{g_m R_{\text{sh}}}{1 + r_{bb'}/r_{b'e}}$$

In general, $r_{b'e} \gg r_{bb'}$ and, therefore, we can approximate this by

$$\mathbf{A}_{i\,\text{mid}} = g_m R_{\text{sh}}$$

Note that there is no minus sign associated with $\mathbf{A}_{i\,\text{mid}}$ because of the assumed positive direction of I_2.

High-Frequency Region

Let us compute the high-frequency response assuming that the input impedance to the next stage is purely resistive. If we use the model of Fig. 12-17a to analyze the circuit, we find that simplifications, which are very similar to those used in the derivation of the voltage gain, can be used and a model that is essentially the same as that of Fig. 12-17b results. However, the capacitance is now given by

$$C'_{\text{sh}} = C_{b'e} + C_{b'c}\left(1 + \frac{R_{\text{sh}}}{r_{b'e}} + g_m R_{\text{sh}}\right) \tag{12-109}$$

Using this model, we have

$$\mathbf{V}_{b'e} = \frac{\mathbf{I}_1 r_{b'e}}{1 + j\omega r_{b'e} C_{\text{sh}}} \tag{12-110a}$$

$$\mathbf{I}_2 = \frac{g_m \mathbf{V}_{b'e} R_{\text{sh}}}{R_i} \tag{12-110b}$$

where the parameters are defined in Eqs. 12-84 and 12-91. Manipulating, we obtain

$$\mathbf{A}_{i\,\text{high}} = \frac{g_m R_{\text{sh}} r_{b'e}/R_i}{1 + j\omega r_{b'e} C'_{\text{sh}}}$$

Normalizing with respect to $A_{i\,\text{mid}}$ yields

$$\frac{\mathbf{A}_{i\,\text{high}}}{\mathbf{A}_{i\,\text{mid}}} = \frac{1}{1 + j\omega r_{b'e} C'_{\text{sh}}} \tag{12-111}$$

The upper half-power frequencies are characterized by

$$\omega_2 = 1/r_{b'e} C'_{\text{sh}} \tag{12-112a}$$

or

$$f_2 = 1/2\pi r_{b'e} C'_{\text{sh}} \tag{12-112b}$$

$$\frac{\mathbf{A}_{i\,\text{high}}}{\mathbf{A}_{i\,\text{mid}}} = \frac{1}{1 + j\omega f/f_2} = \frac{1}{\sqrt{1 + (f/f_2)^2}} e^{-j\tan^{-1} f/f_2} \tag{12-113}$$

If we compare the half-power frequency of the voltage gain given by Eq. 12-93 with that given by Eq. 12-112, we see that they differ.

Now let us determine the current gain when we consider that the input impedance of the next stage is given by Fig. 12-18. Thus, we use the model of Fig. 12-19 with C_{sh} replaced by C'_{sh} (see Eq. 12-109). Then, $\mathbf{V}_{b'e}$ is given by Eq. 12-110a and the ratio $\mathbf{V}_i/\mathbf{V}_{b'e}$ is given by Eq. 12-95b. Also

$$\frac{\mathbf{I}_2}{\mathbf{V}_2} = \frac{-1}{r_{bb'2} + r_{b'e2}} \frac{1 + j\omega r_{b'e2} C_{\text{sh}2}}{1 + j\omega R_{p2} C_{\text{sh}2}} \tag{12-114}$$

where

$$\frac{1}{R_{p2}} = \frac{1}{r_{bb'2}} + \frac{1}{r_{b'e2}} \tag{12-115}$$

Manipulating and normalizing with respect to $\mathbf{A}_{i\,\text{mid}}$, we have

$$\frac{\mathbf{A}_{i\,\text{high}}}{\mathbf{A}_{i\,\text{mid}}} = \frac{(1 + j\omega r_{b'e2} C_{\text{sh}2})}{(1 + j\omega r_{b'e} C'_{\text{sh}})(1 + j\omega C_{\text{sh}2} R'_{\text{sh}})} \tag{12-116}$$

If the two stages are identical and we assume that $C_{\text{sh}2} \approx C'_{\text{sh}}$ then

$$\frac{\mathbf{A}_{i\,\text{high}}}{\mathbf{A}_{i\,\text{mid}}} = \frac{1}{(1 + j\omega R'_{\text{sh}} C_{\text{sh}2})} \tag{12-117}$$

Either of these relations can easily be plotted using the procedure discussed in Sec. 12-2.

Low-Frequency Region

In the low-frequency region, we use the model of Fig. 12-20. Then, proceeding as before, we have

$$\frac{\mathbf{A}_{i\,\text{low}}}{\mathbf{A}_{i\,\text{mid}}} = \frac{1}{1 - jf_1/f} \tag{12-118}$$

where f_1 is given by Eq. 12-104b.

Direct Coupled Amplifier

If we compute the current gain of the amplifier of Fig. 12-14b, the results are essentially the same as the ones just discussed except that $R_B \to \infty$, and the midfrequency response is flat down to 0 Hz.

Let us now consider an example that will illustrate the relations developed in this section. In the next section, we shall discuss the significance of these expressions.

Example

The transistor used in the amplifier of Fig. 12-14 has the following parameter values.

$$\begin{aligned} r_{bb'} &= 100 \text{ ohms} \\ r_{b'e} &= 900 \text{ ohms} \\ r_{b'c} &= 10^7 \text{ ohms} \\ r_{ce} &= 10^5 \text{ ohms} \\ C_{b'e} &= 100 \text{ pF} \\ C_{b'c} &= 3 \text{ pF} \\ g_m &= 50{,}000\ \mu\text{mho} \end{aligned}$$

The parameters of the circuit are

$$\begin{aligned} R_{B1} = R_{B2} &= 10{,}000 \text{ ohms} \\ R_C &= 5000 \text{ ohms} \end{aligned}$$

and, for the amplifier of Fig. 12-14a

$$C_C = 10\ \mu\text{F}$$

This is a large capacitance. We shall discuss its significance in the next section.

Compute $\mathbf{A}_{v\,\text{mid}}, f_2$ assuming a resistive load of 1000 ohms, then compute f_2 assuming an identical transistor load. Then compute f_1 for the circuit of Fig. 12-14a.

To obtain $\mathbf{A}_{v\,\text{mid}}$, we use Eq. 12-85. Therefore,

$$\mathbf{A}_{v\,\text{mid}} = -g_m R_{\text{sh}} \frac{r_{b'e}}{r_{b'e} r_{bb'}}$$

where

$$\frac{1}{R_{\text{sh}}} = \frac{1}{r_{ce}} + \frac{1}{R_C} + \frac{1}{R_B} + \frac{1}{R_i}$$

Hence,

$$\frac{1}{R_{\text{sh}}} = \frac{1}{10^5} + \frac{1}{5000} + \frac{1}{5000} + \frac{1}{1000}$$

$$R_{\text{sh}} = 709.2 \text{ ohms}$$

$$\mathbf{A}_{v\,\text{mid}} = -5 \times 10^{-2}(709.2)\frac{900}{900 \times 100} = 31.9$$

Now let us compute f_2 assuming a resistive load. From Eq. 12-93, we have

$$f_2 = 1/2\pi R_p C_{\text{sh}}$$

where

$$C_{\text{sh}} = C_{b'e} + C_{b'c}\left(1 + \frac{R_{\text{sh}}}{R_p} + g_m R_{\text{sh}}\right)$$

and

$$\frac{1}{R_p} = \frac{1}{r_{b'e}} + \frac{1}{r_{bb'}}$$

$$\frac{1}{R_p} = \frac{1}{900} + \frac{1}{100}$$

$$R_p = 90$$

Substituting, we obtain

$$C_{\text{sh}} = 100 + 3\left(1 + \frac{709.2}{90} + 5 \times 10^{-2} \times 709.2\right)$$

$$C_{\text{sh}} = 100 + 3(1 + 7.88 + 35.46) = 233.0 \text{ pF}$$

Hence,

$$f_2 = \frac{1}{2\pi \times 90 \times 233 \times 10^{-12}} = 7.589 \times 10^6 \text{ Hz} = 7.589 \text{ mHz}$$

Now let us consider that the amplifier drives an identical stage. We assume that Eq. 12-100 is a valid expression, then using Eq. 12-101, we have

$$f_2 = 1/2\pi C_{\text{sh}} R'_{\text{sh}}$$

where

$$R'_{\text{sh}} = \frac{r_{b'e2}(r_{bb'2} + R)}{r_{b'e2} + r_{bb'2} + R}$$

and

$$\frac{1}{R} = \frac{1}{r_{ce}} + \frac{1}{R_C} + \frac{1}{R_B} = \frac{1}{10^5} + \frac{1}{5000} + \frac{1}{5000}$$

$$R = 2439$$

$$R'_{\text{sh}} = \frac{900(100 + 2439)}{900 + 100 + 2439} = 664.5$$

Hence,

$$f_2 = 1/(2\pi \times 233 \times 10^{-12} \times 664.5) = 1.028 \times 10^6 \text{ Hz}$$

Note that this half-power frequency is considerably less than that calculated assuming a resistive load. This is because the capacitive component of the transistor's input admittance reduces the voltage gain at high frequencies

Now let us compute the lower half-power frequency. From Eq. 12-104, we have

$$f_1 = 1/2\pi C_c R_{\text{low}}$$

where

$$R_{\text{low}} = \frac{r_{ce}R_C}{r_{ce} + R_C} + \frac{R_B R_i}{R_B + R_i}$$

$$R_{\text{low}} = \frac{10^5 \times 5000}{10^5 + 5000} + \frac{5000 \times 1000}{5000 + 1000} = 4761.9 + 833.3 = 5595.2$$

Hence,

$$f_1 = 1/(2\pi \times 10 \times 10^{-6} \times 5595.2) = 2.84 \text{ Hz}$$

Now let us determine the validity of the approximations we have made. Relation 12-82 states $g_m \gg 1/r_{b'c}$. Let us verify this.

$$50{,}000 \times 10^{-6} \overset{?}{\gg} 1/10^7$$

$$5 \times 10^{-2} \gg 10^{-7}$$

This certainly is true.

Now let us verify Eqs. 12-88.

$$g_m \gg j\omega C_{b'c}$$

and

$$\frac{1}{R_{\text{sh}}}\left(\frac{1}{r_{bb'}} + \frac{1}{r_{b'e}}\right) \gg \omega^2 C_{b'e} C_{b'c}$$

We shall use the frequency $f = 10f_2$ (see the example of Sec. 12-3). Then, for the first expression

$$5 \times 10^{-2} \overset{?}{\gg} 2\pi \times 7.59 \times 10^7 \times 3 \times 10^{-12}$$

$$5 \times 10^{-2} \overset{?}{\gg} 0.143 \times 10^{-2}$$

Thus, the approximation is valid.

Now let us check the second expression.

$$\frac{1}{709.2}\left(\frac{1}{100} + \frac{1}{900}\right) \overset{?}{\gg} (2\pi \times 7.59 \times 10^7)^2 100 \times 10^{-12} \times 3 \times 10^{-12}$$

$$1.567 \times 10^{-5} \overset{?}{\gg} 6.83 \times 10^{-5}$$

Therefore, at $10f_2$, the expression is not true. On the other hand, if we consider the cascade of similar transistors, then $f_2 = 1.03 \times 10^6$ Hz. Now we have

$$1.567 \times 10^{-5} \overset{?}{\gg} (2\pi \times 1.03 \times 10^7)^2 100 \times 10^{-12} \times 3 \times 10^{-12}$$

$$1.567 \times 10^{-5} \gg 1.26 \times 10^{-6}$$

Hence, the approximation is quite accurate here. In general this is the practical case since we usually work with cascaded amplifiers.

Finally, let us check relation 12-98.

$$1 + g_m R_{\text{sh}} \gg \frac{R_{\text{sh}}}{R_p}$$

Now we have

$$36.46 \overset{?}{\gg} 7.88$$

This relation is fairly accurate. Actually we desire that $C_{\text{sh}2} \approx C_{\text{sh}}$. If $C_{\text{sh}2}$ is computed using Eq. 12-97 we obtain $C_{\text{sh}2} = 209.4$ pF. We computed $C_{\text{sh}} = 233$ pF. Hence, they are approximately equal (within 10%).

In the next section we shall discuss the significance of the results obtained in this one.

12-6. FACTORS AFFECTING THE FREQUENCY RESPONSE OF THE ONE-STAGE COMMON-EMITTER TRANSISTOR AMPLIFIER

Let us now discuss the significance of the results derived in the last section. In general, we shall see that the relation between the midband gain and the high-frequency response is a relatively complex one although, when suitable approximations are made, the results appear to be simple. As in the case of the FET, the low-frequency gain is essentially unrelated to these gains. If a direct coupled amplifier is used, then the low-frequency response is not a consideration since the midband amplification extends down to 0 Hz.

We shall start by considering the low-frequency response of the amplifier of Fig. 12-14a. After this we shall discuss the more important mid- and high-frequency response.

The lower half-power frequency is given by (see Eq. 12-104),

$$f_2 = 1/2\pi C_c R_{\text{low}} \tag{12-119}$$

where

$$R_{\text{low}} = \frac{r_{ce} R_C}{r_{ce} + R_C} + \frac{R_B R_i}{R_B + R_i} \tag{12-120}$$

In general, the value of R_{low} will be fixed by other considerations such as midfrequency gain and the location of the quiescent operating point so if we want to vary the lower half-power frequency, C_c must be varied. In particular, if we want to increase the low-frequency bandwidth, C_c must be increased. The value of R_{low} will be small, typically less than 1000 ohms. (This is in comparison to 10^6–10^7 ohms in a MOSFET circuit.) Thus, C_c must be very large if there is to be reasonable low-frequency response. This usually dictates the use of an electrolytic capacitor here. Electrolytic capacitors have large capacitance but relatively small leakage resistance (approximately 100 megohms). However, since the input of R_B in parallel with R_i is small, this presents no problem (see Sec. 12-4). Electrolytic capacitors *cannot* be fabricated within integrated circuits. Of course, if very low frequencies are to be amplified, or if we want to use integrated circuits, then a direct coupled amplifier should be used.

Now let us consider the mid- and high-frequency responses. We shall start with a discussion of the amplifier which drives a resistive load R_i. Then, we shall consider the more important case where the load is another transistor amplifier. The midband gain and upper half-power frequency are given by Eqs. 12-85 and 12-93. Thus, we have

$$\mathbf{A}_{v\,\mathrm{mid}} = -g_m R_{\mathrm{sh}} \frac{r_{b'e}}{r_{bb'} + r_{b'e}} \tag{12-121}$$

$$f_2 = 1/2\pi R_p C_{\mathrm{sh}} \tag{12-122}$$

where

$$\frac{1}{R_{\mathrm{sh}}} = \frac{1}{r_{ce}} + \frac{1}{R_C} + \frac{1}{R_B} + \frac{1}{R_i} \tag{12-123}$$

and

$$\frac{1}{R_p} = \frac{1}{r_{b'e}} + \frac{1}{r_{bb'}} \tag{12-124}$$

These quantities appear to be independent of each other. However this is not true. C_{sh} is dependent upon R_{sh} (see Eq. 12-91). As R_{sh} increases, so does C_{sh}. There is not a constant gain bandwidth product. However as R_{sh} is increased, increasing $\mathbf{A}_{v\,\mathrm{mid}}$, C_{sh} increases, decreasing f_2. Now let us consider cascaded amplifiers. In this case, we have (see Eq. 12-101). (Note the approximation discussed in conjunction with this equation.)

$$f_2 = 1/2\pi C_{\mathrm{sh}} R'_{\mathrm{sh}} \tag{12-125}$$

where

$$\frac{1}{R'_{\mathrm{sh}}} = \frac{1}{r_{b'e}} + \frac{1}{r_{bb'} + R} \tag{12-126}$$

and

$$\frac{1}{R} = \frac{1}{r_{ce}} + \frac{1}{R_C} + \frac{1}{R_B} \tag{12-127}$$

We have assumed here that the two stages are identical. In general, $R \gg r_{bb'}$, so that R'_{sh} can be considered to represent the parallel combination of r_{ce}, R_C, R_B, and $r_{b'e}$. Now consider R_{sh}. It represents the parallel combination of r_{ce}, R_C, R_B, and R_i. However,

$$R_i = r_{bb'} + r_{b'e}$$

and, in general, $r_{b'e} \gg r_{bb'}$. Thus, R_{sh} approximately represents the parallel combination of r_{ce}, R_C, R_B, and $r_{b'e}$. Hence,

$$R'_{\text{sh}} \simeq R_{\text{sh}} \tag{12-128}$$

Now, if we take the gain-bandwidth product, we have

$$|\mathbf{A}_{v\,\text{mid}}|\, f_2 = g_m \frac{R_{\text{sh}}}{R'_{\text{sh}}} \frac{1}{2\pi C_{\text{sh}}} \frac{r_{b'e}}{r_{bb'} + r_{b'e}}$$

Hence,

$$|\mathbf{A}_{v\,\text{mid}}|\, f_2 = \frac{g_m}{2\pi C_{\text{sh}}} \frac{r_{b'e}}{r_{bb'} + r_{b'e}} \tag{12-129}$$

Thus, a figure of merit for the transistor amplifier is the ratio of g_m/C_{sh}. Remember that C_{sh} is influenced by Miller effect, that is, it depends upon R_{sh} (see Eq. 12-91). Therefore, the gain bandwidth product is not constant but will increase as R_{sh} and, hence, $\mathbf{A}_{v\,\text{mid}}$ decrease. Note that the discussion of gain-bandwidth product applies equally well to either the direct coupled amplifier of Fig. 12-14b or to the *RC* coupled amplifier of Fig. 12-14a. Remember that, although this discussion is based upon some relatively weak approximations, it provides a general idea about the relation between gain and bandwidth. In a subsequent section we shall see how these cascaded amplifiers are designed.

12-7. BYPASS CAPACITORS

In Secs. 5-2, 5-3, and 5-8 we demonstrated that resistances inserted in series with the source or emitter leads can be used to provide gate bias for the FET and operating point stabilization for the FET common-source and common-emitter amplifiers. Such resistances must be bypassed (shunted) by capacitors if the circuit's gain is not to be substantially reduced. In this section we shall consider the effect of these bypassed resistances on the circuit's gain. In general, the bypassed capacitances incorporated in such circuits are so large that their use is precluded in integrated circuits. Since the capacitances are large, they essentially act as short circuits in the mid- and high-frequency ranges. Thus, the analysis performed in this section will be in the low-frequency range.

FET Source Impedance

Let us start by considering the normalized response of the common-source FET amplifier of Fig. 12-22a. The model for this circuit is given in Fig. 12-22b.

In general, in circuits of this type

$$R_d \ll R_g \tag{12-130}$$

Hence,

$$\mathbf{Z} = R_d \tag{12-131}$$

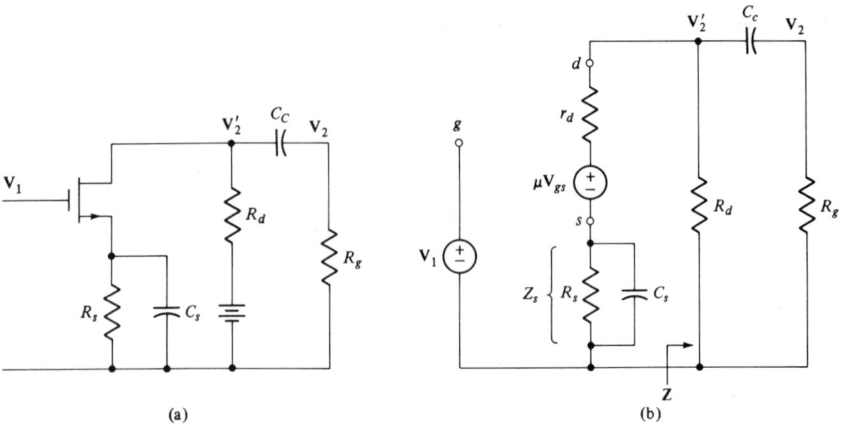

Figure 12-22. (a) A common-source FET amplifier with a source impedance. (b) A model for this amplifier.

We shall start by computing the gain $\mathbf{V}_2'/\mathbf{V}_1$, that is, the gain from input to drain. Using the analysis of Sec. 6-3, we have

$$\mathbf{A}_{v'\,\text{low}} = \frac{-\mu R_d}{r_d + R_d + (1+\mu)\mathbf{Z}_s} \tag{12-132}$$

where

$$\mathbf{Z}_s = \frac{R_s}{1 + j\omega R_s C_s} \tag{12-133}$$

Substituting and manipulating, we obtain

$$\mathbf{A}_{v'\,\text{low}} = \frac{-\mu R_d}{r_d + R_d}\,\frac{1}{1 + \dfrac{R_s(1+\mu)}{r_d + R_d}}\,\frac{1 + jR_sC_s}{1 + j\omega\dfrac{R_sC_s(r_d + R_d)}{r_d + R_d + R_s(1+\mu)}}$$

Note that $\mu = g_m r_d$ and that R_{sh} (see Eq. 12-31), represents the parallel combination of r_d, R_d, and R_g. Since $R_g \gg R_d$, then the parallel combination of R_d and r_d will approximately equal R_{sh}. Hence, using Eq. 12-32, we have

$$\frac{\mathbf{A}_{v\,\text{low}}}{\mathbf{A}_{v\,\text{mid}}} \frac{r_d + R_d}{r_d + R_d + R_s(1+\mu)}\,\frac{1 + j\omega R_sC_s}{1 + j\omega\dfrac{R_sC_s(r_d + R_d)}{r_d + R_d + R_s(1+\mu)}} \tag{12-134}$$

Note that, in the midfrequency region, $|\mathbf{A}_{v\,\text{low}}/\mathbf{A}_{v\,\text{mid}}| = 1$.

As the frequency decreases, this ratio does not approach zero. Its minimum value is given by

$$\left|\frac{\mathbf{A}_{v'\,\text{low}}}{\mathbf{A}_{v\,\text{mid}}}\right|_{\text{min}} = \frac{r_d + R_d}{r_d + R_d + R_s(1+\mu)} \tag{12-135}$$

We shall normalize the result. Let

$$f_{s1} = 1/2\pi R_s C_s \tag{12-136a}$$

and

$$f_{s2} = \frac{r_d + R_d + R_s(1+\mu)/(r_d + R_d)}{2\pi R_s C_s} = \left[\frac{r_d + R_d + R_s(1+\mu)}{r_d + R_d}\right] f_{s1} \tag{12-136b}$$

Note that $f_{s2} > f_{s1}$. Hence,

$$\frac{\mathbf{A}_{v'\,\text{low}}}{\mathbf{A}_{v\,\text{mid}}} = \frac{f_{s1}}{f_{s2}} \frac{1 + jf/f_{s1}}{1 + jf/f_{s2}} \tag{12-137}$$

A plot of this expression is shown in Fig. 12-23. Note that the phase angle is positive and approaches zero at sufficiently low or high frequencies.

Now let us obtain the frequency response of the entire stage. Since $R_g \gg R_d$, the output circuit consisting of C_c and R_g has no effect on V_2'. Also

$$\frac{\mathbf{V}_2}{\mathbf{V}_2'} = \frac{1}{1 - j\omega(1/R_g C_c)}$$

Since $R_g \gg R_d$, then $R_g \approx R_{\text{low}}$ (see Eq. 12-63). Hence,

$$\frac{V_2}{V_2'} = \frac{1}{1 - j(1/\omega R_{\text{low}} C_c)} = \frac{1}{1 - jf_1/f} \tag{12-138}$$

(see Eq. 12-45). Hence, for the overall amplifier

$$\frac{\mathbf{A}_{v\,\text{low}}}{\mathbf{A}_{v\,\text{mid}}} = \frac{f_{s1}}{f_{s2}} \frac{1 + jf/f_{s1}}{1 + jf/f_{s2}} \frac{1}{1 - jf_1/f} \tag{12-139}$$

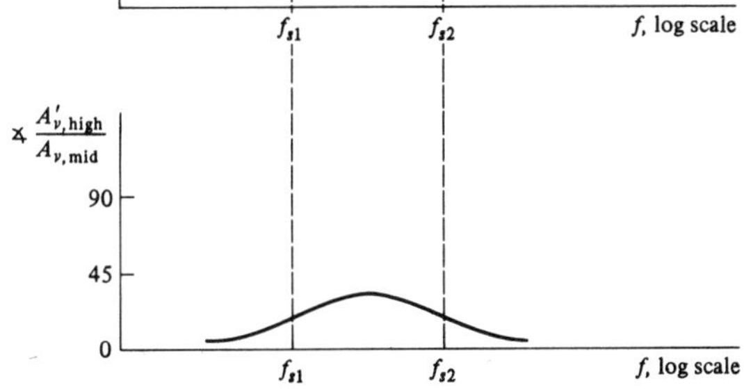

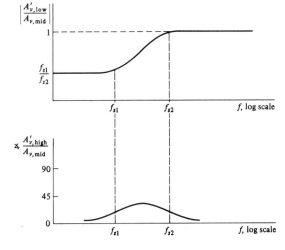

Figure 12-23. Amplitude and phase plots of $\mathbf{A}_{v\,\text{low}}/\mathbf{A}_{v\,\text{mid}}$ for a FET amplifier with a bypassed source resistance.

The magnitude of the response on a decibel basis is sketched in Fig. 12-24. Note that the shape of the curve can change somewhat depending upon the relative values of f_1 and f_{s1} and f_{s2}.

Transistor Emitter Impedance

Now let us consider the transistor circuit of Fig. 12-25a. A model for one stage of this amplifier is shown in Fig. 12-25b. Note that we have replaced the portion of the model consisting of the current generator $g_m V_{b'e}$ in parallel with r_{ce} by its Thévenins equivalent. Then, applying mesh analysis to the circuit, we obtain

$$\mathbf{V}_1 = (r_{bb'} + r_{b'e} + \mathbf{Z}_E)\mathbf{I}_1 + \mathbf{Z}_E\mathbf{I}'_2 \tag{12-140a}$$

$$g_m \mathbf{V}_{b'e} r_{ce} = \mathbf{Z}_E\mathbf{I}_1 + (r_{ce} + \mathbf{Z}_E + \mathbf{Z})\mathbf{I}'_2 \tag{12-140b}$$

where

$$\mathbf{V}_{b'e} = I_1 r_{b'e} \tag{12-140c}$$

and

$$\mathbf{Z}_E = \frac{R_E}{1 + j\omega C_E R_E} \tag{12-140d}$$

Substitution and manipulation yields

$$\frac{\mathbf{I}'_2}{\mathbf{V}_1} = \frac{g_m r_{ce} r_{b'e} - Z_E}{r_{ce}[r_{bb'} + r_{b'e} + \mathbf{Z}_E(1 + g_m r_{b'e})] + \mathbf{Z}(r_{bb'} + r_{b'e} + \mathbf{Z}_E) + \mathbf{Z}_E(r_{bb'} + r_{b'e})} \tag{12-141}$$

In general,

$$g_m r_{ce} r_{b'e} \gg |\mathbf{Z}_E| \tag{12-142a}$$

and

$$r_{ce}[r_{bb'} + r_{b'e} + \mathbf{Z}_E(1 + g_m r_{b'e})] \gg |\mathbf{Z}(r_{bb'} + r_{b'e} + Z_E) + \mathbf{Z}_E(r_{bb'} + r_{b'e})| \tag{12-142b}$$

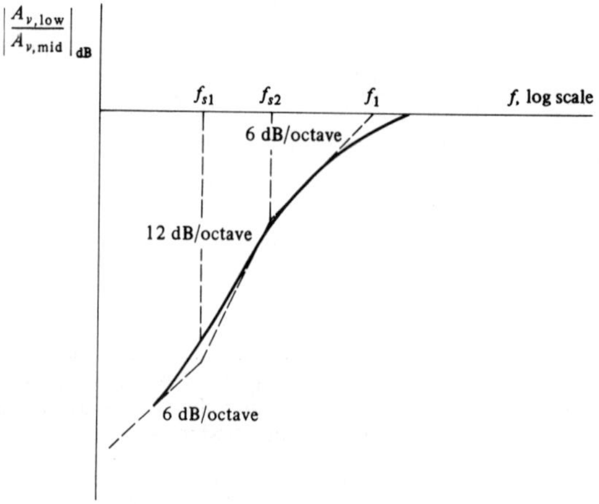

Figure 12-24. Typical low-frequency response of a *RC* coupled common-source FET amplifier with a source bypass capacitance. The asymptotes are shown dashed.

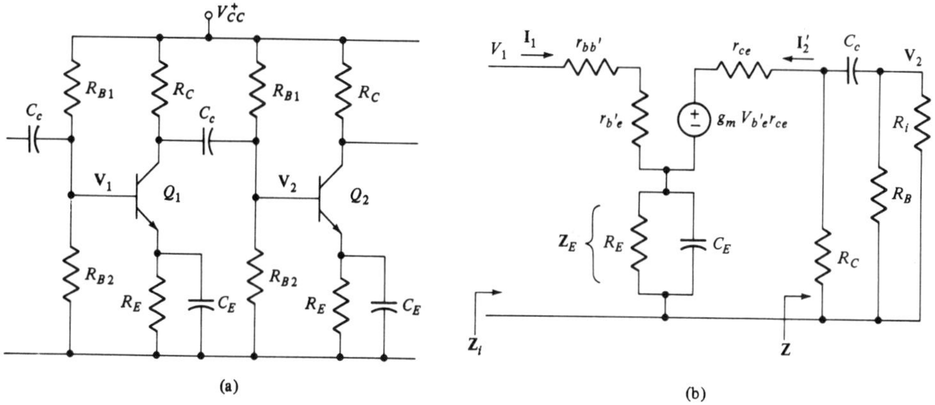

Figure 12-25. (a) A common-emitter amplifier with a bypassed emitter stabilization resistance. (b) Its model.

Hence, we have

$$\frac{\mathbf{I}_2'}{\mathbf{V}_1} = \frac{g_m r_{b'e}}{r_{bb'} + r_{b'e} + \mathbf{Z}_E(1 + g_m r_{b'e})}$$

Substituting Eq. 12-140d and manipulating, we have

$$\frac{\mathbf{I}_2'}{\mathbf{V}_1} = \frac{g_m r_{b'e}}{r_{bb'} + r_{b'e}} \frac{f_{E1}}{f_{E2}} \frac{1 + jf/f_{E1}}{1 + jf/f_{E2}} \tag{12-143}$$

where

$$f_{E1} = 1/2\pi R_E C_E \tag{12-144a}$$

and

$$f_{E2} = f_{E1}\left[1 + \frac{R_E(1 + g_m r_{b'e})}{r_{bb'} + r_{b'e}}\right] \tag{12-144b}$$

In general, $f_{E2} > f_{E1}$. If we solve for the ratio $\mathbf{V}_2/\mathbf{I}_2'$, we obtain

$$\frac{\mathbf{V}_2}{\mathbf{I}_2'} = -R_{\text{sh}}' \frac{1}{1 - j(1/\omega R_{\text{low}}' C_c)} \tag{12-145}$$

where

$$\frac{1}{R_{\text{sh}}'} = \frac{1}{R_C} + \frac{1}{R_B} + \frac{1}{R_i} \tag{12-146a}$$

and

$$R_{\text{low}}' = R_C + \frac{R_B R_i}{R_B + R_i} \tag{12-146b}$$

In general, $r_{ce} \gg R_c$. Comparing this with Eqs. 12-84, 12-103 ,and 12-104 yields

$$\frac{\mathbf{V}_2}{\mathbf{I}_2'} = -R_{\text{sh}} \frac{1}{1 - jf_1/f} \tag{12-147}$$

Hence, combining Eqs. 12-147 and 12-143, and normalizing with respect to $\mathbf{A}_{v\,\mathrm{mid}}$ (see Eq. 12-85), we get

$$\frac{\mathbf{A}_{v\,\mathrm{low}}}{\mathbf{A}_{v\,\mathrm{mid}}} = \frac{f_{E1}}{f_{E2}} \cdot \frac{1 + jf/f_{E1}}{1 + jf/f_{E2}} \cdot \frac{1}{1 + jf_1/f} \tag{12-148}$$

The curves of Figs. 12-23 and 12-14 characterize this response as well as that for the previously discussed FET amplifier.

We have made an approximation here. We have assumed that the input impedance of the next stage was a pure resistance, equal to the midband resistance R_i. Actually, when there is a bypassed emitter resistance, this will not be the case in the *low*-frequency region. For instance, let us obtain $\mathbf{Z}_i$, the input impedance of this stage. Solving Eqs. 12-140 for $\mathbf{V}_1/\mathbf{I}_1$ and using inequality 12-142, we obtain

$$\mathbf{Z}_i = r_{bb'} + r_{b'e} + \mathbf{Z}_E(1 + g_m r_{b'e}) \tag{12-149}$$

In general, $g_m r_{b'e}$ is a large number (approximately 100). Note that $g_m r_{b'e} = \beta_0$ (see Eq. 6-141). Hence, $|\mathbf{Z}_i|$ can be appreciably larger than $R_i = r_{bb'} + r_{b'e}$ and $|\mathbf{Z}_i|$ can become very large in the low-frequency region. We have ignored this in our analysis but any error introduced is of the safe side since (see Fig. 12-25a) if the input impedance of Q_2 is greater than R_i, then $|\mathbf{V}_2|$ will be larger than we have calculated. Thus, if we use these equations in design, the resultant amplifier will have better low-frequency response than calculated. Let us consider a numerical example for the transistor amplifier.

Example

The transistor used in the amplifier of Fig. 12-25 has the following parameter values.

$$r_{bb'} = 100 \text{ ohms}$$
$$r_{b'e} = 900 \text{ ohms}$$
$$r_{b'c} = 10^7 \text{ ohms}$$
$$r_{ce} = 5 \times 10^5 \text{ ohms}$$
$$C_{b'e} = 100 \text{ pF}$$
$$C_{b'c} = 3 \text{ pF}$$
$$g_m = 50{,}000\ \mu\text{mhos}$$

The parameters of the circuit are

$$R_{B1} = R_{B2} = 10{,}000 \text{ ohms}$$
$$R_C = 5000 \text{ ohms}$$
$$R_E = 1000 \text{ ohms}$$
$$C_c = 10\ \mu\text{F}$$
$$C_E = 100\ \mu\text{F}$$

Find $\mathbf{A}_{v\,\mathrm{mid}}$, f_1, f_{E1}, and f_{E2}.

The parameter and element values (with the exception of R_E and C_E) are the same as those used in the example of Sec. 12-5. Hence,

$$\mathbf{A}_{v\,\text{mid}} = 31.9$$

$$R_{\text{low}} = 5595.2$$

and

$$f_1 = 2.84 \text{ Hz}$$

Now

$$f_{E1} = 1/2\pi R_E C_E$$

$$f_{E1} = 1/(2\pi \times 1000 \times 100 \times 10^{-6}) = 1.59 \text{ Hz}$$

$$f_{E2} = \left[1 + \frac{R_E(1 + g_m r_{b'e})}{r_{bb'} + r_{b'e}}\right] f_{E1}$$

$$f_{E2} = \left[1 + \frac{1000(5 \times 10^{-2} \times 900)}{900 + 100}\right](1.59) = (46)(1.59) = 73.1 \text{ Hz}$$

Note that the low-frequency response will start to fall off at 73.1 Hz (see Fig. 12-24). Actually, it will be about 3 dB down at this frequency. Thus, if very good low-frequency response is desired, very large emitter bypass capacitances are required. Fortunately, electrolytic capacitances can be used here. In general, emitter (or source in the case of FET amplifiers) bypass capacitors *cannot* be included within an integrated circuit chip. If stabilization is required with integrated circuits, then other forms of bias stabilization should be used (see Sec. 5-8).

Let us verify that the inequalities 12-142 are satisfied. These are

$$g_m r_{ce} \gg |\mathbf{Z}_E|$$

and

$$r_{ce}[r_{bb'} + r_{b'e} + Z_E(1 + g_m r_{ce})] \gg |Z(r_{bb'} + r_{b'e} + Z_E) + Z_E(r_{bb'} + r_{b'e})|$$

To verify the first one, we shall use the maximum value of $|\mathbf{Z}_E|$, which is R_E.

$$50{,}000 \times 10^{-6} \times 500{,}000 \overset{?}{\gg} 1000$$

$$25{,}000 \overset{?}{\gg} 1000$$

Thus, this is true. To verify the second inequality, we shall use the minimum value of $\mathbf{Z}_E$, which is zero, on the left-hand side of the inequality and its maximum value on the right-hand side. Similarly, we shall use the maximum value of $\mathbf{Z} = R_C$. Hence,

$$500{,}000[100 + 900] \overset{?}{\gg} |\,5000(100 + 900 + 1000) + 1000(100 + 900)|$$

$$5 \times 10^8 \overset{?}{\gg} 1.1 \times 10^7$$

This is also true. Therefore, both inequalities are valid and the approximations made using them are accurate.

Let us compute the input impedance using Eq. 12-149. In the midfrequency region

$$\mathbf{Z}_i = r_{bb'} + r_{b'e} = 100 + 900 = 1000 \text{ ohms}$$

At very low frequencies, $\mathbf{Z}_E = 1000$ ohms. Hence,

$$\begin{aligned}\mathbf{Z}_i &= r_{bb'} + r_{b'e} + (1 + g_m r_{b'e})\mathbf{Z}_E \\ &= 100 + 900 + 1000(1 + 5 \times 10^{-2} \times 900) = 47000 \text{ ohms}\end{aligned}$$

Thus, the emitter impedance can have a large effect on Z_i. Of course, the purpose of the bypass capacitance is to keep $|\mathbf{Z}_E|$ small so that these effects do not occur for any of the input frequencies.

12-8. SOURCE FOLLOWER AMPLIFIER

In Sec. 6-11 we discussed the source follower amplifier and demonstrated that it had an extremely high input impedance. In particular, its input capacitance was extremely small. Some uses for this amplifier were discussed in that section. In subsequent sections we shall discuss other applications for the common drain or source follower amplifier. Now we shall determine its frequency response. Much of this analysis was performed in Sec. 6-11 and we shall use those results here. A typical source follower amplifier and its model are shown in Fig. 12-26. Note that we have included a capacitor C_i in the model. This accounts for the input capacitance of the next stage, and so forth. As in Sec. 12-3, we can break the analysis into three regions. In the midfrequency region the parasitic capacitances C_{gd}, C_{ds}, C_{gs}, and C_i can all be considered to be open circuits while C_c can be considered to be a short circuit. In the high-frequency region, C_c can be ignored, but the parasitic capacitances must be considered. Similarly, in the low-frequency region, the parasitic capacitance can be ignored while the coupling capacitance must be considered.

Midfrequency Region

In the midfrequency, we have (see Eq. 6-117a),

$$\mathbf{A}_{v\,\text{mid}} = g_m R_{\text{shs}} \tag{12-150}$$

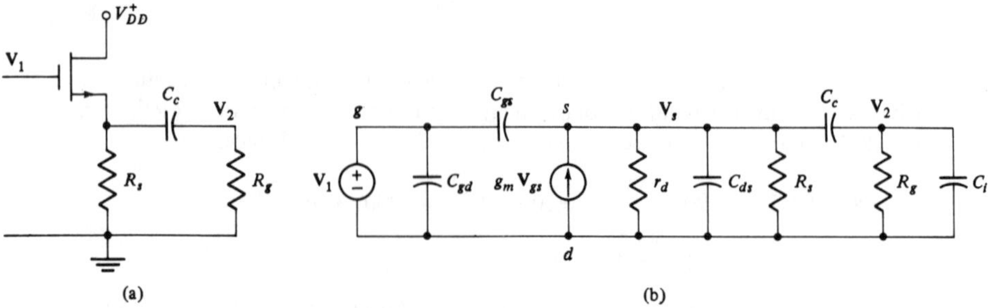

Figure 12-26. (a) A source follower amplifier. (b) A model for this amplifier.

where

$$\frac{1}{R_{\text{shs}}} = g_m + \frac{1}{r_d} + \frac{1}{R_s} + \frac{1}{R_g} \tag{12-151}$$

Note that R_{shs} represents the parallel combination of r_d, R_s, R_g, and a ficticious resistance $1/g_m$. Thus,

$$R_{\text{shs}} < \frac{1}{g_m} \tag{12-152}$$

so that the gain will be less than unity. In general, we want the gain to be as close to unity as possible so we usually design the circuit so that

$$g_m \gg \frac{1}{r_d} + \frac{1}{R_s} + \frac{1}{R_g} \tag{12-153}$$

High-Frequency Region

The high-frequency gain is given by (see Eq. 6-116)

$$\mathbf{A}_{v\,\text{high}} = \frac{g_m + j\omega C_{gs}}{(1/R_{\text{shs}}) + j\omega(C_{gs} + C_{gd} + C_i)} \tag{12-154}$$

In general,

$$g_m \gg \omega C_{gs} \tag{12-155}$$

over frequencies of interest. Again, if we omit the $j\omega C_{gs}$ term from the numerator, we are ignoring the direct transmission component (see Sec. 12-3). Then, using relation 12-155, and manipulating, we obtain

$$\frac{\mathbf{A}_{v\,\text{high}}}{\mathbf{A}_{v\,\text{mid}}} = \frac{1}{1 + jf/f_2} \tag{12-156}$$

where

$$f_2 = 1/2\pi R_{\text{shs}} C_{\text{shs}} \tag{12-157a}$$

and

$$C_{\text{shs}} = C_{gs} + C_{ds} + C_i \tag{12-157b}$$

Thus, $\mathbf{A}_{v\,\text{high}}/\mathbf{A}_{v\,\text{mid}}$ has the same form as Eq. 12-39 for the common-source amplifier.

Low-Frequency Region

In the low-frequency region, an analysis similar to ones that we have used before yields

$$\frac{\mathbf{A}_{v\,\text{low}}}{\mathbf{A}_{v\,\text{mid}}} = \frac{1}{1 + jf_1/f} \tag{12-158}$$

where

$$f_1 = 1/2\pi C_c R_{\text{low}\,s} \tag{12-159a}$$

and

$$R_{\text{low}\,s} = R_g + \frac{1}{g_m + (1/r_d) + (1/R_s)} \tag{12-159b}$$

Again, this has the same form as $\mathbf{A}_{v\,\text{low}}/\mathbf{A}_{v\,\text{mid}}$ for the common-source amplifier (see Eq. 12-45). Let us now illustrate these results with a numerical example.

Example

The FET used in the amplifier of Fig. 12-26c has the following parameter values.

$$g_m = 10{,}000\ \mu\text{mhos}$$
$$r_d = 500{,}000\ \text{ohms}$$
$$C_{gd} = 0.25\ \text{pF}$$
$$C_{gs} = 3\ \text{pF}$$
$$C_{ds} = 1.5\ \text{pF}$$

The elements of the circuit are

$$R_s = 10{,}000\ \text{ohms}$$
$$R_g = 10^6\ \text{ohms}$$
$$C_c = 0.01\ \mu\text{F}$$

Let us assume that $C_i = 27.5$ pF. (This value is used so that we can compare the results with the example of Sec. 12-3.) Find the values of $\mathbf{A}_{v\,\text{mid}}$, f_1, and f_2.

From Eqs. 12-150 and 12-151, we have

$$\mathbf{A}_{v\,\text{mid}} = g_m R_{\text{shs}}$$

$$\frac{1}{R_{\text{shs}}} = g_m + \frac{1}{r_d} + \frac{1}{R_s} + \frac{1}{R_g} = 10{,}000 \times 10^{-6} + \frac{1}{500{,}000} + \frac{1}{10{,}000} + \frac{1}{10^6}$$

$$R_{\text{shs}} = 98.98\ \text{ohms}$$

$$\mathbf{A}_{v\,\text{mid}} = 10^{-2} \times 98.98 = 0.9898$$

From Eqs. 12-156 and 12-157

$$f_2 = 1/2\pi C_{\text{shs}} R_{\text{shs}}$$

$$C_{\text{shs}} = C_{gs} + C_{ds} + C_i = 3 + 1.5 + 27.5 = 32\ \text{pF}$$

$$f_2 = \frac{1}{2\pi \times 32 \times 10^{-12} \times 98.98} = 5.025 \times 10^7\ \text{Hz}$$

Now let us calculate f_1. Using Eq. 12-159, we have

$$f_1 = 1/2\pi C_c R_{\text{low}\,s}$$

$$R_{\text{low}\,s} = R_g + \frac{1}{g_m + (1/r_d) + (1/R_s)} = 10^6 + \frac{1}{10^{-2} + (1/500{,}000) + (1/10{,}000)}$$

$$= 10^6 + 99$$

$$R_{\text{low}\,s} \simeq 10^6 \text{ ohms}$$

In general,

$$R_{\text{low}\,s} \simeq R_g$$

Thus,

$$f_1 = 1/(2\pi \times 0.01 \times 10^{-6} \times 10^6) = 15.9 \text{ Hz}$$

Let us compare the results of this example with those of the example of Sec. 12-3 which used the same FET and comparable parameter values. We shall start by discussing the high-frequency region. There we had $f_2 = 5.59 \times 10^5$ Hz. Thus, the source follower has an upper half-power frequency which is almost 100 times as high as that of the common-source amplifier. Actually, this should be expected since the midband gain is smaller. When we consider cascaded amplifier stages, we shall see how the source follower, with its very low input capacitance can be used to improve the frequency response of cascaded stages. We shall see that this is true even though the gain of the source follower is less than unity. Note that the low-frequency response of the source follower is essentially the same as that for the common-source amplifier.

We can use direct coupling between the source follower and a subsequent stage. In this case, the results can be modified as discussed in Sec. 12-3.

In the example of this section we used $R_s = 10{,}000$ ohms so that the results could be compared with those of Sec. 12-3. Actually, a smaller value of R_s could be used without substantially changing the results.

The direct voltage across R_s produces a bias which may be undesirable. (Actually, it may be used to offset positive input bias if the source follower is used in a direct coupled cascade.) If it is desirable to eliminate the effects of such bias, then the circuit of Fig. 6-18 can be used. Note that (see Eq. 6-123) the impedance R_G will act as a very high impedance.

12-9. EMITTER FOLLOWER AMPLIFIER

Now let us consider the gain of the emitter follower amplifier. We shall see that many of the ideas of the last section are applicable here. A typical emitter follower amplifier and its model are shown in Fig. 12-27. Again, in general, we can analyze the low-, mid-, and high-frequency regions separately. In the low- and midfrequency regions, $\mathbf{Z}_i$, the input impedance of the next stage, can be considered to be purely resistive. In the high-frequency region we shall assume that it is both resistive and of the form given by Fig. 12-18.

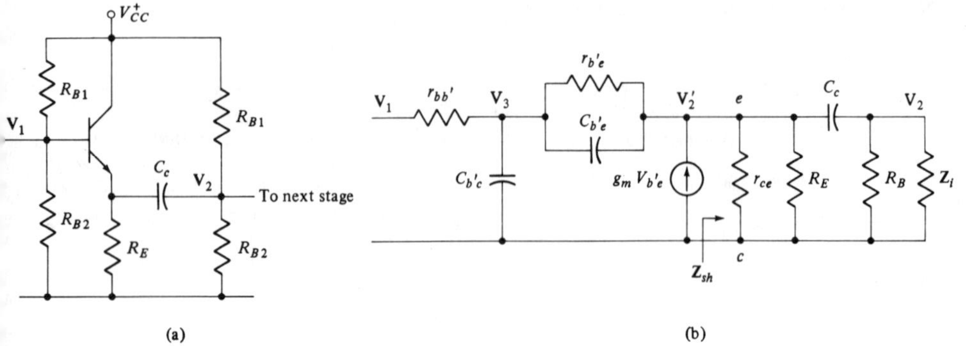

Figure 12-27. (a) An emitter follower amplifier. (b) Its model.

Midfrequency Region

If we analyze the circuit of Fig. 12-27, assuming that C_c is a short circuit, and that $C_{b'c}$ and $C_{b'e}$ are open circuit, we obtain

$$\mathbf{A}_{v\,\text{mid}} = \frac{g_m + 1/r_{b'e}}{g_m + (1/R_{\text{sh}})(1 + r_{bb'}/r_{b'e}) + 1/r_{b'e}} \tag{12-160}$$

where

$$\frac{1}{R_{\text{sh}}} = \frac{1}{r_{ce}} + \frac{1}{R_E} + \frac{1}{R_B} + \frac{1}{R_i} \tag{12-161}$$

In general, g_m for transistors is high so that

$$g_m \gg \frac{1}{r_{b'e}} \tag{12-162}$$

Thus, Eq. 12-160 reduces to

$$\mathbf{A}_{v\,\text{mid}} = \frac{g_m}{g_m + (1/R_{\text{sh}})(1 + r_{bb'}/r_{b'e})} \tag{12-163}$$

Often,

$$g_m \gg \frac{1}{R_{\text{sh}}}\left(1 + \frac{r_{bb'}}{r_{b'e}}\right) \tag{12-164}$$

in which case

$$\mathbf{A}_{v\,\text{mid}} \simeq 1 \tag{12-165}$$

High-Frequency Region

For the high-frequency model we assume that C_c is a short circuit. We also assume that $\mathbf{Z}_i = R_i$, a pure resistance. Analysis of this circuit yields

$$\mathbf{A}_{v\,\text{high}} = \frac{g_m + \dfrac{1}{r_{b'e}} + j\omega C_{b'e}}{g_m + \dfrac{1}{r_{b'e}} + \dfrac{1}{R_{\text{sh}}}\left(1 + \dfrac{r_{bb'}}{r_{b'e}}\right) - \omega^2 C_{b'e} C_{b'c} r_{bb'} + j\omega\left[C_{b'e}\left(1 + \dfrac{r_{bb'}}{R_{\text{sh}}}\right) + C_{b'c} r_{bb'}\left(g_m + \dfrac{1}{r_{b'e}} + \dfrac{1}{R_{\text{sh}}}\right)\right]} \tag{12-166}$$

Let us assume that, at all frequencies of interest

$$g_m \gg \left|\frac{1}{r_{b'e}} + j\omega C_{b'e}\right| \tag{12-167a}$$

and

$$g_m + \frac{1}{R_{\text{sh}}}\left(1 + \frac{r_{bb'}}{r_{b'e}}\right) \gg \omega^2 C_{b'e} C_{b'c} r_{bb'} \tag{12-167b}$$

Then, we have

$$\mathbf{A}_{v\,\text{high}} = \frac{g_m}{g_m + \dfrac{1}{r_{b'e}} + \dfrac{1}{R_{\text{sh}}}\left(1 + \dfrac{r_{bb'}}{r_{b'e}}\right) + j\omega\left[C_{b'e}\left(1 + \dfrac{r_{bb'}}{R_{\text{sh}}}\right) + C_{b'c} r_{bb'}\left(g_m + \dfrac{1}{r_{b'e}} + \dfrac{1}{R_{\text{sh}}}\right)\right]} \tag{12-168}$$

Normalization yields

$$\frac{\mathbf{A}_{v\,\text{high}}}{\mathbf{A}_{v\,\text{mid}}} = \frac{1}{1 + jf/f_2} \tag{12-169}$$

where

$$f_2 = 1/2\pi R_{\text{sh}E} C_{\text{sh}E} \tag{12-170}$$

and

$$\frac{1}{R_{\text{sh}E}} = g_m + \frac{1}{r_{b'e}} + \frac{1}{R_{\text{sh}}}\left(1 + \frac{r_{bb'}}{r_{b'e}}\right) \tag{12-171a}$$

$$C_{\text{sh}E} = C_{b'e}\left(1 + \frac{r_{bb'}}{R_{\text{sh}}}\right) + C_{b'c} r_{bb'}\left(g_m + \frac{1}{r_{b'e}} + \frac{1}{R_{\text{sh}}}\right) \tag{12-171b}$$

The following approximations are useful at times. If

$$g_m \gg \frac{1}{r_{b'e}} + \frac{1}{R_{sh}}\left(1 + \frac{r_{bb'}}{r_{b'e}}\right) \tag{12-172a}$$

$$1 \gg \frac{r_{bb'}}{R_{sh}} \tag{12-172b}$$

$$g_m \gg \frac{1}{r_{b'e}} + \frac{1}{R_{sh}} \tag{12-172c}$$

then

$$R_{shE} = \frac{1}{g_m} \tag{12-173a}$$

$$C_{shE} = C_{b'e} + C_{b'c}\, g_m r_{bb'} \tag{12-173b}$$

Now let us consider the voltage gain when the load is a common-emitter amplifier (see Fig. 12-18). Now we can still use Eq. 12-168 to obtain the gain but R_{sh} must be replaced by $\mathbf{Z}_{sh}$ where

$$\mathbf{Z}_{sh} = \frac{R_{sh}(1 + j\omega C_{sh2} R_{p2})}{1 + j\omega C_{sh2}\dfrac{r_{b'e2}(r_{bb'2} + R)}{r_{b'e2} + r_{bb'2} + R}} \tag{12-174}$$

(see Eqs. 12-95b, 12-95c, and 12-95d). This equation is tedious to manipulate. At times, the following approximations are valid over the frequencies of interest.

$$g_m \gg \left|\frac{1}{\mathbf{Z}_{sh}}\left(1 + \frac{r_{bb'}}{r_{b'e}}\right)\right| \tag{12-175a}$$

$$g_m \gg \left|\frac{1}{r_{b'e}} + \frac{1}{\mathbf{Z}_{sh}}\right| \tag{12-175b}$$

$$1 \gg \left|\frac{r_{bb'}}{\mathbf{Z}_{sh}}\right| \tag{12-175c}$$

In this case, the expression for the normalized gain reduces to Eq. 12-169 where R_{shE} and C_{shE} are approximately given by Eqs. 12-173a and 12-173b, respectively.

Low-Frequency Region

Usually in the low-frequency region $g_m \gg 1/\mathbf{Z}_{sh}$ (see Fig. 12-27b). In this case the normalized low-frequency response is given by

$$\frac{\mathbf{A}_{v\,\text{low}}}{\mathbf{A}_{v\,\text{mid}}} = \frac{1}{1 + jf_1/f} \tag{12-176}$$

where

$$f_1 = 1/2\pi C_c R_{\text{low}\,E} \tag{12-177}$$

$$\frac{1}{R_{\text{low}\,E}} = \frac{1}{R_B} + \frac{1}{R_i} \tag{12-178}$$

(we assume that $g_m \gg 1R_{\text{low}\,E}$). If response down to very low frequency is desired, or when integrated circuit amplifiers are fabricated, direct coupled amplifiers can be used.

Example

The transistor used in the amplifier of Fig. 12-27 has the following parameter values.

$$\begin{aligned} r_{bb'} &= 100 \text{ ohms} \\ r_{b'e} &= 900 \text{ ohms} \\ r_{b'c} &= 10^7 \text{ ohms} \\ r_{ce} &= 10^5 \text{ ohms} \\ C_{b'e} &= 100 \text{ pF} \\ C_{b'c} &= 3 \text{ pF} \\ g_m &= 50{,}000\ \mu\text{mho} \end{aligned}$$

The elements of the circuit are

$$\begin{aligned} R_{B1} = R_{B2} &= 10{,}000 \text{ ohms} \\ R_E &= 1000 \text{ ohms} \\ C_c &= 10\ \mu\text{F} \end{aligned}$$

Compute $\mathbf{A}_{v\,\text{mid}}$, f_2, assuming a load of 1000 ohms, f_2, assuming a common-emitter transistor whose input impedance is that calculated in the example of Sec. 11-5, and f_1.

Let us start by computing $\mathbf{A}_{v\,\text{mid}}$ using Eq. 12-160 and then we shall verify the approximate relations of Eqs. 12-163 and 12-165.

$$\mathbf{A}_{v\,\text{mid}} = \frac{g_m + 1/r_{b'e}}{g_m + (1/R_{\text{sh}})(1 + r_{bb'}/r_{b'e}) + 1/r_{b'e}}$$

where $1/R_{\text{sh}}$ is given by Eq. 12-161 as

$$\frac{1}{R_{\text{sh}}} = \frac{1}{100{,}000} + \frac{1}{1000} + \frac{1}{5000} + \frac{1}{1000}$$

$$R_{\text{sh}} = 452.5 \text{ ohms}$$

$$\mathbf{A}_{v\,\text{mid}} = \frac{5 \times 10^{-2} + 1/900}{5 \times 10^{-2} + (1/452.5)(1 + 100/900) + 1/900} = \frac{0.05 + 0.0011}{0.05 + 0.00246 + 0.0011}$$

$$= 0.954$$

If we use Eq. 12-163, we have

$$\mathbf{A}_{v\,\mathrm{mid}} = \frac{0.05}{0.05 + 0.00246} = 0.953$$

Thus, the result is very accurate. Note that even Eq. 12-165 is a good approximation here.

Now let us compute the upper half-power frequency assuming a resisitive load. Then, using Eqs. 12-170 and 12-171, we obtain

$$\frac{1}{R_{\mathrm{sh}E}} = g_m + \frac{1}{r_{b'e}} + \frac{1}{R_{\mathrm{sh}}}\left(1 + \frac{r_{bb'}}{r_{b'c}}\right) = 0.05 + \frac{1}{900} + \frac{1}{542.5}\left(1 + \frac{100}{900}\right)$$

$$R_{\mathrm{sh}E} = 18.667$$

$$C_{\mathrm{sh}E} = C_{b'e}\left(1 + \frac{r_{bb'}}{R_{\mathrm{sh}}}\right) + C_{b'c}r_{bb'}\left(g_m + \frac{1}{r_{b'e}} + \frac{1}{R_{\mathrm{sh}}}\right)$$

$$C_{\mathrm{sh}E} = 100\left(1 + \frac{100}{452.5}\right) + 3(100)\left(0.05 + \frac{1}{900} + \frac{1}{452.5}\right) = 138 \text{ pF}$$

Then,

$$f_2 = 1/(2\pi \times 18.667 \times 138 \times 10^{-12}) = 6.17 \times 10^7 \text{ Hz}$$

Note that this frequency is approximately 10 times greater than that for the corresponding common-emitter amplifier whose gain was calculated in the example of Sec. 12-5. Of course, the midband gain of the emitter follower that we are considering here is much less.

Now let us consider that the amplifier drives a common-emitter amplifier. Then, the "load" impedance Z_i will be of the form of Fig. 12-18 with $r_{bb'2} = 100$ ohms, $r_{b'e2} = 900$ ohms and the capacitance is given by $C_{\mathrm{sh}2} \simeq 233$ pF. These are the values used in the example of Sec. 12-5. As long as Eqs. 12-175 are satisfied, the value of f_2 calculated for the resistive load will approximately apply here also. In this case,

$$\mathbf{Z}_i = 100 + \frac{900}{1 + j\omega 900(233 \times 10^{-12})}$$

The minimum value that $|\mathbf{Z}_i|$ can have is 100. Using this value, Eqs. 12-175a and 12-175b yield

$$0.05 \overset{?}{\gg} \frac{1}{100}\left(1 + \frac{100}{900}\right) = 0.011$$

and

$$0.5 \overset{?}{\gg} \frac{1}{900} + \frac{1}{100} = 0.011$$

These are only fair approximations. We shall see that the value of f_2 used previously will also be somewhat in error. We can use the calculated value of f_2 in Eq. 12-169 and obtain accurate results if the maximum value of f is limited. For instance, if we want $|\mathbf{Z}| \geqq 200$, (i.e., $10g_m$) then $f \leqq 4.3 \times 10^6$ Hz. This is much less than the value of f_2 that we just calculated for the resistive load. However, Eq. 12-169 can be used providing that we restrict f to less than 4.3×10^6 Hz. Usually emitter follower amplifiers are cascaded with common-emitter amplifiers. The high-frequency bandwidth of the common-emitter amplifier will, in general, be very much less than that of the source follower. In such cases, the useful range of frequencies is determined by the common-emitter stages and so Eq. 12-169 can be used to characterize the response of the emitter follower over most frequencies of interest.

Now let us obtain f_1. Using Eqs. 12-177 and 12-178, we have

$$R_{\text{low}\,E} = \frac{R_B R_i}{R_B + R_i} = \frac{5000(1000)}{5000 + 1000} = 833 \text{ ohms}$$

$$f_1 = \frac{1}{2\pi \times 10 \times 10^{-6} \times 833} = 19.1 \text{ Hz}$$

Emitter Follower Input Admittance

Let us compute the input admittance of the common-collector (emitter follower) amplifier (see Fig. 12-28). Proceeding as in Sec. 6-14, (for the common-emitter amplifier) we obtain

$$\mathbf{Z}_i = r_{bb'} + Z_i'$$

where

$$\mathbf{Y}_1' = \frac{1}{\mathbf{Z}_i'} = \frac{1 - A_v'}{r_{b'e}} + j\omega C_{b'c} + C_{b'e}(1 - A_v') \qquad (12\text{-}179)$$

and

$$\mathbf{A}_v' = \frac{V_2'}{V_3} \qquad (12\text{-}180)$$

If we are in the midband region, then

$$\mathbf{A}_v' = g_m R_{\text{sh}}$$

Note that, as we have discussed in the example, the bandwidth of the emitter follower is often much greater than that of the overall amplifier. In such cases, all frequencies of interest will lie within the *emitter follower's* midband region and the input admittance will be represented by Fig. 12-28 over all frequencies of interest. Note that the input

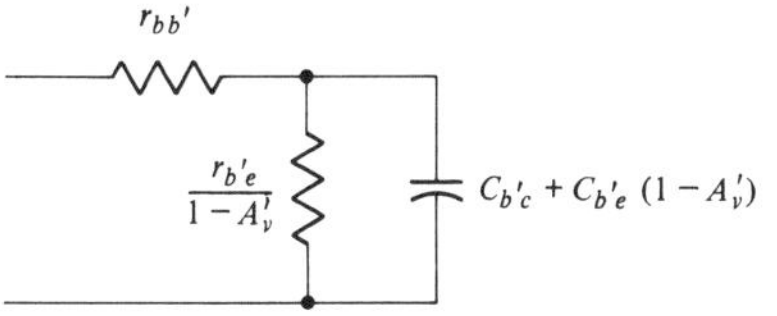

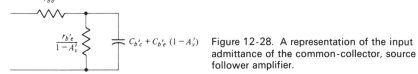

Figure 12-28. A representation of the input admittance of the common-collector, source follower amplifier.

impedance of the emitter follower will be much higher than that of a common-emitter amplifier. For instance, for the previous example,

$$\frac{r_{b'e}}{1 - A_v} = \frac{900}{1 - 0.954} = 19565$$

Thus, the low-frequency input resistance is

$$r_{bb'} + \frac{r_{b'e}}{1 - A_v} = 19665 \text{ ohms}$$

which is much greater than that of the common-emitter amplifier (i.e., 1000 ohms). The "input" capacitance is given by

$$C_{b'c} + C_{b'e}(1 - A_v) = 3 + 100(1 - 0.954) = 7.6 \text{ pF}$$

which is very much less than that of the common-emitter amplifier (233 pF).

12-10. COMMON-BASE AMPLIFIER

Now let us consider the common-base transistor amplifier. A typical common-base amplifier and its model are shown in Figures 12-29a and 12-29b. The impedance $\mathbf{Z}_i$ represents the input impedance of the next stage or the load. As in Sec. 12-5, we can break the analysis into three regions. In the low- and midfrequency regions, $C_{b'e}$ and $C_{b'c}$ can be considered to be open circuits and $\mathbf{Z}_i$ is a pure resistance R_i. In the midfrequency region, $C_{b'c}$ and $C_{b'e}$ can be considered to be open circuits, C_c is considered to be a short circuit, and $\mathbf{Z}_i$ is the pure resistance R_i. In the high-frequency region, C_c can be considered to be a short circuit. In all of the following analysis, we shall assume that $r_{b'c}$ is an open circuit.

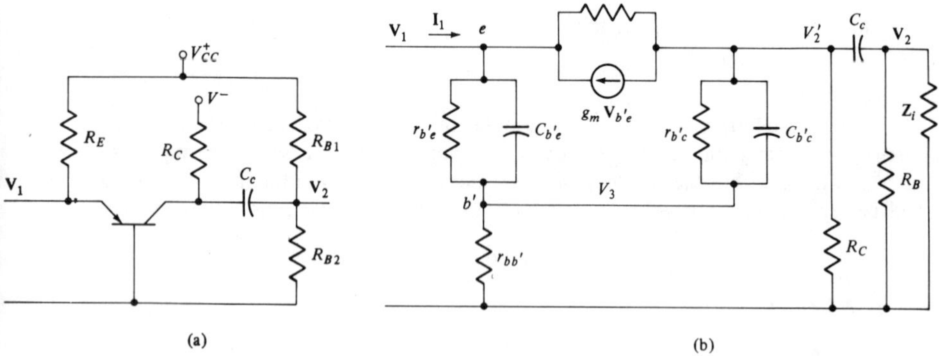

Figure 12-29. (a) A common-base amplifier. (b) Its model. Note that R_E is omitted since it is in parallel with $\mathbf{V}_1$.

Midfrequency Region

If we analyze the circuit of Figure 12-29b, assuming that $C_{b'e}$ and $C_{b'c}$ are open circuits and that C_c is a short circuit, we obtain

$$\mathbf{A}_{v\,\text{mid}} = \frac{g_m R_{\text{sh}} r_{b'e}}{r_{bb'} + r_{b'e}} + \frac{R_{\text{sh}}}{r_{ce}} \tag{12-181}$$

where

$$\frac{1}{R_{\text{sh}}} = \frac{1}{r_{ce}} + \frac{1}{R_C} + \frac{1}{R_B} + \frac{1}{R_i} \tag{12-182}$$

and we have assumed that $r_{b'c}$ can be considered to be an open circuit. In general,

$$\frac{g_m r_{b'e}}{r_{bb'} + r_{b'e}} \gg \frac{1}{r_{ce}}$$

so that we have

$$\mathbf{A}_{v\,\text{mid}} = g_m R_{\text{sh}} \frac{r_{b'e}}{r_{bb'} + r_{b'e}} \tag{12-183}$$

High-Frequency Region

We now assume that C_c is a short circuit. We shall also assume that $Z_i = R_i$, a pure resistance. Then, we obtain

$$\mathbf{A}_{v\,\text{high}} = \frac{\dfrac{g_m}{r_{bb'}} + \dfrac{1}{r_{ce}}\left(\dfrac{1}{R_P}\right) - \omega^2 C_{b'e} C_{b'c} + j\omega\left[g_m C_{b'c} + \dfrac{1}{r_{ce}}(C_{b'e} + C_{b'c}) + \dfrac{1}{r_{b'e}} C_{b'c}\right]}{\dfrac{1}{R_{\text{sh}}}\left(\dfrac{1}{R_P}\right) - \omega^2 C_{b'e} C_{b'c} + j\omega\left[\dfrac{1}{R_{\text{sh}}}(C_{b'e} + C_{b'c}) + \left(\dfrac{1}{r_{bb'}} + \dfrac{1}{r_{b'e}}\right) C_{b'c} + g_m C_{b'c}\right]} \tag{12-184}$$

where $1/R_P = 1/r_{bb'} + 1/r_{b'e}$ (see Eq. 12-89). In general,

$$g_m \gg 1/r_{ce} \tag{12-185a}$$

$$g_m C_{b'c} \gg 1/r_{ce}(C_{b'e} + C_{b'c}) \tag{12-185b}$$

$$g_m \gg 1/r_{b'e} \tag{12-185c}$$

Also, over most frequencies of interest

$$\frac{g_m}{r_{bb'}} \gg \omega^2 C_{b'e} C_{b'c} \tag{12-185d}$$

$$\frac{1}{R_{\text{sh}}}\left(\frac{1}{R_P}\right) \gg \omega^2 C_{b'e} C_{b'c} \tag{12-185e}$$

Then, Eq. 12-184 becomes

$$\mathbf{A}_{v\,\text{high}} = \frac{\dfrac{g_m}{r_{bb'}} + j\omega(g_m C_{b'c})}{\dfrac{1}{R_{\text{sh}}}\left(\dfrac{1}{R_p}\right) + j\omega\left[\left(g_m + \dfrac{1}{R_p} + \dfrac{1}{R_{\text{sh}}}\right)C_{b'c} + \dfrac{1}{R_{\text{sh}}}C_{b'e}\right]}$$

Manipulating and substituting Eq. 12-183 we obtain

$$\frac{\mathbf{A}_{v\,\text{high}}}{\mathbf{A}_{v\,\text{mid}}} = \frac{1 + j\omega r_{bb'}C_{b'c}}{1 + j\omega R_P\left[\left(g_m R_{\text{sh}} + \dfrac{R_{\text{sh}}}{R_p} + 1\right)C_{b'c} + C_{b'e}\right]} \tag{12-186}$$

In general, the numerator of this expression will remain approximately unity up to those frequencies where the denominator has become very large. Thus, over all frequencies of interest we can write

$$\frac{\mathbf{A}_{v\,\text{high}}}{\mathbf{A}_{v\,\text{mid}}} = \frac{1}{1 + jf/f_2} \tag{12-187}$$

where

$$f_2 = \{2\pi R_P[(g_m R_{\text{sh}} + R_{\text{sh}}/R_P + 1)C_{b'c} + C_{b'e}]\}^{-1} \tag{12-188}$$

Note that this is exactly the same as Eq. 12-93b for the common-emitter amplifier.

We have assumed a resistive load here. Suppose instead that the load is a common-emitter amplifier. Then, Eq. 12-184 will still be valid but now R_i must be replaced by the impedance given by Fig. 12-18. This will again lead to results similar to those obtained for the common-emitter amplifier which drives another common-emitter stage.

Low-Frequency Region

If we again assume that inequality 12-185c is valid, we obtain, for the normalized low-frequency gain

$$\frac{\mathbf{A}_{v\,\text{low}}}{\mathbf{A}_{v\,\text{mid}}} = \frac{1}{1 - jf_1/f} \tag{12-189}$$

where

$$f_1 = 1/2\pi R_{\text{low}\,B} C_c \tag{12-190a}$$

$$R_{\text{low}\,B} = \frac{r_{ce}R_C}{r_{ce} + R_C} + \frac{R_B R_i}{R_B + R_i} \tag{12-190b}$$

Of course, when integrated circuit amplifiers are fabricated, direct coupled amplifiers can be used and there will be no low-frequency falloff.

Example

The transistor used in the amplifier of Figure 12-29a has the following parameter values.

$$r_{bb'} = 100 \text{ ohms}$$
$$r_{b'e} = 900 \text{ ohms}$$
$$r_{b'c} = 10^7 \text{ ohms}$$
$$r_{ce} = 10^5 \text{ ohms}$$
$$C_{b'e} = 100 \text{ pF}$$
$$C_{b'c} = 3 \text{ pF}$$
$$g_m = 50{,}000\ \mu\text{mho}$$

The elements of the circuit are

$$R_{B1} = R_{B2} = 10{,}000 \text{ ohms}$$
$$R_C = 5000 \text{ ohms}$$
$$C_C = 10\ \mu\text{F}$$

Compute $\mathbf{A}_{v\,\text{mid}}$, f_2, and f_1, assuming a load of 1000 ohms.

$$\frac{1}{R_{\text{sh}}} = 10^{-5} + \frac{1}{5000} + \frac{1}{5000} + \frac{1}{1000}$$
$$R_{\text{sh}} = 709.22 \text{ ohms}$$

$$\mathbf{A}_{v\,\text{mid}} = 50{,}000 \times 10^{-6} \times 709.22 \times \frac{900}{1000} = 31.9$$

Assuming a resistive load

$$\frac{1}{R_P} = \frac{1}{100} + \frac{1}{900}, \qquad R_P = 90.0$$

$$f_2 = \left\{2\pi \times 90.0\left[\left(50 \times 10^{-3} \times 709.22 + \frac{709.22}{90.0} + 1\right)3 \times 10^{-12} + 100 \times 10^{-12}\right]\right\}^{-1}$$

$$f_2 = 7.59 \times 10^6 \text{ Hz}$$

Now let us compute the lower half-power frequency

$$R_{\text{low}} = \frac{10^5 \times 5000}{5000 + 10^5} + \frac{5000 \times 1000}{5000 + 1000} = 4761.9 + 833.33 = 5595.2 \text{ ohms}$$

$$f_1 = 1/(2\pi \times 5595.2 \times 10 \times 10^{-6}) = 2.84 \text{ Hz.}$$

If we compare these results with those of Sec. 12-5 for a comparable common-emitter amplifier, we see that the results are the same for both amplifiers. *The results when either amplifier drives another common-emitter amplifier will also be the same.* (This assumes that the parallel combination of R_C and R_B is a much smaller resistance than r_{ce}.) In practical situations, a common-base amplifier is not used to drive another common-base stage because the input impedance of the common-base amplifier is so low that the voltage gain of the first common-base amplifier in the cascade would be less than one.

A common-base amplifier has an additional useful property. In the common-emitter amplifier, the parameters $r_{bc'}$ and $C_{b'c}$ feed back a signal from input to output. The value of $r_{b'c}$ is so large that this presents no problems at low frequencies. However, at high frequencies, the feedback through $C_{b'c}$ can result in problems such as Miller effect (see Sec. 6-14). In the common-base amplifier, the feedback is through r_{ce} which is large enough so that it usually presents no problems. There is also feedback to the point b' through the paralleled $r_{b'c}$ and $C_{b'c}$. However, in the common-base circuit, b' is connected to ground through the small resistance $r_{bb'}$. Thus, the feedback voltage and, hence, the effect of the feedback is greatly reduced.

Input Admittance of the Common-Base Amplifier

The input admittance of the common-base amplifier is given by (see Fig. 12-29b)

$$\mathbf{Y}_i = \frac{\mathbf{I}_1}{\mathbf{V}_1}$$

where

$$I_1 = -g_m(\mathbf{V}_3 - \mathbf{V}_1) + \left(\frac{1}{r_{b'e}} + j\omega C_{b'e}\right)(\mathbf{V}_1 - \mathbf{V}_3) + \frac{1}{r_{ce}}(\mathbf{V}_1 - \mathbf{V}_2) \qquad (12\text{-}191)$$

Now solving for $\mathbf{V}_3$ and substituting in Eq. 12-191 and manipulating, we have

$$\mathbf{Y}_i = \left(g_m + \frac{1}{r_{b'e}} + j\omega C_{b'e}\right) \qquad (12\text{-}192)$$

$$\left[1 - \frac{\dfrac{r_{bb'}}{r_{bb'} + r_{b'e}} - \omega^2 R_P R_{\text{sh}} C_{b'e} C_{b'c} + j\omega R_P\left[\left(g_m R_{\text{sh}} + \dfrac{R_{\text{sh}}}{r_{b'e}} + \dfrac{R_{\text{sh}}}{r_{b'c}}\right)C_{b'c} + C_{b'e}\right]}{1 - \omega^2 R_P R_{\text{sh}} C_{b'e} C_{b'c} + j\omega R_P\left[\left(g_m R_{\text{sh}} + \dfrac{R_{\text{sh}}}{R_P} + 1\right)C_{b'c} + C_{b'e}\right]}\right] + \frac{1 - \mathbf{A}_v}{r_{ce}}$$

At midfrequencies, this becomes

$$\mathbf{Y}_i = \left(g_m + \frac{1}{r_{b'e}}\right)\frac{r_{b'e}}{r_{bb'} + r_{b'e}} + \frac{1 - \mathbf{A}_{v\,\text{mid}}}{r_{ce}} \qquad (12\text{-}193)$$

For the parameters of the previous example we have

$$\mathbf{Y}_i = \left(50{,}000 \times 10^{-6} + \frac{1}{900}\right)\left(\frac{900}{1000}\right) + \frac{1 - 31.9}{10^5}$$

$$\mathbf{Y}_i = 0.046 - 0.000309 = 0.0457 \text{ mhos}$$

or

$$\mathbf{Z}_i = 21.886 \text{ ohms}$$

This very low input impedance indicates why common-base circuits are not cascaded.

In general

$$g_m \gg \frac{1}{r_{b'e}}$$

and

$$g_m \frac{r_{b'c}}{r_{bb'} + r_{b'e}} \gg \frac{1 - A_v}{r_{ce}}$$

Thus, the midfrequency input admittance can be expressed as

$$\mathbf{Y}_i = g_m \frac{r_{b'e}}{r_{bb'} + r_{b'e}} \qquad (12\text{-}194)$$

12-11. INPUT AND OUTPUT IN A CASCADE OF AMPLIFIERS

Thus far, we have discussed the gain of single stages. These stages will be used to make up a cascaded amplifier. Before discussing the design of a cascaded amplifier, let us consider the input and output stages of such a cascade.

A typical FET input stage is shown in Fig. 12-30a. The previously developed relations computed the gain of an amplifier stage from its input to its output. If we are to use these relations, then we must compute V_1 in terms of V_s.

A model for the input circuit is shown in Fig. 12-30b. From this, we have

$$\frac{\mathbf{V}_1}{\mathbf{V}_s} = \frac{1}{1 + jf/f_2} \qquad (12\text{-}195)$$

where

$$f_2 = 1/2\pi R_1 C_i \qquad (12\text{-}196)$$

Note that C_i represents the input capacitance of the FET amplifier (including Miller effect).

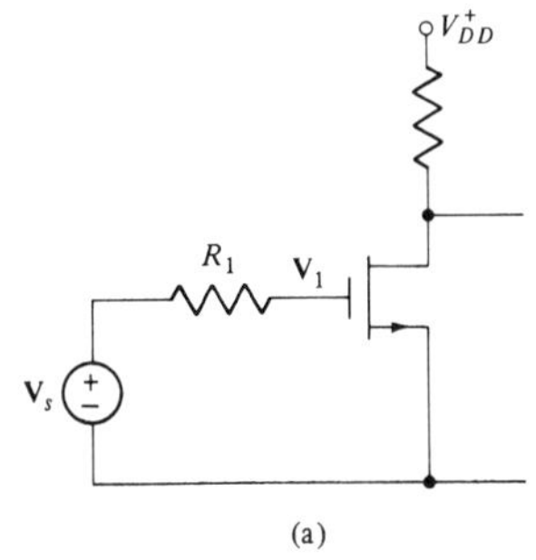

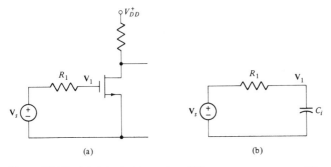

Figure 12-30. (a) A typical input to a FET common-source amplifier. (b) Its model.

Now let us consider the input circuit of a common-emitter transistor amplifier (see Fig. 12-31). In the mid- and high-frequency regions, it is convenient to replace the portion of the circuit which lies to the left of terminals ab by its Thévenin's equivalent. This is shown in Fig. 12-31b where

$$\frac{1}{R_B} = \frac{1}{R_{B1}} + \frac{1}{R_{B2}} \tag{12-197a}$$

$$\frac{1}{R_T} = \frac{1}{R_1} + \frac{1}{R_B} \tag{12-197b}$$

and

$$\mathbf{V}_T = \frac{\mathbf{V}_i R_B}{R_1 + R_B} \tag{12-197c}$$

Now we can use the previously developed relations for voltage gain with the proviso that $\mathbf{V}_1$ is replaced by $\mathbf{V}_T$ and that $r_{bb'}$ is replaced by

$$r_{bb'T} = R_1 + r_{bb'} \tag{12-198}$$

(see Fig. 12-31b).

If the coupling capacitor C_c of Fig. 12-31a is included, then the low-frequency response of the amplifier must be multiplied by

$$\frac{\mathbf{A}'_{v\,\mathrm{low}}}{\mathbf{A}_{v\,\mathrm{mid}}} = \frac{1}{1 - jf_1/f} \tag{12-199}$$

where

$$f_1 = 1/2\pi R_{\mathrm{low}\,i} C_c \tag{12-200a}$$

and

$$R_{\mathrm{low}\,i} = R_1 + \frac{R_B R_i}{R_B + R_i} \tag{12-200b}$$

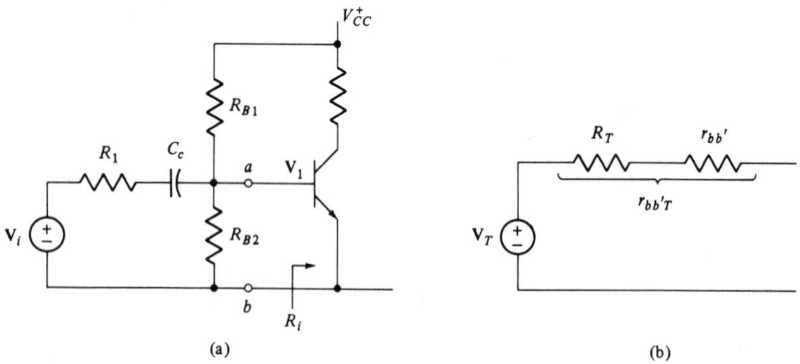

Figure 12-31. (a) A typical input to a common-emitter transistor amplifier. (b) A model useful in the mid- and high-frequencies.

This relation can be derived in a manner similar to that used for the other low-frequency gain expressions.

Let us turn our attention to the output stage. The load impedance can often be considered to be a resistance. In all the amplifiers that we have considered, we have made provision for such a load. At times, the load resistance is shunted by a capacitance. Such loads have also been discussed in the case of the FET amplifier. In the case of the transistor amplifier, we have considered more complex loads. The inclusion of a capacitance can be analyzed using the previously used analysis procedures.

12-12. BANDWIDTH OF CASCADED AMPLIFIER STAGES

When amplifier stages are cascaded, the overall gain is the product of the gains of the individual stages. As a prelude to the design of amplifiers, let us discuss the response of identical cascaded stages (although we shall see that cascaded stages are often not identical). For instance, suppose that we have an amplifier whose normalized (high-frequency) response is given by

$$\frac{\mathbf{A}_{v\,\mathrm{high}}}{\mathbf{A}_{v\,\mathrm{mid}}} = \frac{1}{1 + jf/f_2} = \frac{1}{\sqrt{1 + (f/f_2)^2}}\, e^{-j\tan^{-1} f/f_2} \tag{12-201}$$

Now suppose that we form a cascade of n such stages. Then, for the overall amplifier

$$\frac{\mathbf{A}_{v\,\mathrm{high}\,T}}{\mathbf{A}_{v\,\mathrm{mid}\,T}} = \frac{1}{(1 + jf/f_2)^n} = \frac{1}{[1 + (f/f_2)^2]^{n/2}}\, e^{-jn\tan^{-1} f/f_2} \tag{12-202}$$

or, on a decibel basis,

$$\left|\frac{\mathbf{A}_{v\,\mathrm{high}\,T}}{\mathbf{A}_{v\,\mathrm{mid}\,T}}\right|_{\mathrm{dB}} = -10n \log_{10}\left[1 + \left(\frac{f}{f_2}\right)^2\right] \tag{12-203}$$

A plot of this expression is shown in Fig. 12-32. Note that the break points of the asymptote all occur at $f = f_2$. The slope of the asymptotes are $-6n$ dB/octave $= -20n$ dB/decade.

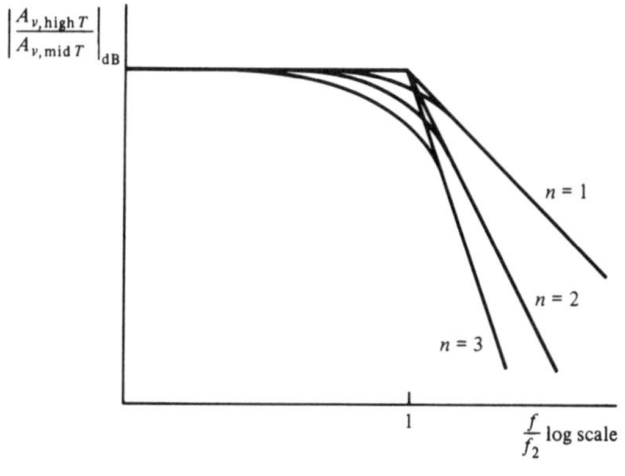

Figure 12-32. Plots of Eq. 12-186 for n = 1, 2, and 3.

Table 12-1 NORMALIZED OVERALL HALF-POWER BANDWIDTH VERSUS NUMBER OF STAGES

n	f_{2T}/f_2
1	1.00
2	0.644
3	0.510
4	0.435
5	0.386
6	0.350
7	0.323
8	0.301
9	0.283
10	0.268

Let us determine f_{2T}, the half-power bandwidth of the cascaded amplifier. This is obtained by solving

$$\left[1 + \left(\frac{f_{2T}}{f_2}\right)^2\right]^{n/2} = \sqrt{2}$$

Then,

$$f_{2T} = f_2\sqrt{2^{1/n} - 1} \tag{12-204}$$

Note that, as n increases, the half-power bandwidth decreases. This is illustrated in Table 12-1[2].

If identical amplifier stages are cascaded, the bandwidth of the overall amplifier will be less than that of a single stage. However, increasing the number of stages can actually increase the bandwidth of an amplifier. Let us reconcile these two apparently contradictory statements. Suppose that we are dealing with amplifiers whose gain bandwidth products are constant. Consider that the (overall) amplifier specifications call for a midband gain of 100 and a half-power bandwidth of 1×10^6 Hz = 1 MHz. Assume that we can build this amplifier with a single stage and that it just meets the specifications, that is, the gain bandwidth of the device is 100×10^6 Hz = 100 MHz.

Now suppose that we construct the amplifier using two stages. Now the gain of each stage is *reduced* from 100 to 10. Thus, the bandwidth of each stage has *increased* to $f_2 = 10 \times 10^6$ Hz = 10 MHz. When two identical stages are cascaded, the overall half-power bandwidth is 0.644 times that of a single stage. Thus, the half-power bandwidth of the overall amplifier is now 6.44×10^6 Hz = 6.44 MHz. Hence, if the overall gain is held constant, increasing the number of stages can increase the bandwidth of the amplifier.

As the number of stages is increased, the bandwidth does not increase continuously. If the overall gain is held constant and the number of stages is increased then, in general,

[2] G. E. Valley, Jr. and H. Wallman, *Vacuum Tube Amplifiers* (New York: McGraw-Hill, 1948).

f_{2T} *will increase and then decrease.* It can be shown (see Prob. 12-55) that the maximum value of f_{2T} occurs when the gain per stage is approximately given by

$$\sqrt{\varepsilon} = 1.649 \quad \text{or} \quad 4.343 \text{ dB} \tag{12-205}$$

In the next section we shall see that, unless extremely large bandwidth is required, the gain per stage is usually greater than this value in order to reduce the number of stages in the amplifier.

We have assumed in this discussion that the gain-bandwidth product is a constant. In general, this is not the case. However, we often work with amplifiers wherein an increase in high-frequency bandwidth accompanies a reduction in midband gain. In such cases, using additional stages to increase gain is a helpful procedure. These ideas will be considered in the next two sections where the design of broadband amplifiers will be discussed in detail.

12-13. DESIGN OF BROADBAND FET AMPLIFIERS

We shall now discuss the design of broadband FET amplifiers. We shall concentrate on the mid- and high-frequency response since the related design procedures are applicable to both integrated and discrete circuits. However, we shall also discuss the low-frequency design.

Design Specifications. Let us design an amplifier with the following specifications. There is to be a well-defined midband region where $|\mathbf{A}_{v\,\text{mid}}| = 1000$. The high-frequency response is to be characterized by $|\mathbf{A}_v/\mathbf{A}_{v\,\text{mid}}| \geqq 0.95$, for all $f \leqq 10^6$ Hz. The low-frequency response is to be characterized by $|\mathbf{A}_v/\mathbf{A}_{v\,\text{mid}}| \geqq 0.8$ for $f \geqq 20$ Hz. The load resistance is 10^6 ohms shunted by 1 pF. The generator impedance is 1000 ohms.

The first step in the design is to choose the FET's to be used. One factor that enters into this choice is the magnitude of the output voltage that is desired. We have not specified it here and we assume that the voltages are low level (e.g., a volt or less). If a large output voltage were specified, then the output FET would have to be capable of handling such a swing. Such "large" FET's usually do not have very high gain-bandwidth products. Thus, a FET might be chosen for the output stage while other FET's with higher gain-bandwidth products would be chosen for the other stages of the amplifier. The design of high-level stages will be discussed in Chapter 15. In the design of this amplifier, we shall assume identical FET's in each stage.

Note that voltage swings and gain-bandwidth products are not the only criteria used in choosing an FET. Operating voltage and current levels and cost are some other considerations.

Now let us assume that we have chosen to construct the amplifier with depletion MOSFET's which have the following specifications.

$$g_m = 10{,}000\ \mu\text{mho}$$
$$r_d = 10^5 \text{ ohms}$$
$$C_{gs} = 2 \text{ pF}$$
$$C_{gd} = 0.25 \text{ pF}$$
$$C_{ds} = 1 \text{ pF}$$

The coordinates of the quiescent operating point are

$$V_{DSQ} = 15 \text{ V}$$
$$I_{DQ} = 1 \text{ mA}$$
$$V_{GSQ} = -1 \text{ V}$$

(Note that a reasonable value of V_{GSQ} would be 0 V. We have chosen -1 V here so that the design of the source bypass capacitance can be illustrated.)

Design procedures are often tedious. Often, there are no formulae that can be solved to uniquely specify the design. There are usually several solutions that meet the specifications, and the one that is chosen may be picked on the basis of size, weight, cost, and so forth.

The first step in our design procedure is to determine the minimum number of stages that can be used. It is probably simplest to use a cut and try procedure here. Let us try one stage first.

We must start by considering the effect of the generator impedance. We shall ignore the resistance. From Eq. 12-195, we have (see Fig. 12-30a)

$$\frac{V_1}{V_g} = \frac{1}{1 + jf/f_{2i}}$$

where

$$f_{2i} = 1/2\pi R_s C_{\text{sh}i}$$
$$C_{\text{sh}i} = C_{gs} + (1 - \mathbf{A}_v)C_{gd} \tag{12-206}$$

and R_s is the generator resistance. To be on the safe side, we shall substitute $\mathbf{A}_{v\,\text{mid}}$ in Eq. 12-206. Since we are only using one stage, $\mathbf{A}_{v\,\text{mid}} = 1000$. Substituting, we obtain

$$C_{\text{sh}i} = 2 + 0.25(1 + 1000) = 252.25 \text{ pF}$$

Then,

$$f_{2i} = 1/[2\pi(1000)252.25 \times 10^{-12}] = 0.631 \text{ MHz}$$

so that, at $f = 10^6$ Hz,

$$\left|\frac{V_1}{V_g}\right| = \frac{1}{\sqrt{1 + (1/0.631)^2}} = 0.534$$

The high input capacitance causes the design using one stage to fail. We should now proceed to the design using two stages. However, before doing this, for illustrative purposes, let us consider the single-amplifier stage. From Eq. 12-69 we have

$$\mathbf{A}_{v\,\text{mid}} f_2 = g_m/2\pi C_{\text{sh}}$$

Here

$$C_{\text{sh}} = C_{gd} + C_{ds} + C_{\text{load}}$$
$$C_{\text{sh}} = 0.25 + 1 + 1 = 2.25 \text{ pF} \tag{12-207}$$

Note that the Miller effect does not come into play here since a succeeding amplifier stage is not driven. Then,

$$f_2 = \frac{10{,}000 \times 10^{-6}}{2\pi \times 1000 \times 2.25 \times 10^{-12}} = 707{,}355 \text{ Hz}$$

At $f = 10^6$ Hz, $|\mathbf{A}_v/\mathbf{A}_{v\,\text{mid}}|$ will be less than 0.707 since the frequency is greater than f_2. Thus, the circuit could not be built using only one stage even if $R_s = 0$ so that there was no input loss. There is another reason why the circuit cannot be built using only one stage $\mu = g_m r_d = 1000$. Thus this is the maximum midband gain that occurs when R_d and R_{load} are infinite.

Now let us attempt the design using two stages. Now the gain per stage becomes

$$\sqrt{1000} = 31.623$$

Then, for the input

$$C_{\text{sh}i} = 2 + 0.25(1 + 31.623) = 10.16 \text{ pF}$$

Note that this value has decreased because $|\mathbf{A}_{v\,\text{mid}}|$ has decreased. Then,

$$f_{2i} = 1/(2\pi \times 1000 \times 10.16 \times 10^{-12}) = 15.66 \text{ MHz}$$

For the last stage, C_{sh} is the same as before. Hence,

$$f_{22} = \frac{10{,}000 \times 10^{-6}}{2\pi \times 31.623 \times 2.25 \times 10^{-12}} = 22.37 \text{ MHz}$$

Now we must compute C_{sh} for the first stage.

$$C_{\text{sh}i} = C_{gd} + C_{ds} + C_{gs} + (1 - \mathbf{A}_{v\,\text{mid}})C_{gd}$$

where the last two terms represent C_i for stage 2. Then,

$$C_{\text{sh}} = 0.25 + 1 + 2 + 0.25(1 + 31.623) = 11.41 \text{ pF}$$

Hence,

$$f_{21} = \frac{10{,}000 \times 10^{-6}}{2\pi \times 31.623 \times 11.41 \times 10^{-12}} = 4.41 \text{ MHz}$$

Then, at a frequency of 10^6 Hz, we have

$$\left|\frac{\mathbf{A}_v}{\mathbf{A}_{v\,\text{mid}}}\right| = \frac{1}{\sqrt{1 + (1/15.66)^2}} \cdot \frac{1}{\sqrt{1 + (1/4.41)^2}} \cdot \frac{1}{\sqrt{1 + (1/22.37)^2}}$$

$$\left|\frac{\mathbf{A}_v}{\mathbf{A}_{v\,\text{mid}}}\right| = (0.998)(0.975)(0.999) = 0.972$$

This is greater than 0.95. Thus, the design can be achieved with two stages. A typical two-stage RC coupled amplifier is shown in Fig. 12-33. Note that parasitic capacitances are *not* shown in schematic diagrams. Note also that we have ignored the input R_g in the mid-frequency calculations. This can be done since we assume that $R_g \gg R_s$.

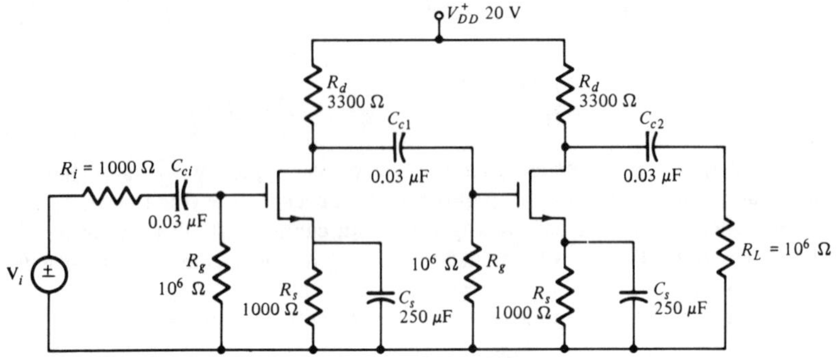

Figure 12-33. A two-stage *RC* coupled FET amplifier.

We can now calculate all the resistances and power supply voltages for this amplifier. From Eq. 12-32, we have

$$R_{sh} = \frac{\mathbf{A}_{v\,\text{mid}}}{g_m} = \frac{31.623}{10{,}000 \times 10^{-6}} = 3162.3 \text{ ohms}$$

Now,

$$\frac{1}{R_{sh}} = \frac{1}{r_d} + \frac{1}{R_d} + \frac{1}{R_g}$$

Let us choose $R_g = 10^6$ ohms. Actually, the largest practical R_g should be used so that the sizes of the coupling capacitors are minimized. Then, substituting, we obtain

$$\frac{1}{R_d} = \frac{1}{R_{sh}} - \frac{1}{r_d} - \frac{1}{R_g} = \frac{1}{3162.3} - \frac{1}{10^5} - \frac{1}{10^6}$$

$$R_d = 3276.3 \text{ ohms}$$

This is not a standard value of resistance. Suppose that we use

$$R_d = 3300 \text{ ohms}$$

Now, $|\mathbf{A}_{v\,\text{mid}}|$ will be (slightly) larger than specified. The values of f_{22} and f_{21} will be reduced. These new values should be computed and $|\mathbf{A}_v/\mathbf{A}_{v\,\text{mid}}|$ should be checked at 10^6 Hz to make sure that the specifications are met. In this case, they are.

The value of $|\mathbf{A}_{v\,\text{mid}}|$ will be larger than specified. This is usually all right. Often, a *gain control* is incorporated so that the gain can be varied (reduced). A typical gain control is shown in Fig. 12-34. One R_g is replaced by a *potentiometer.* This is a resistor with a sliding contact. Thus, Fig. 12-34 represents a variable voltage divider so that $\mathbf{V}_b$ will range from 0 to $\mathbf{V}_a$ V, depending upon the position of the tap. Therefore, the amplifier's gain can be varied from 0 to its maximum value. The gain control is usually placed toward the front of the amplifier. In this way, large signals can be reduced before they overload the amplifier (i.e., drive it into nonlinear regions).

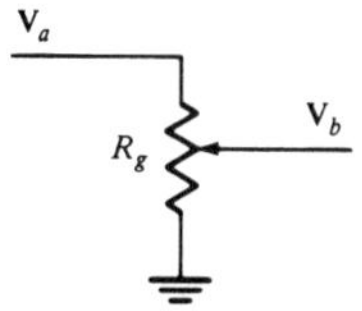

Figure 12-34. A simple gain control.

The value of R_s is determined from the quiescent gate-to-source bias. Often, when depletion MOSFET's are used, $V_{GSQ} = 0$ and $R_s = 0$. In this case, we deliberately have chosen $V_{GSQ} = 1$ V for illustrative purposes. Thus,

$$R_s = \frac{-V_{GSQ}}{I_{DQ}} = \frac{1}{1 \times 10^{-3}} = 1000 \text{ ohms}$$

Now let us determine the required value of the power supply voltage

$$V_{DD} = I_D R_d + V_{DSQ} - V_{GSQ} = 10^{-3}(3300) + 15 + 1 = 19.3 \text{ V}$$

In general, if a 20-V power supply were used, the shift in operating point, and so forth would be small. Thus we shall specify $V_{DD} = 20$ V.

Now let us determine the sizes of the coupling and bypass capacitors. They are functions of the low-frequency specifications. The normalized low-frequency gain of a single stage is given by Eq. 12-139. Rather than work with this relatively complex equation, we shall use a procedure that allows us to work with simple expressions in several steps.

At the start we shall assume that the bypass capacitors act as short circuits. We shall consider their effect subsequently. There are three coupling capacitors. We have added one in series with the input in order to protect the amplifier from any large direct voltage applied to the input terminals. Because of the large value of R_g and R_{load}, we have, for each stage

$$R_{\text{low}} = 10^6 \text{ ohms}$$

(see Eq. 12-63). We shall assume that the three coupling capacitors are equal. Thus,

$$\left|\frac{\mathbf{A}_{v\,\text{low}\,T}}{\mathbf{A}_{v\,\text{mid}\,T}}\right| = \left[\frac{1}{\sqrt{1 + (f_1/f)^2}}\right]^3$$

The subscript T indicates that the gain is for the complete amplifier and not just for a single stage. Thus, at 20 Hz,

$$\left[\frac{1}{1 + (f_1/20)^2}\right]^{3/2} = 0.8$$

Solving, we obtain

$$f_1 = 8.01 \text{ Hz}$$

Substitution in Eq. 12-44 yields

$$C_c = \frac{1}{2\pi \times 8.01 \times 10^6} = 0.020\ \mu\text{F}$$

If we were to use coupling capacitors which are exactly this size, then, in order to meet the design specifications, we would require infinite bypass capacitors. This is because we have assumed that there was no loss in low-frequency response due to the bypass capacitors. Thus, we shall increase the size of the coupling capacitors so that the loss due to the coupling capacitors at 20 Hz will be less than the allowable loss and some loss due to the bypass capacitors will be allowed. Let us try

$$C_c = 0.03\ \mu\text{F}$$

Then,

$$f_1 = 1/(2\pi \times 0.03 \times 10^{-6} \times 10^6) = 5.31\ \text{Hz}$$

Then, at 20 Hz,

$$\left[\frac{1}{1 + (5.31/20)^2}\right]^{3/2} = 0.903$$

This is the "loss" due to the coupling capacitor. Then, the allowable loss due to the bypass capacitor is

$$\frac{0.8}{0.903} = 0.886$$

Hence, (see Eq. 12-137),

$$\left[\frac{f_{s1}}{f_{s2}}\sqrt{\frac{1 + (20/f_{s1})^2}{1 + (20/f_{s2})^2}}\right]^2 = 0.886 \tag{12-208}$$

Note that there are two bypassed source resistors so the expression to the left of the equals sign is squared. From Eq. 12-136b, we have

$$f_{s2} = \left[\frac{10^5 + 3300 + 1000(1 + 1000)}{10^5 + 3300}\right] f_{s1}$$

Note that

$$\mu = g_m r_d = 1000$$

Thus,

$$f_{s2} = 10.69 f_{s1}$$

Substituting in Eq. 12-208 and manipulating, we obtain

$$f_{s1} = 0.739\ \text{Hz}$$

Then, substituting in Eq. 12-136a, we have

$$C_s = 1/(2\pi \times 0.739 \times 1000) = 215.3\ \mu\text{F}$$

Although this is a large capacitance, it can easily be realized using an electrolytic capacitor. Of course, 215.3 μF is not a commonly available size. Then, let us use

$$C_s = 250\ \mu\text{F}$$

Note that the value of C_s can be reduced by increasing C_c, and vice versa. Thus, several designs could be tried and an "optimum" choice could be made. Note that a point is reached where any increase in C_c will only make an insignificant change in the value of C_s.

Miller Effect Compensation

The upper half-power frequency of the first stage is considerably less than that of the second. This is because the Miller effect increases the input capacitance of the second stage which increases the shunt capacitance of the first stage. Note that if there were more than two stages, each stage but the last would have its upper half-power frequency reduced by Miller effect. If the specifications on the gain and bandwidth of the amplifier call for both very high midband gain and broad bandwidth, then, because of the Miller effect, the amplifier may have to be constructed with very many stages, or the design may actually fail. There are several procedures that can be used to diminish the importance of the Miller effect. If dual gate FET's are used, then C_{gd} will be greatly diminished. A typical value for C_{gd} is 0.02 pF for dual gate FET's. In very broadband amplifiers, the use of dual gate FET's is dictated.

There is another procedure that can be used to offset the Miller effect. Suppose that each common-source FET amplifier is cascaded with a source follower. Then, R_{shs} (see Eq. 12-151 is very low so f_2 for the source follower will be very high even if it is loaded by the input capacitance of a common-source amplifier. The input capacitance of the source follower is very low so that the C_{sh} for the common-source amplifier will be low. Thus, very good high-frequency response can be obtained even though extra amplifier stages that do not provide gain are included. Let us illustrate this.

Suppose that we construct a cascade which consists of alternate source follower and common-source amplifiers. The input stage should be a source follower. The output could be either a source follower or a common-source amplifier. Now let us consider the response of a source follower, common-source pair. Assume that the source follower used in the example of Sec. 12-8 is used. (This has the same g_m as the FET that we are considering here.) Thus,

$$\mathbf{A}_{v\,\text{mid}} = 0.9898$$

and

$$R_{\text{shs}} = 98.98 \text{ ohms}$$

Now, for the source follower, the input capacitance is

$$C_{is} = C_{gd} + C_{gs}(1 - \mathbf{A}_v) \tag{12-209}$$

we shall use the capacitances given earlier in this section. Therefore

$$C_{is} = 0.25 + 2(1 - 0.9898) = 0.2704 \text{ pF}$$

From the previous design, we required an $\mathbf{A}_{v\,\text{mid}} = 31.623$. Since the source follower results in a loss, the common-source amplifier would have to supply a gain of

$$\mathbf{A}'_{v\,\text{mid}} = \frac{31.623}{0.9898} = 31.95$$

This is just a very slight increase in the gain. Now the input admittance of the common-source amplifier is

$$C_i = C_{gs} + C_{gd}(1 - \mathbf{A}_v) = 2 + 0.25(1 + 31.95) = 10.24 \text{ pF}$$

Now let us compute the upper half-power frequency for each stage. For the common-source amplifier,

$$C_{\text{sh}} = C_{gd} + C_{ds} + C_{is}$$

$$C_{\text{sh}} = 0.25 + 1 + 0.27 = 1.52 \text{ pF}$$

Then,

$$f_2 = \frac{10{,}000 \times 10^{-6}}{2\pi \times 31.95 \times 1.52 \times 10^{-12}} = 32.8 \times 10^6 \text{ Hz} = 32.8 \text{ MHz}$$

This represents a very great increase in high-frequency bandwidth over a common-source amplifier which is cascaded with an identical common-source stage. However, now each common-source amplifier has been replaced by a common-source, source follower pair. Hence, we must also consider the frequency response of the source follower amplifier.

$$C_{\text{shs}} = C_{gs} + C_{ds} + C_i$$

$$C_{\text{shs}} = 2 + 1 + 10.24 = 13.24 \text{ pF}$$

Then

$$f_{2s} = 1/2\pi R_{\text{shs}} C_{\text{shs}} = 1/(2\pi \times 98.98 \times 13.24 \times 10^{-12}) = 121.4 \text{ MHz}$$

Thus, the overall normalized response of a single stage is given by

$$\frac{\mathbf{A}'_v}{\mathbf{A}_{v\,\text{mid}}} = \frac{1}{(1 + jf/32.8 \times 10^6)} \frac{1}{1 + jf/121.4 \times 10^6}$$

To obtain the upper half-power frequency of this combination, we must solve

$$\frac{1}{\sqrt{1 + (f_{2T}/32.8 \times 10^6)^2}} \frac{1}{\sqrt{1 + (f_{2T}/121.4 \times 10^6)^2}} = \frac{1}{\sqrt{2}}$$

Doing this, we obtain

$$f_{2T} = 30.76 \text{ MHz}$$

If we compare this with $f_{21} = 4.41$ MHz of the design example, we see that, in this case, the half-power frequency of the source follower, common-source *pair* is about seven times as large as that of the single common-source stage. Thus, the use of this pair should be considered when amplifiers with extremely large overall gain-bandwidth product are desired. This is especially true in the case of integrated circuits, where the extra source follower stages can be added without substantially increasing the cost of the chip. Note that dual gate FET's can be used as the active devices in the source follower, common-source pair.

12-14. DESIGN OF BROADBAND TRANSISTOR AMPLIFIERS

Now let us discuss the design of broadband amplifiers that use bipolar junction transistors as their active elements. As in Sec. 12-12, we shall stress mid- and high-frequency design. However, low-frequency design will be included.

Design Specifications

We will design an amplifier that meets the following specifications. There is to be a well-defined midband region where $|\mathbf{A}_{v\,\text{mid}}| = 1000$. The high-frequency response is to be characterized by $|\mathbf{A}_v/\mathbf{A}_{v\,\text{mid}}| \geqq 0.95$ for all $f \leqq 10^6$ Hz. The low-frequency response is to be characterized by $|\mathbf{A}_v/\mathbf{A}_{v\,\text{mid}}| \geqq 0.8$ for $f \geqq 20$ Hz. The load resistance is 1600 ohms and the generator resistance is 1000 ohms.

We must start by choosing the transistors that are to be used. As we discussed in the last section, the signal level will influence the choice of transistors. We shall assume that a low-level amplifier is desired. Again, if a high-level output is specified, then the transistor used for the output stage will be "larger" than the other transistors.

Let us assume that a transistor with the following specifications has been picked.

$$g_m = 75{,}000\ \mu\text{omhs}$$

$$r_{bb'} = 100\ \text{omhs}$$

$$r_{b'e} = 1500\ \text{ohms}$$

$$r_{b'c} = 10^7\ \text{ohms}$$

$$r_{ce} = 100{,}000\ \text{ohms}$$

$$C_{b'e} = 25\ \text{pf}$$

$$C_{b'c} = 0.5\ \text{pf}$$

The coordinates of the quiescent operating point are

$$I_{BQ} = 20\ \mu\text{A}$$

$$I_{CQ} = 2\ \text{mA}$$

$$V_{CEQ} = 5\ \text{V}$$

This transistor has lower capacitance than most in order to obtain the desired high-frequency response, that is, it is a special high-frequency transistor.

In a subsequent chapter, we shall discuss that amplifiers of this type may not require bias stabilization circuits. However, we shall include such a specification here to illustrate the design of the bypass capacitor circuit. We shall require that $S \leqq 5$. Actually, we should specify all the stabilization factors (see Secs. 5-7 and 5-8). We only specify one here (see Sec. 15-9.) The value of R_B $(1/R_B = 1/R_{B1} + 1/R_{B2})$ will affect the input voltage $\mathbf{V}_1$ between the base of the first transistor and ground (see Fig. 12-31a). Thus, we must know R_B before we can proceed with the design. The value for R_B depends upon the chosen value of R_E. If R_E is made large, then R_B will be large, which is desirable since $\mathbf{V}_1$ will be increased and the amplification from point a (see Fig. 12-31a) to the output need be less. However, too large a value of R_E will result in an excessive power supply voltage. Thus, several trial designs using different values of R_E may be necessary. (For reasons of brevity, we shall make only one trial.) From Eq. 5-65, we have

$$S = \frac{1 + \beta_F}{1 + \beta_F R_E/(R_B + R_E)} \tag{12-210}$$

We shall assume that $\beta_F = \beta_0$ so that $\beta_F = g_M r_{b'e} = 75{,}000 \times 10^{-6} \times 1500 = 112.5$. Then, substituting, we obtain

$$5 = \frac{113.5}{1 + 112.5R_E/(R_B + R_E)}$$

Manipulation yields

$$R_B = 4.18R_E$$

As a first trial, let us choose

$$R_E = 1000 \text{ ohms}$$

Then,

$$R_B = 4180 \text{ ohms}$$

Then (see Fig. 12-31b) we obtain, for the Thévenin equivalent circuit,

$$\mathbf{V}_T = \frac{\mathbf{V}_i R_B}{R_B + R_g} = \frac{4180\mathbf{V}_i}{4180 + 1000} = 0.807\,\mathbf{V}_i \tag{12-211}$$

$$R_T = \frac{R_B R_i}{R_B + R_i} = \frac{4180 \times 1000}{4180 + 1000} = 807 \text{ ohms} \tag{12-212}$$

Then, $r_{bb'T}$ for the first stage (see Fig. 12-31b) is given by

$$r_{bb'T} = R_T + r_{bb'} = 807 + 100 = 907 \text{ ohms}$$

Since V_T is equal to 0.807 times the generator voltage, we must design the amplifier so that the midband voltage gain from the V_T generator to the load is given by

$$|\mathbf{A}_{V\,\text{mid}\,T}| = \frac{1000}{0.807} = 1239 \tag{12-213}$$

although the transistor amplifier does not have a constant gain, high-frequency bandwidth product. A reduction in midband gain will be accompanied by an increase in bandwidth. Thus, design procedures of the type discussed in the last section are useful here also. Therefore, let us start the design by attempting to realize the amplifier using only one stage. From Eq. 12-85, we have

$$\mathbf{A}_{v\,\text{mid}} = -g_m R_{\text{sh}} \frac{r_{b'e}}{r_{bb'T} + r_{b'e}}$$

Hence,

$$R_{\text{sh}} = \frac{1239(907 + 1500)}{75{,}000 \times 10^{-6} \times 1500} = 26{,}509 \text{ ohms}$$

where, for a single-stage amplifier

$$\frac{1}{R_{sh}} = \frac{1}{r_{ce}} + \frac{1}{R_C} + \frac{1}{R_{load}}$$

R_{sh} must be less than 1600 ohms (R_{load}). Hence, the design cannot be achieved with a single stage. Note that we have not considered the high-frequency response. In this case, the parameters of the transistor and the specified load resistance were such that one stage simply could not provide enough midband gain.

At this point, we should attempt to design the amplifier using two stages. However, for illustrative purposes, let us assume that R_{load} was specified as a larger value so that one stage could provide enough midband gain and see if the high-frequency response specifications could be met. Then, from Eq. 12-91 we have

$$C_{sh} = C_{b'e} + C_{b'c}\left(1 + \frac{R_{sh}}{R_p} + g_m R_{sh}\right)$$

where, for the one-stage amplifier,

$$\frac{1}{R_p} = \frac{1}{r_{bb'T}} + \frac{1}{r_{b'e}} = \frac{1}{907} + \frac{1}{1500}$$

$$R_p = 565.2 \text{ ohms}$$

Then,

$$C_{sh} = 25 + 0.5\left(1 + \frac{26{,}509}{565.2} + 75{,}000 \times 10^{-6} \times 26{,}509\right)$$

$$C_{sh} = 1043 \text{ pF}$$

Note the very large value of C_{sh}, which is produced by the very high gain. Then,

$$f_2 = 1/2\pi R_p C_{sh} = 1/(2\pi \times 565.2 \times 1043 \times 10^{-12}) = 0.27 \times 10^6 \text{ Hz}$$

This is less than 1 MHz. Thus, the design requirements could not be met with one stage even if R_{low} were not restricted to a small value.

Now let us try two stages. We shall assume that the gain per stage is equal. Then, for each stage,

$$\mathbf{A}_{v\,mid} = \sqrt{1239} = 35.20$$

Note that it may be desirable to make the gain of the second stage greater than that of the first. We shall see that the second stage has a much better high-frequency response because it does not drive a capacitive load. However, to simplify the calculations here we shall make the gain per stage equal. If the design failed, then it would be desirable to repeat the two-stage design with the gain of the second stage greater than that of the first. Then, proceeding, we have

$$R_{sh1} = \frac{35.20(907 + 1500)}{75{,}000 \times 10^{-6} \times 1500} = 753.1 \text{ ohms}$$

and, for the second stage

$$R_{sh2} = \frac{35.20(100 + 1500)}{75{,}000 \times 10^{-6} \times 1500} = 500.6 \text{ ohms}$$

Now let us consider the high-frequency response. For the second stage, we have (see Eq. 12-91)

$$C_{sh2} = C_{b'e} + C_{b'c}\left(1 + \frac{R_{sh}}{R_{p2}} + g_m R_{sh}\right)$$

where

$$\frac{1}{R_{p2}} = \frac{1}{r_{bb'}} + \frac{1}{r_{b'e}} = \frac{1}{100} + \frac{1}{1500}$$

$$R_{p2} = 93.75 \text{ ohms}$$

$$C_{sh2} = 25 + 0.5\left(1 + \frac{500.6}{93.75} + 75{,}000 \times 10^{-6} \times 500.6\right) = 46.9 \text{ pF}$$

Then, (see Eqs. 12-93 and 12-94), the upper half-power frequency for the second stage is given by

$$f_{22} = 1/2\pi R_p C_{sh} = 1/(2\pi \times 93.75 \times 46.9 \times 10^{-12}) = 36.19 \text{ MHz}$$

Thus, the normalized high-frequency gain of the second stage is

$$\left|\frac{\mathbf{A}_{v\,\text{high}}}{\mathbf{A}_{v\,\text{mid}}}\right| = \frac{1}{1 + jf/36.19 \times 10^6}$$

Now let us consider the first stage. It is loaded by the second stage. Hence, Eq. 12-96 is applicable here. Then, for this stage,

$$\frac{\mathbf{A}_{v\,\text{high}}}{\mathbf{A}_{v\,\text{mid}}} = \frac{1 + j\omega C'_{sh2} R_{p2}}{(1 + j\omega C_{sh1} R_{p1})(1 + j\omega C'_{sh2} R'_{sh2})} \tag{12-214}$$

Note that we have added a prime to C_{sh2} from Eq. 12-96 to avoid confusing it with C_{sh2}, which was just calculated. Then, (see Eq. 12-97)

$$C'_{sh2} = C_{b'e2} + C_{b'c2}(1 + g_m R_{sh2}) = 25 + 0.5(1 + 75{,}000 \times 10^{-6} \times 500.6) = 44.27 \text{ pF}$$

For the first stage,

$$R_{p1} = 565.2$$

Hence,

$$C_{sh} = 25 + 0.5\left(1 + \frac{753.1}{565.2} + 75{,}000 \times 10^{-6} \times 753.1\right) = 54.4 \text{ pF}$$

We must now calculate the value of $R_{sh'}$ given by Eq. 12-95e, but to do this we must determine R (see Eq. 12-95d). The values of R_C and R_B are not yet known. However, we can calculate R using the relation

$$\frac{1}{R_{sh1}} = \frac{1}{R_{i2}} + \frac{1}{R} \tag{12-215}$$

Hence,

$$\frac{1}{R} = \frac{1}{753.1} - \frac{1}{1600}$$

$$R = 1422.8 \text{ ohms}$$

Then,

$$R_{sh'} = \frac{r_{b'e2}(r_{bb'2} + R)}{r_{b'e2} + r_{bb'2} + R} = \frac{1500(100 + 1422.8)}{1500 + 100 + 1422.8} = 755.7$$

Then, substituting in Eq. 12-96 and manipulating, we have, for the first stage,

$$\frac{\mathbf{A}_{v\,\text{high}}}{\mathbf{A}_{v\,\text{mid}}} = \frac{1 + jf/38.4 \times 10^6}{(1 + jf/5.18 \times 10^6)(1 + jf/4.76 \times 10^6)}$$

Thus, for the entire amplifier, the high-frequency response is

$$\frac{\mathbf{A}_{v\,\text{high}\,T}}{\mathbf{A}_{v\,\text{mid}\,T}} = \frac{1 + jf/38.4 \times 10^6}{(1 + jf/36.19 \times 10^6)(1 + jf/5.18 \times 10^6)(1 + jf/4.76 \times 10^6)}$$

At $f = 10^6$ Hz, we have

$$\left|\frac{\mathbf{A}_{v\,\text{high}\,T}}{\mathbf{A}_{v\,\text{mid}\,T}}\right| = \sqrt{\frac{1 + (1/38.4)^2}{[1 + (1/36.19)^2][1 + (1/5.18)^2][1 + (1/4.76)^2]}} = 0.961$$

Thus, the design has been achieved with two stages. Note that, as we discussed earlier, the high-frequency response of the second stage is much better than that of the first stage. Therefore, if the design had failed, an attempt to design the amplifier using two stages should be repeated, now with the gain of the second stage greater than that of the first. (Actually several trials might be needed to determine how the gain should be distributed.)

Now let us calculate the various resistance values. For the second stage

$$\frac{1}{R_{sh2}} = \frac{1}{r_{ce}} + \frac{1}{R_{C2}} + \frac{1}{R_{\text{load}}}$$

$$\frac{1}{R_{C2}} = \frac{1}{500.6} - \frac{1}{100{,}000} - \frac{1}{1600}$$

$$R_{C2} = 733.9$$

For the first stage,

$$\frac{1}{R_{sh1}} = \frac{1}{r_{ce}} + \frac{1}{R_{C1}} + \frac{1}{R_B} + \frac{1}{R_i}$$

$$\frac{1}{R_{C1}} = \frac{1}{753.1} - \frac{1}{100{,}000} - \frac{1}{4180} - \frac{1}{1600}$$

$$R_{C1} = 2204.5 \text{ ohms}$$

Then, let us use

$$R_{C2} = 750 \text{ ohms}$$

$$R_{C1} = 2200 \text{ ohms}$$

Now let us calculate the power supply voltages and the values of R_{B1} and R_{B2}. From Eq. 5-35, we have

$$V_{CC} = V_{CEQ} + I_{BQ}R_E + I_{CQ}(R_C + R_E)$$

Then, for stage 1, we have

$$V_{CC1} = 5 + 20 \times 10^{-6} \times 1000 + 2 \times 10^{-3}(2200 + 1000) = 11.42 \text{ V}$$

For stage 2, we have

$$V_{CC2} = 5 + 20 \times 10^{-6} \times 1000 + 2 \times 10^{-3}(750 + 1000) = 8.52 \text{ V}$$

Thus, two different power supply voltages are required. It is not uncommon for different stages of an amplifier to use different power supply voltages. In this case, a single power supply voltage of

$$V_{CC} = 10 \text{ V}$$

could possibly be used. Since a considerable shift in the operating point will result, the characteristics of the transistors should be checked at this new operating point. Let us

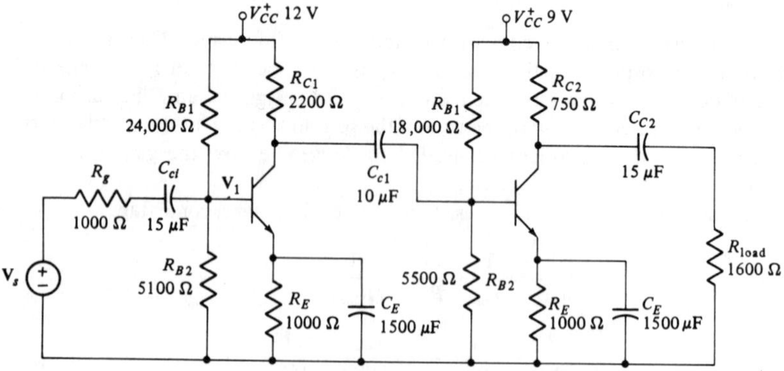

Figure 12-35. A two-stage *RC* coupled transistor amplifier. See text for a discussion of the electrolytic capacitors.

assume that two different power supply voltages are used, $V_{CC1} = 12$ V, $V_{CC2} = 9$ V (see Fig. 12-35). Alternatively, it may be possible to change R_{load} so that R_{C2} could be increased. Then, the values of V_{CC1} and V_{CC2} would approach each other.

Equation 5-35 shall be used to obtain R_{B1}. For the first stage, we have

$$R_{B11} = \frac{V_{CC1}R_B}{I_{BQ}(R_B + R_E) + I_{CQ}R_E} = \frac{12 \times 4180}{20 \times 10^{-6}(4180 + 1000) + 2 \times 10^{-3} \times 1000}$$

$$= 23{,}845 \text{ ohms}$$

Then,

$$\frac{1}{R_{B21}} = \frac{1}{R_B} - \frac{1}{R_{B11}} = \frac{1}{4180} - \frac{1}{23{,}845}$$

$$R_{B21} = 5069 \text{ ohms}$$

We shall use

$$R_{B11} = 24{,}000 \text{ ohms}$$

$$R_{B21} = 5100 \text{ ohms}$$

Proceeding similarly for stage 2, we have

$$R_{B12} = 17{,}884 \text{ ohms}$$

$$R_{B22} = 5459 \text{ ohms}$$

We shall use

$$R_{B12} = 18{,}000 \text{ ohms}$$

$$R_{B22} = 5500 \text{ ohms}$$

We must now determine the values of the coupling and bypass capacitances, which involves the low-frequency specifications. The normalized low-frequency gain for each amplifier stage is given in Eq. 12-148. As in the case of the FET amplifier of the last section we shall break the design into two parts and start by assuming at the start that the source bypass capacitors are infinite. Subsequently we shall consider their effect. The normalized low-frequency response due to the coupling capacitors is given by Eqs. 12-103 to 12-105. For each stage, we have

$$f_1 = 1/2\pi R_{\text{low}} C_c$$

There are three "stages" here since we have included a coupling capacitor in the input stage. Thus,

$$R_{\text{low}\,i} = R_g + \frac{R_B R_i}{R_B + R_i} = 1000 + \frac{4180 \times 1600}{4180 + 1600} = 2157 \text{ ohms} \tag{12-216a}$$

$$R_{\text{low}\,1} = \frac{r_{ce} R_{C1}}{r_{ce} + R_{C1}} + \frac{R_B R_i}{R_B + R_i} = \frac{100{,}000 \times 2200}{100{,}000 + 2200} + \frac{4180 \times 1600}{4180 + 1600} = 3310 \text{ ohms} \tag{12-216b}$$

$$R_{\text{low}\,2} = \frac{r_{cc} R_{C2}}{r_{cc} + R_{C2}} + R_{\text{load}} = \frac{100{,}000 \times 750}{100{,}000 + 750} + 1600 = 2344 \text{ ohms} \tag{12-216c}$$

Let us have the same f_1 for all three stages. Then,

$$\left[\frac{1}{1+(f_1/20)^2}\right]^{3/2} = 0.8$$

Solving, we have

$$f_1 = 8.01 \text{ Hz}$$

The largest coupling capacitance will be C_{ci}. Let us calculate its value.

$$C_{ci} = 1/2\pi f_1 R_{\text{low}\,i} = 1/(2\pi \times 8.01 \times 2157) = 9.21\ \mu\text{F}$$

Corresponding values can be calculated for C_{c1} and C_{c2}. If these are used, then infinite bypass capacitors would be required. Let us increase the coupling capacitors' value. Suppose that we use

$$C_{ci} = 15\ \mu\text{F}$$

Then,

$$f_1 = 1/(2\pi \times 2157 \times 15 \times 10^{-6}) = 4.92 \text{ Hz}$$

Then, the loss due to the coupling capacitors is

$$\left[\frac{1}{1+(4.92/20)^2}\right]^{3/2} = 0.916$$

Hence, the allowable loss due to the emitter bypass circuit is

$$0.8/0.916 = 0.873$$

Then, using Eq. 12-148, we have

$$\left[\frac{f_{E1}}{f_{E2}}\sqrt{\frac{1+(20/f_{E1})^2}{1+(20/f_{E2})^2}}\right]^2 = 0.873$$

where

$$f_{E1} = 1/2\pi R_E C_E$$

and

$$f_{E2} = \left[1 + \frac{R_E(1+g_m r_{b'e})}{r_{bb'} + r_{b'e}}\right] f_{E1}$$

$$f_{E2} = \left[1 + \frac{1000(1 + 75{,}000 \times 10^{-6} \times 1500)}{100 + 1500}\right] f_{E1} = 71.9 f_{E1}$$

Note that we are making an approximation here. The emitter impedance will cause the input impedance of the transistor to increase as the frequency is decreased. This will tend to offset the falloff in gain at low frequencies. In general, if the falloff in gain is small, then this effect will not be large. In any event, if we ignore this effect, our design will be on the safe side. That is, the amplifier will better than meet specifications. Because of this approximation, we use $r_{bb'} = 100$ for the first stage as well as for the second one. Thus, we have

$$\left[\frac{1}{71.9}\sqrt{\frac{1 + (20/f_{E1})^2}{1 + (20/71.9f_{E1})^2}}\right]^2 = 0.873$$

Solving, we obtain

$$f_{E1} = 0.106 \text{ Hz}$$

Hence,

$$C_E = 1501\ \mu\text{F}$$

We shall use

$$C_E = 1500\ \mu\text{F}$$

(The slight reduction in C_E will be more than offset by the increase in the coupling capacitance.) This is a large value. However, electrolytic capacitors of this size are available. The size of C_E can be reduced somewhat if larger coupling capacitors were used. An alternative approach is to use a smaller R_E but this will then reduce R_B and, thus, complicate the mid- and high-frequency designs. As we discussed, amplifiers of this type often do not require much, or any, stabilization so a higher stability factor could be tolerated. Now R_E could be reduce while maintaining an acceptable R_B. Note that (see Sec. 5-8) there are other forms of stabilization that can be used which do not require an emitter resistor. These can be used when a high degree of stabilization is required. Hence, the problem of this large, electrolytic capacitor can be eliminated. (Note that 1500 μF low-voltage electrolytic capacitors are not uncommon elements.) Let us assume that we use the 1500-μF capacitor. Then, let us calculate the coupling capacitances.

The value of f_1 that we are using is $f_1 = 4.92$ Hz. Hence,

$$C_{c1} = 1/2\pi R_{\text{low }1} f_1 = 1/(2\pi \times 3310 \times 4.92) = 9.8\ \mu\text{F}$$

$$C_{c2} = 1/2\pi R_{\text{low }2} f_1 = 1/(2\pi \times 2344 \times 4.92) = 13.8\ \mu\text{F}$$

Then, we should use

$$C_{c1} = 10\ \mu\text{F}$$

$$C_{c2} = 15\ \mu\text{F}$$

The value of $C_{ci} = 15\ \mu$F has already been chosen. All of the coupling capacitors will be electrolytic capacitors. The final design is shown in Fig. 12-35.

Use of Common-Emitter, Emitter Follower Pairs

In the previous design example, we saw that the half-power frequency of the second stage was much greater than that of the first. This is because the first amplifier stage had to drive the capacitive input of the second stage. The frequency response can often be improved by alternating common-emitter amplifiers and emitter follower amplifiers. This is analogous to the common-source, source follower pairs discussed in the last section. If the amplifier input is a source follower, then its high-input impedance may prove desirable. Also, if the load is highly capacitive, then the low R_{sh} of the source follower may also help to improve the high-frequency response.

Let us illustrate these ideas by considering a cascade of a common-emitter amplifier and an emitter follower. For instance, suppose that we use the transistor from the previous design in an emitter follower where $\mathbf{A}_{v\,\mathrm{mid}} = 0.98$. Then (see Eq. 12-163),

$$0.98 = \frac{75{,}000 \times 10^{-6}}{75{,}000 \times 10^{-6} + (1/R_{sh})(1 + 100/1500)}$$

Solving, we have

$$R_{sh} = 696.8 \text{ ohms}$$

Then, (see Eq. 12-171)

$$C_{shE} = 25\left(1 + \frac{100}{696.8}\right) + 0.5 \times 100\left(75{,}000 \times 10^{-6} + \frac{1}{1500} + \frac{1}{696.8}\right)$$

$$C_{shE} = 32.4 \text{ pF}$$

$$\frac{1}{R_{shE}} = 75{,}000 \times 10^{-6} + \frac{1}{1500} + \frac{1}{696.8}\left(1 + \frac{100}{1500}\right)$$

$$R_{shE} = 13.0 \text{ ohms}$$

Then,

$$f_2 = 1/2\pi R_{shE} C_{shE} = 1/(2\pi \times 13 \times 32.4 \times 10^{-12}) = 378 \text{ MHz}$$

This is very much greater than the half-power frequency of a common-emitter amplifier stage. Actually, we have ignored the loading effect of the succeeding common-emitter stage on the source follower but, if approximations 12-175 are valid, then this is allowable. Note that g_m is large enough in this case so that approximations 12-175 will be valid. Now let us consider the gain of the common-emitter stage that is loaded by the source follower.

In order to make a valid comparison here we shall ignore the generator resistance. Now we shall compare the responses of typical stages in a cascade, that is, we shall compare the response of a common-emitter stage of gain 35.20 when it is loaded with a similar common-emitter stage with a common-emitter, emitter follower pair of overall gain 35.20.

Equation 12-200 is still valid for the common-emitter stage cascaded with a source follower but now C'_{sh2} and R_{p2} refer to the input of the emitter follower amplifier. The other quantities must be recalculated to account for the modification just discussed. Let us calculate the necessary quantities. From Fig. 12-28, we have

$$\frac{1}{R_{p2}} = \frac{1}{r_{bb'}} + \frac{1}{r_{b'e}/(1 - A_v)} \tag{12-217a}$$

and

$$C'_{sh2} = C_{b'c} + C_{b'e}(1 - A'_v) \tag{12-217b}$$

Substituting, we obtain

$$\frac{1}{R_{p2}} = \frac{1}{100} + \frac{1}{1500/(1 - 0.98)}$$

$$R_{p2} = 99.9$$

$$C'_{\text{sh}2} = 0.5 + 25(1 - 0.98) = 1.0\ p\text{F}$$

Before substituting in Eq. 12-200, we must calculate the new value of $R_{\text{sh}'}$, $C_{\text{sh}1}$, and R_{p1}. Let us start by calculating a new value of $R_{\text{sh}1a}$. (We have added the subscript a to differentiate it from the previously calculated value.) The gain of the stage is

$$\frac{35.20}{0.98} = 35.9$$

Then,

$$R_{\text{sh}1a} = \frac{35.9(100 + 1500)}{75{,}000 \times 10^{-6} \times 1500} = 510.6 \text{ ohms}$$

Also,

$$\frac{1}{R_{p1a}} = \frac{1}{100} + \frac{1}{1500}$$

$$R_{p1a} = 93.7$$

Then,

$$C_{\text{sh}1a} = 25 + 0.5\left(1 + \frac{510.6}{93.7} + 75{,}000 \times 10^{-6} \times 510.6\right) = 47.4 \text{ pF}$$

In addition,

$$R'_{\text{sh}} = \frac{[r_{b'e2}/(1 - A_{v2})](r_{bb'2} + R)}{[r_{b'2}/(1 - A_{v2})] + r_{bb'2} + R} \tag{12-218}$$

and

$$\frac{1}{R} = \frac{1}{R_{\text{sh}1a}} - \frac{1}{R_{i2}}$$

The subscript 2 refers to the emitter follower.

$$\frac{1}{R} = \frac{1}{510.6} - \frac{1}{100 + 1500/0.02}$$

Thus,

$$R = 514.1 \text{ ohms}$$

Hence,

$$R'_{\text{sh}} = \frac{(1500/0.02)(100 + 514.1)}{(1500/0.02) + 100 + 514.1} = 609.1 \text{ ohms}$$

Then, substituting in Eq. 12-214 we obtain, for the normalized high-frequency response of the common-emitter stage,

$$\frac{\mathbf{A}_{v\,\text{high}}}{\mathbf{A}_{v\,\text{mid}}} = \frac{1 + jf/1593 \times 10^6}{(1 + jf/35.8 \times 10^6)(1 + jf/261 \times 10^6)}$$

Then, the overall frequency response of the common-emitter, emitter follower amplifier cascade is

$$\frac{\mathbf{A}'_{v\,\text{high}}}{\mathbf{A}'_{v\,\text{mid}}} = \frac{1 + jf/1593 \times 10^6}{(1 + jf/35.8 \times 10^6)(1 + jf/261 \times 10^6)(1 + jf/378 \times 10^6)}$$

The upper half-power frequency of the combination is approximately

$$f'_2 = 35.8 \text{ Mhz}$$

We must compare this with f_2 for a common-emitter stage of gain 35.20 in a cascade of common-emitter stages, then, proceeding as before, we have

$$\frac{\mathbf{A}_{v\,\text{high}}}{\mathbf{A}_{v\,\text{mid}}} = \frac{1 + jf/38.3 \times 10^6}{(1 + jf/36.2 \times 10^6)(1 + jf/6.74 \times 10^6)}$$

The half-power frequency of this single common-emitter amplifier is approximately

$$f_2 = 6.74 \text{ MHz}$$

Thus, the common-emitter, emitter follower pair has considerably better high-frequency response. Hence, the use of these pairs should always be considered when a broadbanded integrated circuit amplifier is to be built since the extra stages can be easily fabricated.

Direct Coupled Amplifiers

The direct coupled amplifier of Fig. 12-14b can be used when integrated circuit amplifiers or amplifiers with very low-frequency response are to be built. In this case, emitter stabilization is usually not used. The mid- and high-frequency design now proceeds as before except that R_B is absent. If other bias stabilization circuits are used, their effect on gain should be considered (see Sec. 5-8).

12-15. THE CASCODE AMPLIFIER PAIR

In the last section we discussed the advantage of the cascaded emitter follower, common-emitter pair. In this section we shall discuss some other pairs called *cascode* amplifiers. The usual form of the cascade is a cascade of common-emitter and common-base stages, although, at times, emitter follower, common-base cascodes are used. Cascodes are often used in integrated circuit amplifiers. We shall consider these in subsequent chapters.

A simple cascode amplifier is shown in Fig. 12-36. We have drawn a direct coupled amplifier here. The diodes act as a constant voltage source, which properly biases the emitter-base junction of Q_2. Further consideration of the biasing of cascode amplifiers will be discussed when the biasing integrated circuit amplifiers are discussed in Chapter 14. In this section we shall compute the voltage gain of this pair of stages. After we obtain the gain of these stages we shall be in a position to discuss why these pairs are used. For

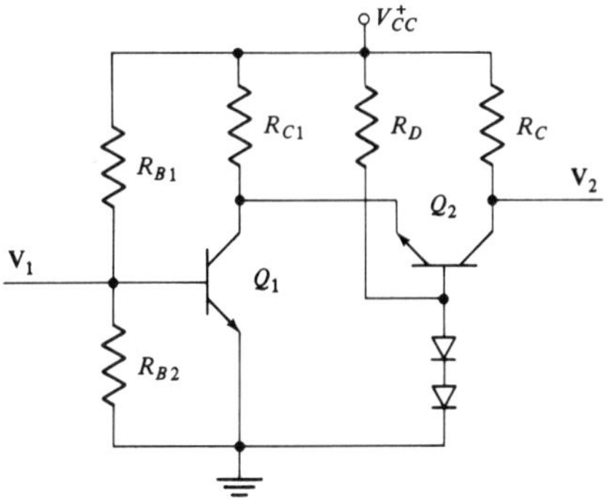

Figure 12-36. A direct coupled cascode amplifier.

purposes of comparison, we shall use transistors whose parameters are the same as those used in Sec. 12-14.

$$g_m = 75{,}000\ \mu\text{mho}$$
$$r_{bb'} = 100 \text{ ohms}$$
$$r_{b'e} = 1500 \text{ ohms}$$
$$r_{b'c} = 10^7 \text{ ohms}$$
$$r_{ce} = 100{,}000 \text{ ohms}$$
$$C_{b'e} = 25 \text{ pF}$$
$$C_{b'c} = 0.5 \text{ pF}$$

Again, to aid in comparison, we shall use R_C such that the gain of the cascode is 35.2, which is the gain of a single stage of the amplifier in the last section.

The low-frequency input impedance of the common-base amplifier is given by Eq. 12-193. In general, we shall approximate the high-frequency input impedance by

$$\mathbf{Y}_i = g_m + j\omega C_{b'e} \tag{12-219}$$

We shall assume that, at all frequencies of interest (to be on the safe side) $C_{b'e}$ is added in parallel with $C_{b'c}$ of the first stage so that, for the common-emitter stage, we shall use

$$C_{b'c} = 25.5 \text{ pF}$$

The midband voltage gain of the common-emitter amplifier is given by Eq. 12-85 where

$$\frac{1}{R_{\text{sh}}} = \frac{1}{Y_i} + \frac{1}{r_{ce}} + \frac{1}{R_{C1}} = 75 \times 10^{-3} + \frac{1}{100{,}000} + \frac{1}{R_{C1}}$$
$$R_{\text{sh}} = 13.33 \text{ ohms}$$

(Note that we have assumed that $R_{C1} \gg 1/g_m$. In fact $R_{\text{sh}} \approx 1/g_m = 1/Y_i$. Since the input admittance of the common-base amplifier is very low.)

$$\mathbf{A}_{v\,\text{mid}} = -75 \times 10^{-3} \times 13.33 \times \frac{1500}{1600} = -0.9373$$

Now let us compute the upper half-power frequency for this amplifier. From Eqs. 12-89, 12-90, and 12-93, we have

$$\frac{1}{R_P} = \frac{1}{r_{bb'}} + \frac{1}{r_{b'e}} = \frac{1}{100} + \frac{1}{1500}$$

$$R_P = 93.75 \text{ ohms}$$

$$C_{sh} = C_{b'e} + C_{b'c}\left(1 + \frac{R_{sh}}{R_P} + g_m R_{sh}\right) = 25 + 25.5\left(1 + \frac{13.33}{93.75} + 75 \times 10^{-3} \times 13.33\right)$$

$$C_{sh} = 79.62 \text{ pF}$$

Note that this capacitance is small because R_{sh} is so small. Then,

$$f_2 = 1/2\pi C_{sh} R_{sh} = 1/(2\pi \times 79.62 \times 10^{-12} \times 13.33) = 150.0 \times 10^6 \text{ Hz}$$

Now let us compute the voltage gain and upper half-power frequency of the common-base stage. From Eqs. 12-182 and 12-183, we have

$$\frac{1}{R_{sh}} = \frac{1}{r_{ce}} + \frac{1}{R_C}$$

We assume that R_C is such that the gain of the two stages is 35.2. Thus, the gain of the second stage is 35.2/0.9373 = 37.55.

$$A_{v\,\text{mid}\,2} = g_m R_{sh} \frac{r_{b'e}}{r_{bb'} + r_{b'e}} = 37.55$$

Hence,

$$R_{sh} = 534.0 \text{ ohms}$$

The upper half-power frequency is given by Eq. 12-188. Substituting, we obtain

$$\frac{1}{R_P} = \frac{1}{100} + \frac{1}{1500}$$

$$R_P = 93.75$$

$$f_{22} = \left\{2\pi(93.75)\left[\left(75 \times 10^{-3} \times 534.0 + \frac{534.0}{93.75} + 1\right)0.5 \times 10^{-12} + 25 \times 10^{-12}\right]\right\}^{-1}$$

$$f_{22} = 35.10 \times 10^6 \text{ Hz}$$

The overall half-power frequency is determined by the half-power frequencies of both stages. However, $f_{21} \gg f_{22}$. Hence.

$$f_{2T} = f_{22} = 35.10 \times 10^6 \text{ Hz}$$

Let us compare this with the second stage of the amplifier of Sec. 12-14. (The second stage is used since it does not drive a capacitive load.) There $f_2 = 36.19 \times 10^6$ Hz. This is very slightly greater than f_{2T}. This is because the gain of the common-base stage of the cascode must be slightly greater than the second stage of the example of Sec. 12-14.

(The gain of the output stage of the cascode is made greater to offset the slight loss in the first stage of the cascode.)

It may appear as though the cascode has no advantages over the single common-emitter stage but this will not always be the case. The cascode has some important advantages. For instance, consider the cascade of this section. The gain of its first stage is less than unity. Thus, its input capacitance will be small since the Miller effect will be unimportant. As discussed in Sec. 12-10, in most cases the input capacitance loading on the common-base stage will have essentially the same effect as it does on a common-emitter stage of comparable gain. Note that we used a resistive load in our calculations.

Now suppose that we compare a cascade of cascode stages with a cascade of common-emitter stages. In general, the high-frequency response of the cascode amplifier will be superior because of the reduced Miller effect. (Note that in the common-emitter cascade of Sec. 12-14, the half-power frequency of the first stage is very much less than that of the second stage.)

There is another, related, advantage of the cascode. In Sec. 12-10 we discussed that the common-base stage had very small feedback from output to input. There are many circumstances when we want to reduce this feedback. (Some of these applications will be discussed in Chapter 18.) Cascodes are often used in such cases.

Cascode pairs, in contrast to single common-base stages, can effectively be cascaded. This is because the common-emitter input stage of the cascode raises the input impedance to reasonable values.

An emitter follower can also be used as the first stage in a cascode. This results in a much higher input impedance but there is a loss in gain. The maximum voltage gain of an emitter follower is 1 and its output impedance is approximately $1/g_m$. Similarly, the input impedance of a common-base circuit is approximately $1/g_m$. Thus, the maximum voltage gain of an emitter follower driving a comparable common-base stage is 0.5. Therefore, common-emitter input stages are only used in cascodes when very high input impedance is required.

12-16. POLES AND ZEROS

We have characterized amplifiers by their frequency response. That is, we have considered the amplitude and phase of the amplification as functions of ω. There is another procedure that can be used. We can consider the response of the amplifier as a function of time to a given input signal. This is called *time domain* analysis where the previous procedure was called *frequency domain* analysis.

Our time domain analysis shall be based upon the Laplace transform which we shall introduce in a simple and nonrigorous way. For those readers who are familiar with the Laplace transform, this will be a review.

In all of our analyses the only time that ω appeared was as the term $j\omega$. For instance, for a capacitor

$$\mathbf{Z}_C = \frac{1}{j\omega C}$$

$$\mathbf{Y}_C = j\omega C$$

Then, let us make the substitution

$$s = j\omega \tag{12-220}$$

Hence,

$$\mathbf{Z}_C = \frac{1}{sC}$$

$$\mathbf{Y}_C = sC$$

In any expression for the amplification, we can replace ω by s/j. Note that the j's will combine so that the coefficients of the final expression will be real numbers. For instance, Eq. 12-39 can be written as

$$\frac{\mathbf{A}_{v\,\text{high}}}{\mathbf{A}_{v\,\text{mid}}} = \frac{1}{1 + s/\omega_2} \tag{12-221}$$

Similarly, Eq. 12-89 can be written as

$$\mathbf{A}_{v\,\text{high}} = \frac{-\dfrac{1}{r_{bb'}}(g_m - sC_{b'c})}{s^2 C_{b'e}C_{b'c} + s\left[\dfrac{1}{R_{\text{sh}}}(C_{b'e} + C_{b'c}) + \left(\dfrac{1}{r_{bb'}} + \dfrac{1}{r_{b'e}}\right)C_{b'c} + g_m C_{b'c}\right] + \dfrac{1}{R_{\text{sh}}}\left(\dfrac{1}{r_{bb'}} + \dfrac{1}{r_{b'e}}\right)} \tag{12-222}$$

In general, no matter how complex the amplifier, the amplification can be written in the general form

$$\mathbf{A}(s) = \frac{a_n s^n + a_{n-1}s^{n-1} + \cdots + a_1 s + a_0}{b_m s^m + b_{m-1}s^{m-1} + \cdots + b_1 s + b_0} \tag{12-223}$$

Note the (s) following the $\mathbf{A}$, which *indicates that* $\mathbf{A}$ *is a function of the variable* s. The a_i, $i = 1, 2, 3, \ldots, n$ and the b_k, $k = 1, 2, \ldots, m$, are real numbers that are independent of ω or s. They depend only upon the parameters of the amplifier circuit such as resistance, capacitance, or transconductance.

Poles and Zeros. We can always factor a polynomial and express it in terms of its roots and a constant multiplier. Thus we can write Eq. 12-223 in the following way.

$$\mathbf{A}(s) = K\frac{(s - s_1)(s - s_3)\cdots(s - s_{2n-1})}{(s - s_2)(s - s_4)\cdots(s - s_{2m})} \tag{12-224}$$

Note that the roots of the numerator are given odd numbered subscripts while the roots of the denominator are given even numbered subscripts. The roots need not be real. They can be complex or imaginary. Since the coefficients of Eq. 12-223 are real, the roots must occur in complex conjugate pairs.

The constant K of Eq. 12-224 does not affect the shape of the frequency response plot. All of the shape information is conveyed by the location of the roots of the numerator and denominator. These roots are often given by a two-dimensional plot (see Fig.

12-37.) The axis of imaginary numbers is labeled $j\omega$. Note that if s is replaced by $j\omega$, then the expression for the frequency response results. The roots of the numerator are marked with circles while the roots of the denominator are marked with x's. If $\mathbf{A}(s)$ is evaluated at a root of the numerator, its value will be zero. For this reason, the roots of the numerator called *zeros*. If $\mathbf{A}(s)$ is evaluated at a root of the denominator, its magnitude will be infinite. The roots of the denominator are called *poles*. The diagram of Fig. 12-37 is called a *pole-zero diagram* or a *pole-zero plot*. The entire plane is called the *s plane*. The $j\omega$ axis divides it into a *right-half plane* and a *left-half plane*. We shall discuss the significance of these half-planes in the next section.

Frequency Response Plots from the Pole-Zero Diagram

The frequency response can be obtained directly from the pole-zero diagram by a simple graphical procedure. Let us consider it. To obtain the frequency response from $\mathbf{A}(s)$, we replace s by $j\omega$. Hence, using Eq. 12-224, we obtain

$$A(j\omega) = K\frac{(j\omega - s_1)(j\omega - s_3)\cdots(j\omega - s_{2n-1})}{(j\omega - s_2)(j\omega - s_4)\cdots(j\omega - s_{2m})} \tag{12-225}$$

Thus,

$$|A(j\omega)| = K\frac{|j\omega - s_1||j\omega - s_3|\cdots|j\omega - s_{2n-1}|}{|j\omega - s_2||j\omega - s_4|\cdots|j\omega - s_{2m}|} \tag{12-226a}$$

$$\begin{aligned}\measuredangle A(j\omega) = {} & \measuredangle(j\omega - s_1) + \measuredangle(j\omega - s_3) + \cdots + \measuredangle(j\omega - s_{2n-1}) \\ & -[\measuredangle(j\omega - s_2) + \measuredangle(j\omega - s_4) + \cdots + \measuredangle(j\omega - s_{2m})]\end{aligned} \tag{12-226b}$$

If the pole-zero plot is available, then these magnitudes and angles can be obtained by a simple graphical procedure. (This procedure will not include the value of K.) Consider Fig. 12-38. The point s_k, which could represent the location of a pole or a zero is shown. Now suppose that we draw a vector from s_k to a point on the $j\omega$ axis called $j\omega_0$. The length of the vector is $|j\omega_0 - s_k|$ and its angle is $\measuredangle(j\omega_0 - s_k)$. Now let us see how the frequency response at a frequency ω_0 can be determined from a pole-zero diagram such as that of Fig. 12-37. Draw vectors from each pole and zero to the point

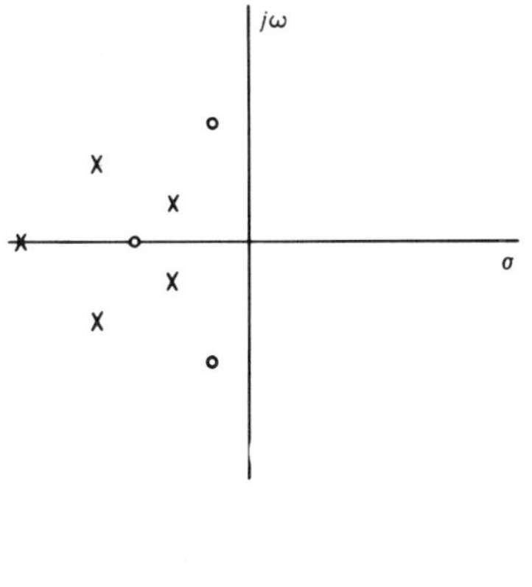

Figure 12-37. A typical pole-zero diagram.

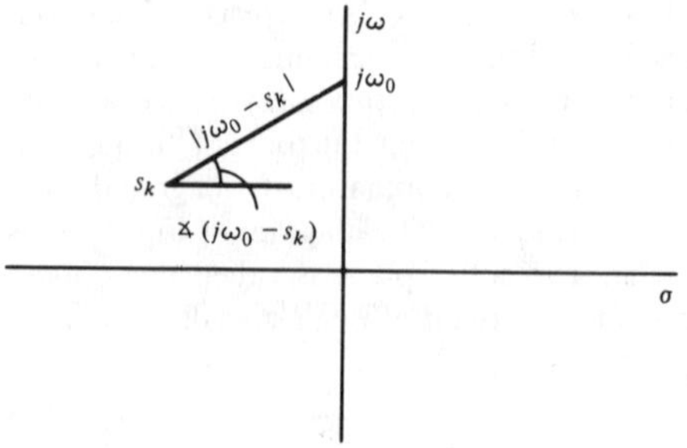

Figure 12-38. A graphical construction useful in obtaining a frequency reponse from a pole-zero diagram.

$j\omega_0$. The magnitude of the amplification (with the exception of the constant multiplier) is found by taking the product of the lengths of all the vectors drawn from the zeros to $j\omega_0$ and then dividing this number by the product of the lengths of all the vectors drawn from the poles to $j\omega_0$. The phase shift is equal to the sum of all the angles of the vectors drawn from the zeros to $j\omega_0$ minus the sum of all the angles of the vectors drawn from the poles to $j\omega_0$. Note that there may be multiple poles and/or zeros. When this graphical procedure is used, then each multiple pole or zero is counted as several single poles or zeros. For instance, if there is a double pole at s_k, then in computing magnitude, the square of the length of the vector from s_k to ω_0 would be used. The angle of this vector would be subtracted twice when the angle of the amplification was computed.

This graphical procedure can be used to illustrate that certain poles and zeros have more effect on the frequency response than others. For instance, suppose that we are computing the frequency response for a range of frequencies, that is, consider that ω_0 "moves" along the $j\omega$ axis. If a pole is near the $j\omega$ axis at s_k, then as $j\omega_0$ passes near the point s_k, $|j\omega_0 - s_k|$ and $\measuredangle(j\omega_0 - s_k)$ will change rapidly. If s_k is far from $j\omega_0$, then these quantities will vary much less rapidly. Thus, the variation in the frequency response is determined primarily by the poles and zeros closest to the range of $j\omega_0$ under consideration. At times, the variations due to the far removed poles and zeros can be neglected.

Let us consider the pole-zero diagrams for some typical amplifiers (see Fig. 12-39). Figure 12-39a is the pole-zero diagram for Eq. 12-221 which represents a simple high-frequency response. When $\omega_0 \ll \omega_2$, the response is flat. As ω_0 increases, the length of the vector increases and the magnitude of the response falls off.

In Fig. 12-39b the pole-zero diagram for the more complex high-frequency response of Eq. 12-222 is plotted. The response falls off as the frequency is increased because there is one more pole than zero. If

$$\omega_{2b} \gg \omega_{2a} \tag{12-227a}$$

$$\omega_{2c} \gg \omega_{2a} \tag{12-227b}$$

then, over much of the frequency range, the response can be computed by only considering the pole at $s = -\omega_{2a}$ and ignoring the other pole and zero.

A typical low-frequency response is given by Eq. 12-105. Manipulating this equation, we obtain

$$\frac{\mathbf{A}_{v\,\text{low}}}{\mathbf{A}_{v\,\text{mid}}} = \frac{s}{s + \omega_1} \tag{12-228}$$

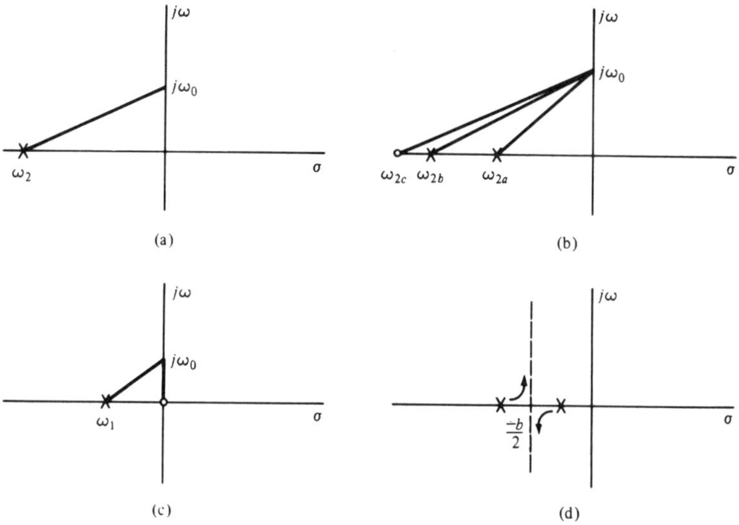

Figure 12-39. Some typical pole-zero diagrams. (a) Simple high-frequency response. (b) More complex high-frequency response. (c) Low-frequency response. (d) For Eq. 12-214. If $b^2 > 4c$ then the poles lie on σ axis. If $b^2 < 4c$, then the poles lie on dashed line.

The pole-zero diagram for the expression is drawn in Fig. 12-39c. There is a zero at the origin. This causes the response to become 0 at $\omega_0 = 0$. As ω_0 increases, the lengths and angles of the vectors drawn from the zero and from the pole approach each other. Thus, the response becomes flat.

Let us consider one other form of pole-zero diagram. Suppose that we are working with an amplification of the form

$$\mathbf{A}(s) = \frac{K}{s^2 + bs + c} \tag{12-229}$$

The poles occur at

$$s_{1,2} = \frac{-b \pm \sqrt{b^2 - 4c}}{2}$$

Let us assume that b and c are positive. Then, the poles s_1 and s_2 will lie in the left-half plane. Suppose that c is a variable. If

$$b^2 > 4c \tag{12-230a}$$

then the poles lie on the negative real axis on either side of the point $s = -b/2$. If

$$b^2 = 4c \tag{12-230b}$$

then there is a double pole at $s = -b/2$. If

$$b^2 < 4c \tag{12-230c}$$

then the poles are no longer real but are complex and lie at $-b/2 \pm j\sqrt{c - b^2/4}$. This is illustrated in Fig. 12-39d. In the next section, we shall discuss the significance of the location of the poles and zeros.

12-17. TRANSIENT RESPONSE

The output of an amplifier consists of a signal, which is a function of time, in response to an input signal, which also is a function of time. The ultimate reason for studying the frequency response of an amplifier is to determine the distortion in the output signal (see Sec. 12-1). Thus, we should consider the distortion on a time basis. The response of an amplifier on a time domain basis is called its *transient response*. In this section we shall discuss a method for obtaining the transient response of an amplifier and for considering the distortion on a time domain basis.

We shall use the Laplace transform of the amplification (function of s) which was developed in the last section. As we mentioned there, this will be a simple, nonrigorous discussion. If you are familiar with the Laplace transform, then this section will serve as a review.

A function of time $f(t)$ can be transferred into a function of $\mathbf{F}(s)$ by an integral called the direct Laplace transform integral

$$\mathbf{F}(s) = \int_0^\infty f(t)e^{-st}\,dt \tag{12-231}$$

The Laplace transform of the output waveform of an amplifier can be obtained by multiplying the amplification $\mathbf{A}(s)$ by $\mathbf{F}(s)$. This Laplace transform can be converted into a function of time by a process called the inverse Laplace transform. We shall not be concerned with the mathematical process of taking the Laplace transform and its inverse here. Instead, we shall use Table 12-2 to obtain this conversion. The function $u(t)$ represents the unit step (see Fig. 12-40) where

$$\begin{aligned} u(t) &= 1 \qquad t > 0 \\ &= 0 \qquad t < 0 \end{aligned} \tag{12-232}$$

We can observe some facts about a function of time by considering the pole(s) of its Laplace transform. For instance, poles in the left-half plane are transforms of functions of time which decay exponentially. Similarly, if the poles lie in the right-half plane, the function will increase exponentially. Simple poles on the $j\omega$ axis lead to functions of time that do not either build up or decrease. For instance, a pair of simple poles at $\pm j\omega_0$ lead to sinusoidal functions of time. Multiple poles of order $n + 1$ on the $j\omega$ axis lead to functions that increase with time as t^n where n is an integer.

Now let us determine the time response of an amplifier. Suppose that we have the amplifier whose gain is given by Eq. 12-221.

$$\mathbf{A}_v(s) = \frac{\omega_2 \mathbf{A}_{v\,\text{mid}}}{s + \omega_2} \tag{12-233}$$

Table 12-2 THE LAPLACE TRANSFORM OF SOME COMMON FORMS

$f(t)$	$\mathbf{F}(s)$
$u(t)$	$\frac{1}{s}$
$u(t) \sin \omega_0 t$	$\frac{\omega_0}{s^2 + \omega_0^2} = \frac{\omega_0}{(s + j\omega_0)(s - j\omega_0)}$
$u(t) \cos \omega_0 t$	$\frac{s}{s^2 + \omega_0^2} = \frac{s}{(s + j\omega_0)(s - j\omega_0)}$
$u(t)e^{-at} \sin \omega_0 t$	$\frac{\omega_0}{(s + a)^2 + \omega_0^2} = \frac{\omega_0}{(s + a + j\omega_0)(s + a - j\omega_0)}$
$u(t)e^{-at} \cos \omega_0 t$	$\frac{s}{(s + a)^2 + \omega_0^2} = \frac{s}{(s + a + j\omega_0)(s + a - j\omega_0)}$
$u(t)e^{-at}$	$\frac{1}{s + a}$
$u(t)e^{at}$	$\frac{1}{s - a}$
$u(t)t$	$\frac{1}{s^2}$

Let us determine the response of this amplifier to an input signal $v_1(t) = u(t)e^{-at}$. The Laplace transform of $v_1(t)$ is $1/(s + a)$ (see Table 12-2). That is,

$$\mathbf{V}_1(s) = \frac{1}{(s + a)} \tag{12-234}$$

The Laplace transform of the output voltage is

$$\mathbf{V}_2(s) = \mathbf{V}_1(s)\mathbf{A}_v(s) \tag{12-235}$$

Hence,

$$\mathbf{V}_2(s) = \left(\frac{\mathbf{A}_{v\,\text{mid}}}{s + a}\right)\left(\frac{\omega_2}{s + \omega_2}\right) \tag{12-236}$$

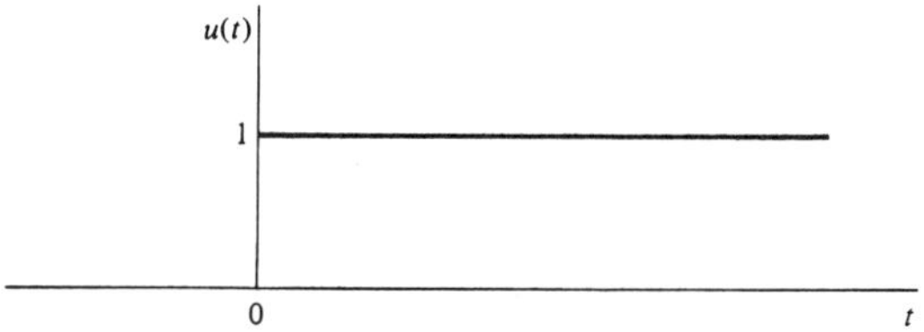

Figure 12-40. The unit step function.

This function is not in Table 12-2. However, functions such as this can be expanded in a series so that each term contains only one pole. For instance, we can write

$$\mathbf{V}_2 = \frac{[\omega_2/(\omega_2 - a)]\mathbf{A}_{v\,\text{mid}}}{s + a} + \frac{[\omega_2/(a - \omega_2)]A_{v\,\text{mid}}}{s + \omega_2} \tag{12-237}$$

Each of these terms is in Table 12-2. Hence, the output time signal is

$$v_2(t) = u(t)\mathbf{A}_{v\,\text{mid}} \frac{\omega_2}{\omega_2 - a}(e^{-at} - e^{-\omega_2 t}) \tag{12-238}$$

Unit Step Response

In an ideal amplifier, if $v_1(t)$ is its input signal, then $Kv_1(t)$ should be its output signal. If the output signal is not equal to a constant multiplied by the input signal, then distortion has occurred. If the input signal is irregular, then the output will also be an irregular function of time. Then, unless tedious measurements are made, it will be difficult to determine the distortion. On the other hand, if a simple input signal is used, then the distortion will be readily apparent. An input waveform that is commonly used for testing the amplifier is the unit step response (see Fig. 12-40) since any departure of the output from a step response will be easily seen.

Let us consider the unit step response of some typical amplifiers. For instance, suppose we consider the amplifier of Eq. 12-233 which has a single pole leading to a simple high-frequency response falloff.

$$\mathbf{A}_v(s) = \frac{\omega_2 \mathbf{A}_{v\,\text{mid}}}{s + \omega_2} \tag{12-239}$$

where $f_2 = \omega_2/2\pi$ is the upper half-power frequency. The Laplace transform of the unit step response of this amplifier is

$$V_2(s) = \frac{1}{s}\mathbf{A}_v(s) = \frac{\omega_2 \mathbf{A}_{v\,\text{mid}}}{s(s + \omega_2)} = \frac{\mathbf{A}_{v\,\text{mid}}}{s} - \frac{\mathbf{A}_{v\,\text{mid}}}{s + \omega_2} \tag{12-240}$$

Then, using Table 12-2, we have

$$v_2(t) = \mathbf{A}_{v\,\text{mid}}\, u(t)(1 - e^{-\omega_2 t}) \tag{12-241}$$

This is plotted in Fig. 12-41. Note that the response rises asymptotically to $\mathbf{A}_{v\,\text{mid}}$.

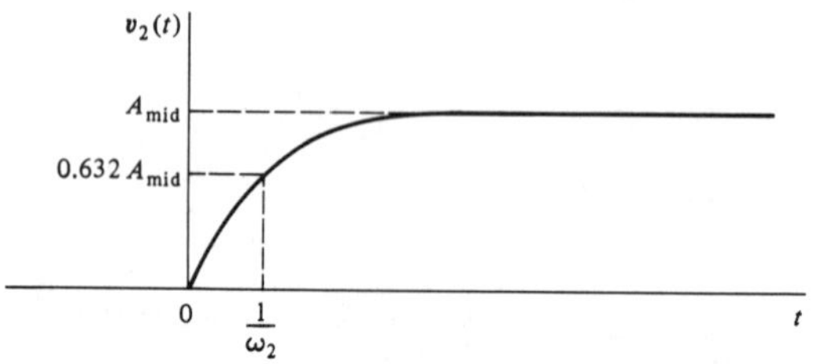

Figure 12-41. A plot of the unit step response of the amplifier characterized by Eq. 12-224.

It is usually convenient to normalize the unit step response by dividing the output by $\mathbf{A}_{v\,\text{mid}}$. We shall call this normalized unit step response $b(t)$. Then, in this case

$$b(t) = u(t)(1 - e^{-\omega_2 t}) \tag{12-242}$$

A plot of this normalized unit step response is shown in Fig. 12-42. The output exponentially rises to 1. At time $t = 1/\omega_2 = 2\pi f_2$, the response has risen to 63.2% of its final value. Increasing the upper half-power frequency causes $b(t)$ to rise to its final value more rapidly. Thus, as ω_2 increases, $b(t)$ more closely approximates a unit step. In general, if we want amplifiers to respond very rapidly, then they must have a broad high-frequency response.

Let us now investigate the effect of low-frequency falloff upon the unit step response. The normalized low-frequency response of a simple RC coupled stage is (see Eq. 12-228)

$$\frac{\mathbf{A}_{v\,\text{high}}}{\mathbf{A}_{v\,\text{mid}}} = \frac{s}{s + \omega_1} \tag{12-243}$$

Thus, the Laplace transform of the unit step response is given by

$$B(s) = \frac{1}{s}\frac{\mathbf{A}_{v\,\text{high}}}{\mathbf{A}_{v\,\text{mid}}} = \frac{\omega_1}{s + \omega_1} \tag{12-244}$$

Then, the unit step response is

$$b(t) = u(t)e^{-\omega_1 t} \tag{12-245}$$

A plot of this expression is given in Fig. 12-43. The response decays exponentially from 1 to 0. At $t = 1/\omega_1 = 1/2\pi f_1$, the response has fallen off to 36.8% of its initial value. As ω_1 is decreased, the rate of falloff is decreased. Although Fig. 12-43 does not look like a unit step, note that as $\omega_1 \to 0$, $b(t)$ does approach the unit step.

The scales of Figs. 12-42 and 12-43 are usually very different. The rise of the unit step is usually measured in microseconds (10^{-6} s) or nanoseconds (10^{-9} s). The decay of the unit step is measured in tenths of a second or in seconds. Of course, this implies that

$$\omega_2 \gg \omega_1 \tag{12-246}$$

that is, that there is a well-defined midband region.

Now let us consider the unit step response of an amplifier that has both a low-frequency and a high-frequency falloff. That is, its normalized amplification is

$$\frac{\mathbf{A}_v(s)}{\mathbf{A}_{v\,\text{mid}}} = \frac{s}{s + \omega_1}\frac{\omega_2}{s + \omega_2} \tag{12-247}$$

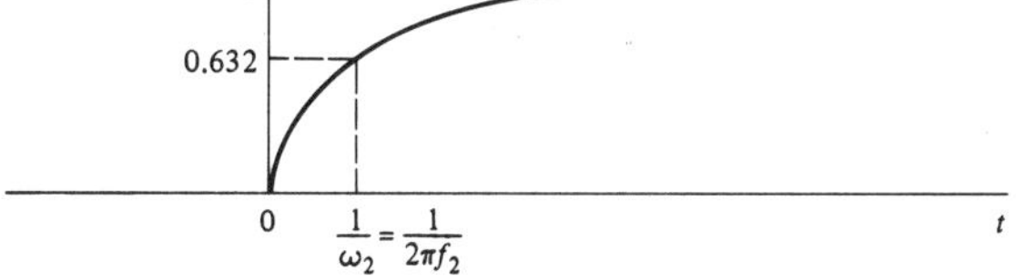

Figure 12-42. A plot of the normalized unit step response of the amplifier characterized by Eq. 12-224.

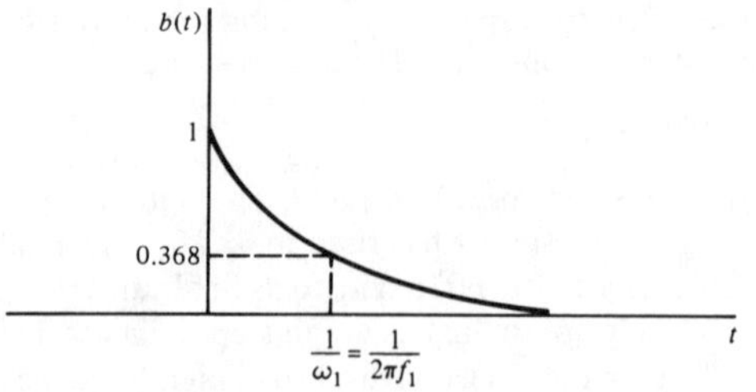

Figure 12-43. A plot of the normalized unit step response of the amplifier characterized by Eq. 12-228.

where we assume that inequality 12-246 is satisfied. The transformed, normalized unit step response is given by

$$\mathbf{B}(s) = \frac{1}{s}\frac{\mathbf{A}_v(s)}{\mathbf{A}_{v\,\text{mid}}}\frac{\omega_2}{(s+\omega_1)(s+\omega_2)} = \frac{\omega_2}{\omega_2-\omega_1}\frac{1}{s+\omega_1} + \frac{\omega_2}{\omega_1-\omega_2}\frac{1}{s+\omega_2}$$

Hence,

$$b(t) = \left(\frac{\omega_2}{\omega_2-\omega_1}e^{-\omega_1 t} - \frac{\omega_2}{\omega_2-\omega_1}e^{-\omega_2 t}\right)u(t) \tag{12-248a}$$

We assume that inequality 12-246 is satisfied. Typically, ω_2 will be 10^6 or more times larger than ω_1. Thus,

$$\frac{\omega_2}{\omega_2+\omega_1} \simeq 1$$
$$b(t) = u(t)(e^{-\omega_1 t} - e^{-\omega_2 t}) \tag{12-248b}$$

Since $\omega_2 \gg \omega_1$, $e^{-\omega_2 t}$ will essentially decay to 0 before $e^{-\omega_1 t}$ has changed a measurable amount from unity. Hence, for

$$t \ll \frac{1}{\omega_1}$$
$$b(t) = u(t)(1 - e^{-\omega_2 t}) \tag{12-249a}$$

Similarly, for $t \gg 1/\omega_2$, $e^{-\omega_2 t}$ has become almost 0 and Eq. 12-248b can be written as

$$b(t) = u(t)e^{-\omega_1 t} \tag{12-249b}$$

A plot of $b(t)$ is shown in Fig. 12-44. Note that the time scale changes in this figure. In an amplifier with a well-defined midband region, the buildup of the unit step response is determined almost entirely by the high-frequency response of the amplifier while the decay of the unit step response is determined almost entirely by the low-frequency response of the amplifier.

In most practical amplifiers, there is a well-defined midband region. In such cases, the buildup and decay of the unit step response are essentially independent of each other and can be studied separately. We shall now do this and develop some simple figures of merit that are used to rate amplifiers' unit step response.

Rise of the Unit Step Response

In the examples we have considered, the normalized unit step response rises exponentially to unity. This need not be the case. If the amplifier contains complex conjugate

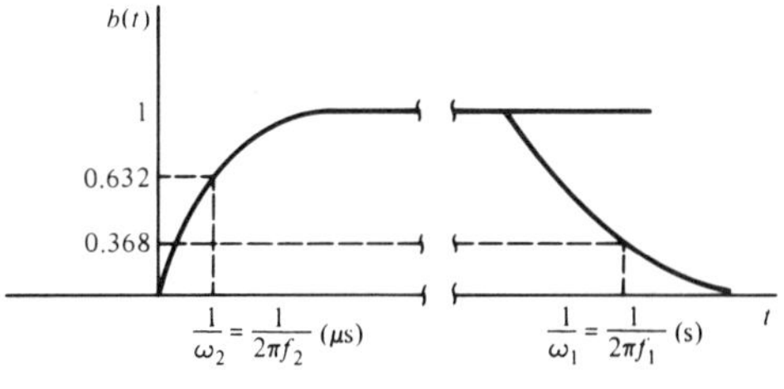

Figure 12-44. A plot of the normalized unit step response of the amplifier characterized by Eq. 12-232.

poles, then the response may exhibit a decayed sinusoidal oscillation about unity. Such a general unit step response is shown in Fig. 12-45.

An important criterion in predicting the rise of the unit step response is the time required for the response to rise to its final value. Many responses rise exponentially to unity. Thus, in theory, the response time is infinite. In practice, however, once the response becomes sufficiently close to unity, it can be considered to have "reached" it. Therefore, to rate the response, the time it takes for the response to reach a value close to 1 is chosen. Usually, this is 0.9. This is called the 90% *rise time*. In Sec. 12-1 we discussed that, if an amplifier only introduced delay, this did not distort the signal. In such cases, delay time should not be included in the rise time. To account for delay in the rise time in a simple way, the time required for the input to rise to 0.1 is often not included in the rise time. The time required for $b(t)$ to rise from 0.1 to 0.9 is then considered to be the rise time of the amplifier. This is called the 10–90% *rise time*. It is illustrated in Fig. 12-45 and is mathematically expressed as

$$\tau_r = \text{time for } b(t) \text{ to reach } 0.9 - \text{time for } b(t) \text{ to reach } 0.1 \tag{12-250}$$

In digital circuits, the total time for a circuit to respond to a pulse is of importance. In this case, delay time is detrimental and should be included in the figure of merit. Hence, we use the 90% rise time

$$\tau_p = \text{time for } b(t) \text{ to reach } 0.9 \tag{12-251}$$

as the criterion for digital circuits.

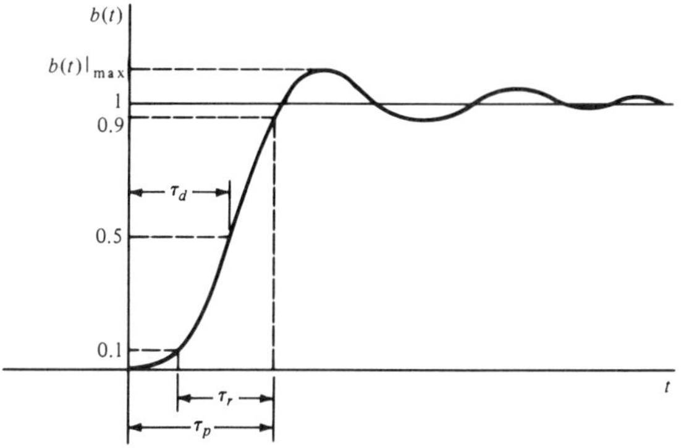

Figure 12-45. A general normalized unit step response.

The time τ_d (see Fig. 12-45) which is the time required for $b(t)$ to reach 0.5, is arbitrarily defined as the *delay time*.

In defining figures of merit in this way, we are attempting to characterize a curve by a few numbers. This has its limitations but these figures of merit are often useful.

The other figure of merit that is used to characterize the normalized unit step response is the *overshoot*, δ_o. This is defined as

$$\delta_o = \max b(t) - 1 \tag{12-252}$$

If $\delta_o > 0$, then the unit step response overshoots its final value of 1 and decays back toward it, usually in a damped sinusoidal fashion.

In amplifier circuits, there is often a tradeoff between rise time and overshoot. That is, by varying the parameters of certain circuits, we can reduce the rise time at the expense of increased overshoot. (This is illustrated in Sec. 17-8.)

Let us consider the significance of rise time and overshoot in terms of a practical amplifier. Suppose that one line of a television picture consists of a series of black and white bars. A train of pulses such as that of Fig. 12-46 would be transmitted. The response of the video amplifier is shown in Fig. 12-46b. (To simplify the diagram, we have not shown any overshoot here.) Thus, the television picture will not instantaneously switch from black to white but there will be a transition gray area which is only a very small part of each bar. Now consider Fig. 12-46c where we have shortened the length of the bars. The amplifier output is shown in Fig. 12-46d. The rise time remains unchanged but

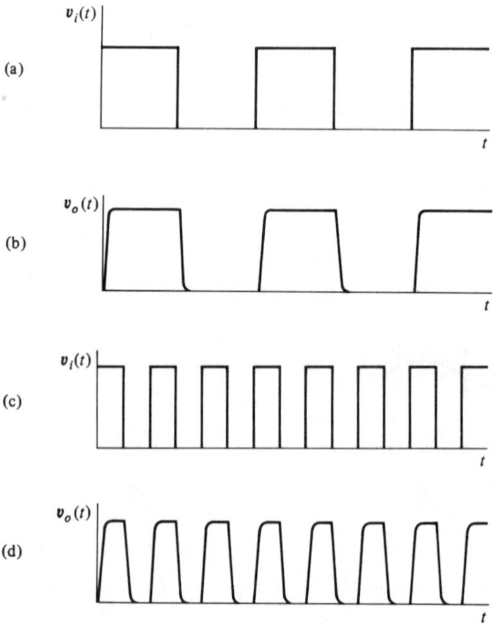

Figure 12-46. A response of an amplifier to a train of high-frequency pulses. (a) Input. (b) Output. (c) Higher frequency input. (d) Output for higher frequency input.

now it occupies more of the time of the pulse. The television image no longer appears as black or white squares. The gray region occupies a large part of the area. In effect, the black and white squares have been smeared. Thus, the number of black or white squares per picture that can be transmitted is limited. If the rise time is reduced, then the number of black and white squares that can be transmitted per picture without severe smearing is increased. Therefore, the rise time of the video amplifier is related to the *resolution* of the picture (i.e., the amount of fine detail it can present).

We have not illustrated the effect of overshoot here. Overshoot would manifest itself as a fringing of varying intensity lines about the transition from black to white.

Slew Rate. Another quantity that is related to the speed of response of an amplifier is the *slew rate* or *slewing rate.* Let us consider it. In Fig. 12-41 we illustrate a non-normalized unit step response. The output voltage rises to a maximum value of $\mathbf{A}_{v\,\text{mid}}$. Now suppose that, instead of applying an input $u(t)$, we apply $Vu(t)$, that is, the input voltage is multiplied by the constant V. The maximum output voltage is now $V\mathbf{A}_{v\,\text{mid}}$. Thus (see Eq. 12-241),

$$v_2(t) = V\mathbf{A}_{v\,\text{mid}}(1 - e^{-\omega_2 t}) \tag{12-253}$$

Then,

$$\frac{dv_2(t)}{dt} = V\mathbf{A}_{v\,\text{mid}}\,\omega_2 e^{-\omega_2 t} \tag{12-254}$$

This slope has its maximum value when $t = 0$. Let us call this S_l

$$S_l = V\mathbf{A}_{v\,\text{mid}}\,\omega_2 \tag{12-255}$$

In theory, as V increases, S_l will increase linearly. Thus, by increasing V, we can increase S_l without limit. However, this is not the case. *Eventually, the amplifier will saturate.* The maximum value of S_l is called the slew rate of the amplifier. In Sec. 14-13 we shall consider the slew rate in greater detail.

Decay of the Unit Step Response

A typical decay in the unit step response is shown in Fig. 12-43. One figure of merit for such decay would be the time that elapses before the normalized unit step response falls off to 0.9. The longer this 90% *fall time*, the better the response.

Another criterion is more commonly used. Let us consider it. Often, the amplifier is to amplify pulses wherein the longest pulse duration T_1 is known. In Fig. 12-47a, we show an amplifier driven by a train of pulses T_1. The period of the pulse is T where we assume $T > T_1$. The *normalized* response is shown in Fig. 12-47b. During the pulse, the response falls off. The total amount of the falloff in the normalized response is called the *sag*. Note that we have assumed that T is large enough so that the response returns to zero before the next pulse occurs. In general, for a given amplifier, as the pulse duration increases, the sag increases. Conversely, improving the low-frequency response (i.e., reducing f_1) reduces the sag.

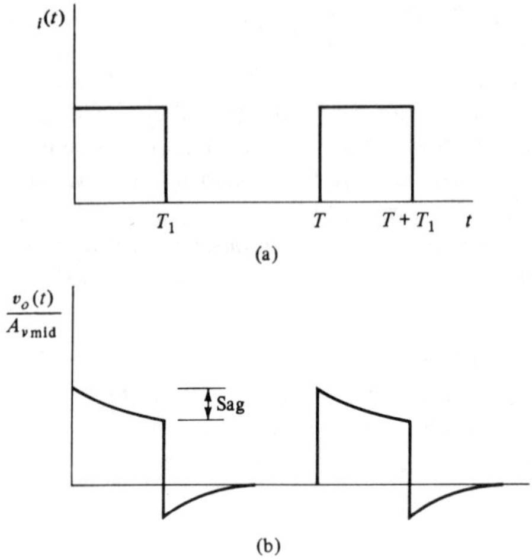

Figure 12.47. A response of an amplifier to a train of low-frequency pulses. (a) Input. (b) Normalized response.

12-18. NOISE—AMPLIFIER SENSITIVITY

It may seem as though any signal, no matter how small, can be amplified to usable values (subject to bandwidth restrictions) but this is not the case. Very small signals can be amplified by very high gain amplifiers. However, the output signal, in addition to containing the amplified input signal, will contain a random component called *noise*. At times, the noise component is large enough to obscure the signal. It is often this noise that places practical limits on the amplification of an amplifier.

Resistor Noise—Johnson Noise

The electrons in a resistance are always randomly moving because of thermal excitation. The net current at any instant of time will not exactly be zero. This gives rise to a random voltage across the resistance. Since the motion is random, the waveform of the voltage cannot be predicted but some fact have been ascertained. Let us assume that we are concerned with the noise voltage across a resistance R. The noise power will be proportional to the absolute temperature of the resistance. The noise is uniform in any bandwidth $\Delta f = f_2 - f_1$ unless the frequency is extremely high (i.e., close to heat or light frequencies). The rms voltage will be proportional to the square root of the power. In general, a detailed analysis shows that the rms noise voltage is given by

$$V_n = 2\sqrt{keTR\,\Delta f} \qquad (12\text{-}256)$$

where

T = temperature (°K)

R = resistance (ohms)

Δf = bandwidth (Hz)

e = charge of electron

K = Boltzmann constant (eV/°K)

Since the noise is uniform at all frequencies, it is called *white noise* by analogy to white light.

Shot—Schottky Noise

We have previously assumed that, under quiescent conditions, the current in a device such as a transistor or FET is constant. Actually, current consists of the flow of discrete charge carriers. Thus, if we very closely examine this "constant" current, we see that it fluctuates slightly. This fluctuation leads to a random noise component called *shot* or *Schottky noise*. In general, the noise current is given by

$$I_n = \sqrt{2eI_Q\,\Delta f} \tag{12-257}$$

where I_Q is the quiescent current through the device. If the current is supplied to a load resistance R_L, then a rms noise component I_nR_L will appear across the resistance in addition to the resistance Johnson noise

Noise Due to the Amplifier Signal Source

The input to an amplifier is usually supplied by a transducer such as an antenna or a microphone. These are also sources of noise. Such devices have an effective resistance (called a radiation resistance) which is indicative of the energy they can radiate or pick up. Let us consider the example of an antenna. It can be shown that the average antenna noise is a function of its radiation resistance and the average temperature of the antenna. (The average temperature depends upon the temperature of all spaces within the radiation pattern of the antenna and the shape of the radiation pattern.) If we do not want to have an output that is obscured by noise, then the smallest signal that can be amplified is limited by the noise produced in the source.

Noise Figure

The minimum signal that an amplifier can amplify without its being obscured by noise is called the *sensitivity* of the amplifier. If amplifiers produced no noise, then the sensitivity would only depend upon the noise produced "by" the source (antenna, etc.). Unfortunately, all amplifiers produce noise, often much more than that of the source.

To rate an amplifier in terms of the noise it produces, a quantity called the *noise figure* (NF) is used. One definition of this is

$$\text{NF} = 10\log_{10}\frac{P_{No}}{A_P P_{Ni}} \tag{12-258}$$

where

$$P_{No} = \text{total output noise power}$$

$$P_{Ni} = \text{noise power of the source}$$

$$A_P = \text{power gain of the amplifier}$$

Then, NF in decibels represents the ratio of the total output noise power to the noise power that would be produced if the amplifier were noiseless.

Another definition of noise figure is used. It is equivalent to Eq. 12-258 if the input and output impedances of the amplifier are equal and resistive.

$$\text{NF} = 20 \log_{10} \frac{V_{No}}{A_v V_{Ni}} \tag{12-259}$$

where

V_{No} = rms total noise output voltage

V_{Ni} = rms noise produced by source

A_v = voltage gain

To obtain the lowest noise, the bandwidth should be no larger than required by the input signal.

The value of the noise voltage and current are not important in themselves, it is the *ratio* of the signal to the noise. For this reason, we define voltage and power *signal to noise ratios.* These are

$$S_v = \frac{V_s}{V_N} \tag{12-260a}$$

$$S_p = \frac{P_S}{P_N} \tag{12-260b}$$

where V_S and V_N are the rms values of the signal and noise voltage power, respectively, and P_S and P_N are the average signal and noise powers, respectively. The subscripts i and o are then appended to these quantities to indicate input and output, respectively. For instance,

$$A_v = \frac{V_{So}}{V_{Si}} \tag{12-261}$$

Manipulating Eq. 12-259, we obtain

$$\text{NF} = 20 \log_{10} S_{Vi} - 20 \log_{10} S_{Vo} \tag{12-262}$$

Thus, the noise figure in decibels is the difference between the input signal to noise ratio in decibels, and the output signal to noise ratio in decibels. Let us now consider some noise that is produced by transistors and FET's.

Transistor Noise

Transistor noise is produced by effects in *addition* to both Johnson noise in its ohmic resistances and Schottky noise. The motion of the charge carriers across the base is a random one. This randomness contributes an additional noise component to the transistor. In addition, there is a random recombination of free electrons and holes which contributes to the noise.

There is another mechanism that leads to noise in the transistor since some minority carriers recombine in the base and become base current while the majority of the minority carriers diffuse to the collector-base junction and contribute to the collector current. The division is on a random basis and contributes to the noise. It is called *partition noise.*

All of the above discussed noise mechanisms lead to white noise. There is also a noise voltage that varies approximately as $1/f$. This is called *excess noise* or *flicker effect noise.* Its mechanism is not completely understood. However, it is thought to be due to effects that occur on the surface of the transistor.

The noise produced by a transistor varies widely with frequency. At low frequencies, the noise figure is high because of flicker effect. The noise falls off as the frequency is increased and then remains constant over a wide range of frequencies. At high frequencies, the noise figure deteriorates because the gain falls off. This reduction in gain reduces the output signal more than it does output noise. Manufacturers often supply curves showing the noise figure as a function of frequency for particular transistors.

FET Noise

In addition to the Johnson noise and the Schottky noise, FET noise is produced by several effects. There is an extremely small component of current from the gate to the channel. This introduces a noise component. In addition, surface phenomena lead to an approximately $1/f$ flicker effect. In general, the noise figure of the FET is very low and, often, FET's are superior to transistors as low noise devices.

PROBLEMS

12-1. Discuss frequency distortion. What properties must an amplifier have if it is to be free of frequency distortion?

12-2. An amplifier's gain is given by

$$\mathbf{A} = \frac{100}{1 + j(f/10^6)}$$

Plot the magnitude and phase of this amplification.

12-3. What is the 90% bandwidth of the amplifier of Prob. 12-2? What is the half-power bandwidth? Use a normalized response plot to obtain your results.

12-4. The amplifier of Fig. 12-4 has a voltage gain of 100. $R_1 = R_2 = 10{,}000$ ohms. Express the voltage, current, and power gain in decibels.

12-5. Repeat Prob. 12-4 but now assume that $R_1 = 10{,}000$ ohms, $R_2 = 100$ ohms. Comment on the appropriateness of using decibel notation in this case.

12-6. Plot the magnitude of the gain of the amplifier of Prob. 12-2 on a decibel basis.

12-7. Sketch the magnitude of the gain of the following amplifier on a decibel basis.

$$\mathbf{A} = \frac{100(1 + jf/10^4)}{(1 + jf/2 \times 10^4)(1 + jf/6 \times 10^4)^4}$$

12-8. Repeat Prob. 12-7 but now plot the curve accurately. Compare this curve with the one sketched in Prob. 12-7.

12-9. The FET used in the amplifier of Fig. 12-8a has the following parameter values.

$$g_m = 15{,}000\ \mu\text{mhos}$$
$$r_d = 500{,}000\ \text{ohms}$$
$$C_{gd} = 0.2\ \text{pF}$$
$$C_{gs} = 2\ \text{pF}$$
$$C_{ds} = 1.5\ \text{pF}$$

The elements of the circuit are $R_d = 10{,}000$ ohms, $R_g = 10^6$ ohms, and $C_c = 0.25\ \mu$F. Compute $\mathbf{A}_{v\,\text{mid}}$, f_1, and f_2. Sketch the response on a decibel basis. Assume that the amplifier is cascaded with an identical stage.

12-10. Repeat Prob. 12-9 but now assume that R_g represents the load (i.e., there is no next stage). Compare your results with those of Prob. 12-9.

12-11. Repeat Prob. 12-9 but now assume that $R_d = 5000$ ohms.

12-12. Repeat Prob. 12-10 but now assume that $R_d = 5000$ ohms.

12-13. Compare the results of Prob. 12-9 with those of Prob. 12-11. Why does the gain-bandwidth product appear to vary from Prob. 12-9 to Prob. 12-11?

12-14. The FET whose characteristics are given in Prob. 12-9 is used in the amplifier of Fig. 12-8c. The elements of the circuit are $R_d = 10{,}000$ ohms, $R_g = 900{,}000$ ohms, and $R_1 = 100{,}000$ ohms. Compute $\mathbf{A}_{v\,\text{mid}}$ and f_2. Sketch the response on a decibel basis. Assume that the amplifier is cascaded with an identical stage.

12-15. Repeat Prob. 12-14 but now assume that R_g represents the load (i.e., there is no next stage). Compare your results with those of Prob. 12-14.

12-16. Repeat Prob. 12-14 but now assume that $R_d = 50{,}000$ ohms.

12-17. Repeat Prob. 12-15 but now assume that $R_d = 50{,}000$ ohms.

12-18. Compare the results of Probs. 12-14 to 12-17. Comment on the ideas of a constant-gain bandwidth product.

12-19. The transistor used in the amplifier of Fig. 12-14a has the following parameter values.

$$r_{bb'} = 80\ \text{ohms}$$
$$r_{b'e} = 1200\ \text{ohms}$$
$$r_{b'c} = 10^7\ \text{ohms}$$
$$C_{b'e} = 120\ \text{pF}$$
$$C_{b'c} = 2\ \text{pF}$$
$$r_{ce} = 600{,}000\ \text{ohms}$$
$$g_m = 75{,}000\ \mu\text{mho}$$

The elements of the circuit are

$$R_C = 10{,}000\ \text{ohms}$$
$$R_{B1} = 20{,}000\ \text{ohms}$$
$$R_{B2} = 25{,}000\ \text{ohms}$$
$$C_c = 50\ \mu\text{F}$$

Compute $\mathbf{A}_{v\,\text{mid}}$, f_1, and f_2 for the stage. Sketch the frequency response on a decibel basis. Assume that this amplifier is cascaded with an identical one.

12-20. Repeat Prob. 12-19 but now assume that instead of driving an identical stage, a 1280-ohm resistive load is driven.

12-21. Repeat Prob. 12-19 but now assume that $R_C = 2000$ ohms.

12-22. Repeat Prob. 12-20 but now assume that $R_C = 2000$ ohms.

12-23. Repeat Prob. 12-19 but now assume that $C_c = 20\ \mu\text{F}$.

12-24. The transistor whose parameters are given in Prob. 12-19 is used in the circuit of Fig. 12-14b, where $R_C = 5263$ ohms. Compute $\mathbf{A}_{v\,\text{mid}}$ and f_2 for this circuit. Sketch the frequency response on a decibel basis. Assume that this amplifier is cascaded with an identical one.

12-25. Repeat Prob. 12-24 but now assume that, instead of driving an identical stage, the load is a 1280-ohm resistance.

12-26. Repeat Prob. 12-24 but now assume that $R_C = 2000$ ohms.

12-27. Repeat Prob. 12-25 but now assume that $R_C = 2000$ ohms.

12-28. Repeat Prob. 12-19 but now work in terms of the current gain.

12-29. Repeat Prob. 12-20 but now work in terms of the current gain.

12-30. Repeat Prob. 12-21 but now work in terms of the current gain.

12-31. Repeat Prob. 12-22 but now work in terms of the current gain.

12-32. Repeat Prob. 12-24 but now work in terms of the current gain.

12-33. Repeat Prob. 12-25 but now work in terms of the current gain.

12-34. Compare the results of Prob. 12-19 and Prob. 12-21. Comment on the idea of a gain-bandwidth product here.

12-35. Comment on the usefulness of a gain-bandwidth product even if $|\mathbf{A}_{v\,\text{mid}}|\,f_2$ is not constant.

12-36. Repeat Prob. 12-34 for the results of Probs. 12-24 and 12-26.

12-37. Repeat Prob. 12-34 for the results of Probs. 12-25 and 12-27.

12-38. Repeat Prob. 12-34 for the results of Probs. 12-28 and 12-30.

12-39. Repeat Prob. 12-34 for the results of Probs. 12-29 and 12-31.

12-40. The FET whose parameters are given in Prob. 12-9 is used in the circuit of Fig. 12-22a. The elements of the circuit are

$$R_d = 10{,}000 \text{ ohms}$$
$$R_g = 10^6 \text{ ohms}$$
$$R_s = 100 \text{ ohms}$$
$$C_c = 0.25\ \mu\text{F}$$
$$C_s = 50\ \mu\text{F}$$

Compute $\mathbf{A}_{v\,\text{mid}}$, f_1, f_{s1}, and f_{s2}. Sketch the response on a decibel basis. Use this to determine the actual frequency where $|\mathbf{A}_{v\,\text{low}}/\mathbf{A}_{v\,\text{mid}}| = 0.707$.

12-41. Repeat Prob. 12-40 but now assume that $C_s = 1000\ \mu\text{F}$.

12-42. The transistor whose parameters are given in Prob. 12-19 is used in the circuit of Fig. 12-25a. The elements of the circuit are

$$R_C = 10{,}000 \text{ ohms}$$
$$R_{B1} = 20{,}000 \text{ ohms}$$
$$R_{B2} = 25{,}000 \text{ ohms}$$
$$R_E = 1500 \text{ ohms}$$
$$C_c = 50\ \mu\text{F}$$
$$C_E = 500\ \mu\text{F}$$

Compute $\mathbf{A}_{v\,\text{mid}}$, f_1, f_{E1}, and f_{E2}. Sketch the response on a decibel basis. Use this sketch to determine the actual frequency where $|\mathbf{A}_{v\,\text{low}}/\mathbf{A}_{v\,\text{mid}}| = 0.707$.

12-43. Repeat Prob. 12-42 but now assume that $C_E = 2000\ \mu F$.

12-44. The FET whose parameters are given in Prob. 12-9 is used in the circuit of Fig. 12-26a. The parameters of the circuit are

$$R_s = 500 \text{ ohms}$$
$$R_g = 10^7 \text{ ohms}$$
$$C_c = 0.01\ \mu F$$

Compute $\mathbf{A}_{v\,\mathrm{mid}}$, f_1, and f_2 for this amplifier.

12-45. Repeat Prob. 12-44 but now assume that the common-emitter amplifier of Prob. 12-9 is connected to the right of R_g in Fig. 12-26a.

12-46. Repeat Prob. 12-45 but now assume that $R_s = 2000$ ohms.

12-47. The transistor whose parameters are given in Prob. 12-19 is used in the circuit of Fig. 12-27a. The parameters of the circuit are

$$R_E = 500 \text{ ohms}$$
$$R_{B1} = 20{,}000 \text{ ohms}$$
$$R_{B2} = 20{,}000 \text{ ohms}$$
$$C_c = 50\ \mu F$$

Compute $\mathbf{A}_{v\,\mathrm{mid}}$, f_2, and f_1 for the amplifier. Use $R_i = 1280$ ohms.

12-48. Repeat Prob. 12-47 but now assume that the transistor amplifier of Prob. 12-19 is connected to the right of R_{B1} and R_{B2} in Fig. 12-27a.

12-49. The transistor whose parameters are given in Prob. 12-19 is used in the circuit of Fig. 12-29a. The parameters of the circuit are

$$R_E = 1000 \text{ ohms}$$
$$R_C = 20{,}000 \text{ ohms}$$
$$R_{B1} = 20{,}000 \text{ ohms}$$
$$R_{B2} = 20{,}000 \text{ ohms}$$
$$C_C = 50\ \mu F$$

Compute $\mathbf{A}_{v,\,\mathrm{mid}}$, f_2, and f_1 for the amplifier.

12-50. The capacitor C_c of the FET amplifier of Fig. 12-30a is 20 pF. Compute $\mathbf{V}_1/\mathbf{V}_s$ as a function of frequency for the amplifier

$$R_1 = 1000 \text{ ohms}$$

12-51. Repeat Prob. 12-50 but now assume that $R_1 = 10{,}000$ ohms.

12-52. The amplifier shown in Fig. 12-31a is the same as that of Prob. 12-19. In addition,

$$R_1 = 1000 \text{ ohms}$$
$$C_c = 50\ \mu F$$

Compute $\mathbf{V}_2/\mathbf{V}_i$ as a function of frequency for this amplifier. $\mathbf{V}_2$ is the output of the amplifier (see Fig. 12-14a).

12-53. Repeat Prob. 12-52 but now assume that $R_1 = 100$ ohms.

12-54. Twelve amplifier stages each of whose gain is given by $4.6/(1 + jf/10^6)$ are cascaded. Determine the midband gain and half-power bandwidth of the overall amplifier.

12-55. An amplifier is composed of n identical stages whose gain-bandwidth products are constant and equal. Demonstrate that, if the midband gain of the overall amplifier is constant, then the maximum value of half-power bandwidth of the overall amplifier occurs when the midband gain of the identical stages is equal to $\sqrt{e}$(4.343 dB). Hint: Use the approximation $2^{1/n} - 1 \simeq (\ln 2)/n$.

12-56. Design a broadband FET amplifier to meet the following specifications: $|\mathbf{A}_{v\,\text{mid}}| = 1500$; at $f = 1.3 \times 10^6$ Hz, $|\mathbf{A}_v/\mathbf{A}_{v\,\text{mid}}| \geqq 0.93$; at $f = 10$ Hz, $|\mathbf{A}_v/\mathbf{A}_{v\,\text{mid}}| \geqq 0.9$. The load impedance is 10^7 ohms shunted by 1 pF, and the generator resistance is 1000 ohms. Use a coupling capacitor in series with the input. The gain of all stages should be equal. Use depletion MOSFET's with the following specifications.

$$g_m = 15{,}000\ \mu\text{mhos}$$
$$r_d = 10^5\ \text{ohms}$$
$$C_{gs} = 2\ \text{pF}$$
$$C_{gd} = 0.3\ \text{pF}$$
$$C_{ds} = 1\ \text{pF}$$

The coordinates of the quiescent operating point are

$$V_{DSQ} = 10\ \text{V}$$
$$I_{DQ} = 1\ \text{mA}$$
$$V_{GSQ} = -1\ \text{V}$$

12-57. Repeat Prob. 12-56 but now make the gain of the output stage larger than that of the other stages to improve the high-frequency response.

12-58. Modify the design of Prob. 12-56 by including a source follower between the stages. Use the same number of common-source stages. Compare the high-frequency response with that of the amplifier of Prob. 12-56. Make $\mathbf{A}_{v\,\text{mid}} \geqq 0.98$ for the source follower.

12-59. Repeat Prob. 12-56 but now assume that the low-frequency specification is replaced by $\mathbf{A}_v/\mathbf{A}_{v\,\text{mid}} = 1$ at low frequencies down to 0 Hz. Assume that $V_{GSQ} = 0$ and that the requirements for an input coupling capacitor is removed.

12-60. Design a transistor amplifier to meet the following specifications. There is to be a well-defined midband region, $|\mathbf{A}_{v\,\text{mid}}| = 1500$; for $f = 1.3 \times 10^6$ Hz, $|\mathbf{A}_v/\mathbf{A}_{v\,\text{mid}}| \geqq 0.9$; for $f = 20$ Hz, $|\mathbf{A}_v/\mathbf{A}_{v\,\text{mid}}| \geqq 0.85$. The load impedance is 2500 ohms. The generator impedance is 100 ohms. Use a coupling capacitor in series with the input. The stability factor S should be less than 10. (For simplicity, we shall not give the other stability factors.) Use transistors with the following specifications.

$$g_m = 180{,}000\ \mu\text{mhos}$$
$$r_{bb'} = 80\ \text{ohms}$$
$$r_{b'e} = 1500\ \text{ohms}$$
$$r_{b'c} = 10^7\ \text{ohms}$$
$$r_{ce} = 10^5\ \text{ohms}$$
$$C_{b'e} = 30\ \text{pF}$$
$$C_{b'c} = 0.6\ \text{pF}$$

The coordinates of the quiescent operating point are

$$V_{CEQ} = 5\ \text{V}$$
$$I_{CQ} = 1.0\ \text{mA}$$
$$I_{BQ} = 3.5\ \mu\text{A}$$

12-61. Repeat Prob. 12-60 but now make the gain of the output stage greater than that of the other stage(s) to improve the high-frequency response.

12-62. Modify the design of Prob. 12-60 by incorporating a source follower stage after each common-emitter stage. Use the same number of common-emitter stages as in Prob. 12-60. Compare the high-frequency response with that of Prob. 12-60.

12-63. Repeat Prob. 12-60 but now assume that the low-frequency specification is replaced by $\mathbf{A}_v/\mathbf{A}_{v\,\text{mid}} = 1$ down to 0 Hz. Also assume that the specifications on S and the input coupling capacitor are removed.

12-64. Modify the design of Prob. 12-60 by replacing each common-emitter stage with a cascode (i.e., common-emitter, common-base cascade). Use the same number of common-emitter stages as in Prob. 12-60. Compare the high-frequency response with that of Prob. 12-60.

12-65. The amplification of an amplifier is given by

$$\frac{\mathbf{A}}{\mathbf{A}_{\text{mid}}} = [(1 + jf/2.3 \times 10^6)(1 + jf/4.2 \times 10^6)(1 - j15/f)]^{-1}$$

Determine the poles and zeros of this amplifier and draw the pole-zero diagram. Use the pole-zero diagram to draw curves of amplitude and phase response for this amplifier.

12-66. The amplification of an amplifier is given by

$$\frac{\mathbf{A}}{\mathbf{A}_{\text{mid}}} = \frac{1 + jf/256 \times 10^6}{(1 + jf/132 \times 10^6)(1 + jf/2.2 \times 10^6)(1 + jf/32 \times 10^6)}$$

We want to plot $|\mathbf{A}/\mathbf{A}_{\text{mid}}|$ and $\measuredangle\, \mathbf{A}/\mathbf{A}_{\text{mid}}$ for those frequencies where $1 \geqq |\mathbf{A}/\mathbf{A}_{\text{mid}}| \geqq 0.1$. Use the pole-zero diagram to simplify the expression and plot the appropriate curves.

12-67. Determine the response of an amplifier whose gain is

$$\mathbf{A} = \frac{1}{1 + j\omega/10^6}$$

to an input signal $u(t) \sin 10^6 t$.

12-68. Determine the unit step response of the amplifier of Prob. 12-67.

12-69. Determine the unit step response of the amplifier whose Laplace transformed amplification is

$$\mathbf{A}(s) = \frac{s}{(s + 2)}$$

12-70. Determine the unit step response of an amplifier whose normalized gain is

$$\mathbf{A} = [(1 + jf/10^6)(1 - j10/f)]^{-1}$$

12-71. Determine the 10–90% rise time of an amplifier whose normalized gain is

$$\mathbf{A} = \frac{1}{1 + jf/f_2}$$

That is, relate the 10–90% rise time to f_2. Note that this relationship only applies to this particular response.

12-72. The normalized unit step response of an amplifier is given by

$$\mathbf{A}(s) = \frac{10^6}{s^2 + bs + 10^6}$$

Determine the rise time and overshoot when $b = 2 \times 10^3$.

12-73. Repeat Prob. 12-72 but now use $b = 10^3$. Compare your answer with that of Prob. 12-72.

12-74. Determine the unit step response of the amplifier of Prob. 12-65.

12-75. An amplifier whose normalized amplification is

$$\mathbf{A} = \frac{1}{1 - jf_1/f}$$

is to amplify pulses whose duration is 1 s. If $f_1 = 0.2$, determine the sag.

12-76. Repeat Prob. 12-75 but now use $f_1 = 0.05$.

12-77. Repeat Prob. 12-75 but now use a pulse of 0.4-s duration.

12-78. Discuss the mechanisms whereby noise is produced in a junction transistor.

12-79. Repeat Prob. 12-78 for a FET.

12-80. Obtain the noise figure of an amplifier, defined by Eq. 12-258, in terms of its power signal to noise ratio.

BIBLIOGRAPHY

Chirlian, P. M. *Electronic Circuits: Physical Properties, Analysis and Design.* New York: McGraw-Hill, 1971, Chapter 9.

Gray, P. E. and Searle, C. L. *Electronic Principles: Physics, Models, and Circuits.* New York: Wiley, 1969, Chapters 14–16.

Millman, J. and Halkias, C. C. *Integrated Electronics: Analog and Digital Circuits and Systems.* New York: McGraw-Hill, 1972, Chapter 12.

Chapter 13

Operational Amplifiers Applications

The term *operational amplifier* is commonly applied to a general class of high-gain, direct coupled, monolithic integrated circuit amplifiers. These amplifiers can be easily used in many applications. An operational amplifier is fabricated on a single chip. Indeed, chips are available which contain several operational amplifiers. In this chapter we shall discuss applications of operational amplifiers. In the next, we shall consider their actual circuitry and limitations. There are some aspects of operational amplifiers which cannot be completely discussed until feedback amplifiers are considered. Of course, the entire discussion could be deferred until then. However, we shall not do so because we can discuss many important applications of operational amplifiers at this time. It is desirable for the reader to understand these applications as soon as possible since operational amplifiers are widely used.

We shall begin by considering an ideal operational amplifier, and then discuss many of their applications. Additional aspects and applications of operational amplifiers will be pointed out as we progress through the rest of the book.

13.1 THE IDEAL OPERATIONAL AMPLIFIER—THE QUASI-IDEAL OPERATIONAL AMPLIFIER

An operational amplifier is a high-gain, direct coupled amplifier. In this section we shall introduce this amplifier by assuming that it is ideal. This will allow us to obtain an overall picture of the functions of the operational amplifier. We shall also consider a more practical form of idealized operational amplifiers here. In the next chapter, we shall discuss the practical limitations of operational amplifiers.

The block diagram for a typical operational amplifier is shown in Fig. 13-1a. There are two inputs labeled $\mathbf{V}_1$ and $\mathbf{V}_2$. The output is given by

$$\mathbf{V}_o = \mathbf{A}_v(\mathbf{V}_2 - \mathbf{V}_1) \tag{13-1}$$

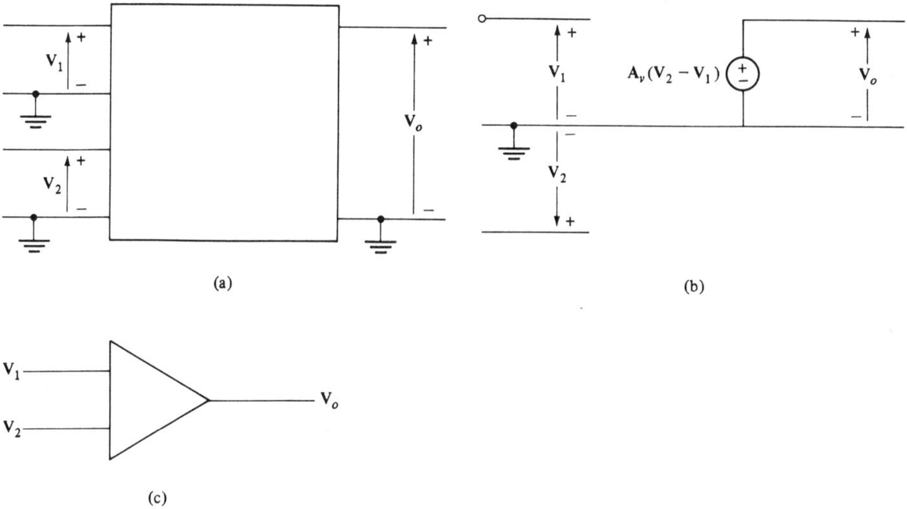

Figure 13-1. (a) A block diagram for an operational amplifier. (b) Its model. (c) Its schematic diagram.

$\mathbf{A}_v$ is the voltage gain of the operational amplifier and $\mathbf{V}_1$ and $\mathbf{V}_2$ are called the *inverting* and *noninverting* inputs, respectively. Note that $\mathbf{V}_o$ is proportional to the negative of $\mathbf{V}_1$. Hence, the signal that is applied to the $\mathbf{V}_1$ input is shifted in-phase by 180°, that is, it is inverted. The model for this amplifier is shown in Fig. 13-1b. In the ideal case, the input impedance is infinite while the output impedance is zero.

Note that one lead is common to both inputs and the output. This is the ground lead. Since the ground lead is common to all ports of the circuit, it is often omitted when schematic representations are drawn. Thus, the schematic representation for an operational amplifier is as shown in Fig. 13-1c. A practical operational amplifier must be connected to a power supply. The actual chip has leads to allow this to be done. These leads are often omitted from the block diagram.

We have assumed a voltage gain $\mathbf{A}_v$ for the operational amplifier. Ideal operational amplifiers are often assumed to have infinite gain. Let us suppose that this is the case and that the input signals are such that the output voltage is finite. Since the gain is infinite, the potential difference $\mathbf{V}_1 - \mathbf{V}_2$ must be differentially small, (i.e., essentially zero). In practical operational amplifiers, $\mathbf{A}_v$ is often so large that the potential difference $\mathbf{V}_1 - \mathbf{V}_2$ is extremely small.

The Quasi-ideal Operational Amplifier

Let us now consider a more practical form of operational amplifier. This will still be an ideal form since we shall assume that some of the practical problems associated with operational amplifiers are nonexistent. These problems will be discussed in subsequent sections and in the next chapter.

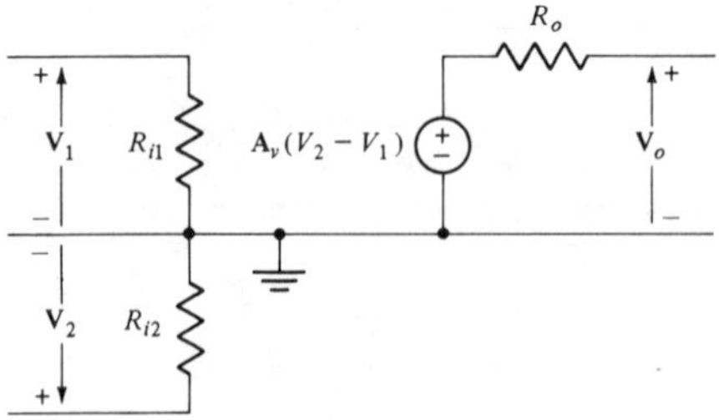

Figure 13-2. An operational amplifier model that takes input and output resistance into account.

The input impedance will not be infinite but will be a finite number. In practical operational amplifiers, the input impedance for each input usually exceeds 100,000 ohms, and is often much larger. The output impedance is nonzero but is usually less than several hundred ohms. Thus, a model for an operational amplifier that takes input and output impedance into account is as shown in Fig. 13-2.

The ideal operational amplifier will be linear, that is, v_o will be a linear function of $v_1 - v_2$. (Note that we are using instantaneous rather than complex voltages here.) Of course, in an actual operational amplifier, just as in any amplifier, the response is not *exactly* linear, but the response is usually *very* linear over a region where $|v_2 - v_1|$ is small. A typical curve of v_o versus $v_2 - v_1$ is given in Fig. 13-3. Note that the scale for $v_2 - v_1$ is in millivolts while that for v_o is in volts. For the quasi-ideal operational amplifier we shall assume that the response is given by the three confluent straight line segments as shown. Note that this approximation is quite accurate. That is, the amplifier is linear if it is not saturated. In this case, if $v_2 - v_1 \geqq v_{\alpha 1}$, then the output v_o saturates at the positive value V_{A1}. Similarly, if $v_2 - v_1 \leqq v_{\alpha 2}$, then the output voltage v_o saturates at the negative voltage $-V_{A2}$. Many operational amplifiers are symmetric so that

$$V_{A1} = V_{A2} = V_A \tag{13-2a}$$

and

$$V_{\alpha 1} = V_{\alpha 2} = V_\alpha \tag{13-2b}$$

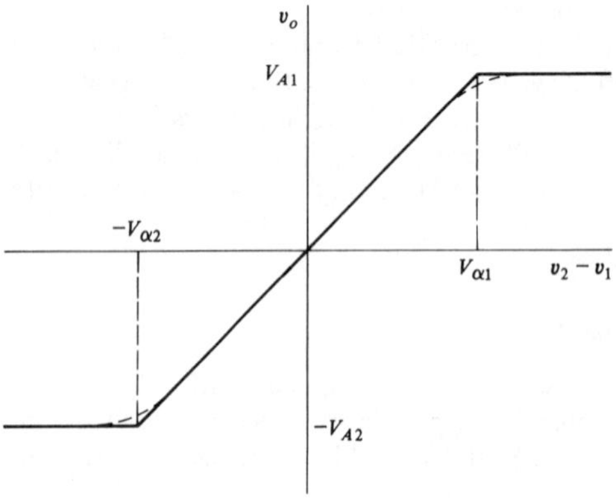

Figure 13-3. A curve of v_o versus $v_2 - v_1$ for a typical operational amplifier. The scales on the axes are different.

The value of V_A depends upon the power supply voltage. Typically, V_A ranges from 5 to 15 V. The value of V_α is in the order of millivolts or less.

Example

An operational amplifier has a voltage gain $\mathbf{A}_v = 50{,}000$ ohms. The maximum output voltage is 5 V. Compute the value of V_α.

$$v_o = \mathbf{A}_v(v_2 - v_1)$$

When $v_2 - v_1 = V_\alpha$, v_o will equal its maximum value. Hence,

$$V_\alpha = 5/50{,}000 = 10^{-4}\ \text{V}$$

Note that $|v_2 - v_1|$ must be kept very small if linear operation is to result.

13-2. THE SIMPLE INVERTING AMPLIFIER

In this and the following sections we shall discuss practical applications of operational amplifier circuits. In the next chapter we shall consider the circuits of the operational amplifiers themselves and discuss some problems associated with operational amplifiers.

A basic application is to simply provide amplification. It might seem as though we could just use the operational amplifier itself with no additional circuitry. However, there are several reasons why this is not done. For one thing, different applications call for amplifiers with different gains. It would be impractical to manufacture very many operational amplifiers to supply a very large selection of gains.

There is another more important reason why an operational amplifier is not used without external circuitry to provide amplification. The manufacturing tolerances are such that the gains of operational amplifiers that are fabricated under the "same" conditions will actually be widely different. For instance, the nominal gain of an operational amplifier could be 10,000. However, the gains of actual samples might vary between 5000 and 15,000. In addition, the gain of an operational amplifier will change if its power supply voltage or operating temperature changes.

For these reasons it is desirable to build an amplifier whose gain is essentially independent of the gain of the operational amplifier. Let us demonstrate how this can be done. Consider the amplifier of Fig. 13-4. This is a form of *feedback* amplifier. In Chapter 17, we shall discuss feedback amplifiers in detail. For the time being, we shall just calculate the gain of the circuit. Note that the noninverting input is grounded in Fig. 13-4. Hence,

$$\mathbf{V}_2 = 0 \tag{13-3}$$

Let us assume that $\mathbf{Z}_i$, the input impedance of the operational amplifier, is infinite. We shall discuss the validity of this assumption subsequently. Since $\mathbf{Z}_i = 0$, then the current through both R_1 and R_2 is equal to $\mathbf{I}$. Then, we have

$$\mathbf{I} = \frac{\mathbf{V}_{i1} - \mathbf{V}_1}{R_1} = \frac{\mathbf{V}_1 - \mathbf{V}_o}{R_2} \tag{13-4}$$

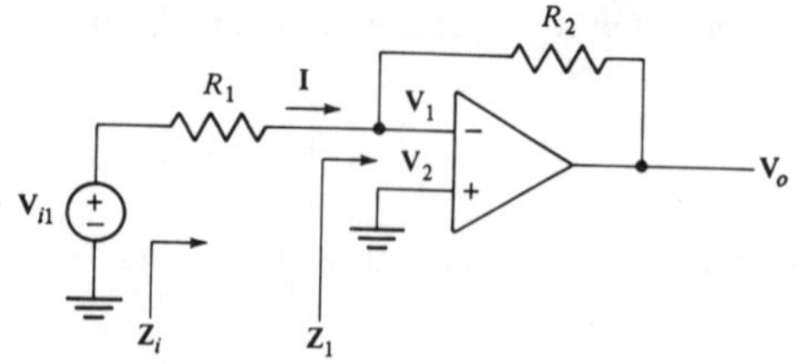

Figure 13-4. A simple inverting amplifier.

From Eq. 13-1, we have

$$\mathbf{V}_o = -\mathbf{V}_1\mathbf{A}_v \tag{13-5}$$

Substituting in Eq. 13-4 and manipulating, we obtain

$$\frac{R_2}{R_1}\mathbf{V}_{i1} = -\mathbf{V}_o\left[1 + \frac{1}{\mathbf{A}_v}\left(1 + \frac{R_2}{R_1}\right)\right] \tag{13-6}$$

For most operational amplifiers, $|\mathbf{A}_v|$ is very large whereas, as we shall see, R_2/R_1 is only moderate in size. Thus, the following approximation is valid.

$$1 \gg \left|\frac{1}{\mathbf{A}_v}\left(1 + \frac{R_2}{R_1}\right)\right| \tag{13-7}$$

Note that, as we have discussed in Chapter 12, $\mathbf{A}_v$ will fall off with frequency so that at high enough frequencies, 13-7 will no longer be valid. We assume here that we are working at sufficiently low frequencies so that this is not the case. Then, using inequality 13-7, Eq. 13-6 becomes

$$\mathbf{V}_o = -\frac{R_2}{R_1}\mathbf{V}_{i1}$$

Hence, the voltage gain of the overall circuit is

$$\mathbf{K}_v = \frac{\mathbf{V}_o}{\mathbf{V}_{i1}} = -\frac{R_1}{R_1} \tag{13-8}$$

The gain of the overall amplifier is essentially independent of $\mathbf{A}_v$, the operational amplifier gain. This is the result that we desire. Of course, this depends upon approximation 13-7 being valid.

The magnitude of the gain is given by R_2/R_1. In general this number will be much less than $|\mathbf{A}_v|$. Note that this is necessary if approximation 13-7 is to be valid. Since $\mathbf{V}_o = -\mathbf{A}_v\mathbf{V}_1$, then

$$|\mathbf{V}_1| \ll |\mathbf{V}_{i1}| \tag{13-9}$$

Actually, $|\mathbf{V}_1|$ will be very small. Its value is usually almost zero. Note that if this is not the case then $|\mathbf{V}_1| > |\mathbf{V}_\alpha|$ (see Fig. 13-3) and the amplifier will saturate. Thus, $|\mathbf{V}_1| \simeq 0$. In this case, the input $\mathbf{V}_1$ is said to be at *virtual ground*. This can be a helpful idea. For instance, suppose that we want to calculate the input impedance $\mathbf{Z}_i$ for the overall amplifier (see Fig. 13-4). This is given by

$$\mathbf{Z}_i = \frac{\mathbf{V}_{i1}}{\mathbf{I}}$$

Substituting Eq. 13-4 and manipulating, we have

$$\mathbf{Z}_i = \frac{R_1}{(1 - \mathbf{V}_1/\mathbf{V}_{i1})} \tag{13-10}$$

However, we assume that $\mathbf{V}_1$ is at virtual ground. Hence,

$$\left|\frac{\mathbf{V}_1}{\mathbf{V}_{i1}}\right| \ll 1$$

Therefore, Eq. 13-10 becomes

$$\mathbf{Z}_i = R_1 \tag{13-11}$$

The idea of the virtual ground is often a convenient one to use when the noninverting input is grounded. However, it cannot be used indiscriminately. For instance, if we assume that $\mathbf{V}_1 = 0$, the input impedance $\mathbf{Z}_i$ can be obtained easily. On the other hand, if $\mathbf{V}_1$ is really zero, then $\mathbf{V}_o = 0$ and the amplifier output is zero.

Example

We want to design an operational amplifier circuit that has a voltage gain $\mathbf{K}_v = -50$. The input impedance of the operational amplifier $\mathbf{Z}_i$ is to be 1000 ohms.

The design relations that we shall use are

$$\mathbf{K}_v = \frac{-R_2}{R_1}$$

and

$$\mathbf{Z}_i = R_1$$

Then,

$$R_1 = 1000 \text{ ohms}$$

Hence,

$$R_2 = 50 \times R_1 = 50{,}000 \text{ ohms}$$

In the derivation of the gain of the amplifier of Fig. 13-4 we assumed that the input impedance of the operational amplifier was infinite. Let us now demonstrate that for all practical cases this is a valid approximation for the circuit of Fig. 13-4. Consider the circuit of Fig. 13-5, which represents a portion of the amplifier circuit. Let us compute the input impedance $\mathbf{Z}_a$. Let us start by assuming that $\mathbf{Z}_1$, the input impedance of the

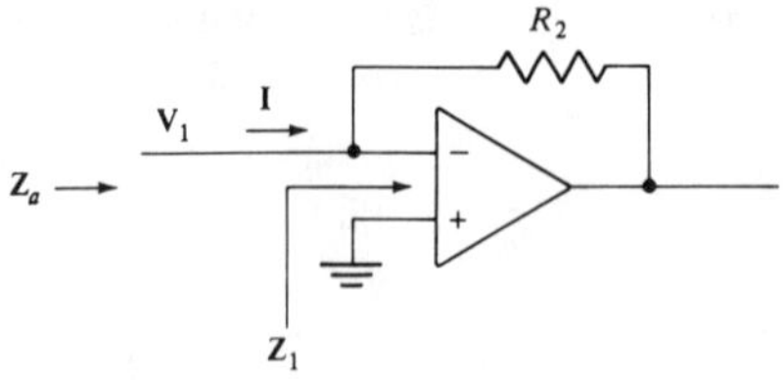

Figure 13-5. A circuit used to calculate the input impedance of a portion of the operational amplifier circuit.

operational amplifier itself, is infinite. (If $\mathbf{Z}_1$ is not infinite, then the actual input impedance will be the parallel combination of $\mathbf{Z}_a$ and $\mathbf{Z}_1$.) Then,

$$\mathbf{Z}_a = \frac{\mathbf{V}_1}{I} \tag{13-12}$$

Substituting Eq. 13-4 and manipulating, we have

$$\mathbf{Z}_a = \frac{R_2}{1 - \mathbf{V}_o/\mathbf{V}_1} \tag{13-13}$$

Substituting Eq. 13-1 we have

$$\mathbf{Z}_a = \frac{R_2}{1 + \mathbf{A}_v} \tag{13-14}$$

Assume that $\mathbf{A}_v$ is a large positive number. Then, $\mathbf{Z}_a$ will, in general, be small. For instance, if $\mathbf{A}_v = 10{,}000$ and $R_2 = 50{,}000$ ohms, then $\mathbf{Z}_a = 5$ ohms. In general, $\mathbf{Z}_1$ will be 100,000 ohms or more. Hence, the parallel combination of $\mathbf{Z}_1$ and $\mathbf{Z}_a$ will essentially equal $\mathbf{Z}_a$. Thus, the assumption that $\mathbf{Z}_1$ can be considered infinite is a valid one for this circuit.

In Eq. 13-14 we again see a manifestation of Miller effects (see Sec. 6-10). Whenever we have an impedance connected between the input and output of an amplifier with a large negative gain, the effective input impedance is greatly reduced.

Sensitivity of $\mathbf{K}_v$ to Changes in $\mathbf{A}_v$

Equation 13-8 implies that $\mathbf{K}_v$, the gain of the circuit of Fig. 13-4, is independent of $\mathbf{A}_v$. Actually, this is not excatly true since the relation 13-7 is only approximate. Let us now see how much $\mathbf{K}_v$ varies when $\mathbf{A}_v$ varies. Manipulating Eq. 13-6 we obtain

$$\mathbf{K}_v = \frac{\mathbf{V}_o}{\mathbf{V}_{i1}} = -\frac{R_2/R_1}{1 + \mathbf{A}_v^{-1}(1 + R_2/R_1)} \tag{13-15}$$

Now suppose that $\mathbf{A}_v$ changes to $\mathbf{A}_v + \Delta\mathbf{A}_v$. The amplifier gain then becomes $\mathbf{K}_v + \Delta\mathbf{K}_v$ where

$$\mathbf{K}_v + \Delta\mathbf{K}_v = \frac{-R_2/R_1}{1 + [1/(\mathbf{A}_v + \Delta\mathbf{A}_v)](1 + R_2/R_1)} \tag{13-16}$$

Substituting Eq. 13-15 and manipulating, we have

$$\Delta \mathbf{K}_v = \frac{\left(\dfrac{R_2}{R_1}\right)\left(1 + \dfrac{R_2}{R_1}\right)\dfrac{\Delta \mathbf{A}_v}{\mathbf{A}(\mathbf{A} + \Delta \mathbf{A})}}{\left[1 + \dfrac{1}{\mathbf{A}_v}\left(1 + \dfrac{R_2}{R_1}\right)\right]\left[1 + \dfrac{1}{\mathbf{A}_v + \Delta \mathbf{A}_v}\left(1 + \dfrac{R_2}{R_1}\right)\right]} \tag{13-17}$$

We shall assume that $\Delta \mathbf{A}_v$ will be small enough so that, in addition to 13-7 the following is also true.

$$\left|\frac{1}{\mathbf{A}_v + \Delta \mathbf{A}_v}\left(1 + \frac{R_2}{R_1}\right)\right| \ll 1 \tag{13-18}$$

Then, Eq. 13-17 becomes

$$\Delta \mathbf{K} = \frac{(R_2/R_1)(1 + R_2/R_1)(\Delta \mathbf{A}_v)}{\mathbf{A}_v(\mathbf{A}_v + \Delta \mathbf{A}_v)} \tag{13-19}$$

$\mathbf{K}_v = -R_2/R_1$. Substituting and manipulating, we have

$$\frac{\Delta \mathbf{K}_v}{\mathbf{K}_v} = \frac{\Delta \mathbf{A}_v}{\mathbf{A}_v} \frac{1 - \mathbf{K}_v}{\mathbf{A}_v(1 + \Delta \mathbf{A}_v/\mathbf{A}_v)} \tag{13-20}$$

The term $\Delta \mathbf{K}/\mathbf{K}_v$ represents the fractional change in $\mathbf{K}_v$. ($100 \times |\Delta \mathbf{K}/\mathbf{K}_v|$ would be the percent change.) Thus, Eq. 13-18 relates the fractional change in $\mathbf{K}_v$ to the fractional change in $\mathbf{A}_v$. The ratio

$$\mathbf{S}_{\mathbf{A}_v}^{\mathbf{K}_v} = \frac{\Delta \mathbf{K}_v/\mathbf{K}_v}{\Delta \mathbf{A}_v/\mathbf{A}_v} \tag{13-21}$$

is called the *sensitivity*. Note that an ideal sensitivity would be zero. Then, $\mathbf{A}_v$ could change without changing $\mathbf{K}_v$. (Sensitivity can be defined on a differential basis as well as on a finite change basis. We shall discuss this in greater detail in Sec. 17-3. Manipulating Eq. 13-20 we have

$$\mathbf{S}_{\mathbf{A}_v}^{\mathbf{K}_v} = \frac{1 - \mathbf{K}_v}{\mathbf{A}_v(1 + \Delta \mathbf{A}_v/\mathbf{A}_v)} = \frac{1 + R_2/R_1}{\mathbf{A}_v(1 + \Delta \mathbf{A}_v/\mathbf{A}_v)} \tag{13-22}$$

Note that the sensitivity depends very much upon the ratio of the gain of the overall amplifier $\mathbf{K}_v$ to the gain of the operational amplifier $\mathbf{A}_v$. Let us illustrate the use of these relations.

Example

It is desired to build an amplifier whose gain $\mathbf{K}_v = -100$. It is known that an operational amplifier's gain can depart from its nominal value by 50%. This is to result in no more than a 1% change in $|\mathbf{K}_v|$. What is the minimum value that $|\mathbf{A}_v|$ can have?

$$\frac{\Delta \mathbf{K}_v}{\mathbf{K}_v} = -0.01$$

$$\frac{\Delta \mathbf{A}_v}{\mathbf{A}_v} = -0.5$$

We take negative changes in $\mathbf{A}_v$ since they will produce the greatest change in $\mathbf{K}_v$. Substituting in Eq. 13-20, we obtain

$$\frac{0.01}{0.5} = \frac{1 + 100}{\mathbf{A}_v(1 - 0.5)}$$

Solving, we name

$$\mathbf{A}_v = 10{,}100$$

Thus, we must choose an operational amplifier whose nominal gain is 10,100. Note that a 50% change is rather large. Thus, an $\mathbf{A}_v \geqq 10{,}000$ would probably be a valid choice here.

Note how the specification of sensitivity causes the designer to specify the value of the operational amplifier gain. The previously developed expressions for gain and input impedance did not contain the value of $\mathbf{A}_v$. However, the magnitude of $\mathbf{A}_v$ is actually an important design quantity.

13-3. NONINVERTING AMPLIFIER CONFIGURATIONS

In this section we shall discuss some additional basic amplifier forms that utilize operational amplifiers. Let us start by considering a noninverting amplifier. It might appear that this could be obtained by modifying the amplifier of Fig. 13-4 so that the noninverting input of the operational amplifier is used and the inverting input is grounded. However, we shall see in Chapter 17 that this will result in an undesirable form of feedback that will lead to improper operation. (Actually, the amplifier circuit will oscillate.) An amplifier circuit that *can* be used is shown in Fig. 13-6. The pertinent equations are

$$\mathbf{V}_o = \mathbf{A}_v(\mathbf{V}_2 - \mathbf{V}_1) \tag{13-23a}$$

$$\mathbf{V}_2 = \mathbf{V}_{i2} \tag{13-23b}$$

$$\mathbf{V}_1 = \frac{\mathbf{V}_o R_1}{R_1 + R_2} \tag{13-23c}$$

Solving for the voltage gain $\mathbf{K}_v = \mathbf{V}_o/\mathbf{V}_{i2}$, we obtain

$$\mathbf{K}_v = \frac{\mathbf{A}_v}{1 + \mathbf{A}_v R_1/(R_1 + R_2)} \tag{13-24}$$

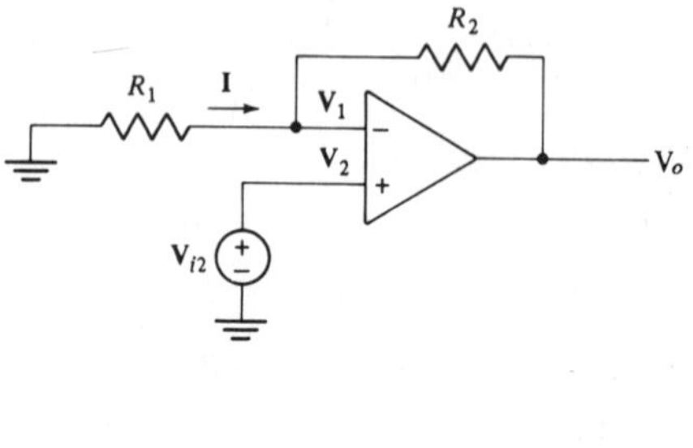

Figure 13-6. A noninverting amplifier.

In general,

$$\left| \frac{\mathbf{A}_v R_1}{R_1 + R_2} \right| \gg 1 \tag{13-25}$$

Hence,

$$\mathbf{K}_v = 1 + \frac{R_2}{R_1} \tag{13-26}$$

Again, if $\mathbf{A}_v$ is sufficiently large, the voltage gain is essentially independent of it.

The input impedance of this amplifier is equal to the input impedance of the noninverting terminal of the operational amplifier. Thus, it ranges from 100,000 ohms to extremely large values depending upon the operational amplifier.

The sensitivity of $\mathbf{K}_v$ to changes in $\mathbf{A}_v$ can be computed as in the last section. Doing this we obtain

$$\mathbf{S}_{\mathbf{A}_v}^{\mathbf{K}_v} = \frac{\Delta\mathbf{K}/\mathbf{K}_v}{\Delta\mathbf{A}/\mathbf{A}_v} = \frac{\mathbf{K}_v}{\mathbf{K}_v + \mathbf{A}_v(1 + \Delta\mathbf{A}_v/\mathbf{A}_v)} = \frac{1 + R_2/R_1}{\mathbf{K}_v + \mathbf{A}_v(1 + \Delta\mathbf{A}_v/\mathbf{A}_v)} \tag{13-27}$$

This relation is essentially the same as that of Eq. 13-22, since $|\mathbf{A}_v| \gg |\mathbf{K}_v|$, in general. Hence the implications of Eq. 13-27 are the same as those of Eq. 13-22.

The Voltage Follower

In Sec. 6-4 we discussed the source follower. It is desirable for its gain to be as close to unity as possible. Its input impedance was high and its output impedance was low. The operational amplifier allows us to achieve gains that are extremely close to unity. The output impedance of the operational amplifier circuits we have been discussing are usually very low. We shall consider this in Sec. 13-5. Thus, they can be excellent impedance matching or isolation devices. If special high-input impedance operational amplifiers are used, then the input impedance can be extremely high. The output impedance can be very small, much less than that of a source follower if the appropriate circuit is used.

Consider Fig. 13-6 and Eq. 13-26. If we set $R_2 = 0$ and $R_1 = \infty$, then $\mathbf{K}_v = 1$ and the circuit of Fig. 13-7 results. Let us analyze the circuit directly. We have

$$\mathbf{V}_o = \mathbf{A}_v(\mathbf{V}_2 - \mathbf{V}_1) = \mathbf{A}_v(\mathbf{V}_{i2} - \mathbf{V}_o)$$

Manipulating, we obtain

$$\mathbf{K}_v = \frac{\mathbf{V}_o}{\mathbf{V}_{i2}} = \frac{\mathbf{A}_v}{\mathbf{A}_v + 1} \tag{13-28}$$

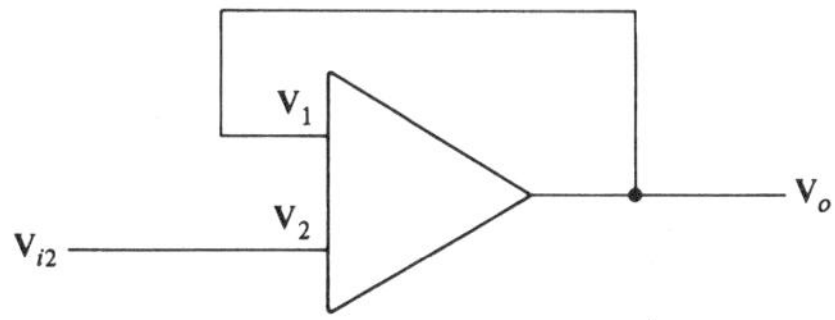

Figure 13-7. A voltage follower.

Since $|\mathbf{A}_v| \gg 1$, we have

$$\mathbf{K}_v \simeq 1 \tag{13-29}$$

Hence, we have achieved the desired gain of unity.

13-4. THE DIFFERENTIAL AMPLIFIER—THE BALANCED AMPLIFIER

There are times when we want to build an amplifier whose output is the difference of two signals. Such a circuit is called a *differential amplifier* or a *balanced amplifier*. The operational amplifier itself is one such amplifier [i.e., $\mathbf{V}_o = \mathbf{A}_v(\mathbf{V}_2 - \mathbf{V}_1)$]. However (see Sec. 13-1), we want to stabilize the gain and also be able to set specific gains. A circuit that accomplishes this is shown in Fig. 13-8. It is essentially a combination of Figs. 13-4 and 13-6. The resistances R_3 and R_4 are included to adjust the noninverting gain. The pertinent equations are

$$\frac{\mathbf{V}_{i1} - \mathbf{V}_1}{R_1} = \frac{\mathbf{V}_1 - \mathbf{V}_o}{R_2} \tag{13-30a}$$

$$\mathbf{V}_2 = \frac{\mathbf{V}_{i2} R_4}{R_3 + R_4} \tag{13-30b}$$

Utilizing these equations and Eq. 13-1, and manipulating, we obtain

$$\frac{\mathbf{V}_{i1}}{R_1} - \frac{\mathbf{V}_{i2}}{R_1}\left[\frac{1 + R_1/R_2}{1 + R_3/R_4}\right] = -\frac{\mathbf{V}_o}{R_2}\left[1 + \frac{1}{\mathbf{A}_v}\left(1 + \frac{R_2}{R_1}\right)\right] \tag{13-31}$$

If the inequality 13-7 is valid, then

$$\frac{\mathbf{V}_{i1}}{R_1} - \frac{\mathbf{V}_{i2}}{R_1}\left[\frac{1 + R_1/R_2}{1 + R_3/R_4}\right] = -\frac{\mathbf{V}_o}{R_2} \tag{13-32}$$

Now suppose that we adjust R_3 and R_4 such that

$$\frac{R_3}{R_4} = \frac{R_1}{R_2} \tag{13-33}$$

Then,

$$\mathbf{V}_o = \frac{R_2}{R_1}(\mathbf{V}_{i2} - \mathbf{V}_{i1}) \tag{13-34}$$

Thus, we have achieved the desired result.

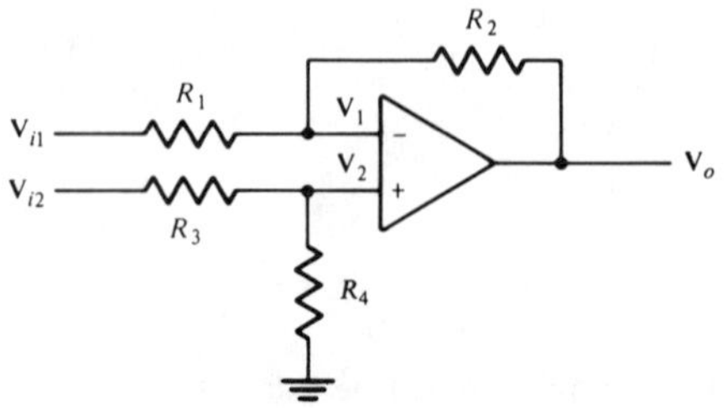

Figure 13-8. A differential, or balanced amplifier.

Let us consider an application for this amplifier. Suppose that we have an impedance measuring bridge such as that shown in Fig. 13-9. Assume that $\mathbf{Z}_d$ is an unknown impedance and that $\mathbf{Z}_a$, $\mathbf{Z}_b$, and $\mathbf{Z}_c$ are known variable impedances. The known resistors are adjusted for *null*. This occurs when

$$\mathbf{V}_{ab} = \mathbf{V}_a - \mathbf{V}_b = 0 \tag{13-35}$$

When this condition is met, then the following condition holds.

$$\frac{\mathbf{Z}_a}{\mathbf{Z}_b} = \frac{\mathbf{Z}_c}{\mathbf{Z}_d} \tag{13-36a}$$

or, equivalently,

$$\mathbf{Z}_d = \frac{\mathbf{Z}_b}{\mathbf{Z}_a}\mathbf{Z}_c \tag{13-36b}$$

Thus, to measure $\mathbf{Z}_d$, the impedances $\mathbf{Z}_a$, $\mathbf{Z}_b$, and $\mathbf{Z}_c$ are adjusted for null and the value of $\mathbf{Z}_d$ is then calculated using Eq. 13-36b. It is assumed that $\mathbf{Z}_a$, $\mathbf{Z}_b$, and $\mathbf{Z}_c$ are calibrated so that their values are known.

A simple detector can be used to sense the null. For instance, if the measurements are made at $f = 0$ (i.e., dc), then a dc voltmeter can be used to detect if $\mathbf{V}_{ab} = 0$. The null can be determined more accurately if the voltage is amplified. For instance, suppose that we have a detector that can detect signals as small as 0.01 V. Any signal whose magnitude is less than this appears as a null. Thus, the value of $\mathbf{Z}_d$ will be somewhat in error since there will be a range of values that show a null. Now suppose that we amplify the signal by 100 before we apply it to the null detector. Now we can detect signals as small as 0.0001 V. Hence, the accuracy has been improved.

We cannot simply amplify $\mathbf{V}_{ab}$ since neither point a nor point b is grounded. The usual amplifier has one input terminal grounded; this is called an *unbalanced input.* One lead of the generator $\mathbf{V}_i$ is also usually grounded. Thus, if we connected terminals a and b to the input of an amplifier such as that of Fig. 13-4, either $\mathbf{Z}_b$ or $\mathbf{Z}_d$ would be "shorted out."

Now consider the amplifier of Fig. 13-8. Suppose that the resistors are adjusted so that the input impedance viewed by $\mathbf{V}_{i1}$ is equal to that viewed by $\mathbf{V}_{i2}$. Both of these inputs are above ground. This is said to be a *balanced* input. If such a balanced amplifier is connected to points a and b of Fig. 13-9, satisfactory operation will result. However, there is one problem that arises. The impedances $\mathbf{Z}_a$, $\mathbf{Z}_b$, $\mathbf{Z}_c$, and $\mathbf{Z}_d$ now become part of the amplifier. Their values will affect the gain. The amplifier design could take the

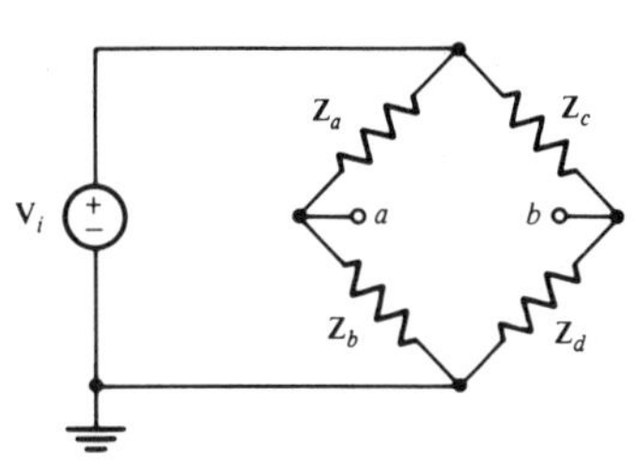

Figure 13-9. An impedance measuring bridge.

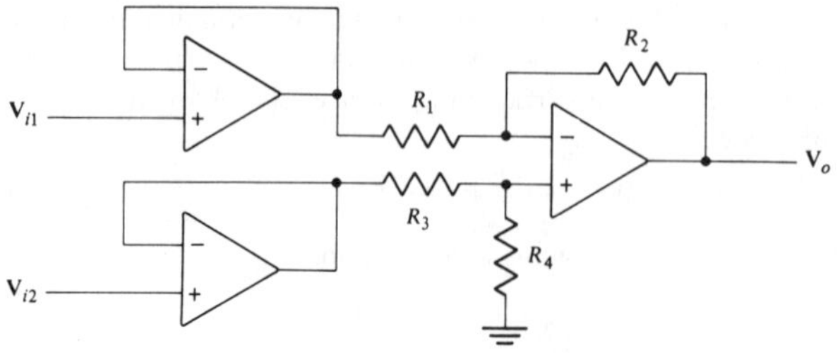

Figure 13-10. A balanced amplifier whose gain is not affected by the impedance of the sources.

bridge impedance input into account. However, this complicates the design and causes the amplification to depend upon the bridge values. Another circuit can be used to eliminate this problem. It is shown in Fig. 13-10. It is essentially the amplifier of Fig. 13-8 with two voltage followers added to isolate the inputs. We assume that the input impedance of the voltage follower is high enough so that it does *not* disturb the circuit being measured. The output impedance of the voltage follower should be added to R_1 and R_3. However, these output impedances are often so low in comparison with R_1 and R_3 that they can be ingored.

If the amplifier of Fig. 13-10 is used as a null detector, then it should be adjusted so that the gain from inputs 1 and 2 are exactly equal in magnitude. This can be accomplished by connecting the two impedances together and applying a signal. This then causes

$$\mathbf{V}_{i1} = \mathbf{V}_{i2}$$

Under these circumstances the output should be zero. However, due to the tolerances of the resistances, and because of the fact that the integrated circuits are not exactly balanced, this will not be exactly true. Resistances R_3 and/or R_4 should be adjusted until $\mathbf{V}_o$ actually becomes zero. The amplifier is then properly adjusted.

It may appear as though the circuit of Fig. 13-10 uses very many components. This is true if we count up the individual transistor diodes, and so forth. However, inexpensive integrated circuit chips can be obtained which contain four operational amplifiers. Thus, the circuit of Fig. 13-10 can be built using one integrated circuit chip and four external resistors.

13-5. OUTPUT IMPEDANCE

Let us now demonstrate that the output impedances of the operational amplifier circuits that we have considered are very low. We shall use the amplifier circuit of Fig. 13-4 here. However, similar results would be obtained with the other circuits that we have considered. The operational amplifier shall be represented by the model of Fig. 13-2. The input resistance R_{i2} will be short-circuited to ground and hence can be ignored. As we discussed in Sec. 13-2, the Miller effect causes R_{i1} to be shunted by a very small resistance. Hence, R_{i1} can be ignored. Therefore, the model of Fig. 13-11 can be used in the analysis of Fig. 13-4.

We shall calculate the output impedance using the Thévinin theorem. That is, we shall determine the open-circuit output voltage $\mathbf{V}_{OC}$ and the short circuit output current $\mathbf{I}_{SC}$ and then take their ratio. We start by computing $\mathbf{V}_{OC}$. From Fig. 13-11 we have

$$\mathbf{V}_{i1} + \mathbf{A}_v\mathbf{V}_1 = \mathbf{I}(R_1 + R_2 + R_o) \tag{13-37a}$$

$$\mathbf{V}_1 = \mathbf{V}_{i1} - \mathbf{I}R_1 \tag{13-37b}$$

and

$$\mathbf{V}_{OC} = \mathbf{V}_{i1} - \mathbf{I}(R_1 + R_2) \tag{13-37c}$$

Manipulating, we obtain

$$\mathbf{V}_{OC} = \frac{-\mathbf{V}_{i1}(\mathbf{A}_v R_2 - R_o)}{\mathbf{A}_v R_1 + R_1 + R_2 + R_o} \tag{13-38}$$

In general,

$$|\mathbf{A}_v R_2| \gg R_o \tag{13-39a}$$

and

$$|\mathbf{A}_v R_1| \gg R_1 + R_2 + R_o \tag{13-39b}$$

Thus,

$$\mathbf{V}_{OC} = -\mathbf{V}_i \frac{R_2}{R_1} \tag{13-40}$$

This gives the same value of voltage gain as was calculated previously.

Now let us calculate the short circuit current. For this purpose we include the dashed line in Fig. 13-11.

$$\mathbf{I}_{SC} = \frac{\mathbf{V}_{i1}}{R_1 + R_2} - \frac{\mathbf{A}_v\mathbf{V}_1}{R_o} \tag{13-41a}$$

where

$$\mathbf{V}_1 = \frac{\mathbf{V}_{i1}R_2}{R_1 + R_2} \tag{13-41b}$$

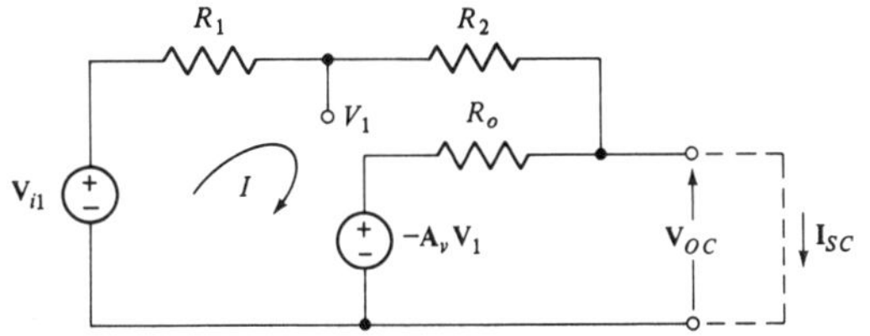

Figure 13-11. A model used to calculate the output impedance of the amplifier of Fig. 13-4.

Note that because of the short circuit, the voltage across the output terminals is zero. Substituting Eq. 13-41b into Eq. 13-41a and manipulating, we obtain

$$\mathbf{I}_{SC} = \mathbf{V}_i\left[\frac{1}{R_1 + R_2} - \frac{\mathbf{A}_v R_2}{R_o(R_1 + R_2)}\right] \tag{13-42}$$

In general, $|\mathbf{A}_v|$ will be very large and $R_2 > R_o$, so that

$$\frac{|\mathbf{A}_v| R_2}{R_o} \gg 1 \tag{13-43}$$

Hence,

$$\mathbf{I}_{SC} = -\frac{\mathbf{V}_i \mathbf{A}_v R_2}{R_o(R_1 + R_2)} \tag{13-44}$$

Taking the ratio of Eq. 13-40 to Eq. 13-42 yields

$$\mathbf{Z}_o = R_o \frac{1 + R_2/R_1}{\mathbf{A}_v} \tag{13-45}$$

Remember that the voltage gain of the circuit is $\mathbf{K}_v = -R_2/R_1$. Substituting, we obtain

$$\mathbf{Z}_o = R_o \frac{1 - \mathbf{K}_v}{\mathbf{A}_v} \tag{13-46}$$

As we have seen, $\mathbf{A}_v$ is usually very much greater than $\mathbf{K}_v$. Hence, $\mathbf{Z}_o$ will be very much less than R_o, which is the output resistance of the operational amplifier acting alone. Let us illustrate some typical values with an example.

Example

The amplifier of Fig. 13-4 has a gain of $\mathbf{K}_v = -50$. The gain of the operational amplifier is $\mathbf{A}_v = 10{,}000$ and its output resistance is $R_o = 1000$ ohms. Compute the output impedance of the amplifier circuit.

Substituting in Eq. 13-46 we have

$$\mathbf{Z}_o = 1000\left(\frac{1 + 50}{10{,}000}\right) = 5.1 \text{ ohms}$$

This is a pure resistance since we have assumed $\mathbf{A}_v$ to be real. At higher frequencies, $\mathbf{A}_v$ will fall off and no longer be real. In such cases, the output impedance will increase in magnitude and become complex.

Note that the output resistance is very small. If the ratio $|\mathbf{K}_v/\mathbf{A}_v|$ decreases, the output impedance becomes even smaller. For circuits such as the voltage follower (see Sec. 13-3), the output resistance is extremely low (typically 0.30 ohm or less).

13-6. THE SUMMER OR ADDER CIRCUIT

There are many applications when we wish to add several signals. For instance, when audio recordings are made there are usually several microphones placed at various points about the stage. The signals from each of these are then added to form the final signal. All the signals are not weighted equally. That is, they are multiplied by different constant values before they are combined. A circuit that accomplishes this multiplication by a constant and addition is called an *adder* or *summer*. We shall consider other applications for such circuits subsequently.

A very simple summer circuit is shown in Fig. 13-12. This circuit can be analyzed by applying the superposition theorem. Doing this we obtain

$$\mathbf{V}_o = \frac{R_{21}}{R_{11} + R_{21}}\mathbf{V}_{i1} + \frac{R_{22}}{R_{12} + R_{22}}\mathbf{V}_{i2} + \frac{R_{23}}{R_{13} + R_{23}}\mathbf{V}_{i3} + \cdots + \frac{R_{2n}}{R_{1n} + R_{2n}}\mathbf{V}_{in} \tag{13-47}$$

where

$$\frac{1}{R_{21}} = \frac{1}{R_{12}} + \frac{1}{R_{13}} + \cdots + \frac{1}{R_{1n}} + \frac{1}{R_2'} \tag{13-48a}$$

$$\frac{1}{R_{22}} = \frac{1}{R_{11}} + \frac{1}{R_{13}} + \cdots + \frac{1}{R_{1n}} + \frac{1}{R_2'} \tag{13-48b}$$

$$\vdots$$

In general, R_{2j} represents the parallel combination of all the resistances of the network except the one connected to input j.

At first glance, Eq. 13-47 seems to indicate the circuit of Fig. 13-12 adequately performs the desired summing operation. However, it suffers from two problems. The constant multipliers $R_{2j}/(R_{jj} + R_{2j})$ are all less than one. Thus, the circuit cannot provide amplification. A problem which, at times, is much more troublesome is that the

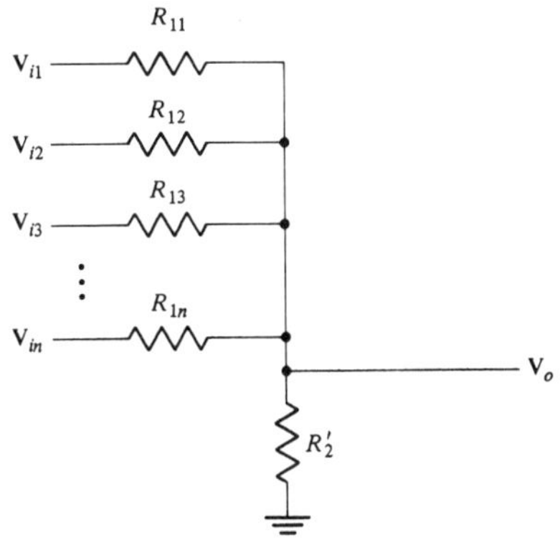

Figure 13-12. A very simple summer that has some practical problems.

coefficients of the input voltages all interact. For instance, suppose that we want to change the constant multiplier of $\mathbf{V}_{i1}$. This is

$$\frac{R_{21}}{(R_{11} + R_{21})}$$

We can adjust this by changing R_{11}. However, this will change $R_{22}, \ldots, R_{2n}$. Hence, all the constant multipliers will change. This interaction makes gain adjustment very tedious.

The problem of interaction can be alleviated by making R_2' very small. If R_2' is very much less than all the other resistances, then

$$R_{2j} \simeq R_2'$$

Equation 13-47 then becomes

$$\mathbf{V}_o = \frac{R_2'}{R_{i1} + R_2'}\mathbf{V}_{i1} + \frac{R_2'}{R_{i2} + R_2'}\mathbf{V}_{i2} + \cdots + \frac{R_2'}{R_{in} + R_2'}\mathbf{V}_{in} \tag{13-49}$$

The interaction is eliminated, but the output voltage becomes very small because R_2' is so small.

Let us see how these difficulties can be eliminated by using the operational amplifier circuit of Fig. 13-13. Proceeding as in Sec. 13-2, we have

$$\mathbf{I} = \frac{\mathbf{V}_{i1} - \mathbf{V}_1}{R_{11}} + \frac{\mathbf{V}_{i2} - \mathbf{V}_1}{R_{12}} + \frac{\mathbf{V}_{i3} - \mathbf{V}_1}{R_{13}} + \cdots + \frac{\mathbf{V}_{in} - \mathbf{V}_1}{R_{1n}} = \frac{\mathbf{V}_1 - \mathbf{V}_o}{R_2}$$

Utilizing the relation that $\mathbf{V}_o = -\mathbf{A}_v\mathbf{V}_1$, and manipulating, we obtain

$$\frac{\mathbf{V}_{i1}}{R_{11}} + \frac{\mathbf{V}_{i2}}{R_{12}} + \cdots + \frac{\mathbf{V}_{in}}{R_{1n}} = -\frac{\mathbf{V}_o}{R_2}\left[1 + \frac{1}{\mathbf{A}_v}\left(\frac{R_2}{R_{11}} + \frac{R_2}{R_{12}} + \cdots + \frac{R_2}{R_{1n}}\right)\right] \tag{13-50}$$

In most practical circuits, $|\mathbf{A}_v|$ will be so large that

$$1 \gg \left|\frac{1}{\mathbf{A}_v}\left(\frac{R_2}{R_{11}} + \frac{R_2}{R_{12}} + \cdots + \frac{R_2}{R_{1n}}\right)\right| \tag{13-51}$$

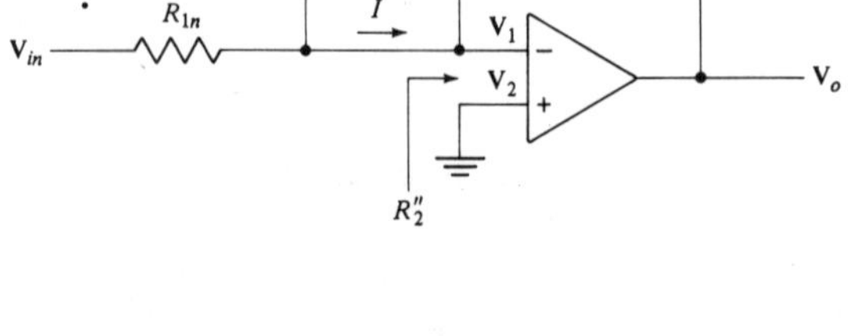

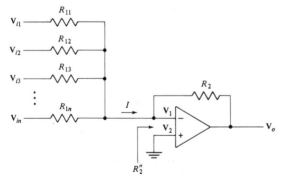

Figure 13-13. A practical summer.

Hence, we can write

$$\mathbf{V}_o = -\left[\frac{R_2}{R_{i1}}\mathbf{V}_{i1} + \frac{R_2}{R_{i2}}\mathbf{V}_{i2} + \cdots + \frac{R_2}{R_{in}}\mathbf{V}_{in}\right] \tag{13-52}$$

Note that we have achieved the desired result. We can adjust the constant multipliers simply by changing the appropriate R_{ij} and there is no interaction. The overall gain can be adjusted by changing R_2. Note that the circuit can also provide gain. Thus, the circuit of Fig. 13-13 overcomes all the objections to that of Fig. 13-12.

Let us see how the problems of the circuit of Fig. 13-12 are eliminated in Fig. 13-13. The circuit of Fig. 13-13 is essentially the same as that of Fig. 13-12. The input resistance R_2'' of Fig. 13-13 serves the same function as R_2' in Fig. 13-12. From Eq. 13-14, we have

$$R_2'' = \frac{R_2}{1 + \mathbf{A}_v}$$

This will be a very small number and explains why the interaction problem is eliminated. This small value of R_2' causes $\mathbf{V}_1$ to be very small. However, the output value $\mathbf{V}_o$ is not small because of the amplification of the operational amplifier. Let us consider the design of a simple summer.

Example

Obtain a summing amplifier that achieves the following output.

$$\mathbf{V}_o = -[3\mathbf{V}_{i1} + 5\mathbf{V}_{i2} + \mathbf{V}_{i3}] \tag{13-53}$$

From Eq. 13-52 we have

$$\frac{R_2}{R_{i1}} = 3$$

$$\frac{R_2}{R_{i2}} = 5$$

$$\frac{R_2}{R_{i3}} = 1$$

There are three equations with four unknowns. Thus, we have some freedom of choice here. Manipulating, we obtain

$$3R_{i1} = 5R_{i2} = R_{i3} = R_2$$

We can then choose one of the resistances. Note that $\mathbf{V}_1$ will be at virtual ground. Thus, the input impedance measured from input k is R_{ik}. This can aid in the choice. Suppose that we desire the minimum imput resistance to be 10,000 ohms. Then, choose

$$R_{i2} = 10{,}000 \text{ ohms}$$

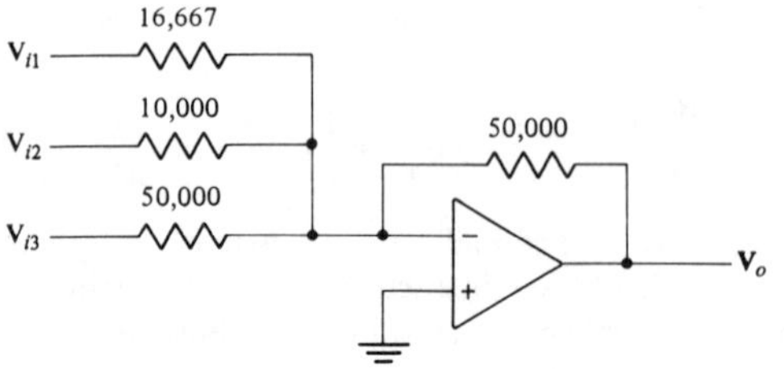

Fig. 13-14. A summer that realizes Eq. 13-53. All resistor values are in ohms.

Then,

$$R_{i1} = 16{,}667 \text{ ohms}$$

$$R_{i3} = 50{,}000 \text{ ohms}$$

$$R_2 = 50{,}000 \text{ ohms}$$

A circuit for this amplifier is shown in Fig. 13-14.

A resistance of 16,667 ohms is not a standard one. If great accuracy is not required, then the closest available standard resistance value can be used. Of course, if great accuracy is needed, then a precision resistance will have to be used. A simple solution is to use variable resistances and adjust them to the appropriate values. However, the process of adjusting components can prove costly if a large number of amplifiers are to be built.

13-7. THE INTEGRATOR

The original operational amplifier was not an integrated circuit device. In fact, it used vacuum tubes. These operational amplifiers were also high-gain, direct coupled amplifiers. They were used in analog computers to solve such things as integral or differential equations. In an analog computer, this is done by fabricating a circuit whose equation is the same as the one to be solved. The output signal is then the same as the desired equation solution. This can then be recorded. The analog computer had building blocks that performed mathematical *operations.* The operational amplifier was an important part of the most building blocks. The digital computer has replaced the analog computer for many applications. However, analog computations are still performed in applications where very precise operation is not needed. In addition, mathematical operations are used to perform such operations as waveshaping and frequency equalizing. In this section we shall consider a circuit that performs the mathematical operation of integration.

A simple circuit that approximates an integrator is shown in Fig. 13-15. The circuit only functions approximately. Suppose that

$$|V_o| \ll |V_i| \tag{13-54}$$

then

$$i = \frac{v_i}{R} \tag{13-55}$$

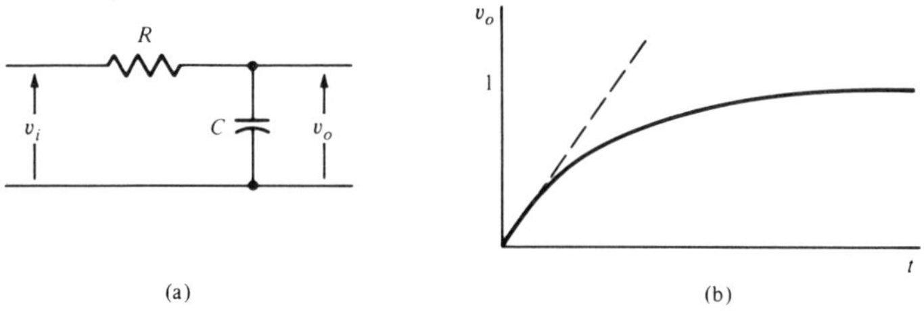

Figure 13-15. (a) A simple integrator. (b) v_o for this circuit when v_i is a unit step.

hence

$$v_o = \frac{1}{RC} \int v_i \, dt \tag{13-56}$$

and we achieve the desired integration of the input signal. This circuit only functions properly if inequality 13-54 is valid. For instance, suppose that $v_i(t)$ represents a unit step.

$$u(t) = 0, \quad t < 0$$
$$\quad 1, \quad t > 0$$

Then, ideally we would have

$$v_o(t) = \int_0^t 1 \, dt = t$$

This is represented by the dashed curve of Fig. 13-15b. However, the unit step response of the circuit of Fig. 13-15a is given by the solid curve of Fig. 13-15b. Hence, the approximation is valid only for small values of time. When v_o becomes large, inequality 13-54 is no longer valid and Eq. 13-55 no longer represents the current and Eq. 13-56 is thus in error.

If we increase R or C, this will reduce the voltage across C and hence, the circuit will function as an accurate integrator for longer periods of time. There are two problems that occur here. Increasing R or C reduces the output voltage which may be undesirable. In addition, if very large R or C is required, it may be costly to obtain the components.

An operational amplifier circuit can resolve many of these difficulties (see Fig. 13-16). We shall compute the gain of this circuit using the techniques developed in Sec. 13-2, except that we shall work on an instantaneous basis.

$$i = \frac{v_i - v_1}{R} = C \frac{d(v_1 - v_o)}{dt} \tag{13-57}$$

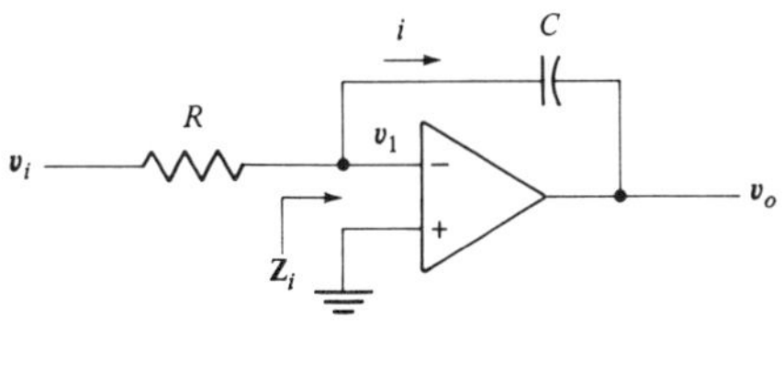

Figure 13-16. An integrator circuit.

Using the relation $v_o = -Av_i$ and manipulating, we have

$$\frac{v_i}{R_1} = -C\frac{dv_o}{dt} - \frac{1}{A_v}\left(\frac{v_o}{R} + C\frac{dv_o}{dt}\right) \tag{13-58}$$

We assume here that A_v is a real positive number. Let us also assume that it is large enough so that

$$\left|C\frac{dv_o}{dt}\right| \gg \left|\frac{1}{A_v}\left(\frac{v_o}{R} + C\frac{dv_o}{dt}\right)\right| \tag{13-59}$$

If this is true then we can rewrite Eq. 13-58 as

$$v_o = -\frac{1}{RC}\int v_i\, dt \tag{13-60}$$

Thus, the circuit functions as an integrator. Note that the inequality 13-59 is not as clear cut as some of the others that we have considered (e.g., relation 13-7). In relation 13-59 the inequality depends upon the signal and its derivative as well as upon the parameters of the circuit. For instance, suppose that the input is a unit step. After a long enough time, the output will approach a constant so that dv_o/dt becomes very small. In such cases, no matter how large A_v is, eventually inequality 13-59 will become untrue and the results will become inaccurate.

Suppose that we build the integrators of Fig. 13-15 and 13-16 using the same values of R and C and compare them. If we look at Eqs. 13-56 and 13-60, it seems as though the results will be the same. This is not the case. For instance, if a unit step is applied, the output of the operational amplifier integrator will follow the desired linear curve for a much longer time, and for correspondingly much larger values of v_o. Let us see why. Earlier in this section we demonstrated that the circuit of Fig. 13-15a would function more accurately if C were made larger. Now let us consider the input impedance $\mathbf{Z}_i$ of the amplifier of Fig. 13-16. If we proceed as in the derivation of Eq. 13-14, we obtain

$$\mathbf{Z}_i = 1/j\omega C(1 + A_v) \tag{13-61}$$

If we assume that A_v is a real number, then this impedance appears as a capacitance of value

$$C_{\text{eff}} = C(1 + A_v) \tag{13-62}$$

Thus, if we want to calculate v_1 in Fig. 13-16, we could use the circuit of Fig. 13-15a with C replaced by C_{eff}. However, C_{eff} will be an extremely large capacitance since A_v is very large. This greatly improves the accuracy of the circuit. However, as we have discussed, a large value of C_{eff} causes v_1 to be very small. The output voltage $v_o = -A_v v_1$, however, since A_v is large, the output voltage will not be small. Hence, the circuit of Fig. 13-16 is superior to that of Fig. 13-15b since the operational amplifier circuit allows us to obtain the advantages of a large capacitor without having to actually use one, and without causing the output voltage to be very small.

In this circuit we have used an operational amplifier with a capacitor connected between the inverting input and output to act as an extremely large capacitance. It might appear as though this procedure would be widely used to obtain large capacitance. However, it can only be used in a limited number of applications. If the voltage across the capacitor becomes large, then the operational amplifier will saturate (see Fig. 13-3). Once the amplifier saturates, its voltage gain becomes small and we no longer have a large value for C_{eff}. Many (but not all) applications requiring large capacitances involve signals that contain relatively large direct components of voltage. (For instance, consider the bypass capacitor discussed in Sec. 12-7.) The direct component of voltage will saturate the operational amplifier and it will not function properly. In such cases, we cannot use an operational amplifier-capacitor circuit to obtain a large capacitance.

Initial Value of v_o

In some applications it is desirable to specify the value of v_o at some time which we shall call $t = 0$. The circuit of Fig. 13-16 can be modified to accomplish this (see Fig. 13-17). The direct voltage V_o is connected across the capacitor C as shown. At $t = 0$ the switch is opened. Since the voltage across the capacitor cannot change instantaneously at $t = 0+$, the time just after the switch is opened, we have

$$v_o - v_1 = V_0$$

Substituting Eq. 13-5, we obtain

$$v_o\left(1 + \frac{1}{A_v}\right) = V_0$$

Since

$$1 \gg \left|\frac{1}{A_v}\right|$$

$$v_o|_{t=0+} = V_0 \tag{13-63}$$

Then, we have established the initial value of v_o. The switch can be an electronic one of the type we shall discuss in Sec. 13-13. In the next section we shall discuss an application for a circuit of this type.

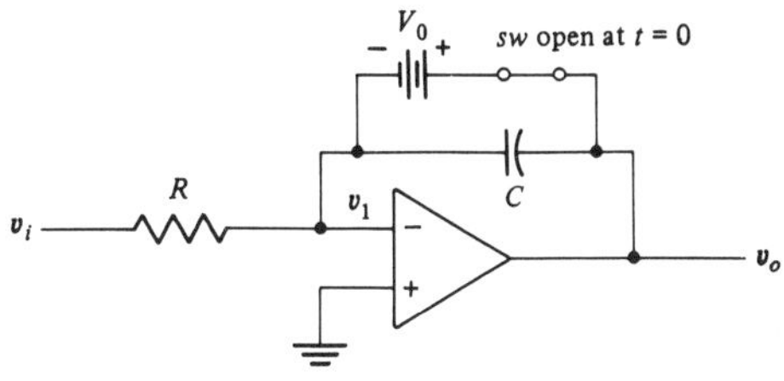

Figure 13-17. An integrator circuit that allows the initial value of v_o to be established.

13-8. SIMPLE ANALOG COMPUTER

Let us demonstrate how some of the circuits we have discussed can be used to simulate (solve) a simple differential equation. Suppose that we have

$$\frac{d^2v(t)}{dt^2} + 10\frac{dv(t)}{dt} + 2v(t) = u(t) \tag{13-64}$$

and we wish to determine the solution for v. The problem is not completely stated since we must also specify initial conditions. Suppose that these are

$$v(0) = 4 \tag{13-65a}$$

and

$$\left.\frac{dv(t)}{dt}\right|_{t=0} = 6 \tag{13-65b}$$

Now let us obtain a circuit that has $v(t)$ as its output. We start by rewriting Eq. 13-64 in the following way.

$$\frac{d^2v(t)}{dt^2} = -10\frac{dv(t)}{dt} - 2v(t) + u(t) \tag{13-66}$$

Now let us assume that we have a voltage equal to $d^2v(t)/dt^2$. Of course, we actually do not, but we shall see that we can surmount this difficulty subsequently. Now consider the diagram of Fig. 13-18. Assume for the moment that the connection ab is broken, and that we input a voltage equal to d^2v/dt^2 at point a. Then the two integrators will have outputs of $-dv(t)/dt$ and $v(t)$, respectively, as shown. The batteries and switches will establish the specified initial values of these variables.

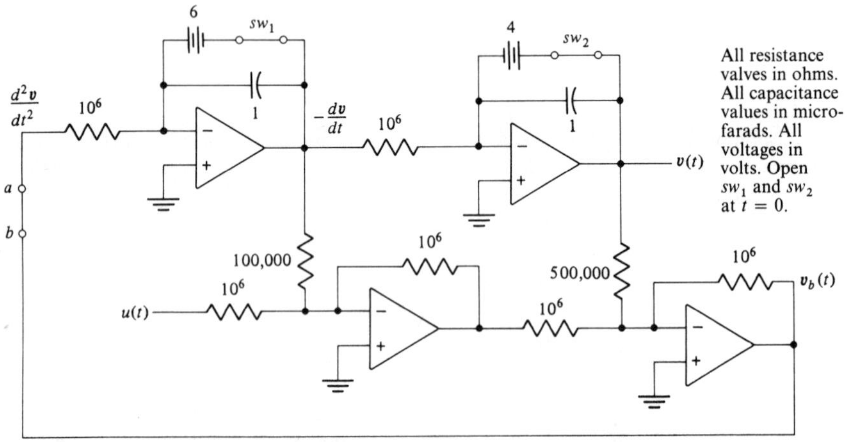

Figure 13-18. A simple analog computer circuit that solves Eq. 13-64.

Now consider the lower portion of the circuit that consists of two summers. Using the results of Sec. 13-6, we have

$$v_b = -10\frac{dv(t)}{dt} - 2v(t) + u(t)$$

where we assume that a unit step voltage $u(t)$ is applied to the circuit at the point shown.

Now suppose that we make the connection between points a and b. This forces d^2v/dt^2 to equal v_b. Thus, Eq. 13-66 must be satisfied. Hence, the differential equation that characterizes this circuit is the same as the given one. Therefore, if at $t = 0$, we open switches 1 and 2 and apply the unit step, the voltage $v(t)$ will be the solution to the desired differential equation. This can then be recorded on an oscilloscope. Thus, we have obtained our desired solution.

13-9. THE DIFFERENTIATOR

At times it is useful to have a circuit whose output signal is the derivative of its input waveform. This can be used in analog computations and wave shaping as well as in other applications. We shall discuss such circuits in this section. Many of the ideas considered here will parallel those of Sec. 13-7 and, hence, many of the details will be omitted here.

A simple RC differentiating circuit is given in Fig. 13-19. The current i is given by

$$i = C\frac{d(v_i - v_o)}{dt}$$

if

$$|v_o| \ll |v_i| \tag{13-67}$$

Then, the voltage across the resistance will be much less than that across the capacitance and we can write

$$i = C\frac{dv_i}{dt} \tag{13-68}$$

Hence,

$$v_o = RC\frac{dv_i}{dt} \tag{13-69}$$

In order to ensure that inequality 13-67 is satisfied, for most inputs, we must make either or both R and C very small. This results in very small values of v_o. Just as in the case

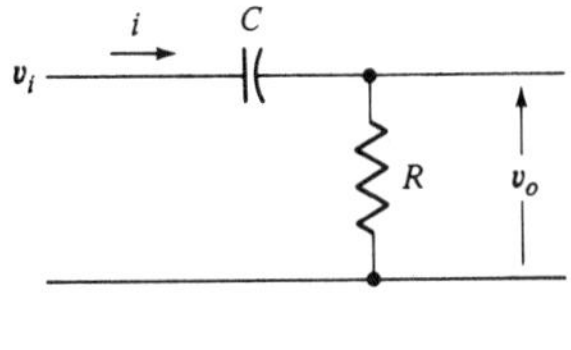

Figure 13-19. A simple RC differentiator circuit.

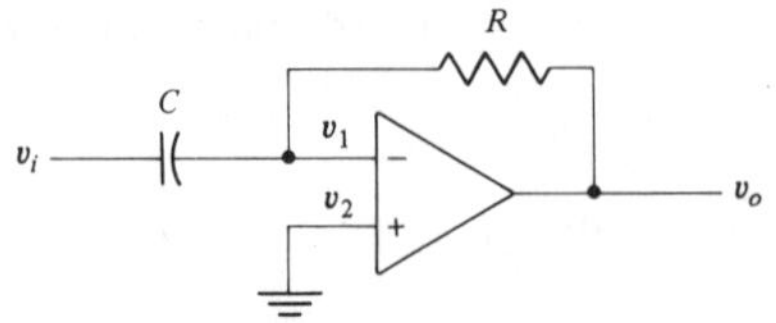

Figure 13-20. An operational amplifier differentiator circuit.

of the integrator, we can use an operational amplifier to avoid this problem. The circuit is shown in Fig. 13-20. Analyzing this circuit as before, we have

$$C\frac{dv_i}{dt} = -\frac{v_o}{R} - \frac{1}{A_v}\left(\frac{v_o}{R} + C\frac{dv_o}{dt}\right)$$

If

$$\left|\frac{v_o}{R}\right| \gg \left|\frac{1}{A_v}\left(\frac{v_o}{R} + C\frac{dv_o}{dt}\right)\right| \tag{13-70}$$

then

$$v_o = -RC\frac{dv_i}{dt} \tag{13-71}$$

Thus, we have achieved the desired result. The circuit of Fig. 13-19 serves as a model for this one since the input impedance of the operational amplifier with the feedback resistor R is a resistance $R/(1 + A_v)$. Now we have an extremely small effective resistance, but the output voltage is not very small because of the gain provided by the operational amplifier.

At times, interference spikes appear on signal lines because of stray capacitive coupling to other signal lines. These spikes are often small enough so that they do not obscure the signal but their derivatives can be large. In such cases the use of a differentiator can aggrevate the interference problem.

13-10. THE LOGARITHMIC AMPLIFIER

Let us now consider an amplifier that responds logarithmically to an input signal. Although such amplifiers are nonlinear, they are useful when wide ranges of signals are to be worked with. For instance, using the logarithmic frequency axes of Fig. 12-3, both low-frequency and high-frequency responses can be displayed. In a similar way, if we use a logarithmic voltage amplifier, we can construct a voltmeter that will give a reasonable deflection for low voltage levels but will not go "off-scale" for high values. A meter that responds logarithmically is also useful for making audio measurements since the ear is also a logarithmic device. Thus, the meter responds in a way similar to that of the ear.

Logarithmic amplifiers are used for applications other than fabricating meters. For instance, very wide dynamic signals are compressed into a much smaller range when amplified by a logarithmic amplifier. The resulting signals will then not saturate or cut off subsequent amplifiers. Of course, nonlinear distortion is introduced by such operation. However, in some systems, such nonlinearity is not important. In addition, in other systems, the signals are then amplified by an exponential amplifier which, when combined with the response of the logarithmic amplifier, removes the nonlinear distortion.

Let us now consider the logarithmic amplifier of Fig. 13-21. The transistor that is connected in a common-base configuration replaces the normal R_2 feedback resistor. Thus, as long as the collector-base junction is reverse biased, $I_C \simeq -I_E$ since I_B will be small. We shall assume that the transistor is characterized by Eq. 2-5.

Then,

$$i_C = c_{21}(e^{V_{eb}/kT} - 1) + c_{22}(e^{v_{CB}/kT} - 1) \tag{13-72}$$

$$v_{EB} = v_o \tag{13-73a}$$

and

$$v_{CB} \simeq 0 \tag{13-73b}$$

Note that $v_{CB} = v_1$ which is very small (i.e., it is at virtual ground). Then, we can approximate i_C by

$$i_C = c_{22}(e^{v_{EB}/kT} - 1) \tag{13-74}$$

Proceeding as in our previous operational amplifier analysis, we have

$$(v_i - v_1)/R = i_C = c_{22}(e^{v_o/kT} - 1) \tag{13-75}$$

Noting that $v_1 = -v_o/A_v$, we obtain

$$\frac{v_i}{R} = -\frac{v_o}{A_v R} + c_{22}(e^{v_o/kT} - 1) \tag{13-76}$$

We assume that A_v is large enough so that

$$\left|\frac{v_o}{A_v R}\right| \ll c_{22}(e^{v_o/kT} - 1) \tag{13-77}$$

We also assume that v_o will be a positive value such that

$$e^{v_o/kT} \gg 1 \tag{13-78}$$

This will be true in the active region of the transistor. Then,

$$v_i = Rc_{22}e^{v_o/kT}$$

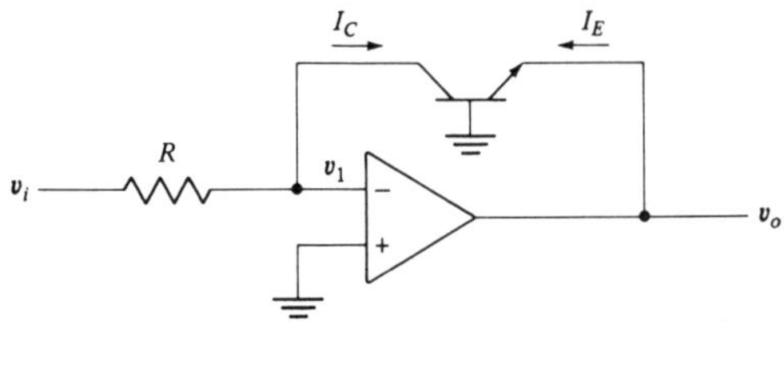

Figure 13-21. A logarithmic amplifier.

Manipulating, we have

$$v_o = \frac{1}{kT} \ln \frac{v_i}{c_{22} R} \tag{13-79}$$

Thus, the desired logarithmic response has been obtained.

We assumed in this analysis that the collector-base junction was reverse biased and that the emitter-base junction was forward biased. This implies that v_i is positive. Hence, v_1 will be (slightly) positive and v_o will be negative, achieving the desired result. If v_i becomes negative, improper operation will result. In fact, the transistor will be operated backward with emitter-base junctions reverse biased and the collector-base junction forward biased. With most transistors, there are only small "reverse collector" currents in this backward configuration. This is somewhat equivalent to making R_2 very large in Fig. 13-4. In such cases, v_1 can become large enough to damage the transistor.

13-11. THE COMPARATOR

We shall now consider an operational amplifier circuit called a *comparator* that is not used to amplify signals, but to determine if a voltage is greater or less than a given reference level. Later in this chapter we shall show that such a circuit has many digital applications. Other applications will be considered in this section.

The block diagram for a comparator and its idealized characteristics are given in Fig. 13-22a. Note that a C is included in the comparator symbol to differentiate it from that for an operational amplifier. A reference voltage is connected between the + terminal and ground. The input voltage connected to the − terminal is compared with this reference voltage. If $v_i < v_R$, then $v_o = V_C$. If $v_i > v_R$, then $v_o = V_D$. That is, if v_o is less than the reference, the output voltage is V_C; if v_i becomes greater than the reference, then v_o switches to V_D. In Fig. 13-22 we have V_C positive and V_D negative. This need not be the case. They can be any two different voltage levels. (Note that if the input were connected to the + terminal and the reference to the − terminal, the circuit would function as a comparator but the output polarity would be reversed.)

Let us now consider some simple applications of the comparator. Suppose that we wish to construct a frequency meter, that is, a device that indicates the frequency of the

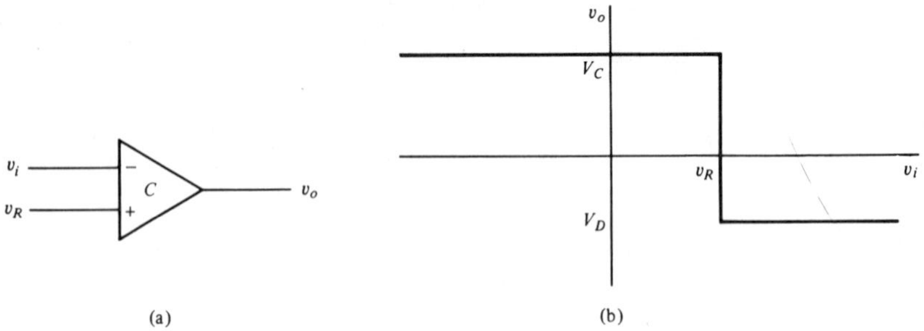

Figure 13-22. The comparator. (a) Its block diagram (the ground connections are omitted). (b) Its idealized characteristics.

applied signal. If we are dealing with waveforms of the same amplitude and shape (e.g., sinusoid whose rms value is 10 V), then the signal can be applied to a circuit such as that of Fig. 13-15a. As the frequency is increased, the rms value of the voltage across the capacitor will decrease. A voltmeter that reads this voltage can then be calibrated in terms of the signal frequency. A problem arises when the signal's amplitude or waveshape changes. Now the output voltage will change even if there has been no change in frequency. A comparator can be used to eliminate these problems by converting all waveforms to a standard shape. (We shall assume in this discussion that all waveforms are periodic and cross zero in the middle of these periods.) Consider Fig. 13-23a, which represents the input waveform that is applied to an ideal comparator with $V_R = 0$ and $V_C = -V_D$. The output waveform will be as shown in Fig. 13-23b. Thus, when an arbitrarily shaped signal is applied to an ideal comparator, the output will be a square wave of amplitude V_C. Therefore, no matter what input waveform is applied, the output waveshape will always be the same. The only variation will be its frequency. Hence, this waveform can be applied to the previously discussed frequency measuring circuit to determine the frequency.

Let us consider another application of a comparator. Here it is used in a *power conditioning circuit* that is used to efficiently reduce a dc voltage level to a smaller value. In addition, this circuit provides voltage regulation, that is, it compensates for changes in the supply voltage or in the load current in such a way that the output voltage remains relatively constant.

Let us start by just considering the problem of reducing a direct voltage to a smaller one. A simple circuit that will accomplish this is shown in Fig. 13-24a. The resistor R is chosen so that the voltage drop in it causes V_L to be the required value. There are two problems with this circuit. It is inefficient in that power is dissipated in R; it provides no voltage regulation in that if R_L or V changes, V_L will also change.

Now consider the simple power conditioning circuit of Fig. 13-24b. The controlled switch works in the following way. Suppose that we desire the value of V_L to be V_R V.

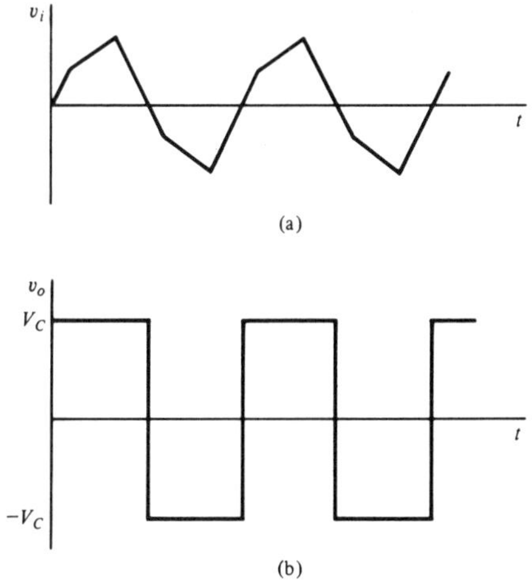

Figure 13-23. (a) A periodic waveform applied to the input of an ideal symmetric comparator with $V_R = 0$. (b) The output waveform.

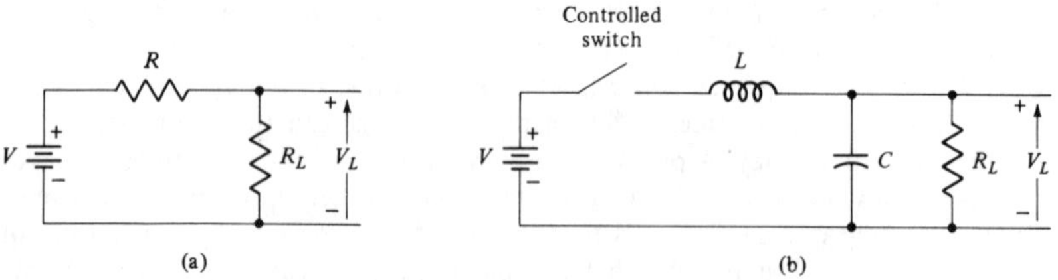

Figure 13-24. (a) A simple circuit that will reduce a direct voltage. (b) A much more efficient circuit. Its operation is described in the text.

The value of V_L is sensed. If it is less than V_R, then the switch is closed. This permits the capacitor to be charged. The inductor L serves to reduce voltage fluctuations; we shall discuss this in Sec. 22-6. If V_L rises above V_R then the controlled switch is opened. The capacitor then discharges through R_L and the voltage falls off. Ideally the controlled switch would have zero resistance and open and close in zero time. This results in efficient operation. When the switch is open, the voltage across it is high but the current is zero. When the switch is closed, the current may be high but the voltage across it is low (ideally zero). Hence, the power dissipated by the switch is low (ideally zero). In addition, this circuit provides regulation, that is, it automatically compensates for change in R_L or V. (This assumes that V is always greater than the desired value of V_L.)

Let us see how we can implement the controlled switch electronically. We shall use a transistor which shall be either cut off or saturated. This will approximate the switch. Note that we avoid the use of the active region here since then there would be both significant voltage across *and* current through the switch (transistor) and the power dissipation would be high. (In Chapter 22 we shall discuss voltage regulators that do use transistors in their active regions. However, here we are concerned with efficiency.) We must derive a circuit that can be used to switch the transistor from saturation to cutoff. A comparator will accomplish this (see Fig. 13-25a). The comparator functions in the following way. If v_L is greater than V_R, then v_o is a negative or zero value. The base-emitter voltage of the transistor will be cut off. This corresponds to an open switch in Fig. 13-24b. Now suppose that V_L becomes less than V_R. The comparator is such that v_o then becomes a large positive value which is greater than V_L. Now v_{BE} is sufficiently

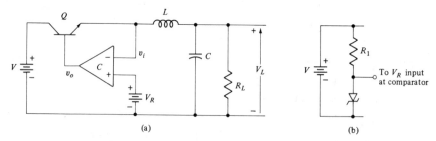

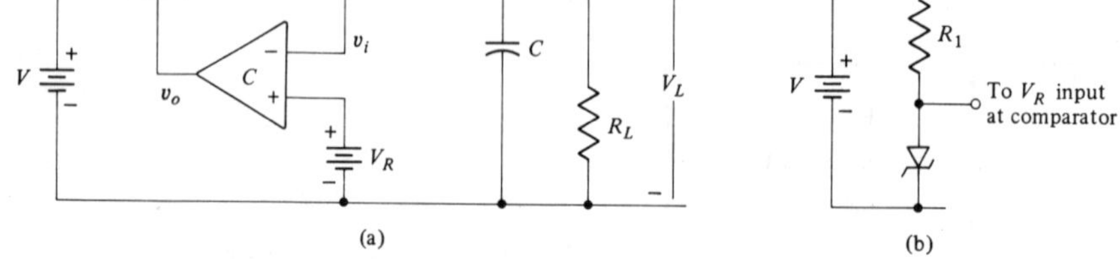

Figure 13-25. (a) A power conditioning circuit. (b) The actual circuit used to obtain the reference voltage V_R.

positive so that the transistor Q saturates. This corresponds to the closed switch condition. Thus, the circuit functions as it should.

We have shown a battery supplying the reference voltage. Actually, a Zener diode (see Sec. 1-6) circuit such as that of Fig. 13-25b is usually used to provide the reference voltage.

Now let us see how we can actually obtain a comparator. An operational amplifier by itself provides a simple one. For instance, consider the circuit of Fig. 13-26. We shall assume that the operational amplifier is characterized by the curve of Fig. 13-3 where

$$V_{A1} = V_{A2} = V_A \tag{13-80a}$$

and

$$V_{1\alpha} = V_{2\alpha} = V_\alpha \tag{13-80b}$$

Remember that V_A is typically in the range of 5 to 15 V, whereas V_α is 0.001 V or less. Now suppose that

$$v_i > V_R + V_\alpha \tag{13-81}$$

Then, the amplifier will be saturated and $v_o = -V_A$. On the other hand, if

$$v_1 < V_R - V_\alpha \tag{13-82}$$

then the output voltage will be $v_o = +V_A$. Since V_α is very small, the circuit functions as a comparator. A problem arises if

$$V_R - V < v_i < V_R + V_\alpha \tag{13-83}$$

The operational amplifier is now operating in its linear regions and v_o is not $\pm V_A$. For some applications, the range given by relation 13-83 is so small that it can be ignored and the circuit functions in a satisfactory manner. On the other hand, there may be occasions when it is not. For instance, consider the power conditioning circuit of Fig. 13-25a. Suppose that V_L is very close to V_R, such that Eq. 13-83 is satisfied. Then, the value of v_o could be such that the transistor Q is in its active region. The resulting current could keep V_L constant and the transistor would remain in its active region. This would result in inefficient operation. This inefficiency would manifest itself as excess power dissipated in the transistor. If the circuit is only designed to operate in the saturation or cutoff regions, then this excess power dissipation could result in the transistor's being burned out. In such cases, the simple comparator of Fig. 13-26 would not be acceptable. In the next section we shall discuss a comparator that does not have this problem.

In the comparator of Fig. 13-26, v_o became negative when v_i was greater than V_R and v_o became positive when v_i was less than V_R. There may be occasions when we want

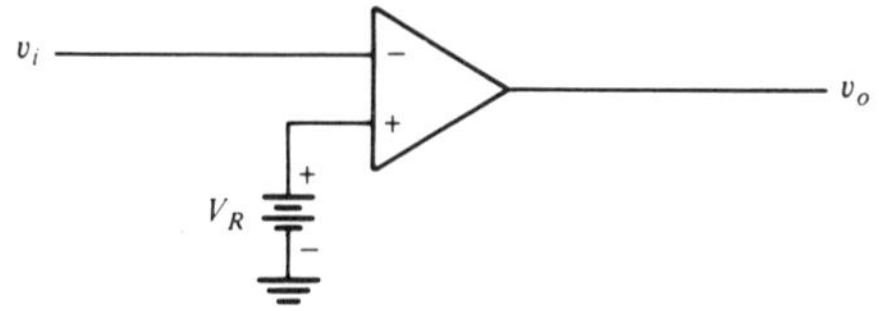

Figure 13-26. A simple operational amplifier comparator.

the polarity to reverse. That is, v_o should become positive when $v_i > V_R$, and so forth. In such cases, the reference should be connected to the inverting terminal and v_i should be connected to the noninverting terminal.

13-12. THE SCHMITT TRIGGER-REGENERATIVE COMPARATOR

As we discussed in the last section, the output of the simple comparator could remain in a region between the desired value of V_A and $-V_A$ (see Eqs. 13-81 to 13-83, and that this could result in undesirable operation, which could actually cause some circuits to fail. In this section we shall discuss a circuit called a *Schmitt trigger* or a *regenerative comparator* which does not have this problem. That is, we shall obtain a comparator that cannot remain in an intermediate state but switches from one level to another in a manner similar to a toggle switch.

Consider the circuit of Fig. 13-27. The voltage v_2 is no longer a fixed reference voltage but depends upon both the values of V_R and v_o. The voltage v_2 is given by

$$v_2 = \frac{v_o R_1}{R_1 + R_2} + \frac{V_R R_2}{R_1 + R_2} \tag{13-84}$$

Suppose that v_i is small or negative so that $v_i \ll v_2$. Then, the amplifier will be saturated so that $v_o = V_A$. Then

$$v_2 = \frac{V_A R_1}{R_1 + R_2} + \frac{V_R R_2}{R_1 + R_2} \tag{13-85}$$

Now suppose that we increase v_i (in a positive direction). The value of v_o will remain unchanged at V_A until $v_i = v_1$ becomes large enough so that

$$v_2 - v_1 = V_\alpha \tag{13-86}$$

The operational amplifier will then enter the linear region and v_o will decrease. Then, v_2 will no longer be given by Eq. 13-85. The value of v_2 will now be given by Eq. 13-84 where v_o is less than V_A. Thus, v_2 will decrease. This in turn results in v_o decreasing further, which will further decrease v_2, which, in turn, will further decrease v_o. This process will continue until v_o reaches $-V_A$ and the amplifier again saturates. Therefore, even if v_i only increases enough just to start the transition and then stops changing, the output of the amplifier will switch "completely" from V_A to $-V_A$, which is the desired form of operation.

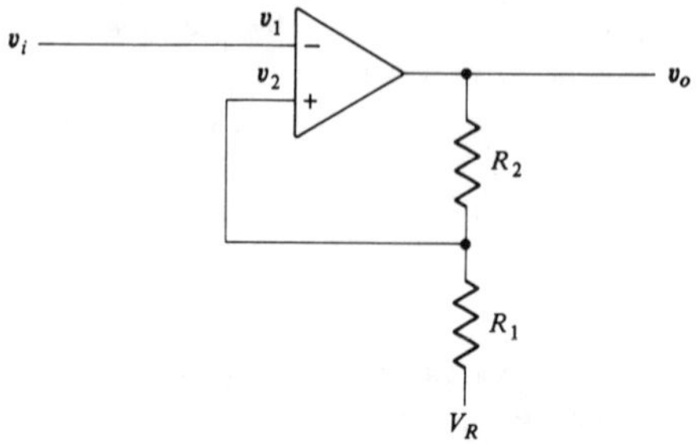

Figure 13-27. An operational amplifier Schmitt trigger.

Actually this switching action will only take place if the amplification A_v is large enough so that the small changes in v_2 are amplified sufficiently. In order to compute the required value of A_v, relatively complex computations must be performed. We shall discuss such calculations in Chapter 17 where we consider feedback. The result of these calculations is, however, simple. The circuit will function properly provided that

$$\frac{A_v R_1}{R_1 + R_2} > 1 \tag{13-87}$$

As long as A_v satisfies this condition the transition will take place as indicated. We have discussed the transition for V_A to $-V_A$ which takes place when v_i is increased. In a similar way there is a transition from $-V_A$ to V_A when v_i is decreased.

Let us now calculate the value of v_i which causes the circuit to switch. Again let us suppose that v_i is negative so that $v_o = V_A$. Now v_i is increased (positively). The transition takes place when $v_i = V_{i1}$, where V_{i1} is given by

$$V_{i1} - v_2 = -V_\alpha \tag{13-88}$$

(Note that we call the transition voltage V_{i1}.) Substituting Eq. 13-85 and manipulating, we have

$$V_{i1} = -V_\alpha + \frac{V_A R_1}{R_1 + R_2} + \frac{V_R R_2}{R_1 + R_2} \tag{13-89}$$

Now let us suppose that v_i is a large positive value and is then reduced. We shall determine the value of v_i when the transition takes place (we call this V_{i2}). If v_i is large and positive, then $v_o = -V_A$. Thus

$$v_2 = -\frac{V_A R_1}{R_1 + R_2} + \frac{V_R R_2}{R_1 + R_2} \tag{13-90}$$

Now the transition takes place when

$$V_{i2} - v_2 = V_\alpha \tag{13-91}$$

Substituting Eq. 13-90 and manipulating, we have

$$V_{i2} = V_\alpha - \frac{V_A R_1}{R_1 + R_2} + \frac{V_R R_2}{R_1 + R_2} \tag{13-92}$$

Note that the two transitions given by Eqs. 13-89 and 13-92 do not occur at the same values of v_i. A plot of the input-output characteristics of the Schmitt trigger are shown in Fig. 13-28. The curve is called a *hysteresis* curve since it has the form of a magnetic hysteresis loop.

Ideally we would like $V_{i1} = V_{i2} = V_R$. Let us see how we can achieve this. The width of the hysteresis loop is given by

$$V_{i1} - V_{i2} = -2V_\alpha + 2\frac{V_A R_1}{R_1 + R_2} \tag{13-93}$$

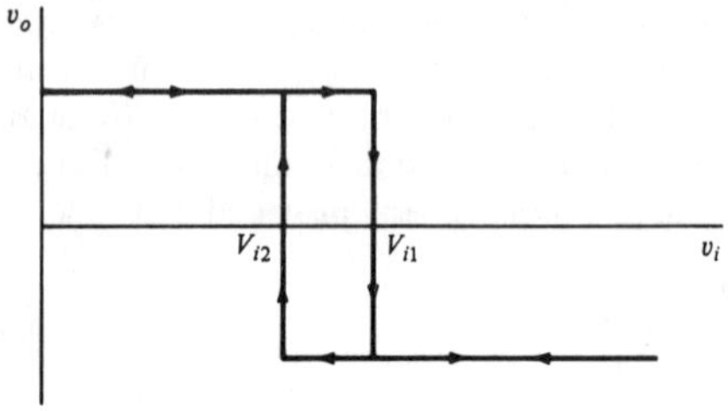

Figure 13-28. The input-output characteristics of the Schmitt trigger.

Often, V_α will be so small that

$$|V_\alpha| \ll \frac{V_A R_1}{R_1 + R_2} \tag{13-94}$$

In this case

$$V_{i1} - V_{i2} = 2\frac{V_A R_1}{R_1 + R_2} \tag{13-95}$$

In such cases we desire to keep $R_1/(R_1 + R_2)$ small. However, we cannot keep it so small that Eq. 13-87 is violated. Actually, if $A_v R_1/(R_1 + R_2)$ is close to unity, the operation can become unreliable since A_v may fluctuate. Thus, it is desirable that $A_v R_1/(R_1 + R_2)$ be substantially greater than unity.

If

$$\frac{R_1}{(R_1 + R_2)} \ll 1 \tag{13-96a}$$

then

$$A_v \gg 1 + \frac{R_2}{R_1} \tag{13-96b}$$

Let us illustrate these ideas with an example.

Example

Obtain a Schmitt trigger that satisfies the following conditions. It is to switch at the following nominal voltages.

$$V_{R(\text{nominal})} = 3 \text{ V}$$

The width of the hysteresis loop is to be less than 0.003 V. We shall use an operational amplifier where $V_A = 5$ V and $A_v = 20{,}000$. Then,

$$V_\alpha = \frac{V_A}{A_v} = 2.5 \times 10^{-4} = 0.00025$$

$$V_{i1} - V_{i2} = -2V_\alpha + \frac{2V_A R_1}{R_1 + R_2} = 0.003$$

$$-0.0005 + \frac{2V_A R_1}{R_1 + R_2} = 0.003$$

Then,

$$\frac{V_A R_1}{R_1 + R_2} = 0.0035$$

Substituting for V_A and manipulating, we have

$$\frac{R_1}{R_1 + R_2} = 7 \times 10^{-4}$$

Let us check that this is a feasible value.

$$\frac{A_V R_1}{R_1 + R_2} = 20{,}000 \times 7 \times 10^{-4} = 14$$

This is considerably larger than 1 and, hence, is acceptable. Then, let us use

$$R_1 = 100 \text{ ohms}$$

Solving for R_2 we obtain

$$R_2 = 142{,}757 \text{ ohms}$$

We can use a somewhat larger value of R_2 and still have inequality 13-87 satisfied. Let us choose

$$R_2 = 150{,}000 \text{ ohms}$$

since this is a commonly available resistance. In this case,

$$\frac{A_v R_1}{R_1 + R_2} = 13.32$$

which is a satisfactory value.

13-13. SAMPLE AND HOLD CIRCUITS

Digital devices are often used to process analog signals. For instance, unwanted components can be removed from an audio signal using a circuit called a *filter*. The filter can be a conventional analog type consisting of resistors, inductors, and capacitors. Another procedure would be to sample the analog signal at discrete intervals of time. It can be shown that if this is done rapidly enough, no information is lost. The analog signal is then converted into a sequence of numbers which can be represented in binary. These binary numbers can then be processed by a digital computer which is programmed to filter the signal in the desired way. Usually, a small dedicated computer, called a *digital filter* is used for this purpose. The output of the digital filter is a sequence of binary numbers. These are then converted back to an analog audio signal and the filtering process is complete. It may seem as though digital filtering represents a complex procedure in comparison with analog filtering. However, for certain applications, large-scale integration makes such digital filtering cheaper and smaller than the comparable analog filters.

An analog signal is converted to a digital one by a process called *analog to digital* conversion—A/D conversion. Similarly, the digital signal is converted to an analog signal using *digital to analog*, D/A conversion. We shall discuss D/A and A/D conversion in the next two sections. In this one we shall consider how an analog signal is sampled.

Note that these processes are not only performed in conjunction with digital filtering. For instance, an analog signal can be obtained from a thermometer that senses the temperature of a chemical process. This signal and other analog signals that could represent pressure, time, and so forth, are then converted to digital signals. These are processed by a digital computer, which then outputs a signal that turns on heaters or pumps to ensure that the chemical process proceeds properly. The output signal(s) are analog. For instance, a sinusoidal voltage could be applied to a heater. This is an example of a *digital control process*. In general, sampling and A/D conversion are used in a wide variety of communication and control applications.

Let us now consider the sampling of a signal. The process is illustrated in Fig. 13-29, where the input analog signal is shown in Fig. 13-29a. The sampled output is shown in Fig. 13-29b. Note that the voltage is held constant between sample times. This is done to supply the digital to analog converter with a constant signal to process during each sampling period.

A circuit that performs this function is called a *sample and hold circuit*. A circuit that illustrates its operation is shown in Fig. 13-30a. The switch is closed at the start of each of the sample times and then is very quickly opened. The switch is opened and closed. The time between switch closings is called the *sampling period*. The time that the switch is closed is short in comparison with the sampling period. The time that the switch is closed is much shorter than the highest frequency in $v_i(t)$, so that during the time that the switch is closed, $v_i(t)$ is essentially constant. During the time that the switch is closed, the capacitor C charges to the instantaneous value of v_i. The switch opens and v_o voltage

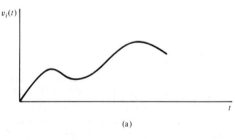

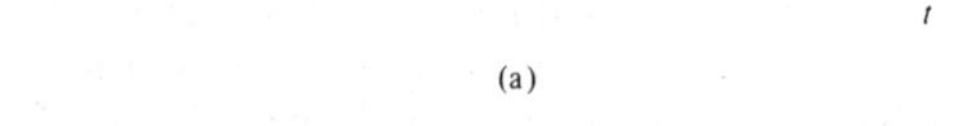

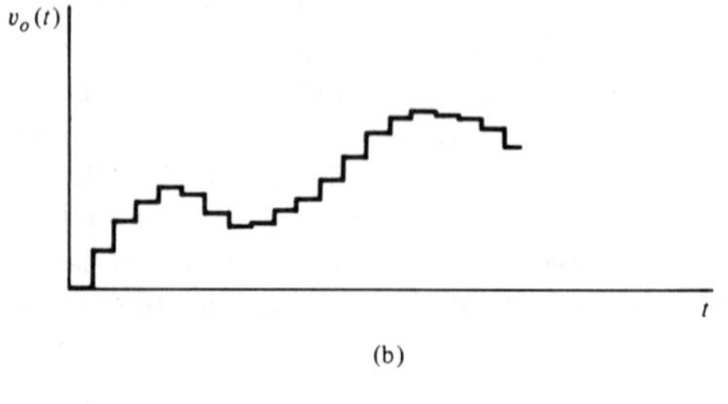

Figure 13-29. Waveforms for a sample and hold circuit. (a) Input. (b) Output.

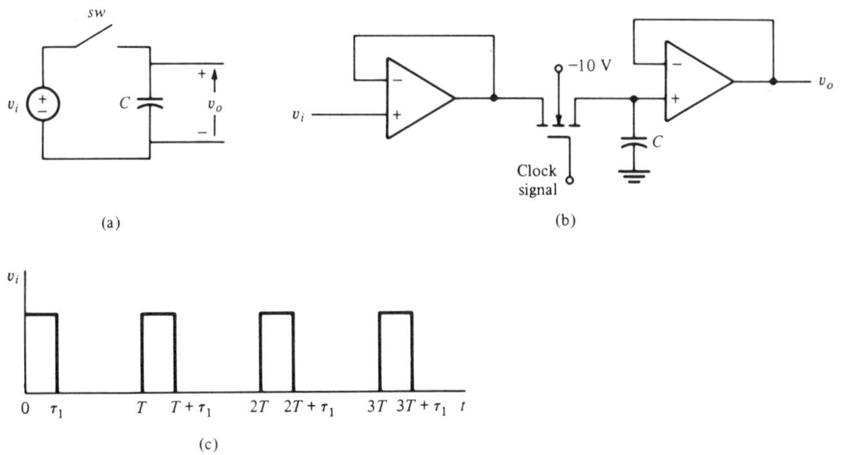

Figure 13-30. (a) An elementary sample and hold circuit. (b) A more practical form of this circuit. (c) The clock signal.

remains at this value until the switch closes at the next sampling period. The voltage across the capacitor again becomes equal to the new value of $v_i(t)$. Thus, the circuit functions as it should.

There are several problems associated with this simple circuit. For one thing, we must have a switch that can open and close rapidly enough. Secondly, the capacitor C must be able to be charged and discharged rapidly through v_i. This assumes that the internal impedance of the input generator is very low. This may not always be the case. Finally, we have assumed that the voltage v_o remains constant when the switch is open. This requires that no current be drawn from C from any external circuit. Again this may not always be the case. The circuit of Fig. 13-30b resolves these problems. The enhancement MOSFET is used as a switch. It is controlled by the clock signal of Fig. 13-30c. When the clock pulse is present, the FET is switched on and acts as a low resistance. During these times when the clock pulse is absent, the FET is cut off and acts as a high impedance. Thus, we have obtained the desired switching action. Note that the substrate is connected to a large negative voltage to isolate it from the circuit.

The voltage follower at the input provides the low-resistance generator required to charge C. The voltage follower has a very low output impedance (see Sec. 13-5). Thus, the capacitor C can be charged and discharged very quickly. Note that the operational amplifier, just as any amplifier, has a finite switching speed (see Sec. 12-15). This will limit the rate at which the capacitor can be charged and discharged. This and other problems associated with practical operational amplifiers will be discussed in the next chapter.

The output voltage follower isolates the capacitor from the external circuit. A high input impedance operational amplifier is used here. Often, such devices use MOSFET's as their input devices. Hence, the input impedance is extremely high and the capacitor does not discharge significantly between clock pulses.

13-14. DIGITAL TO ANALOG CONVERTERS

Let us now discuss circuits that perform digital to analog conversion. (In the next section we shall consider analog to digital conversion.) We shall work with D/A conversion circuits that use operational amplifiers. Actually, single-chip D/A converters can be purchased. However, this discussion will illustrate procedures of D/A conversion which actually can be implemented on a single chip. (In addition, the use of operational amplifiers will be illustrated.)

A simple D/A converter is shown in Fig. 13-31. Let us assume that we are working with a four-bit binary number. That is, there is a four-bit register with four output lines, each of which corresponds to a bit. In a positive logic system, if the voltage on a line is high, then its corresponding bit is a 1. If the voltage is low, then the bit is a 0. In Fig. 13-31, there are four simple switches shown. Actually, they are electronic switches which we shall discuss later in this section. Each switch is controlled by one bit line. When the bit corresponding to a switch is a 1, then the switch is "thrown" to the up position. If the bit is a 0, then the switch is "thrown" down.

Now let us consider the operation of the circuit. It basically consists of the summer of Sec. 13-6. When a switch is up, the corresponding input becomes V. When a switch is down, that input becomes zero. Now suppose that the binary number is

$$b_3 b_2 b_1 b_0 \tag{13-97}$$

If $b_j = 1$, then sw_j is up; if $b_j = 0$, then sw_j is down. Then, from Eq 13-52, we obtain

$$v_o = -\frac{VR_2}{R_1}\left[b_3 + \frac{b_2}{2} + \frac{b_1}{4} + \frac{b_0}{8}\right]$$

Manipulating, we have

$$v_o = -\frac{VR_2}{8R_1}[8b_3 + 4b_2 + 2b_1 + b_0] \tag{13-98}$$

By adjusting $VR_2/8R_1$ we can adjust the level of the output voltage. Remember that the b_j's are either 1 or 0. Thus, the output voltage v_o will be proportional to the binary number given in 13-97. The constant of proportionality is $VR_2/8R_1$.

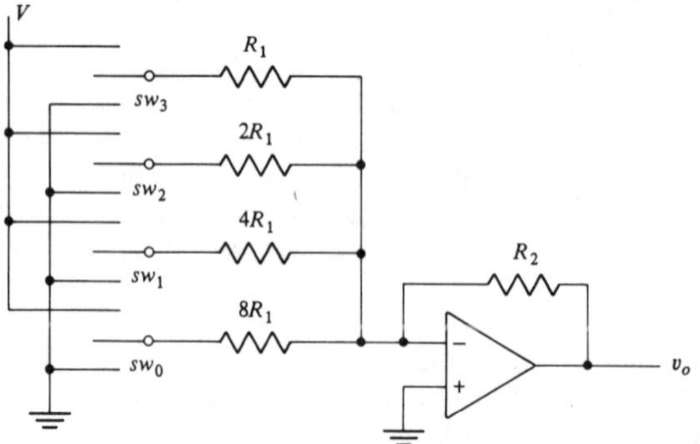

Figure 13-31. A simple digital to analog converter.

Let us discuss a simple circuit using FET's which implements the switches sw_k electronically (see Fig. 13-32). When b_k is a 1, then F_1 will be on and F_2 will be off. Note that the NOT gate inverts the signal to F_2. Then the left end of the resistor will be effectively connected to the supply voltage V.

On the other hand, if b_k is a 0, then F_1 will be cut off and F_2 will be on and effectively connect the left end of the resistor to ground. Hence, the switch functions as it should.

We have not shown the substrate connections for the FET. If they are discrete devices then there is no problem and the substrates can be connected to their respective sources. In an integrated circuit, suitable isolation should be used.

There is a problem associated with the switch. The resistance of a saturated FET is not zero. Hence, this resistance should be added to that of the resistance $2^{3-k}R_1$. Normally, the resistor R_1 is made sufficiently large so that the FET's "on resistance" can be ignored.

If we attempt to use the D/A converter in systems with many bits, a problem arises. The ratio of the smallest to largest resistance becomes very large. In discrete circuits this may not be a problem. However, when integrated circuits are used this can be a great problem since very large resistances cannot be conveniently fabricated. In the circuit of Fig. 13-31, the input resistances are equal to $2^{3-k}R_1$. Hence, if k is large, some resistances can become large. In Fig. 13-33 we illustrate a D/A converter that does not require large resistances even if the number of bits is large.

Let us demonstrate that this circuit functions as a D/A converter. The switches in the converter are located at the input to the operational amplifier. They connect "their" end of their resistors either to the inverting input of the operational amplifier or to ground. The inverting input is at virtual ground so that as far as the ladder network is concerned, the switching does not change the current in it. The currents in the ladder network divide as shown. This can be seen by studying Fig. 13-34 where we have redrawn the ladder. The input resistances at pertinent points of the network are shown. Note that these are either R_1 or $2R_1$. The input resistance of the ladder is R_1. Hence, the input current is

$$I_1 = \frac{V_1}{R_1}$$

At node a the current will divide equally into two currents of $I_1/2$. Again, at node b, the currents divide equally into components of $I_1/4$. Proceeding in this way we obtain the current distribution shown in Fig. 13-33.

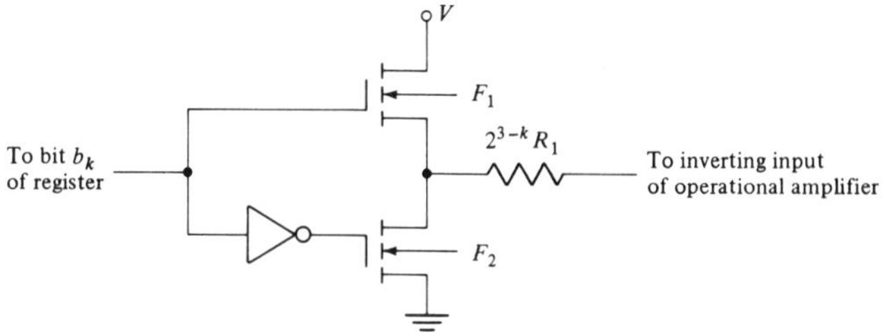

Figure 13-32. A FET switch that can be used with the D/A converter of Fig. 13-31. The substrate connections are not shown.

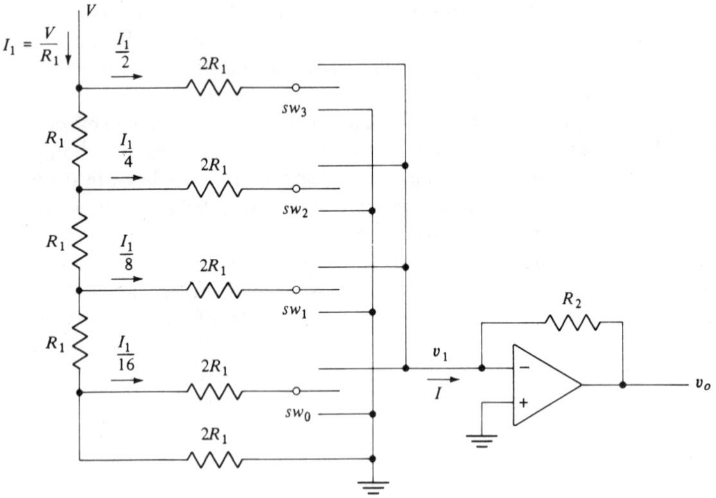

Figure 13-33. A digital to analog converter that does not require a large resistance ratio.

The switches are controlled by the input binary number (see 13-97). When b_j is a 1, then sw_j is in the up position. Similarly, when b_j is a 0, then sw_j is in the down position. When a switch is in the up position, then its component of current contributes to I. Otherwise, it does not. Then, proceeding as in Sec. 13-1, we obtain

$$I = \frac{V - v_1}{R_1}\left[\frac{1}{2}b_3 + \frac{1}{4}b_2 + \frac{1}{8}b_1 + \frac{1}{16}b_0\right] = \frac{v_1 - v_o}{R_2} \tag{13-99}$$

Assuming that A_v is very large so that $v_o \gg v_1$, we have

$$v_o = -\frac{R_2 V}{16R_1}[8b_3 + 4b_2 + 2b_1 + b_0] \tag{13-100}$$

Thus, we have achieved the desired D/A conversion.

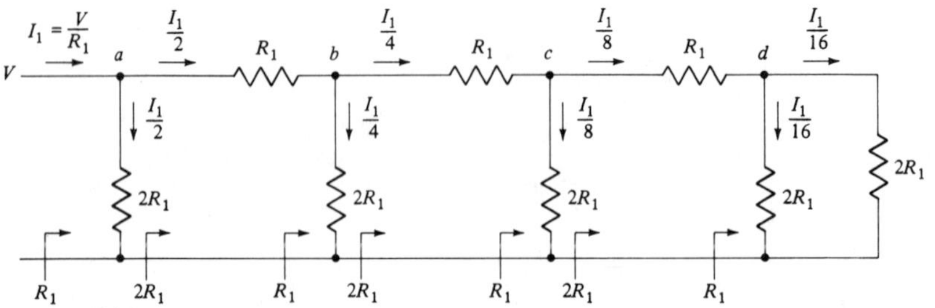

Figure 13-34. The ladder network of Fig. 13-33.

We have considered D/A conversion procedures in this section which have used operational amplifiers. If these circuits are fabricated in an integrated circuit chip, then an amplifier that may not have the same configuration as an operational amplifier will be used. For instance, it may not have as many stages and will not have a noninverting input.

Ratings of D/A Converters

There are several pertinent ratings of D/A converters that should be considered.

Voltage Levels. We have indicated arbitrary levels for the voltage V and the input voltage. Actually these are limited and are specified by the manufacturer. If a D/A converter is built using discrete components then the resistance ratio can be varied. In an integrated circuit device, these are chosen by the manufacturer and cannot be varied by the user. Hence, the variation of the voltages is the only way that the output level can be varied.

Resolution. The smallest step size that can be made in the output voltage is determined by the number of bits that the D/A converter can accommodate. This is usually termed the resolution. For instance, the converter of Figs. 13-31 and 13-33 accommodates four bits. There are then $2^4 = 16$ possible levels. The resolution in one part is 16 or 6.25%. Most D/A converters use many more bits and have considerably better resolution.

Linearity. An ideal D/A converter would be linear. That is, the output voltage would be a linear function of the input binary number. All D/A converters depart somewhat from ideal linearity. Several factors that introduce this nonlinearity are: the resistor values are not exact; the electronic switches are not ideal switches and they contribute "extra" resistance to the circuit.

Accuracy. The actual output voltage of a D/A converter departs for the ideal value. The factors that contribute to lack of linearity also contribute to a lack of accuracy. In addition, there are factors that do not affect linearity but do affect accuracy. For instance, if the voltage V drifts, the output voltage will drift. A change in the resistance R_2 of Figs. 13-31a or 13-33 will change the output voltage but will not change the linearity. Practical operational amplifiers have problems associated with them which affect accuracy. We shall discuss these problems and the procedures used to reduce their effects in the next chapter. The accuracy is also affected by operating conditions. For instance, changes in temperature will change the values of the resistance as well as the characteristics of the amplifier. This will, in turn, change the output. These temperature effects are usually stated in terms of a *temperature sensitivity*. For instance, a typical D/A converter will have a temperature sensitivity of ± 50 parts per million per degree Celsius. This is written as ± 50 ppm/°C and represents a change of $\pm 0.005\%$ in output voltage for each degree Celsius change. Note that there are D/A converters whose temperature sensitivity is only 1–2 ppm/°C.

Transient Response. When the digital output to a D/A converter changes, the output does not change instantaneously. The response has a rise time and possibly an overshoot associated with it (see Sec. 12-15). These quantities should be specified. Any time delay associated with the converter is undesirable so that 10–90% rise times are *not* used. A general figure of merit called the settling time is used. This is the time that elapses from the time that the digital input switches to the time that the output becomes and remains within a specified "closeness" to its final value. There is no "standard of closeness" here. Typically, settling time is measured from the time the input switches to the time that the response remains with 0.2% of final value. A typical settling time is 500 ns (500×10^{-6} s).

13-15. ANALOG TO DIGITAL CONVERTERS

We shall now consider circuits that perform analog to digital conversion. There are a great many such circuits, and in this section we shall limit our discussion to those A/D circuits that utilize circuits of the type we have already discussed.

Comparator A/D Converter

Let us start our discussion by considering the *comparator* A/D converter shown in Fig. 13-35. The interconnection of resistors forms a voltage divider that establishes the

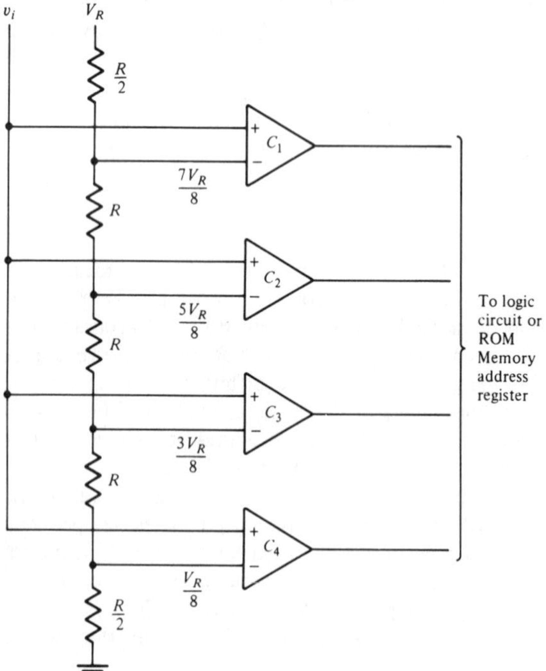

Figure 13-35. A comparator A/D converter.

reference voltage input to each comparator. These reference voltages are $7V_R/8$, $5V_R/8$, $3V_R/8$, and $V_R/8$. By observing the outputs of the comparator we can then determine the voltage level to within the resolution of the device. For instance, suppose that the comparator voltage levels are such that when v_i is greater than the reference input, the output is a 1; otherwise it is a 0. Then, if the output of C_1 and C_2 correspond to 0's while the output of C_3 and C_4 correspond to 1's, then

$$\frac{3V_R}{8} < v_i \leqq \frac{5V_R}{8} \tag{13-101a}$$

Similarly, if the output of C_1, C_2, and C_3 correspond to 0's while that of C_4 corresponds to a 1,

$$\frac{V_R}{8} < v_i \leqq \frac{3V_R}{8} \tag{13-101b}$$

Thus, by observing the comparators' output we can determine the input voltage to within the resolution of the device. In this case, the resolution is $V_R/4$. If more comparators are used, then the resolution is improved. For instance, with eight comparators, the resolution is $V_R/8$.

In general, when we deal with A/D converters, there is a resolution error. We must work with a finite number of bits, that is, a finite number of binary numbers that are used to represent an infinite set of voltage levels. Note that there is an infinite set of voltage levels even if the input is bounded (e.g., it lies between 0 and 10 V). The error produced by attempting to represent an infinite set of levels by a finite set is called a *quantization error*. For instance, suppose that we use binary numbers to represent the five possible levels for the comparator of Fig. 13-35. (Note that $v_i < V_R/8$ is one level.) These numbers are 000, 001, 010, 011, and 100. Note that the comparator outputs do not give us the binary numbers directly. These outputs can be used as inputs to a decoder logic circuit (see Sec. 11-1). The output of the decoder then gives us the desired binary number. Alternatively, we can use the comparator outputs to address the memory location in a ROM. Each memory location stores the appropriate binary number. For instance, the decoder or ROM is such that if $v_i < V_R/8$, the binary output will be 000. If $V_R/8 \leqq v_i \leqq 3V_R/8$, the binary output will be 001, and so forth.

The nominal voltage at the input of the A/D converter will be given by

$$V_{\text{nominal}} = \frac{\beta V_R}{4} \tag{13-102}$$

where β is the decimal representation of the binary number output. For instance, if the binary number is 001, this represents $0.25V_R$ V. Let us consider the quantization error. If the binary output is 000 then v_i can range from 0 to $V_R/8$ V, while the nominal output is 0. Then, the maximum quantization error is $V_R/8$. Suppose that the binary output is 001. The nominal voltage is $V_R/4$. The actual v_i can range from $V_R/8$ to $3V_R/8$. Again the maximum error is $V_R/8$. Proceeding in this way we can demonstrate that the maximum quantization error is $V_R/8$. Of course, the quantization error can be reduced by using more comparators and thus more bits.

Counting A/D Converter

Another form of A/D converter is shown in Fig. 13-36. Its basic operation is as follows. (For the time being, ignore the voltage V_a.) Clock pulses are applied to a counter through an AND gate. The counter's output is connected to a D/A converter. Hence, its voltage output is proportional to the count of the counter. The input signal v_i and the D/A converter output is connected to the comparator as shown. When the D/A converter output becomes greater than v_i, the output of the comparator switches from a 0 to a 1. One input to the AND gate now becomes a 0 and the clock pulses no longer can reach the counter. The clock input of the register becomes a 1 so that it stores the count. This is then the digital representation of v_i. When the start signal is given, the counter is reset and the process is repeated.

The voltage V_a is added as shown to reduce the quantization error of this circuit. V_a is a fixed voltage which is equal to one-half of the voltage change in the output of the D/A converter due to a change in the least significant bit of the counter. Let us consider this. The voltage v_R is

$$v_R = \frac{\beta V_R}{16}$$

(see Eq. 13-100) where β is the decimal representation of the counter's binary output. Then, v_R can take on the following values: 0, $V_R/16, 2V_R/16, \ldots, 15V_R/16$.

Suppose that $V_a = 0$ and v_i is very slightly greater than $V_R/16$. The A/D converter will indicate an output of $2V_R/16$, since the comparator will not switch until $v_i < v_R$. Hence, the maximum error is given by $2V_R/16 - V_R/16 = V_R/16$.

Now suppose that $V_a = V_R/32$ is added to the circuit. The voltage v_B then can take on the following allowable values; $V_R/32, 3V_R/32, \ldots, 31V_R/32$. However, the output of the register is interpreted as though v_a were not present. Now suppose that v_i is again slightly greater than $V_R/16$. The A/D converter will now indicate a voltage of $V_R/16$ reducing the error. In general, the inclusion of V_a halves the maximum error.

The counting A/D converter of Fig. 13-36 requires that V_R be reset to zero for each measurement. Hence, if v_i is large there must be many clock pulses before a result is

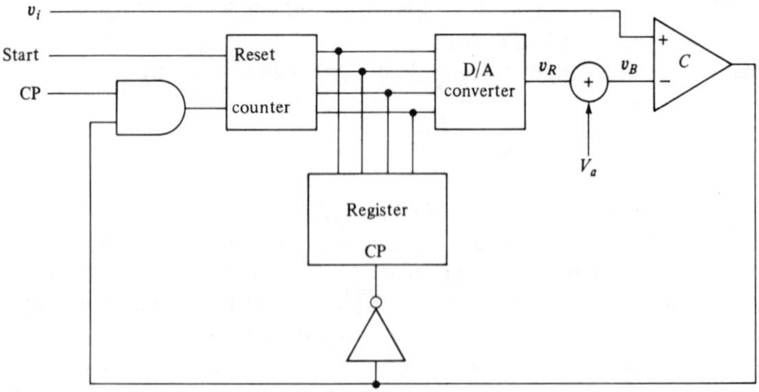

Figure 13-36. A counting A/D converter.

obtained. Usually v_i is a continuous function of time which is applied to a sample and hold circuit (see Sec. 13-13), and the binary representation is obtained. The rate at which the signal can be sampled is limited by the speed of the A/D converter. Most signals are slowly changing so that one sample is close in value to the next. Thus, it wastes time to have to reduce v_R to 0 and count back up to the "sample magnitude." To speed up the operation, the circuit can be modified. The counter is changed so that it can either count up or count down. The mode of counting is controlled by the output of the comparator. When $v_i < v_R$ the counter will count down. Similarly, when $v_i > v_R$, the counter will count up. No reset signals are given in this case. The counter output is sampled periodically to obtain a sequence of digital readouts.

Suppose that v_i is a constant. Then v_R will be increased until $v_R > v_i$. Then, the counting direction will be reversed and v_R will be reduced by one step. Now $v_i < v_R$ and the direction of counting will again be reversed. The output will then oscillate about the final value. This oscillation will only take place in the least significant bit which can be ignored when the binary output is taken. That is, this bit is not supplied to the output register.

Now suppose that v_i changes slightly. The starting value of v_R will be close to v_i. Thus, v_R will come close to v_i in fewer clock periods than if v_R were reset to 0. Hence, the operation is speeded. This type of A/D converter is called a *tracking converter* or a *servo converter*.

The Successive Approximation A/D Converter

We shall now consider an A/D converter that goes through a sequence of approximations to obtain the digital representation of the input voltage v_i. We assume, as before, that the input is obtained from a sample and hold circuit so that v_i is constant during the time that the A/D conversion is taking place. We shall illustrate this procedure using four bits to represent the voltage. At the start these bits are unknown. Let us call them

$$x_3 x_2 x_1 x_0 \tag{13-103}$$

We start by making the most significant bit 1 and the others 0. That is, we try

$$1000$$

This number is inputted to a D/A converter and its output v_R is compared with v_i. If $v_R > v_i$, then this number is too large and we now know that the most significant bit (i.e., x_3) is a 0. If $v_R < v_i$, similarly we know that the most significant bit is a 1. Hence, after the first trial, we have ascertained the first bit. That is, we have

$$b_3 x_2 x_1 x_0 \tag{13-104a}$$

where the x_j's are still unknown.

Next we set $x_2 = 1$ with x_1 and x_0 as zeros. Now the input to the A/D converter is

$$b_3 100$$

where b_3 was established previously. Again this number is inputted to the A/D converter and its output v_R is compared with v_i. If $v_R > v_i$ then the second significant bit is changed to a 0 and if $v_i > v_R$ then it remains a 1. Hence, after the second measurement we have

$$b_3 b_2 x_1 x_0 \tag{13-104b}$$

where only x_1 and x_0 are unknowns. This process is repeated until all the bits are found.

A block diagram for a circuit that performs the successive approximation is shown in Fig. 13-37. The logic circuit is such that on successive clock pulses, it provides the proper binary number to the A/D converter. That is, one bit is tested per clock pulse. The logic circuit also receives an input from the comparator which indicates the result of the test. If the comparator output is a 1, then the bit being tested is unchanged. If the comparator output is a 0, then the bit under test is changed to a 0. This process is repeated until all bits are determined. The fixed voltage v_a serves the same function as it did in the circuit of Fig. 13-36.

After the entire successive approximation procedure is completed, the logic circuit outputs a 1 to the CP terminal of the output register which then records the digital representation of the input voltage.

Dual Slope A/D Converter

We shall now consider the *dual slope* A/D converter which is extensively used in digital voltmeters. We shall discuss the reason for this subsequently. The block diagram for this A/D converter is shown in Fig. 13-38. This circuit makes use of both the integrator and the comparator. Let us consider some aspects of the circuit and then consider its operation. There are two electronic switches sw_1 and sw_2 that are controlled by the logic circuitry. The logic circuitry also resets the counter. Now let us consider the operation of the circuit. At the start, i.e., at $t = 0$, a read signal is given. This causes the logic circuit to establish the following sequence of operations: The counter is reset; sw_1 is thrown up to the v_i input and sw_2 is opened. Assume that sw_2 was closed prior to this. Thus, $v_c(0) = 0$. The output of the integrator is then given by

$$v_c = -\frac{1}{RC}\int_0^t v_i\,dt = -\frac{v_i t}{RC} \tag{13-105}$$

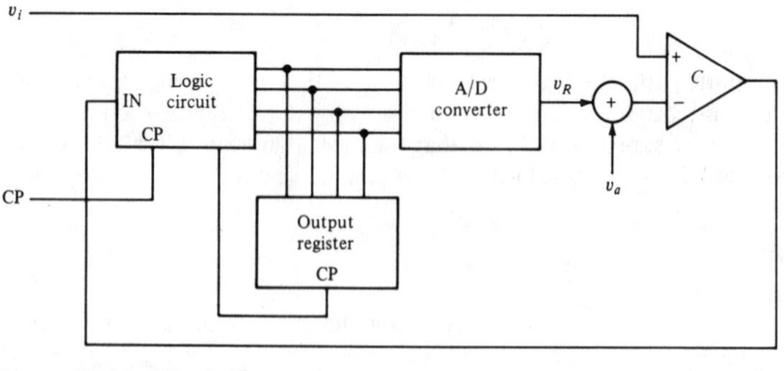

Figure 13-37. Block diagram for a successive approximation A/D converter.

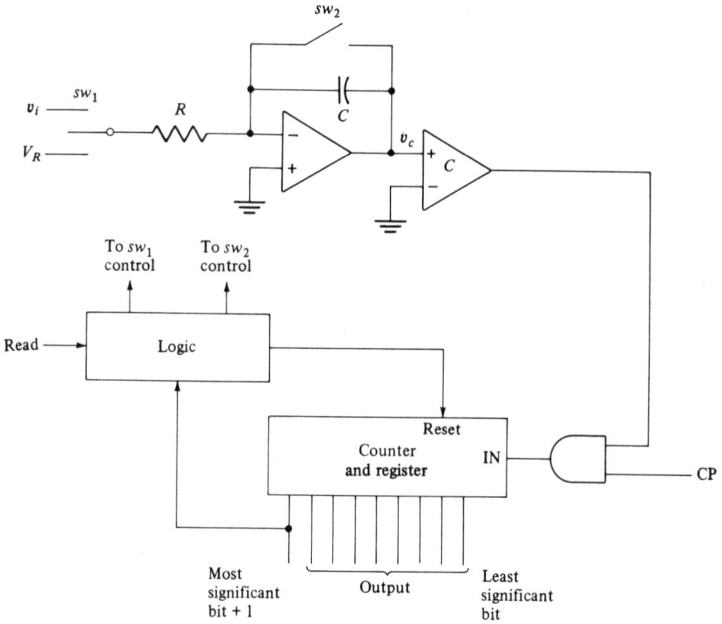

Figure 13-38. The block diagram of a dual slope A/D converter.

Remember that v_i is a constant obtained from a sample and hold circuit. Thus, it remains constant during the integration and v_c will have the form shown in Fig. 13-39 for $0 \leqq t \leqq T_1$. This voltage is applied to the comparator. The reference voltage is 0. Hence, the output of the comparator becomes a positive voltage. This is adjusted to be the level of a 1. This voltage is one input of the AND gate. Thus, the output of the AND gate will be the same as the clock pulse. The counter then counts the clock pulses. This process continues until the leftmost bit (called the most significant bit $+1$) becomes a 1. All other bits are now zero. At this instant, called T_1, sw_1 is thrown to $-V_R$. This is a stable known *negative* reference voltage. From Fig. 13-39, we have

$$v_c(T_1) = -\frac{v_i T_1}{RC} \tag{13-106}$$

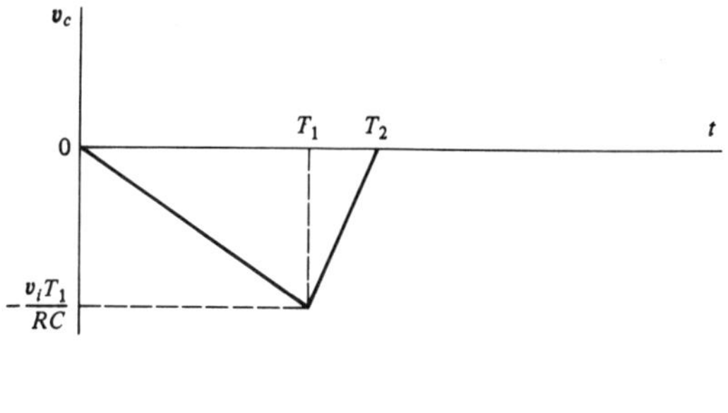

Figure 13-39. The output voltage of the integrator of the dual slope A/D converter of Fig. 13-38.

The integrator now integrates a fixed known negative voltage. At $t = T_1$, Eq. 13-106 gives the initial value of the integration. Hence, for $t > T_1$ (and we shall see also for $t < T_2$) we have

$$v_c = -\frac{v_i T_1}{RC} - \frac{1}{RC}\int_{T_1}^{t} - v_R\, dt = -\frac{v_i T_1}{RC} + \frac{v_R(t - T_1)}{RC} \tag{13-107}$$

Thus, (see Fig. 13-39) the voltage rises linearly toward zero. When v_c becomes slightly greater than 0, the output of the comparator becomes negative (or 0). This prevents the clock pulses from reaching the counter. At $t = T_1$ all the output bits were zero (the leftmost bit is not used as an output bit). Hence, the count of the output bits is proportional to the time $T_2 - T_1$. Therefore, by reading the counter output, which is stored in the register, we can determine, $T_2 - T_1$. Now consider Eq. 13-107. When $v_c = 0$, then $t = T_2$. Hence,

$$0 = -\frac{v_i T_1}{RC} + \frac{v_R(T_2 - T_1)}{RC}$$

Manipulating, we have

$$T_2 - T_1 = \frac{v_i}{v_R} T_1 \tag{13-108}$$

The time T_1 is actually a known. It is the time required for the counter to count from 00...0 to 10...0. Suppose that there are N output bits ($N + 1$ total bits). Then this represents 2^N counts and the clock period is known. Suppose that T_C is the clock period. For instance, in Fig. 13-30, $T_C = T$. Then

$$T_1 = 2^N T_C \tag{13-109}$$

Then, substituting in Eq. 13-108 we have

$$v_i = v_R \frac{T_2 - T_1}{2^N T_C} \tag{13-110}$$

At T_1 all the output bits were equal to 0. Hence, $T_2 - T_1$ is proportional to the final count of the output bits. Let us call this count α. Then,

$$T_2 - T_1 = \alpha T_C$$

Substituting in Eq. 13-109, we obtain

$$v_i = \frac{v_R}{2^N} \alpha \tag{13-111}$$

Thus, by reading the final count on the output bits we can determine v_i. Note that by proper adjustment of v_R we can cause the counter output to read v_i directly. Suppose that $v_R = 2$. Hence,

$$v_i = 2^{-(N-1)}\alpha \tag{13-112}$$

Multiplying or dividing by a power of two is simply equivalent to shifting to the right or to the left. Hence, by shifting the counter output $N - 1$ bits to the left, we then obtain a direct reading of the voltage v_i. (Of course, the binary number must be converted to a base 10 number.) This is the procedure used in most digital voltmeters.

The dual slope A/D converter is especially useful in low-level voltage measurements. The input signal is averaged. Thus, if there are any high-frequency noise or interference components, they will be averaged out. Another advantage is accuracy. Note that this circuit does not require any precision resistors for its accuracy. For instance, the RC product cancels out of the relations, as does the clock pulse time T_C. Note that the clock pulse generator must be relatively stable so that T_C does not change during the measuring interval. However, this is a short time and it is relatively simple to obtain the desired stability.

Comparison of A/D Converter Speeds

Of all the A/D converters considered in this section, the comparator A/D converter is the fastest. It also requires a great deal of hardware. In particular, many comparators must be used. The successive approximation counters are somewhat slower. However, much less hardware is required. The counting A/D converters are the slowest. However, as we have noted, the dual slope A/D converter, which is a counting converter, has characteristics which make it widely used in digital voltmeters. This is an application where very high speed is not required.

PROBLEMS

13-1. Describe what is meant by an ideal operational amplifier.

13-2. How does the operational amplifier whose characteristics are given in Fig. 13-3 differ from an ideal one?

13-3. The quasi-ideal operational amplifier whose characteristics are given in Fig. 13-3 has the following parameter values.

$$V_{A1} = V_{A2} = 15 \text{ V}$$
$$V_{\alpha 1} = V_{\alpha 2} = 0.001 \text{ V}$$

What is the voltage gain $\mathbf{A}_v$ of this amplifier?

13-4. Discuss the differences between the ideal and the quasi-ideal operational amplifiers.

13-5. The operational amplifier of the circuit of Fig. 13-4 has the following parameters values: $\mathbf{A}_v = 10{,}000$, $\mathbf{Z}_{in} = 10{,}000$ ohms. The parameters of the circuit are $R_1 = 10{,}000$ ohms, $R_2 = 20{,}000$ ohms. Compute the voltage gain $\mathbf{K}_v = \mathbf{V}_o/\mathbf{V}_{i1}$ of this circuit.

13-6. Compute the impedances $\mathbf{Z}_i$ and $\mathbf{Z}_1$ (see Fig. 13-4) for the amplifier circuit of Prob. 13-5.

13-7. If, in the circuit of Prob. 13-5, $\mathbf{V}_{i1} = 1.0$ V what is the value of $\mathbf{V}_1$?

13-8. Discuss the concept of a virtual ground. Discuss when this is a useful idea and when it cannot be used.

13-9. Design an inverting operational amplifier that meets the following specifications: $\mathbf{K}_v = -25$, $\mathbf{Z}_i = 20{,}000$ ohms. Assume that an operational amplifier with an $\mathbf{A}_v = 30{,}000$ is used.

13-10. Repeat Prob. 13-9 but now assume that $\mathbf{A}_v = 50{,}000$.

13-11. Design an inverting operational amplifier that meets the following specifications.

$$\mathbf{K}_v = -25$$
$$\mathbf{Z}_i = 20{,}000$$
$$S_{\mathbf{A}_v}^{\mathbf{K}_v} = 0.001$$

What is the minimum $\mathbf{A}_v$ that can be used? Assume that $\mathbf{A}_v$ will change by no more than 20%.

13-12. The amplifier circuit of Fig. 13-6 has the following parameter values. $\mathbf{R}_2 = 20{,}000$ ohms; $\mathbf{R}_1 = 8000$ ohms, $\mathbf{A}_v = 30{,}000$. Compute the voltage gain $\mathbf{K}_v$ for this circuit.

13-13. Repeat Prob. 13-12 but now assume that $\mathbf{A}_v = 10{,}000$.

13-14. Obtain a relation for the sensitivity $\mathbf{S}_{\mathbf{A}_v}^{\mathbf{K}_v}$ of the amplifier circuit of Fig. 13-6.

13-15. Design a noninverting amplifier that meets the following specifications.

$$\mathbf{K}_v = 10$$
$$\mathbf{S}_{\mathbf{A}_v}^{\mathbf{K}_v} = 0.001$$

What is the smallest value of $\mathbf{A}_v$ that can be used? Assume that $\mathbf{A}_v$ will change by no more than 20%

13-16. The voltage follower of Fig. 13-7 uses an operational amplifier which is characterized by Fig. 13-3 where $V_{A1} = V_{A2} = 15$ V and $V_{\alpha 1} = V_{\alpha 2} = 0.001$ V. What is the maximum value that v_{i2} can have if the amplifier is not to saturate?

13-17. Design a voltage follower that meets the following specifications.

$$\mathbf{K}_v \geqq 0.998$$
$$\mathbf{S}_{\mathbf{A}_v}^{\mathbf{K}_v} \leqq 0.001$$

Assume that $\mathbf{A}_v$ changes by no more than 20%.

13-18. The parameters of the amplifier circuit of Fig. 13-8 are

$$R_1 = 10{,}000 \text{ ohms}$$
$$R_2 = 50{,}000 \text{ ohms}$$
$$R_3 = 10{,}000 \text{ ohms}$$
$$R_4 = 100{,}000 \text{ ohms}$$

Obtain an expression for $\mathbf{V}_o$ in terms of $\mathbf{V}_{i1}$ and $\mathbf{V}_{i2}$.

13-19. Derive an expression for the sensitivity $\mathbf{S}_{\mathbf{A}_v}^{\mathbf{V}_o}$ for the amplifier of Fig. 13-8. Assume that $\mathbf{V}_{i2} = 0$.

13-20. Repeat Prob. 13-19 but now assume that $\mathbf{V}_{i1} = 0$.

13-21. Design a balanced amplifier (see Fig. 13-8) that meets the following specifications.

$$\mathbf{V}_o = 20(\mathbf{V}_{i2} - \mathbf{V}_{i1})$$

The input impedances "viewed" by $\mathbf{V}_{i1}$ and $\mathbf{V}_{i2}$ are each to be 10,000 ohms. Use an operational amplifier where $\mathbf{A}_v = 10{,}000$.

13-22. Design a balanced amplifier (see Fig. 13-8) that meets the following specifications.

$$\mathbf{V}_o = 20(\mathbf{V}_{i2} - \mathbf{V}_{i1})$$
$$\mathbf{S}_{\mathbf{A}_o}^{\mathbf{V}_o} \leqq 0.0001$$

The input impedances viewed by $\mathbf{V}_{i2}$ and $\mathbf{V}_{i1}$ are each to be 10,000 ohms. What is the smallest value that $\mathbf{A}_v$ can have? Assume that $\mathbf{A}_v$ changes by no more than 20%.

13-23. The sensitivity to null of the bridge circuit of Fig. 13-9 is to be increased by a factor of 10 by the incorporation of an operational amplifier circuit. Design such an amplifier circuit.

13-24. The operational amplifier of Prob. 13-5 has an output impedance of 1000 ohms. What is the output impedance of the overall circuit?

13-25. Repeat Prob. 13-24 but now assume that $\mathbf{A}_v$ has been doubled.

13-26. Discuss the difference between the summer (adder) circuits of Figs. 13-12 and 13-13.

13-27. Design a summer that produces the sum

$$\mathbf{V}_o = -(2\mathbf{V}_{i1} + 5\mathbf{V}_{i2} + 3\mathbf{V}_{i3})$$

Use an operational amplifier whose $\mathbf{A}_v = 20{,}000$. The input impedance, for any input terminal, is to be equal to or greater than 10,000 ohms

13-28. Discuss the error in the design of Prob. 13-27 produced because $\mathbf{A}_v$ is finite.

13-29. Compare the integrator circuit of Fig. 13-15a with that of Fig. 13-16. In general, why will the circuit of Fig. 13-16 be more accurate?

13-30. The parameters of the integrator circuit of Fig. 13-16 are: $C = 1\ \mu\text{F}$, $R = 10^6$ ohms. The input voltage is

$$v_i = 1 \sin t \text{ V}.$$

If $\mathbf{A}_v$ is infinite, what will be the value of v_o?

13-31. Repeat Prob. 13-30 but now assume that $\mathbf{A}_v = 10{,}000$.

13-32. Repeat Prob. 13-30 but now assume that $\mathbf{A}_v = 100$.

13-33. What is the effective input capacitance (viewed at $\mathbf{Z}_i$ of Fig. 13-16) of the amplifier of Prob. 13-31? Why is the circuit not often used to simulate large capacitances?

13-34. Discuss the establishment of the initial values of the output voltage of an integrator.

13-35. Design an analog computer circuit that solves the following differential equation.

$$\frac{d^2y}{dx^2} - 3\frac{dy}{dx} + 2y = 5u(t)$$

The initial conditions are

$$y(0) = 1 \qquad \left.\frac{dy}{dt}\right|_{t=0} = -2$$

13-36. Design an analog computer circuit that solves the following differential equation

$$3\frac{d^3y}{dt^2} + 2\frac{d^2y}{dx^2} + 4\frac{dy}{dx} = 6y = 2 \sin 3t$$

The initial conditions are

$$y(0) = 1$$

$$\left.\frac{dy}{dt}\right|_{t=0} = 0$$

$$\left.\frac{d^2y}{dt^2}\right|_{t=0} = 10$$

13-37. Compare the differentiating circuits of Figs. 13-19 and 13-20. In general, why will the circuit of Fig. 13-20 be more accurate?

13-38. The parameters of the differentiating circuit of Fig. 13-20 are $C = 1\ \mu\text{F}$, $R = 10^6$ ohms. The input voltage is

$$v_i = 1 \sin t \text{ V}$$

If $\mathbf{A}_v$ is infinite, what will be the value of v_o?

13-39. Repeat Prob. 13-38 but now assume that $\mathbf{A}_v = 10{,}000$.

13-40. Repeat Prob. 13-38 but now assume that $\mathbf{A}_v = 100$.

13-41. Discuss some uses for a logarithmic amplifier.

13-42. A voltage 1 sin t is applied to the ideal comparator of Fig. 13-22. If $V_R = 0$ and $V_C = -V_D = 10$ V, plot the waveform.

13-43. Repeat Prob. 13-42 but now set $V_R = 0.5$.

13-44. Discuss the operation of the power conditioning circuit of Fig. 13-25a.

13-45. How does the comparator of Fig. 13-26 differ from an ideal one?

13-46. In Fig. 13-27, $R_1 = 100$ ohms, $R_2 = 100{,}000$ ohms, and $V_R = 2$ V. The operational amplifier has an $\mathbf{A}_v = 10{,}000$. Plot a curve of v_o versus v_i showing the hysteresis loop. The parameters of the operational amplifier are $V_A = 10$ V, $V_\alpha = 0.001$ V.

13-47. Repeat Prob. 13-46 but now assume $V_\alpha = 0$.

13-48. Repeat Prob. 13-46 but now assume $V_R = 1$ V.

13-49. Design a Schmitt trigger comparator whose nominal reference voltage is 3 V. The hysteresis loop is to be no wider than 0.001 V. Use an operational amplifier with the following characteristics: $\mathbf{A}_v = 50{,}000$, $V_A = 10$ V.

13-50. What is the minimum value of $\mathbf{A}_v$ which can be used for the operational amplifier of Prob. 13-49?

13-51. Repeat Prob. 13-49 but now make the nominal reference voltage 1 V.

13-52. Discuss the operation of the sample and hold circuit of Fig. 13-30b.

13-53. Discuss the need for sample and hold circuits.

13-54. Design a digital to analog converter of the type shown in Fig. 13-31, whose output voltage is given by

$$v_o = \tfrac{1}{15}(b_5 b_4 b_3 b_2 b_1 b_0)\ \text{V}$$

where $b_5 b_4 b_3 b_2 b_1 b_0$ represents a five-bit binary number.

13-55. Discuss the design of the electronic switches in the D/A converter of Prob. 13-54.

13-56. Repeat the design of Prob. 13-54 now using a D/A converter of the type shown in Fig. 13-33.

13-57. What is the resolution of the D/A converter of Prob. 13-54?

13-58. Discuss and compare the resolution and accuracy of a D/A converter.

13-59. Discuss the factors that limit the rate of response of a D/A converter.

13-60. Discuss the operation of the comparator A/D converter.

13-61. Design an A/D converter that converts a signal that can vary between 0 and 10 V into a six-bit binary number. Use a comparator A/D converter.

13-62. Discuss the operation of the counting A/D converter (see Fig. 13-36).

13-63. Repeat the design of Prob. 13-61 but now use a counting A/D converter of the type shown in Fig. 13-36.

13-64. Repeat the design of Prob. 13-61 but now use a counting A/D converter that counts up and counts down.

13-65. Discuss the operation of the successive approximation A/D converter.

13-66. Repeat the design of Prob. 13-61 but now use a successive approximation A/D converter.

13-67. Discuss the operation of the dual slope A/D converter.

13-68. Repeat the design of Prob. 13-61 but now use a dual slope A/D converter.

13-69. Why is a dual slope A/D converter usually used as the A/D converter in a digital voltmeter?

BIBLIOGRAPHY

Glaser, A. B. and Subak-Sharpe, G. F. *Integrated Circuit Engineering*. Reading, Mass.: Addison-Wesley, 1977, Chapter 13.

Gray, P. R. and Meyer, R. G. *Analysis and Design of Analog Integrated Circuits*. New York: Wiley, 1977, Chapter 6.

Grinich, V. H. and Jackson, H. G. *Introduction to Integrated Circuits*. New York: McGraw-Hill, 1975, Chapters 9 and 10.

Holt, C. A. *Electronic Circuits Digital and Analog*. New York: Wiley, 1978, Chapter 14.

Chapter 14

Operational Amplifier Circuitry—The Practical Operational Amplifier

In this chapter we shall discuss the circuits used in operational amplifiers. This will provide greater understanding of their operation and indicate their limitations and the practical problems that arise in their use.

14-1. THE FET DIFFERENTIAL INPUT STAGE

We shall start our discussion of operational amplifier circuitry by considering the differential input stage. Most operational amplifiers use junction transistors as their active elements. Some use FET's as their input stages to obtain a high impedance input. We shall consider the FET stage first because of its simpler model. Many operational amplifiers that use FET's do not use them as differential amplifiers but to drive a junction transistor differential amplifier. Nevertheless, we shall start our discussion with a FET amplifier since its model is simpler and it will aid our discussion of the transistor amplifier.

The basic MOSFET differential amplifier is shown in Fig. 14-1a. Its model is given in Fig. 14-1b. An analysis of this model yields

$$u(\mathbf{V}_{gs2} - \mathbf{V}_{gs1}) = 2(R_d + r_d)\mathbf{I}_1 + (R_d + r_d)\mathbf{I}_2 \tag{14-1a}$$

$$u\mathbf{V}_{gs2} = (R_d + r_d)\mathbf{I}_1 + (R_d + r_d + R)\mathbf{I}_2 \tag{14-1b}$$

where

$$\mathbf{V}_{gs1} = \mathbf{V}_1 - \mathbf{I}_2 R \tag{14-2a}$$

$$\mathbf{V}_{gs2} = \mathbf{V}_2 - \mathbf{I}_2 R \tag{14-2b}$$

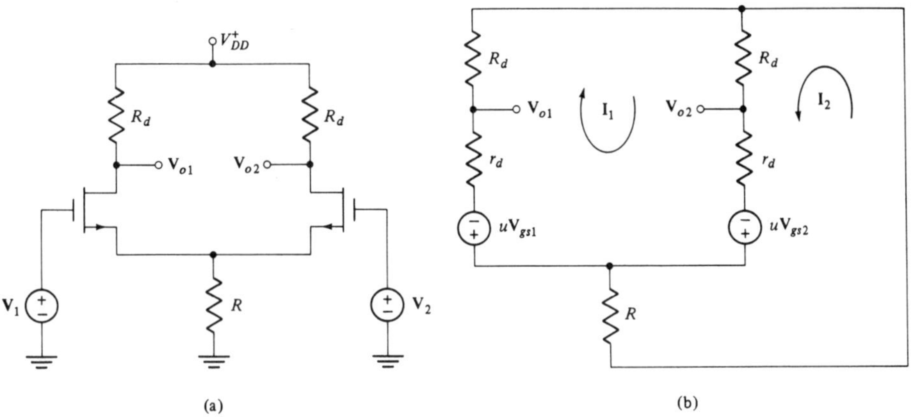

Figure 14-1. (a) A MOSFET differential amplifier. (b) Its model.

Substituting, and manipulating we obtain

$$\mathbf{I}_1 = \frac{u(\mathbf{V}_2 - \mathbf{V}_1)[R_d + r_d + R(1+u)]}{(R_d + r_d)[R_d + r_d + 2R(1+u)]} - \frac{u\mathbf{V}_2}{R_d + r_d + 2R(1+u)} \tag{14-3a}$$

$$\mathbf{I}_2 = \frac{u(\mathbf{V}_1 + \mathbf{V}_2)}{R_d + r_d + 2R(1+u)} \tag{14-3b}$$

The output voltages are given by

$$\mathbf{V}_{o1} = \mathbf{I}_1 R_d \tag{14-4a}$$

$$\mathbf{V}_{o2} = -(\mathbf{I}_1 + \mathbf{I}_2)R_d \tag{14-4b}$$

Hence, we have

$$\mathbf{V}_{o1} = \frac{uR_d(\mathbf{V}_2 - \mathbf{V}_1)[R_d + r_d + R(1+u)]}{(R_d + r_d)[R_d + r_d + 2R(1+u)]} - \frac{u\mathbf{V}_2 R_d}{R_d + r_d + 2R(1+u)} \tag{14-5a}$$

$$\mathbf{V}_{o2} = \frac{uR_d(\mathbf{V}_1 - \mathbf{V}_2)[R_d + r_d + R(1+u)]}{(R_d + r_d)[R_d + r_d + 2R(1+u)]} - \frac{u\mathbf{V}_1 R_d}{R_d + r_d + 2R(1+u)} \tag{14-5b}$$

The output of an ideal differential amplifier will be proportional to $\mathbf{V}_2 - \mathbf{V}_1$. However, each of these voltages has an "extra" second component that produces an error. Let us see what can be done to make this error term very small.

Suppose that R is large enough so that

$$R(1+u) \gg R_d + r_d \tag{14-6}$$

Then, the expression for $\mathbf{V}_{o1}$ becomes

$$\mathbf{V}_{o1} = \frac{uR_d}{2(R_d + r_d)}(\mathbf{V}_2 - \mathbf{V}_1) - \frac{u\mathbf{V}_2 R_d}{2R(1 + u)} \tag{14-7}$$

(There is a similar form for $\mathbf{V}_{o2}$.) The first term has a coefficient $uR_d/2(R_d + r_d)$ while the second one has a coefficient $uR_d/2R(1 + u)$. The ratio of these two coefficients is

$$\rho_1 = \frac{R_d + r_d}{R(1 + u)} \tag{14-8}$$

Then, if R is made very large, the error term can become extremely small. Note that we cannot unequivocally state that the second term will be small in comparison with the first, since $\mathbf{V}_2 - \mathbf{V}_1$ may be zero, or very small while $\mathbf{V}_1$ and $\mathbf{V}_2$ are large. In a practical case we can make R large enough so that for most applications the magnitude of the second term is very small. We shall consider this in greater detail in Sec. 14-14.

If we consider that R is large enough so that the second terms of Eqs. 14-5 can be ignored, we have

$$\mathbf{V}_{o1} = \frac{uR_d}{2(R_d + r_d)}(\mathbf{V}_2 - \mathbf{V}_1) \tag{14-9a}$$

and

$$\mathbf{V}_{o2} = \frac{uR_d}{2(R_d + r_d)}(\mathbf{V}_1 - V_2) \tag{14-9b}$$

Then, this circuit functions as a differential amplifier.

We require that R be very large if the circuit is to function properly but the direct voltage drop across R will then become very large. We can overcome this by increasing V_{DD}. However, with typical values of R, V_{DD} would have to be increased excessively. The large direct component of voltage across R also results in an excessively large V_{GSQ} for the FET's. Thus, their operating point will be incorrect. To eliminate these undesirable effects we would like to replace R with a device that has a low direct voltage drop but yet resists change in the current through it. Therefore, it acts as a large resistance for signals. The current generator of Fig. 14-2, where I is a direct current, can provide such a circuit. First let us show that this circuit can be used. If the resistor R of Fig. 14-1a is replaced by the current generator of Fig. 14-2, the model of Fig. 14-1b will be unchanged since no signal currents pass through the current generator. If an ideal current generator is used, then R will be infinite. This is an ideal situation as far as $\mathbf{V}_{o1}$ and $\mathbf{V}_{o2}$ are concerned. However, the current I can be such that the direct voltage drop across the current generator is small; therefore the aforementioned bias problems do not arise.

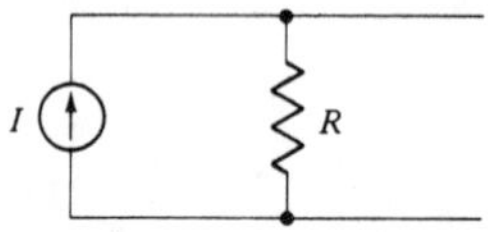

Figure 14-2. A current generator.

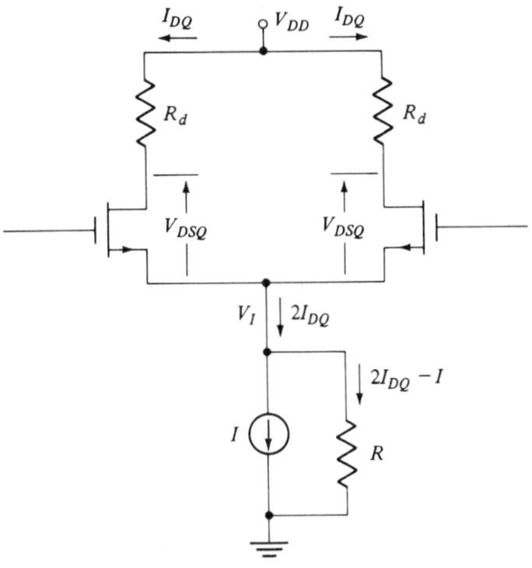

Figure 14-3. The direct voltages and currents for a MOSFET differential amplifier that contains a current generator.

Let us consider this. In the circuit of Fig. 14-3 we have replaced the resistor R by the current generator of Fig. 14-2 and labeled the pertinent direct quantities. The voltage drop V_I across the current generator is given by

$$V_I = (2I_{DQ} - I)R \tag{14-10}$$

Thus, by making I close to $2I_{DQ}$ we can make $|V_I|$ small even if R is very large.

Integrated circuits allow us to implement such current generators in an inexpensive way. We shall consider this implementation in Sec. 14-5.

The circuits we have discussed have output voltages that are positive with respect to ground. At times, we desire a circuit whose output voltage can swing both positive and negative with respect to ground. This can be accomplished by using two power supplies as shown in Fig. 14-4. The operation of this circuit is essentially the same as that of the previous one except that the direct voltage levels have been shifted with respect to ground. Usually, V_{DD}^+ and $|V_{DD}^-|$ will be half that of V_{DD}^+ in Fig. 14-1a.

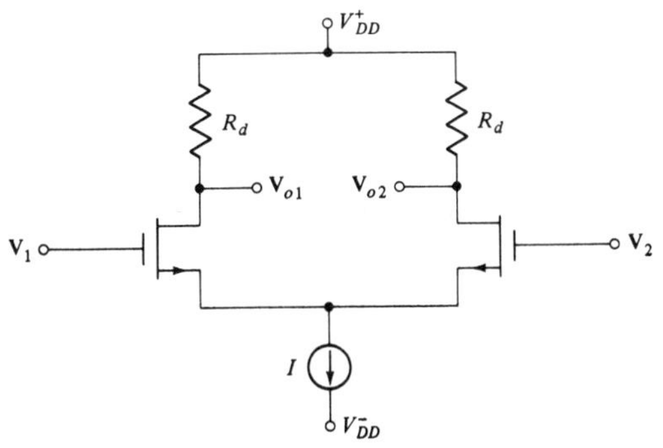

Figure 14-4. A modification of the circuit of Fig. 14-1a that uses two power supplies.

14-2. THE JUNCTION TRANSISTOR—DIFFERENTIAL INPUT STAGE

An elementary form of differential input stage that uses junction transistors is shown in Fig. 14-5a. We have introduced two power supplies so that the output voltage can swing both positive and negative with respect to ground (see Sec. 14-1). If this is not necessary, then only one power supply need be used and the terminal marked V_{EE}^{-} should be connected to ground.

The model for this amplifier is shown in Fig. 14-5b. We have used the low-frequency hybrid-pi model here. As is usually the case, we have assumed that $r_{b'c}$ is infinite. Let us start by obtaining some pertinent relationships.

$$\mathbf{V}_{b'e1} = \frac{(\mathbf{V}_1 - \mathbf{V}_E)r_{b'e}}{r_{bb'} + r_{b'e}} \tag{14-11a}$$

$$\mathbf{V}_{b'e2} = \frac{(\mathbf{V}_2 - \mathbf{V}_e)r_{b'e}}{r_{bb'} + r_{b'e}} \tag{14-11b}$$

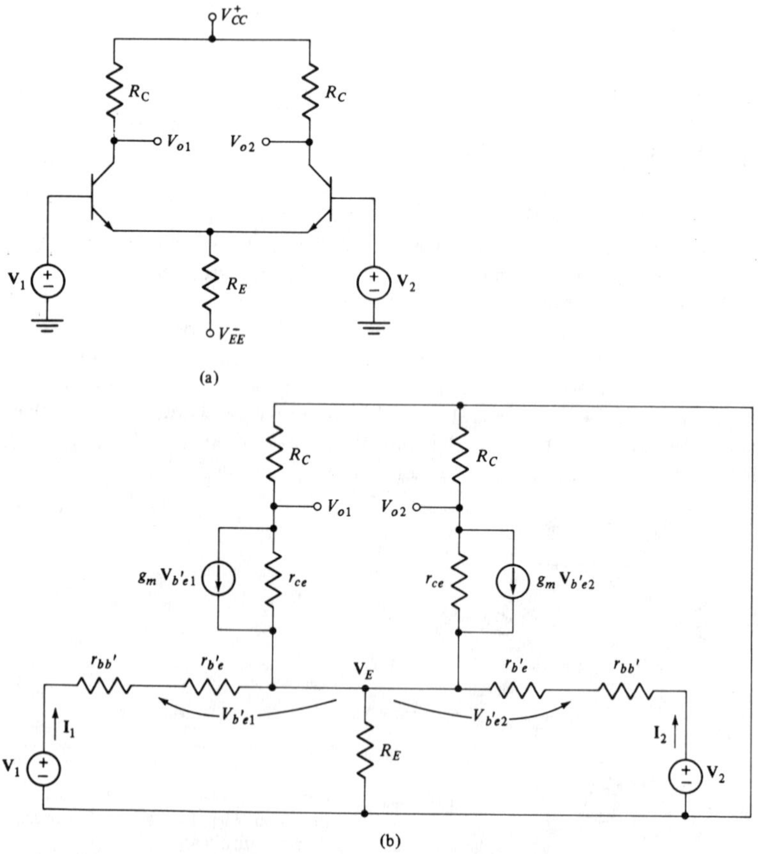

Figure 14-5. (a) A simple junction transistor differential input stage. (b) Its model.

Applying nodal analysis to the output nodes, we obtain

$$-g_m \mathbf{V}_{b'e1} = \mathbf{V}_{o1}\left(\frac{1}{R_C} + \frac{1}{r_{ce}}\right) - \frac{1}{r_{ce}}\mathbf{V}_E \tag{14-12a}$$

$$-g_m \mathbf{V}_{b'e2} = \mathbf{V}_{o2}\left(\frac{1}{R_C} + \frac{1}{r_{ce}}\right) - \frac{1}{r_{ce}}\mathbf{V}_E \tag{14-12b}$$

We shall find it convenient to make the following substitutions.

$$r_b = r_{bb'} + r_{b'e} \tag{14-13a}$$

$$r_c = r_{ce} + R_C \tag{14-13b}$$

Now let us convert the $g_m \mathbf{V}_{b'e}$ current generator shunted by r_{ce} into a voltage generator. After combining r_{ce} and R_C in series, we shall convert back to a current generator. Doing this and converting the other voltage generators to current generators, we obtain the model shown in Fig. 14-6. The nodal equation for this circuit is

$$\frac{\mathbf{V}_1}{r_b} + g_m \frac{r_{ce}}{r_c}\mathbf{V}_{b'e1} + g_m \frac{r_{ce}}{r_c}\mathbf{V}_{b'e2} + \frac{\mathbf{V}_2}{r_b} = \mathbf{V}_E\left(\frac{1}{R_E} + \frac{2}{r_c} + \frac{2}{r_b}\right) \tag{14-14}$$

Substituting Eqs. 14-11 and manipulating, we obtain

$$\mathbf{V}_E = \frac{(\mathbf{V}_1 + \mathbf{V}_2)}{2}\left[\frac{r_c + g_m r_{ce} r_{b'e}}{r_b r_c/2R_E + r_b + r_c + g_m r_{ce} r_{b'e}}\right] \tag{14-15}$$

In general, the following approximations are true

$$g_m r_{b'e} r_{ce} \gg r_c \tag{14-16a}$$

$$g_m r_{b'e} r_{ce} \gg r_c + r_b \tag{14-16b}$$

Hence,

$$\mathbf{V}_E = \frac{\mathbf{V}_1 + \mathbf{V}_2}{2}\left[\frac{g_m r_{ce} r_{b'e}}{r_b r_c/2R_E + g_m r_{ce} r_{b'e}}\right] \tag{14-17}$$

Now let us assume that the value of R_E is chosen sufficiently large that

$$g_m r_{ce} r_{b'c} \gg \frac{r_b r_c}{2R_E} \tag{14-18}$$

In this case we can write

$$\mathbf{V}_E = \frac{\mathbf{V}_1 + \mathbf{V}_2}{2} \tag{14-19}$$

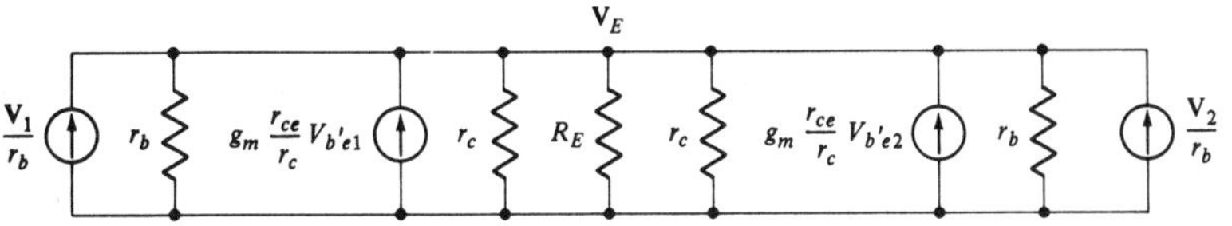

Figure 14-6. A modification of the model of Fig. 14-5b.

Substituting this result and Eq. 14-11a into Eq. 14-12a, we obtain

$$\mathbf{V}_{o1} = \frac{g_m r_{b'e}}{2r_b(1/R_C + 1/r_{ce})}(\mathbf{V}_2 - \mathbf{V}_1) + \frac{1}{2r_{ce}(1/R_C + 1/r_{ce})}(\mathbf{V}_1 + \mathbf{V}_2) \quad \text{(14-20a)}$$

Similarly,

$$\mathbf{V}_{o2} = \frac{g_m r_{b'e}}{2r_b(1/R_C + 1/r_{ce})}(\mathbf{V}_1 - \mathbf{V}_2) + \frac{1}{2r_{ce}(1/R_C + 1/r_{ce})}(\mathbf{V}_1 + \mathbf{V}_2) \quad \text{(14-20b)}$$

The output(s) consist of two terms, one proportional to $(\mathbf{V}_2 - \mathbf{V}_1)$ and the other proportional to $(\mathbf{V}_1 + \mathbf{V}_2)$. The output ideally should consist only of the term proportional to $(\mathbf{V}_2 - \mathbf{V}_1)$. Let us consider the magnitude of the "error" term. We shall use $\mathbf{V}_{o1}$ in this discussion. The coefficient of $(\mathbf{V}_2 - \mathbf{V}_1)$ is

$$\mathbf{A}_1 = \frac{g_m r_{b'e}}{2r_b(1/R_C + 1/r_{ce})} \quad \text{(14-21a)}$$

and the coefficient of $(\mathbf{V}_2 + \mathbf{V}_1)$ is

$$\mathbf{A}_2 = \frac{1}{2r_{ce}(1/R_C + 1/r_{ce})} \quad \text{(14-21b)}$$

Taking the ratio of these coefficients, we obtain

$$\frac{\mathbf{A}_2}{\mathbf{A}_1} = \frac{r_b}{g_m r_{b'e} r_{ce}} \quad \text{(14-21c)}$$

Let us consider some representative values for these numbers. We shall use the typical bipolar junction transistor parameters given in Sec. 6-12. These are $g_m = 50{,}000\ \mu$mho, $r_{b'e} = 900$ ohms, $r_{bb'} = 100$ ohms, $r_{ce} = 10^5$ ohms. Substituting in Eq. 14-21c, we have

$$\frac{\mathbf{A}_2}{\mathbf{A}_1} = \frac{(900 + 100)}{50{,}000 \times 10^{-6} \times 900 \times 10^5} = 2.22 \times 10^{-4}$$

Thus, $\mathbf{A}_1$ will be several thousand times as large as $\mathbf{A}_2$ and in many cases we can state

$$\mathbf{V}_{o1} = \frac{g_m r_{b'e}(\mathbf{V}_2 - \mathbf{V}_1)}{2r_b(1/R_C + 1/r_{ce})} \quad \text{(14-22a)}$$

$$\mathbf{V}_{o2} = \frac{g_m r_{b'e}(\mathbf{V}_1 - \mathbf{V}_2)}{2r_b(1/R_C + 1/r_{ce})} \quad \text{(14-22b)}$$

Note that the term which is proportional to $(\mathbf{V}_1 + \mathbf{V}_2)$ will actually be larger than that predicted by Eq. 14-21. There are several reasons for this. First, $\mathbf{V}_E$ as given by Eq. 14-19 is not exact. The value of $\mathbf{V}_E$ given by Eq. 14-17 should be used to compute $\mathbf{A}_2$ more accurately. The second reason is that the two transistors and the two R_C's will not be identical. This imbalance can contribute substantially to the $(\mathbf{V}_1 + \mathbf{V}_2)$ component. We shall discuss this further in Sec. 14-14. The fact that $|\mathbf{A}_1| \gg |\mathbf{A}_2|$ does mean that the magnitude of the second term of Eq. 14-19 will be much less than the first one (see Sec. 14-1).

Use of Current Generator to Replace R_E

Equation 14-17 indicates that R_E must be very large if proper operation is to result. In Sec. 14-1 we showed that this could be accomplished without introducing an unduly large voltage drop if R_E were replaced by a current generator. Figure 14-7 shows such a circuit for the transistor amplifier. The actual realization of the current generator will be discussed in Sec. 14-5.

Input Impedance

Let us now compute the input impedance of the differential amplifier. From Fig. 14-5 we have

$$\mathbf{Z}_{i1} = \left.\frac{\mathbf{V}_1}{\mathbf{I}_1}\right|_{\mathbf{V}_2=0} \tag{14-23a}$$

$$\mathbf{Z}_{i2} = \left.\frac{\mathbf{V}_2}{\mathbf{I}_2}\right|_{\mathbf{V}_1=0} \tag{14-23b}$$

and

$$\mathbf{I}_1 = \frac{\mathbf{V}_1 - \mathbf{V}_E}{r_b}$$

Substituting Eq. 14-19 and manipulating, we obtain

$$\mathbf{Z}_{i1} = 2r_b \tag{14-24a}$$

Similarly,

$$\mathbf{Z}_{i2} = 2r_b \tag{14-24b}$$

Let us now do an example that illustrates the relative magnitudes of the quantities we have been discussing.

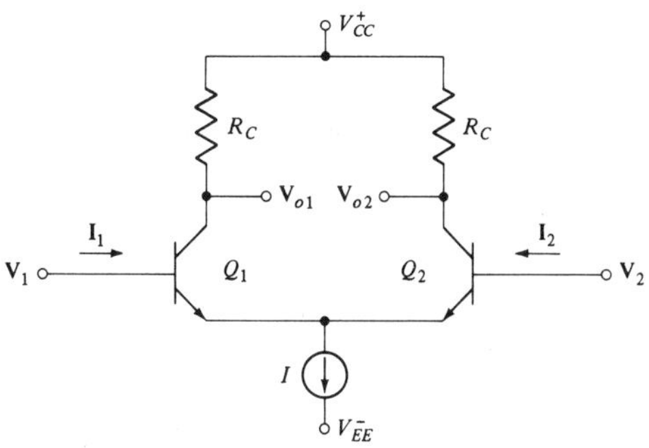

Figure 14-7. A modification of the circuit of Fig. 14-5a where R_E is replaced by a current generator.

Example

The parameters of the transistors used in the differential amplifier of Fig. 14-5a are

$$r_{bb'} = 100 \text{ ohms}$$
$$r_{b'e} = 900 \text{ ohms}$$
$$g_m = 75{,}000\ \mu\text{mho}$$
$$r_{ce} = 100{,}000 \text{ ohms}$$

The parameters of the circuit are

$$R_C = 10{,}000 \text{ ohms}$$
$$R_E = 100{,}000 \text{ ohms (effective)}$$

Compute $\mathbf{V}_{o1}$ and $\mathbf{Z}_{i1}$ for this amplifier.

Let us start by checking the approximations. From Eqs. 14-16a and 14-16b, we have

$$g_m r_{b'e} = 75 \times 10^{-3} \times 900 = 67.5 \gg 1$$
$$g_m r_{b'e} r_{ce} = 75 \times 10^{-3} \times 900 \times 10^5 = 6.75 \times 10^6$$
$$r_c + r_b = 100{,}000 + 10{,}000 + 900 + 100 = 111{,}000$$

Then, $6.75 \times 10^6 \gg 0.111 \times 10^6$ and, hence, the approximations are valid. Now let us see if R_E is large enough (see Eq. 14-18).

$$\frac{r_b r_c}{2R_E} = \frac{10^3 \times 1.1 \times 10^5}{2 \times 10^5} = 550$$
$$6.75 \times 10^6 \gg 550$$

Hence, inequality 14-18 is satisfied and $\mathbf{V}_{o1}$ is approximately given by Eq. 14-22a.

$$\mathbf{V}_{o1} = \frac{75 \times 10^{-3} \times 900(\mathbf{V}_2 - \mathbf{V}_1)}{2 \times 1000(1/10{,}000 + 1/100{,}000)}$$
$$\mathbf{V}_{o1} = -306.8(\mathbf{V}_1 - \mathbf{V}_2)$$

The input resistance is given by

$$\mathbf{Z}_i = 2r_b = 2000 \text{ ohms}$$

The voltage gain of the amplifier stage in this example is high but the input impedance is not. It is desirable for general purpose amplifiers to have high input impedances. We shall consider such high input impedance amplifiers in Sec. 14-4.

14-3. THE CASCODE DIFFERENTIAL AMPLIFIER

In Sec. 12-15 we discussed the cascode amplifier pair and its advantages. The cascode pair can be used to replace each common-emitter "stage" in a differential amplifier. Such an amplifier is shown in Fig. 14-8. Compare this with the common-emitter amplifier

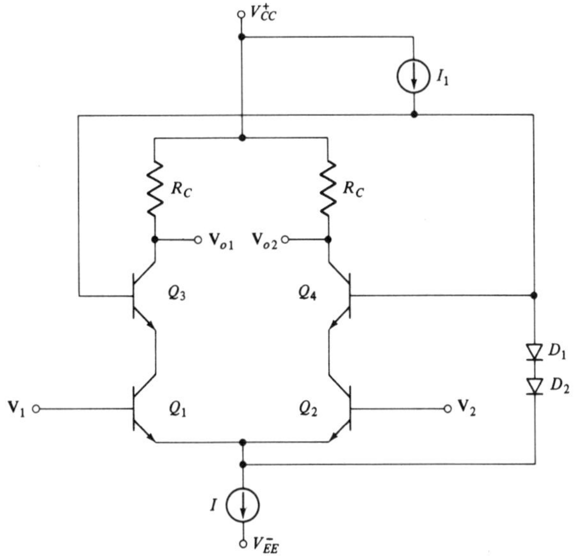

Figure 14-8. A differential amplifier that uses cascode amplifiers.

of Fig. 14-7. The common-emitter stage consisting of transistor Q_1 is replaced by the cascode consisting of Q_1 and Q_3. To obtain the proper bias we connect the base of the output stage to a fixed direct voltage supply. This is shown in Fig. 14-8. In this case, the current generator I_1 and the voltage drop across the forward biased diodes D_1 and D_2 establishes the required fixed voltage supply.

The small signal model for a cascode pair is similar to that for a common-emitter transistor except that the coupling between input and output is greatly reduced at high frequencies. Thus, the analysis of the cascode amplifier is similar to that of the last section and will not be repeated here.

14-4. HIGH-INPUT IMPEDANCE STAGES

Operational amplifiers are usually required to have high input impedances, typically 10^6 ohms or more. The input impedance of an ordinary common-emitter differential amplifier of the type discussed in the last section does not meet this requirement. In this section we shall discuss several procedures that are used to substantially increase the input impedance of the operational amplifier.

Emitter Follower Input Stages

In order to increase the input impedance of the operational amplifier, emitter follower stages are often added to the differential amplifier. Such an input is shown in Fig. 14-9. Assume, for the time being, that the resistors R_B are omitted from the diagram. As we discussed in Sec. 6-8, the input impedance of an emitter follower circuit can be in excess

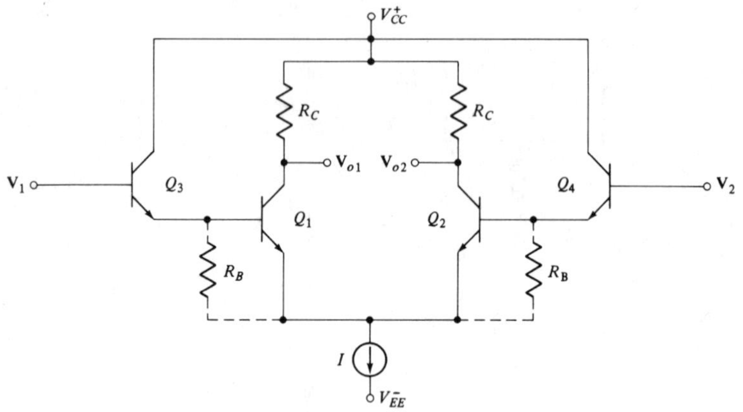

Figure 14-9. A differential amplifier with emitter follower inputs.

of 10^6 ohms, whereas its gain is close to unity (e.g., 0.995). Thus, the circuit of Fig. 14-8 provides the desired high-input impedance while still functioning as a differential amplifier.

The computation of the small signal gain from input 1 (i.e., V_1) to the base of Q_1, or from input 2 to the base of Q_2, follows that of Sec. 6-8. However, there is one important fact that should be noted. For economic reasons, when the integrated circuit is fabricated, transistors Q_1, Q_2, Q_3, and Q_4 will all have essentially the same characteristics. If Q_1 and Q_2 are operated "normally" then the emitter currents of Q_3 and Q_4 will be very small. If the emitter current is very low then the parameters of Q_3 and Q_4 cause both the voltage gain and the input impedance of the emitter follower to fall off. (In Fig. 6-24 we show the variation of some parameters with I_{CQ}.) To prevent this from occurring, the resistors R_B are added to the circuit (see Fig. 14-9). Now the emitter current of Q_3 (or Q_4) can be greater than the base current of Q_1 (or Q_2) and the falloff in gain and input impedance does not occur.

The addition of the resistance R_B does tend to reduce the gain since not all of the output signal current of Q_3 (Q_4) enters the base of Q_1 (Q_2). To prevent this from happening, the circuit of Fig. 14-10 is used. Here the resistors R_B are replaced by current generators. These have a very high (ideally infinite) impedance as far as the signals are concerned. Hence, they do not cause the gain to be reduced.

Bias Current Cancellation

The input current of the differential amplifier consists of both signal components and bias components. It is desirable to make both of these negligibly small. A circuit that accomplishes this is shown in Fig. 14-11 where we have added the current generators i_{a1} and i_{a2} to the basic circuit of Fig. 14-7. The input currents are given by

$$i_1 = i_{B1} - i_{a1} \tag{14-25a}$$

$$i_2 = i_{B2} - i_{a2} \tag{14-25b}$$

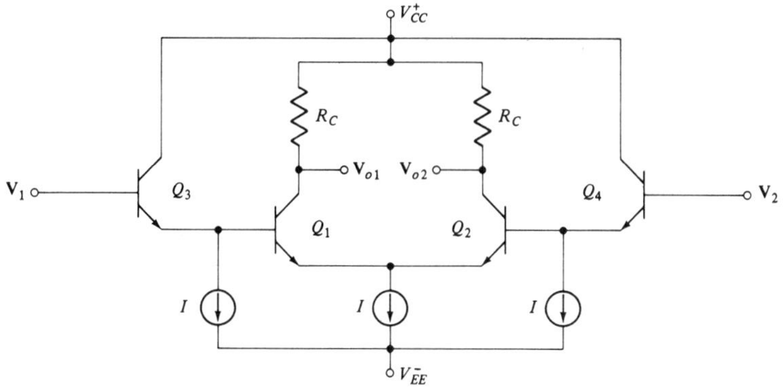

Figure 14-10. A modification of Fig. 14-8 that uses current generators in place of the resistors R_B.

Now suppose we could devise a circuit that caused the currents of the current generators i_{a1} and i_{a2} to vary with i_{B1} and i_{B2}, respectively, so that

$$i_{a1} = i_{B1} \tag{14-26a}$$

$$i_{a2} = i_{B2} \tag{14-26b}$$

Then, i_1 and i_2 would be zero and the input impedance would become infinite and there would also be no input bias currents.

The circuit of Fig. 14-12 provides such controlled current generators. The basic circuit is the cascode differential amplifier of Fig. 14-8. Let us consider its modification. In the circuit of Fig. 14-8 the forward bias voltages of two diodes are used to establish the fixed voltage drop between the base of Q_3 and the emitter of Q_1. (We shall confine our discussion to the left-hand transistors. Of course, similar statements apply to the right-hand pair.) In this circuit there are three diodes D_3, D_4, and D_5 instead of two. This increases the voltage. However, this is compensated for by the diode D_1, which adds an

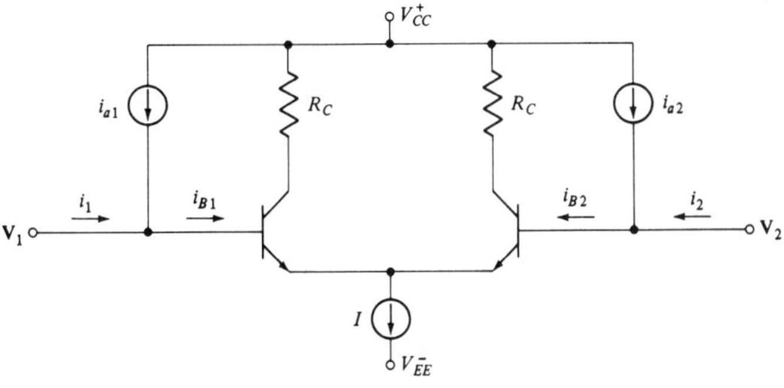

Figure 14-11. An illustration of the basic ideas of an input bias current cancellation procedure.

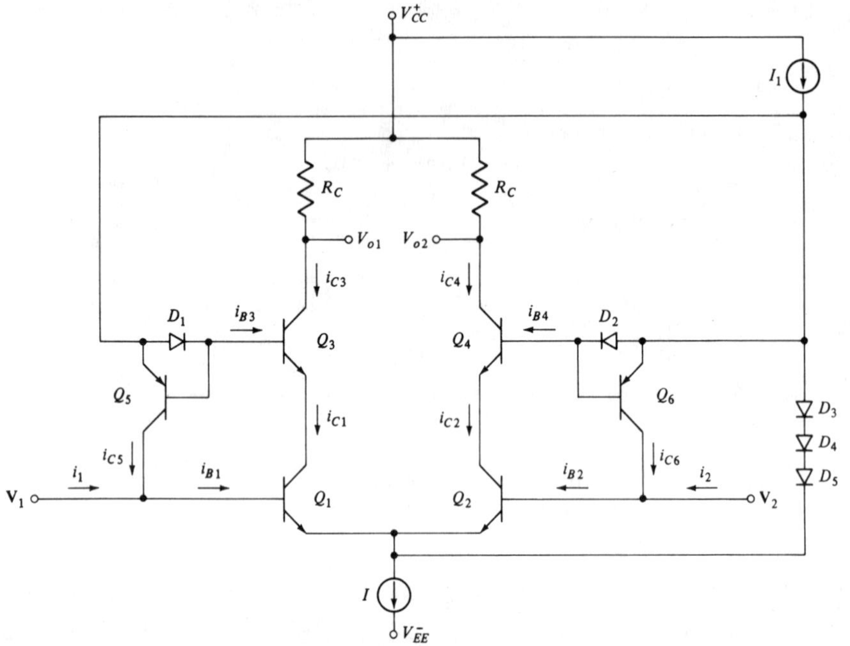

Figure 14-12. An amplifier that uses input bias current cancellation to increase input impedance.

additional voltage drop so that the voltage between the base of Q_3 and the emitter of Q_1 is the same as in the circuit of Fig. 14-8.

Let us now consider the bias current cancellation of this circuit. We shall assume that the β's of all the transistors are high so that for each transistor $I_C \gg I_B$. Hence, the emitter and collector currents of each transistor are essentially the same. Therefore,

$$i_{C3} = i_{C1} \tag{14-27}$$

The numerical subscript will indicate the transistor whose current or voltage we are considering.

In the linear region, $i_B \simeq i_C/\beta$. Thus, if the transistors are identical

$$i_{B3} = i_{B1} \tag{14-28}$$

We must now demonstrate that

$$i_{C5} = i_{B1} \tag{14-29}$$

To do this we redraw the circuit consisting of D_1 and Q_5. The diode D_1 is actually fabricated by constructing a transistor and connecting its collector to its base. This circuit is shown in Fig. 14-13. We assume that D_1 is a high β transistor so that

$$i_{CD1} \simeq i_{B3} \tag{14-30}$$

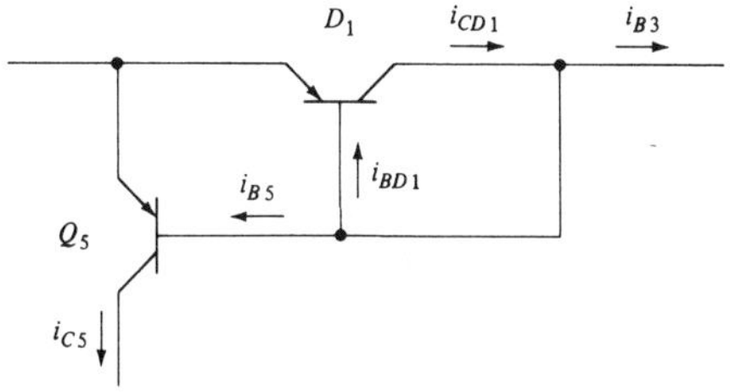

Figure 14-13. A detail of the circuit of Fig. 14-12 showing the actual structure of the diode D_1.

From Fig. 14-13 we see that

$$v_{EBD1} = v_{EB5} \tag{14-31}$$

Thus, the base current is

$$i_{BD1} \simeq i_{B5} \tag{14-32}$$

We assume that the base and collector currents are related by β and that all transistors have the same β's. Hence,

$$i_{C5} = i_{B3} \tag{14-33}$$

Thus, from Eq. 14-28 we have

$$i_{C5} = i_{B1} \tag{14-34}$$

This is the result we desire. If all the transistors are identical and if the β's are infinite then the input currents would be zero. Actually there is some mismatch between transistors and the β's are finite. Because of this, the input currents are not zero. However, this circuit typically reduces them to between 5 and 20% of their uncompensated values.

Use of Super Beta Transistors

The value of the base current is approximately given by I_C/β. Hence, if β is made very large, then i_B will be small so the input impedance will be high. It is possible to fabricate transistors with extremely high values of β (2000 to 5000). These are called *super beta* transistors. These can then be used to obtain high input impedance. A typical circuit using super beta transistors is the cascode differential amplifier (see Fig. 14-8). Thus the transistors Q_1 and Q_2 would be super beta transistors.

The extremely high values of β are achieved by making the base extremely narrow. Breakdown considerations then limit v_{CB} for these transistors to 2 to 4 V. The collector currents of these transistors are usually in the order of 1 μA. Super beta transistors can only be used in those circuits where the collector base voltage is kept small.

The transistors are operated with the emitter-base junction forward biased so that v_{BE} is small. Thus, if the value of v_{CE} is limited, then v_{CB} will also be small. The circuit of Fig. 14-8 is designed to limit the value of v_{CE} for Q_1 and Q_2. Let us assume that the voltage drop across a forward biased diode, or emitter-base junction is 0.8 V. Then, because of D_1 and D_2, the bases of Q_3 and Q_4 are at a potential which is 1.6 V above the emitters of Q_1 and Q_2. In addition,

$$v_{BE3} = V_{BE4} \simeq 0.8 \text{ V} \tag{14-35}$$

Hence, v_{CE1} and v_{CE2} will be about 0.8 V. Thus, v_{CB1} and v_{CB2} will be limited as desired. The direct power supplies are adjusted so that, with zero signal applied, the two inputs are at ground potential.

FET Input Operational Amplifiers

Another procedure for obtaining extremely high-input impedance operational amplifiers is to use FET's as the input stage. Before considering a typical input stage, let us discuss some problems that arise in such circuits. For economic reasons it is desirable that the FET's be fabricated at the same time as the junction transistors. This makes it desirable to use JFET's. In such cases, the JFET's are such that their drain to source voltage must be limited to relatively small values if breakdown is to be avoided. The circuit of Fig. 14-14a accomplishes this by limiting V_{DS}. We assume that the transistors are of high β so that their base currents are much smaller than their collector currents. Hence, for each junction transistor, $I_C \simeq I_E$. Then, the voltage drop across the resistor R is established by the current generator I_2. This voltage drop is $I_2 R$. Then, for the *FET*, $V_{DS} = I_2 R + V_{BEA} - V_{EBB}$. Since the emitter-base junctions of both transistors are forward biased, the magnitudes of these base-emitter voltages are approximately equal. Hence

$$V_{DS} \approx I_2 R_1 \tag{14-36}$$

Thus, by appropriately choosing I_2 and R_1 we can limit V_{DS}. Note that Q_B is a *p-n-p* transistor.

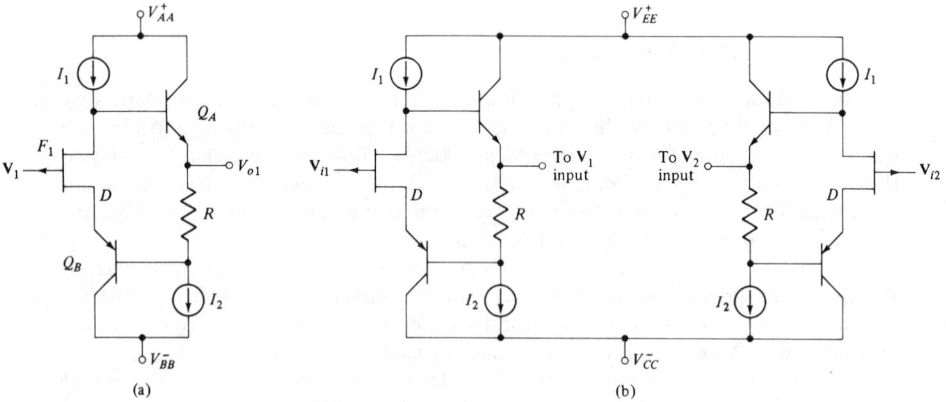

Figure 14-14. (a) A circuit that limits $V_{DS,\max}$ for the FET input transistor. (b) This circuit used as a differential amplifier input.

Now let us consider the amplifier circuit itself. F_1 essentially acts as a source follower amplifier. Transistor Q_A then is an emitter follower that "impedance matches" the output of the FET stage to the following stage. Note that Q_B prevents v_{BEA} from increasing v_{DS1}.

Now let us consider the actual differential amplifier circuit (see Fig. 14-14b). Two circuits of the type shown in Fig. 14-14a are used here. The leads marked "to $\mathbf{V}_1$ input" and "to $\mathbf{V}_2$ input" are connected to the inputs of a bipolar junction transistor differential amplifier. Thus, we have achieved the desired high input impedance. Note that the differential amplifier often uses *p-n-p* transistors because of the voltages of the circuit.

MOSFET Input's

The JFET provides a high impedance input. However, even higher input impedance can be obtained using MOSFET's. A typical MOSFET differential amplifier is shown in Fig. 14-1a. Operational amplifiers are often constructed using such circuits. In such cases MOSFET's are often used throughout the amplifier.

14-5. CURRENT SOURCES

In the previous sections of this chapter we discussed the need for current sources. Let us now consider some actual circuits used in realizing current sources.

The simplest current source consists only of a transistor operated so that its base current is constant. Such a circuit is shown in Fig. 14-15. If $V \gg |v_{BE}|$, then $I_B \simeq V/R$. The collector current will then ideally be βI_B independent of v_{CE}. Actually this simple circuit must be modified for a number of reasons. Foremost is temperature stability. As the operating temperature changes, the parameters of the transistor will shift and $I = I_C$ will change. Hence, the current generator current will vary with temperature. In addition, the current I will be somewhat dependent upon V_{CE} so that the current generator will not be ideal since its internal resistance will not be infinite. This can be seen by studying the low-frequency, small-signal model of Fig. 14-16. (Note that we have assumed that $r_{b'c}$ is so large that it can be considered to be an open circuit.) The impedance looking into the collector-emitter terminals (assuming that i_B is constant) is r_{ce}. Thus, this is the effective resistance of the current generator.

In order to stabilize I against changes in temperature, the Widlar circuit (see Sec. 5-8) can be used. (Actually the nomenclature is somewhat confusing here since, as we shall see, there is a modification of this circuit also called the Widlar current source.) The circuit is shown in Fig. 14-17a. Using the discussion of Sec. 5-8, we have

$$V_{BE1} = V_{BE2} \tag{14-37a}$$

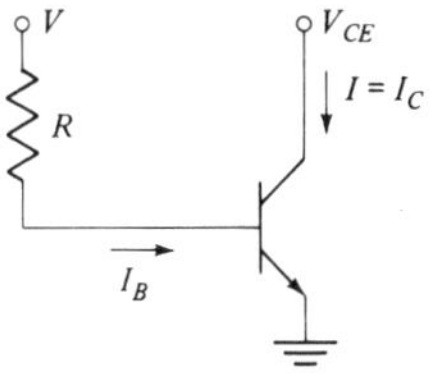

Figure 14-15. An elementary current source which is not often used for the reasons discussed in the text.

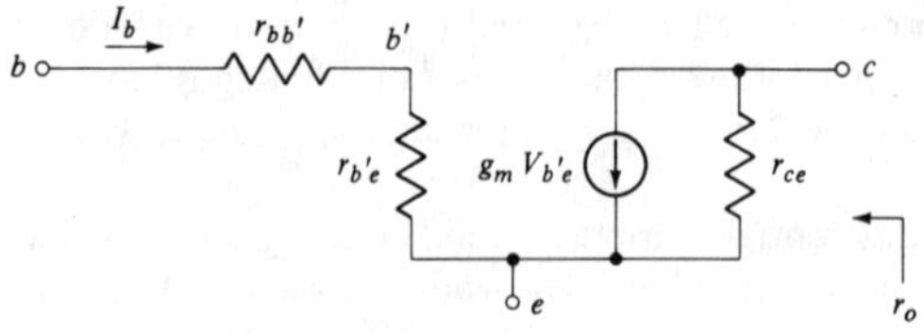

Figure 14-16. A low-frequency model of the transistor used to calculate r_o. It is assumed that $r_{b'c}$ is large enough that it can be ignored.

Hence, if the two transistors are *identical*,

$$I_{B1} = I_{B2} \tag{14-37b}$$

Let us assume that I_C is independent of V_{CE}. We shall discuss this further subsequently. Then,

$$I_{C1} = I_{C2} \tag{14-37c}$$

If

$$V \gg V_{CE1} \tag{14-38}$$

then I_{ref} will be essentially independent of the parameters of the transistor. Note that V_{CE1} will be small since Q_1 is a forward biased diode. We assume that the transistors have large values of β so that

$$I_{C1} = I_{ref} \tag{14-39}$$

Then, under the idealized conditions that we have been considering, I_{C2} will be independent of V_{CE2}. Hence,

$$I = I_{ref} \tag{14-40}$$

and we have achieved a stabilized current source. Note that I_{ref} is independent of temperature. Hence, I will be also (this is discussed in Sec. 5-8). Note that Fig. 14-17b is equivalent to that of Fig. 14-17a. It is often drawn this way.

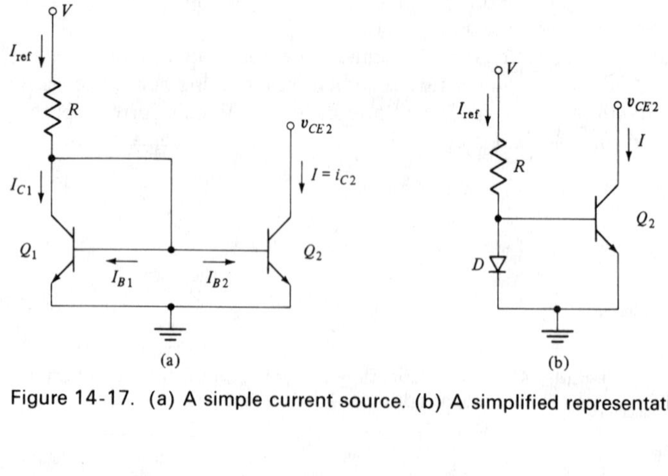

Figure 14-17. (a) A simple current source. (b) A simplified representation of this source.

We can again use the incremental model of Fig. 14-16 to obtain the effective resistance of the current source. Proceeding as before we have

$$r_o = r_{ce} \tag{14-41}$$

We can relate the resistance r_o to the operating point of the transistor. If i_{C2} were independent of v_{CE2}, then r_o would be infinite. The actual curve of i_{C2} versus v_{CE2} for a typical transistor is shown in Fig. 14-18. In the ideal case, i_{C2} becomes constant when v_{CE2} becomes greater than V_{CEA}. (Note that r_o is the reciprocal of the slope of the curve.) In a practical case, the curve is not horizontal and r_O is finite. It can be shown that if $v_{CE} > V_{CEA}$ (i.e., in the region to the right of the knees), the value of i_C can be approximated by

$$i_C = I_{CO}\left(1 + \frac{v_{CE}}{V_A}\right)e^{v_{BE}/V_T} \tag{14-42}$$

where I_{CO} is the collector cutoff current. (We assume here that we are dealing with a silicon transistor.) V_A is a constant parameter called the *Early voltage*. Typically, for *n-p-n* transistors, it lies in the range of 100–150 V. Ideally it would be infinite. Remember that $V_T = T/11{,}600$ where T is the temperature in degrees Kelvin. The effective resistance r_o can be found using the following calculation

$$\frac{1}{r_o} = \left.\frac{di_C}{dv_{CE}}\right|_{v_{BE}=V_{BEQ}} \tag{14-43}$$

Hence,

$$r_o = \frac{V_A}{I_{CO}}\, e^{-V_{BEQ}/V_T} \tag{14-44}$$

Let us now simplify this expression. In general,

$$|v_{CE}| \ll V_A \tag{14-45}$$

Therefore,

$$i_C \simeq I_{CO}\, e^{v_{BE}/V_T} \tag{14-46}$$

Then, substituting in Eq. 14-44 we obtain

$$r_o = \left.\frac{V_A}{i_C}\right|_{i_C=I_{CQ}} = \frac{V_A}{I_{CQ}} \tag{14-47}$$

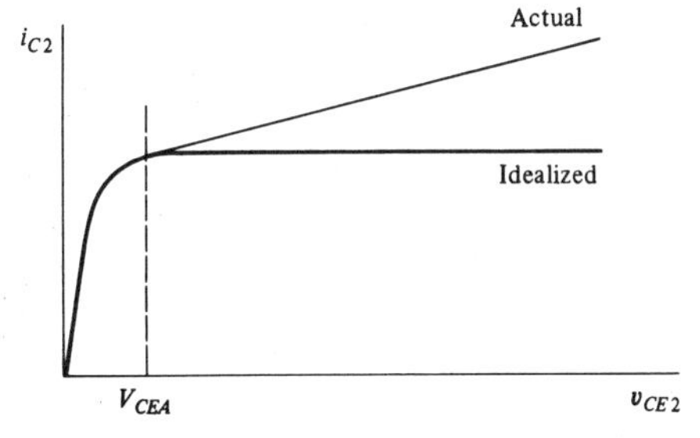

Figure 14-18. A plot of $i_{C2} = I$ versus v_{CE2} for the transistor Q_2 of Fig. 14-17.

Note that it is permissible to substitute Eq. 14-46 *after* the differentiation has been performed. If it had been done before we would compute $r_o = \infty$.

Example

The current source of Fig. 14-17 provides a current $I = 10^{-3}$ A = 1 mA. The effective resistance of the current source is 100,000 ohms. Find V_A and $r_{b'c}$ for the transistor.

From Eq. 14-47,

$$V_A = r_o I_{CQ} = 10^{-3} \times 10^5 = 100 \text{ V}$$

$$r_o = r_{b'c} = 100{,}000 \text{ ohms}$$

We have assumed that $I_{\text{ref}} = I_{C2} = I_C$. However, Eq. 14-42 indicates that this may not always be the case. Consider Fig. 14-17a. v_{CE1} (for Q_1) will, in general, be small since R will be a large resistance while v_{CE2} may be relatively large. Then, from Eq. 14-42, since $v_{BE1} = v_{BE2}$ and we assume that Q_1 and Q_2 are identical,

$$\frac{i_{C1}}{i_{C2}} = \frac{1 + v_{CE1}/V_A}{1 + v_{CE2}/V_A} \tag{14-48}$$

For instance, suppose that $V_A = 120$ V, $v_{CE1} = 0.8$ V, and $v_{CE2} = 15$ V. Then,

$$\frac{i_{C1}}{i_{C2}} = \frac{1 + 0.8/120}{1 + 15/120} = 0.895$$

Thus, i_{C1} and i_{C2} may not be exactly equal, although they may not differ substantially.

The current generators used in the input stages of operational amplifiers are often required to produce very small currents. A typical value is 5 μA (5×10^{-6} A). In order to obtain this low current, the resistance R of Fig. 14-17 must be large. For instance, in Fig. 14-17, if $V = 30$ V and $I = 5$ μA, then

$$R = \frac{30 - 0.8}{5 \times 10^{-6}} = 5.84 \times 10^6 \text{ ohms}$$

where we have assumed a voltage drop of 0.8 V across the forward biased diode. In an integrated circuit, a large resistance requires a large area of the chip. This is undesirable since it limits the number of components that can be placed on the chip. We shall next consider a circuit that does not require a large resistance to obtain a small value of current.

Widlar Current Source

The circuit that we shall consider is that of Fig. 14-19. It is also called a Widlar current source. It is essentially the same as the circuit of Fig. 14-17 except that the resistor R_E is added to the circuit. We shall see that the inclusion of this resistance allows us to use *less total resistance* in the circuit. This means that less area of the chip is utilized for resistance. In addition, we shall see that the effective output resistance of this current generator can be *much* greater than that of the simple current source of Fig. 14-17.

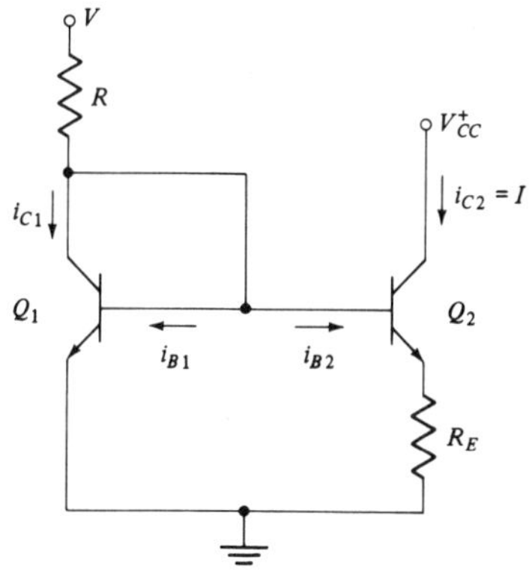

Figure 14-19. A Widlar current source.

Let us obtain some design equations to use with this circuit. From Eq. 14-42 we have (assuming identical transistors)

$$\frac{i_{C1}}{i_{C2}} = e^{(v_{BE1} - v_{BE2})/V_T}\left[\frac{1 + v_{CE1}/V_A}{1 + v_{CE2}/V_A}\right] \tag{14-49}$$

From Fig. 14-19, we have

$$v_{BE1} - v_{BE2} = i_{C2} R_E$$

Hence, substituting in Eq. 14-49 and manipulating, we have

$$R_E = \frac{V_T}{i_{C2}} \ln\left[\frac{i_{C1}}{i_{C2}} \cdot \frac{(1 + v_{CE2}/V_A)}{(1 + v_{CE1}/V_A)}\right] \tag{14-50}$$

Let us illustrate the use of this equation.

Example

Design a Widlar current source of the type shown in Fig. 14-19. The specifications are

$$I = i_{C2} = 5\ \mu\text{A}$$

$$V_{CE} = 15\ \text{V}$$

$$V = 30\ \text{V}$$

It is desired that $i_{C1}/i_{C2} = 10$. The transistors are identical and $V_A = 120$ V. Assume an operating temperature of $T = 300°$K.

From Eq. 14-50 we have

$$R_E = \frac{V_T}{i_{C2}} \ln\left[\frac{i_{C1}}{i_{C2}} \cdot \frac{(1 + v_{CE2}/V_A)}{(1 + v_{CE1}/V_A)}\right]$$

v_{CE1} is not known. However, it will be small. Let us approximate it as 0.8 V. V_{CE2} is also not known. We shall assume that the voltage drop across R_E is small so that $v_{CE1} \simeq$ 15 V. (This must subsequently be verified.) Thus,

$$R_E = \frac{0.02586}{5 \times 10^{-6}} \ln 10 \frac{(1 + 15/120)}{(1 + 0.8/120)}$$

$$R_E = 12{,}484 \text{ ohms}$$

The voltage drop across R_E is $12{,}484 \times 5 \times 10^{-6} = 0.062$ V. Hence, the assumption that $v_{CE} = 15$ V is justified. Then,

$$R = \frac{V - 0.8}{5 \times 10^{-5}} = \frac{30 - 0.8}{5 \times 10^{-5}} = 584{,}000 \text{ ohms}$$

The circuit of Fig. 14-17 required a resistance of 5.84×10^6 ohms whereas this one only uses a total resistance of 584,000 + 12,484 = 596,484 ohms. The circuit of Fig. 14-19 uses approximately one-tenth the resistance of that of Fig. 14-17. Thus, the resistances occupy approximately one-tenth the area of those of Fig. 14-17.

Now let us compute the effective resistance of the current generator of Fig. 14-19. The incremental model for this circuit is given in Fig. 14-20a. It is assumed here that the effective resistance of the forward biased diode Q_1 is small. (Any resistance can be added to $r_{bb'}$.) In Fig. 14-20b we have modified this circuit by replacing the current generator with a voltage generator. Analyzing this circuit, we obtain

$$r_o = \frac{V}{I} = r_{ce} + R_E + \frac{(g_m r_{b'e} r_{ce} - R_E)R_E}{R_E + r_{bb'} + r_{b'e}}$$

In general,

$$g_m r_{b'e} r_{ce} \gg R_E$$

Hence,

$$r_o = r_{ce} + R_E + \frac{g_m r_{b'e} r_{ce} R_E}{R_E + r_{bb'} + r_{b'e}} \tag{14-51a}$$

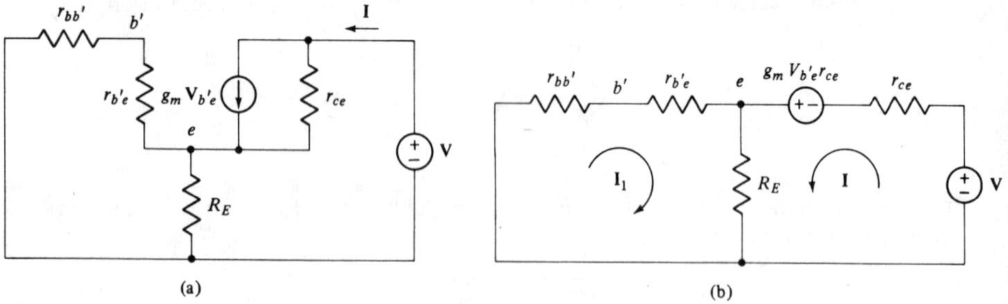

Figure 14-20. (a) The model used to calculate the effective generator resistance of the Widlar current source of Fig. 14-19. (b) A modification of this circuit.

Since

$$g_m r_{b'e} = \beta_o$$

Eq. 14-51a can be written as

$$r_o = r_{ce} + R_E + \frac{\beta_o r_{ce} R_E}{R_E + r_{bb'} + r_{b'e}} \tag{14-51b}$$

Let us consider an example.

Example

The parameters of the transistor used in the circuit of Fig. 14-19 are

$$g_m = 75{,}000\ \mu\text{mho}$$
$$r_{bb'} = 100 \text{ ohms}$$
$$r_{b'e} = 100 \text{ ohms}$$
$$r_{ce} = 100{,}000 \text{ ohms}$$

The resistances are

$$R = 584{,}000$$
$$R_E = 12{,}484$$

Compute the effective resistance of the current generator.

Substituting in Eq. 14-51a we have

$$r_o = 100{,}000 + 12{,}484 + \frac{75 \times 10^{-3} \times 900 \times 100{,}000 \times 12{,}484}{12{,}484 + 100 + 900} = 6.36 \times 10^6 \text{ ohms}$$

The comparable circuit of Fig. 14-17 had a r_o of 100,000 ohms. The inclusion of the emitter resistance increases r_o by a factor of about 64 in this case. Hence, it is a superior current generator.

The Wilson Current Source

Another high-impedance current source, called the *Wilson current source*, is shown in Fig. 14-21a. A model used to calculate the resistance r_o of this current source is shown in Fig. 14-21b. Analyzing this circuit we obtain

$$r_o = \frac{g_m r_{b'e} r_{ce}}{2 + (r_{bb'} + r_{b'e})/R} = \frac{\beta r_{ce}}{2 + (r_{bb'} + r_{b'e})/R} \tag{14-52}$$

where we have assumed that g_m is very much greater than $1/(r_{bb'} + r_{b'e})$, $1/r_{ce}$, and $1/R$. If

$$R \gg r_{bb'} + r_{b'e}$$

then

$$r_o = g_m r_{b'e} r_{ce}/2 = \beta r_{ce}/2 \tag{14-53}$$

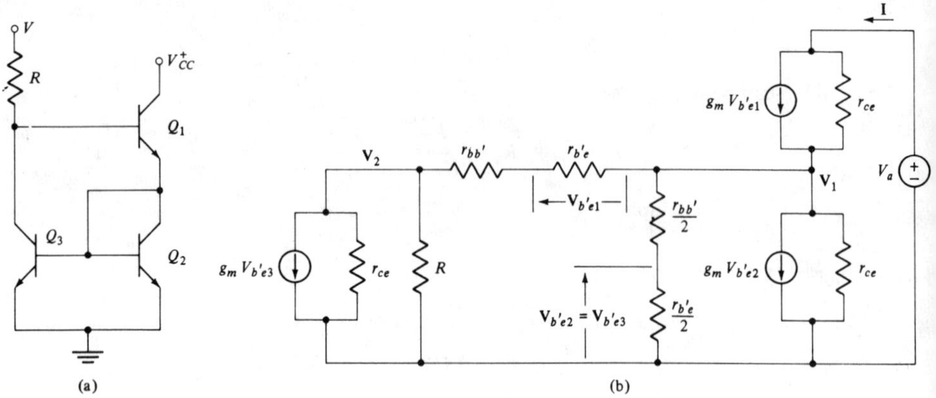

Figure 14-21. (a) The Wilson current source. (b) A model used to calculate r_o for the current source.

If we compare this result with Eq. 14-51, which gives r_o for the Widlar circuit, we see that if $R_E < r_{bb'} + r_{b'e}$, then the Wilson circuit has a larger value of r_o than does the Widlar circuit. In the Widlar circuit, a large value of R_E can result in a large voltage drop across it if the source current I is large. In the Wilson circuit R_E is replaced by the diode Q_2 and, hence, the voltage drop across it is limited to about 0.8 V.

Multiple Current Sources

At times, circuits require more than one current source (e.g., see Fig. 14-10). There are circumstances when we require them to be the same. Usually, the current-source current is controlled using a diode connected transistor. We can build several current sources which use only a single control diode. For instance, Fig. 14-22 illustrates such a multiple source using the simple circuit of Fig. 14-17 as a basis. The emitter-base voltages of Q_{2a}, Q_{2b}, and Q_{2c} are each established by the single diode connected transistor Q_1. Thus we have established three current sources. Note that the bases of all the transistors are connected together. They are fabricated as a common electrode.

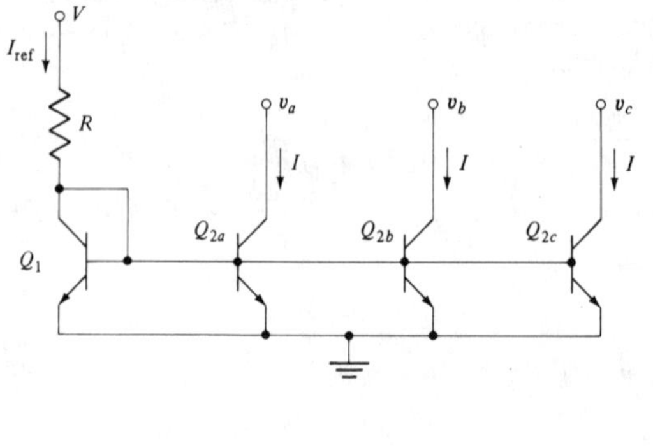

Figure 14-22. A multiple current source based on the current source of Fig. 14-17.

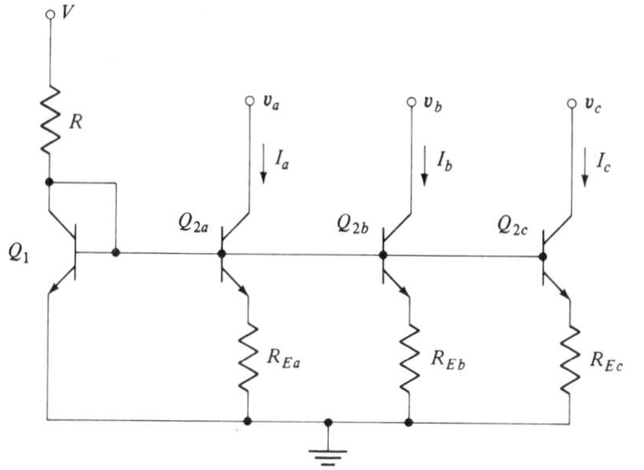

Figure 14-23. A multiple current source based on the Widlar current source of Fig. 14-19.

Suppose that we want to construct two current sources, one with a current I and the other with a current $2I$. This can be accomplished using the circuit of Fig. 14-22 by connecting the collector leads of Q_{2b} and Q_{2c} together. Actually, Q_{2b} and Q_{2c} would not be fabricated as two separate transistors. Instead, one transistor whose cross-sectional area is twice that of Q_1 would be constructed. (Note that in the original analysis of Fig. 14-17 we assumed that Q_1 and Q_2 were identical.) The magnitudes of the current-source currents can thus be varied by varying the areas of the transistors.

We can also easily vary the value of the current by incorporating emitter resistors. In this case, the multiple current source is modeled after the source of Fig. 14-19. Such a Widlar multiple current source is shown in Fig. 14-23. Since R_{Ea}, R_{Eb}, and R_{Ec} are not necessarily equal, the currents of the different sources can be made to differ.

The inclusion of these emitter resistors also increases the effective r_o of each of the current sources, which is another advantage of the circuit of Fig. 14-23.

14-6. USE OF CURRENT SOURCES AS LOAD IMPEDANCES

In general the gain of an amplifier stage increases as its load resistance increases. For instance (see Eq. 14-22), the gain increases as R_C increases. We do not always want to maximize the gain because of high-frequency considerations (see Secs. 12-12 and 12-13). However, very high-gain operational amplifiers are often built where the high-frequency response is of secondary importance. In such cases the use of very large load resistances becomes desirable.

If we simply increase R_C (or R_d in the case of a FET amplifier) several problems arise. If I_{CQ} is the quiescent collector current, then there will be a quiescent voltage drop $I_{CQ}R_C$. If R_C is large, then this voltage will be large, necessitating the use of high-power supply voltages and increasing the power dissipation within the integrated circuits. Also when integrated circuits are used, large resistances occupy large areas on the chip, which is another disadvantage.

If we replace the resistors by current sources, these disadvantages are eliminated. The voltage drop across the current source need not be large but it resists change in current. Thus, it has a large effective resistance for signals (see Sec. 14-5). Also in general, a simple current source can be fabricated in a smaller area than a large resistance. Therefore, the use of current sources as loads is a practical procedure when very high-gain, low-frequency amplifiers are fabricated.

In Fig. 14-24 we have redrawn the differential amplifier of Fig. 14-7 with the loads replaced by current sources. Let us consider this circuit. The transistors Q_1 and Q_2 serve the same function as the transistors Q_1 and Q_2 of Fig. 14-7. Transistor Q_3 and diode Q_4 in conjunction with R_1 and R_E form a Widlar current source, which functions as the current generator I of Fig. 14-7. Transistors Q_5 and Q_6 with diode Q_7 and resistor R_2 form the current source loads. Note that *p-n-p* transistors are used here since we desire to connect all the emitters of the current source transistors to the "ground potential." Of course, the V_{CC}^+ potential is not at ground for direct current, but it is for signals. We have used the simple current source of Fig. 14-22 here since, under quiescent conditions,

$$I_{11} = I_{12} \tag{14-54}$$

In addition, the $\mathbf{V}_{o1}$ and $\mathbf{V}_{o2}$ leads will be connected to the inputs of other amplifier stages whose input resistances will not, in general, be extremely high. Thus, it is not necessary that the resistance of the current generator be extremely high.

The current generators are fabricated so that, ideally

$$I_{11} = I_{12} = \frac{I}{2} \tag{14-55}$$

In this case, when there is no signal, $\mathbf{V}_{o1} = \mathbf{V}_{o2}$.

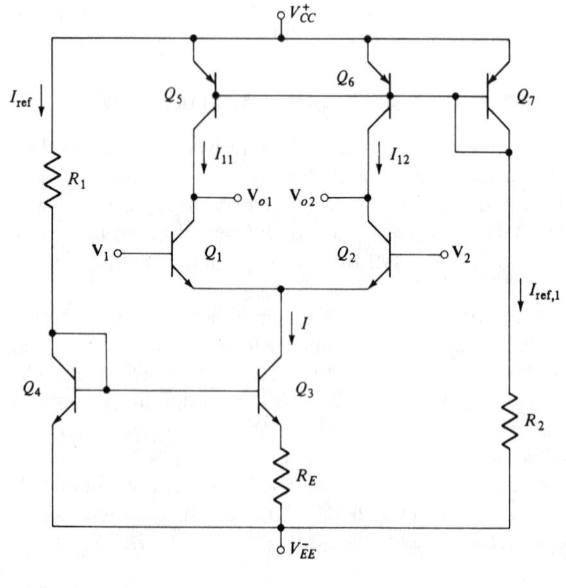

Figure 14-24. A differential amplifier using current source loads.

There is a problem associated with this circuit. Let us assume that V_{CC} and V_{EE} are adjusted so that $\mathbf{V}_{o1} = \mathbf{V}_{o2} = 0$ when $\mathbf{V}_1 = \mathbf{V}_2$. Assume for purposes of this discussion that there are two identical resistors R_L connected between the outputs and ground. Now suppose that $I_{\text{ref, 1}}$ is not equal to I_{ref} because the circuit parameter values are not fabricated exactly equal. Then,

$$I_{11} = I_{12} \neq I/2$$

In this case, current will be forced to be in either the $\mathbf{V}_{o1}$ or $\mathbf{V}_{o2}$ lead, or in both of them. Hence, a voltage will be developed across one or both R_L. Then, even though $\mathbf{V}_1 = \mathbf{V}_2$, there will be a direct component of output. This is termed an *offset* voltage. Such offset voltages are undesirable since, if they are large enough, they can bias subsequent stages into undesirable regions. Even if the offset voltages are not that large, they are undesirable since they indicate that an input is present when it may not exist. Note that offset voltage can be produced by various imbalances in the circuit. For instance, if Q_1 and Q_2 are not identical, an offset may be produced. However, Q_1 and Q_2 are transistors that are fabricated at the same time and so they will tend to be very similar. On the other hand, Q_3 and Q_4 are *n-p-n* transistors and Q_5, Q_6, and Q_7 are *p-n-p* transistors. The *p-n-p* and *n-p-n* transistors are not fabricated at the same time and are very likely to have different characteristics. We shall next discuss a circuit where the balance problem is eliminated. Note that offset problems exist in operational amplifiers even if they do not have current source loads. We shall discuss these problems in Sec. 14-15.

Now let us consider the circuit of Fig. 14-25 where Q_5 and Q_6 constitute the current source load. The reference current is now a function of i_{C1}. Let us start our analysis of

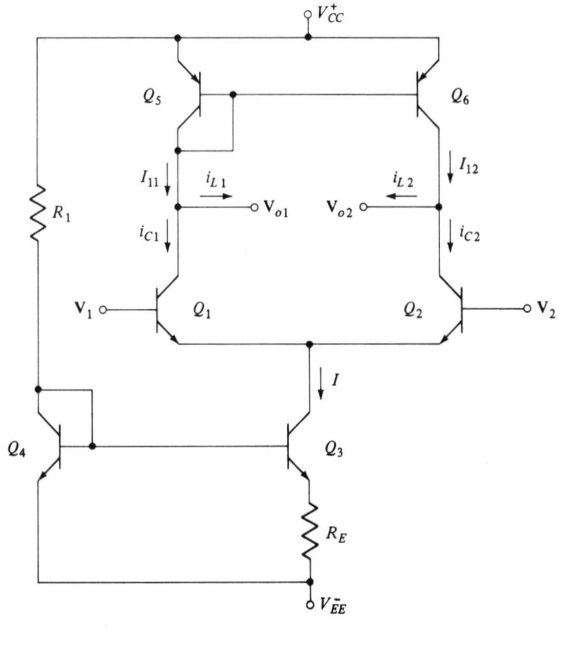

Figure 14-25. An improvement over the circuit of Fig. 14-24 which can be used when a single ended output is used. Note that $\mathbf{V}_{o1}$ cannot be used as an output.

this circuit by assuming that $i_{L1} = i_{L2} = 0$, that is, the loads are open circuits. Then, if the current source is ideal

$$I_{11} = I_{12} \tag{14-56}$$

and

$$I_{11} + I_{12} = I \tag{14-57}$$

If I varies, I_{11} and I_{12} will *automatically adjust themselves.* Note that the current generator transistor Q_2 acts as a very high load impedance for Q_2 and, hence, the gain to output $\mathbf{V}_{o2}$ will be high. However, Q_5 is actually a forward biased diode. If we consider it as a transistor, its effective resistance for small signals is less than $1/g_M$. Hence, Q_1 has a very small load resistance and the gain to $\mathbf{V}_{o1}$ is very small and is *not* used as an output signal.

A small signal model for this circuit is given in Fig. 14-26. We have assumed here that the effective resistance of the emitter current source is very large and can be ignored. Before we analyze this circuit, let us simplify it. That part of the circuit between $\mathbf{V}_{o1}$ and ground acts as a simple resistance. To compute it we have redrawn this part of this circuit in Fig. 14-27. Its input admittance is given by

$$\frac{1}{r} = \frac{\mathbf{I}}{\mathbf{V}} \tag{14-58}$$

where

$$\mathbf{V}_{b'e5} = \frac{\mathbf{V}r_{b'e}}{r_{bb'} + r_{b'e}}$$

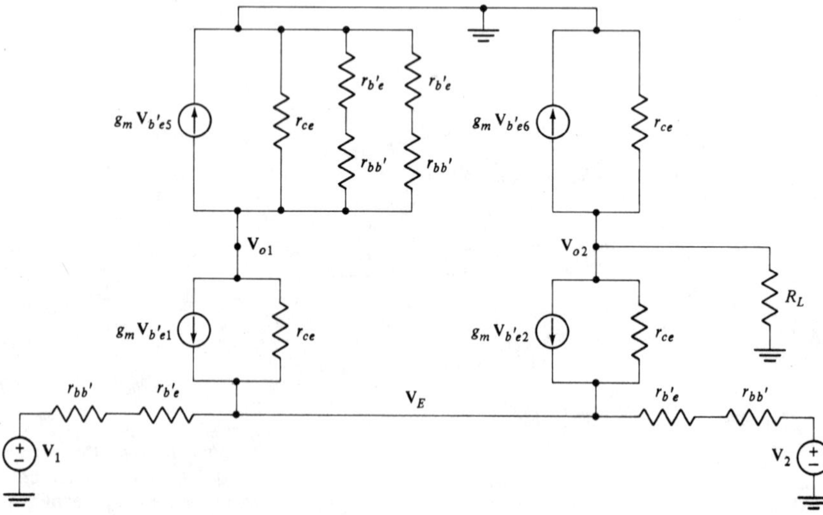

Figure 14-26. A small signal model for the circuit of Fig. 14-25. It is assumed that the emitter-current source resistance is extremely large.

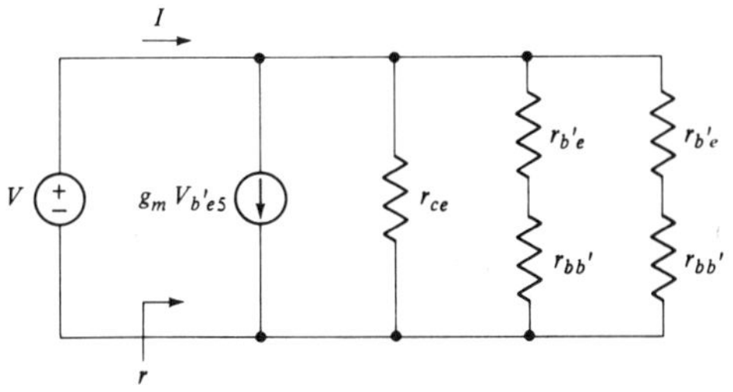

Figure 14-27. A circuit used to simplify a portion of Fig. 14-26.

Then,

$$\mathbf{I} = \left[\frac{g_m r_{b'e}}{r_{bb'} + r_{b'e}} + \frac{1}{r_{ce}} + \frac{2}{r_{bb'} + r_{b'e}}\right]\mathbf{V}$$

Hence,

$$\frac{1}{r} = \frac{g_m r_{b'e}}{r_{bb'} + r_{b'e}} + \frac{1}{r_{ce}} + \frac{2}{r_b} \tag{14-59}$$

where

$$r_b = r_{bb'} + r_{b'e}$$

The resistance r then replaces the circuit between $\mathbf{V}_{o1}$ and ground in Fig. 14-26. Now analyzing this modified figure, we have

$$-g_m \mathbf{V}_{b'e1} = \left(\frac{1}{r} + \frac{1}{r_{ce}}\right)\mathbf{V}_{o1} - 0\mathbf{V}_{o2} - \frac{1}{r_{ce}}\mathbf{V}_E \tag{14-60a}$$

$$-g_m \mathbf{V}_{b'e6} - g_m \mathbf{V}_{b'e2} = 0\mathbf{V}_{o1} + \left(\frac{1}{R_L} + \frac{2}{r_{ce}}\right)\mathbf{V}_{o2} - \frac{1}{r_{ce}}\mathbf{V}_E \tag{14-60b}$$

$$\frac{\mathbf{V}_1}{r_b} + \frac{\mathbf{V}_2}{r_b} + g_m \mathbf{V}_{b'e1} + g_m \mathbf{V}_{b'e2} = -\frac{1}{r_{ce}}\mathbf{V}_{o1} - \frac{1}{r_{ce}}\mathbf{V}_{o2} + \left(\frac{2}{r_b} + \frac{2}{r_{ce}}\right)\mathbf{V}_E \tag{14-60c}$$

where

$$\mathbf{V}_{b'e1} = \frac{(\mathbf{V}_1 - \mathbf{V}_E)r_{b'e}}{r_{bb'} + r_{b'e}} \tag{14-61a}$$

$$\mathbf{V}_{b'e2} = \frac{(\mathbf{V}_2 - \mathbf{V}_E)r_{b'e}}{r_{bb'} + r_{b'e}} \tag{14-61b}$$

$$\mathbf{V}_{b'e6} = \mathbf{V}_{b'e5} = \frac{\mathbf{V}_{o1} r_{b'e}}{r_{bb'} + r_{b'e}} \tag{14-61c}$$

Substituting and manipulating to eliminate $\mathbf{V}_E$, we have

$$g_m'(\mathbf{V}_1 - \mathbf{V}_2) = \left(g_m' - \frac{1}{r} - \frac{1}{r_{ce}}\right)\mathbf{V}_{o1} + \left(\frac{1}{R_L} + \frac{2}{r_{ce}}\right)\mathbf{V}_{o2} \tag{14-62a}$$

$$\left(g_m' + \frac{1}{r_b}\right)(\mathbf{V}_1 + \mathbf{V}_2) - Xg_m'\mathbf{V}_2 = \left(g_m'X - \frac{1}{r_{ce}}\right)\mathbf{V}_{o1} + \left(\frac{X}{R_L} + \frac{2X - 1}{r_{ce}}\right)\mathbf{V}_{o2} \tag{14-62b}$$

where

$$g'_m = \frac{g_m r_{b'e}}{r_{bb'} + r_{b'e}} \tag{14-63a}$$

and

$$X = \frac{2(g'_m + 1/r_b + 1/r_{ce})}{g'_m + 1/r_{ce}} \tag{14-63b}$$

Solving for $\mathbf{V}_{o2}$ we obtain

$$\mathbf{V}_{o2} = \left\{\mathbf{V}_1\left[-g'_m\left(g'_m X - \frac{1}{r_{ce}}\right) + \left(g'_m + \frac{1}{r_b}\right)\left(g'_m - \frac{1}{r} - \frac{1}{r_{ce}}\right)\right]\right.$$
$$\left. + \mathbf{V}_2\left[g'_m\left(g'_m X - \frac{1}{r_{ce}}\right) + \left(g'_m - Xg_m + \frac{1}{r_b}\right)\left(g'_m - \frac{1}{r} - \frac{1}{r_{ce}}\right)\right]\right\} \Big/$$
$$\left\{\left(g'_m - \frac{1}{r} - \frac{1}{r_{ce}}\right)\left(\frac{X}{R_L} + \frac{2X - 1}{r_{ce}}\right) - \left(g'_m X - \frac{1}{r_{ce}}\right)\left(\frac{1}{R_L} + \frac{2}{r_{ce}}\right)\right\} \tag{14-64}$$

This is a complex expression. Let us make some approximations to simplify it. We shall assume that g_m is large enough so that

$$g'_m \gg \frac{1}{r_{ce}} \tag{14-65a}$$

$$g'_m \gg \frac{1}{r_b} \tag{14-65b}$$

$$\frac{1}{r} \simeq g'_m \tag{14-65c}$$

$$X \simeq 2 \tag{14-65d}$$

Using these relations we obtain

$$\mathbf{V}_{o2} = \frac{g'_m(\mathbf{V}_1 - \mathbf{V}_2)}{1/R_L + 2/r_{ce}} \tag{14-66}$$

or, equivalently,

$$\mathbf{V}_{o2} = \frac{g_m r_{b'e}(\mathbf{V}_1 - \mathbf{V}_2)}{r_b(1/R_L + 2/r_{ce})} \tag{14-67}$$

Let us compare this with Eq. 14-22b which gives $\mathbf{V}_{o2}$ for the simple differential amplifier of Fig. 14-5. Before doing this we must make the circuits equivalent. The circuit of Fig. 14-5 did not have external load resistances. Thus, we must modify Eq. 14-22b by including a R_L in parallel with R_C. Hence, Eq. 14-22b becomes

$$\mathbf{V}_{o2R} = \frac{g_m r_{b'e}(\mathbf{V}_1 - \mathbf{V}_2)}{2r_b(1/R_C + 1/R_L + 1/r_{ce})} \tag{14-68}$$

Note that the $1/R_C$ term is missing from Eq. 14-67 and does not reduce the gain. This is because it is replaced by the high effective impedance of the current source load. Also, the single load resistance does not reduce the gain as much as the two load resistances that we have now "added" to Fig. 14-5.

The simple amplifier of Fig. 14-5 had an error term in its output proportional to $(\mathbf{V}_1 + \mathbf{V}_2)$ (see Eqs. 14-20). Equation 14-67 seems to indicate that the circuit of Fig. 14-25 does not have this error. However, this is not the case. If we studied the more exact expression of Eq. 14-64 we would see that such an error term is present. However, the error is usually much less when the circuit of Fig. 14-25 is used. Note that we cannot always use this circuit since there are occasions when we wish *both* the $\mathbf{V}_{o2}$ and $\mathbf{V}_{o1}$ outputs.

Example

Compare the output of the circuits of Figs. 14-5 and 14-25 using transistors with the following parameter values.

$$r_{bb'} = 100 \text{ ohms}$$

$$r_{b'e} = 900 \text{ ohms}$$

$$g_m = 75{,}000\ \mu\text{mhos}$$

$$r_{ce} = 100{,}000 \text{ ohms}$$

The parameters of the circuit are

$$R_L = 1000 \text{ ohms}$$

and for Fig. 14.5

$$R_C = 10{,}000 \text{ ohms}$$

Substituting in Eq. 14-67 for the circuit of Fig. 14-25, we have

$$\mathbf{V}_{o2} = \frac{75 \times 10^{-3} \times 900(\mathbf{V}_1 - \mathbf{V}_2)}{1000(1/1000 + 2/100{,}000)} = 66.2(\mathbf{V}_1 - \mathbf{V}_2)$$

Substituting in Eq. 14-68 for the circuit of Fig. 14-5, we have

$$\mathbf{V}_{o2} = \frac{75 \times 10^{-3} \times 900}{2 \times 1000(1/10{,}000 + 1/1000 + 2/100{,}000)} = 30.1(\mathbf{V}_1 - \mathbf{V}_2)$$

Thus, the gain of the circuit with the current source load is considerably larger.

The current source load can be considered to be an active load. This is analogous to the active pull-up circuit discussed in Sec. 9-7. We can consider this another way. The increased gain is due to the activity of the load.

14-7. CASCADED DIFFERENTIAL AMPLIFIERS—dc STABILITY

Often operational amplifiers have only one differential amplifier, which is the first stage and the output of this stage is a single signal whose voltage is proportional to $(\mathbf{V}_2 - \mathbf{V}_1)$ (e.g., Fig. 14-9). That is, the differential amplifier can accept a *balanced* input and it converts to a *single ended* output. Note that a *single ended signal* is measured between a single lead and ground whereas a balanced signal is measured between two leads. The magnitude of the voltage between either of these leads and ground is equal. However, these two voltages differ in phase by 180°.

As stated, most differential input stages utilize only one single ended output. However, some operational amplifiers use a cascade of (balanced) differential amplifier stages. Let us consider the reason for this.

Because of temperature or power supply voltage fluctuations, the effective bias of each stage of the amplifier will drift slowly. These shifts act as very low-frequency signals. For instance, the period of the fluctuation can be on the order of several minutes or more. The stabilization procedures discussed in Secs. 14-5 and 5-8 are usually used so that the effective fluctuations are small, but the fluctuations do exist and the amplifier cannot "tell them apart" from low-frequency signals. If the overall gain is extremely large, then the amplifier may actually saturate or cut off as a result of bias drift. Suppose that we are working with a very high-gain amplifier (e.g., $\mathbf{A}_v = 10^6$). Then, if the input bias shifts by only 0.2×10^{-5} V, the output voltage should shift by 20 V. Probably under these circumstances, the amplifier would saturate or cut off. The effects of drift can be minimized by cascading differential amplifier stages. We shall now discuss this.

Consider the amplifier of Fig. 14-28, which consists of the cascade of two differential amplifier stages. The first stage consists of the transistors Q_1 and Q_2 and their load resistance, R_C. The second stage, which has a single ended output, consists of transistors Q_3 and Q_4 and their active (current source) loads consisting of Q_5 and Q_6. Transistors Q_7, Q_8, and Q_9 form the "emitter" current sources. Note that the first stage uses a passive load (i.e., the resistors R_C) because both outputs $\mathbf{V}_{11}$ and $\mathbf{V}_{12}$ are desired.

Now let us suppose that a temperature change causes $\mathbf{V}_{11}$ and $\mathbf{V}_{12}$ to drift. Both transistors Q_1 and Q_2 are in extremely close proximity (i.e., in the same chip) so their temperatures will be essentially equal and the drift in $\mathbf{V}_{11}$ and $\mathbf{V}_{12}$ will be almost the same. Let us call this shift in voltage δ. Hence, $\mathbf{V}_{11}$ becomes $\mathbf{V}_{11} + \delta$ and $\mathbf{V}_{12}$ becomes $\mathbf{V}_{12} + \delta$. The next stage is also a differential amplifier so that its output voltage is proportional to the difference between $\mathbf{V}_{11}$ and $\mathbf{V}_{12}$. Hence, we can write

$$\mathbf{V}_o = \mathbf{A}_v[\mathbf{V}_{22} + \delta - (\mathbf{V}_{11} + \delta)] = A_v(\mathbf{V}_{22} - \mathbf{V}_{11}) \tag{14-69}$$

The effects of drift in the first stage have been *cancelled*. Actually, the drifts in $\mathbf{V}_{11}$ and $\mathbf{V}_{12}$ are not exactly equal. Thus, the effects of drift are not exactly cancelled, but they are made very small.

The effects of drift of the operating points of Q_3 and Q_4 are *not* cancelled. In order to have these drifts cancelled, the second stage would have to be modified to provide a differential output, and this would have to drive a third differential amplifier stage.

The voltage gains of the individual stages are usually high so the use of a pair of stages such as those shown in Fig. 14-28 can reduce the effective drift in the output voltage by a factor of 200 or more.

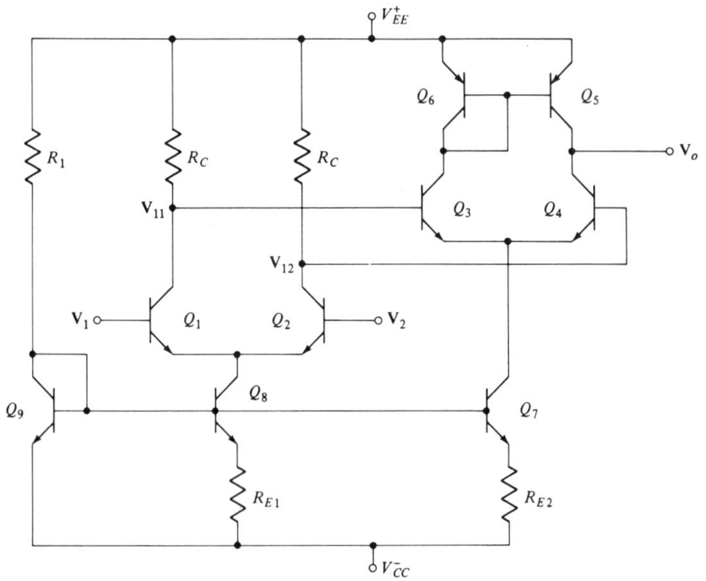

Figure 14-28. A cascade of two differential amplifier stages which tends to cancel the effect of drift in the first stage.

In Chapter 12 we considered high-gain *RC* coupled amplifiers but did not worry about the drift in the output voltage. Remember that the drift in operating point acts as a very low-frequency signal. The gain of *RC* coupled amplifiers is usually small at very low frequencies. Hence, the drift is not amplified and the problem does not exist in *RC* coupled amplifiers.

14-8. OUTPUT STAGES

In this section we shall discuss the output stages of operational amplifiers. We shall only consider relatively low-level output stages here. The next chapter shall contain a complete discussion of high-level output stages.

Let us start by presenting some elementary requirements for the output stage. Ideally, when the input signals are zero (or when $\mathbf{V}_1 = \mathbf{V}_2$), the output voltage should be 0 V. When $\mathbf{V}_2 - \mathbf{V}_1$ is positive, the output voltage should swing positively with respect to ground, and when $\mathbf{V}_2 - \mathbf{V}_1$ is negative, the output voltage should be negative with respect to ground. The output voltage is single ended (unbalanced). That is, one lead is the ground.

Let us now consider some circuits that can be used to achieve these objectives. Consider the simple circuit of Fig. 14-7. It provides a single ended output. However, the output voltage will not be zero when $\mathbf{V}_1 = \mathbf{V}_2$. The dc level can be shifted by using a circuit called a *level shifting circuit*. A typical one is shown in Fig. 14-29a. Transistors

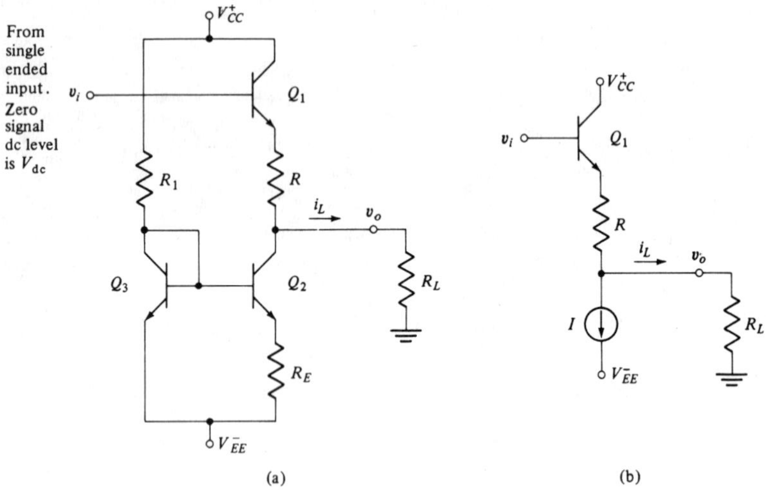

Figure 14-29. (a) A dc voltage level shifter. (b) A simplified representation of this circuit.

Q_2 and Q_3 and resistors R_1 and R_E form a current generator. Thus, the circuit can be represented by the simplified form shown in Fig. 14-29b. Therefore, the circuit basically consists of an emitter follower which has a current source load.

Let us see how the circuit functions and how the various element values are chosen. The input signal v_i is taken from a single ended signal such as V_o of Fig. 14-28. Suppose that the dc level of this signal is V_{dc}. That is, when the input signals are zero (or $\mathbf{V}_1 = \mathbf{V}_2$), $v_i = V_{dc}$. Note that all voltages are expressed with respect to ground. In these calculations we shall assume that, for a transistor operating in the active region, $v_{BE} \simeq 0.7$ V. (This will vary but will always be close to 0.7 V.)

We must now choose the magnitude of the current generator current I. The load current swings symmetrically about 0. When Q_1 is cut off,

$$i_L = -I \tag{14-70}$$

Hence, the maximum load current swing is $\pm I$. Therefore, I is equal to the specified value of maximum load current.

When there is no input signal present ($v_i = V_{dc}$) under this condition we desire that

$$v_o = 0$$

In this case,

$$i_L = 0$$

Hence,

$$V_{dc} - v_{BE} - IR = 0 \tag{14-71}$$

Solving for R we obtain

$$R = (V_{dc} - V_{BE})/I \tag{14-72}$$

This value of R will result in $v_o = 0$ when $v_i = V_{dc}$.

Example

Determine the value of R in the circuit of Fig. 14-29 if

$$V_{dc} = 8 \text{ V}$$

and

$$I = 1 \text{ mA}$$

Substituting in Eq. 14-72, we obtain

$$R = \frac{8 - 0.7}{10^{-3}} = 7300 \text{ ohms}$$

Let us consider the voltage gain of this circuit. The voltage gain of the emitter follower will be close to unity and its output impedance will be very low (i.e., very much less than R). The effective resistance r_o of the current generator I will be much greater than R. Hence, the output resistance of the circuit will be R (or R in parallel with r_o). Therefore, if a load resistance R_L is connected between the v_o terminal and ground, the voltage gain will be given by

$$\mathbf{A}_v = \frac{R_L}{R + R_L} \tag{14-73}$$

The circuit of Fig. 14-29 is inefficient. For instance, suppose that no signal is present (or that the signal levels are low). The constant current I will be through Q_1, Q_2, R, and R_E. In addition, an equal current will be through R_1 and Q_3. Then, the power dissipated within the integrated circuit chip will be

$$P_D = 2I(V_{CC} + V_{EE}) \tag{14-74}$$

If the maximum output current is not very small, then I will be large and the dissipation will be excessive. We shall now discuss the circuit of Fig. 14-30, which introduces

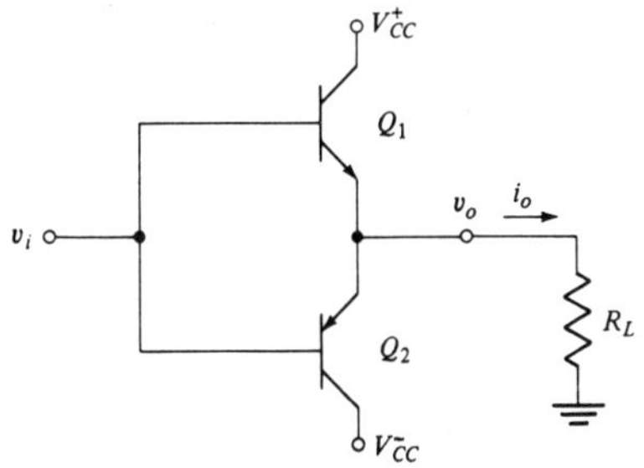

Figure 14-30. A basic class B push-pull output stage.

less dissipation and, thus, is more suitable to use at higher power levels (although it is usually not used at power output levels exceeding 1–2 W). In Fig. 14-30 we assume that v_i is level shifted so that it swings about 0 V. The circuit of Fig. 14-29 can be used for this purpose. (Note that the power dissipated by the level shifter will now be small since I can be very small because the current levels are low.) Consider Fig. 14-30. Q_1 is a *n-p-n* transistor while Q_2 is a *p-n-p* transistor. The values of the positive and negative power supplies are equal. Thus, when both transistors are operating symmetrically, v_o will be 0. Hence, when $v_i = 0$, $v_{BE1} = v_{BE2} = 0$ since $v_o = 0$ and thus, *both* transistors will be cut off. Under these conditions no power will be dissipated by the circuit so it is much more efficient than that of Fig. 14-29.

Now suppose that v_i becomes positive. Q_2 will remain cut off but now Q_1 will conduct so i_o will be positive. On the other hand, if v_i becomes negative, then Q_1 will be cut off and Q_2 will conduct and i_o and v_o will be negative. This circuit is called a *push-pull* amplifier. We shall discuss it in great detail in the next chapter. It is also called a class B amplifier since if v_i is sinusoidal, i_c for each transistor is zero for half a cycle. This will also be discussed in the next chapter.

In Fig. 14-31 we plot v_o versus v_i (i.e. the transfer characteristic) for this amplifier. (For the moment, ignore the discontinuity near the origin.) When v_i is positive, Q_1 conducts; v_o will be positive and increases as v_i increases until Q_1 saturates. Beyond that point, v_o no longer increases with v_i. Similarly, when v_i is negative, Q_2 conducts and v_o is negative. Each transistor, when it is conducting, is an emitter follower. Hence, the nonzero slopes of Fig. 14-31 will be essentially unity if the load resistance is sufficiently large.

Consider the discontinuity near the origin, which is called *crossover distortion*, and can be the source of considerable distortion. That is, the shape of v_o will be considerably different from that of v_i. The reason for the crossover distortion is that the transistors do not conduct unless $v_{BE} \geqq V_{BE\gamma} \simeq 0.6$ V for the *n-p-n* transistor or $|v_{BE}| \geqq |V_{BE\gamma}| \simeq 0.6$ V for the *p-n-p* transistor.

Consider the circuit of Fig. 14-32, which eliminates the crossover distortion. The current sources cause each diode voltage to be slightly greater than $|V_{BE\gamma}|$. Hence, if $v_i = 0$, then both Q_1 and Q_2 will conduct. However, they will conduct equally. Hence, v_o and i_o will be 0. Now suppose that v_i increases positively. This will increase the current through Q_1 and decrease it through Q_2. Similarly, if v_i becomes negative, the current

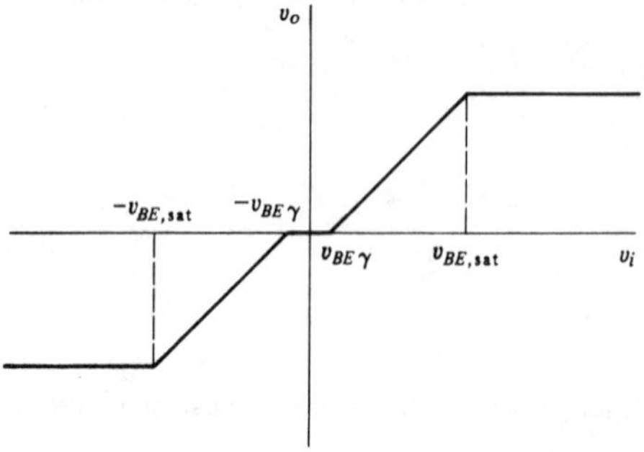

Figure 14-31. Idealized transfer characteristics of the amplifier of Fig. 14-30.

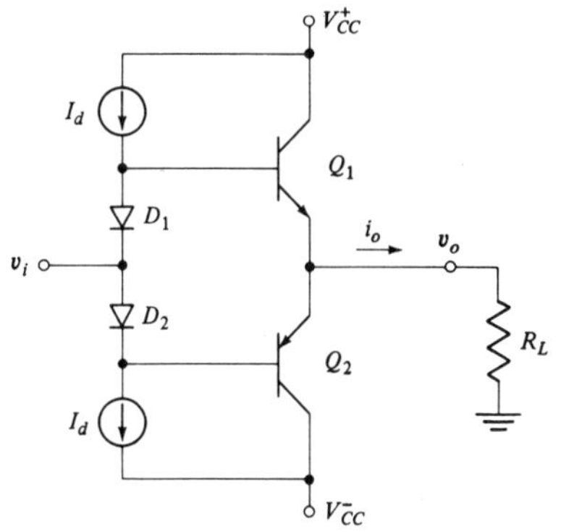

Figure 14-32. A circuit that eliminates the effect of crossover distortion.

through Q_2 would increase while that through Q_1 would decrease. Note that $v_{BE} = v_i - v_o$ so that $v_{BE} \neq v_i$. However, when v_i becomes positive, i_o increases positively. When v_i becomes negative, the converse occurs. Note that when $v_i = 0$, the bias is such that the transistors are *not* cut off. However, under these conditions i_{C1} and i_{C2} are small so that the dissipation is small.

If we consider the small signal behavior of Fig. 14-32, we still have two emitter followers. Thus, the idealized transfer characteristics are as shown in Fig. 14-33. The slope of the curve is very close to unity if the load resistance is large enough.

One problem encountered with circuits of this type is that if R_L becomes too small, the currents through the transistor can become excessive. At times, the output terminals of an amplifier are accidentally short-circuited. If there is an input signal present, the output current can become large enough to destroy the transistors. Fuses cannot be used as a protection since the transistors "blow out" faster than the fuses so the circuit must be protected electronically. A circuit that has short circuit protection is shown in Fig. 14-34. The two resistors R_E are small resistances which are considerably less than the rated R_L so that they do not substantially affect the operation. Under normal operating conditions, the voltage drops across the resistances R_E are so small that Q_3 and Q_4 are cut off and the circuit functions essentially as that of Fig. 14-32.

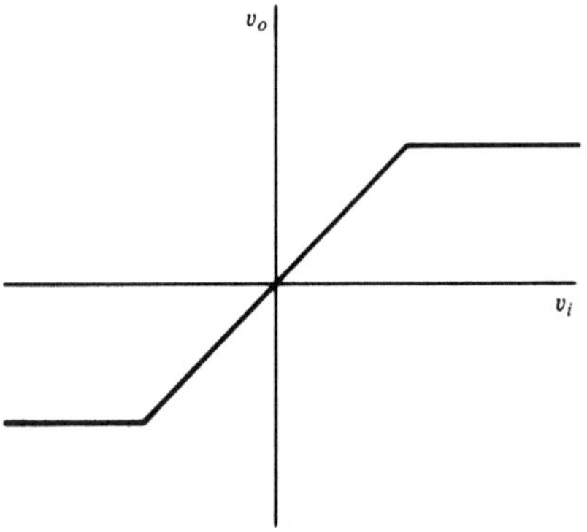

Figure 14-33. The idealized transfer characteristics of the amplifier of Fig. 14-32.

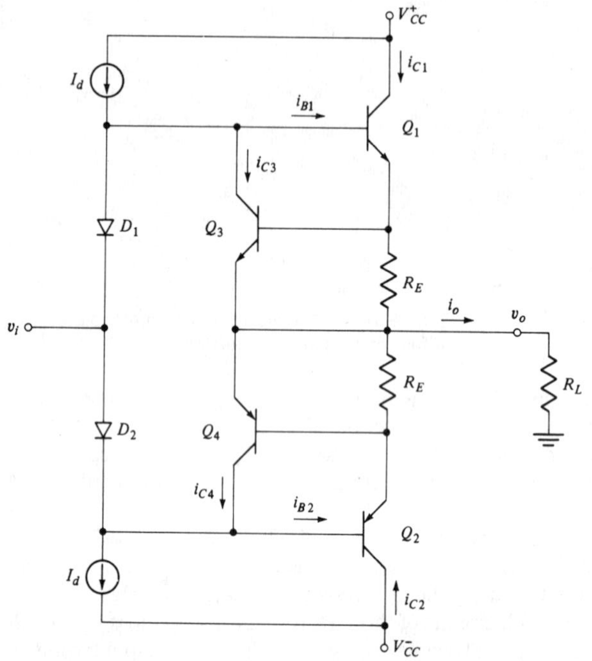

Figure 14-34. A modification of the circuit of Fig. 14-33 that provides short circuit protection.

Now suppose that the output is shorted to ground. The currents in Q_1 and Q_2 will tend to become excessive. The voltage drop across the resistors R_E will rise, turning on Q_3 and Q_4. The currents i_{C3} and i_{C4} will now be nonzero, and reduce the base currents i_{B1} and i_{B2}. This causes i_{C1} and i_{C2} to decrease. In a properly designed circuit Q_1 and Q_2 will not be overloaded. In general, the collector current of a transistor is much greater than its base current. Then, under conditions of overload, transistors Q_3 and Q_4 greatly reduce i_{B1} and i_{B2} and protect the circuit.

Example

In the circuit of Fig. 14-34 we want to turn transistors Q_3 and Q_4 on if the collector current exceeds 10 mA. Find the value of R_E that accomplishes this.

For a typical transistor $V_{BE\gamma} = 0.6$ V.

$$R_E = \frac{V_{BE\gamma}}{I_{C,\max}} = \frac{0.6}{10 \times 10^{-3}} = 60 \text{ ohms}$$

Let us see if this value of R_E is suitable. Let us calculate the minimum value of R_L which will be used. Assume that the output voltage swing is ± 10 V. Under normal operating conditions, the maximum load current swing will be about ± 8 mA. Note that we obtain this value by taking 80% of the maximum allowed collector current. Then, the load resistance is

$$R_L = 10/8 \times 10^{-3} = 1250 \text{ ohms}$$

Thus, R_L will be about 20 times as large as R_E so the voltage drop across the resistors R_E will not be excessive.

In the next chapter we shall considėr push-pull circuits that operate at much higher power levels, and much smaller values of R_L and R_E will be used. In such cases, we shall discuss why it is desirable to use stages that consist of all *n-p-n* transistors. We shall see how the circuit of Fig. 14-34 is modified in such cases.

Let us now consider a modification of this circuit (see Fig. 14-35). The circuit consisting of Q_1, Q_2, Q_3, and Q_4 is the basic push-pull output circuit that we have discussed. The input voltage v_i applied to the base of Q_5 varies the voltage v_a. Let us describe the operation of this circuit in terms of v_a. The diodes D_1 and D_2 are included to eliminate or reduce crossover distortion. Suppose that v_a is zero. The base of Q_1 will be raised above ground by the voltage drops across D_1 and D_2 so Q_1 will be on, and v_o will be positive. Hence, the emitter of Q_2 will be above ground. The magnitude of this voltage will be sufficient to turn Q_2 on. This will tend to reduce v_o. However, v_o cannot become small enough for Q_2 to be cut off. In general, under these conditions, $v_o \simeq V_{BE\gamma}$. Note that both Q_1 and Q_2 are conducting with Q_1 conducting more current than Q_2. Now suppose that v_a increases positively. Then Q_1 will conduct still more current. In fact, it acts as an emitter follower. The positive v_a will tend to cut off Q_2 but the increase in v_o

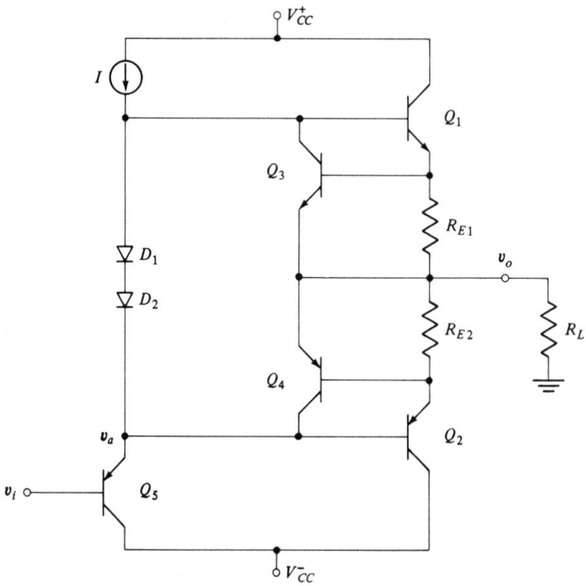

Figure 14.35. Another form of class B output stage.

will nullify this effect. Note that since Q_1 acts as an emitter follower, the increase in v_o will almost equal the increase in v_a so the value of v_{BE2} will remain almost unchanged. Hence, i_{C2} will remain small but nonzero. Similarly, when v_a increases negatively, Q_2 acts as an emitter follower and conducts heavily, whereas i_{C1} remains equal to its value when $v_a = 0$. Since neither transistor ever becomes cut off, crossover distortion is eliminated.

A practical form of this circuit is shown in Fig. 14-36. Note that the current source is realized by transistors Q_6, Q_7, and the resistor R. Diode D_1 is replaced by the diode connected transistor Q_{D1}. On the other hand, diode D_2 is replaced by the transistor Q_{D2}. This circuit functions in essentially the same way as did the diodes D_1 and D_2 of Fig. 14-35. That is, Q_{D1} and the emitter-base junction of Q_{D2} maintain the difference of potential between the bases of Q_1 and Q_2 equal to the voltage drop across two forward biased diodes.

The reader may ask why fabricate the circuit in this way and not just use two diode connected transistors. It is done basically because it simplifies the integrated circuit fabrication. Note that Q_3, Q_{D1}, and Q_{D2} all have their collectors connected together. Thus, they can be the same electrode and need not be isolated. If D_1 and D_2 of Fig. 14-35 were both fabricated using diode connected transistors, the collector of D_2 would have to be isolated from that of D_1, since D_1 and D_2 are connected in series. This would increase the complexity of the integrated circuit fabrication. Note that, in general, integrated circuits may have circuits that appear complex but which actually result in simpler circuit fabrication.

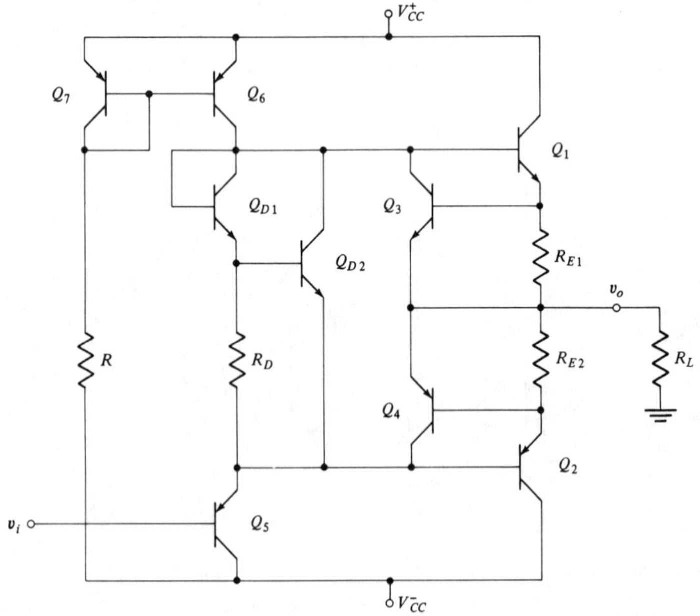

Figure 14-36. A practical form of the circuit of Fig. 14-35.

14-9. BIAS ANALYSIS OF A COMPLETE OPERATIONAL AMPLIFIER

In this section we shall consider procedures for obtaining the quiescent operating points of all the devices in a complete operational amplifier. It might seem logical to start by determining the quiescent operating point of the devices of the first stage and then use these to determine the quiescent operating points of the next stage. Proceeding in this way we could determine the quiescent operating points of all the devices in the amplifier. *However, this procedure will not yield practical results.* Let us consider the reason for this. Assume that we calculate the voltage between collector and ground for one of the transistors in the input differential amplifier stage. Suppose that this voltage actually is 10.0 V. However, because of minor inaccuracies, we calculate it to be 10.1 V. This is only a 1% error and is probably more accurate than we can calculate. Now consider that the gain of the amplifier from the point in question to the output is 1000. The resulting error in the output voltage will be 100 V. Actually, no practical operational amplifier can handle such a voltage level and, hence, according to our calculations, the output transistor would either be saturated or cut off. Thus, the actual error in the operating points of many of the devices will be large. (Note that if the *actual* input bias drifted by 0.1 V, the amplifier would actually saturate.) In the usual operational amplifier circuit, a feedback circuit of the type shown in Fig. 13-4 is used. This reduces the gain to $-R_2/R_1$ but stabilizes the operation. If v_o increases positively, the resulting signal fed back to the input tends to diminish the increase. This tends to stabilize the output voltage against changes in bias (as well as other quantities such as $\mathbf{A}_v$). We shall assume that the direct voltage and current levels are stabilized and that the output voltage is zero (because the input signal is zero) and then work backward through the amplifier. That is, we shall assume that the output voltage is zero and compute the operating point of the output stage. These quantities will then be used to compute the operating point of the next to last stage, and so forth.

In Fig. 14-37 we show a simple complete operational amplifier. We have deliberately not included too many stages so as not to obscure the analysis with repetitive details. The amplifier consists of an output stage such as that shown in Fig. 14-36 and an input stage which is a differential amplifier with current source load of the type shown in Fig. 14-25. The output impedance of this stage is high so we have made the next stage an emitter follower (Q_7). This is done because the input impedance of the emitter follower is high and, thus, the output voltage of the first stage is not reduced by a small load resistance. The level shifter consisting of transistor Q_{19} and resistor R_3 is incorporated into this stage. This is necessary since the collector of transistor Q_2 must be at a relatively large positive voltage with respect to ground while the base of transistor Q_{14} will be at a negative potential. (Subsequent calculations will illustrate this.)

The stage consisting of Q_8 and its current source load Q_9 provides another stage of amplification and serves as an additional level shifter to provide the proper voltage level at the base of Q_{14}.

The diode connected transistors are shown as such in this schematic. The subscript D is added to these transistors to indicate that they are diode connected. Note that in many schematic drawings, the diode connected transistors are simply drawn as diodes.

In order to analyze this circuit with complete accuracy we should use the graphical characteristics of each transistor but this would result in extremely tedious calculations.

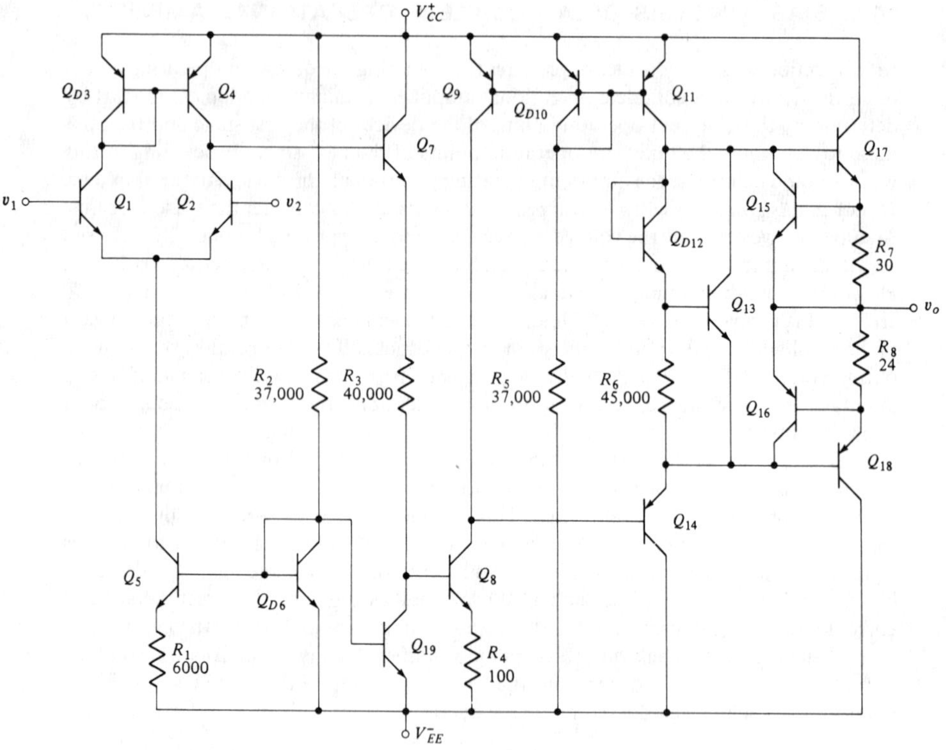

Figure 14-37. A simple complete operational amplifier. Resistance values are given in ohms.

In addition, such characteristics are often not available for integrated circuit operational amplifiers. Even when graphical characteristics are available, they are only approximate. Thus, we shall make some approximations here which enable us to obtain the quiescent operating points to within 10–15%. (The graphical characteristics may be no more accurate than this.) We shall discuss the approximations at the end of this section. Of course, if we wish to compute the nonlinear distortion, then graphical characteristics *must* be used. We shall consider such nonlinear analysis in the next chapter.

Let us now consider some of the approximations that we shall make. First we shall assume that

$$i_C = \beta_F i_B \tag{14-75}$$

In addition, we shall assume that i_C and v_{BE} are related by Eq. 14-42 and that the Early voltage V_A is sufficiently large so that

$$V_A \gg v_{CE}$$

Hence, Eq. 14-42 can be written as

$$i_C = I_{C0}\, e^{v_{BE}/V_T} \tag{14-76}$$

As a first step in analyzing the operational amplifier, we replace all current source circuits (e.g., transistors) by ideal current sources so that the simpler circuit of Fig. 14-38 results. This represents a further approximation since the current sources are not ideal.

The first step in the analysis is to determine the currents produced by the current generators. The schematic actually does not provide all the information necessary to do this. For instance, consider current generator I_{11}. This current is actually the collector current of Q_{11} (see Fig. 14-37). In the basic analysis of this current generator (see Sec. 14-5) we assumed that i_{C11} and i_{CD10} were the same. (Note that we have added the transistors' numbers to the subscripts.) However, as we subsequently discussed, the ratio i_{C11}/i_{CD10} depended upon the ratio of the cross-sectional areas of the transistors. In the present analysis, we assume that this information is also known. Manufacturers do not usually supply such information in their handbooks. However, the ordinary user of an

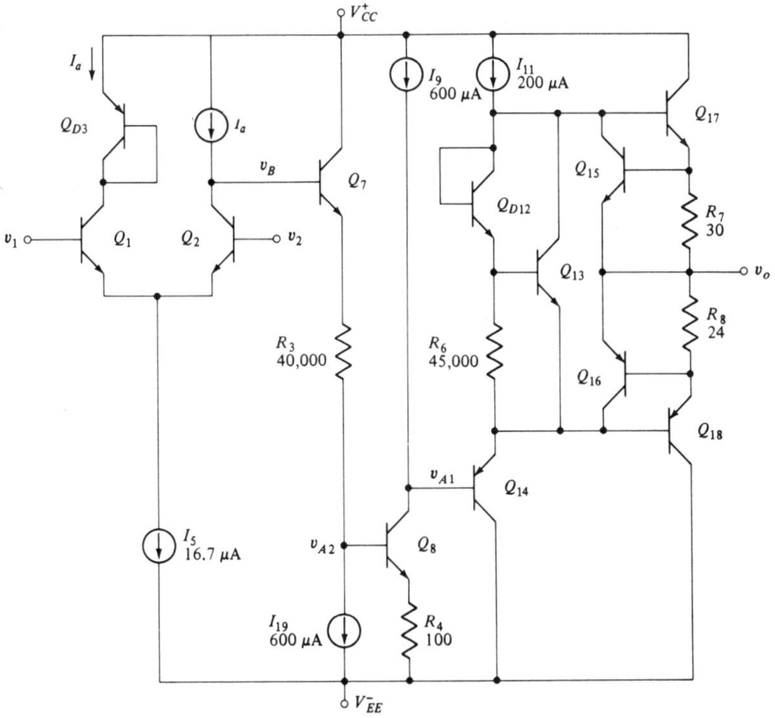

Figure 14-38. A modification of the circuit of Fig. 14-37 where the current source circuits have been replaced by ideal current sources.

operational amplifier does not usually make these calculations. Of course, such information would be available to or could be specified by the designer of the integrated circuit.

Let us now calculate the current source values assuming that we know all the pertinent information.

We shall assume the following values.

$$V_{CC}^{+} = 15 \text{ V}$$

$$V_{EE}^{-} = -15 \text{ V}$$

$$R_1 = 6000 \text{ ohms}$$

$$R_2 = 37{,}000 \text{ ohms}$$

$$R_3 = 40{,}000 \text{ ohms}$$

$$R_4 = 100 \text{ ohms}$$

$$R_5 = 37{,}000 \text{ ohms}$$

$$R_6 = 45{,}000 \text{ ohms}$$

We shall calculate the values of the other resistances so that desired objectives are obtained.

The current generator I_5 is formed by Q_5, Q_{D6}, and the resistors R_1 and R_2. From Eq. 14-50 we have, if V_A is sufficiently large and the transistors are identical,

$$R_E = \frac{V_T}{I_5} \ln \frac{I_{CD6}}{I_5} \tag{14-77}$$

We can calculate I_{CD6} using the following relation

$$I_{CD6} = (V_{CC}^{+} - V_{EE}^{-} - V_{CED6})/R_2$$

V_{CED6} is actually the voltage drop across a conducting diode. We shall approximate it as 0.8 V. Then,

$$I_{CD6} = \frac{15 + 15 - 0.8}{37{,}000} = 0.789 \text{ mA}$$

Then, substituting in Eq. 14-77 and manipulating

$$I_5 = \frac{0.0259}{6000} \ln \frac{0.789 \times 10^{-3}}{I_5}$$

where we have used $T = 300°\text{K}$ to evaluate $V_T = T/11{,}600$.

$$I_5 = 4.31 \times 10^{-6} \ln \frac{0.789 \times 10^{-3}}{I_5}$$

This is a transcendental equation that must be solved by trial and error procedures. Doing this we obtain

$$I_5 = 16.7 \ \mu\text{A}$$

If the current generator I_a functions ideally, then

$$I_a = \frac{I_5}{2} = 8.35\ \mu\text{A}$$

Let us assume that R_5 is equal to R_2. Then, the current through Q_{D10} will also be 0.789 mA. Q_9 and Q_{11} form simple current sources. From Sec. 4-5, if all transistors are of equal cross-sectional area, then $I_{C9} = I_{C11} = I_{CD10}$. Actually, this is not the case because the transistors Q_9 and Q_{11} are constructed with cross-sectional areas less than that of Q_{D10}. Let us assume that we desire

$$I_9 = 600\ \mu\text{A}$$

and

$$I_{11} = 200\ \mu\text{A}$$

Then we have the following ratios of cross-sectional area.

$$\frac{A_9}{A_{D10}} = \frac{600}{789} = 0.760$$

$$\frac{A_{11}}{A_{D10}} = \frac{200}{789} = 0.253$$

Similarly, let us assume that

$$\frac{A_{19}}{A_{D6}} = 0.760$$

Hence,

$$I_{19} = 600\ \mu\text{A}$$

We now have determined the values of all the current generators. Proceeding in the converse manner, with some freedom of choice, we could determine the resistance values and transistor cross-sectional areas from a specification of the desired current generator values.

Let us now analyze the output stage of the amplifier. The resistors R_7 and R_8 are small resistances whose only function is to turn transistors Q_{15} and Q_{16} on in the event of an overload. Under quiescent conditions, the voltage drop across them is very small and, for the purposes of this analysis they can be considered to be short circuits. Similarly, under quiescent conditions, Q_{15} and Q_{16} will be cut off and not affect the circuit.

To actually analyze the output stage, we shall make use of Eqs. 14-75 and 14-76. Note that v_{BE} is taken as positive when the emitter-base junction is forward biased. As stated earlier in this section we shall assume that

$$v_o = 0 \tag{14-78}$$

Now let us obtain some relations among the currents in the output circuit. Let us start by summing voltage drops around a closed loop. Neglecting the small voltages across R_7 and R_8, we have

$$v_{BE12} + v_{BE13} = v_{BE17} + |v_{BE18}| \tag{14-79}$$

Note that we take the magnitude of v_{BE18} since Q_{18} is a *p-n-p* transistor and, hence, its v_{BE} is defined as opposite in polarity to the v_{BE}'s of the *n-p-n* transistors. Substituting Eq. 14-76 and manipulating, we have

$$V_T \ln \frac{I_{C12}}{I_{CO12}} + V_T \ln \frac{I_{C13}}{I_{CO13}} = V_T \ln \frac{I_{C17}}{I_{CO17}} + V_T \ln \left| \frac{I_{C18}}{I_{CO18}} \right| \tag{14-80}$$

Under quiescent conditions

$$I_{C17} = |I_{C18}| \tag{14-81}$$

Actually (see Sec. 14-8), the quiescent values of I_{C17} and $|I_{C18}|$ do differ slightly but the difference is small, so Eq. 14-81 is essentially correct. Then, substituting Eq. 14-81 into Eq. 14-80 and manipulating, we have

$$I_{C17} = |I_{C18}| = \sqrt{I_{C12} I_{C13}} \sqrt{\frac{I_{CO17} I_{CO18}}{I_{CO12} I_{CO13}}} \tag{14-82}$$

If all other conditions are equal (e.g. doping and temperature) then the I_{CO} of two transistors are proportional to their cross-sectional areas. Usually, the output transistors are larger since they have to provide larger current swings and must dissipate greater power. Typically their areas are three times as large as those of the other transistors. Thus, we have approximately

$$I_{CO17} = |I_{CO18}| = 3I_{CO12} = 3I_{CO13} \tag{14-83}$$

This ratio will depend upon the type of operational amplifier used. We have used 3 as a typical value.

Now let us calculate I_{C12} and I_{C13}. The value of $v_{BE12} = v_{BE13} \simeq 0.65$ V, which is typical for a conducting transistor. The current through R_6 is then 0.65/45,000 = 14.4 μA. The current i_{CD12} will equal this current plus i_{B13}. We assume that β is high so that this base current can be neglected. Also, if β_{D12} is high then

$$I_{CD12} = 14.4\ \mu\text{A}$$

If we also assume that the base currents of Q_{17} and Q_{18} are negligible, then all of I_{11} passes through Q_{D12} and Q_{D13}. Then,

$$I_{C13} = 200 - 14.4 = 185.6\ \mu\text{A}$$

Substituting in Eq. 14-82 and using Eq. 14-83 we have

$$I_{C17} = |I_{C18}| = 3\sqrt{14.4 \times 185.6} = 155\ \mu\text{A}$$

We assumed that the betas of the transistor were large enough so that the base currents could be ignored in the previous calculation. If $\beta = 100$, then the base current will be in the range 1–2 μA and thus will not be large enough to substantially affect the computations.

Let us now calculate the values of R_7 and R_8. Let us assume that we wish to start limiting the current through Q_{17} and Q_{18} when it exceeds 20 mA. Hence, Q_{15} and Q_{16} should turn on if the currents exceed this value. Assuming that $v_{BE\gamma} = 0.6$ V, we have

$$R_7 = \frac{0.6}{20 \times 10^{-3}} = 30 \text{ ohms}$$

Actually, because of the asymmetry in the circuit discussed in the last section, R_8 is usually made about 20% less than R_7.

$$R_8 = 24 \text{ ohms}$$

Note that when the quiescent conditions were calculated, we assumed that the voltage drop across these resistances could be neglected. The actual drop is $155 \times 10^{-6} \times 30 = 0.00465$ V. Hence, our assumption was valid.

Let us now compute the remaining operating points. We start by computing v_{BE14}. Since we can ignore the base currents in comparison with the collector current, we have $i_{C14} = 200\ \mu$A. Then,

$$v_{BE14} = V_T \ln \left| \frac{I_{C14}}{I_{CO14}} \right| \tag{14-84}$$

In order to solve this equation we must know the value of I_{CO14}. A typical value for the (nonoutput) transistors of an integrated circuit is 0.3×10^{-14} A. Then, substituting, we have

$$v_{BE14} = \frac{300}{11{,}600} \ln \frac{200 \times 10^{-6}}{0.3 \times 10^{-14}} = 0.645 \text{ V}$$

We wish to determine the potential v_{A1} above ground. Again neglecting the drop in R_8, we have

$$v_{A1} = -(v_{BE14} + v_{BE18})$$

(Note that $v_o = 0$.) We know that $|I_{C18}| = 155\ \mu$A. In addition (see Eq. 14-83),

$$|I_{CO18}| = 0.9 \times 10^{-14}$$

$$v_{BE18} = \frac{300}{11{,}600} \ln \frac{155 \times 10^{-6}}{0.9 \times 10^{-14}} = 0.610 \text{ V}$$

$$v_{A1} = -(0.645 + 0.610) = -1.255 \text{ V}$$

This value of v_{A1}, then, subject to approximations, produces an output of 0 V.

We can also state that

$$i_{C8} = 600\ \mu\text{A}$$

This again assumes that the beta of Q_{14} is high so that its base current can be neglected. We must now assume that we know the value of beta for Q_8. (At the end of this section we shall make some observations about all the approximations that we have made.)

A typical value is

$$\beta_8 = 250$$

Then,

$$i_{B8} = \frac{600 \times 10^{-6}}{250} = 2.4\ \mu\text{A}$$

Hence,

$$v_{BE8} = \frac{300}{11{,}600} \ln \frac{600 \times 10^{-6}}{0.3 \times 10^{-14}} = 0.672 \text{ V}$$

Now let us calculate the voltage drop across the 100-ohm bias stabilizing resistance R_4.

$$v_{R4} = 600 \times 10^{-6} \times 100 = 0.06 \text{ V}$$

The voltage v_{A2} is then

$$v_{A2} = v_{R4} + v_{BE8} - V_{EE} = 0.06 + 0.672 - 15 = -14.27$$

Also

$$v_{CE19} = 0.06 + 0.672 = 0.732 \text{ V}$$

Again, assuming that beta is large, we have

$$I_{C7} = 600 \ \mu\text{A}$$

Then,

$$v_{BE7} = V_T \ln \frac{I_{C7}}{I_{C07}} = 0.0259 \ln \frac{600 \times 10^{-6}}{0.3 \times 10^{-14}} = 0.674 \text{ V}$$

Now let us determine the voltage v_B. If the input stage is to function properly, then the collector must be a relatively large positive voltage with respect to ground.

$$v_B = v_{BE7} + I_{19} R_3 + v_{A2}$$

$$v_B = 0.674 + 600 \times 10^{-6} \times 40{,}000 - 14.27 = 10.404 \text{ V}$$

This is a satisfactory value.

Note that as far as signal quantities are concerned, the emitter follower (Q_7) presents a high impedance load to the first stage since its load impedance consisting of R_3 and the input impedance of Q_8 is high. Note that the input impedance of Q_8 is approximately $\beta \times 100 \simeq 25{,}000$ ohms.

We have already calculated that the bias current for the first stage is

$$i_{C1} = i_{C2} = 16.7/2 = 8.35 \ \mu\text{A}$$

Thus, we have computed the pertinent bias currents.

Some Comments Concerning the Approximation Made in This Analysis

We have used numerous approximations in the quiescent analysis of this section. This analysis was performed to provide the reader, and operational amplifier user, with a feel for the quiescent levels within an operational amplifier. However, in a sense, the analysis of this section should not be performed. The actual integrated circuit designer would have more specific information (i.e., graphical characteristics) about the transistor and, hence, would not have to make all of the approximations. The user of the integrated circuit would not be concerned with the internal biases and thus would not perform this analysis. It was included since it does provide some insight into the operation of the operational amplifier.

14-10. THE SIGNAL ANALYSIS OF A COMPLETE OPERATIONAL AMPLIFIER

We shall now consider the procedures for calculating the low-frequency gain of the complete operational amplifier of Fig. 14-37. We have considered small-signal analysis for individual circuits in detail previously. Here we shall apply these individual analyses to the complete circuit of Fig. 14-37.

The input stage is the same as that of Fig. 14-25 and its small-signal model is drawn in Fig. 14-26. The output voltage of this first stage is given by Eq. 14-67. Thus, the input signal applied at the base of Q_7 is

$$\mathbf{V}_b = \frac{g_m r_{b'e}(\mathbf{V}_1 - \mathbf{V}_2)}{(r_{bb'} + r_{b'e})(1/R_L + 2/r_{ce})} \tag{14-85}$$

where R_L is the input impedance of the emitter follower Q_7. Typically, this will be in excess of 10^6 ohms (see Sec. 6-8). Hence,

$$\frac{2}{r_{ce}} \gg \frac{1}{R_L} \tag{14-86}$$

and Eq. 14-85 can be approximated by

$$\mathbf{V}_b = \frac{g_m r_{b'e} r_{ce}(\mathbf{V}_1 - \mathbf{V}_2)}{2(r_{bb'} + r_{b'e})} \tag{14-87}$$

The voltage gain of the emitter follower will be very close to unity and we shall approximate it as such. However, R_3 and the input resistance of Q_8 act as a voltage divider. Hence the gain of the stage is

$$\mathbf{A}_{v7} = \frac{R_{i8}}{(R_3 + R_{i8})}$$

The next stage, consisting of transistor Q_8, is a common-emitter amplifier with an unbypassed emitter resistor R_4. The gain of such an amplifier stage was analyzed in Sec. 12-7. Manipulating these results, we have

$$\mathbf{A}_{v8} = \frac{-g_m R_{\text{sh}} r_{b'e}/(r_{bb'} + r_{b'e})}{1 + R_4[(1 + g_m r_{b'e})/(r_{bb'} + r_{b'e})]} \tag{14-88}$$

where

$$\frac{1}{R_{\text{sh}}} = \frac{1}{r_{ce}} + \frac{1}{R_{i14}} \tag{14-89}$$

Transistor Q_{14} is an emitter follower stage that drives the emitter followers Q_{17} and Q_{18} so its input resistance R_{i14} will be large and we shall assume that

$$R_{\text{sh}} \simeq r_{ce}$$

Hence,

$$\mathbf{A}_{v8} = \frac{-g_m r_{ce} r_{b'e}/(r_{bb'} + r_{b'e})}{1 + R_4[(1 + g_m r_{b'e})/(r_{bb'} + r_{b'e})]} \tag{14-90}$$

The remaining amplifier stages consisting of Q_{14}, Q_{18}, and Q_{19} are emitter followers and we shall approximate their gains as unity. This assumes that a sufficiently large load resistance is connected to the output terminal. Then,

$$\mathbf{A}_v = -\left[\frac{g_m r_{b'e} r_{ce}}{2(r_{bb'} + r_{b'e})}\right]\left[\frac{g_m r_{ce} r_{b'e}/(r_{bb'} + r_{b'e})}{1 + R_4[(1 + g_m r_{b'e})/(r_{bb'} + r_{b'e})]}\right]\left[\frac{R_{i8}}{R_3 + R_{i8}}\right] \quad (14\text{-}91)$$

(Note that we have assumed that all the transistors have the same parameters.)

Example

For the operational amplifier under consideration

$$g_m = 75{,}000 \ \mu\text{mho}$$
$$r_{b'e} = 900 \text{ ohms}$$
$$r_{bb'} = 100 \text{ ohms}$$
$$r_{ce} = 30{,}000 \text{ ohms}$$

(The value of r_{ce} is chosen on the low side to account for shunt resistances that have been neglected.)

$$R_4 = 100 \text{ ohms}$$
$$R_3 = 40{,}000 \text{ ohms}$$

Computer $\mathbf{A}_v$ for this amplifier.

$$\beta = g_m r_{b'e} = 75 \times 10^{-3} \times 900 = 67.5$$

The input impedance $R_{i8} \simeq \beta \times R_4 + r_{bb'} + r_{b'e}$.

$$R_{i8} = 67.5 \times 100 + 100 + 900 = 7750$$

$$\mathbf{A}_v = -\left(\frac{75 \times 10^{-3} \times 900 \times 0.3 \times 10^5}{1000 \times 2}\right)$$
$$\times \left[\frac{75 \times 10^{-3} \times 0.3 \times 10^5 \times \dfrac{900}{1000}}{1 + 100\left(\dfrac{1 + 75 \times 10^{-3} \times 900}{1000}\right)}\right]\left(\frac{7750}{40{,}000 + 7750}\right)$$

$$\mathbf{A}_v = -(1012.5)(258)(0.162) = -42{,}318$$

We have approximated the gain of the operational amplifier here. Somewhat more accurate results could be obtained if we replaced each transistor by its small-signal model. However, the results would still not be totally accurate since the parameters of the transistor in an integrated circuit are not exactly known. For instance, these will vary widely from sample to sample. Thus, the approximate analysis will be as accurate as the "exact" one. In general, manufacturers specify typical, maximum, and minimum values of $\mathbf{A}_v$. Each operational amplifier is checked and those that fall within allowable limits are accepted and the others rejected. Therefore, it becomes reasonable to make approximations of the type used in this section when dealing with operational amplifiers.

14-11. THE DARLINGTON TRANSISTOR—COMPOUND TRANSISTORS

Often we wish to fabricate transistors with special characteristics such as extremely high β or, equivalently, with α very close to unity. It may be difficult and/or costly to fabricate such a transistor. However, it is often possible to obtain the desired operation from the interconnection of two transistors. In such a case, the two transistors are treated as though they are a single one. Such an interconnection is called a *compound transistor*.

To illustrate a compound transistor consider the configuration of Fig. 14-39. This is termed a *Darlington* connection or a *Darlington transistor*. The current $i_{B'}$, $i_{C'}$, and $i_{E'}$ are the "base," "emitter," and "collector" currents, respectively, for the compound transistor.

This compound transistor has an extremely high beta. Let us consider this. Writing currents for this circuit, we have

$$i_{C1} = \beta_{F1} i_{B1} = \beta_{F1} i_{B'} \tag{14-92a}$$

$$-i_{E1} = i_{B2} = i_{B1} + i_{C1} = (1 + \beta_{F1}) i_{B'} \tag{14-92b}$$

$$i_{C2} = \beta_{F2} i_{B2} = \beta_{F2}(1 + \beta_{F1}) i_{B'} \tag{14-92c}$$

$$i_{C'} = i_{C1} + i_{C2} = \beta_{F1} i_{B1} + \beta_{F2}(1 + \beta_{F1}) i_{B'} \tag{14-92d}$$

β_F for the compound transistor is given by $i_{C'}/i_{B'}$. Thus,

$$\beta_{F'} = \beta_{F1} + \beta_{F2} + \beta_{F1}\beta_{F2} \tag{14-93}$$

Thus, the Darlington transistor has a very high β_F. For instance, if $\beta_{F1} = \beta_{F2} = 100$, then $\beta_{F'} = 10{,}200$.

At times, external resistances are connected to "internal" leads of the compound transistor to provide bias. For instance, such a resistance could be connected to the base of Q_2.

Compound transistors can be used in either discrete or integrated circuits. Of course, they are especially attractive in integrated circuits where the addition of an extra transistor does not increase the size or cost appreciably.

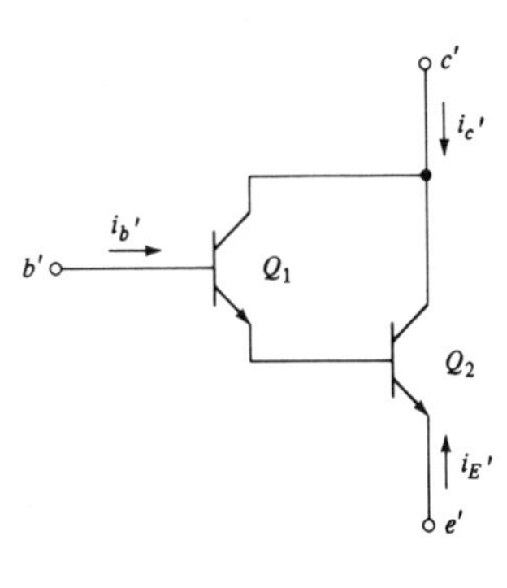

Figure 14-39. A Darlington compound transistor.

14-12. THE FREQUENCY RESPONSE OF OPERATIONAL AMPLIFIERS

Let us now consider procedures for obtaining the frequency response of operational amplifiers. In Chapter 12 we discussed the frequency response of various types (e.g., common-base, common-emitter, common-collector, common-source) of unbalanced amplifiers. These analyses can be directly applied to the single ended stages of the operational amplifier. However, we must develop results for the differential input stages and also for the output stage. In this analysis we shall utilize the aproximations developed in Chapter 12.

Let us start by considering the differential amplifier of Fig. 14-5a, where R_E is actually realized using a current source. We shall use the approximation to the hybrid-pi model which was developed in Chapter 12 and shown in Fig. 12-17b. We repeat it in Fig. 14-40 for convenience. The capacitor C_{sh} is given by (see Eq. 12-91)

$$C_{sh} = C_{b'e} + C_{b'c}\left(1 + \frac{R_{sh}}{R_p} + g_m R_{sh}\right) \tag{14-94}$$

Let us relate these quantities to the parameters of Fig. 14-5a. R_{sh} represents the parallel combination of r_{ce}, R_C, and any resistance connected to the output terminal. R_P is the parallel combination of $r_{bb'}$ and $r_{b'e}$.

The model of Fig. 14-40 is the same as the low-frequency model used in Fig. 14-5 except that $r_{b'e}$ is replaced by the parallel combination of $r_{b'e}$ and C_{sh}. Thus, to obtain the high-frequency response, we need only replace $r_{b'e}$ by $r_{b'e}/(1 + j\omega r_{b'e}C_{sh})$ in any analysis using the model of Fig. 14-5.

Let us now obtain the high-frequency response for the amplifier of Fig. 14-5. If we assume that the various approximations discussed in Sec. 14-2 are valid, then the output voltage can be obtained by modifying Eq. 14-22 as discussed. Doing this we have

$$\mathbf{V}_{o2} = \frac{\left(\dfrac{g_m r_{b'e}}{1 + j\omega r_{b'e}C_{sh}}\right)(\mathbf{V}_1 - \mathbf{V}_2)}{2\left(r_{bb'} + \dfrac{r_{b'e}}{1 + j\omega r_{b'e}C_{sh}}\right)\left(\dfrac{1}{R_C} + \dfrac{1}{r_{ce}}\right)}$$

Manipulating, we obtain

$$\mathbf{V}_{o2} = \frac{g_m r_{b'e}(\mathbf{V}_1 - \mathbf{V}_2)/[2(r_{bb'} + r_{b'e})(1/R_C + 1/r_{ce})]}{1 + j\omega[r_{bb'}r_{b'e}/(r_{bb'} + r_{b'e})]C_{sh}} \tag{14-95}$$

We can write this as

$$\mathbf{V}_{o2} = \mathbf{A}_v(\mathbf{V}_1 - \mathbf{V}_2)$$

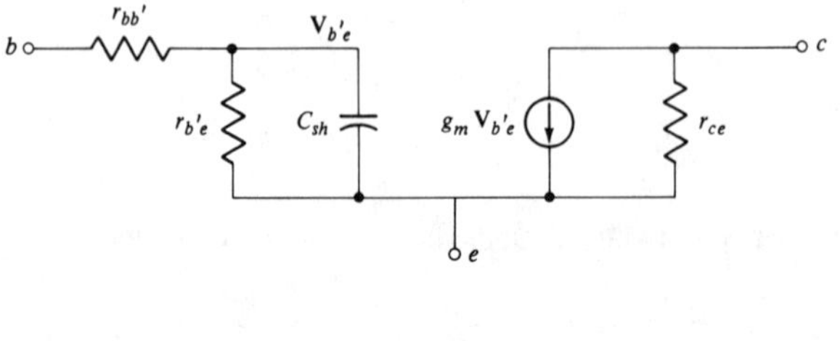

Figure 14-40. The model used in the high-frequency analysis of the operational amplifier.

Then,

$$\mathbf{A}_v = \frac{g_m r_{b'e} R_{\text{sh}}/2(r_{bb'} + r_{b'e})}{1 + j\omega R_P c_{\text{sh}}} \tag{14-96}$$

where

$$\frac{1}{R_{\text{sh}}} = \frac{1}{R_C} + \frac{1}{r_{ce}} \tag{14-97a}$$

and

$$\frac{1}{R_P} = \frac{1}{r_{bb'}} + \frac{1}{r_{b'e}} \tag{14-97b}$$

The mid- and low-frequency value of $\mathbf{A}_v$ is

$$\mathbf{A}_{v\,\text{mid}} = \frac{g_m R_{\text{sh}} r_{b'e}}{2(r_{bb'} + r_{b'e})} \tag{14-98}$$

and the normalized high-frequency response is

$$\frac{\mathbf{A}_{v\,\text{high}}}{\mathbf{A}_{v\,\text{mid}}} = \frac{1}{1 + j(f/f_2)} \tag{14-99}$$

where

$$f_2 = 1/2\pi R_P C_{\text{sh}} \tag{14-100}$$

If we compare these equations with Eqs. 12-85 and 12-92 to 12-94, we see that the midband gain of the common-emitter differential amplifier is one-half of that of the comparable differential amplifier and the normalized high-frequency response is identical. Of course, the analyses of this section assume that the approximations of Sec. 14-2 still hold. Some of these approximations are frequency dependent and will *not* hold over all frequencies. However, they usually are valid over frequencies of interest and, hence, the results obtained here are valid. Note that we have not considered the loading of this stage by a common-emitter stage. We shall see that this analysis follows that given in Sec. 12-5. In addition, as we have seen, the stage following the differential amplifier stage is often an emitter follower. Its loading can usually be ignored (see Sec. 12-13). If the differential amplifier is followed by a common-emitter stage then the analysis will follow that of Sec. 12-5.

Let us now consider another procedure that is very helpful when differential amplifiers are considered. The response of a differential amplifier is proportional to $(\mathbf{V}_1 - \mathbf{V}_2)$. For purposes of analysis, instead of assuming that two independent signals are applied to the inverting and noninverting inputs, let us assume that $(\mathbf{V}_1 - \mathbf{V}_2)/2$ is applied to the inverting input and that $(\mathbf{V}_2 - \mathbf{V}_1)/2$ is applied to the noninverting input. The difference between the two inputs is $\mathbf{V}_1 - \mathbf{V}_2$ as before so that the output should be ideally unchanged. However, we shall now demonstrate that the models and analyses are greatly simplified when these special inputs are applied.

The model for a typical differential amplifier is shown in Fig. 14-41a. If we assume that the approximations of Sec. 14-2 are valid, then V_E is one-half the sum of the two input signals. Hence,

$$\mathbf{V}_E = \frac{1}{2}\left[\frac{\mathbf{V}_1 - \mathbf{V}_2}{2} + \frac{\mathbf{V}_2 - \mathbf{V}_1}{2}\right] = 0 \tag{14-101}$$

Since $\mathbf{V}_E = 0$ there is no current through R_E. Hence, we can replace it with any value resistance *without changing any of the voltages and currents in the remainder of the circuit.* Let us then replace it by a short circuit. In this case, the model can be redrawn as shown in Fig. 14-41b. Now the two halves of the circuit are decoupled. That is, these are two isolated models. Each of these models is essentially the same as that for a conventional common-emitter stage, except that the input voltage is $(\mathbf{V}_1 - \mathbf{V}_2)/2$ or $(\mathbf{V}_2 - \mathbf{V}_1)/2$.

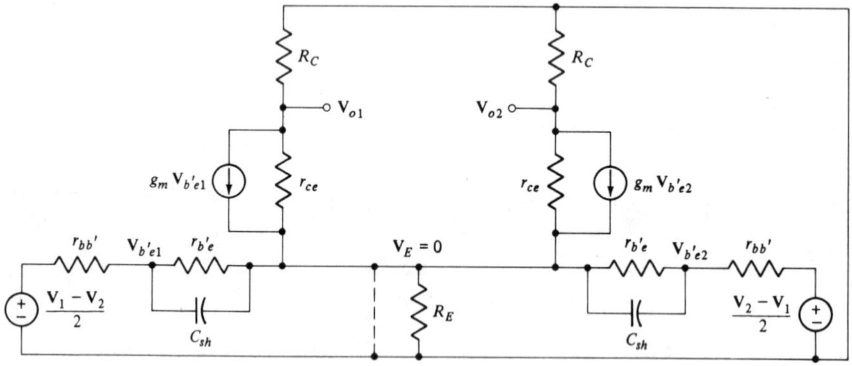

(a)

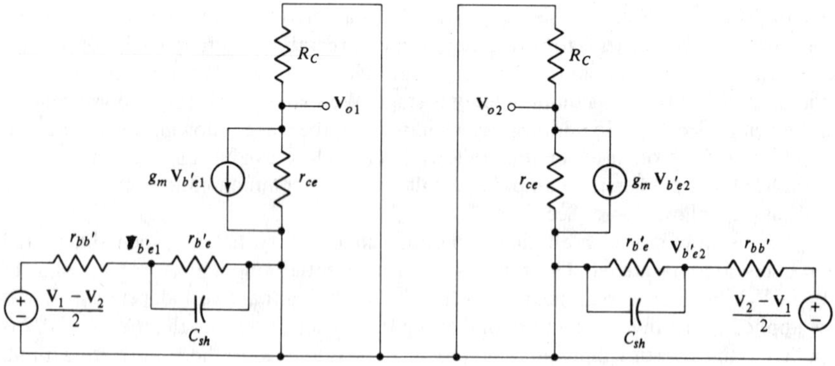

(b)

Figure 14-41. (a) A model for a differential amplifier with special inputs. (b) The model broken into two isolated models.

Thus, we can now apply the pertinent calculations and results of Chapter 12 to differential amplifiers.

If we use the model of Fig. 14-41b to obtain the mid- and high-frequency responses of the differential amplifier, the results of Eqs. 14-96 to 14-100 are obtained. This indicates that this model is as accurate as the previously obtained one. This procedure of analyzing a differential amplifier as a single ended amplifier with one input of $\pm(\mathbf{V}_1 - \mathbf{V}_2)/2$ can also be applied to FET differential amplifiers.

Let us now consider the analysis of the output stages. We can approximate the typical output as two push-pull class B emitter follower stages driving the load. That is, in this approximation, one emitter follower is on for exactly one-half of the cycle and the other one is on for exactly the other half cycle. Thus, in the linear analysis of the gain and frequency response, we can assume that the output is a single-emitter following stage.

Analysis of Complete Operational Amplifiers

When the complete operational amplifier is analyzed, then we can utilize the models and results developed in Chapter 12. Thus, the response will be that of a cascade of common-emitter and emitter follower stages. Therefore, the normalized frequency response of a typical operational amplifier will be of the form

$$\frac{\mathbf{A}_{v\,\text{high}}}{\mathbf{A}_{v\,\text{mid}}} = \frac{1}{(1 + jf/f_{21})(1 + jf/f_{22}) \cdots (1 + jf/f_{2n})} \tag{14-102}$$

A sketch of $|\mathbf{A}_{v\,\text{high}}/\mathbf{A}_{v\,\text{mid}}|_{\text{dB}}$ is shown in Fig. 14-42. We have assumed here that there are four effective stages. The pole zero diagram (see Sec. 12-12) for this amplifier is shown in Fig. 14-43.

Note that there are additional effects that, at times, must be considered. For example, the typical emitter follower has a low output impedance. Hence the input capacitance of the next stage will not seriously affect the response unless very high frequencies are used. However, consider Q_7 of Fig. 14-37. It is an emitter follower but its

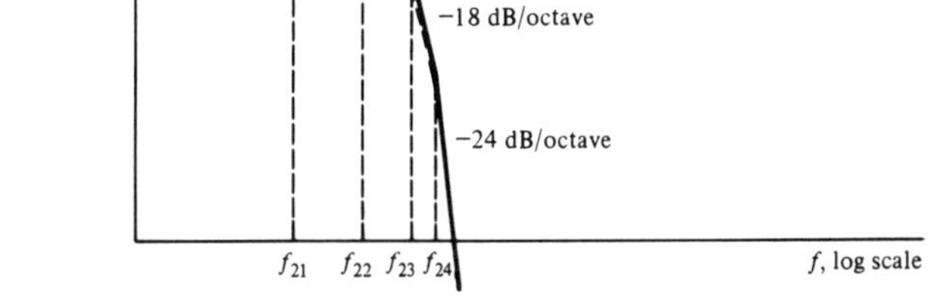

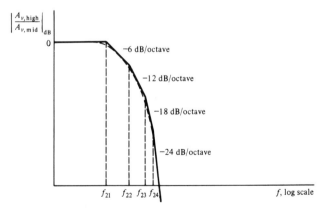

Figure 14-42. A plot of $|\mathbf{A}_{v\,\text{high}}/\mathbf{A}_{v\,\text{mid}}|_{\text{dB}}$ for a four-stage operational amplifier.

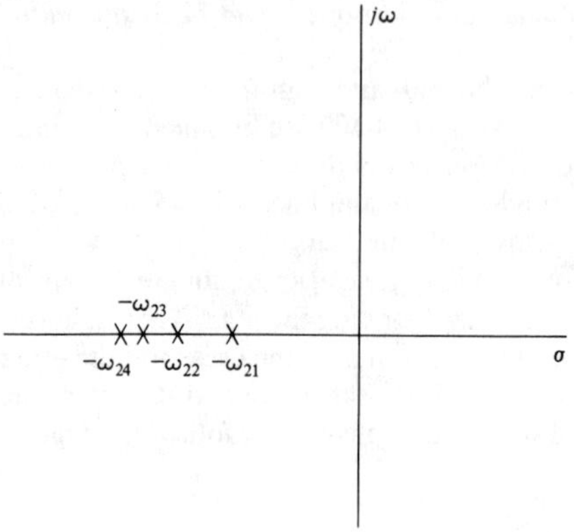

Figure 14-43. A pole-zero diagram for the amplifier whose frequency response is given in Fig. 14-42.

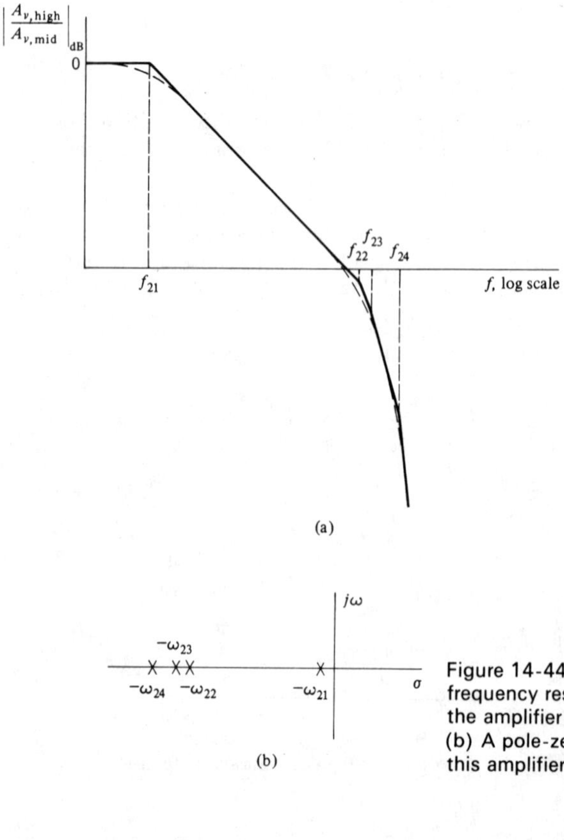

Figure 14-44. (a) A frequency response plot for the amplifier of Eq. 14-103. (b) A pole-zero diagram for this amplifier.

output impedance is increased by the presence of R_3. Since R_3 is large, the effective output impedance of the emitter follower will be high and the capacitive loading of the next stage can seriously affect the (high) frequency response at much lower frequencies.

There are many operational amplifiers wherein one of the upper half-power frequencies is very much less than all the others. For instance, suppose that

$$\frac{\mathbf{A}_{v\,\mathrm{high}}}{\mathbf{A}_{v\,\mathrm{mid}}} = \frac{1}{(1 + jf/f_{21})(1 + jf/f_{22})(1 + jf/f_{23})(1 + jf/f_{24})} \tag{14-103}$$

where

$$f_{21} \ll f_{22} \tag{14-104a}$$

$$f_{21} \ll f_{23} \tag{14-104b}$$

$$f_{21} \ll f_{24} \tag{14-104c}$$

Then the frequency response plot and pole-zero diagram will be as shown in Fig. 14-44. For most frequencies of interest (where the gain is appreciable)

$$\frac{\mathbf{A}_{v\,\mathrm{high}}}{\mathbf{A}_{v\,\mathrm{mid}}} \simeq \frac{1}{1 + jf/f_{21}} \tag{14-105}$$

The pole zero diagram for this amplifier is shown in Fig. 14-44b. One pole is much closer to the $j\omega$ axis than all the others so it dominates the frequency response (see Sec. 12-12). When a single pole dominates in this way, it is termed a *dominant pole.* In the next section we shall see how such dominant poles are established in operational amplifiers.

14-13. SLEWING RATE

Thus far in this chapter and in Chapter 12 we have considered frequency and/or transient response on a linear basis. For instance, we did not consider the effects of saturation or cutoff. In this section we shall discuss the effects of nonlinearities. In addition, we shall present a procedure that is, at times, used to establish a single dominant pole in operational amplifiers (see Sec. 14-12).

Let us start by considering the representation for an operational amplifier shown in Fig. 14-45a. We have broken the amplifier up into two subamplifiers, which provide the voltage gains $\mathbf{A}_{v1}$ and $\mathbf{A}_{v2}$. It is assumed that a capacitor C has been added as shown. This causes the input capacitance of the second "stage" to become (see Eq. 13-62).

$$C_{\mathrm{in}} = C(1 + \mathbf{A}_{v2}) \tag{14-106}$$

Since $\mathbf{A}_{v2}$ will, in general, be a large negative number, C_{in} will be very large.

Now let us calculate v_o. The model we shall use is shown in Fig. 14-45b. This will be used to obtain the voltage v_a. The output voltage is $\mathbf{A}_v = v_o$. The resistance r_o is the output resistance of the first "stage." The capacitance C can be actually incorporated within the integrated circuit chip although, at times, it is added externally. It may appear to be poor design to incorporate such a capacitance since it degrades the high-frequency response of the amplifier. From many viewpoints, it is poor design. However, as we shall see in Chapter 16 where we discuss feedback amplifiers, the incorporation of such

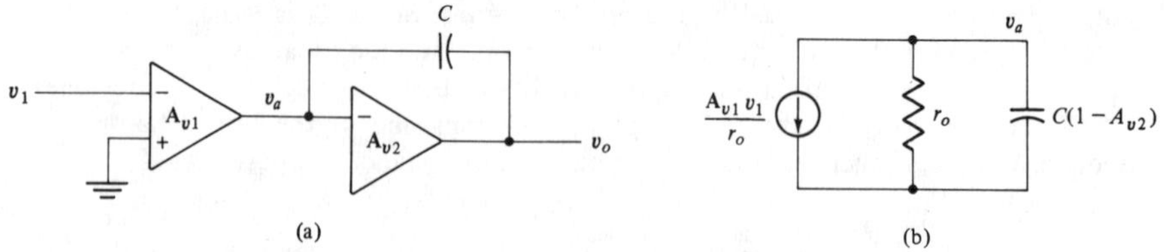

Figure 14-45. (a) A representation of a particular operational amplifier. (b) A model used to calculate V_a.

a capacitor that introduces a single dominant pole simplifies feedback amplifier design for those who are unfamiliar with its details.

The effect of shunt capacitance on frequency and transient response has been studied in Chapter 12. We shall now take some of the nonlinearities into account. All the stages of the amplifier will affect both the frequency and transient response, but since C_{in} is so large, its effect will predominate. Thus a dominant pole has been introduced. Therefore, when we consider the frequency or transient response, the only capacitor that we need consider is C_{in}.

We shall now obtain a quantity called the *slewing rate* or the *slew rate* ρ_s. This is defined as the maximum slope that the step response can have.

Proceeding as in Sec. 12-15 and using Fig. 14-45b we have, for the step response

$$v_a = -\mathrm{A}_{v1} V_i(1 - e^{-t/r_o C_{in}}) \tag{14-107}$$

Note that the input is

$$v_i(t) = V_i u(t) \tag{14-108}$$

As before, $u(t)$ represents the unit step. Then $v_0 = -\mathrm{A}_{v2} V_a$. Hence,

$$v_o = \mathrm{A}_{v1}\mathrm{A}_{v2} V_i(1 - e^{-t/r_o C_{in}}) \tag{14-109}$$

Then,

$$\frac{dv_o}{dt} = \frac{\mathrm{A}_{v1}\mathrm{A}_{v2} V_i}{r_o C_{in}} e^{-t/r_o C_{in}} \tag{14-110}$$

The maximum value of the slope occurs at $t = 0$ and is

$$\left.\frac{dv_o}{dt}\right|_{max} = \frac{\mathrm{A}_{v1}\mathrm{A}_{v2} V_i}{r_o C_{in}} \tag{14-111}$$

It appears as though this result can be made as large as desired simply by increasing V_i. As long as the amplifier functions linearly, this is true. However, all amplifiers will saturate, or cut off, when their input signal becomes large enough. Let us assume that the saturation occurs in the $\mathbf{A}_{v1}$ subamplifier. We shall represent it in the following way. The current generator $\mathrm{A}_{v1} v_1/r_o$ will linearly vary with v_1 until the current $\mathrm{A}_{v1} v_1/r_o$ becomes I_{max}. It will then increase no further. In other words, I_{max} defines the saturation value of the output current of the first subamplifier. Under the conditions of saturation, the term $A_{v1}V_i/r_o$ in Eq. 14-110 or 14-111 must be replaced by I_{max}. Hence, the maximum value of $dv_o/dt|_{max}$ is

$$\rho_s = \frac{I_{max}A_{v2}}{C_{in}} \tag{14-112}$$

This is then the slewing rate of the amplifier. Its units are volts per second or volts per microsecond.

The slewing rate is a measure of the maximum rate at which an amplifier can be driven from saturation to cutoff. For instance, if an operational amplifier is used as a comparator, it cannot switch instantaneously. If the output changes from $-V_A$ to V_A, then the time required for this to occur is greater than T where

$$T = 2V_A\rho_s \tag{14-113}$$

The slewing rate also affects the sinusoidal steady state response of the amplifier. For instance, if

$$v_i = V_{i,\,max}\sin\omega t$$

then, on a phasor basis

$$\mathbf{V}_a = -\frac{A_{v1}V_{i,\,max}}{1 + j\omega C_{in}r_o} \tag{14-114}$$

or, equivalently,

$$|\mathbf{V}_{a,\,max}| = \frac{A_{v1}V_{i,\,max}}{\sqrt{1 + \omega^2C_{in}^2r_o^2}} \tag{14-115}$$

The current supplied by the A_{v1} amplifier cannot exceed I_{max}. Any attempt to make it do this will result in clipping of the signal. Hence, the magnitude of Eq. 14-115 is limited. Its maximum value is obtained by substituting I_{max} for $A_v V_{1\,max}/r_o$. Hence,

$$|V_{o,\,max}|_{max} = \frac{A_{v2}I_{max}r_o}{\sqrt{1 + \omega^2C_{in}^2r_o^2}} \tag{14-116}$$

Note that this value falls off with frequency. Thus, if we are not to distort (clip) the output signal, the maximum allowable input signal is limited and this value falls off with frequency. Often, when we consider such limits, the frequency is high enough so that

$$\omega^2C_{in}^2r_o^2 \gg 1 \tag{14-117}$$

In this case, Eq. 14-116 becomes

$$|V_{o,\,max}|_{max} = \frac{\rho_s}{\omega} \tag{14-118}$$

Thus, the maximum value of the peak value of an undistorted output sinusoidal signal varies directly with the slewing rate and inversely with frequency. Hence, the signal levels must be reduced if the frequency is increased. Therefore it is important to know the slewing rate if we are to operate at high frequencies.

We have approximated the operational amplifier by the model of Fig. 14-45. In many cases such a dominant pole approximation is valid. If it is not, then the response of all the individual stages must be considered in determining the frequency and transient response. In addition, the saturation of the amplifier can take place in several stages simultaneously. In such cases, the computation of the slewing rate becomes an extremely complex procedure. Its relation to linear high-frequency behavior is similarly complex. Manufacturers often specify slewing rate based upon experimentally determined measurements.

14-14. COMMON MODE PROBLEMS

The output of an ideal operational amplifier is

$$\mathbf{V}_o = \mathbf{A}_v(\mathbf{V}_2 - \mathbf{V}_1)$$

but in practice, this is not exactly achieved. The output can be characterized by

$$\mathbf{V}_o = \mathbf{A}_2 V_2 - \mathbf{A}_1\mathbf{V}_1 \tag{14-119}$$

where $\mathbf{A}_1$ and $\mathbf{A}_2$ are *not* exactly equal. For instance, the analysis of Sec. 14-2 illustrates this. Actually, in many of our analyses we have made approximations that result in $\mathbf{A}_2$ and $\mathbf{A}_1$ being equal, but if these approximations were not made, then this would not be the case. In addition, in all our previous analyses we have assumed that the two "halves" of the differential amplifier were identical. Of course, this is not exactly true. For instance, the two transistors may have different values of g_m. This is another reason that $\mathbf{A}_1 \neq \mathbf{A}_2$. In general, $\mathbf{A}_1$ and $\mathbf{A}_2$ will be approximately, *but not exactly*, equal. Thus, when signals are applied to both the inverting and noninverting inputs, the output will be somewhat in error.

Let us see how we can characterize this error. Let us write

$$\mathbf{V}_o = \mathbf{A}_d(\mathbf{V}_2 - \mathbf{V}_1) + \mathbf{A}_{\text{cm}}(\mathbf{A}_2 + \mathbf{A}_1) \tag{14-120}$$

where

$$\mathbf{A}_d = (\mathbf{A}_2 + \mathbf{A}_1)/2 \tag{14-121a}$$

and

$$\mathbf{A}_{\text{cm}} = (\mathbf{A}_2 - \mathbf{A}_1)/2 \tag{14-121b}$$

Ideally,

$$\mathbf{A}_{\text{cm}} = 0 \tag{14-122a}$$

and

$$\mathbf{A}_d = \mathbf{A}_v \tag{14-122b}$$

$\mathbf{A}_{\text{cm}}$ is called the *common mode* gain while $\mathbf{A}_d$ is called the *differential mode* gain. It is desirable that $\mathbf{A}_d \gg \mathbf{A}_{\text{cm}}$. For instance, suppose that we are using an operational amplifier to detect the null of a bridge (see Figs. 13-9 and 13-10). If $\mathbf{A}_{\text{cm}} \neq 0$, then an error in the location of the null will occur since there will be an output when $\mathbf{V}_2 = \mathbf{V}_1$. To characterize the difference between $\mathbf{A}_1$ and $\mathbf{A}_2$ a quantity called the *common mode rejection ratio* ρ_{cm} or CMRR is defined. It is

$$\text{CMRR} = \rho_{\text{cm}} = \left|\frac{\mathbf{A}_d}{\mathbf{A}_{\text{cm}}}\right| \tag{14-123}$$

Often, this is expressed in decibels.

$$\text{CMRR}_{\text{dB}} = \rho_{\text{cmdB}} = 20 \log_{10}\left|\frac{\mathbf{A}_d}{\mathbf{A}_{\text{cm}}}\right| \tag{14-124}$$

This is usually a large number, exceeding 50 dB or more.

As an example of the importance of the common mode rejection ratio, let us see how a finite value of ρ_{cm} unbalances the amplifier of Fig. 13-8. Proceeding as in Sec. 13-4 we have

$$\frac{\mathbf{V}_{i1} - \mathbf{V}_1}{R_1} = \frac{\mathbf{V}_1 - \mathbf{V}_o}{R_2} \tag{14-125}$$

$$\mathbf{V}_o = \mathbf{A}_d(\mathbf{V}_2 - \mathbf{V}_1) + \mathbf{A}_{\text{cm}}(\mathbf{V}_2 + \mathbf{V}_1) \tag{14-126}$$

and

$$\mathbf{V}_2 = \mathbf{V}_{i2}\frac{R_4}{R_3 + R_4} \tag{14-127}$$

Manipulating these expressions, we obtain

$$\frac{\mathbf{V}_{i1}}{R_1} - \frac{\mathbf{V}_{i2}}{R_1}\left(\frac{\mathbf{A}_d/\mathbf{A}_{\text{cm}} + 1}{\mathbf{A}_d/\mathbf{A}_{\text{cm}} - 1}\right)\left(\frac{1 + R_1/R_2}{1 + R_3/R_4}\right) = -\frac{\mathbf{V}_o}{R_2}\left[1 + \frac{1}{\mathbf{A}_d - \mathbf{A}_{\text{cm}}}\left(1 + \frac{R_2}{R_1}\right)\right] \tag{14-128}$$

In general,

$$1 \gg \left|\frac{1}{\mathbf{A}_d - \mathbf{A}_{\text{cm}}}\left(1 + \frac{R_2}{R_1}\right)\right| \tag{14-129}$$

Hence,

$$\mathbf{V}_o = \frac{R_2}{R_1}\left[\mathbf{V}_{i2}\left(\frac{\rho_{\text{cm}} + 1}{\rho_{\text{cm}} - 1}\right)\left(\frac{1 + R_1/R_2}{1 + R_3/R_4}\right) - \mathbf{V}_{i1}\right] \tag{14-130}$$

Note that the approximation made due to inequality 14-129 only affects the magnitude of the overall gain, whereas ρ_{cm} affects the difference between the gain $\mathbf{A}_2$ and $\mathbf{A}_1$. Since this affects the difference between two signals that may be nearly equal, it is often more important. If we set

$$\frac{R_1}{R_2} = \frac{R_3}{R_4}$$

then Eq. 14-130 becomes

$$\mathbf{V}_o = -\frac{R_2}{R_1}\left[\mathbf{V}_{i1} - \frac{\rho_{\text{cm}} + 1}{\rho_{\text{cm}} - 1}\mathbf{V}_{i2}\right] \tag{14-131}$$

The error in the output is thus $(\rho_{cm} + 1)/(\rho_{cm} - 1)$. It may seem as though this error could be reduced to zero simply by adjusting the ratio R_1/R_2 and R_3/R_4. However, ρ_{cm} will vary slightly from amplifier to amplifier, depending upon the imbalance in the component values. If we wish to make very accurate measurements on the amplifier and use expensive precision resistors, then this error can be cancelled. On the other hand, if we do not make this measurement, then the common mode error cannot be cancelled in this way. Let us do an example to illustrate the size of this error.

Example

An amplifier has a common mode rejection ratio of 50 dB. Compute the error indicated by Eq. 14-131 if $R_1/R_2 = R_3/R_4$.

$$20 \log_{10} \rho_{cm} = 50$$

$$\rho_{cm} = 316.23$$

Then,

$$\frac{\rho_{cm} + 1}{\rho_{cm} - 1} = 1.0063$$

Hence,

$$\mathbf{V}_o = -\frac{R_2}{R_1}(\mathbf{V}_{i1} - 1.006\mathbf{V}_{i2})$$

The error computed in this example may or may not be significant. For instance, if a very accurate null is needed, the error is significant. Then an operational amplifier with a higher common mode rejection ratio could be chosen or the values of R_3 and R_4 should be carefully adjusted to eliminate the differences in $\mathbf{A}_1$ and $\mathbf{A}_2$. On the other hand, if we use the circuit to mix (combine) two audio signals, then the error is insignificant and can be ignored.

14-15. OFFSET PROBLEMS

In an ideal operational amplifier, if the input voltages are zero or are equal, then the output voltage v_o should be zero. However, in general, there will be departures from this ideal case. For instance, the output may not be zero when the inputs are open circuited. In addition, the v_o may vary with time even though $v_1 = v_2$ or $v_1 = v_2 = 0$. For instance, suppose that the inputs are shorted to ground; the output voltage may be zero and then start to slowly drift about this value. We shall consider such effects in this section.

Input Bias Current

As we discussed in Sec. 14-4, there will be an input bias current with junction transistor input stages. For typical operational amplifiers, each input current is in the range of 10–100 nA (10×10^{-9} to 100×10^{-9} A). This bias current will be in the impedance connected to the input terminal. This is illustrated in Fig. 14-46. We have not shown any

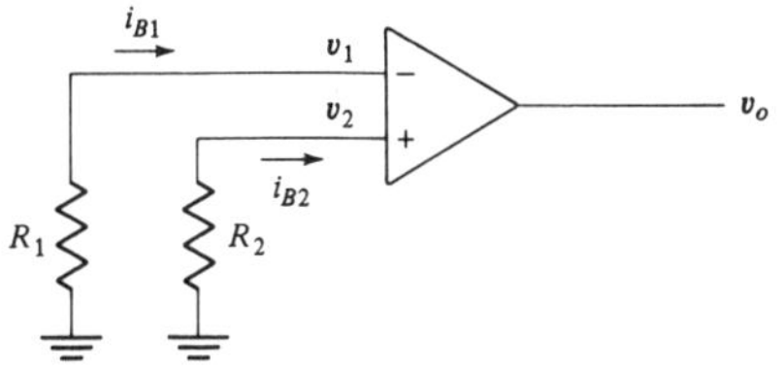

Figure 14-46. An illustration of input bias currents.

external generators in this circuit since we are only concerned with the effects of the bias at this time. Thus,

$$v_1 = -i_{B1}R_1 \tag{14-132a}$$

$$v_2 = -i_{B2}R_2 \tag{14-132b}$$

In an ideal case if

$$R_1 = R_2$$

and $i_{B1} = i_{B2}$, then $v_1 = v_2$ and the output voltage v_o will not be affected. On the other hand, if $R_1 \neq R_2$ and $i_{B1} = i_{B2}$, then an undesired component of voltage will appear in the output. Often, we can make $R_1 = R_2$ so that, if $i_{B1} = i_{B2}$, the input bias currents do not produce a component of output.

The effects of input bias currents can be reduced by reducing them beyond their already low values. For instance, if JFET's are used in the input stage, then the bias currents will be in the range 1×10^{-12} to 1×10^{-12} A. The use of MOSFET inputs reduces the input currents to negligible values.

We have assumed that if $v_1 = v_2$ then $v_o = 0$. Actually, because of common mode problems (see Sec. 14-14), this is not exactly the case. Hence, even if $R_1 = R_2$ there will usually be a small direct component of v_o. Often, this is small and can be ignored. However, in some circuits, even an extremely small direct component causes trouble. Consider the integrator of Fig. 13-16. If v_o is a nonzero value, however small, the circuit functions as though there is a small input, the integral of which can eventually become large. Thus, eventually, there may be a large error component in the output.

Offset Currents

We have thus far assumed that both input bias currents are equal. Although this is approximately true, it is not exact since both input transistors are not identical. Such differences in currents are termed offsets. The *input offset current* is defined as

$$i_{os} = i_{B1} - i_{B2} \tag{14-133}$$

Thus, the input offset current results in an additional component of output voltage.

Usually only a single value of input bias current is specified for an operational amplifier. This is the average of i_{B1} and i_{B2}.

Offset Voltage

We have thus far discussed the component of output voltage that is due to bias currents. However, even if we make R_1 and R_2 zero (see Fig. 14-46), there may still be a component

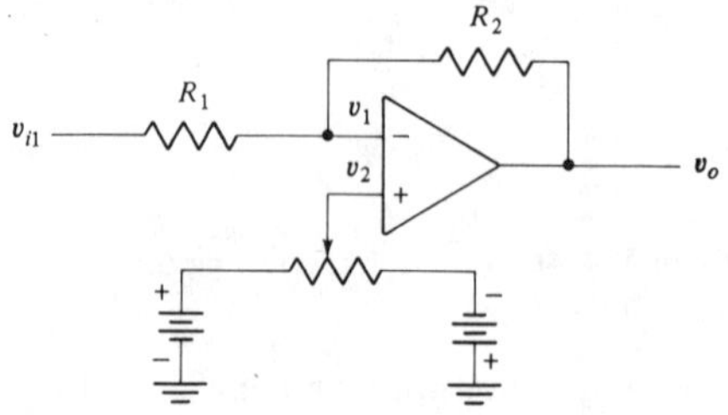

Figure 14-47. A circuit that can be used to cancel static offsets.

of output voltage. This is due to imbalances within the differential amplifier(s) and is termed an *output offset voltage.* We can assume that it is caused by a fictitious input voltage. For instance, if the operational amplifier has a voltage gain $\mathbf{A}_v = 10{,}000$ and the offset output voltage is 0.1 V, then we can assume that the fictitious input that caused this output is $0.1/10{,}000 = 10^{-5}$ V. This is termed the *input offset voltage.*

All of the effects that we have considered in this section result in a direct component appearing in the output voltage v_o. Let us assume, for the time being, that it does not vary with time. In such cases we can cancel this constant output voltage by applying an appropriate input signal. For instance, consider Fig. 14-47 where we have a simple inverting amplifier. The variable resistor and power supply are used to vary v_2 in both magnitude and polarity. This voltage can be adjusted until $v_o = 0$ (with $v_{c1} = 0$). The undesired direct component of output voltage is thus eliminated.

The circuit of Fig. 14-47 suffers from several practical disadvantages. First the value of v_2 needed to null the output voltage is extremely small so it often becomes difficult to adjust R. In addition, the noninverting terminal cannot then be used for signal inputs. To eliminate this, manufacturers often supply an extra terminal where an offset correcting voltage can be applied. This changes a bias of one of the later (i.e., not input) stages of the amplifier. At this point, the gain to the output is reduced so larger, more easily adjustable voltages can be used.

The procedures that we have discussed usually satisfactorily eliminate offset problems. However, there is a complexity that arises. All the effects that we have discussed depend, to some extent, upon temperature and power supply voltage. Then, they drift with time, Thus, the output offset voltage will not remain cancelled. These effects are small and often can be ignored but there are certain critical cases where they cannot. For instance, consider the integrator discussed at the beginning of this section where even an extremely small output voltage can be troublesome. There are special high-quality operational amplifiers where great attention is paid to bias stabilization. Such amplifiers are used in very critical applications. In such cases, the bias stabilization procedures discussed in this chapter and in Chapter 5 are used to ensure that all drifts are kept to an absolute minimum.

14-16. LATCH UP

When excessively large input signals are applied to an amplifier, the active devices (e.g., transistors or FET's) can be driven into either their saturation or cutoff regions. When this occurs, the amplifier no longer functions properly. When the excessive signal is

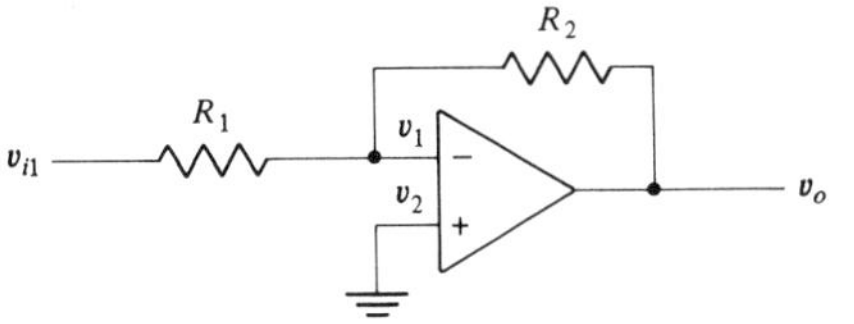

Figure 14-48. A simple operational amplifier feedback circuit.

removed, however, the voltages return to normal and the amplifier again functions properly. (Note that this will not happen instantaneously since amplifiers do not respond instantaneously.)

When the amplifier is used in a feedback configuration, which is typical for an operational amplifier, the situation is more complex. For instance, consider Fig. 14-48. Suppose that v_{i1} is a large positive signal that saturates the amplifier. v_o will be negative and the signal fed back through R_2 will reduce v_1 and tends to eliminate the condition. Of course, if v_{i1} is large enough, the amplifier will still saturate. This type of feedback is called *negative feedback* since the fed back signal is out-of-phase with the input signal.

Suppose that the feedback and input were applied to the noninverting input. This is called *positive feedback*. Now a positive input signal would result in a positive value of v_o and the signal fed back would also be positive. If it were large enough, it would keep the amplifier saturated. Thus, the amplifier would never recover even if the input signal were removed.

It may seem as though the situation just discussed would never occur since the feedback is usually from the output to the inverting terminal. However, this may not be the case. Suppose that one amplifier stage saturates. It no longer functions as an amplifier and signals are just fed through it as though it were a passive element (e.g., a resistor). Assume that the amplifier stage produced a phase inversion. This phase inversion will now be missing. This is equivalent to multiplying the gain of the amplifier by minus unity. Hence, the inverting terminal becomes the noninverting one and vice versa. We now have the positive feedback situation just described and the amplifier may not recover. In this case, a *latch up* is said to have occurred. In general, a latched up amplifier can only be returned to normal operation by turning off the power supply for a short time. Latch up will not always occur for several reasons. The saturation may occur in a stage that does not introduce phase inversion (e.g., an emitter follower). Also, when saturation occurs, the gain of the amplifier decreases greatly and there may not be enough gain to sustain the latch up. In an integrated circuit operational amplifier, latch up is usually caused by a more complex condition. Sometimes, under saturation conditions, there are local feedback loops set up. These are due to parasitic transistors that are "accidentally" established between *p*- and *n*-type regions and the substrate. This local positive feedback results in latch up. Most operational amplifiers are now fabricated in such a way that the parasitic transistors that cause latch up are not introduced. Therefore, operational amplifiers are not subject to latch up under most operating conditions.

14-17. OPERATIONAL AMPLIFIER SPECIFICATIONS

Manufacturers supply data sheets to provide the operational amplifier user with much pertinent information. Some of this data are supplied as maximum ratings. If these ratings are exceeded, the circuit's life may be shortened or the circuit may be destroyed. Other data describes the performance of the operational amplifier. In this section we shall consider the information given by the data sheets.

Maximum Ratings

We shall start by discussing the maximum ratings.

Power Supply Voltage. The maximum magnitudes of the power supply voltages are given. Remember that most operational amplifiers use two power supplies, one positive with respect to ground and the other negative. Both of these values are given.

Differential Input Voltage. The maximum value of $\mathbf{V}_1 - \mathbf{V}_2$ is specified here. Often this is given in terms of the actual (not rated) power supply voltages.

Absolute Input Voltage. The maximum values of $\mathbf{V}_1$ and $\mathbf{V}_2$ are specified. Again, this is often supplied in terms of the actual power supply voltages.

Duration of Output Short Circuit. This rating gives the maximum time that the output can be short-circuited to ground if the circuit is not to be destroyed. Most operational amplifiers have protected outputs so that this time is unlimited. Often, this information is also given for a short circuit between output and either power supply. This time too is often unlimited because of the protective circuits.

Power Dissipation. The maximum average power dissipation within the integrated circuit chip is given. At times, different types of external packaging are used for the same type of chip. One factor that determines temperature rise and, hence, the allowed power dissipation, is the type of package used. If manufacturers supply a particular operational amplifier with various types of packaging, then several power dissipation ratings will be given. We shall discuss this in greater detail in Sec. 15-9.

Storage and Installation Temperatures. There are ratings given which do not directly apply to operation. For instance, the maximum allowable storage temperatures are given. Similarly, the maximum allowable lead temperature during soldering is given. A maximum time for the application of this soldering temperature is also given.

Electrical Characteristics

The following specifications describe the operation of the operational amplifier but they are not maximum ratings (e.g., they do not specify maximum voltages). These quantities will vary between different samples of the same amplifier. Thus, manufacturers usually specify three numbers for each value. One gives the *typical* value encountered, while the other two specify the *maximum* and *minimum* values.

Large-Signal Voltage Amplification or Open Loop Gain. This specifies the voltage gain $\mathbf{A}_v$ for the operational amplifier. The low-frequency value is specified.

Input Offset Voltage. This gives the direct voltage that must be applied between the inverting and noninverting terminals to make the output voltage zero. Note that this is not an exact value but is a typical, or maximum one.

Average Temperature Coefficient of the Input Offset Voltage. The offset voltage will vary with the ambient temperature (see Sec. 14-15). The temperature coefficient provides an indication of how much it will change. The average temperature coefficient is defined as

$$\alpha_{VOF} = \frac{V_{OF}(T_1) - V_{OF}(T_2)}{T_1 - T_2} \tag{14-134}$$

where $V_{OF}(T_1)$ is the offset voltage at ambient temperature T_1, and so forth. The temperatures T_1 and T_2 are the limits of the allowed ambient temperature range. Temperature coefficients are often defined on a differential basis. For instance, we could write

$$\alpha'_{VOF}(T) = \frac{dV_{OF}}{dT} = \lim_{T_2 \to T_1} \frac{V_{OF}(T_1) - V_{OF}(T_2)}{T_1 - T_2} \tag{14-135}$$

α'_{VOF} is the slope of the curve of V_{OF} versus T and is a function of temperature. Normally, the average α_{VOF} as specified by Eq. 14-134 is given.

Input Offset Current. This is the magnitude of the difference between the currents into the inverting and noninverting terminals when the output voltage is zero (see Sec. 14-15). This is not an exact value but a typical or maximum value.

Average Temperature Coefficient of Input Offset Current. This is defined in a manner that is analogous to Eq. 14-134, and is

$$\alpha_{IOF} = \frac{I_{OF}(T_1) - I_{OF}(T_2)}{T_1 - T_2} \tag{14-136}$$

Input Bias Current. This is the average current into the inverting and noninverting terminals when $v_o = 0$.

Common Mode Rejection Ratio. This is the ratio of $\mathbf{A}_d = \mathbf{A}_v$ to $\mathbf{A}_{\text{cm}}$ as defined in Sec. 14-14.

Input Resistance. This is the resistance measured into either of the input terminals with the other terminal grounded.

Maximum Output Voltage. This gives the maximum limits of output voltage swing if there is to be no clipping of the output signal. This is usually specified as a low-frequency value (see Eq. 14-118). It is often defined in terms of the power supply voltage(s).

Slewing Rate. This is the maximum rate at which v_o can change with time (see Sec. 14-13).

Transient Response. The 10–90% rise time is specified. It is assumed that the amplifier is operated linearly. This figure will vary with the external circuitry of the amplifier. For instance (see Fig. 14-48), it will vary with R_1 and R_2. Some manufacturers specify this figure for a variety of values of R_1 and R_2.

Power Supply Sensitivity. This represents the (average) ratio of the change in input offset voltage to the change in power supply voltage. Some manufacturers supply two sensitivities, one for a change in the positive power supply voltage, assuming that the negative power supply is held constant, and the other for a change in the negative power supply voltage assuming that the positive power supply voltage is held constant. Other manufacturers only supply a single figure, which assumes that both power supplies vary simultaneously. These figures provide the designer with an idea of how stable the power supplies need be.

Other Data

In addition to the data that we have discussed, other material is supplied in the manufacturers' data sheets. Let us consider this.

Terminal Connections. The operational amplifier chip is encased in a plastic or ceramic package. The external leads are connected to pins on the package. These pins are specified and numbered. For instance, pins that connect to the inputs $\mathbf{V}_1$ and $\mathbf{V}_2$, the power supply inputs V_{CC}^+ and V_{EE}^-, and the ground connection are given. In addition, other special terminals such as those for offset correction, are indicated. This information is often supplied in the form of a diagram and is called the *pinout*.

Schematic Diagram. The actual circuit configuration, such as that of Fig. 14-37, is also given. This allows the user of the amplifier to understand its actual configuration.

Other Material. In addition to the material discussed, manufacturers also supply additional information such as curves that indicate the frequency response of the amplifier.

Design Information. Manufacturers also supply typical operational amplifier circuits. This information can provide the circuit designer with useful information. For instance, the appropriate circuitry, including element values, used to cancel effects of offset voltages and bias currents are given. Circuits for typical applications are also supplied.

Operational amplifiers are usually used in feedback configurations. These circuits may oscillate, which can prevent them from functioning properly. (In Chapter 16 we shall study this in detail.) The inclusion of appropriate circuitry can stabilize an oscillating circuit. Operational amplifier chips are often manufactured with terminals provided so that such stabilizing circuits can be connected externally. The data sheet often gives typical values for these stabilizing circuits. Note that such stabilization is only applicable in simple cases, usually where large bandwidth is not required.

Amplifiers

LH0024/LH0024C high slew rate operational amplifier

general description

The LH0024/LH0024C is a very wide bandwidth, high slew rate operational amplifier intended to fulfill a wide variety of high speed applications such as buffers to A to D and D to A converters and high speed comparators. The device exhibits useful gain in excess of 50 MHz making it possible to use in video applications requiring higher gain accuracy than is usually associated with such amplifiers.

features

- Very high slew rate – 500 V/μs at Av = +1
- Wide small signal bandwidth – 70 MHz
- Wide large signal bandwidth – 15 MHz
- High output swing – ±12V into 1K
- Offset null with single pot
- Low input offset – 2 mV
- Pin compatible with standard IC op amps

The LH0024/LH0024C's combination of wide bandwidth and high slew rate make it an ideal choice for a variety of high speed applications including active filters, oscillators, and comparators as well as many high speed general purpose applications.

The LH0024 is guaranteed over the temperature range -55°C to +125°C, whereas the LH0024C is guaranteed -25°C to +85°C.

schematic and connection diagrams

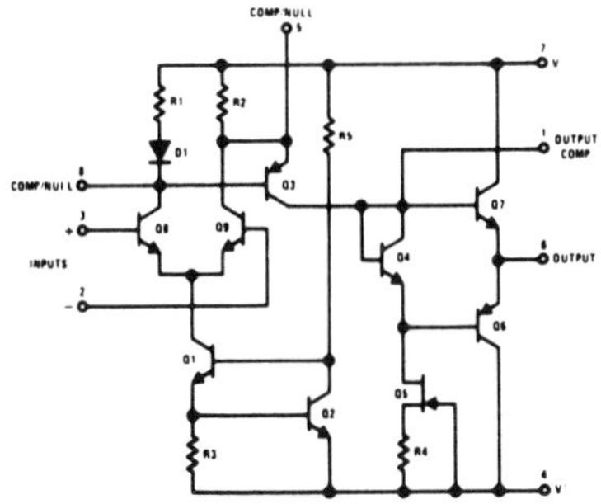

Metal Can Package

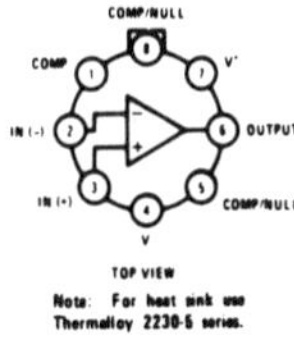

Order Number LH0024H or LH0024CH
See Package 9

typical applications

TTL Compatible Comparator

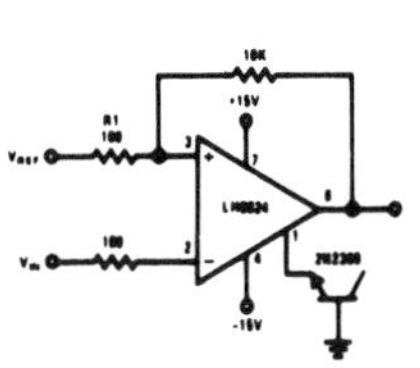

Offset Null

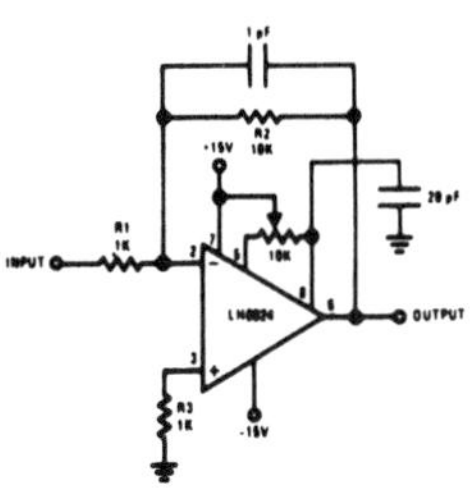

Video Amplifier

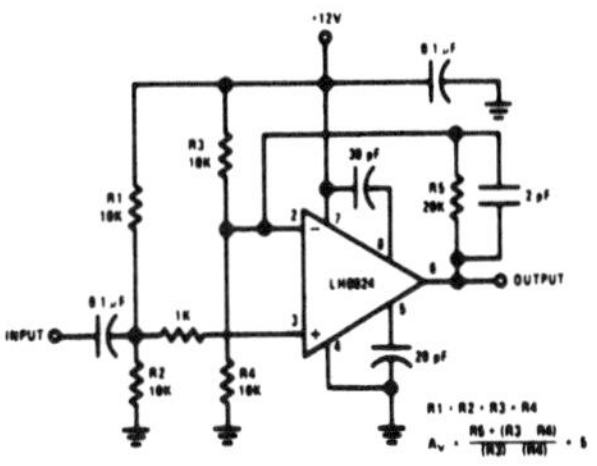

Figure 14-49. Manufacturer's data sheets for the LH0024/LH0024TC high slew rate operational amplifier (Courtesy National Semiconductor Corp.)

absolute maximum ratings

Supply Voltage		±18V
Input Voltage		Equal to Supply
Differential Input Voltage		±5V
Power Dissipation		600 mW
Operating Temperature Range	LH0024	-55°C to +125°C
	LH0024C	-25°C to +85°C
Storage Temperature Range		-65°C to +150°C
Lead Temperature (Soldering, 10 sec)		300°C

dc electrical characteristics (Note 1)

PARAMETER	CONDITIONS	LH0024			LH0024C			UNITS
		MIN	TYP	MAX	MIN	TYP	MAX	
Input Offset Voltage	$R_S = 50\Omega$, $T_A = 25°C$		2.0	4.0		5.0	8.0	mV
	$R_S = 50\Omega$			6.0			10.0	mV
Average Temperature Coefficient of Input Offset Voltage	$V_S = \pm 15V$, $R_S = 50\Omega$ -55°C to 125°C		20			25		μV/°C
Input Offset Current	$T_A = 25°C$		2.0	5.0		4.0	15.0	μA
				10.0			20.0	μA
Input Bias Current	$T_A = 25°C$		15	30		18	40	μA
				40			50	μA
Supply Current			12.5	13.5		12.5	13.5	mA
Large Signal Voltage Gain	$V_S = \pm 15V$, $R_L = 1k$, $T_A = 25°C$	4	5		3	4		V/mV
	$V_S = \pm 15V$, $R_L = 1k$	3			2.5			V/mV
Input Voltage Range	$V_S = \pm 15V$	±12	±13		±12	±13		V
Output Voltage Swing	$V_S = \pm 15V$, $R_L = 1k$, $T_A = 25°C$	±12	±13		±10	±13		V
	$V_S = \pm 15V$, $R_L = 1k$	±10			±10			V
Slew Rate	$V_S = \pm 15V$, $R_L = 1k$, $C_1 = C_2 = 30$ pF, $A_V = +1$, $T_A = 25°C$	400	500		250	400		V/μs
Common Mode Rejection Ratio	$V_S = \pm 15V$, $\Delta V_{IN} = \pm 10V$, $R_S = 50\Omega$		60			60		dB
Power Supply Rejection Ratio	$\pm 5V \leq V_S \leq \pm 18V$, $R_S = 50\Omega$		60			60		dB

Note 1: These specifications apply for $\pm 5V \leq V_S \leq \pm 18V$ and -55°C to +125°C for the LH0024 and -25°C to +85°C for the LH0024C.

frequency compensation

TABLE I

CLOSED LOOP GAIN	C_1	C_2	C_3
100	0	0	0
20	0	0	0
10	0	20 pF	1 pF
1	30 pF	30 pF	3 pF

Frequency Compensation Circuit

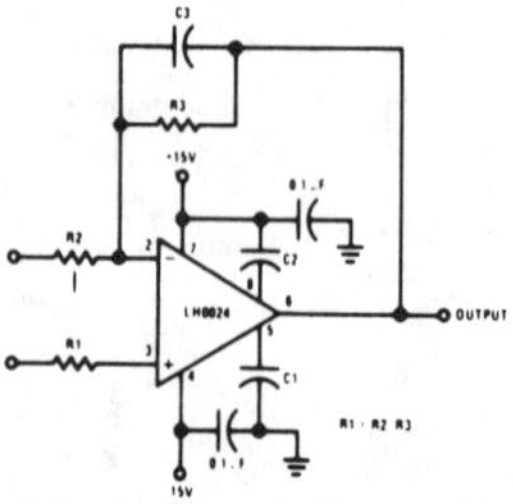

Figure 14-49—(*continued*)

typical performance characteristics

Maximum Power Dissipation

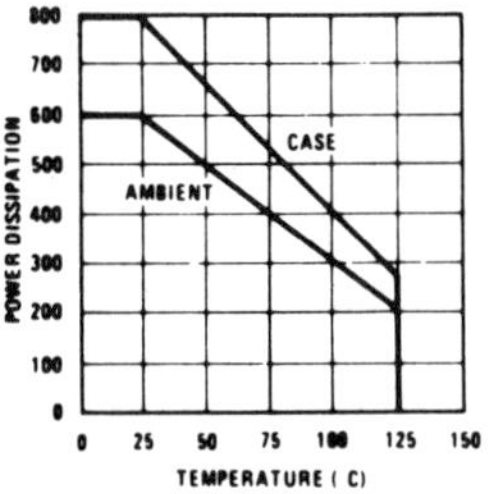

Large Signal Frequency Response

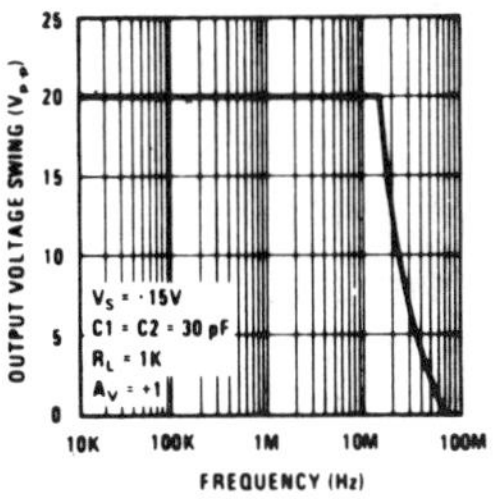

Open Loop Frequency Response

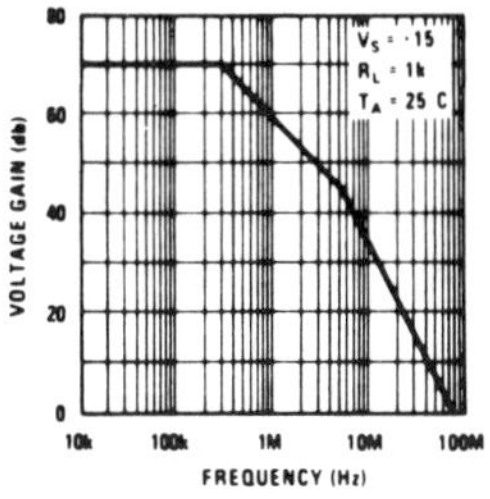

Voltage Follower Pulse Response

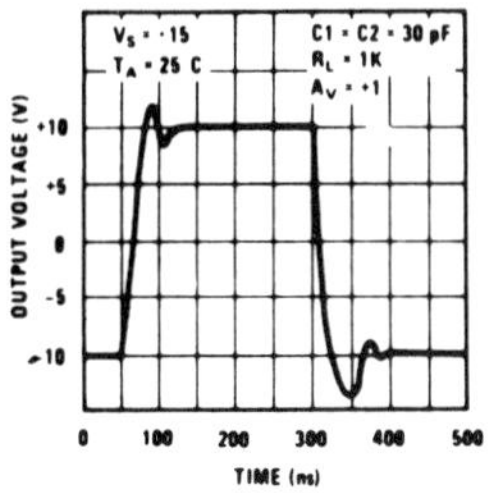

Input Voltage vs Supply Voltage

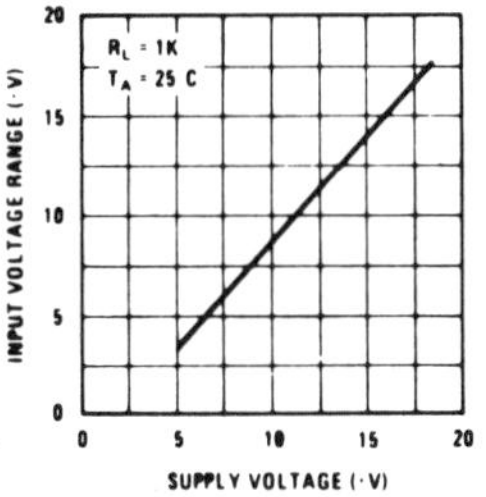

Output Voltage Swing

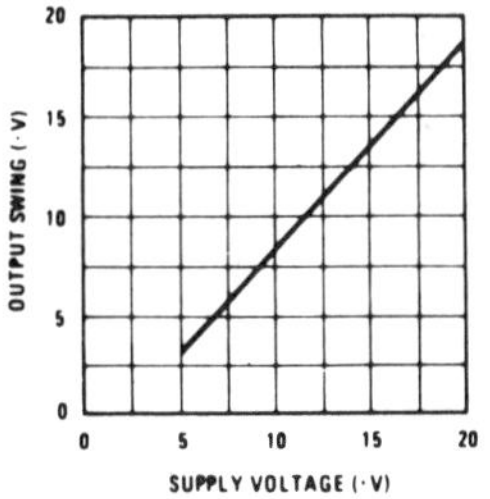

Supply Current vs Supply Voltage

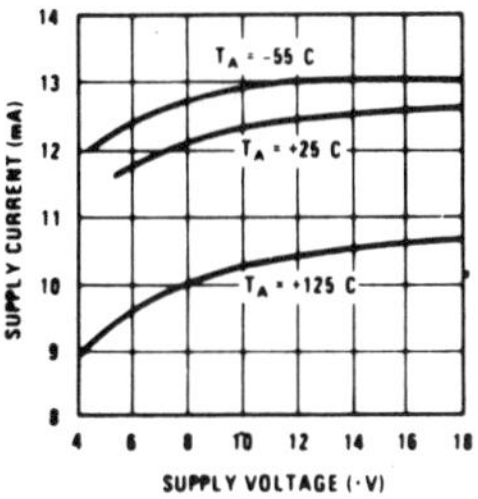

Input Bias Current vs Voltage

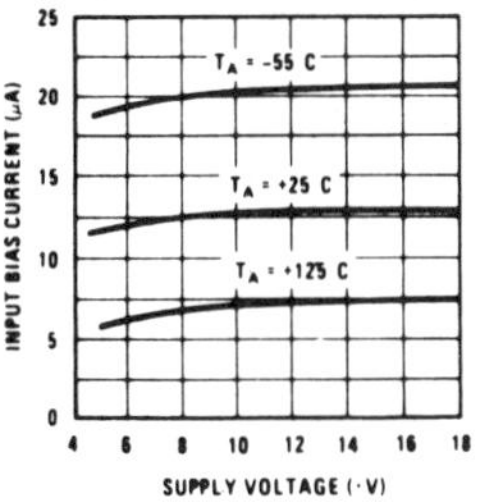

applications information

1. Layout Considerations

The LH0024/LH0024C, like most high speed circuitry, is sensitive to layout and stray capacitance. Power supplies should be by-passed as near the device as is practicable with at least .01 μF disc type capacitors. Compensating capacitors should also be placed as close to device as possible.

2. Compensation Recommendations

Compensation schemes recommended in Table 1 work well under typical conditions. However, poor layout and long lead lengths can degrade the performance of the LH0024 or cause the device to oscillate. Slight adjustments in the values for C1, C2, and C3 may be necessary for a given layout. In particular, when operating at a gain of −1, C3 may require adjustment in order to perfectly cancel the input capacitance of the device.

When operating the LH0024/LH0024C at a gain of +1, the value of R1 should be at least 1K ohm.

The case of the LH0024 is electrically isolated from the circuit; hence, it may be advantageous to drive the case in order to minimize stray capacitances.

3. Heat Sinking

The LH0024/LH0024C is specified for operation without the use of an explicit heat sink. However, internal power dissipation does cause a significant temperature rise. Improved offset voltage drift can be obtained by limiting the temperature rise with a clip-on heat sink such as the Thermalloy 2228B or equivalent.

Figure 14-49—(*continued*)

The information presented on data sheets is for routine design. When complex circuits are to be fabricated, the designer's ingenuity must be used, but the data sheet information does eliminate many simple design tasks.

Typical Manufacturers' Data Sheets

A typical set of data sheets for an LH0024/LH0024C high slew rate operational amplifier is shown in Fig. 14-49. As is common with integrated circuit chips, these are two different amplifiers with similar characteristics which can be used over different temperature ranges. The LH0024 has the wider temperature range. Note that not all manufacturers supply the same data but usually they supply the most pertinent data.

PROBLEMS

14-1. The parameters of the FET's in the circuit of Fig. 14-1a are

$$g_m = 15{,}000\ \mu\text{mho}$$
$$r_d = 10^5\ \text{ohms}$$

The parameters of the circuit are

$$R_d = 10{,}000\ \text{ohms}$$
$$R = 10{,}000\ \text{ohms}$$

Compute the exact values for $\mathbf{V}_{o1}$ and $\mathbf{V}_{o2}$. Compare this with the approximate expressions of Eq. 14-9a and 14-9b.

14-2. Repeat Prob. 14-1 but now use $R = 500$ ohms.

14-3. What practical problems result in the circuit of Fig. 14-1a if R is made too large?

14-4. The FET's in the circuit of Fig. 14-1a are operated at the following operating point.

$$V_{DSQ} = 5\ \text{V}$$
$$I_{DQ} = 1\ \text{mA}$$

The resistor R is to be replaced by a current generator, which is modeled as shown in Fig. 14-2. The value of $R = 100{,}000$ ohms. It is desired that the quiescent voltage drop across the current generator be equal to or less than 2 V. What should be the value of I?

14-5. The parameters of the transistor in the circuit of Fig. 14-5 are

$$g_m = 70{,}000\ \mu\text{mho}$$
$$r_{bb'} = 100\ \text{ohms}$$
$$r_{b'c} = 10^7\ \text{ohms}$$
$$r_{ce} = 10^5\ \text{ohms}$$

The parameters of the circuit are

$$R_C = 10{,}000\ \text{ohms}$$
$$R_E = 10{,}000\ \text{ohms}$$

Compute the exact expressions for $\mathbf{V}_{o1}$ and $\mathbf{V}_{o2}$. Compare these with the approximate ones given by Eq. 14-22.

14-6. Compute the input impedance of the amplifier of Prob. 14-5.

14-7. Repeat Prob. 14-5 but now use $R_E = 500$ ohms.

14-8. The transistors in the circuit of Fig. 14-5a are operated at the following operating point.

$$V_{CEQ} = 5 \text{ V}$$
$$I_{CQ} = 1 \text{ mA}$$

The resistor R_E is to be replaced by a current generator, which can be modeled as shown in Fig. 14-2. The value of R is to be 100,000 ohms. It is desired that the quiescent voltage drop across the current generator be equal to or less than 1 V. What is the minimum value that I can have?

14-9. Compute the voltage gain of the cascode differential amplifier of Fig. 14-8.

14-10. Discuss the need for high-input impedance in an operational amplifier.

14-11. Compute the input impedance of the emitter follower, input differential amplifier stage of Fig. 14-9.

14-12. Compute the voltage gain of the amplifier of Fig. 14-9.

14-13. Discuss the circuit of Fig. 14-10. Compare it with the circuit of Fig. 14-9.

14-14. Repeat Prob. 14-11 for the circuit of Fig. 14-10.

14-15. Repeat Prob. 14-12 for the circuit of Fig. 14-10.

14-16. Discuss the operation of the input bias current cancelling circuit of Fig. 14-11.

14-17. Discuss how the circuit of Fig. 14-12 implements the ideas discussed in Prob. 14-16.

14-18. Compute the voltage gain of the circuit of Prob. 14-12.

14-19. Discuss super beta transistors. Why and how are they used in operational amplifiers?

14-20. Discuss the FET input differential amplifier of Fig. 14-14b.

14-21. Compute the voltage gain of the circuit of Fig. 14-14b.

14-22. It is desired to obtain an operational amplifier with the highest possible input impedance. What type of input stage should be used?

14-23. The current source of Fig. 14-15 is to be modeled using the model of Fig. 14-2. Determine the parameters of the model in terms of the parameters of the transistor and its operating point.

14-24. Why is the circuit of Fig. 14-17 used rather than that of Fig. 14-15?

14-25. Relate I to I_{ref} in the circuit of Fig. 14-17.

14-26. The transistors in Fig. 14-17 have the following parameter and operating values.

$$V_A = 200 \text{ V}$$
$$V_{CE1} = 0.9 \text{ V}$$
$$V_{CE2} = 20 \text{ V}$$

What is the ratio I/I_{ref}?

14-27. What are the advantages of the Widlar current source of Fig. 14-19 over the circuit of Fig. 14-17?

14-28. Design a Widlar current source of the type shown in Fig. 14-19, which meets the following specifications.

$$I = 10 \ \mu\text{A}$$
$$V = 30 \text{ V}$$
$$V_{CC} = 10 \text{ V}$$

It is desired that $I_{\text{ref}}/I = 5$. Assume that the transistors are identical and that $V_A = 150$ V. The operating temperature is 300°K.

14-29. Repeat Prob. 14-28 but now assume that $T = 330°K$.

14-30. For the circuit of Prob. 14-28, how does the operation change if the temperature increases to 330°K? Compare the operation with the circuit of Fig. 14-29.

14-31. The parameters of the transistor used in the design of Prob. 14-28 are

$$g_m = 75{,}000\ \mu\text{mho}$$
$$r_{bb'} = 100 \text{ ohms}$$
$$r_{b'e} = 1000 \text{ ohms}$$
$$r_{ce} = 100{,}000 \text{ ohms}$$

Compute the effective resistance of the current generator.

14-32. Repeat Prob. 14-31 for the current generator of Prob. 14-29.

14-33. Compute an exact expression for the output resistance of the Wilson current source of Fig. 14-21a.

14-34. The transistor whose parameters are given in Prob. 14-31 is used in the circuit of Fig. 14-21a. What is the effective resistance of this current source?

14-35. Discuss the operation of the multiple current source of Fig. 14-22.

14-36. Repeat Prob. 14-35 for the multiple Widlar current source of Fig. 14-23.

14-37. Discuss the operation of the circuit of Fig. 14-24. Why is this circuit not usually used?

14-38. Discuss the operation of the differential amplifier with a current source load of Fig. 14-25.

14-39. The parameters of the transistor used in the circuit of Fig. 14-25 are the same as those of Prob. 14-31. In addition

$$R_E = 1000 \text{ ohms}$$

It is desired that $\mathbf{V}_{o2} = 700(\mathbf{V}_1 - \mathbf{V}_2)$. What is the smallest value that R_L (the load resistance connected externally to the v_{o2} terminal) can have?

14-40. A direct coupled amplifier consists of a cascade of six stages, each with a gain of 10. Because of changes in power supply voltages, the input voltages of the first stage drifts by 0.0001 V. Compute the change in the output voltage assuming that the amplifier is ideal.

14-41. Discuss the procedures used to eliminate drift in direct coupled amplifiers.

14-42. How does the circuit of Fig. 14-28 improve the dc stability of an operational amplifier?

14-43. Compute the gain of the circuit of Fig. 14-28.

14-44. Discuss the operation of the circuit of Fig. 14-29a.

14-45. For the level shifter of Fig. 14-29a, we desire that $v_o = 0$ when $v_i = 6$ V. The current generator produces a current of 1 mA. Determine the value of R so that the desired results are achieved.

14-46. Design the current generator in the circuit of Prob. 14-45. Assume that $V_{CE} = 15$ V.

14-47. Compute the voltage gain of the circuit of Fig. 14-29.

14-48. Describe the operation of the circuit of Fig. 14-30.

14-49. Compute the voltage gain of the circuit of Fig. 14-30.

14-50. Compare the circuits of Figs. 14-30 and 14-32. Why is the latter one used?

14-51. Describe the operation of the overload protective circuit of Fig. 14-34.

14-52. The output transistors in the circuit of Fig. 14-34 can safely pass collector currents of 25 mA. Design the protective circuit so that this current value will not be exceeded.

14-53. Compute the voltage gain of the circuit of Fig. 14-34.

14-54. Describe the operation of the circuit of Fig. 14-35.

14-55. Compute the voltage gain of the circuit of Fig. 14-35.

14-56. Describe the operation of the circuit of Fig. 14-36. Use the discussion of Prob. 14-54.

14-57. Compute the voltage gain of the circuit of Fig. 14-36.

14-58. Describe the operation of the complete operational amplifier of Fig. 14-37.

14-59. When the bias voltages of the complete operational amplifier are calculated, why do we not start at the input and work toward the output?

14-60. Obtain all pertinent bias quantities for the complete operational amplifier of Fig. 14-37. Use the parameter values given in the text but now use

$$V_{CC}^{+} = 20 \text{ V}$$
$$V_{EE}^{-} = -20 \text{ V}$$

14-61. Repeat Prob. 14-60 but now use

$$R_1 = 6500 \text{ ohms}$$
$$R_2 = 40{,}000 \text{ ohms}$$

14-62. Repeat Prob. 14-60 but now use

$$V_{CC}^{+} = 10 \text{ V}$$
$$V_{EE}^{-} = -10 \text{ V}$$

14-63. Compute the voltage gain of the operational amplifier of Fig. 14-37. Use the parameter values of Prob. 14-31.

14-64. The transistors in the Darlington transistor of Fig. 14-39 have the parameters given in Prob. 14-31. What is the beta of the compound transistor?

14-65. Compute the frequency response of the operational amplifier of Fig. 14-37. Assume that the transistors have the following parameter values.

$$g_m = 75{,}000 \ \mu\text{mho}$$
$$r_{bb'} = 100 \text{ ohms}$$
$$r_{b'e} = 1000 \text{ ohms}$$
$$r_{b'c} = 10^8 \text{ ohms}$$
$$r_{ce} = 100{,}000 \text{ ohms}$$
$$C_{b'e} = 100 \text{ pF}$$
$$C_{b'e} = 3 \text{ pF}$$

14-66. Compare the low-frequency results of Prob. 14-65 with those of Prob. 14-63.

14-67. Repeat Prob. 14-65 but now double $C_{b'e}$ and $C_{b'c}$.

14-68. Discuss the concept of a dominant pole.

14-69. Draw the frequency response for a "four-stage" operational amplifier with poles at $s = -1000$, -10^5, -10^6, and -2×10^6.

14-70. Identify the dominant pole in Prob. 14-69.

14-71. Discuss how the circuit of Fig. 14-45 can be used to establish a dominant pole.

14-72. The amplifier of Fig. 14-45 has the following characteristics.

$$\mathbf{A}_{v1} = 10$$
$$\mathbf{A}_{v2} = 1000$$
$$C = 20 \text{ pF}$$

In addition, $\mathbf{A}_{v1} v_1 / r_o |_{\max} = 1$ mA. What is the slewing rate of the amplifier?

14-73. Why is the concept of slewing rate not used in conjunction with ideal linear amplifiers?

14-74. Assume that the input to the amplifiers of Prob. 14-72 is a sinusoid of frequency f. Determine an expression for the peak output signal versus frequency if clipping is not to result.

14-75. Repeat Prob. 14-74 but now obtain the peak input signal.

14-76. Determine the common mode rejection ratio for the amplifier of Prob. 14-1.

14-77. Repeat Prob. 14-76 for the circuit of Prob. 14-5.

14-78. An operation amplifier output is ideally to be $10{,}000(\mathbf{V}_2 - \mathbf{V}_1)$. For the actual amplifier, when $\mathbf{V}_2 = \mathbf{V}_1 = 0.01$ V, V_o is to be less than 0.0001 V. All signals are sinusoidal and rms values are given. If these results are to be achieved, what is the smallest value that the common mode rejection ratio can have?

14-79. The amplifier of Fig. 13-8 has the following parameter values.

$$R_1 = 10{,}000 \text{ ohms}$$
$$R_2 = 50{,}000 \text{ ohms}$$
$$R_3 = 10{,}000 \text{ ohms}$$
$$R_4 = 50{,}000 \text{ ohms}$$

The output voltage is

$$\mathbf{V}_o = \mathbf{K}[\mathbf{V}_{i2}(1 + \delta) - \mathbf{V}_{i1}]$$

We desire that $|\delta| \leq 0.0001$. What is the smallest value that the common mode rejection ratio can have?

14-80. Discuss the effects of input bias currents. Use Fig. 14-46 in your discussion.

14-81. Discuss the concept of offset current.

14-82. Discuss the concept of offset voltage.

14-83. Discuss how the circuit of Fig. 14-47 can compensate for offset effects.

14-84. In a practical operational amplifier, how are offset voltages compensated for?

14-85. Discuss the concept of latch up.

14-86. How is latch up avoided in an operational amplifier?

14-87. Obtain data sheets for several operational amplifiers. Discuss all the ratings given.

BIBLIOGRAPHY

Glaser, A. B. and Subak-Shoupe, G. E. *Integrated Circuit Engineering*. Reading, Mass.: Addison-Wesley, 1977.

Gray, P. R. and Meyer, R. C. *Analysis and Design of Analog Integrated Circuits*. New York: Wiley, 1977, Chapters 5, 6, and 7.

Heuhne, K. *Getting More Out of an Integrated Operational Amplifier Data Sheet*, Motorola Semiconductor Products—In Application Note AN–273A.

Holt, C. A. *Electronic Circuits, Digital and Analog*. New York: Wiley, 1978, Chapter, 14.

Chapter 15

Untuned Power Amplifiers

In this chapter we shall consider circuits that are designed to supply appreciable power to a load. In such cases, the signal levels are usually so large that the nonlinearities of the circuit must be taken into account. Such amplifiers are called *large-signal amplifiers* or *power amplifiers*. In this chapter we shall consider amplifiers that operate over a relatively broad range of frequencies.

We shall start with a general discussion of amplifier efficiency and then consider specific amplifier circuits.

15-1. THE EFFICIENCY OF IDEAL AMPLIFIERS

When we deal with amplifiers that supply appreciable amounts of power, we must become concerned with the efficiency of these amplifiers. If an amplifier is inefficient then, of course, it requires more energy to run it and it is more expensive to run. Additionally, there is another reason for considering efficiency. An amplifier takes energy from the power supply. Some of this is converted to signal power which is supplied to the load. The remainder is dissipated in the form of heat. Much of this heat must be dissipated by the active devices (e.g., transistors and FET's). In general, the cost and size of a device increases as its rated dissipation increases. In addition, if the dissipation is large, special ventilation procedures must be used. At times, cooling fans are required. If there are extremely large amounts of heat to dissipate, then water cooling must be used. Thus, high-efficiency amplifiers are, in general, smaller, simpler, and less costly than low-efficiency ones. The present "bookshelf" audio amplifiers would not be practical if low-efficiency circuits were used.

In this section we shall consider the maximum efficiency available from several classes of amplifier circuits. These theoretical maximum efficiencies will be greater than those actually achieved in practice but these results will serve as useful indications of amplifier performance.

In order to provide complete generality in our discussion, we shall use the generalized device introduced in Sec. 5-11 which can be used to represent either a transistor or a FET.

In this section we shall calculate the maximum *output circuit efficiency*. We define output circuit efficiency as

$$\eta_2 = \frac{\text{signal power delivered to load}}{\text{power supplied by power supply}} \tag{15-1}$$

Let us now define several types of operation. The definitions, assuming sinusoidal operation, are: class A, where current is in the active device for the entire period; class B, where current is in the device for one half-period; class AB, where current is in the device for more than one half-period but less than a full period; and class C, where the current is in the device for less than one half-period.

We start by analyzing the amplifier of Fig. 15-1a and assume that it is operated class A. We also assume that the device has the idealized characteristics shown in Fig. 15-1b, and that the input is

$$x_i = X_{iQ} + X_{i,\max} \sin \omega t \tag{15-2}$$

where X_{iQ} represents the quiescent input bias. Then, the output current is given by $\sqrt{2}$

$$i_o = I_{oQ} + \sqrt{2} I_{o,\text{rms}} \sin \omega t \tag{15-3}$$

The power supplied by the power supply is

$$P_{oo} = V_{oo} I_{oQ} \tag{15-4}$$

This is independent of the signal level. To obtain maximum efficiency, we must, then, obtain the maximum output power. We assume that the operation is restricted so that no distortion results (i.e., there is no clipping due to saturation or cutoff). For the load line drawn in Fig. 15-1d, we use

$$X_{i,\max} = 2\,\Delta X$$

Hence, the maximum output current is

$$I_{o,\max} = 2I_{oQ} \tag{15-5}$$

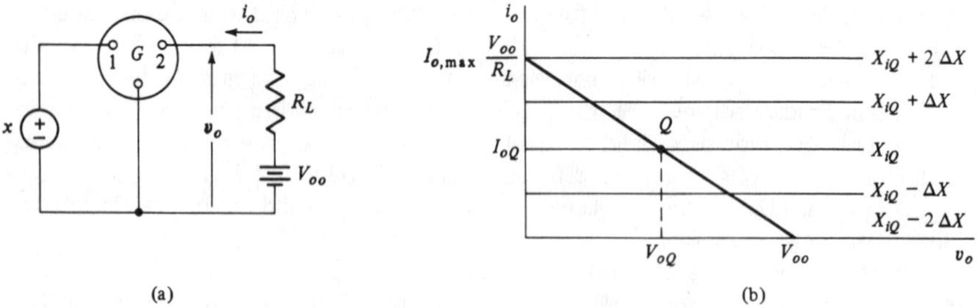

Figure 15-1. (a) A simple amplifier circuit. (b) The idealized output characteristics of the generalized device and load line.

and the minimum output current is

$$I_{o,\min} = 0$$

Thus

$$I_{o,\mathrm{rms}} = (I_{o,\max} - I_{o,\min})/2\sqrt{2}$$

Proceeding similarly for the voltage, we obtain the output power.

$$P_2 = (I_{o,\max} - 0)(V_{oo} - 0)/8 \tag{15-6}$$

Hence, the output circuit efficiency is

$$\eta_2 = \frac{(I_{o,\max} - 0)(V_{oo} - 0)}{8V_{oo}I_{oQ}} \times 100 \tag{15-7}$$

Substituting Eq. 15-5, we obtain

$$\eta_2 = 25\% \tag{15-8}$$

This efficiency is very low. One reason is that the direct component of i_o (i.e., I_{oQ}) is through the load resistance and dissipates power in it. Note that this is *not* signal power.

We can eliminate this power by using a transformer as shown in Fig. 15-2. (In subsequent sections of this chapter we shall see how this can be accomplished *without* using a transformer.) We assume that the resistance of the transformer to direct current will be zero. However, at signal frequencies it has an input resistance

$$R_{\mathrm{ac}} = \left(\frac{n_1}{n_2}\right)^2 R_L$$

where n_1/n_2 is the turns ratio of the transformer.

The dc load line is the vertical line drawn on the characteristic of Fig. 15-2b. Then, as before

$$P_{oo} = V_{oo}I_{oQ} \tag{15-9}$$

Again, this is independent of signal.

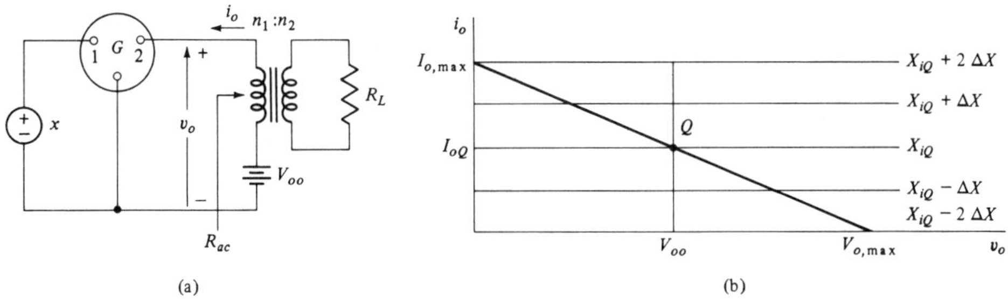

Figure 15-2. (a) A simple transformer coupled amplifier. (b) Idealized output characteristics of the generalized device and load line.

The turns ratio of the transformer is chosen so that we can obtain the maximum swing in both voltage and current. Hence,

$$I_{o,\max} = 2I_{oQ} \tag{15-10a}$$

$$V_{o,\max} = 2V_{oo} \tag{15-10b}$$

Substituting into Eq. 15-6 and manipulating, we have

$$\eta_{2,\max} = \frac{(2I_{oQ} - 0)(2V_{oo} - 0)}{8V_{oo}I_{oQ}} \tag{15-11}$$

$$\eta_{2,\max} = 50\% \tag{15-12}$$

The maximum efficiency has been doubled but the operation of this circuit still leaves much to be desired. Typically, audio amplifiers supply maximum power for only a small percent of time. For instance, suppose that $P_{\max} = 100$ W and a symphony is being amplified. The output power will approach 100 W only during crescendos. For most of the time, the power output will be low, 5 watts or less. Nevertheless, the power supplied by the power supply will be constant. Thus, the actual efficiency will be very low. Let us consider this. Suppose that $P_{\max} = 100$ W. Then $P_{oo} = 200$ W. Now if

$$P_2 = 5$$

P_{oo} will remain constant and then the efficiency will be

$$\eta_2 = \frac{5}{200} \times 100 = 2.5\%$$

Thus, for much of the time the efficiency will be very low.

Another quantity of interest is P_{OD}, the power dissipated by the "output circuit" of the device.

$$P_{OD} = P_{oo} - P_2 \tag{15-13}$$

This dissipation will be maximum when $P_2 = 0$. Hence, for our 100-W amplifier, the maximum P_{OD} is $P_{OD} = 200$ W. Note that for the usual audio amplifier, we must use an output device that is able to dissipate this maximum value since there may be long periods of time when $P_2 = 0$ or is very small.

All class A amplifiers suffer from the low-efficiency, high-dissipation conditions that we have discussed. The situation is greatly improved if we shift to class *B* operation. This can be accomplished in the circuit of Fig. 15-2a by adjusting the quiescent input bias X_{iQ} so that the device is just cut off. The output characteristic and load line for this amplifier is shown in Fig. 15-3. The output will then be a half-sinusoid.

$$i_o = \begin{cases} I_{o,\max} \sin \omega t & 0 \leq \omega t \leq \pi \\ 0 & \pi \leq \omega t \leq 2\pi \end{cases}$$

The direct component of the current is

$$I_{OA} = \frac{1}{2\pi} \int_0^{\pi} i_o \, d\omega t$$

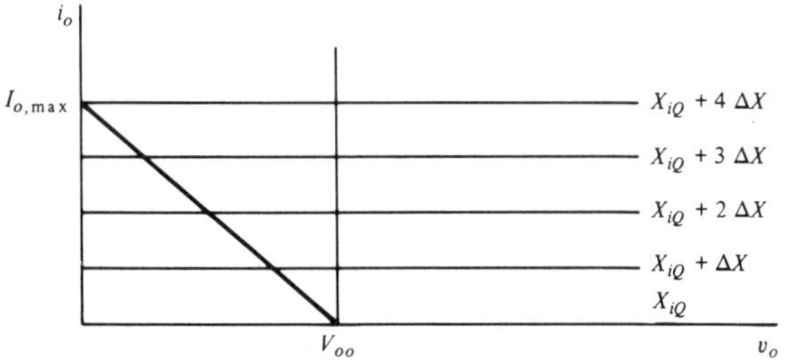

Figure 15-3. Idealized output characteristics with load line drawn for a class B amplifier.

Substituting for i_o and integrating, we have

$$I_{OA} = I_{o,\max}/\pi \tag{15-14}$$

Hence, the average power supplied by the power supply is

$$P_{oo} = V_{oo} I_{o,\max}/\pi \tag{15-15}$$

Note that now P_{oo} varies with the signal level.

The instantaneous current is a sinusoid for half a cycle. Hence,

$$\eta_{2,\max} = \frac{(V_{oo} - 0)(I_{o,\max} - 0)\frac{1}{4}}{V_{oo}/I_{o,\max}/\pi}$$

$$\eta_{2,\max} = \frac{\pi}{4} \times 100 = 78.5\% \tag{15-16}$$

This efficiency is considerably higher than for the class A case. The situation is dramatically improved at lower power levels. For instance, suppose that we have zero input signal. Then,

$$P_{oo} = 0$$

and we do not have the high-dissipation, low-efficiency condition that we encountered for the class A amplifiers. At low-signal levels, the dissipation will be relatively small.

If we use class C operation, then maximum efficiency will increase still further. In fact, it can theoretically approach 100%. Class C operation cannot be used for audio amplifiers although it is often used with tuned power amplifiers.

Let us now consider efficiencies of practical amplifiers. If we did not use idealized characteristics, then the swings in the output signals would be limited by the knees of the curves and the output power would be reduced with a corresponding reduction in the efficiency. Actually, the knees in the characteristic of transistors and FET's are relatively close to the i_o axis so the actual efficiencies are relatively close to the theoretical ones. For instance, the actual maximum efficiency of a practical transistor class B amplifier can easily be 50%, or higher. With class C amplifiers, maximum efficiencies of 85 to 90% or higher can be obtained.

The calculations performed in this section were based on sinusoidal signals. If certain other waveforms are used, the efficiencies can be higher. For instance, if square waves are used, the circuit of Fig. 15-2a, with class A operation, can have efficiencies that approach 100% but for most audio applications, square waves do not represent typical signals, and power analysis and design should be based upon sinusoidal signals.

15-2. THE SINGLE ENDED AMPLIFIER

In this section we shall discuss a simple form of power amplifier called the *single ended amplifier* which was once widely used. Even though it has, in large part, now been replaced by other circuits that we shall consider in the next sections, we shall discuss the single ended amplifier here since it is simple and will enable us to develop procedures that we shall use in the more complex circuits.

If we deal with common-emitter transistor amplifiers or common-source transistor amplifiers, the developments in Chapter 5 apply directly. Let us briefly review the pertinent results and then consider the somewhat more complex graphical analysis of source follower and emitter follower circuits. We shall consider class A amplifiers in this section. Class B and class AB amplifiers will be considered later.

Suppose that the output characteristics and ac load line for the amplifier of Fig. 15-2a are as drawn in Fig. 15-4. The maximum and minimum values of output current are as marked there. Let us start by neglecting distortion. Then, the average signal power output is given by

$$P_2 = (V_{o,\max} - V_{o,\min})(I_{o,\max} - I_{o,\min})/8 \tag{15-17}$$

The rms output voltage and current are given by

$$V_2 = \frac{(V_{o,\max} - V_{o,\min})}{2\sqrt{2}} \tag{15-18a}$$

and

$$I_2 = \frac{(I_{o,\max} - I_{o,\min})}{2\sqrt{2}} \tag{15-18b}$$

The power supplied by the power supply is

$$P_{oo} = V_{oo} I_{oQ} \tag{15-19}$$

The dissipation within the output circuit of the device is

$$P_{OD} = P_2 - P_{oo} \tag{15-20}$$

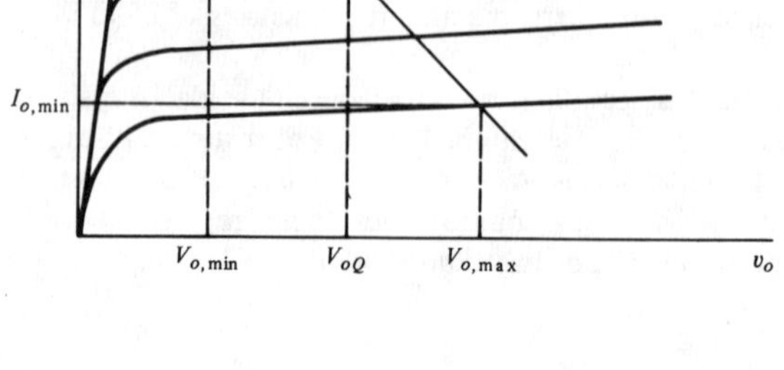

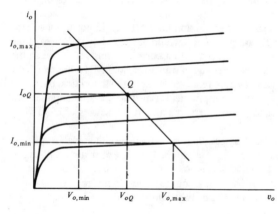

Figure 15-4. Output characteristics and load line for a simple power amplifier.

We have assumed that there is no external resistance other than the effective resistance of the load and that this resistance is zero for dc. This may not always be the case. For instance, there could be an emitter stabilizing resistance present. Then, the voltage drop across it and the power dissipated in it must be taken into account.

If there is distortion, then we use the procedure of Sec. 5-13 to calculate

$$i_o = I_{oA} + \sqrt{2}(I_{o1} \cos \omega t + I_{o2} \cos 2\omega t + I_{o3} \cos 3\omega t) + I_{o4} \cos 4\omega t + \cdots) \quad (15\text{-}21)$$

Now the signal power output is

$$P_2 = I_{o1} R_{ac} \quad (15\text{-}22)$$

where R_{ac} is the resistance viewed into the transformer. The power supplied by the power supply is

$$P_{oo} = V_{oo} I_{oA} \quad (15\text{-}23)$$

and the dissipation within the output circuit of the device is given by

$$P_{oD} = P_{oo} - (I_{o1}^2 + I_{o2}^2 + I_{o3}^2 + I_{o4}^2 + \cdots)R_{ac} \quad (15\text{-}24)$$

Note that even though the harmonic power is not considered usable output power, it still must be subtracted from P_{oo} to obtain P_{OD}.

Source Follower Power Amplifier

Let us now discuss the analysis of the source follower power amplifier of Fig. 15-5. The analysis of this circuit is complicated by the fact that v_{GS} is not equal to v_1, but depends upon v_2. From Fig. 15-5 we have

$$v_{GS} = v_1 - v_2 \quad (15\text{-}25)$$

To analyze this circuit we shall express the characteristic curves as a function of v_1 rather than of v_{GS}. It should be stressed that *this analysis will only be valid for a particular value of R_{ac} and a particular operating point.* That is, a set of characteristics that is *only* valid for one particular set of operating conditions will be obtained.

The output characteristics for the FET used in the amplifier of Fig. 15-5 are drawn in Fig. 15-6. The dc and ac load lines are drawn there. Since the load is in series with the FET, the load line is drawn as in the case of the common-source amplifier. That is (neglecting distortion), it passes through the quiescent operating point and has a slope

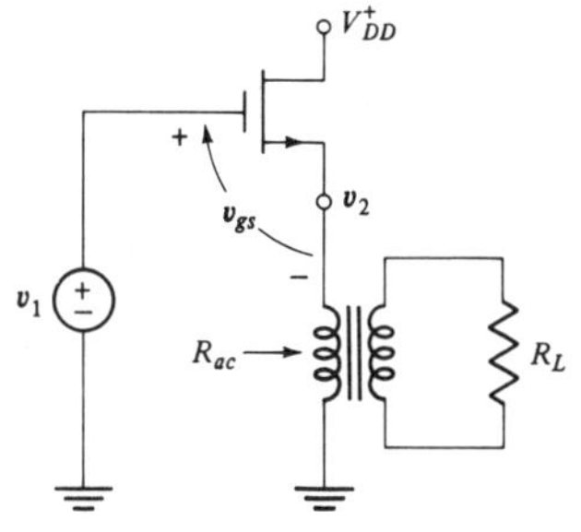

Figure 15.5 A simple source follower amplifier.

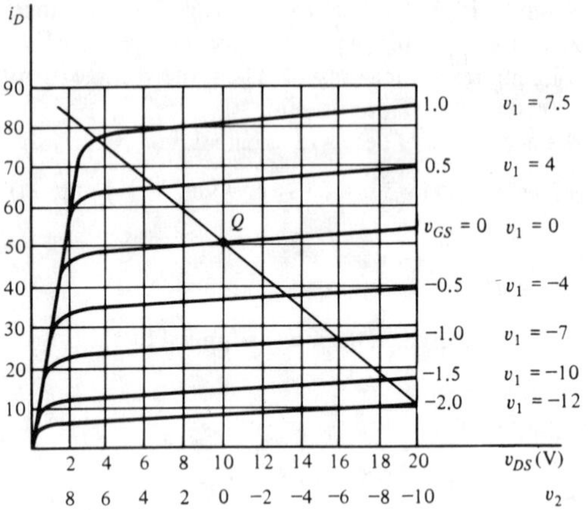

Figure 15-6. Characteristics for the source follower amplifier of Fig. 15-4.

of $-1/R_{ac}$. The primary difference between this analysis and the previous ones is that the *output* values affect v_{GS} as indicated in Eq. 15-25.

Another difference in this analysis is that v_{DS} is not the output voltage.

$$v_2 = V_{DD} - v_{DS} \tag{15-26}$$

Let us assume that

$$V_{DD} = 10 \text{ V}$$

and

$$R_{ac} = 250 \text{ ohms}$$

Then,

$$v_2 = 10 - v_{DS}$$

We have drawn a separate v_2 axis on Fig. 15-6. Remember that this axis only applies to the case where $V_{DD} = 10$ V. If we change V_{DD} then this axis must be changed.

The load line is drawn though the quiescent operating point.

$$R_{ac} = \frac{10}{40} \times 10^{-3} = 250 \text{ ohms}$$

We must now relate the values of v_{GS} to the input voltage. Equation 15-25 is used here. The intersection of the load line with a particular characteristic curve gives the actual operating point for the value of v_{GS} equal to the value specified on the characteristic curve (when $V_{DD} = 10$ V and $R_{ac} = 250$ ohms). The value of v_2 can then be read from the axis and, hence, v_1 determined, for instance, where $v_{GS} = 0$, $v_{DS} = 10$ V, and $v_2 = 0$ V. Then,

$$v_1 = 0 - 0 = 0 \text{ V}$$

Similarly, when $v_{GS} = -0.5$ V, $v_2 = -3.5$ V. Hence,

$$v_1 = -0.5 - 3.5 = -4 \text{ V}$$

Proceeding in this way we determine all the values for v_1 shown in Fig. 15-6.

We can now determine $V_{2,\max}$, $V_{2,\min}$, and so forth, and determine P_2, P_{oo}, P_{OD}, and the harmonic distortions as before. For instance, when $v_1 = 7.5$ V, $i_D = 77$ mA, $v_{DS} = 3.5$ V, and $v_2 = 6.5$ V.

Several facts should be noted here. Even though the characteristics are plotted for equal increments of v_{GS}, the increments in v_1 are *not* equal. This is because of the nonlinearities of the characteristics. For instance, the characteristics "squeeze together" when v_{GS} becomes negative. There is a corresponding compression of the values of v_i. Thus, this circuit inherently reduces distortion because of the feedback present. In Chapter 17 we shall consider this in great detail. Note that the compression of the "input characteristics" may require us to use interpolation.

Example

The FET whose characteristics are supplied in Fig. 15-6 is used in the circuit of Fig. 14-5 where

$$v_i = 4 \sin \omega t \text{ V}$$

$$R_{ac} = 250 \text{ ohms}$$

and

$$V_{CC} = 10 \text{ V}$$

Compute P_2, P_{oo}, and P_{OD}. Neglect distortion in this analysis.

The load line and specifications of v_i are as shown in Fig. 15-6. Then,

$$V_{2,\min} = -3.3 \text{ V} \qquad I_{o,\min} = 37 \text{ mA}$$

$$V_{2,\max} = 3.3 \text{ V} \qquad I_{o,\max} = 64 \text{ mA}$$

Then,

$$P_2 = (3.3 + 3.3)(64 - 37) \times 10^{-3}/8 = 0.0223 \text{ W}$$

The quiescent current is

$$I_{DQ} = 51 \text{ mA}$$

Hence, the power supplied by the power supply is

$$P_{oo} = 10 \times 51 \times 10^{-3} = 0.51 \text{ W}$$

The dissipation within the FET is

$$P_{OD} = 0.51 - 0.0223 = -0.488 \text{ W}$$

The output circuit efficiency is

$$\eta_2 = \frac{0.0223}{0.51} \times 100 = 4.37\%$$

If the signal level is increased, then the efficiency will increase.

Emitter Follower Amplifier

We shall now consider the analysis of the emitter follower amplifier shown in Fig. 15-7. We have included a generator resistance here. (It could be neglected in the case of the FET amplifier because of the extremely high input impedance of the FET).

To aid in the analysis of this circuit we shall replace the input portion of the circuit by its Thévenin equivalent (see Fig. 15-7b). Here,

$$v_T = \frac{v_g R_B + V_{CC} R_g}{R_B + R_g} \tag{15-27a}$$

$$\frac{1}{R_T} = \frac{1}{R_B} + \frac{1}{R_G} \tag{15-27b}$$

Analyzing this circuit we have the following

$$v_2 = V_{CC} - v_{CE} \tag{15-28}$$

$$i_B = \frac{v_T - v_{BE} - v_2}{R_T} \tag{15-29}$$

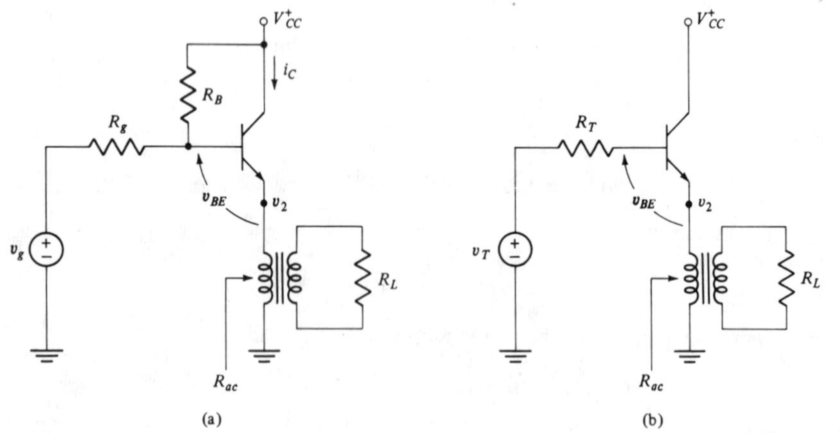

Figure 15-7. (a) A simple emitter follower amplifier. Only a simple bias circuit is shown. (b) A modification where the input is replaced by its Thévenin equivalent.

We now proceed in a manner that is analogous to the analysis used for the FET source follower. That is, we obtain graphical characteristics for the emitter follower amplifier which are valid only for a particular set of V_{DD}, R_G, and R_B. Let us illustrate how these characteristics are obtained by performing a numerical analysis. Assume that the emitter follower amplifier of Fig. 15-7a has the following parameter values.

$$V_{CC} = 5 \text{ V}$$

$$R_B = 18{,}000 \text{ ohms}$$

$$R_G = 18{,}000 \text{ ohms}$$

$$R_{ac} = 12.5 \text{ ohms}$$

Using the transistor characteristics that are given in Fig. 15-8, we shall obtain the characteristics necessary to analyze this amplifier.

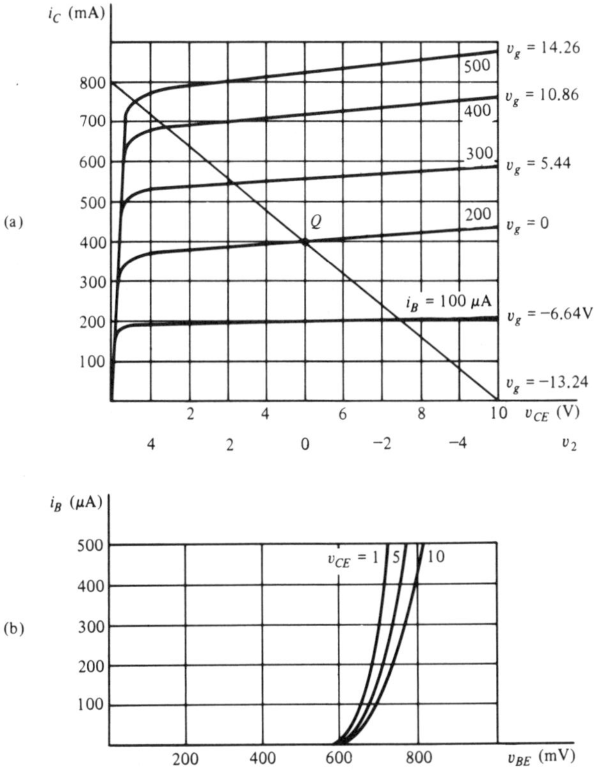

Figure 15-8. Characteristics for the emitter follower amplifier of Fig. 15-7. (a) Output. (b) Input.

Substituting in Eqs. 15-27 to 15-29, we have

$$v_T = \tfrac{1}{2}(v_g + 5)$$

$$R_T = 9000 \text{ ohms}$$

$$v_2 = 5 - v_{CE} \tag{15-30}$$

$$i_B = \frac{\tfrac{1}{2}(v_g + 5) - v_{BE} - v_2}{9000} \tag{15-31}$$

We use Eq. 15-30 to establish a v_2 axis adjacent to the v_{CE} axis (see Fig. 15-8).

We must now determine the values of v_g that correspond to the values of i_B which are used in the output characteristics. Manipulating Eq. 15-31 we obtain

$$v_G = 2(9000i_B + v_{BE} + v_2) - 5 \tag{15-32}$$

Next we draw the load lines. The quiescent base current is given by

$$I_{BQ} = \left.\frac{V_T - v_{BEQ}}{R_T}\right|_{v_g=0}$$

$$I_{BQ} = \frac{2.5 - 0.7}{9000} = 200\ \mu\text{A}$$

The value of v_{BEQ} used above was estimated. Let us check to see if it is correct. The dc load line is drawn vertically from the V_{CC} point. Thus,

$$V_{CEQ} = 5 \text{ V}$$

We obtain V_{BEQ} using I_{BQ}, V_{CEQ} Fig. 15-8b.

$$V_{BEQ} = 0.705 \text{ V}$$

which is very close to our assumed value. The ac load line is then drawn through the quiescent operating point with slope $-1/R_{ac} = -1/12.5$.

We can now obtain the necessary information to solve for v_g using Eq. 15-32. For instance, suppose that $i_B = 100\ \mu$A. The intersection of the load line with the $i_B = 100\ \mu$A curve yields $v_2 = -2.4$ V and $v_{CE} = 7.4$ V. The values of $i_B = 100\ \mu$A and $v_{CE} = 7.4$ V now enable us to obtain v_{BE} from Fig. 15-8b. In this case we have $v_{BE} = 0.68$ V. Then, substitution in Eq. 15-32 yields

$$v_g = -6.64 \text{ V}$$

This value is then marked on the $i_B = 100\ \mu$A curve. Proceeding in this way we then compute the following table. These values are marked on the output characteristics of Fig. 15-8a. We now can analyze the amplifier.

i_B (μA)	v_g (V)
0	−13.74
100	−6.64
200	0
300	5.44
400	10.86
500	14.26

Assume that

$$v_g = 13.74 \sin \omega t$$

and obtain the output voltage swing. From the characteristics we see that when $v_g = -13.74$, $v_2 = -5$, $v_{CE} = v_{CE,\max} = 10$ V, $I_C = I_{c,\min} = 0$ mA. When $v_g = 13.74$ we must interpolate between the $v_g = 10.86$ V and the $v_g = 14.26$ V curves. Doing this we obtain

$$v_2 = 4.2 \text{ V}, \qquad v_{CE,\min} = 0.8 \text{ V}, \qquad I_{C,\max} = 740 \text{ mA}$$

Then,

$$P_2 = [(10 - 0.8)(740 - 0) \times 10^{-3}]/8 = 0.851 \text{ W}$$

Note that, just as in the case of the source follower, this circuit tends to reduce distortion. For instance, in the region of the knees of the curves, the values of v_g also become closer together and tend to cancel the distortion. Of course, the distortion is not completely cancelled and the equations of Sec. 5-13 can be used to compute the actual percent harmonic distortion.

We have considered the basic analysis of power amplifiers here. In subsequent sections we shall use these procedures to analyze and design practical amplifier circuits.

15-3. THE LOUDSPEAKER AS A LOAD IMPEDANCE

Most audio amplifiers use a loudspeaker as a load. In this section we shall consider the impedance presented to the amplifier by the loudspeaker. The basic loudspeaker construction consists of a coil of wire called the *voice coil*, which is attached to a movable cone. The coil is mounted in a magnetic field set up by a permanent magnet. When current is passed through the voice coil, it deflects in the magnetic field and moves the cone. This in turn interacts with the air in its vicinity and sets up a sound wave. The determination of the actual acoustic characteristics of the loudspeaker is an extremely complex problem which we shall not consider here. The loudspeaker does not have an ideal frequency response so that it introduces frequency distortion. In addition, it also introduces nonlinear distortion. These distortions degrade the quality of the system and low-distortion loudspeakers are as important as low-distortion amplifiers.

Let us consider the load impedance presented by the loudspeaker. The impedance of a loudspeaker measured at dc ($f = 0$ Hz) is that of a very small resistance. This is simply the resistance of the voice coil which can usually be approximated to be 0 ohms.

Now suppose that we supply an audio signal to the loudspeaker. Sound will be radiated so electrical energy must be supplied. Thus, there will now be a resistive component of the input impedance. This is ideally a constant resistance called the *nominal resistance* of the loudspeaker. The actual input impedance of a loudspeaker is a complex number that varies with frequency. For purposes of analysis we shall assume that, at signal frequencies, the loudspeaker acts as a pure resistance which is equal to the nominal resistance. Typically, this resistance is 4, 8, or 16 ohms. The resistance for dc is almost zero. Thus, the input impedance of an ideal loudspeaker is similar to that of an ideal transformer with a resistive load.

15-4. THE COMPLEMENTARY SYMMETRY PUSH-PULL AMPLIFIER—GRAPHICAL ANALYSIS

In Sec. 14-8, we discussed the class B push-pull amplifier. That circuit is called a *complementary symmetry* amplifier since it uses a *n-p-n* transistor and a *p-n-p* transistor that have matched (or symmetrical) characteristics. In this section we shall consider the graphical analysis of these amplifiers. The complementary symmetry amplifier is usually not used when the power output is high. In the next section we shall discuss circuits that are suitable for high-power output.

We shall start our analysis with a push-pull amplifier that uses FET's in a source follower configuration. With present FET's, this amplifier would only be capable of low-power output but the analysis is relatively simple and will provide the basis for the more complex analyses to follow.

The amplifier circuit is shown in Fig. 15-9. Note that F_1 is a *n*-channel FET while F_2 is a *p*-channel FET. Loudspeakers cannot pass substantial quantities of direct current. Thus, when there is no input signal present, we desire that $v_L = 0$. If the circuit is balanced, then, under quiescent conditions, $i_{D1} = |i_{D2}|$, so $i_L = 0$ and $v_L = 0$.

We must now determine a procedure to analyze this circuit. The drain current through a FET can be expressed as a function of its v_{GS} and v_{DS}, so for F_1 we can write

$$i_{D1} = f_1(v_{GS1}, v_{DS1}) \tag{15-33}$$

Similarly, for F_2

$$i_{D2} = f_2(v_{GS2}, v_{DS2}) \tag{15-34}$$

Note that f_1 and f_2 are commonly supplied, not as mathematical relations, but as graphical characteristics (e.g., the output characteristics) and we shall ultimately utilize these characteristics. For the time being, however, it is more convenient for us to use the functional notation. Now let us relate f_1 and f_2. We assume complementary symmetry, so the characteristics for f_1 and f_2 are equal in magnitude and only differ in sign.

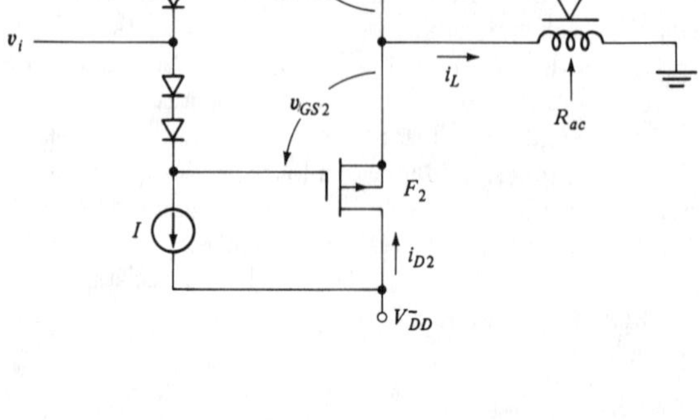

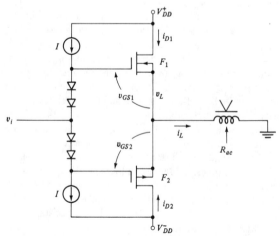

Figure 15-9. A complementary symmetry source follower push-pull amplifier.

For instance, in Fig. 15-10 we show the output characteristics for a pair of complementary symmetric FET's. Thus, the functions f_1 and f_2 are the same if we make the appropriate sign changes. In practice, we can write

$$f_2(v_{GS2}, v_{DS2}) = -f_1(-v_{GS2}, -v_{DS2}) \tag{15-35}$$

Therefore, we have

$$i_{D1} = f_1(v_{GS1}, v_{DS1}) \tag{15-36a}$$

$$i_{D2} = -f_1(-v_{GS2}, -v_{DS2}) \tag{15-36b}$$

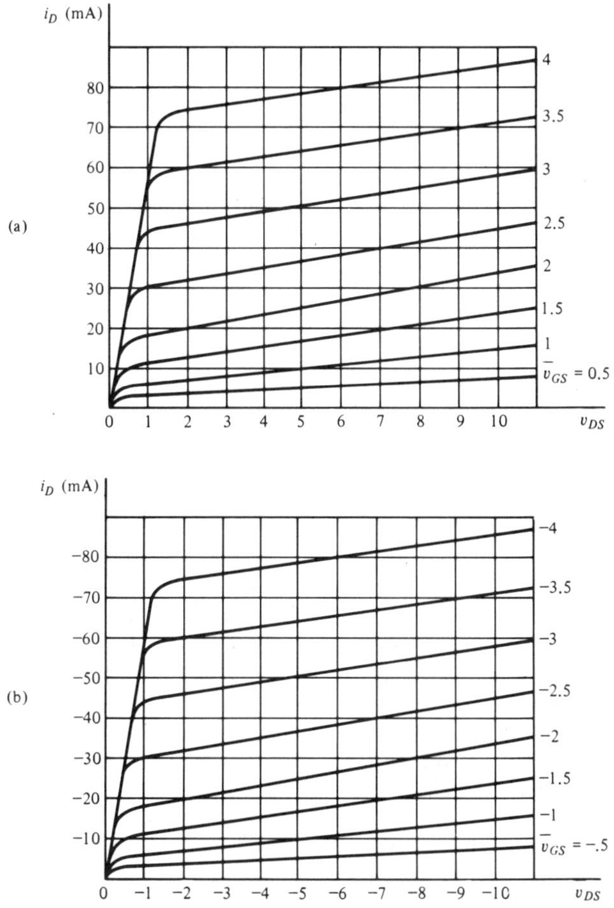

Figure 15-10. Output characteristics of complementary symmetry FET's. (a) *n* channel. (b) *p*-channel.

Then, from Fig. 15-9 we obtain

$$i_L = i_{D1} + i_{D2} = f_1(v_{GS1}, v_{DS1}) - f_1(-v_{GS2}, -v_{DS2}) \tag{15-37}$$

Now let us express v_{GS2} and v_{DS2} in terms of the voltages of F_1. The current generator I produces a direct voltage drop across the diodes. Let us call these V_{GS1Q} and V_{GS2Q}. The circuit is such that

$$V_{GS1Q} = -V_{GS2Q}$$

Then,

$$v_{GS1} = V_{GS1Q} + v_i - v_L \tag{15-38a}$$

$$v_{GS2} = -V_{GS1Q} + v_i - v_L \tag{15-38b}$$

The drain to source voltages are given by

$$v_{DS1} = V_{DD} - v_L \tag{15-39a}$$

$$v_{DS2} = -V_{DD} - v_L \tag{15-39b}$$

Note that $V_{DD}^- = -V_{DD}$ and $V_{DD}^+ = V_{DD}$. Manipulating, we obtain

$$v_{DS2} = -2V_{DD} + v_{DS1} \tag{15-40a}$$

Similarly,

$$v_{GS2} = -2V_{GS1Q} + v_{GS1} \tag{15-40b}$$

The substitution of Eqs. 15-38 and 15-40 into Eq. 15-37 yields

$$i_L = f_1(V_{GS1Q} + v_1 - v_L, v_{DS1}) - f_1(V_{GS1Q} - v_1 + v_L, 2V_{DD} - v_{DS1}) \tag{15-41a}$$

and

$$i_L = f_1(v_{GS1}, v_{DS1}) - f_1(2V_{GSQ} - v_{GS1}, 2V_{DD} - v_{DS1}) \tag{15-41b}$$

Equations 15-41 express i_L in terms of the applied voltage, the output voltage, and the voltages of F_1. We can consider that i_L describes the characteristics of a fictitious device which produces the same output voltage and current as does the push-pull amplifier. Such a fictitious device is called a *composite device*, and Eqs. 15-41 describe its characteristics.

Now let us draw the graphical characteristics for the composite device. These characteristics will depend not only upon the characteristics of the FET's, they will also depend upon V_{GSQ} and V_{DD} and R_{ac}. Hence, they are valid for only one set of operating conditions. (This is similar to the discussion of Sec. 15-2). To draw the characteristics we use Eq. 15-41b. For instance, choose a pair of values v_{GS1} and v_{DS1}. Read two currents from the characteristics which correspond to $v_{GS} = v_{GS1}, v_{DS} = v_{DS1}$ and $v_{GS} = 2V_{GSQ} - v_{GS}, v_{DS} = 2V_{DD} - v_{DS1}$. Now subtract the two currents. This then gives the value of i_L which corresponds to the chosen v_{GS1} and v_{DS1}. The procedure can be simplified by the graphical construction shown in Fig. 15-11. We must subtract currents that correspond to drain to source voltages of v_{DS1} and $2V_{DD} - v_{DS1}$. We position the characteristics so that these values are aligned. Note that we have drawn two sets of characteristics so that

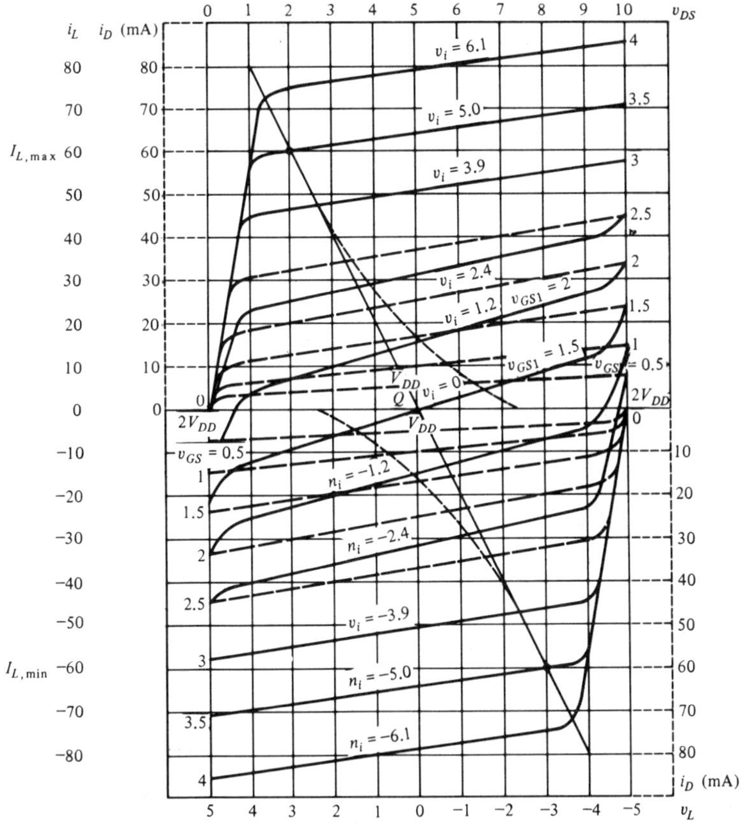

Figure 15-11. Composite characteristics for the amplifier of Fig. 15-9.

the voltage $2V_{DD}$ on one is aligned with 0 on the other. Let us illustrate the procedure with a numerical example. Assume that

$$V_{DD} = 5 \text{ V}$$

$$V_{GSQ} = 1.5 \text{ V}$$

$$R_{ac} = 50 \text{ ohms}$$

Then we obtain two sets of output characteristics for F_1 and position them so that the v_{DS} axes align as discussed. In these curves we have plotted the individual device characteristics with dotted lines.

Now choose a value of v_{GS1}. We start with $v_{GS1} = 1.5$ V. Then, from Eq. 15-41b we have

$$i_L = f(1.5, v_{DS1}) - f(1.5, 10 - v_{DS1})$$

Hence, use both the $v_{GS} = 1.5$ V curves. The curves for the composite device labeled $v_{GS1} = 1.5$ V then results.

Now we choose a new value of $v_{GS1} = 2$ V. Then, substituting in Eq. 15-41b, we obtain

$$i_L = f_1(2, v_{DS1}) - f_1(1, 10 - v_{DS1})$$

We now subtract the $v_{GS} = 1$ V curve from the $v_{GS} = 2$ V curve. The curve on the composite characteristics labeled $v_{GS1} = 2$ V then results.

If we proceed in this way for all values of $v_{GS1} = 0.5, 1, 1.5, \ldots, 4$, the complete composite device output characteristic will be obtained. Note that when $v_{GS1} > 2.5$, $i_{D2} = 0$ and, hence, the composite device characteristic coincides with one for the individual device.

We must label the composite device characteristics in terms of v_i rather than in terms of v_{GS1}. The procedure for doing this is similar to that discussed in the last section. We start by drawing the load line. The load has a dc resistance of 0 ohms and an ac resistance of 50 ohms. To draw the load line we must label the axes in terms of i_L and v_L. The value of v_L is given by (see Eq. 15-39a)

$$v_L = V_{DD} - v_{DS1} \tag{15-42}$$

Substituting in this equation, we obtain the axis labeled v_L in Fig. 15-11. (V_L varies from -5 to $+5$ V here.)

The load current is given by Eq. 15-37. Hence, the i_L axis is as shown in Fig. 15-11. Under quiescent conditions, $i_L = 0$ and $v_L = 0$. Hence, the quiescent operating point of the *composite* device is as shown on the v_{DS} axis in Fig. 15-11. The ac load line is then drawn through this point with a slope equal to $-1/R_{ac}$.

The intersection of the ac load line with each composite characteristic gives the values of v_L which result when v_{GS1} is equal to the value specified for the composite characteristic in question. Then, using Eq. 15-38a we can obtain the value of v_i which corresponds to the v_{GS1} in question. For instance, if $v_{GS1} = 2$ V, then $v_L = 0.7$ V and

$$v_i = 2 - 1.5 + 0.7 = 1.2 \text{ V}$$

Doing this for each curve on the composite characteristic, we obtain the final set of composite characteristics shown in Fig. 15-11. The composite characteristic is now complete and we can use it to obtain the output signal. For instance, suppose that

$$v_i = 5 \cos \omega t \text{ V} \tag{15-43}$$

Then, the maximum and minimum values will be as marked on the curve. Then, the output power is given by

$$\begin{aligned} P_2 &= (V_{L,\max} - V_{L,\min})(I_{L,\max} - I_{L,\min})/8 \\ P_2 &= [3 - (-3)][60 \times 10^{-3} - (-60 \times 10^{-3})]/8 = 0.09 \text{ W} \end{aligned} \tag{15-44}$$

Note that we have used the composite curves for $v_i = 5$ and $v_i = -5$ V to obtain the data.

If we want to perform a five-point analysis to compute the harmonic distortion (see Sec. 5-13), we then would use the curves for $v_i = 5, 2.5, 0, -2.5$, and -5 V to obtain the desired information. (Note that we would have to interpolate to obtain the data from the ± 2.5-V curves.)

The output waveform from the push-pull circuit is symmetric so the second harmonic distortion is zero (see Eq. 5-100c). In general, we shall show (in Sec. 15-6) that, because of symmetry, all the even harmonic distortions will be zero in a push-pull circuit. This *cancellation of the even harmonic distortion* is an important advantage of push-pull circuits.

The load line is the locus of operation of the composite device. Of course, it is a straight line. Let us now obtain the locus of operation of the individual devices. This is obtained by "working backward." Each point on the composite characteristic is obtained from the subtraction of two currents. These are the actual currents through the FET's. (Actually it is the negative of i_{D2}.) The current defined by the intersection of the load line with the appropriate composite characteristics gives an instantaneous operating point for the composite device. The two currents used to obtain this point give the currents of the FET's. Thus, we can project up and down to the appropriate curves to obtain the operating points of the FET's. The connection of these points gives the locus of operation of the individual FET's and is shown by the dashed lines in Fig. 15-11. Note that each FET is cut off for part of the cycle. Hence, this amplifier operates class AB.

The lower characteristic in Fig. 15-11 is for a *n*-channel FET. To obtain the actual operating voltage and currents for F_2, the values must be multiplied by -1.

Junction Transistor Amplifiers

Let us now consider the analysis of the emitter follower push-pull amplifier shown in Fig. 15-12. The basic ideas of this amplifier were discussed in Sec. 14-8. We shall now consider its graphical analysis, which follows that for the FET amplifier. That is, we shall

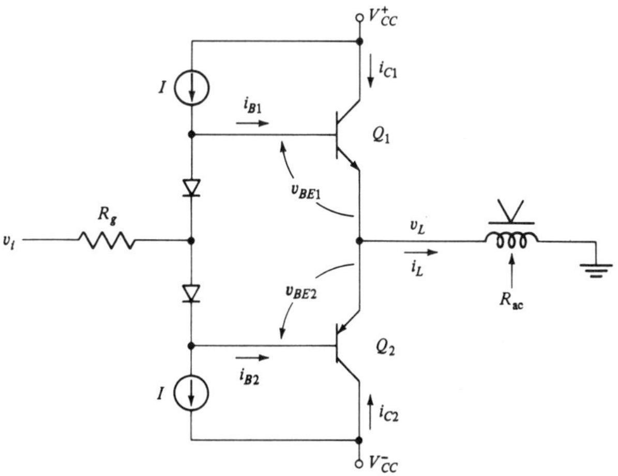

Figure 15-12. A complementary symmetry, emitter follower push-pull amplifier. Note that two power supplies are used $V_{CC}^{-} = -V_{CC}^{+} = V_{CC}$

obtain the composite characteristics and, from them, obtain the output information. For bipolar junction transistors, the analysis is complicated by the fact that we must obtain the base current and, hence, the input characteristics must be used. The ideas of Sec. 9-2 will be applied here.

The output characteristics of transistors Q_1 and Q_2 can be expressed as

$$i_{C1} = f_1(i_{B1}, v_{CE1}) \tag{15-45a}$$

$$i_{C2} = f_2(i_{B2}, v_{CE2}) \tag{15-45b}$$

Since we have complementary symmetry,

$$f_2(i_{B2}, v_{CE2}) = -f_1(-i_{B2}, -v_{CE2}) \tag{15-46}$$

Note that these relations are essentially the same as Eqs. 15-35 and 15-36. The load current is given by

$$i_L = -(i_{E1} + i_{E2})$$

In general, we can assume that β is large, so that

$$i_E = -i_C$$

Hence,

$$i_L = i_{C1} + i_{C2} \tag{15-47}$$

Now, proceeding as in the derivation of Eqs. 15-37 to 15-41, we have

$$i_L = f_1(i_{B1}, v_{CE1}) - f_1(-i_{B2}, -v_{CE2}) \tag{15-48}$$

$$i_L = f_1(i_{B1}, v_{CE1}) - f_1(-i_{B2}, 2V_{CC} - v_{CE1}) \tag{15-49}$$

We must now determine i_{B1} and i_{B2} as a function of v_i. We shall write the *magnitude* of the voltage drop across the diode as V_D. Then, from Fig. 15-12, we have

$$i_{B2} + i_{B1} = (v_i + V_D - v_{BE1} - v_L)/R_g \tag{15-50a}$$

$$i_{B1} + i_{B2} = (v_i - V_D - v_{BE2} - v_L)/R_g \tag{15-50b}$$

Under quiescent conditions

$$v_i = 0 \tag{15-51}$$

$$v_L = 0 \tag{15-52}$$

By symmetry

$$I_{B1Q} = -I_{B2Q} \tag{15-53}$$

Hence,

$$V_{BE1Q} = V_D \tag{15-54a}$$

$$V_{BE2Q} = -V_D \tag{15-54b}$$

In addition, we can write

$$V_{CE1Q} = V_{CC} \tag{15-55a}$$

$$V_{CE2Q} = -V_{CC} \tag{15-55b}$$

Then, using these equations and Eq. 15-54 we can obtain I_{B1Q} and I_{B2Q} from the input characteristics. Let us write

$$i_{B1} = I_{B1Q} + i_{b1} \tag{15-56a}$$

$$i_{B2} = -I_{B1Q} + i_{b2} \tag{15-56b}$$

and

$$v_{BE1} = v_{BE1Q} + v_{be1} \tag{15-57a}$$

$$v_{BE2} = -V_{BE1Q} + v_{be2} \tag{15-57b}$$

The *signal* voltages across the diodes are zero. Hence,

$$v_{be1} = v_{be2} \tag{15-58}$$

Now let us assume that

$$i_{b1} = i_{b2} \tag{15-59}$$

This implies that the variation of i_{B1} and i_{B2} about their quiescent operating points is the same. We shall demonstrate that this assumption is valid subsequently.

Then

$$i_{B2} = -I_{B1Q} + i_{B1} \tag{15-60}$$

This equation is approximately correct as long as i_{B2} does not change sign. If it does then replace Eq. 15-6a by $i_{B2} = 0$. Substituting in Eq. 15-49 we have

$$i_L = f_1(I_{B1Q} + i_{b1}, v_{CE1}) - f_1(I_{B1Q} - i_{B1}, 2V_{CC} - v_{CE1}) \tag{15-61}$$

This relation has the same form as Eq. 15-41a and, hence, the procedure for drawing the composite characteristic follows that for the FET. Now we match curves of $I_{B1Q} + i_{b1}$ with those for $I_{B1Q} - i_{b1}$. Let us illustrate this procedure with an example. Note that we still must relate the values of i_B to those of v_i.

Assume that, in the circuit of Fig. 15-12,

$$V_{CC} = 10 \text{ V } (V_{CC}^{+} = 10 \text{ V}, V_{CC}^{-} = -10 \text{ V})$$

$$R_g = 20 \text{ ohms}$$

$$R_{ac} = 7.5 \text{ ohms}$$

$$V_D = 0.7 \text{ V}$$

We require the input characteristics (see Fig. 15-14) to obtain the input quantities. Using the values of V_{CC} and v_D, we have

$$I_{B1Q} = 3.0 \text{ mA}$$

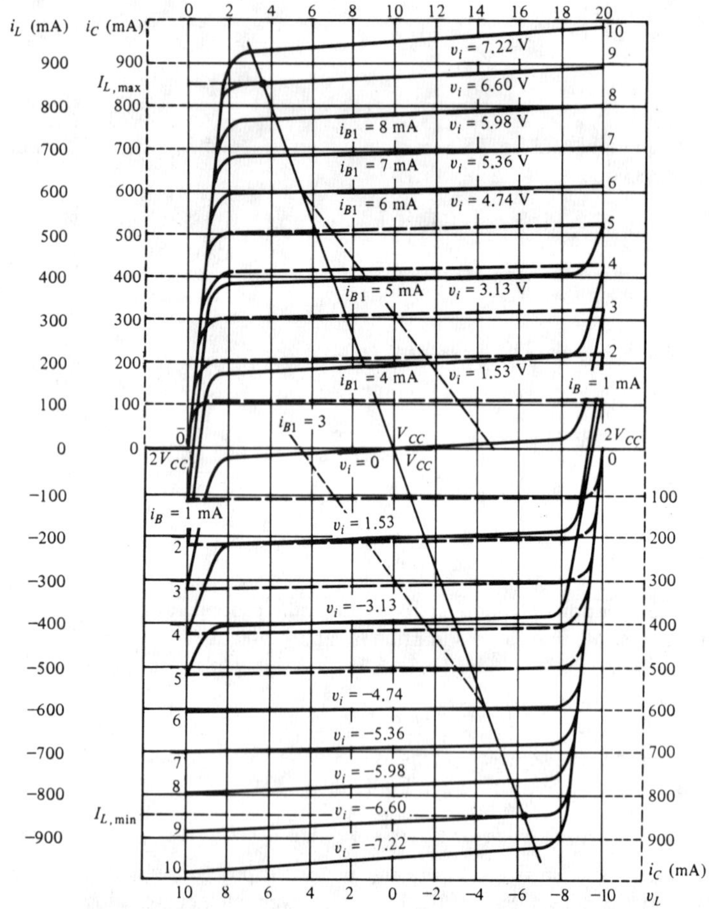

Figure 15-13. Composite characteristics for the amplifier of Fig. 15-12.

We now use Eq. 15-61 to plot the composite characteristics. This is done in Fig. 15-13 for increments of i_{B1} of 1 mA. Note that when $i_{B1} > 3$ mA, i_{B2} does not change sign since Q_2 is now cut off and $i_{B2} = 0$.

Now we must calculate the value of v_i which corresponds to the value of i_{b1} used to plot the composite characteristic. From Eq. 15-50, we have

$$v_i = (i_{B1} + i_{B2})R_g - V_D + v_{BE1} + v_L \tag{15-62}$$

Let us now draw the load line. It passes through the point Q with a slope $-1/R_{\text{ac}} = -1/7.5$. Now we can obtain the value of v_L which corresponds to i_{B1}. Now we can draw the locus of operation for each transistor as in the case of the FET amplifier. It is shown by the dashed curve in Fig. 15-13. (Note that for part of each cycle, the current

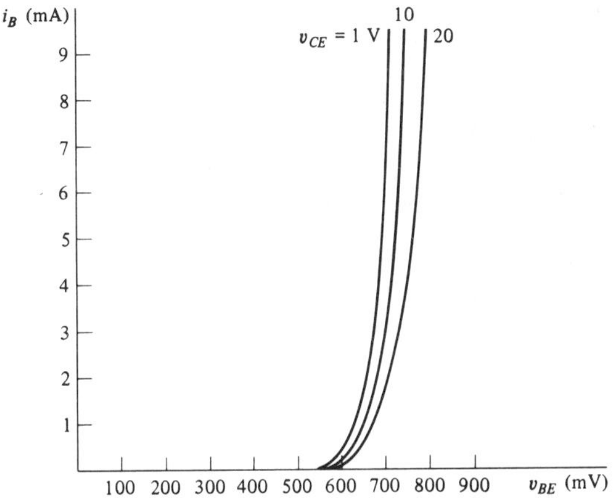

Figure 15-14. Input characteristics for the *n-p-n* transistor of Fig. 15-12.

through each transistor becomes zero so the operation is class AB.) We can now find v_{CE1} that corresponds to i_{B1}. The input characteristic can then be used to find v_{BE1}. Equation 15-60 and the restrictions following it can then be used to obtain i_{B2}. All of the calculated values can then be substituted in Eq. 15-62 to obtain v_i.

Now let us obtain the output power neglecting distortion if

$$v_i = 6.6 \cos \omega t \text{ V}$$

Then,

$$P_2 = (V_{L,\text{max}} - V_{L,\text{min}})(I_{L,\text{max}} - I_{L,\text{min}})/8$$

Substituting, we obtain

$$P_2 = [6.4 - (-6.4)][0.850 - (-0.850)]/8 = 2.72 \text{ W}$$

The lower characteristic is for a *n-p-n* transistor. To actually obtain the operating voltages and currents for Q_2, all quantities should be multiplied by -1.

Note that the spacing between the composite characteristic curve is greater for values of $-4.74 \leqq v_i \leqq 4.74$ than it is for $|v_i| > 4.74$. This constitutes a distortion. However, we shall see in Sec. 15-6 that this distortion is greatly reduced by the feedback of the common-emitter stages, That is, the spacing of the value of v_i on the composite characteristic tends to offset the varied spacing of the composite characteristics. Note that, as in the case of the FET amplifiers, the output is symmetric so the even harmonic distortion is zero.

We assumed that $i_{b1} = i_{b2}$. Let us study the input characteristic to see if this approximation is valid. From these characteristics we see that i_B varies approximately linearly about its quiescent value. Consequently, the increase in i_{B1} will be essentially equal to the decrease in i_{B2} and so $i_{b1} = i_{b2}$. These curves depart from linearity for small values of i_B, but then the value of i_C will be small and thus it will not substantially affect the composite characteristic. Similarly, the value of v_i calculated by Eq. 15-62 will be accurate. (Also note that if R_g is small, the value of i_B will have little effect on v_i.)

15-5. THE QUASICOMPLEMENTARY SYMMETRY PUSH-PULL AMPLIFIER

The complementary symmetry push-pull amplifier uses matched, but complementary, devices. That is, the output stage consists of a *n*-channel FET and a matching *p*-channel FET or a *n-p-n* and a matching *p-n-p* transistor. Both devices have the same characteristics except for a change in sign. Often, it would be an advantage to use two identical (rather than complementary) devices. This makes matching them less of a problem since devices from the same production run can be picked. In the case of integrated circuits this is especially important. For instance, if both transistors were *n-p-n* then, since they were fabricated at the same time, the chance that they will be matched is very good. In integrated circuits it is also desirable to use *n-p-n* transistors for the output stages since *p-n-p* transistors fabricated in integrated circuits can only handle a limited amount of power.

Power FET's are, at the present time, fabricated as *n*-channel enhancement MOS devices called *VMOS FET's*. The V stands for vertical, or "V," since a V-shaped "cut" is etched into the surface of the substrate. This improves the heat dissipating ability of the transistor and, thus, its power handling ability. Let us now see how push-pull amplifiers can be fabricated using identical output devices.

The complementary symmetry push-pull amplifier discussed in the last section had no even harmonic distortion. The push-pull circuits that we shall develop here will also have this advantage. In fact, we shall see that they function in essentially the same way as the complementary symmetry push-pull amplifiers. Such amplifiers are called *quasicomplementary symmetry* push-pull amplifiers since they act as complementary symmetry amplifiers but do not use complementary symmetry devices.

VMOS Push-Pull Amplifiers

We shall start our discussion with the VMOS quasicomplementary symmetry amplifier (see Fig. 15-15). Note that this circuit requires two input signals v_i and $-v_i$. These are 180° out-of-phase. Such signals can be supplied by a circuit called a *phase inverter* or a *phase splitter*. The differential amplifiers of Secs. 14-1 to 14-3 can be used as phase inverters. If one input is grounded, then one output of the differential amplifier will be $A_v V_1$ and the other will be $-A_v V_1$ so the required 180° phase difference is obtained.

To simplify the diagram we have also assumed that the input bias voltages are applied through the input leads. (We shall subsequently discuss a more practical circuit.) Then

$$v_{GS1Q} = v_{GS2Q} \tag{15-63}$$

Note that under quiescent conditions, $v_i = 0$. Also, from Fig. 15-15, we have

$$i_L = i_{D1} - i_{D2} \tag{15-64}$$

Then, proceeding as in Sec. 15-4, we obtain

$$i_L = f_1(v_{GS1}, v_{DS1}) - f_1(v_{GS2}, v_{DS2}) \tag{15-65}$$

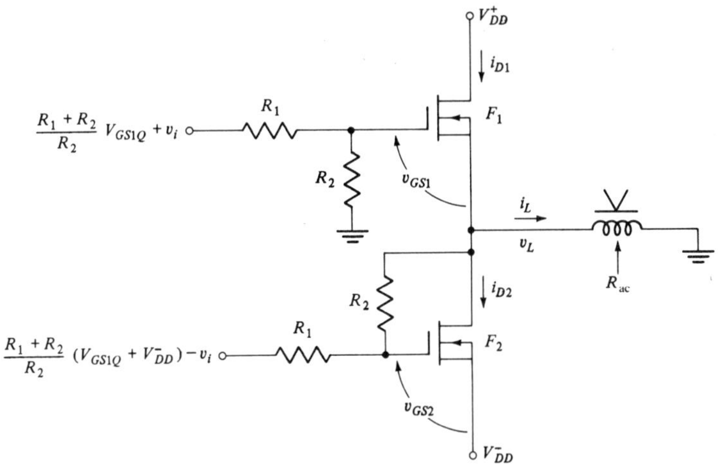

Figure 15-15. A basic quasicomplementary symmetry VMOS push-pull amplifier. Note that there are two power supplies V_{DD}^{+} and V_{DD}^{-}. $V_{DD}^{+} = -V_{DD}^{-} = V_{DD}$.

From Fig. 15-15, we can write

$$v_{DS1} = V_{DD} - v_L \tag{15-66a}$$

$$v_{DS2} = v_L + V_{DD} \tag{15-66b}$$

Note that $V_{DD}^{-} = -V_{DD}$. Then, manipulating, we have

$$v_{DS2} = 2V_{DD} - v_{DS1} \tag{15-66c}$$

Now let us compute the gate to source voltages.

$$v_{GS1} = V_{GS1Q} + \frac{R_2}{R_1 + R_2} v_i - v_L \tag{15-67a}$$

$$v_{GS2} = V_{GS1Q} - \frac{R_2}{R_1 + R_2} v_i + v_L \frac{R_1}{R_1 + R_2} \tag{15-67b}$$

From Eq. 15-41a we see that we would like to be able to express these quantities as $V_{GS1Q} + v_i - v_L$ and $V_{GS1Q} - v_i + v_L$, respectively. The coefficients of v_L differ in Eqs. 15-67a and 15-67b. To remedy this situation, let us choose

$$R_1 \gg R_2 \tag{15-68}$$

Now we have

$$v_{GS1} = V_{GS1Q} + v_i' - v_L \tag{15-69a}$$

$$v_{GS2} = V_{GS1Q} - v_i' + v_L \tag{15-69b}$$

where

$$v_i' = \frac{R_2}{R_1 + R_2} v_i \tag{15-70}$$

Then, substituting Eqs. 15-69 and 15-66c into Eq. 15-65, we obtain

$$i_L = f_1(V_{GS1Q} + v_i' - v_L, v_{DS1}) - f_1(V_{GS1Q} - v_i' + v_L, 2V_{DD} - v_{DS1}) \qquad (15\text{-}71)$$

This is essentially the same relation as that of Eq. 15-41a so the procedure used to draw the composite characteristics of Fig. 15-11 apply here. In fact, if, for the circuit of Fig. 15-15

$$V_{DD} = 5 \text{ V}$$

$$V_{GS1Q} = 1.5 \text{ V}$$

$$R_{ac} = 50 \text{ ohms}$$

then the characteristics of Fig. 15-11 apply exactly for this amplifier. The input signal given on these characteristics now must be expressed in terms of v_i'. The actual input signal must be $(R_1 + R_2)/R_2$ times as large as v_i'. This seems to require that the stage that drives the push-pull amplifier be capable of providing relatively large voltage swings, but we shall see that this need not be the case.

Before considering an actual amplifier circuit let us discuss why the resistances R_1 and R_2 are introduced in the circuit of Fig. 15-15. The amplifier can be considered to consist of a source follower (F_1) and a common-source stage (F_2). The emitter follower has the inherent feedback that we discussed in Secs. 15-2 and 15-4. The common-source stage does not have this feedback so we include the resistors R_1 and R_2 in the common-source stage so that the feedback is introduced. Thus, the common-source stage functions in the same way as the source follower stage. The incorporation of the resistors also reduces the effective signal level. To balance this, the resistors R_1 and R_2 are also included in the source follower stage.

In Fig. 15-16 we show the push-pull amplifier with typical driver stages. The transistors Q_3 and Q_4 together with emitter resistors R_E provide the driver circuits with high-output impedance. This provides the large value of R_1 needed. The current generators I are used to establish the bias values. Note that the gain of the amplifier stages Q_3 and Q_4 will not be high because R_2 will be small. On the other hand, these amplifiers can provide moderate gain. Consequently, the signal levels need not be excessive. We can construct a junction transistor amplifier that is analogous to Fig. 15-16. We shall next consider an alternate procedure that can be used.

The Junction Transistor Quasicomplementary Symmetry Amplifier

Now let us consider a quasicomplementary symmetry amplifier that uses *n-p-n* transistors. A basic one is shown in Fig. 15-17. This circuit is the same as the true complementary symmetry circuit of Fig. 15-12 except that now the pair of transistors Q_2 and Q_3 replace the single *p-n-p* transistor. It may seem as though we are not accomplishing anything here since Q_3 itself is a *p-n-p* transistor, but it is not difficult to obtain low-power *p-n-p* transistors, even in integrated circuits. Problems arise when we want to obtain a high-power *p-n-p* transistor. In this circuit, Q_2 is a high-power *n-p-n* transistor while Q_3 is a low-power *p-n-p* transistor.

Now let us demonstrate that Q_2 and Q_3 together are equivalent to a high-power *p-n-p* transistor that is complementary symmetric to Q_2. Consider Fig. 15-18. We want

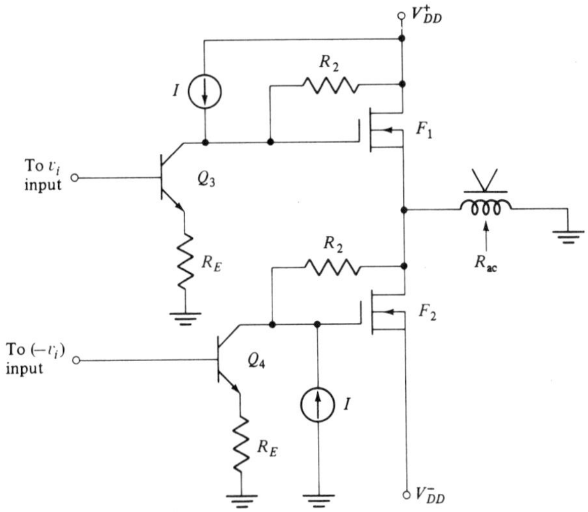

Figure 15-16. A quasi-complementary symmetry VMOS push-pull amplifier. Note that two power supplies are used $V_{DD}^{+} = -V_{DD}^{-} = V_{DD}$.

to show that the circuit of Fig. 15-18a functions in the same way as the *p-n-p* transistor of Fig. 15-18b, when either of them is to be connected into the same circuit. That is, assume that there are two identical circuits except that one contains Q_P and the other contains the Q_2, Q_3 pair. We will show that both function equivalently. If the conditions external to points *a*, *b*, and *d* are the same, then

$$v_{BE3} = v_{BEP} \tag{15-72}$$

and

$$v_{CE3} - v_{BE2} = v_{CEP} \tag{15-73}$$

In general, in the active region, which is the one we are concerned with when we draw composite characteristics.

$$|v_{CE}| \gg |v_{BE}|$$

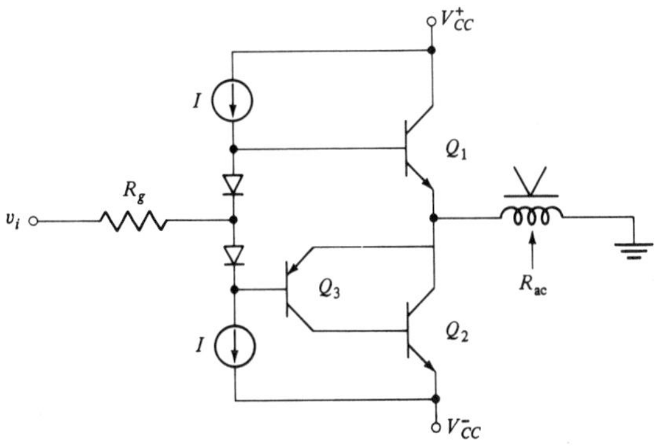

Figure 15-17. A quasi-complementary symmetry transistor amplifier. Note that there are two power supplies $V_{CC}^{+} = -V_{CC}^{-} = V_{CC}$.

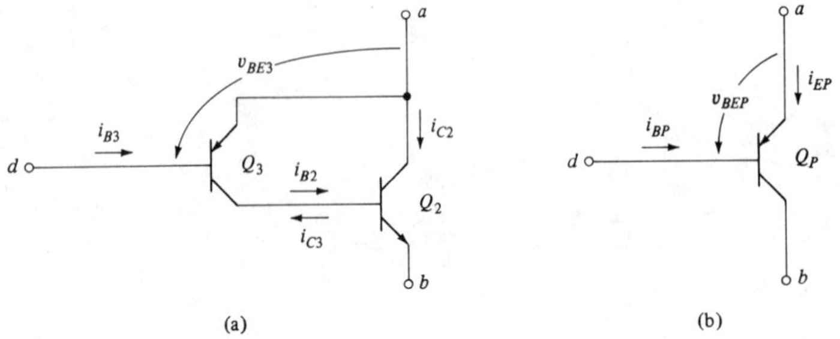

Figure 15-18. (a) A two transistor pair that is equivalent to a high-power *p-n-p* transistor. (b) A high-power *p-n-p* transistor.

Hence,

$$v_{CE3} \simeq v_{CEP} \tag{15-74}$$

For Q_3 and Q_P we can write

$$i_{C3} = f_3(v_{BE3}, v_{CE3}) \tag{15-75a}$$

$$i_{CP} = f_P(v_{BEP}, v_{CEP}) \tag{15-75b}$$

Then, substituting Eqs. 15-72 and 15-74, we have

$$i_{C3} = f_3(v_{BEP}, v_{CEP}) \tag{15-76}$$

Transistors Q_3 and Q_P are both *p-n-p* transistors. Assume that they are each fabricated in the same way except that transistor Q_P will have a larger cross-sectional area since it is a power transistor. Thus, we can state

$$f_3 = K_1 f_P \tag{15-77}$$

where K_1 is a constant that is considerably less than one. Hence,

$$i_{C3} = K_1 f_P(v_{BEP}, v_{CEP}) \tag{15-78}$$

Then

$$i_{B2} = -K_1 f_P(v_{BEP}, v_{CEP}) \tag{15-79}$$

The collector current is approximately proportional to the base current. Hence,

$$i_{C2} = K_1 \beta_F f_P(v_{BEP}, v_{CEP}) \tag{15-80}$$

The "constant" β_F actually varies. For instance, β_F falls off greatly to the left of the knees of the output characteristics, that is, in the saturation region. However, the function f_P contains a falloff of i_C with v_{CE}. In addition, we usually do not work in the saturation region since it is a region of high distortion. Thus, the results will be reasonably accurate if we assume that β_F is a constant.

The current that corresponds to $i_{EP} = -i_{CP}$ is $i_{C2} + i_{E3}$. Let us call this i_E'. Then, since $|i_{C2}| \gg |i_{E3}|$

$$i_E' = -K_1 \beta_F f_P(v_{BEP}, v_{CEP}) \tag{15-81a}$$

while

$$i_{EP} = -f_P(v_{BEP}, v_{CEP}) \tag{15-81b}$$

Now let us consider the term $K_1\beta_F$.

$$K_1 = \frac{|i_{C3}|}{|i_{CP}|} = \frac{|i_{B2}|}{|i_{CP}|} \tag{15-82a}$$

In addition,

$$\beta_F \simeq \frac{|i_{C2}|}{|i_{B2}|} \tag{15-82b}$$

We know that Q_2 and Q_P are to be complementary transistors. Then, under symmetric operation conditions we desire that

$$|i_{C2}| = |i_{CP}| \tag{15-83}$$

If these conditions are to be met then we must have

$$K_1 = \frac{1}{\beta_F} \tag{15-84}$$

If this is the case, then substituting in Eq. 15-81, we obtain

$$i'_E = i_{EP} = -f_P(v_{BEP}, v_{CEP}) \tag{15-85}$$

Hence, Q_2 and Q_3 function as the transistor Q_P. This is the relation that we wished to establish. Hence, the circuit of Fig. 15-17 can be analyzed in exactly the same fashion as that of Fig. 15-12. For instance, if, in the circuit of Fig. 15-17,

$$V_{CC} = 10\text{ V } (V_{CC}^+ = 10\text{ V}, V_{CC}^- = -10\text{ V})$$

$$R_g = 20\text{ ohms}$$

$$R_{ac} = 7.5\text{ ohms}$$

$$V_D = 0.7\text{ V}$$

where V_D is the voltage drop across the diodes then Fig. 15-13 represents the composite characteristics for this amplifier. In Fig. 15-17, $|i_{B3}|$ will be less than $|i_{B1}|$. This will introduce some asymmetries into the value of v_i (see Eq. 15-62). However, if R_g is small, then the effect of i_B on v_i will be small. Thus the effect of the asymmetries will be minor.

The reader should note that we have made some approximations in obtaining Eq. 15-85 and some error in the calculations will result. Nevertheless, the results obtained using this analysis are reasonably accurate in computing the distortion and power output.

If the conditions of Eqs. 15-81 to 15-84 are not met then some unbalance will result this can be reduced by driving Q_1 with a transistor that is symmetric with a_3.

The circuit of Fig. 15-18a can be used to replace a *n-p-n* transistor in other complementary symmetry circuits. For instance, in Fig. 15-19, we show a modification of the circuit of Fig. 14-36. This circuit is similar to that of Fig. 15-17. Note that we have added resistors R_{E1} and R_{E2} and transistors Q_4 and Q_5 to provide short circuit protection.

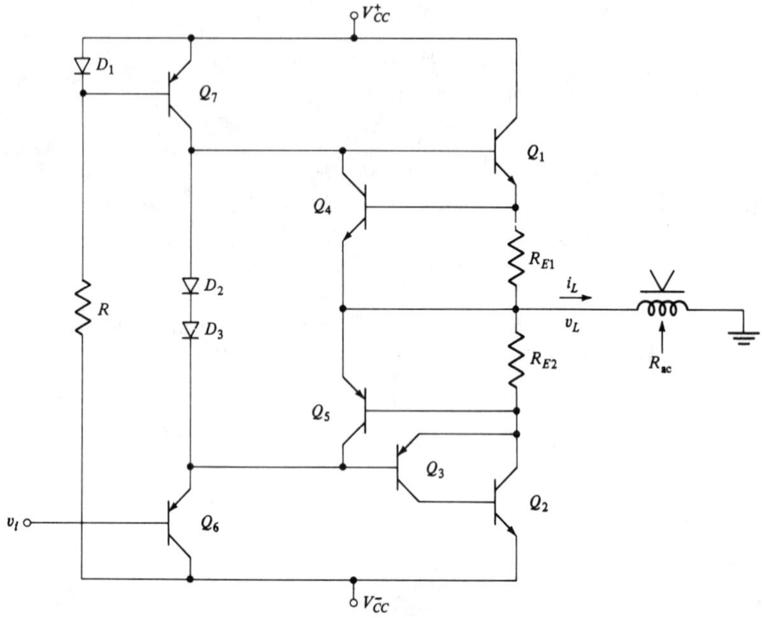

Figure 15-19. A quasicomplementary symmetry amplifier based on the circuit of Fig. 14-36.

Normally these resistors are small enough so that they do not substantially affect the analysis. Remember (see Sec. 14-8) that v_i must be level shifted so that, under quiescent operation, $v_L = 0$.

The short circuit protective circuits can also be added to the circuits of Figs. 15-12 and 15-17 without substantially affecting the operation.

15-6. DISTORTION IN PUSH-PULL AMPLIFIERS

Push-pull amplifiers have numerous advantages. They allow the use of class AB operation with a subsequent increase in efficiency (see Sec. 15-1). They can be easily adjusted so that the quiescent current through the load, which is often a loudspeaker, is zero. This is necessary for proper operation of most loudspeakers. Finally, when the circuit is symmetric, all even harmonic distortion is cancelled. Let us demonstrate that this is so. We shall use the amplifier of Fig. 15-12 in our discussion but it applies to all the push-pull circuits that we have considered. From Eq. 15-47 we have

$$i_L = i_{C1} + i_{C2} \tag{15-86}$$

Now suppose that there is distortion, so that

$$i_{C1} = I_{CA} + \sqrt{2}[I_{C1} \cos \omega t + I_{C2} \cos 2\omega t + I_{C3} \cos 3\omega t + I_{C4} \cos 4\omega t + \cdots] \tag{15-87}$$

The input signal for Q_2 is 180° out-of-phase with that for Q_1. In addition, i_{C2} will be negative while i_{C1} is positive. Hence,

$$i_{C2}(\omega t) = -i_{C1}(\omega t + \pi) \tag{15-88}$$

Therefore,

$$\begin{aligned} i_{C2} = &- \{I_{CA} + \sqrt{2}[I_{C1} \cos(\omega t + \pi) + I_{C2} \cos 2(\omega t + \pi) \\ &+ I_{C3} \cos 3(\omega t + \pi) + I_{C4} \cos 4(\omega t + \pi) + \cdots]\} \end{aligned} \tag{15-89}$$

Substituting in Eq. 15-86, we obtain

$$i_L = 2\sqrt{2}[I_{C1} \cos \omega t + I_{C3} \cos 3\omega t + \cdots] \tag{15-90}$$

Note that the load current contains no even harmonic terms. That is, as we have discussed, the push-pull circuit does not produce any even harmonic distortion. In practice, no push-pull circuit will be perfectly balanced. Hence, there will be some even harmonic distortion present. However, in most well-designed and constructed push-pull circuits, the matching of components will be such that the even harmonic distortion will be very small.

There is another distortion that occurs mainly in class AB push-pull transistor amplifiers. We discussed this briefly at the end of Sec. 15-4. Consider the composite characteristics of Fig. 15-13. Note that the spacing between the composite characteristics that are drawn for $0 \leqq i_{B1} \leqq 4.74$ mA is approximately twice that of the spacing for the characteristics drawn for $i_{B1} > 4.74$ mA. In general, we will find that spacing for the composite characteristics drawn for $0 \leqq i_{b1} \leqq 2I_{BQ}$ will be twice the spacing between the composite characteristics drawn for $i_{b1} > 2I_{BQ}$.

Let us consider the reason for this. When $i_B > 2I_{BQ}$, one transistor will be cut off so that the composite characteristics will coincide with the output characteristics for a single transistor. When $0 \leqq i_{b1} \leqq 2I_{BQ}$, the composite characteristics are obtained by subtracting a negative current from a positive one. Hence, the wider spacing results.

We can avoid this type of distortion by keeping $|i_B| < 2I_{BQ}$, but then the operation becomes class A with all its attendant inefficiencies (see Sec. 15-1). Usually, this is an undesirable solution.

Another way of avoiding this distortion is to operate exactly class B. For instance, for the transistors whose output characteristics are given in Fig. 15-13, we would set $I_{BQ} = 0$. Now one or the other transistor would always be cut off and there would be no actual subtraction of characteristics. That is, we would always have $i_B > 2I_{BQ}$. However, this solution is not acceptable because any slight increase in bias, or drift in operating point could result in the crossover distortion discussed in Sec. 14-8. Thus, to have a practical, efficient amplifier, we must operate class AB and then the distortion caused by the unequal spacing of the composite characteristics will be present. However, the actual distortion is not as bad as might be expected. The feedback introduced by the emitter follower circuit tends to offset the distortion. For instance, in Fig. 15-13, the spacing of the values of v_i on the characteristics that correspond to $0 \leqq i_B \leqq 2I_{BQ}$ is almost twice the spacing of the v_i values on those characteristics that correspond to $i_B > 2I_{BQ}$. This tends to cancel the distortion. In Fig. 15-20 we plot a transfer characteristic v_L versus v_i for the amplifier of Fig. 15-13. This characteristic is very linear and the variation in spacing of the composite characteristic cannot be observed. Thus, when emitter follower

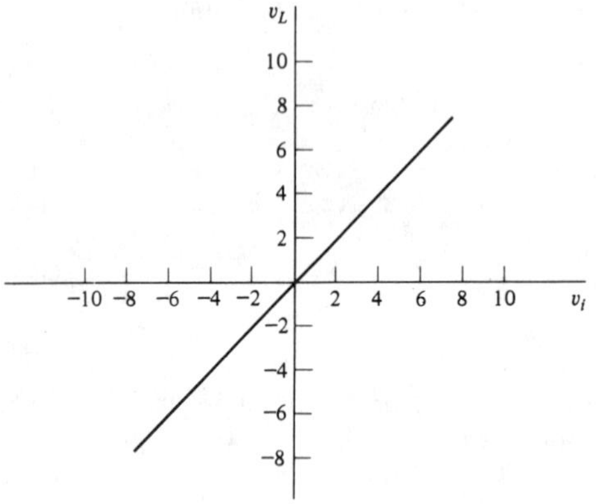

Figure 15-20. Transfer characteristics for the amplifier whose composite characteristics are given in Fig. 15-13.

stages are used, the distortion caused by the unequal spacing that we have discussed is greatly reduced.

If we used a common-emitter stage, then there would be no inherent feedback and the distortion could be large. In this case, the slope of the transfer characteristic for values of v_i which correspond to $0 \leqq i_B \leqq 2I_{BQ}$ would be twice that for values of v_i corresponding to $i_b > 2I_{BQ}$. The earliest transistor amplifiers suffered from this distortion as well as from crossover distortion. The effect of these distortions has been termed *transistor sound, but* as we have discussed, *it is not a problem in a well-designed transistor amplifier* and there is no reason why transistors cannot be used, and indeed are used, in the highest quality audio amplifiers.

When FET's are used as power stages, their composite characteristics do not exhibit the varied spacing that we have discussed here. This is because (see Sec. 15-4) the compression of the FET characteristics for low values of current tends to offset the varied spacing effect. Thus, FET's could be used in common-source as well as in source follower amplifiers. In general, this is not a very important advantage since we desire amplifiers with low-output impedance and source follower (or emitter follower) stages are usually used.

The primary source of distortion in a push-pull amplifier is operation in the saturation region (i.e., near or to the left of the knees of the curves). We shall discuss this in greater detail in the next section. (One source of distortion that we have not considered is the inability of the power supply to provide the required voltages and currents. We shall consider this in the next section.

15-7. DESIGN OF PUSH-PULL AMPLIFIERS

We have thus far considered the analysis of push-pull amplifiers. These analysis techniques can now be used in their design. There are several quantities that must be considered in the design of a power amplifier. These are: the output power P_2, which is the total signal power delivered to the load; the distortion, which is usually expressed as total harmonic distortion and/or as intermodulation distortion (see Sec. 5-13), and the maximum ratings of the transistors or FET's, especially the power dissipation rating.

The design can be broken up into several phases. The first consists of the choice of the circuit to be used. Next, the quiescent operating point of the devices must be picked. It must be verified that the required output and distortion specifications are met and that the ratings are not exceeded. In general, a first trial will not result in the meeting of all requirements, and a second or additional trials may be necessary. The essence of most designs is that there is no clear-cut solution. There will often be several acceptable designs and usually each has differing advantages. One may have better efficiency while another may use less expensive transistors, and so forth. The designer must weigh all alternatives and then choose the design to be used.

Let us now consider the given specifications. In general, these are R_{ac}, the ac load resistance of the loudspeaker or load, P_2, the sinusoidal signal output power, and the maximum total harmonic (and/or intermodulation) distortion. Now we must choose the circuit, then specify the operating point of the devices, which also specifies the power supply voltages, and finally determine the input requirements.

Usually, for high-power audio amplifiers, the choice of circuit is one of the quasi-complementary symmetry push-pull amplifiers. At lower power levels, complementary symmetry audio amplifiers will also be used.

Now let us discuss the actual details of the design of a specific circuit. In Fig. 15-21 we have drawn a composite characteristic and several load lines for a transistor push-pull amplifier of the types discussed in Secs. 15-4 and 15-5. We have drawn different load lines for four values of R_{ac}, the ac load resistances R_1, R_2, R_3, and R_4, where

$$R_4 > R_3 > R_2 > R_1 \tag{15-91}$$

In general, the load resistance is specified and cannot be varied so the load lines in Fig. 15-21 do not represent variations of a single design. However, it is instructional to consider the effect of varying the load resistance. Suppose that we adjust the input signal in order that we keep the maximum values of i_{B1} at 100 mA, so that $i_{B,\max}$ and $v_{B,\max}$ are determined from the intersection of the pertinent load line with the $i_{B1} = 100$ mA characteristic. Let us now consider a plot of P_2 and $\%H_T$ as functions of R_{ac} (see Fig. 15-22). As R_{ac} is increased from 0, P_2 increases and then falls off. The total harmonic distortion increases gradually and then begins to increase rapidly. Now consider Fig. 15-21. As R_{ac} increases, the load lines move toward and then into the knees of the curves. At this point, saturation limits the output and the waveform becomes clipped. For instance, the peaks of a sinusoid would become flattened. This causes the distortion to increase greatly and also limits the output power.

In general, R_{ac} is specified but varying the operating point can produce similar effects. Suppose that V_{CC} is reduced. The right and left ends of the curves will be moved closer together which will have the effect of moving the ends of the load lines closer to the knees of the characteristics, increasing the distortion. This will reduce the output power. In addition, it would also be reduced even if there were no distortion because the voltage swing would be reduced. However, reducing V_{CC} does reduce the dissipation. Similarly, if V_{CC} is increased, the distortion will decrease, and P_2 will increase as will the dissipation. In general, we attempt to obtain the operating conditions that yield minimum dissipation and input power while meeting the specifications on power output and distortion.

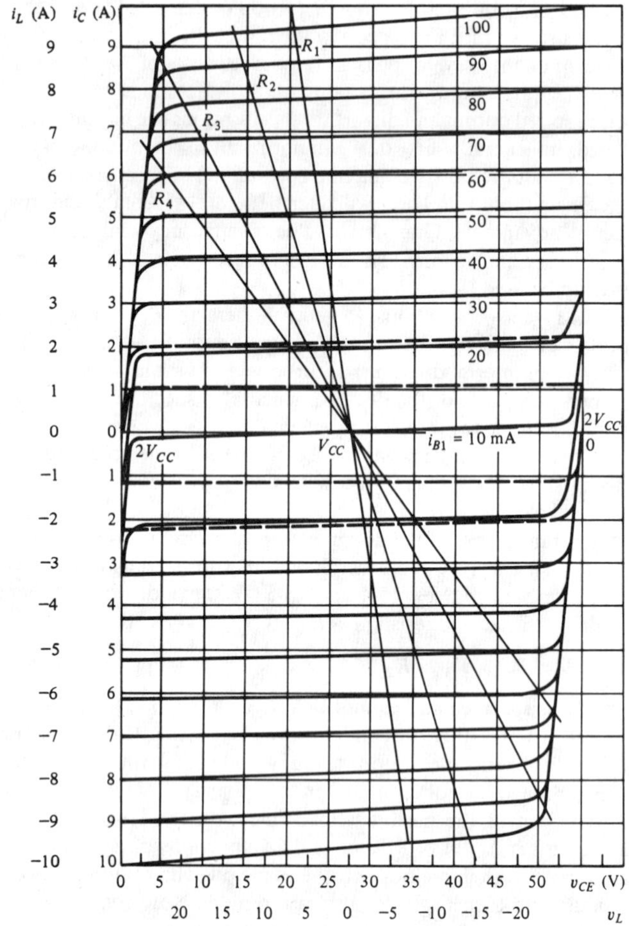

Figure 15-21. A composite characteristic showing different load lines.

The value of I_{CQ} can also be varied. In general, as the operation moves closer to class B, the efficiency increases. However, the operating point must be sufficiently far from cutoff so that crossover distortion is avoided.

In general, several operating points must be tried to determine an optimum design. This is tedious, since new composite characteristics must be drawn each time that the operating point is changed, but it is a necessary aspect of this design.

The maximum ratings of the transistor must not be exceeded. The maximum voltage and current swings can be obtained directly from the locus of operation of the transistor. This is shown in the dashed curve of Fig. 15-13. Note that for class AB operation, the locus lies along a (nonzero) length of the v_{CE} axis. The direct current is also determined from

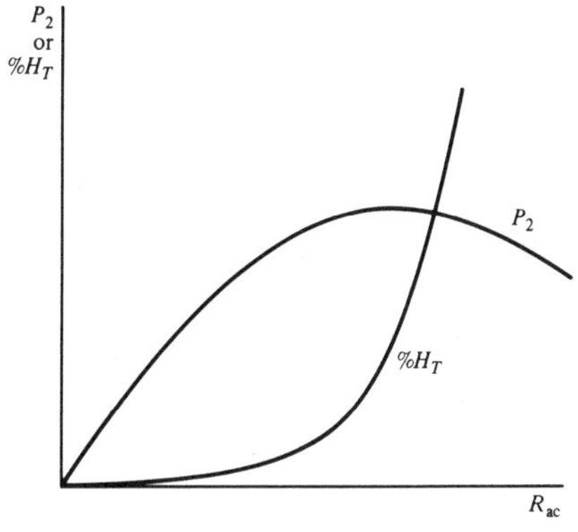

Figure 15-22. A plot of power output and total harmonic distortion versus load resistance for a typical push-pull amplifier.

this locus. That is, the value of I_{CA} is computed, using the five-point computation of Eq. 5-100a. Note that several of these points will be zero since the transistor will be cut off for somewhat less than half a cycle. Then, the power supplied by the power supply is

$$P_{oo} = 2I_{CA}V_{CC} \tag{15-92}$$

Hence, the power dissipated in *each* transistor is

$$P_{oD} = \tfrac{1}{2}(2I_{CA}V_{CC} - P_2) \tag{15-93}$$

If the operation is close to class B, then maximum P_{oD} will occur with maximum signal swing. On the other hand, if the operation is close to class A, then the dissipation is a maximum where P_2 is 0 (or close to it). Thus, P_{oD} may have to be checked at various signal levels. Note (see Sec. 15-6) that the distortion may also have to be checked at low as well as at high signal levels. If there is any series resistance in the circuit, the voltage drop across it and the power dissipated in it must be considered in all calculations.

Transistor manufacturers supply curves wherein maximum values of i_C and v_{CE} are supplied. The operation must be such that i_C and v_{CE} lie within the limits defined by the characteristic. It should be noted that these limitations are a function of the transistor's case temperature. In Sec. 15-9 we shall discuss such thermal considerations.

We have used the junction transistor in our discussion but the design using the VMOS FET's is essentially the same. Under some operating conditions, a reduction in distortion is possible. From Eq. 5-100d we see that the third harmonic distortion component of i_D is given by

$$\sqrt{2}I_{D3} = (I_{D,\max} - I_{D,\min})/6 - (I_{D\alpha} - I_{D\beta})/3 \tag{15-94}$$

In general, saturation (the knees of the curve) compresses $I_{D,\max}$ and $I_{D,\min}$. Similarly, under *some* conditions of operation, the compression of the FET output characteristics for low values of i_D can reduce $I_{D\alpha} - I_{D\beta}$. It is possible that both of these distortion effects will cause

$$I_{D,\max} - I_{D,\min} = 2(I_{D\alpha} - I_{D\beta})$$

In such a case, the third harmonic distortion will become zero. Usually, the total harmonic distortion is small when this occurs.

When a complete audio amplifier is built, the distortion produced in the output stage may actually be significantly *greater* than the actual distortion produced by the overall amplifier. In Chapter 17 we shall discuss feedback amplifiers. We shall demonstrate there that the incorporation of feedback can substantially reduce the distortion. In fact, we have already seen this to some extent where the simple feedback in emitter or source followers significantly reduced the distortion.

One other fact should be noted. Distortion in audio amplifiers is often due, not to the amplifier itself, but to the power supply. For instance, consider the amplifier whose characteristics are given in Fig. 15-21. Suppose that $R_{ac} = R_1$. Then, no significant distortion due to saturation will occur. The maximum value of i_D is 9.6 A. Suppose that the power supply cannot deliver this current without having its voltage fall off excessively. Then this will flatten the peaks of i_L and distortion will result. Thus, it is important to have a power supply that can supply the required maximum current without having the power supply voltage fall off measurably.

15-8. PUSH-PULL AMPLIFIER WITH AN OUTPUT TRANSFORMER

In the design of push-pull amplifiers (or amplifiers in general) it would be very convenient to be able to vary the load resistance (see Sec. 5-7). Unfortunately, this is usually not possible since the load is usually specified. In Sec. 15-1 we considered the ideal transformer and discussed how its input impedance is a multiple of its turns ratio squared. That is, at signal frequencies, the input impedance of a transformer whose turns ratio is $n_1:n_2$ and whose load resistance is R_L, is

$$R_{ac} = \left(\frac{n_1}{n_2}\right)^2 R_L \tag{15-95}$$

(see Fig. 15-2a).

Push-pull amplifiers can utilize transformers to vary the load impedance seen by the active device. Two such circuits are shown in Fig. 15-23. The analysis of these circuits is similar to the analysis of transformerless ones discussed earlier. For instance, let us work with Fig. 15-23a.

$$i_L = \frac{n_1}{n_2}(i_{D1} - i_{D2}) \tag{15-96}$$

where, as in Sec. 15-4, we can write

$$i_{D1} = f_1(v_{GS1}, v_{DS1}) \tag{15-97a}$$

$$i_{D2} = f_1(v_{GS2}, v_{DS2}) \tag{15-97b}$$

The voltage induced in the coil of an ideal transformer is $n\, d\phi/dt$ where ϕ is the magnetic flux of the core. Then, because of this *transformer action*

$$v_{ds1} = -v_{ds2} \tag{15-98}$$

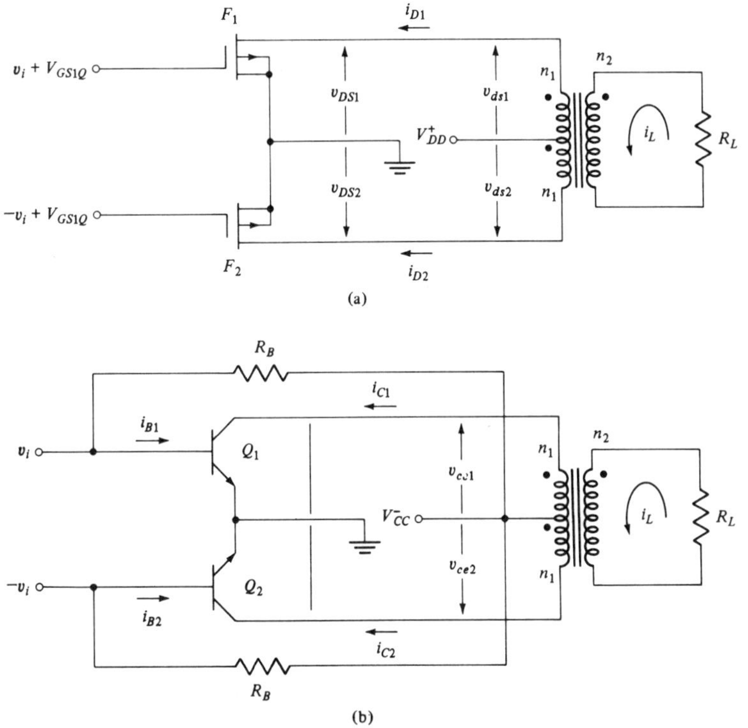

Figure 15-23. Simple circuits illustrating the use of an output transformer with a push-pull circuit.

(Note that we cannot state that this is true because of symmetry since, if it were not for transformer action, distortion could cause $v_{ds1} \neq -v_{ds2}$.) Then, proceeding as in Sec. 15-4,

$$v_{DS1} = V_{DD} + v_{ds1} \tag{15-99a}$$

$$v_{DS2} = V_{DD} + v_{ds2} \tag{15-99b}$$

Substituting Eq. 15-98 and manipulating, we obtain

$$v_{DS2} = 2V_{DD} - v_{DS1} \tag{15-99c}$$

Then, using the values for v_{GS1} and v_{GS2} from Fig. 15-23a, and substituting in Eqs. 15-97 and then into Eq. 15-96, we have

$$i_L = \frac{n_1}{n_2}[f_1(V_{GS1} + v_1, v_{DS1}) - f_1(V_{GS1} - v_1, 2V_{DD} - v_{DS1})] \tag{15-100}$$

This is basically the same form as Eq. 15-41 except that the v_L is missing since there is no inherent feedback in this circuit. Thus, the procedure for drawing the composite characteristic for the amplifier of Fig. 15-23 is essentially the same as that used to draw the composite characteristic of Fig. 15-11. There is one simplification here. Since feedback is missing, no computation of v_i from v_{GS} is necessary. The signal component of v_{GS1} is v_i and the signal component of v_{GS2} is $-v_i$.

Equation 15-96 indicates that the effective load resistance seen by the composite device is that seen looking into a transformer whose turns ratio is $n_1:n_2$. Hence,

$$R_{\text{ac}} = \left(\frac{n_1}{n_2}\right)^2 R_L \tag{15-101}$$

The analysis of the transistor amplifier of Fig. 15-23b is essentially the same as the one we have just considered. We have drawn a common-emitter transistor amplifier in Fig. 15-23b. The amplifier will be subject to the distortion caused by unequal spacing of the composite characteristics discussed in Sec. 15-6. If an emitter follower were used here, most of this distortion would be eliminated.

The transformer is a convenient way of adjusting the load seen by the amplifier to an optimum value. In fact, by having different taps on the secondary, a single transformer can provide several different turns ratios. This allows several values of R_L to be used without changing the R_{ac} seen by the active devices.

The transformer appears to be a very useful device. However, in most audio applications, the transformerless circuits discussed in Secs. 15-4 and 15-5 are used because they do not require a transformer. Transformers have relatively poor frequency response. In fact, a transformer used in a power amplifier that adequately covers the audio frequency range will be large, heavy, and expensive if the amplifier provides 10 W or more.

In Fig. 15-24 we show a model for a practical transformer. It consists of an ideal transformer, with other elements added to make its frequency response approximate that of an actual transformer.

Let us consider the elements of the model. The ideal transformer has an infinite primary inductance. Consequently, in an ideal transformer, if the secondary current is 0, then the primary current must also be zero. The *magnetizing inductors* L_m account for the fact that the actual primary inductance is finite. Note that, as the frequency decreases, the impedance of L_m will decrease, which decreases the voltage across the ideal transformer. Hence, the low-frequency response falls off. If the core of the transformer saturates, L_m becomes small, and in addition the transformer will not function properly.

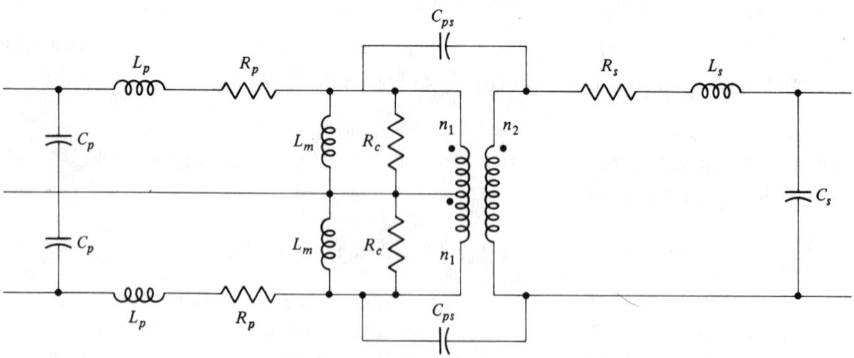

Figure 15-24. Model for a practical transformer.

To prevent this from happening, cores of high-power transformers are large and, consequently, heavy.

The resistors R_C account for core losses (i.e., eddy current and hysteresis loss). That is, the power dissipated in R_C is approximately equal to the core loss. The resistors R_p and R_s account for the resistance of the wires of the primary and secondary windings.

In an actual transformer some flux set up by the primary coil does not link the secondary and vice versa. Such flux does not produce transformer action but does result in a voltage drop equivalent to that produced by an inductance in series with the transformer winding. The *leakage inductances* L_p and L_s account for this voltage drop. At high frequencies, these leakage inductances reduce the output of the transformer.

The capacitors C_{ps}, C_p, and C_s account for the stray capacitance across and between the windings. These capacitances cause the high-frequency performance to further deteriorate. Often, the resistances of the load and generators are small enough so that the effect of these capacitances is minimal. Nevertheless, the high-frequency response falls off because of the leakage inductance.

In general, even in a transformer of excellent quality, which is expensive, large, and heavy, the frequency response is much poorer than that of a simple transistor or FET amplifier. Thus, as we have stated, output transformers are very rarely used in high-quality modern audio amplifiers.

15-9. THERMAL DESIGN—THERMAL STABILITY

When power is dissipated within a device, its temperature tends to rise. The actual increase in temperature depends upon the rate at which the thermal energy can be transferred to the ambient surroundings.

The thermal energy can be removed from transistors or FET's by various means. It can simply be removed by conduction and radiation from the case of the device. This is usually sufficient only if the power dissipation is small. At higher power levels, the surface area of the transistor's or FET's case is not large enough (even for large transistors). This effective surface area must then be increased by mounting the device on a larger surface called a *heat sink*. In this section we shall consider the design of heat sinks. When devices are operated at still higher power levels, the cooling provided by the heat sink can be augmented by a fan, which forces air over the heat sink. At very high power levels, water cooling is used (although usually with devices other than transistors or FET's).

In general, in most audio amplifiers, the output transistors or FET's utilize simple heat sinks. Let us now consider their design. We shall start by introducing the concept of a *thermal resistance* θ. If an average power of P watts is dissipated in a device, and the ambient temperature is T_A, then the temperature of the device will be

$$T_d = P\theta_{DA} + T_A \tag{15-102}$$

where θ_{DA} is the thermal resistance between the device and the ambient temperature. The units of θ_{DA} are degrees Celsius per watt. Note that, in this section, we use the word device to indicate that part of the transistor or FET which is actually dissipating the power (i.e., the collector-base junction of a transistor or the channel of a FET).

Actually, θ_{DA} consists of several resistances in series. There is θ_{DC}, which is the thermal resistance between the internal device and its case. Then there is θ_{CH}, which is the thermal resistance between the case and the heat sink. Finally, there is θ_{HA}, which is the thermal resistance between the heat sink and the ambient temperature. A simple diagram depicting the thermal resistance is shown in Fig. 15-25.

In general, the thermal resistance θ_{DA} can be expressed as

$$\theta_{DA} = \theta_{DC} + \theta_{CH} + \theta_{HA} \tag{15-103}$$

Let us consider values for each of these resistances in turn.

The resistance θ_{DC} is the resistance between the device and its case. This is a function of the internal construction of the device, and can be controlled only during manufacture. This thermal resistance is made low for high-power transistors. Typically, θ_{DC} is made to vary inversely with rated power dissipation. The maximum operating temperature of silicon semiconductors is about 180°C. Thus, the thermal resistance between the case and the device is also made to vary as a function of rated case temperature. In Fig. 15-26, we plot θ_{DC} versus rated power dissipated for typical transistors and FET's. One curve is given for a rated case temperature of 25°C and the other for a rated case temperature of 100°C. These curves are only approximate.

The thermal resistance between the heat sink and the case, θ_{CH}, is a function of several factors. Often, the collector of the transistor is in electrical contact with the case while the heat sink is at ground potential. Thus, an electrical insulator must be placed between the heat sink and the case. Usually, a thin mica spacer is used for this purpose. The thermal resistance of the mica spacer varies directly with its thickness and inversely with its effective area. (This effective area is essentially that of the transistor case.) The thermal resistance is substantially lowered if silicon heat conducting greases are used between the heat sink and the mica and between the mica and the transistor. If this is done, the resistance of a mica spacer 0.05 mm thick with an area of 1 cm^2 is 4°C/W. In general, if the mica spacer is T mm thick and has an area of A cm^2, then

$$\theta_{HC} = \frac{80T}{A} \text{ °C/W} \tag{15-104}$$

This figure is also approximate and will vary with the type of silicon grease used and with the pressure of the mounting screws or rivets.

Now let us consider the resistance between the heat sink and the ambient temperature. Heat is removed from the heat sink by both the processes of conduction and radia-

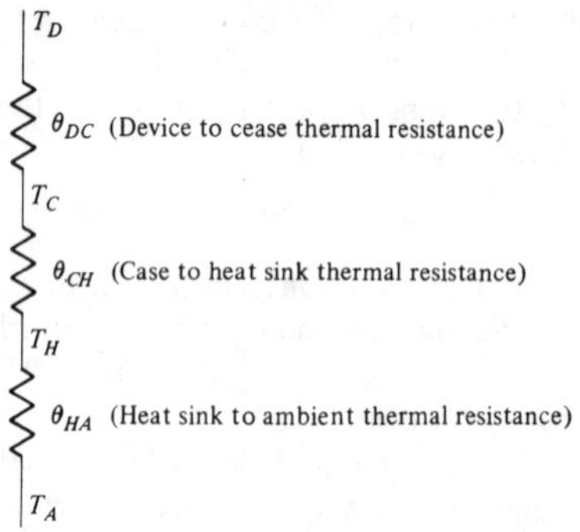

Figure 15-25. A diagrammatic representation of the thermal resistance between a device and the ambient temperature.

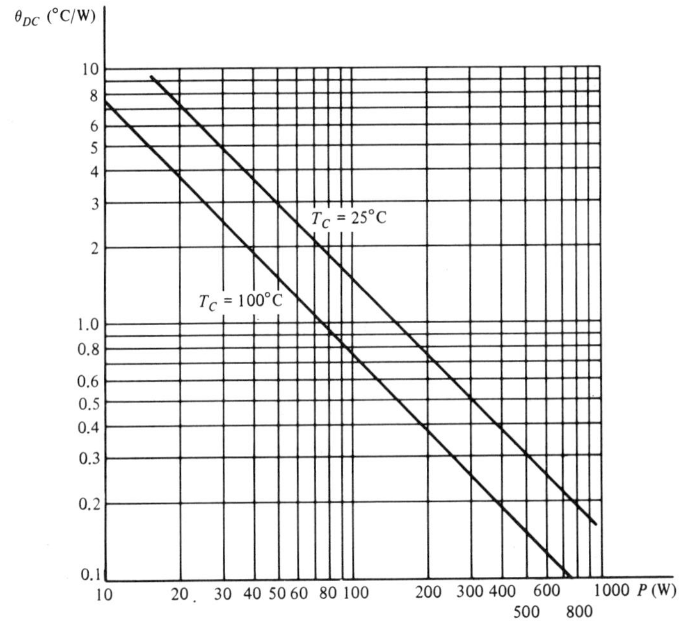

Figure 15-26. A plot of thermal resistance between the device and its case versus rated power dissipation for typical transistors and FET's. Note that this curve is only approximate.

tion. In general, these depend upon the ambient temperature and the temperature of the heat sink. In addition, the temperature of the heat sink will not be constant but will be hotter near the transistor (or FET). In Fig. 15-27, we plot an experimentally measured value of θ_{HA} versus total surface area for a typical heat sink made of 4-mm-thick aluminum sheet which has been painted a dull black. This improves its radiating ability. If an unpainted aluminum sheet is used, the thermal resistance will be increased by about 15%. Note that the area given in Fig. 15-27 is the total area. For instance, a heat sink 2 cm square will have a total area of 8 cm^2. The value of θ_{HA} varies inversely with the total area raised to the 0.439 power. Note that θ_{HA} does not vary inversely with area because of unequal removal of heat from the surface of the heat sink.

Example

A transistor dissipating 15 W is to operate at a case temperature that is not to exceed 100°C when the ambient temperature is equal to or less than 40°C. The area of the transistor that is in contact with the heat sink is 2 cm^2. Design a suitable heat sink and determine the junction temperature.

From Fig. 15-25 we have the following.

$$T_D = T_A + P_D(\theta_{DC} + \theta_{CH} + \theta_{HA}) \tag{15-105}$$

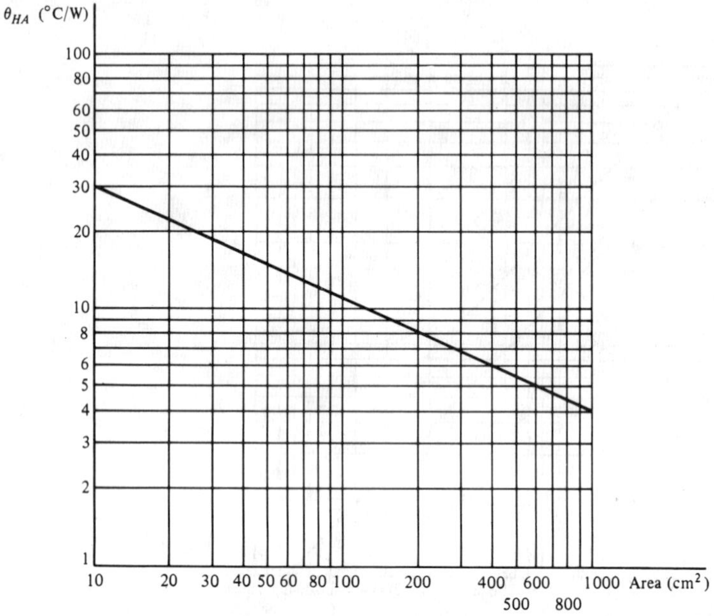

Figure 15-27. Thermal resistance for a dull black aluminum heat sink 4-mm thick versus total surface area.

Similarly, for the case temperature, we have

$$T_C = T_A + P_D(\theta_{CH} + \theta_{HA}) \tag{15-106}$$

Then, substituting the specifications, we have

$$100 = 40 + 15(\theta_{CH} + \theta_{HA})$$

or

$$\theta_{CH} + \theta_{HA} = 4°\text{C/W}$$

We shall assume that there is a mica spacer 0.05 mm thick between the transistor and the heat sink. Then, from Eq. 15-104, we have

$$\theta_{CH} = (80 \times 0.05)/2 = 2°\text{C/W}$$

Then, $\theta_{HA} = 2°$C/W.

The value of 2°C/W is not given in Fig. 15-27. However, from Fig. 15-27 we have that θ_{HA} is proportional to the area raised to the -0.439 power. From 15-27 we see that if $A = 100$ cm², $\theta_{HA} = 11°$C/W. Hence,

$$100/A = (\tfrac{2}{11})^{1/0.439}$$

Thus

$$A = 4858 \text{ cm}^2$$

Hence, the area of one surface is $4858/2 = 2429 \text{ cm}^2$. If we assume a square heat sink, then the length of one side of the square is

$$L = \sqrt{2429} = 49 \text{ cm}$$

From Eqs. 15-105 and 15-106, we have

$$T_D = T_C + \theta_{DC} P_D$$

From Fig. 15-26, we have $\theta_{DC} = 5°\text{C/W}$. Thus,

$$T_D = 100 + 5 \times 15 = 175°\text{C}$$

We have assumed in the previous discussion that the heat sink was a flat piece of aluminum. Heat sinks are often made with cooling fins. This greatly increases the surface area and, thus, the overall size is greatly reduced. The use of a small fan can also greatly reduce the required size of the heat sink.

Thermal Stability

The design that we have performed is based upon a static analysis. However, as we have discussed, transistor amplifiers may be subject to thermal runaway. For instance, suppose that a transistor is operating with $v_{CE} = V_{CE}$ and $i_C = I_C$. Then, the power dissipation in the collector-base junction, which is essentially the total power dissipated within the transistor, is given by

$$P_D = V_{CE} I_C \tag{15-107}$$

Now suppose that there is no resistance in series with the transistor. In that case V_{CE} will remain constant, independent of I_C. Then if P_J increases, the junction temperature T_D will increase. This increases I_C, which causes P_D to increase. This will further increase I_C. This process can repeat itself until the transistor destroys itself. On the other hand, if the external circuitry holds I_C constant, then, if the transistor's temperature increases, V_{CE} will drop and the power will decrease and there is a stable situation. Usually, in power amplifiers, the resistance in series with the transistor is very small. To be on the safe side, we shall assume it to be zero.

Now let us consider how thermal stability affects heat sink design. Equation 15-102 assumed that P and T_D were independent. Let us solve the equation for P and differentiate with respect to T_D. This yields

$$\frac{dP}{dT_D} = \frac{1}{\theta_{DA}}$$

Since we assumed that P and T_D were independent, this represents the stable condition. If $dP/dT_D > 1/\theta_{DA}$, then instability may result. Consequently, we will have a stable design if

$$\frac{dP}{dT_D} < \frac{1}{\theta_{DA}} \tag{15-108}$$

Now let us relate this to the stability factor. Again we shall assume the worst case, that is, where V_{CE} is constant. Then, differentiating Eq. 15-107,

$$\frac{dP}{dT_D} = V_{CE}\frac{dI_C}{dT_D}$$

In Sec. 5-7 we discussed that I_C will vary with I_{CO}, β, and v_{BE}. Often, much of the variation of I_C with temperature can be attributed to the variation of I_{CO} with temperature. All the variation is due to the variation of I_{CO}, and then, to account for other effects, we multiply by 3. Hence,

$$\frac{dP}{dT_D} = 3V_{CE}\frac{dI_C}{dI_{CO}}\cdot\frac{dI_{CO}}{dT_D} \tag{15-109}$$

The quantity dI_C/dI_{CO} is simply the stability factor S. If we assume that all of the variation of I_C with temperature is due to the variation of I_{CO} with temperature, then the partial derivative of Eq. 5-45 can be replaced by total derivatives.) Hence, manipulating Eqs. 15-108 and 15-109, we have, for conditions of thermal stability

$$3V_{CE}\theta_{DA}S\frac{dI_{CO}}{dT_D} < 1 \tag{15-110}$$

It has been experimentally found that

$$\frac{dI_{CO}}{dT_D} = 0.07I_{CO} \tag{15-111}$$

Then, Eq. 15-110 can be written as

$$0.21V_{CE}S\theta_{DA}I_{CO} < 1 \tag{15-112}$$

Example

The transistor in the previous example of this section has a maximum V_{CE} of 30 V. The value of I_{CO} for this transistor is 2×10^{-6} A. Using the heat sink designed in the previous example, determine the maximum stability factor the circuit can have to ensure that there is no thermal runaway.

From the previous example

$$\theta_{DA} = \theta_{DC} + (\theta_{CH} + \theta_{HA}) = 5 + 4 = 9°\text{C/W}$$

Substituting in Eq. 15-112 we obtain

$$S \leqq (0.21 \times 30 \times 9 \times 2 \times 10^{-6})^{-1} = 8818$$

Note that, in this example, we design very much on the safe side, in that the maximum V_{CE} was used. This value of stability factor is very large so we do not have to worry about thermal runaway. On the other hand, with high-power transistors, stability factor is often a prime consideration. For instance, if $I_{CO} = 2$ mA, as it might in a high-power (150-W) transistor, then, for the last example, $S < 8.8$.

In the last example we determine a maximum value of S based in part upon a chosen heat sink area. Alternatively, we can choose a value of S and then determine the minimum heat sink area. This area may then be greater than the area determined from static thermal considerations and thus may determine the heat sink size.

PROBLEMS

15-1. Why is it desirable to have efficient power amplifiers? Discuss all aspects of this topic.

15-2. A device having the output characteristics shown in Fig. 15-28 is used in the class A amplifier of Fig. 15-2a, where $V_{oo} = 6$ V, $X_{iQ} = 3$. What is the value of R_{ac} which gives maximum output circuit efficiency? The operation is to be such that there is no distortion. Compute the value of P_2, the signal power output; P_{OD}, the device dissipation; the input signal; and the output circuit efficiency, η_2.

15-3. Repeat the calculations of P_2, P_{OD}, and η_2 for Prob. 15-2, but now double the value of R_{ac}.

15-4. Repeat the calculations of P_2, P_{OD}, and η_2 for Prob. 15-2 but now halve the value of R_{ac}.

15-5. Repeat Prob. 15-2, but now use $V_{oo} = 4$ V.

15-6. Repeat Prob. 15-2 but now use $X_{iQ} = 2$.

15-7. Repeat the calculations of P_2, P_{OD}, and η_2 for Prob. 15-2, but now halve the input signal.

15-8. Repeat Prob. 15-2 but now assume that X_{iQ} is adjusted so that operation is exactly class B. There is now to be no distortion for values of $x_i \geqq 0$.

15-9. Repeat the calculations of P_2, P_{OD}, and η_2 for Prob. 15-8 but now double R_{ac}.

15-10. Repeat the calculations of P_2, P_{OD}, and η_2 for Prob. 15-8 but now halve R_{ac}.

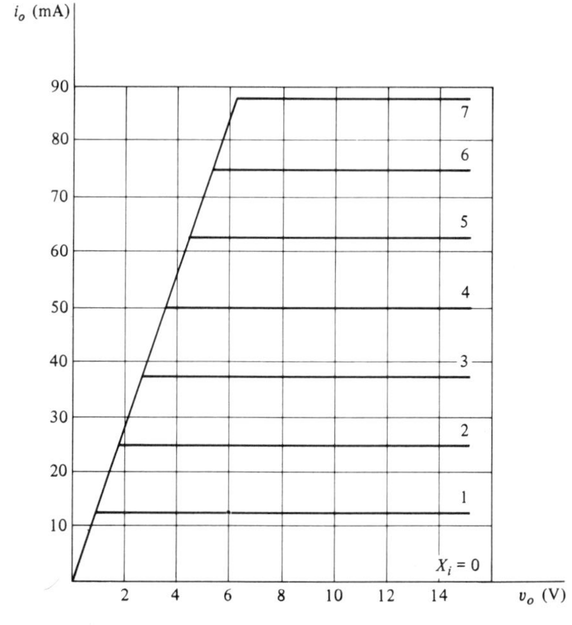

Figure 15-28

15-11. Repeat Prob. 15-8 but now use $V_{oo} = 4$ V.

15-12. Repeat the calculations of P_2, P_{OD}, and η_2 for Prob. 15-8 but now halve the input signal.

15-13. Compare Eqs. 15-20 and 15-24. Discuss the reasons for the differences between these equations.

15-14. The source follower amplifier in Fig. 15-5 is operated with

$$V_{DD} = 12 \text{ V}, \qquad V_{GSQ} = 0, \qquad R_{ac} = 155 \text{ ohms}$$

The characteristics for the FET are given in Fig. 15-6. Modify these characteristics so that they now apply to the amplifier in question. Determine the input voltage that will swing v_{GS} from $+1$ to -1 V. Compute the output power, harmonic distortion, dissipation within the FET, and output circuit efficiency for this input voltage.

15-15. Repeat Prob. 15-14 but now halve the input voltage.

15-16. Repeat Prob. 15-14 but now double R_{ac}.

15-17. Repeat Prob. 15-14 but now halve R_{ac}.

15-18. Repeat Prob. 15-14 but now use $V_{DD} = 4$ V.

15-19. Why is the operation of Prob. 15-18 undesirable? Why is it desirable?

15-20. The transistor whose characteristics are given in Fig. 15-8 is operated in the emitter follower circuit of Fig. 15-7a. The parameters of the circuit are

$$V_{DD} = 5 \text{ V}$$

$$R_B = 18{,}000 \text{ ohms}$$

$$R_G = 18{,}000 \text{ ohms}$$

$$R_{ac} = 6 \text{ ohms}$$

Relabel the characteristics for this set of conditions. Compute the output power, harmonic distortion, transistor output circuit dissipation, and output circuit efficiency for this amplifier. Assume that $v_g = 8.6 \cos \omega t$ V.

15-21. Repeat Prob. 15-20 but now use $R_{ac} = 20$ ohms.

15-22. Repeat Prob. 15-20 but now use $V_{CC} = 6$ V.

15-23. Repeat Prob. 15-20 but now use $V_{CC} = 2$ V.

15-24. Why is the operation of Prob. 15-23 undesirable? Why is it desirable?

15-25. Repeat Prob. 15-20 but now adjust R_B so that $i_{BQ} = 200\ \mu$A.

15-26. Discuss the impedance viewed into the terminals of a loudspeaker.

15-27. Discuss the derivation of Eqs. 15-41

15-28. The FET's whose characteristics are given in Fig. 15-10 are used in the push-pull amplifier of Fig. 15-9. The parameters of the circuit are V_D (the total voltage across the diodes) $= 2$ V, $V_{DD} = 5$ V, and $R_{ac} = 40$ ohms. Draw the composite characteristics for the amplifier. What value of v_i is required to obtain the largest possible swing on the characteristic? For this value, compute the output power, the total harmonic distortion, the dissipation within each FET, and the output circuit efficiency.

15-29. Repeat Prob. 15-28 but now use $R_{ac} = 100$ ohms.

15-30. Repeat Prob. 15-29 but now use $V_D = 3$ V.

15-31. Repeat Prob. 15-29 but now use $V_{DD} = 6.5$ V.

15-32. Compare the results of Probs. 15-28, 15-29, 15-30, and 15-31.

15-33. Why is the even harmonic distortion in the output of a push-pull amplifier zero?

15-34. The transistors whose characteristics are given in Figs. 15-13, 15-14, and 15-29 are used in the circuit of Fig. 15-12 where

$$V_{CC} = 10 \text{ V}$$
$$R_G = 2.834 \text{ ohms}$$
$$R_{ac} = 15 \text{ ohms}$$
$$V_D = 0.7 \text{ V}$$

Draw the composite characteristic for the amplifier. What value of v_i is required to produce the largest possible swing in the output? For this v_i, compute the output power, the total harmonic distortion, the collector-base junction dissipation, and the output circuit efficiency.

15-35. Repeat Prob. 15-34 but now use $R_{ac} = 3$ ohms.

15-36. Repeat Prob. 15-34 but now use $V_{CC} = 12$ V. Estimate the characteristics for values of $v_{CE} >$ 20 V.

15-37. Repeat Prob. 15-34 but now use $V_{CC} = 4$ V.

15-38. The characteristics of the FET's used in the quasicomplementary symmetry push-pull amplifier of Fig. 15-15 are given in Fig. 15-10. Determine all parameters values so that this circuit functions in the same way as that of Prob. 15-28.

15-39. Repeat Prob. 15-38 for the amplifier of Prob. 15-29.

15-40. Repeat Prob. 15-38 for the amplifier of Prob. 15-30.

15-41. Repeat Prob. 15-38 for the amplifier of Prob. 15-31.

15-42. Repeat Prob. 15-38 for the circuit of Fig. 15-16.

15-43. The output characteristics of the output transistor used in the quasicomplementary symmetry push-pull amplifier of Fig. 15-17 are given in Fig. 15-29. The input characteristics are given in Fig. 15-14. Determine all parameter values so that the circuit functions in the same way as that of Prob. 15-34.

15-44. Repeat Prob. 15-43 for the amplifier of Prob. 15-35.

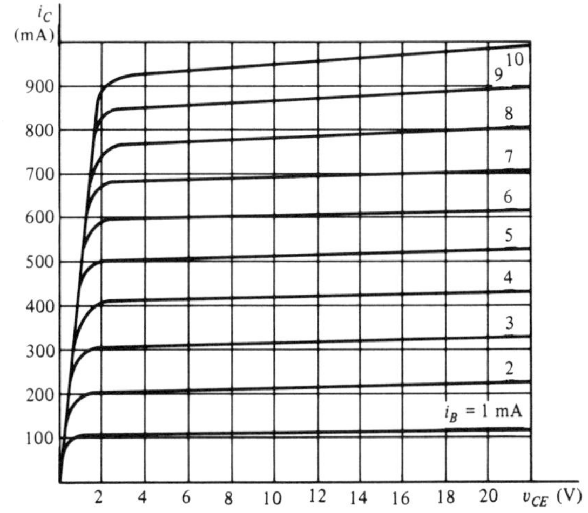

Figure 15-29

15-45. Repeat Prob. 15-43 for the amplifier of Prob. 15-36.

15-46. Repeat Prob. 15-43 for the amplifier of Prob. 15-37.

15-47. Modify the circuit of Prob. 15-43 so that an overload protective circuit is included which limits the maximum collector current to 1 A.

15-48. Discuss the analysis of the amplifier of Fig. 15-19. Illustrate your discussion with an example.

15-49. Demonstrate that an ideal push-pull amplifier will not produce even harmonic distortion.

15-50. Discuss the distortion caused by the unequal spacing of the composite characteristics of transistor amplifiers.

15-51. Why is the distortion discussed in Prob. 15-50 of only limited importance in emitter follower push-pull amplifiers?

15-52. Why is the distortion discussed in Prob. 15-50 of only limited importance in a FET push-pull amplifier?

15-53. Design a complementary symmetry push-pull amplifier whose power output is to be 0.1 W and whose harmonic distortion is not to exceed 10%. Use the FET's whose characteristics are given in Fig. 15-10. Assume that the maximum rated dissipation of the FET's is 0.8 W and $R_{ac} = 48$ ohms.

15-54. Modify the design of Prob. 15-53 so as to obtain maximum power output while still meeting the distortion specification and without exceeding the transistor ratings.

15-55. Design a complementary symmetry push-pull amplifier whose output is 15 W and whose harmonic distortion is not to exceed 10%. Use FET's whose characteristics are the same as those given in Fig. 15-10 except that the v_{CE} axis is multiplied by 5 and i_C axis is multiplied by 30. The maximum ratings of the FET's are $P_{OD} = 120$ W, $|v_{DS,\max}| = 50$ V. Use $R_{ac} = 8$ ohms.

15-56. Modify the design of Prob. 15-53 so as to obtain maximum output power.

15-57. Design a complementary symmetry push-pull amplifier whose power output is to be 2.0 W and whose harmonic distortion is not to exceed 10%. The characteristics of one transistor are given in Fig. 15-29. The maximum rating of the transistor are $P_{OD,\max} = 7.5$ W, $|v_{CE}| \leqq 20$ V, $|i_C| = 1$ A. Use $R_{ac} = 15$ ohms.

15-58. Repeat Prob. 15-57 but now modify the design so that maximum output is obtained.

15-59. Repeat Prob. 15-57 but now use the transistor whose characteristics are given in Fig. 15-30. Now the output power is to be 60 W and $P_{OD,\max} = 190$ W, $|v_{CE}| \leqq 50$ V. Use $R_{ac} = 4$ ohms. Assume that the input characteristics can be obtained from the curve of Fig. 15-14 by multiplying the i_B values by 10, and the v_{CE} values by 5.

15-60. Repeat Prob. 15-59 but now modify the design for maximum output power.

15-61. Repeat the design of Prob. 15-53 but now use a quasicomplementary symmetry amplifier.

15-62. Repeat the design of Prob. 15-54 but now use a quasicomplementary symmetry amplifier.

15-63. Repeat the design of Prob. 15-55 but now use a quasicomplementary symmetry amplifier.

15-64. Repeat the design of Prob. 15-56 but now use a quasicomplementary symmetry amplifier.

15-65. Repeat the design of Prob. 15-57 but now use a quasicomplementary symmetry amplifier.

15-66. Repeat the design of Prob. 15-58 but now use a quasicomplementary symmetry amplifier.

15-67. Repeat the design of Prob. 15-59 but now use a quasicomplementary symmetry amplifier.

15-68. Repeat the design of Prob. 15-60 but now use a quasicomplementary symmetry amplifier.

15-69. Discuss the advantages and disadvantages of transformer coupled output. Why are transformerless amplifiers used in most cases?

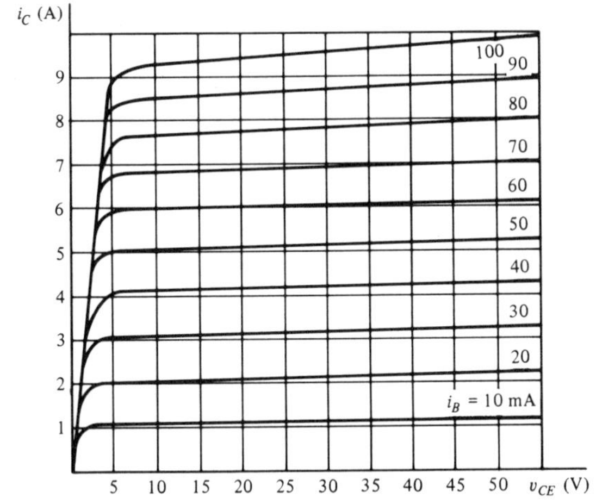

Figure 15-30.

15-70. Draw the composite characteristic for the transformer coupled amplifier of Fig. 15-23a. The output characteristics of the FET's are given in Fig. 15-10a. The parameters of the amplifier are

$$V_{DD} = 5 \text{ volts}$$

$$V_{GSQ} = 1.5 \text{ V}$$

$$R_L = 8 \text{ ohms}$$

$$\frac{n_1}{n_2} = 2.5$$

Compute the output power, harmonic distortion, and P_{OD} if $v_i = 3 \cos \omega t$.

15-71. Repeat Prob. 15-70 if $n_1/n_2 = 4.0$.

15-72. Draw the composite output characteristics for the transformer coupled amplifier of Fig. 15-23b. The output characteristics of the transistor are given in Fig. 15-29. The input characteristics are given in Fig. 15-14. The parameters of the circuit are

$$V_{CC} = 10 \text{ V}$$

$$R_B = 9350 \text{ ohms}$$

$$R_L = 8 \text{ ohms}$$

$$\frac{n_1}{n_2} = 1$$

15-73. Repeat Prob. 15-72, but now use $n_1/n_2 = 2$.

15-74. A transistor dissipates 20 W and is to operate at a case temperature which is not to exceed 100°C. The area of the transistor that is in contact with the heat sink is 4 cm^2. Assume that a silicon greased mica spacer 0.05 mm thick is used between the transistor and the heat sink. Design a suitable heat sink and determine the junction temperature. Use the information given in Figs. 15-26 and 15-27. The ambient temperature is 40°C.

15-75. Repeat Prob. 15-74 but now assume that the case temperature is 25°C and the ambient temperature is 20°C. Assume that the mica spacer can be varied if necessary.

15-76. Repeat Prob. 15-74 but now assume that the area in contact with the heat sink is 10 cm^2.

15-77. Repeat Prob. 15-75 but now assume that the area of the transistor in contact with the heat sink is 10 cm^2.

15-78. The transistor in Prob. 15-74 has a $V_{CE,\max}$ of 20 V and $I_{CQ} = 1\ \mu A$. What is the minimum value that S can have if thermal runaway is to be avoided?

15-79. Repeat Prob. 15-78 but now use $I_{CO} = 1$ mA.

15-80. Compare the results of Probs. 15-78 and 15-79.

BIBLIOGRAPHY

Chirlian, P. M. *Electronic Circuits: Physical Principles, Analysis and Design.* New York: McGraw-Hill, 1971, Chapter 10.

Gray, P. R. and Meyer, R. G. *Analysis and Design of Analog Integrated Circuits.* New York: Wiley, 1977, Chapter 5.

Teeling, J. "Mounting and Heat Sinking Uniwatt Plastic Transistors," Motorola Semiconductor Products Applications Note, AN-472, 1973.

Weber, H. "A Method of Predicting Thermal Stability," Motorola Semiconductor Products Applications Note, AN-182, 1973.

Chapter 16

Feedback Amplifiers

If a signal at the output of any stage of an amplifier affects the input signal of that or any earlier stage, then we say that *feedback* has been introduced. We have seen some of the effects of feedback. For instance, in the operational amplifier circuits discussed in Secs. 13-1 to 13-4, we deliberately introduced feedback to control the gain and to reduce the sensitivity of the voltage gain $\mathbf{K}_v$, the overall gain of the circuit, to changes in $\mathbf{A}_v$, the operational amplifier gain. In Chapter 15 we saw that the feedback introduced by the emitter follower and source follower circuits substantially reduced the nonlinear distortion of the amplifier. Feedback does not always result in improved behavior. For instance, the increased input capacitance due to Miller effect is an undesirable effect of feedback.

If feedback is purposely introduced in complete amplifier circuits, there can be a great improvement in response. The nonlinear distortion can be greatly reduced and the circuit can become relatively insensitive to changes in the parameters of the active devices. In this chapter we shall consider the effects of feedback, whether they be advantageous or disadvantageous. We shall also discuss procedures for properly analyzing and designing feedback amplifiers.

16-1. SOME BASIC IDEAS OF FEEDBACK AMPLIFIERS

A basic form of feedback amplifier is characterized by the block diagram of Fig. 16-1. The $\mathbf{A}_v$ block represents an amplifier of voltage gain $\mathbf{A}_v$. The $\boldsymbol{\beta}$ circuit represents a feedback network. Usually it is a passive circuit. In Fig. 16-1, $\boldsymbol{\beta}$ represents the portion of the output voltage that is fed back to the input. The circle represents a summing point. The voltages are added or subtracted here. (Addition or subtraction is indicated by plus or minus signs.) The actual voltage at the input to the amplifier is $\mathbf{V}_3$.

$$\mathbf{V}_3 = \mathbf{V}_1 + \boldsymbol{\beta}\mathbf{V}_2 \tag{16-1}$$

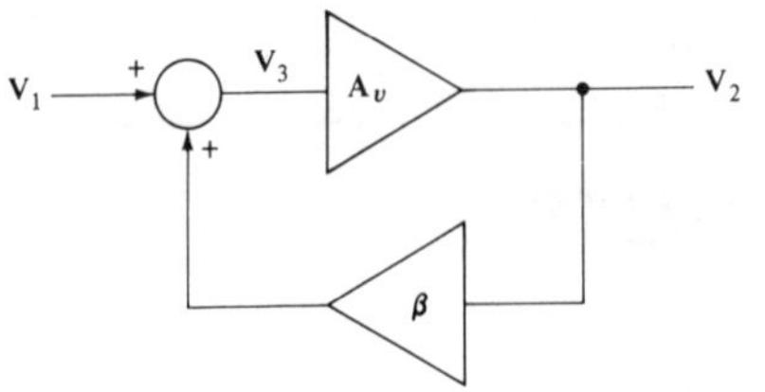

Figure 16-1. Block diagram of a basic form of feedback amplifier.

The amplifier output $\mathbf{V}_2 = \mathbf{A}_v\mathbf{V}_3$. Substituting into Eq. 16-1 and manipulating, we have

$$\mathbf{K}_v = \frac{\mathbf{V}_2}{\mathbf{V}_1} = \frac{\mathbf{A}_v}{1 - \mathbf{A}\boldsymbol{\beta}} \tag{16-2}$$

There are two gains with which we are concerned. One is $\mathbf{K}_v$, the actual gain of the total circuit, and the other is $\mathbf{A}_v$, the gain of the amplifier portion of the circuit.

Many times, in feedback amplifiers, $\boldsymbol{\beta}$ is a real fraction which is established by a simple resistive voltage divider circuit while $\mathbf{A}_v$ is a large negative number which is the gain of an amplifier. Then, if

$$|\mathbf{A}\boldsymbol{\beta}| \gg 1 \tag{16-3}$$

Eq. 16-2 can be approximated by

$$\mathbf{K}_v = -\frac{1}{\boldsymbol{\beta}} \tag{16-4}$$

Note that we saw effects such as this in Secs. 13-1 to 13-4. If $\boldsymbol{\beta}$ is a function of passive elements only, such as resistances, then $\mathbf{K}_v$ will become very independent of the parameters of the active devices. If $\boldsymbol{\beta}$ were such a function and Eq. (14-4) was exactly correct, then there would be no nonlinear or frequency distortion. (Note that nonlinear distortion can be considered to be the variation of gain of an amplifier with the input signal level.)

Note that if Eq. 16-3 is true at some frequency, it will not be true at all frequencies since $|\mathbf{A}_v|$ will fall off as a function of frequency. Also, $|\mathbf{A}_v|$ may change because parameters such as power supply voltage change. In general, Eq. 16-4 will not be exact but, in a well-designed feedback amplifier, the dependence of the overall amplifier's $\mathbf{K}_v$ upon the parameters of the active devices will be greatly reduced. We shall study this effect in great detail in this chapter.

In general, in the type of amplifier that we have been discussing, $\mathbf{A}_v$ will, over most operating frequencies, be a real negative number. Thus, $\mathbf{V}_3 = \mathbf{V}_1 + \boldsymbol{\beta}\mathbf{V}_2$, the actual input to the amplifier, (see Eq. 16-1) will be the difference between two voltages. This is called *negative feedback* since $\boldsymbol{\beta}\mathbf{V}_2$, the signal fed back, is 180° out-of-phase with the input signal. In general, $|\mathbf{V}_1| > |\boldsymbol{\beta}\mathbf{V}_2|$. Let us now consider why $\mathbf{K}_v$ is almost independent of $|\mathbf{A}_v|$. Suppose that $|\mathbf{A}_v|$ increases. Then, the magnitude of $\mathbf{V}_3$ will decrease since the magnitude of the signal subtracted from $\mathbf{V}_1$ will increase. Thus, the voltage input to the amplifier decreases and tends to nullify the increase in $|\mathbf{A}_v|$. A decrease in $|\mathbf{A}_v|$ will tend to be nullified in a similar fashion.

Now let us consider a different amplifier. Suppose that $\mathbf{A}_v$ and $\boldsymbol{\beta}$ are both real positive numbers. This is called *positive feedback* since the input and feedback signals are now in-phase. Suppose that $|\mathbf{A}\boldsymbol{\beta}| < 1$. Then (see Eq. 16-2), $|\mathbf{K}_v|$ will be larger than $\mathbf{A}_v$. The increase in gain is an advantage of positive feedback. However, it is rarely used in practice since the advantages of negative feedback become the disadvantages of positive feedback. The distortion and the dependence of the gain upon the parameters of the amplifier are greater than in the nonfeedback case. Also, positive feedback amplifiers tend to oscillate, which makes them useless as amplifiers.

In the discussion of positive and negative feedback, we did not consider the phase shift of the amplifier. We shall do this subsequently.

We have classified feedback as positive or negative. Let us consider some additional classifications. There is *voltage feedback* and *current feedback*. In voltage feedback, the signal fed back (which can be either a voltage or a current) is proportional to the output voltage, whereas in current feedback, the signal fed back is proportional to the output current. When voltage negative feedback is used, the output voltage tends to become independent of the value of $\mathbf{A}_v$, whereas current negative feedback tends to stabilize the output current. We shall consider the implications of this in greater detail in Sec. 16-6. Block diagrams for voltage and current feedback are shown in Fig. 16-2. Figures 16-2a

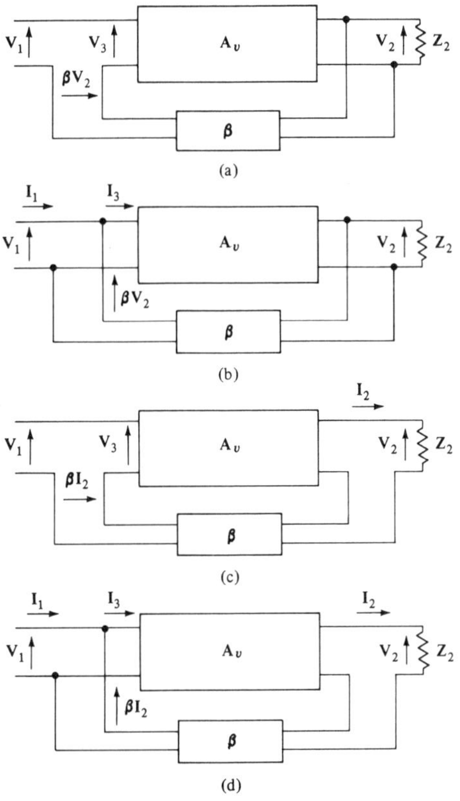

Figure 16-2. (a) Voltage series feedback. (b) Voltage shunt feedback. (c) Current series feedback. (d) Current shunt feedback.

and 16-2b represent voltage feedback since the signal fed back is proportional to the output voltage. Now, look at the inputs to the amplifiers. In Fig. 16-2a the feedback signal is placed in series with the input signal, so

$$\mathbf{V}_3 = \mathbf{V}_1 + \boldsymbol{\beta}\mathbf{V}_2 \tag{16-5}$$

This is called *series feedback.* In Fig. 16-2b, the feedback signal is in parallel (shunt) with the input. Now we consider that the feedback signal is a current that is proportional to the output voltage. This is called *shunt feedback.*

$$\mathbf{I}_3 = \mathbf{I}_2 + \boldsymbol{\beta}\mathbf{V}_2 \tag{16-6}$$

In this case $\boldsymbol{\beta}$ is not dimensionless. Its units are mhos. Note that $\mathbf{V}_3 = \mathbf{V}_1$ in this case. This implies that, if the input generator has no series impedance, then there is no feedback. Note that the amplifier of Fig. 13-4 used voltage shunt feedback. In that case, the resistor R_1 could be considered to be the generator resistance.

In Figs. 16-2c and 16-2d we have examples of current feedback. Now the feedback signal is proportional to the load current. Figure 16-2c is an example of *current series feedback.* Here the feedback signal is a voltage that is proportional to the output current. Figure 16-2d represents *current shunt feedback.* Note that in Fig. 16-2c the units of $\boldsymbol{\beta}$ are ohms while in Fig. 16-2d, $\boldsymbol{\beta}$ is dimensionless.

In later studies of feedback amplifiers, we will consider such things as the input impedance of the amplifier. In this section we have only presented some fundamental definitions.

16-2. TWO VERY SIMPLE FEEDBACK AMPLIFIERS

We shall now illustrate some of the ideas of the last section with two very simple amplifiers. The first is the FET circuit of Fig. 16-3a. Let us use Eq. 16-2 to compute its gain. To compute $\mathbf{A}_v$, the gain of the amplifier portion, break the connection from a to c and insert the dashed connections from a to b. Then,

$$\mathbf{A}_v = -g_m R_{sh} \tag{16-7}$$

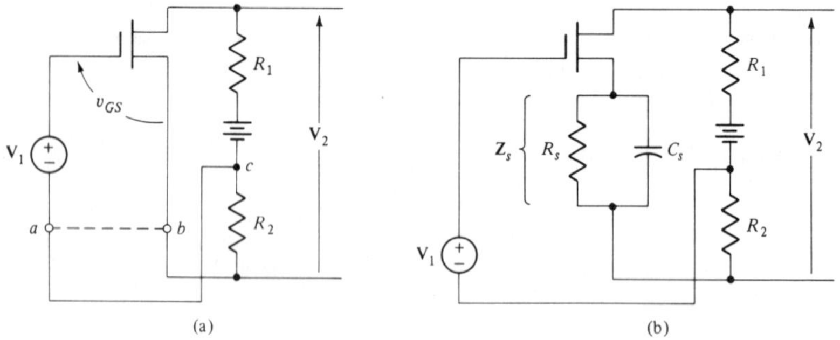

Figure 16-3. (a) Simple, but impractical, feedback amplifier. (b) A modification of this circuit.

where

$$\frac{1}{R_{sh}} = \frac{1}{r_d} + \frac{1}{R_1 + R_2} \tag{16-8}$$

Now consider the original amplifier. $\mathbf{V}_{gs}$ is the input to the amplifier portion. Here

$$\mathbf{V}_{gs} = \mathbf{V}_1 + \frac{1}{R_1 + R_2}\mathbf{V}_2 \tag{16-9}$$

This is voltage feedback since the feedback signal is proportional to the output voltage. It is also series feedback since the feedback voltage is in series with $\mathbf{V}_1$.

From Eq. 16-9, we have

$$\boldsymbol{\beta} = \frac{R_2}{R_1 + R_2} \tag{16-10}$$

Then, substituting Eqs. 16-7 and 16-10 into Eq. 16-2, we obtain

$$\mathbf{K}_v = \frac{-g_m R_{sh}}{1 + g_m R_{sh} R_2/(R_1 + R_2)} \tag{16-11}$$

If

$$\frac{g_m R_{sh} R_2}{(R_1 + R_2)} \gg 1 \tag{16-12}$$

then,

$$\mathbf{K}_v = -\frac{R_1 + R_2}{R_2} = -\left(1 + \frac{R_1}{R_2}\right) \tag{16-13}$$

Do *not* draw the conclusion from this example that Eq. 16-2 is a useful one for computing the gain of a feedback amplifier. It cannot be used for anything but the simplest cases, since $\mathbf{A}_v$ and $\boldsymbol{\beta}$ cannot be identified. For instance, consider the slightly more complex circuit of Fig. 16-3b. We cannot readily identify the gain of the amplifier alone, nor can we easily identify $\boldsymbol{\beta}$. Actually, there are two types of feedback present, voltage feedback, as in Fig. 16-3a, and current feedback. The current through $\mathbf{Z}_s$ produces a feedback signal. Thus, current feedback is also present. Both feedbacks are series feedback.

The procedure used to analyze this amplifier is the same one that we have used in previous chapters. We draw the linear model and analyze it. From Fig. 16-4 we have

$$\mu\mathbf{V}_{gs} = \mathbf{I}(r_d + \mathbf{Z}_s + R_1 + R_2) \tag{16-14a}$$

$$\mathbf{V}_{gs} = \mathbf{V}_1 - \mathbf{I}(R_2 + \mathbf{Z}_s) \tag{16-14b}$$

$$\mathbf{V}_2 = -\mathbf{I}(R_1 + R_2) \tag{16-14c}$$

Manipulating these equations, we obtain

$$\mathbf{K}_v = \frac{-\mu(R_1 + R_2)}{r_d + \mathbf{Z}_s(1 + \mu) + R_1(1 + \mu) + R_2} \tag{16-15a}$$

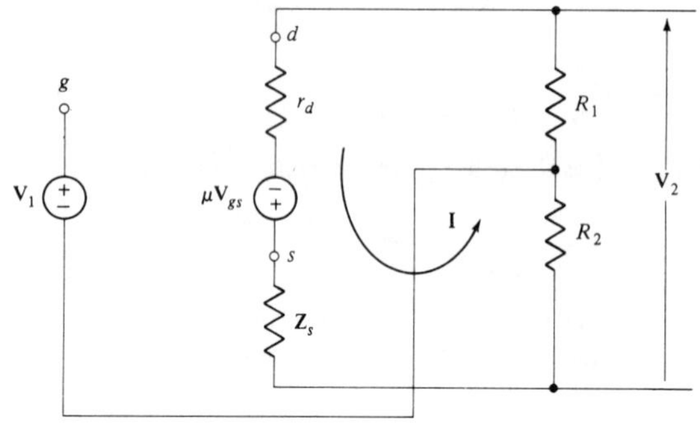

Figure 16-4. A linear model for the circuit of Fig. 16-3b.

Further manipulation yields

$$\mathbf{K}_v = -\frac{\mu(R_1 + R_2)/(r_d + \mathbf{Z}_s + R_1 + R_2)}{1 + \mu(\mathbf{Z}_s + R_2)/(r_d + \mathbf{Z}_s + R_1 + R_2)} \tag{16-15b}$$

If

$$\left|\frac{\mu(\mathbf{Z}_s + R_2)}{r_d + \mathbf{Z}_s + R_1 + R_2}\right| \gg 1 \tag{16-16}$$

then we have

$$\mathbf{K}_v = -\frac{R_1 + R_2}{\mathbf{Z}_s + R_2} \tag{16-17}$$

Note that although Eq. 16-15b was put in the *form* $\mathbf{A}_v/(1 - \mathbf{A}_v\boldsymbol{\beta})$, until the problem was solved, we did not know the formulas of $\mathbf{A}_v$ and $\boldsymbol{\beta}$. For instance, why should $\boldsymbol{\beta}$ be chosen as $(\mathbf{Z}_s + R_2)/(R_1 + R_2)$? We might be able to present some reasons for this *once the answer is known.* However, in general, when we deal with more complex amplifiers, we cannot do this, and linear models will be used to obtain the gain of a feedback amplifier rather than Eq. 16-2. We will follow the procedure indicated here, that is, after the gain is obtained, it will be put into the form of Eq. 16-2. That is, we attempt to write

$$\mathbf{K}_v = \frac{\mathbf{G}}{1 - \mathbf{GB}} \tag{16-18}$$

where $\mathbf{G}$ is a function of the parameters of the active device and $\mathbf{B}$ is not. Then, if

$$|\mathbf{GB}| \gg 1 \tag{16-19}$$

we have

$$\mathbf{K}_v \simeq \frac{-1}{\mathbf{B}} \tag{16-20}$$

and we still obtain the advantages of feedback.

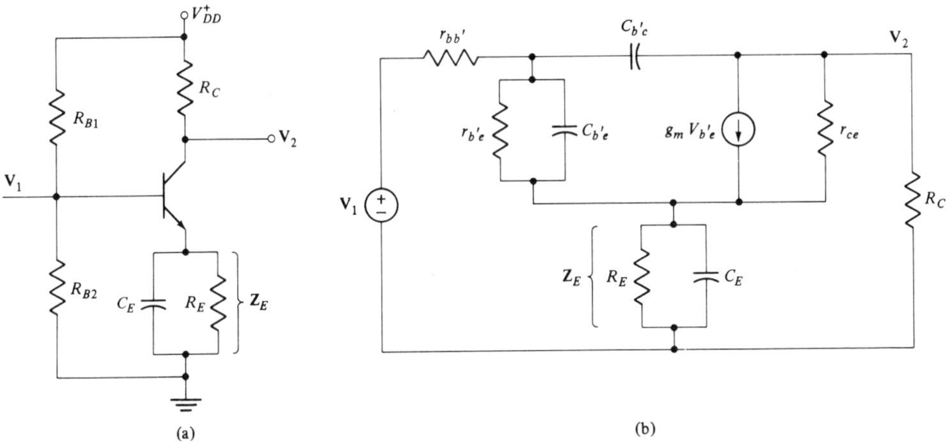

Figure 16-5. (a) A simple transistor amplifier. (b) Its linear model.

The reader may question why Eq. 16-2 was introduced if it is not used to obtain the gain of a feedback amplifier. The answer is that it does provide insight into the behavior of feedback amplifiers. We shall demonstrate this in much of the remainder of the chapter.

The situation that we have described in relation to FET amplifiers is also true in the case of transistor amplifiers. For instance, consider the simple amplifier shown in Fig. 16-5a. Its model is drawn in Fig. 16-5b. There is voltage-shunt feedback through $C_{b'c}$ and current series feedback through $\mathbf{Z}_E$. The appropriate procedure for the analysis of this amplifier is to use the linear model.

In a subsequent section we shall discuss the analysis of complex feedback amplifiers. There we shall consider special procedures for manipulation of the models that specifically aid in the analysis of feedback amplifiers.

16-3. THE EFFECT OF FEEDBACK ON SENSITIVITY— THE IMPORTANCE OF RETURN DIFFERENCE AND LOOP GAIN

Let us see how the incorporation of feedback reduces the sensitivity of the overall voltage gain $\mathbf{K}_v$ to changes in $\mathbf{A}_v$, the gain of the amplifier portion of the circuit. We shall consider the basic feedback structure which has been redrawn in Fig. 16-6 here.

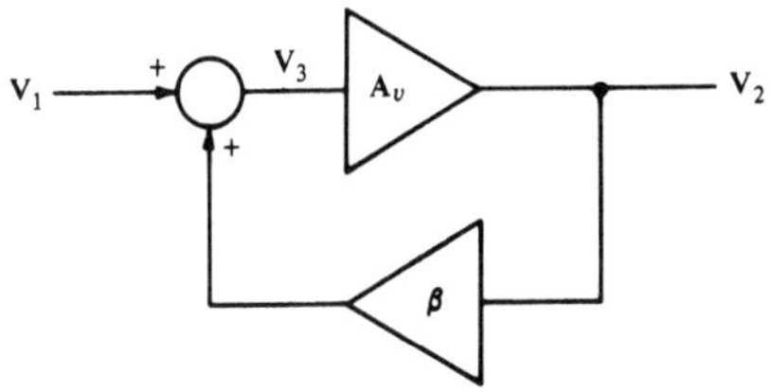

Figure 16-6. The block diagram of a basic feedback amplifier.

We shall define sensitivity in the same way as was done in Sec. 13-2.

$$S_{\mathbf{A}_v}^{\mathbf{K}_v} = \frac{\Delta\mathbf{K}_v/\mathbf{K}_v}{\Delta\mathbf{A}_v/\mathbf{A}_v} \tag{16-21}$$

where $\Delta\mathbf{K}_v$ is the change in $\mathbf{K}_v$ caused by a change $\Delta\mathbf{A}_v$ in $\mathbf{A}_v$. The sensitivity represents the ratio of the fractional change in $\mathbf{K}_v$ to the fractional change in $\mathbf{A}_v$. For instance, if $S_{\mathbf{A}_v}^{\mathbf{K}_v} = 0.1$ and $\mathbf{A}_v$ changes by 25%, then $\mathbf{K}_v$ would only change by 2.5%. Thus, it is desirable to have the sensitivity as small as possible.

For the amplifier of Fig. 16-6,

$$\mathbf{K}_v = \frac{\mathbf{A}_v}{1 - \mathbf{A}_v\boldsymbol{\beta}} \tag{16-22}$$

If $\mathbf{A}_v$ changes by an amount $\Delta\mathbf{A}_v$, then $\mathbf{K}_v$ changes by an amount $\Delta\mathbf{K}_v$. Hence,

$$\mathbf{K}_v + \Delta\mathbf{K}_v = \frac{(\mathbf{A}_v + \Delta\mathbf{A}_v)}{1 - (\mathbf{A}_v + \Delta\mathbf{A}_v)\boldsymbol{\beta}} \tag{16-23}$$

Manipulating Eqs. 16-22 and 16-23 we obtain

$$\frac{\Delta\mathbf{K}_v}{\mathbf{K}_v} = \frac{\Delta\mathbf{A}_v/\mathbf{A}_v}{1 - (\mathbf{A}_v + \Delta\mathbf{A}_v)\boldsymbol{\beta}} \tag{16-24a}$$

or, equivalently,

$$S_{\mathbf{A}_v}^{\mathbf{K}_v} = 1/[1 - (\mathbf{A}_v + \Delta\mathbf{A}_v)\boldsymbol{\beta}] \tag{16-24b}$$

The quantity $1 - \mathbf{A}_v\boldsymbol{\beta}$ is called the *return difference*. Therefore, $1 - (\mathbf{A}_v + \Delta\mathbf{A}_v)\boldsymbol{\beta}$ is the return difference of the feedback amplifier *after* the change in $\mathbf{A}_v$ has occurred. In negative feedback $\mathbf{A}_v\boldsymbol{\beta}$ is often a large negative number so that $1 - \mathbf{A}_v\boldsymbol{\beta}$ and $1 - (\mathbf{A}_v + \Delta\mathbf{A}_v)\boldsymbol{\beta}$ are both large positive numbers. Thus, the sensitivity of the feedback amplifier can be made very small. Note that in the nonfeedback case, $\mathbf{K}_v = \mathbf{A}_v$ so $S_{\mathbf{A}_v}^{\mathbf{K}_v} = 1$. Hence, the return difference represents the improvement in sensitivity due to the incorporation of feedback. In a positive feedback amplifier, the return difference can be very small and, thus, the sensitivity becomes very high.

We have just discussed that the magnitude of the return difference represented the improvement in the sensitivity of a feedback amplifier. We shall subsequently discuss that the return difference represents the improvement due to feedback in many important areas.

Let us now consider the return difference. In Fig. 16-7 we have redrawn the block diagram for the basic feedback amplifier but now we have broken the feedback loop. Now compute the voltage gain

$$\mathbf{L} = \frac{\mathbf{V}_3'}{\mathbf{V}_3} = \mathbf{A}_v\boldsymbol{\beta} \tag{16-25}$$

The quantity $\mathbf{A}_v\boldsymbol{\beta}$ is called the *loop gain*. Note that it represents the gain around the broken feedback loop. (Sometimes this is called the open loop gain. However, open loop gain is also used to represent the gain of the amplifier without feedback, e.g., $\mathbf{A}_v$.)

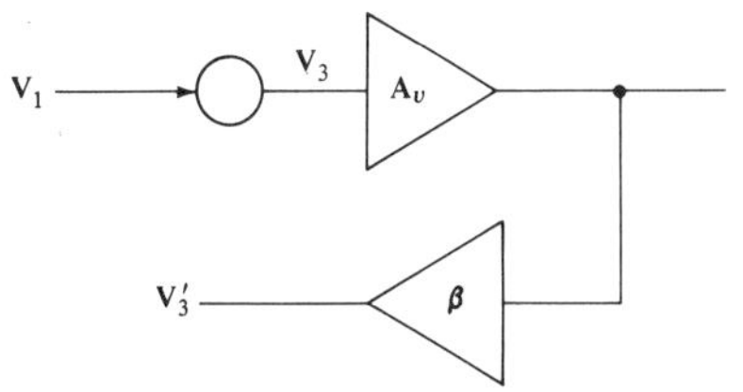

Figure 16-7. The block diagram for the basic feedback amplifier with the feedback loop opened.

The return difference is then given by

$$\mathbf{F} = 1 - \mathbf{A}_v\boldsymbol{\beta} = 1 - \mathbf{L} \tag{16-26}$$

Note that the loop gain can be measured by breaking the feedback loop at the amplifier input, applying a signal there, and then taking the ratio of the signal returned to the $\boldsymbol{\beta}$ circuit output. Suppose that we make the input signal 1 V. Then, $1 - \mathbf{A}_v\boldsymbol{\beta}$ represents the difference between the "input" signal $\mathbf{V}_3$ and the returned signal $\mathbf{V}_3'$. This accounts for the name "return difference."

In negative feedback amplifiers $\mathbf{A}_v\boldsymbol{\beta}$ will be a negative number, usually due to the 180° phase shift of the amplifier. There is another quantity that is defined as the negative of the loop gain. This is called the *return ratio.*

In the last section we discussed how the expression $\mathbf{A}_v/(1 - \mathbf{A}_v\boldsymbol{\beta})$ could not be used in practice since the values of $\mathbf{A}_v$ and $\boldsymbol{\beta}$ cannot be easily identified. However, this is *not* the case for the product $\mathbf{A}_v\boldsymbol{\beta}$. It is important to note that the *loop gain* and, thus, the return difference, can often easily be computed or measured. Thus, the advantage introduced by feedback can be determined. In Sec. 16-12 we shall consider this computation.

16-4. THE EFFECT OF FEEDBACK ON NONLINEAR DISTORTION

Let us now see how feedback affects nonlinear distortion. In order to model the effect of nonlinear distortion in a linear fashion we shall use the signal flow graph of Fig. 16-8. (Note that we have considered a nonfeedback amplifier here.) Nonlinear distortion results in the production of terms such as harmonics, which are not present in the input. The signal $\mathbf{V}_d$ accounts for these extra terms. The output of the amplifier is

$$\mathbf{V}_2' = \mathbf{A}_v\mathbf{V}_1' + \mathbf{V}_d' \tag{16-27}$$

We have added the primes to indicate that this is a nonfeedback case. The distortion is given by

$$\mathbf{D}' = \frac{\mathbf{V}_d'}{\mathbf{A}_v\mathbf{V}_1'} \tag{16-28}$$

Note that the percent distortion is given by $100|D|$.

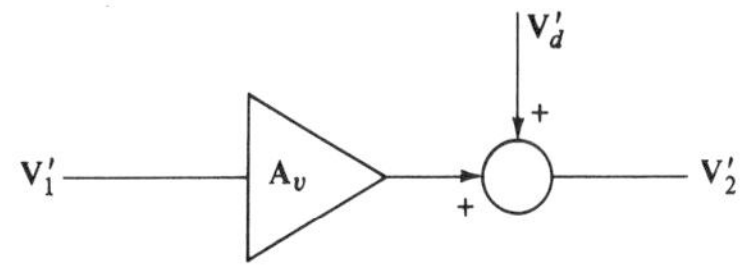

Figure 16-8. A model used to represent the effect of distortion in an amplifier. A nonfeedback amplifier is shown.

Now let us use this model with a feedback amplifier. Care must be used here since the distortion is a function of signal level. We shall assume here that essentially all the nonlinear distortion is produced by the output stage of the amplifier (which is typically the case). Hence, if we adjust the input signals so that the output signals are the same as in the nonfeedback case, then the model of Fig. 16-8 can also be used in a feedback amplifier model with the same value of $\mathbf{V}_d$. Let us restate this in terms of an example. Suppose that we obtain the harmonic distortion of a nonfeedback amplifier when it supplies 100 W of signal power to a load. We now place this amplifier in a feedback configuration and adjust the input signal level so that the same 100 W are again supplied to the load. Now the percent harmonic distortion is compared with the original one to obtain the advantages of feedback. Since the output stage operates at the same levels in both cases, the distortion signals are the same and $\mathbf{V}_d' = \mathbf{V}_d$. Then, the model for the feedback amplifier configuration is given in Fig. 16-9. Analyzing this we obtain

$$\mathbf{V}_2 = \frac{\mathbf{A}_v}{1 - \mathbf{A}_v\boldsymbol{\beta}}\mathbf{V}_1 + \frac{\mathbf{V}_d}{1 - \mathbf{A}_v\boldsymbol{\beta}} \tag{16-29}$$

Hence,

$$\mathbf{D} = \frac{\mathbf{V}_d}{\mathbf{A}_v\mathbf{V}_1} \tag{16-30}$$

Let us take the ratio of Eqs. 16-30 and 16-28 to obtain the advantage gained using feedback.

$$\frac{\mathbf{D}}{\mathbf{D}'} = \frac{\mathbf{V}_1'}{\mathbf{V}_1} \tag{16-31}$$

The input signals $\mathbf{V}_1$ and $\mathbf{V}_1'$ (with and without feedback) must be adjusted so that the output signals are equal. The output signals are given in Eqs. 16-29 and 16-27 so that we have

$$\mathbf{A}_v\mathbf{V}_1' = \frac{\mathbf{A}_v}{1 - \mathbf{A}_v\boldsymbol{\beta}}\mathbf{V}_1 \tag{16-32}$$

Manipulating and substituting in Eq. 16-31 we obtain

$$\frac{\mathbf{D}}{\mathbf{D}'} = \frac{1}{1 - \mathbf{A}_v\boldsymbol{\beta}} \tag{16-33}$$

Thus, the distortion has been reduced by the amount $1 - \mathbf{A}_v\boldsymbol{\beta}$, which is the return difference. (Note that if positive feedback is used and $\mathbf{A}_v\boldsymbol{\beta} < 1$, then the distortion will

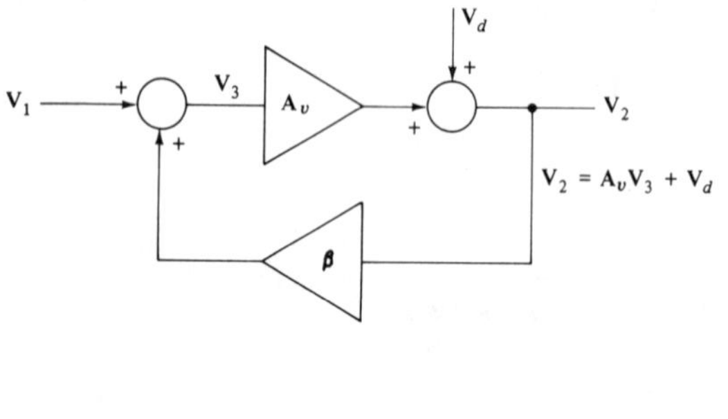

Figure 16-9. The model of Fig. 16-8 used in a feedback configuration.

actually be increased.) We shall assume that negative feedback is used. In this case, the introduction of feedback caused the gain to be reduced so a larger input signal is needed. This may necessitate additional preamplifier stages to amplify the signal. These will usually not produce significant nonlinear distortion since they are operated at low-signal levels. Actually, a well-designed feedback amplifier is *not* obtained by simply taking a nonfeedback amplifier and adding feedback. Rather the entire feedback amplifier should be designed. Let us illustrate this with a simple example. Note that this example only covers a few factors of feedback amplifier design. We shall consider other significant factors subsequently.

Example

Obtain $\mathbf{A}_v$ and $\boldsymbol{\beta}$ for a feedback amplifier that produces 100 W of output with 0.05% distortion. The load is 8 ohms. When the output stage supplies 100 W to an 8-ohm load, in a nonfeedback case, 5% harmonic distortion is produced. The input signal for 100 W of output is to be 1 V.

The output voltage can be found from

$$\frac{\mathbf{V}_2^2}{8} = 100$$

$$\mathbf{V}_2 = 28.3 \text{ V}$$

The input signal is 1 V. Thus,

$$\mathbf{K}_v = \frac{28.3}{1} = 28.3$$

The distortion must be reduced by a factor of 100 to 1 by the feedback. Hence,

$$1 - \mathbf{A}_v\boldsymbol{\beta} = 100$$

$$\mathbf{A}_v\boldsymbol{\beta} = 101$$

Then,

$$\mathbf{K}_v = \frac{\mathbf{A}_v}{1 - \mathbf{A}_v\boldsymbol{\beta}}$$

Hence,

$$\mathbf{A}_v = -2830$$

$$\boldsymbol{\beta} = \frac{101}{2830} = 0.0357$$

16-5. THE EFFECT OF FEEDBACK ON NOISE

In the last section we determined the effect of feedback on nonlinear distortion by considering that an unwanted signal was injected into the output of an amplifier. There are other unwanted signals that occur in an amplifier's output which are not due to nonlinear distortion. These are called *noise*. Noise can manifest itself in many ways.

There is the random noise discussed in Sec. 12-16. Also, no power supply that operates off the 60-Hz power lines produces pure direct current. There are always small sinusoidal voltages present at frequencies of 60 Hz and its harmonics. If these signals are significant, a noise called *hum* results.

The effect of feedback upon noise varies. Let us consider two cases here. Suppose that the only significant amounts of hum are produced by the power supply for the output stage. The discussion of the last section then applies. Now $\mathbf{V}_d$ represents the hum voltage. Thus, provided that the input signal can be increased, the output signal to noise ratio will be reduced by the return difference and feedback can produce a significant advantage.

Note that the incorporation of feedback reduces both the signal and the noise by the same factor (the return difference). Increasing the input signal, or amplifying it, brings the desired output signal back to its original level without increasing the noise.

Now suppose that the noise is the type discussed in Sec. 12-16 and that it is produced in the first amplifier stage and that we cannot increase the input signal. Incorporation of feedback will equally reduce both the signal and the noise. Since we cannot increase the input signal, we must amplify it further. However, the first stage in any amplifier will produce the same noise as before. Hence, the signal to noise ratio at the amplifier input will be unchanged by the incorporation of feedback. Therefore, the signal to noise ratio at the output is unchanged by the incorporation of feedback.

The effect of feedback on noise is actually a complex phenomenon. Feedback may modify the frequency response and actually worsen the noise. Thus, each case must be considered carefully.

16-6. THE EFFECT OF FEEDBACK ON IMPEDANCE LEVELS

The introduction of feedback can greatly change the impedance levels within a device. In this section we shall specifically consider the effect of feedback on input and output impedance. To do this we shall model the nonfeedback portion of the circuit as shown in Fig. 16-10. The input and output impedances are shown there. Note that $\mathbf{A}_{voc}$ represents the gain of the amplifier when the load is an open circuit. This *does not* change if the load $\mathbf{Z}_L$ varies. Of course, the voltage $\mathbf{V}_2$ does vary as a function of load.

Now let us compute the output impedance of the voltage feedback amplifier shown in Fig. 16-11. Note that we have not shown the input connection of the $\mathbf{A}$ and $\boldsymbol{\beta}$ circuits. We shall obtain a relation for output impedance which does not depend upon whether series or shunt feedback is used. We shall call the output impedance $\mathbf{Z}_{ovfb}$ (*vfb* stands for voltage feedback). Then, from Fig. 16-11,

$$\mathbf{Z}_{ovfb} = \frac{\mathbf{V}_{2oc}}{\mathbf{I}_{2sc}} \tag{16-34}$$

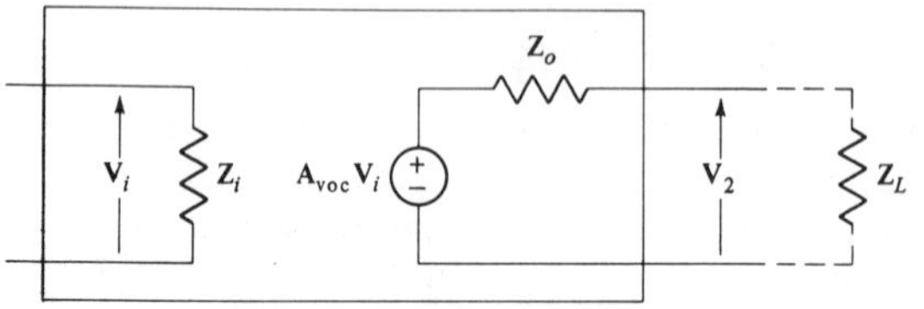

Figure 16-10. Model for an amplifier showing input and output impedance.

When voltage feedback is used, the voltage $\mathbf{V}_i$ is given by

$$\mathbf{V}_i = \mathbf{V}_1 + \boldsymbol{\beta}\mathbf{V}_2 \tag{16-35}$$

where $\mathbf{V}_1$ is the feedback amplifier's input signal and $\mathbf{V}_i$ is the input to the **A** portion of the circuit. Thus, the open circuit output voltage is given by

$$\mathbf{V}_{2oc} = \mathbf{A}_{voc}(\mathbf{V}_1 + \boldsymbol{\beta}\mathbf{V}_{2oc}) \tag{16-36}$$

Manipulation yields

$$\mathbf{V}_{2oc} = \frac{\mathbf{A}_{voc}\mathbf{V}_1}{1 - \mathbf{A}_{voc}\boldsymbol{\beta}} \tag{16-37}$$

(Note that we have assumed that the input impedance of the $\boldsymbol{\beta}$ circuit is infinite so that it does not load down $\mathbf{V}_2$.) When we short-circuit the output, $\mathbf{V}_2$ becomes zero so Eq. 6-35 becomes

$$\mathbf{V}_i = \mathbf{V}_1$$

Hence,

$$\mathbf{I}_{2sc} = \frac{\mathbf{V}_{voc}\mathbf{V}_1}{\mathbf{Z}_o}$$

Substituting in Eq. 6-34, we obtain

$$\mathbf{Z}_{ovfb} = \frac{\mathbf{Z}_o}{1 - \mathbf{A}_{voc}\boldsymbol{\beta}} \tag{16-38}$$

When the voltage feedback is used, the output impedance is equal to $\mathbf{Z}_o$, the output impedance of the nonfeedback amplifier, divided by the return difference *under open-circuit conditions.* Note that this is *not* the actual return difference of the feedback amplifier which is a function of the external load impedance. With negative feedback, voltage feedback amplifiers often have very low output impedance. In an actual feedback amplifier, it may not be possible to determine $\mathbf{Z}_o$, since it may interact with the $\boldsymbol{\beta}$ circuit. Also, the input impedance of the $\boldsymbol{\beta}$ circuit will not be infinite. Thus, Eq. 16-38 may not be useful for actual calculations, but it does indicate the degree to which voltage feedback

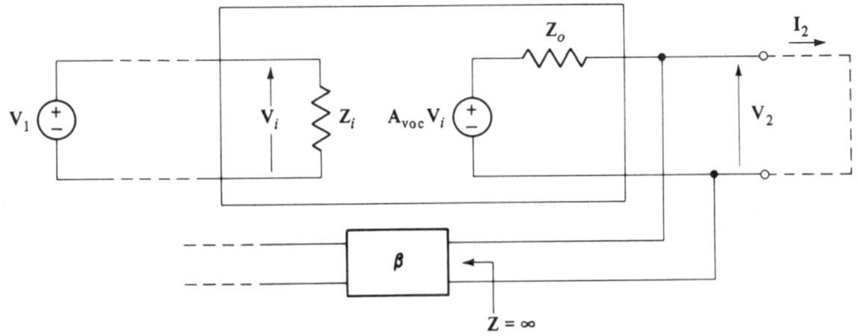

Figure 16-11. A voltage feedback amplifier model.

will reduce output impedance. (Note that the linear model of the actual circuit can always be used to obtain the actual output impedance.)

Now let us consider the case of current feedback (see Fig. 16-12). Now

$$\mathbf{V}_i = \mathbf{V}_1 + \boldsymbol{\beta}\mathbf{I}_2 \tag{16-39}$$

That is, the feedback component of $\mathbf{V}_i$ is proportional to $\mathbf{I}_2$. ($\boldsymbol{\beta}$ now has the dimensions of ohms.) When the output terminals are open circuited, $\mathbf{I}_2 = 0$. Hence,

$$\mathbf{V}_{2oc} = \mathbf{A}_{voc}\mathbf{V}_1 \tag{16-40}$$

When a short circuit is placed across the output, then

$$\mathbf{I}_{2sc} = \frac{\mathbf{A}_{voc}(\mathbf{V}_1 + \boldsymbol{\beta}\mathbf{I}_{2sc})}{\mathbf{Z}_o} \tag{16-41}$$

where we have assumed that the input impedance of the $\boldsymbol{\beta}$ circuit is zero so that it does not affect $\mathbf{I}_2$. Manipulating Eq. 16-41, we have

$$\mathbf{I}_{2sc} = \frac{\mathbf{A}_{voc}\mathbf{V}_1}{\mathbf{Z}_o - \mathbf{A}_{voc}\boldsymbol{\beta}} \tag{16-42}$$

Let us define a dimensionless quantity

$$\boldsymbol{\beta}_1 = \frac{\boldsymbol{\beta}}{\mathbf{Z}_o} \tag{16-43}$$

Then, substituting Eqs. 16-40, 16-42, and 16-43 into Eq. 16-34, we obtain

$$\mathbf{Z}_{oifb} = \mathbf{Z}_o(1 - \mathbf{A}_{voc}\boldsymbol{\beta}_1) \tag{16-44}$$

We shall call $(1 - \mathbf{A}_{voc}\boldsymbol{\beta}_1)$ a *modified return difference under short circuit conditions.* (Note that it occurs in the calculation of $\mathbf{I}_{2sc}$.) Hence, we can state that, when current feedback is used, the output impedance is $\mathbf{Z}_o$ multiplied by the modified return difference under short circuit conditions. (This is *not* a function of $\mathbf{Z}_L$.) The modified return difference, when negative feedback is used, is usually a real positive number, so that current feedback increases the output impedance, often by a substantial amount.

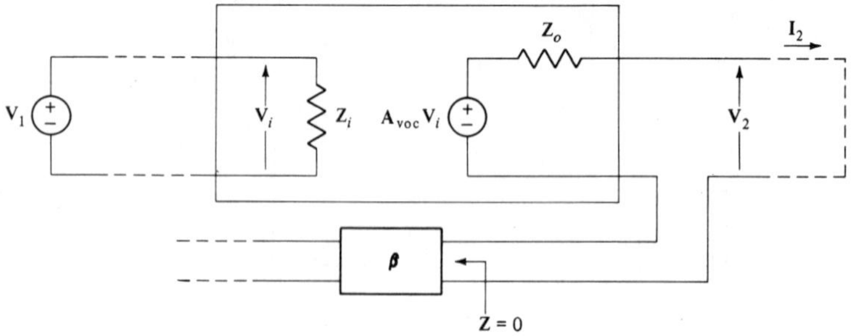

Figure 16-12. A current feedback amplifier model.

Just as Eq. 16-38 cannot be used for computation of $\mathbf{Z}_{ovfb}$, Eq. 16-44 cannot be used for calculation of $\mathbf{Z}_{oifb}$, but again these equations indicate how feedback will affect the impedance and they provide us with an idea of the magnitude of the effect. For instance, we see that voltage negative feedback decreases output impedance whereas current negative feedback increases it. This increase and decrease can be very substantial.

Now let us consider the input impedance of series and shunt feedback amplifiers. We start with the series feedback amplifier of Fig. 16-13. Let us first consider the voltage across the output of the β circuit which we call $\boldsymbol{\beta}\mathbf{X}_2$, where $\mathbf{X}_2 = \mathbf{V}_2$ when voltage feedback is used and $\mathbf{X}_2 = \mathbf{I}_2$ when current feedback is used. Then,

$$\mathbf{I}_1 = \frac{\mathbf{V}_1 + \boldsymbol{\beta}\mathbf{X}_2}{\mathbf{Z}_i} \tag{16-45}$$

The quantity $\mathbf{X}_2$ is proportional to the input voltage $\mathbf{V}_i$. Hence,

$$\mathbf{X}_2 = \mathbf{A}(\mathbf{V}_1 + \boldsymbol{\beta}\mathbf{X}_2) \tag{16-46}$$

Note that $\mathbf{A}$ is not the voltage gain $\mathbf{A}_v$ of the amplifier but depends upon $\mathbf{Z}_o$, the load impedance $\mathbf{Z}_L$, and other circuit elements. Then, solving Eq. 16-46 for $\mathbf{X}_2$ and substituting in Eq. 16-45, we have

$$\mathbf{I}_1 = \frac{\mathbf{V}_1}{\mathbf{Z}_1(1 - \mathbf{A}\boldsymbol{\beta})}$$

The input impedance is given by $\mathbf{V}_1/\mathbf{I}_1$. Hence,

$$\mathbf{Z}_{isefb} = \mathbf{Z}_i(1 - \mathbf{A}\boldsymbol{\beta}) \tag{16-47}$$

In general, with negative feedback, $\mathbf{A}\boldsymbol{\beta}$ will be a negative number, so $\mathbf{Z}_{isefb}$ will be multiplied by a positive number. Hence, the input impedance will be increased when series negative feedback is used. This is similar to the case of the output impedance and current feedback.

Now let us consider the shunt feedback amplifier model of Fig. 16-14. Here we have

$$\mathbf{V}_1 = \mathbf{V}_i = (\mathbf{I}_1 + \boldsymbol{\beta}\mathbf{X}_2)\mathbf{Z}_i \tag{16-48}$$

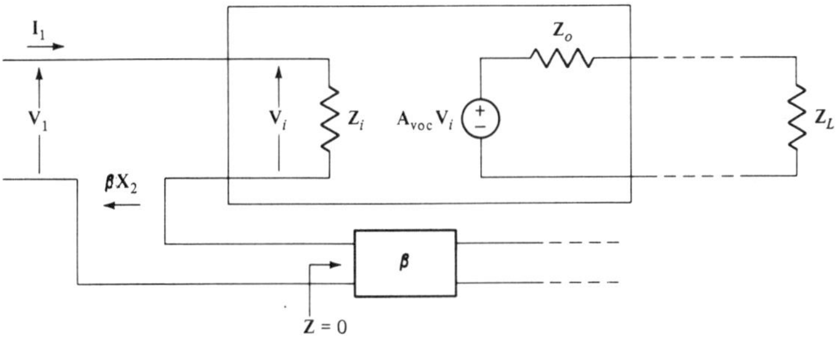

Figure 16-13. A series feedback amplifier model.

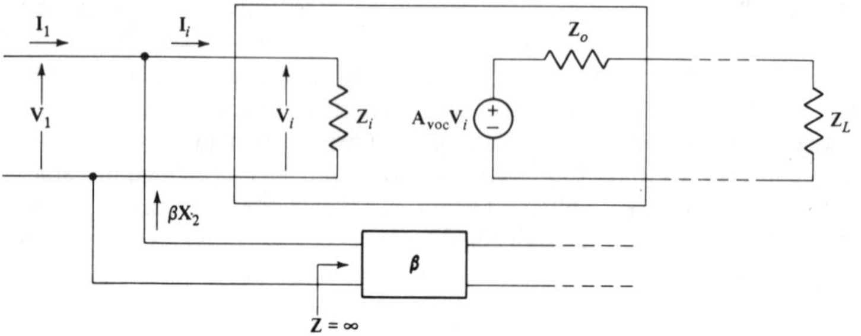

Figure 16-14. A shunt feedback amplifier model.

The output signal will be proportional to $\mathbf{V}_i$ which, in turn, is proportional to $\mathbf{I}_1 + \boldsymbol{\beta}\mathbf{X}_2$. Hence, we can write

$$\mathbf{X}_2 = \mathbf{A}(\mathbf{I}_1 + \boldsymbol{\beta}\mathbf{X}_2) \tag{16-49}$$

Manipulating, we obtain

$$\mathbf{Z}_{ishfb} = \frac{\mathbf{Z}_i}{1 - \mathbf{A}\boldsymbol{\beta}} \tag{16-50}$$

With negative feedback, $\mathbf{A}\boldsymbol{\beta}$ is usually a real negative number (when $\mathbf{Z}_i$ and Z_i are resistive) so that the input impedance is reduced when shunt negative feedback is used.

We have discovered that the impedances which we have discussed where, in general, lowered with both voltage and shunt negative feedback and increased with both current and series negative feedback. Consider the voltage feedback circuit of Fig. 16-11. When the output terminals are short-circuited the feedback signal becomes zero. Similarly consider the shunt feedback of Fig. 16-14 when the input terminals are short-circuited, $\mathbf{V}_i = 0$. Hence, the feedback signal becomes zero. Thus, in both cases, where the incorporation of negative feedback reduced the impedance, short-circuiting the terminals in question eliminates the feedback signal.

In the case of either current or series feedback, the converse occurs. For instance, in Fig. 16-12, when the output terminals are open circuited, $\mathbf{I}_2 = 0$ and the feedback becomes zero. In Fig. 16-13, when the input terminals are open circuited, $\mathbf{I}_1 = 0$, so $\mathbf{V}_i = 0$ and the feedback becomes zero.

In general, the following is true concerning the impedance viewed into a pair of terminals. If short-circuiting them causes the negative feedback signal to become zero, then the incorporation of feedback reduces the impedance. If the negative feedback signal becomes zero when the terminals are open circuited, then the inclusion of feedback has increased the impedance. We have assumed negative feedback in this discussion. For positive feedback, the converse would be true.

16-7. THE EFFECT OF FEEDBACK ON BANDWIDTH

We shall now consider how feedback affects the bandwidth of an amplifier. Let us start our discussion by considering a simple example. Suppose that we are dealing with the basic feedback structure whose block diagram is given by Fig. 16-1b. Thus, the gain of the amplifier is given by

$$\mathbf{K}_v = \frac{\mathbf{A}_v}{1 - \mathbf{A}_v\boldsymbol{\beta}} \tag{16-51}$$

Now let us assume that $\mathbf{A}_v$ is not a constant, but that it varies with frequency. In particular

$$\mathbf{A}_v = \frac{\mathbf{A}_{v\,\text{mid}}}{1 + jf/f_2} \tag{16-52}$$

Thus, the amplifier part of the circuit has a half-power bandwidth f_2. We shall also assume that $\boldsymbol{\beta}$ is a real positive number β, whose magnitude is less than unity, and that $\mathbf{A}_{v\,\text{mid}}$ is a real negative number. Substituting Eq. 16-52 into Eq. 16-51 and manipulating, we have

$$\mathbf{K}_v = \left[\frac{\mathbf{A}_{v\,\text{mid}}}{1 - \beta\mathbf{A}_{v\,\text{mid}}}\right]\left[\frac{1}{1 + j\dfrac{f}{f_2(1 - \mathbf{A}_{v\,\text{mid}}\beta)}}\right] \tag{16-53}$$

The midband gain has been reduced by the return difference $1 - \mathbf{A}_{v\,\text{mid}}\beta$, while the half-power bandwidth has been increased by it. Equation 16-53 indicates that feedback has introduced a simple trade-off of gain for bandwidth. However, this will not always be the case (see Sec. 16-8), and the actual affect of feedback upon gain and frequency response is a complex phenomenon which must be studied for each individual case.

An important fact should be considered. Even though the feedback has improved the bandwidth of the amplifier, it may not have increased the *usable range of frequencies* or *usable bandwidth* that should be applied to the amplifier. In general, this will occur whenever we use feedback to obtain the advantages discussed in Secs. 16-3 to 16-5 and 16-7. To illustrate this, we shall consider an example. Suppose that the amplifier is characterized by Eqs. 16-51 and 16-52, where $f_2 = 10^6$ Hz, $\mathbf{A}_{v\,\text{mid}} = -1000$, and $\beta = 0.1$. Also suppose that, to reduce distortion to acceptable levels, we require that the magnitude of the return difference, $|F|$, be equal to or greater than 70.7. Then, since $\mathbf{F} = 1 - \mathbf{A}\boldsymbol{\beta}$,

$$\mathbf{F} = 1 + \frac{100}{1 + jf/10^6}$$

Now let us determine the frequency where $|\mathbf{F}|$ falls off to 70.7.

$$70.7 = \left|1 + \frac{100}{1 + jf/10^6}\right| = \left|\frac{101 + jf/10^6}{1 + jf/10^6}\right|$$

Solving, we obtain

$$f = 1.02 \times 10^6 \text{ Hz}$$

Thus, the *usable* bandwidth is essentially unchanged by feedback, even though the half-power frequency of the amplifier is given by (see Eq. 16-53)

$$f_2(1 - \mathbf{A}_{v\,\text{mid}}\beta) = 10^6(101) = 101 \text{ MHz}$$

Thus, the amplifier's half-power frequency has increased, but if we are to get the specified advantage of feedback, then we can only apply frequencies of up to 1.02×10^6 Hz. Therefore, the usable range of input frequencies or usable bandwidth is only 1.2×10^6 Hz.

16-8. THE FEEDBACK PAIR

Let us now discuss the effect of feedback on the frequency response of a feedback amplifier where the amplifier part consists of a *pair* of subamplifiers. Each subamplifier might be a single stage or it could be a group of stages, such as an operational amplifier. This is called a *feedback pair.*

In Fig. 16-15a we show a negative feedback pair which uses voltage series feedback with operational amplifiers. Note that the feedback connection is made to the noninverting input of the first stage, resulting in negative feedback. We have drawn two operational amplifiers here for generality. Actually, they could represent single stages. For instance, in Fig. 16-15b we show a similar feedback pair using transistor stages.

Consider Fig. 16-15a.

$$\mathbf{V}_2 = \left(\mathbf{V}_1 - \frac{R_1\mathbf{V}_2}{R_1 + R_2}\right)\mathbf{A}_{v1}\mathbf{A}_{v2} \tag{16-54}$$

Manipulating, we obtain

$$\mathbf{K}_v = \frac{\mathbf{V}_2}{\mathbf{V}_1} = \frac{\mathbf{A}_{v1}\mathbf{A}_{v2}}{1 + [R_1/(R_1 + R_2)]\mathbf{A}_{v1}\mathbf{A}_{v2}} \tag{16-55}$$

Let us call

$$\beta = \frac{R_1}{R_1 + R_2} \tag{16-56}$$

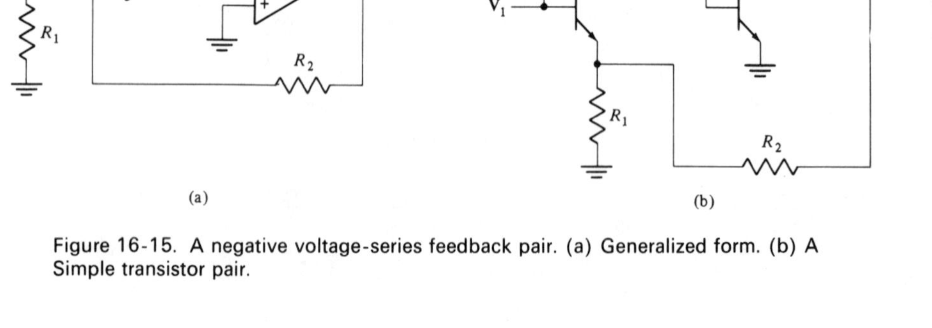

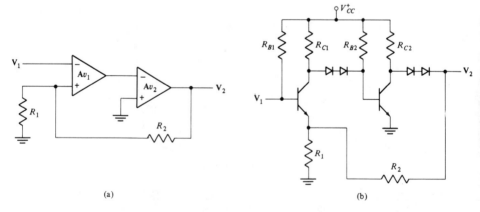

Figure 16-15. A negative voltage-series feedback pair. (a) Generalized form. (b) A Simple transistor pair.

Thus, we can write Eq. 16-55 as

$$\mathbf{K}_v = \frac{\mathbf{A}_{v1}\mathbf{A}_{v2}}{1 + \beta\mathbf{A}_{v1}\mathbf{A}_{v2}} \tag{16-57}$$

Now let us study the frequency response of this feedback pair. Assume that $\mathbf{A}_{v1}$ and $\mathbf{A}_{v2}$ each have simple frequency responses given by

$$\mathbf{A}_{v1} = \frac{\mathbf{A}_{v1\,\mathrm{mid}}}{1 + jf/f_{21}} \tag{16-58a}$$

$$\mathbf{A}_{v2} = \frac{\mathbf{A}_{v2\,\mathrm{mid}}}{1 + jf/f_{22}} \tag{16-58b}$$

Substituting in Eq. 16-57 and manipulating, we have

$$\frac{\mathbf{K}_v}{\mathbf{K}_{v\,\mathrm{mid}}} = \left[1 - \frac{f^2}{(1 + A_o\beta)f_{21}f_{22}} + j\frac{f}{1 + A_o\beta}\left(\frac{1}{f_{21}} + \frac{1}{f_{22}}\right)\right]^{-1} \tag{16-59}$$

where

$$\mathbf{A}_o = \mathbf{A}_{v1\,\mathrm{mid}}\mathbf{A}_{v2\,\mathrm{mid}} \tag{16-60}$$

$$\mathbf{K}_{v\,\mathrm{mid}} = \frac{A_o}{1 + A_o\beta} \tag{16-61}$$

Note that, as β is varied, the *form*, as well as the bandwidth, of the frequency response curves will vary. For instance, in Fig. 16-16 we have plotted curves of $\mathbf{K}_v/\mathbf{K}_{v\,\mathrm{mid}}$ versus β. Note that when $\beta = 0$, there is no feedback. As the magnitude of the loop gain increases, the bandwidth increases. As we saw in Sec. 16-7, the increase can be substantial. However, the response also becomes peaked when β is increased sufficiently.

Let us consider the transient response of the amplifier. Proceeding as in Sec. 12-17, we have

$$\frac{\mathbf{K}_v(s)}{\mathbf{K}_{v\,\mathrm{mid}}} = \left[\frac{s^2}{(1 + A_o\beta)\omega_{21}\omega_{22}} + \frac{s}{1 + A_o\beta}\left(\frac{1}{\omega_{21}} + \frac{1}{\omega_{22}}\right) + 1\right]^{-1} \tag{16-62}$$

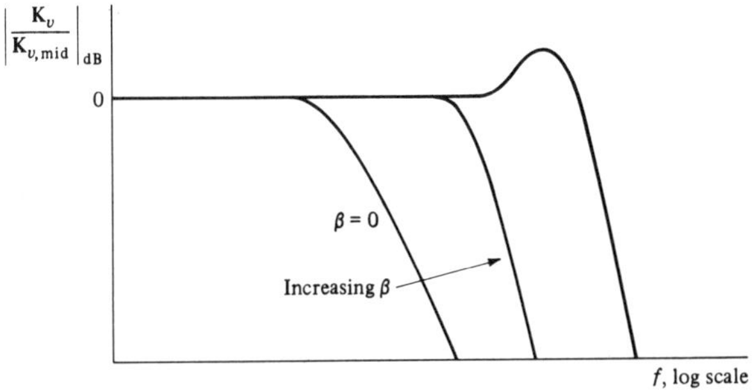

Figure 16-16. A sketch of $|\mathbf{K}_v/\mathbf{K}_{v\,\mathrm{mid}}|_{\mathrm{dB}}$ for the negative voltage-series feedback pair as a function of $\boldsymbol{\beta}$.

The poles of this expression occur at

$$s_{1,2} = -\frac{(\omega_{21} + \omega_{22})}{2} \pm \tfrac{1}{2}\sqrt{(\omega_{21} + \omega_{22})^2 - 4F_o\omega_{21}\omega_{22}} \tag{16-63}$$

where F_o is the return difference measured at *low* frequencies.

$$F_o = 1 + A_o\beta \tag{16-64}$$

Let us determine how the pole locations vary as a function of F_o. When $\beta = 0$ then $F_o = 1$, and

$$s_{1,2} = -\omega_{21}, -\omega_{22} \tag{16-65}$$

These are the poles when there is no feedback. If F_o is very large, (i.e., the loop gain $A_o\beta$ is large) then

$$s_{1,2} = -\frac{(\omega_{21} + \omega_{22})}{2} \pm j\sqrt{F_o\omega_{21}\omega_{22}} \tag{16-66}$$

These are complex conjugate poles. Let us determine the restrictions on F_o if the roots are to be complex. Complex roots will occur when the term within the square root of Eq. 16-63 is negative, which occurs when

$$F_o > \frac{(\omega_{21} + \omega_{22})^2}{4\omega_{21}\omega_{22}} \tag{16-67}$$

A pole-zero diagram is shown in Fig. 16-17. When F_o is small, the poles lie on the negative σ axis. As F_o is increased, the poles move along the axis toward the point $-(\omega_{21} + \omega_{22})/2$.

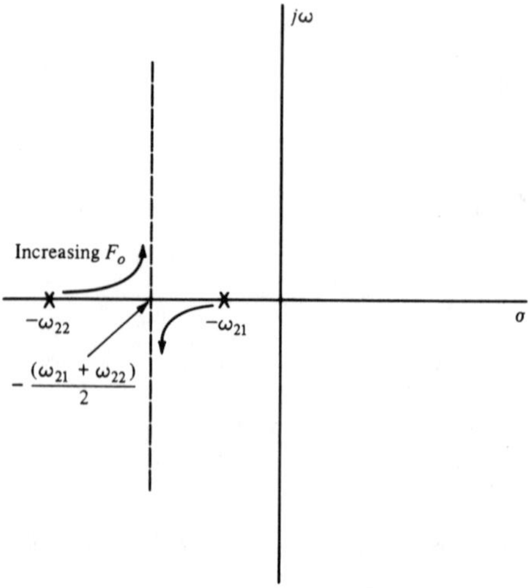

Figure 16-17. Variation of the poles of a feedback pair with F_o. The poles are real if $F_o \leqslant (\omega_{21} + \omega_{22})^2/(4\omega_{21}\omega_{22})$ and lie on the dashed line otherwise.

Increasing F_o beyond the value given in inequality 16-67 results in complex conjugate poles. The normalized unit step response of the feedback pair is given by (see Sec. 12-17)

$$b(t) = u(t)\left[1 + \frac{s_1}{s_2 - s_1} e^{-s_2 t} - \frac{s_2}{s_2 - s_1} e^{-s_1 t}\right] \tag{16-68}$$

In Fig. 16-18 we sketch this response. As F_o is increased, the 10–90% rise time decreases, which is an indication of the increased bandwidth. As F_o is increased further, the rise time decreases still further but overshoot now results. Consider the pole-zero diagram of Fig. 16-17. The overshoot occurs when the poles do not lie on the negative σ axis but become complex conjugate. That is, relation 16-67 defines those values of F_o for which overshoot is to occur.

Example

The individual operational amplifiers in the feedback pair of Fig. 16-15a have the following gains.

$$\mathbf{A}_{v1} = \frac{-100}{1 + j(\omega/10^6)}$$

$$\mathbf{A}_{v2} = \frac{-50}{1 + j(\omega/10^7)}$$

Determine the value of $\beta = R_1/(R_1 + R_2)$ which results in minimum 10–90% rise time without overshoot.

From Eq. 16-67 we have that the maximum value of F_o which will not result in complex conjugate poles is

$$F_o = \frac{(10^6 + 10 \times 10^6)^2}{4(10^6)(10 \times 10^6)} = 3.025$$

$$F_o = 1 + A_o\beta$$

where

$$A_o = \mathbf{A}_{v1\,\text{mid}}\mathbf{A}_{v2\,\text{mid}} = (-100)(-50) = 5000$$

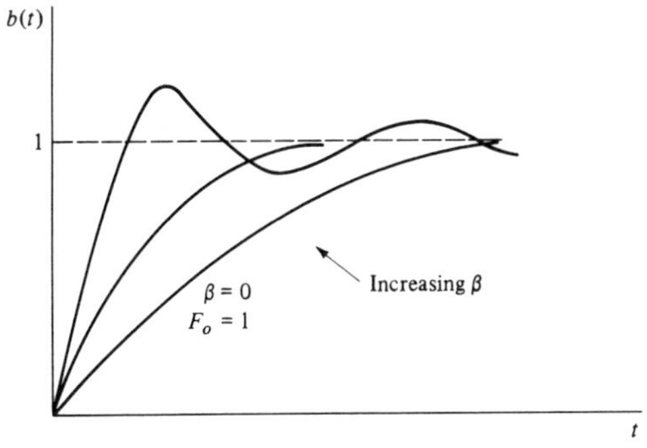

Figure 16-18. The normalized unit step response of a feedback pair.

Therefore,

$$\beta = 0.0005$$

Note that as ω_{21} approaches ω_{22}, F_o approaches 1. That is, when both amplifiers are identical, any feedback will introduce overshoot.

Feedback can be used to modify the frequency and transient response of an amplifier but we must not lose sight of two very important facts. First, as F_o is increased, $\mathbf{K}_{v\,\text{mid}}$ will decrease so there is a trade-off of gain for bandwidth. The second fact is that the increase in bandwidth may not be usable. If the feedback is only introduced to modify the frequency response, then all the bandwidth is usable. On the other hand, if we are using feedback to gain its other advantages, then the discussion at the end of Sec. 16-7 applies and the increased bandwidth is not usable bandwidth.

16-9. USE OF LINEAR MODELS IN GENERAL FEEDBACK AMPLIFIER CALCULATIONS

In this section we shall demonstate the use of linear models in feedback amplifier calculations. Three-stage voltage shunt feedback amplifiers shall be used as examples.

The first example is the FET amplifier of Fig. 16-19a. We have included two capacitors C_1 and C_2 here. These account for the input capacitance of F_1 and for the

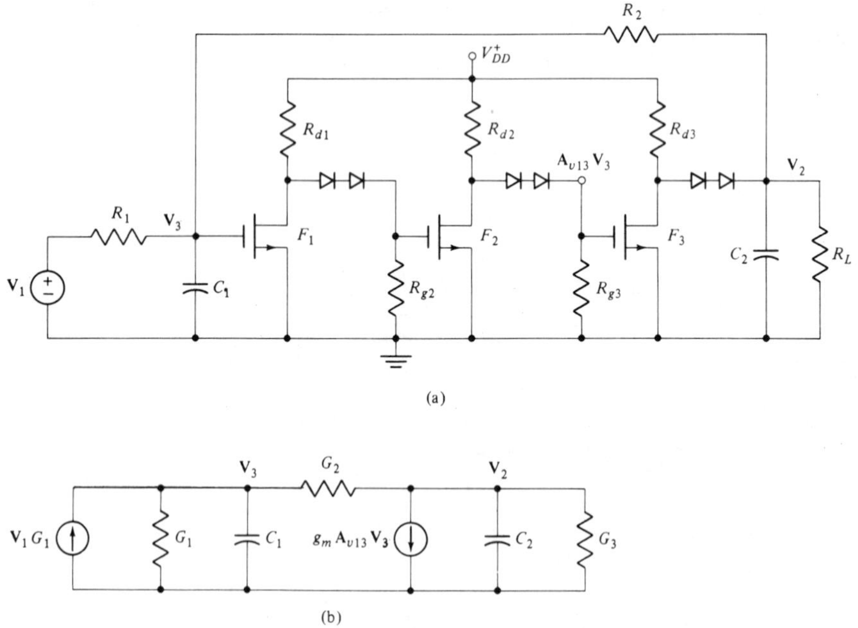

Figure 16-19. (a) A three-stage FET voltage shunt feedback amplifier. (b) Its model.

output and load capacitance of F_3. To simplify the analysis, we shall assume that C_{gs} can be accounted for by increasing C_{in} (Miller effect) and C_{out} (see Sec. 12-3). That is, the effect of C_{gs} as a coupling between input and output, other than in producing Miller effect, will be ignored.

The voltage gain from the gate of the first stage to the gate of the third stage will be written as $\mathbf{A}_{v13}$. The computation of this gain exactly follows that of Sec. 12-3. Note that the feedback does not affect this gain. The feedback manifests itself by affecting $\mathbf{V}_3$. For simplicity, we have assumed that diodes are used to obtain the level shift.

The model for the amplifier of Fig. 16-19a is shown in Fig. 16-19b. Note that $\mathbf{A}_{v13}$ is actually a complex expression for the gain of two stages. The conductance G_3 is given by

$$G_3 = \frac{1}{R_3} = \frac{1}{r_{d3}} + \frac{1}{R_{d3}} + \frac{1}{R_L} \tag{16-69}$$

We have replaced the input generator by its Norton's equivalent.

The procedure of grouping several stages' gain together as $\mathbf{A}_{v13}$ considerably simplifies the model. We only include stages in the grouping which are in cascade without any feedback. In other words, the replaced amplifier is just a simple cascade.

Before we analyze this amplifier, let us consider the transistor amplifier of Fig. 16-20. We have again included the capacitances C_1 and C_2 here. C_2 accounts for any

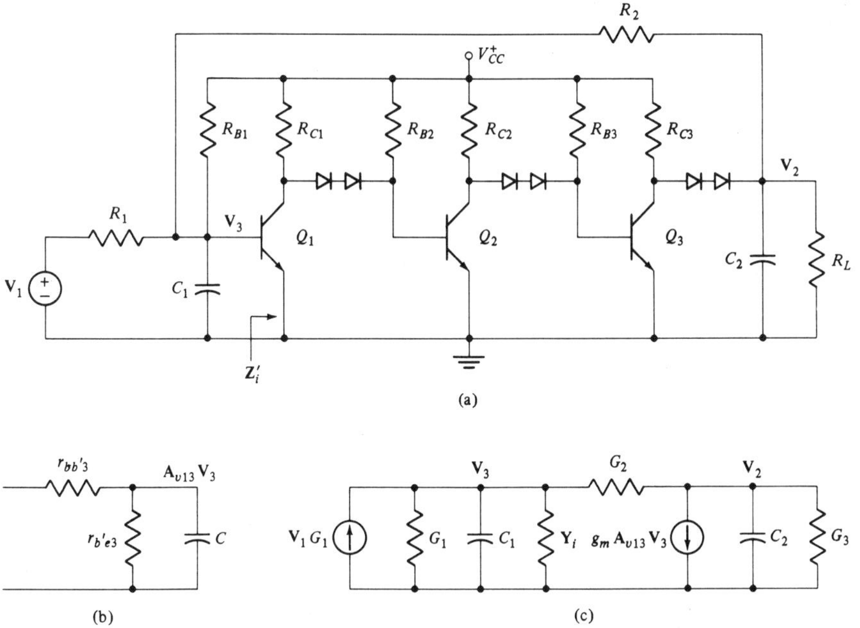

Figure 16-20. (a) A three-stage transistor voltage-shunt feedback amplifier. (b) The input to transistor Q_3. (c) A model for the amplifier.

load capacitance while we have added C_1 for generality. Consider Q_3. We can represent its input impedance by Fig. 16-20b. In this case we call $\mathbf{A}_{v13}$ the voltage gain from the base of Q_1 to the voltage across $r_{b'e3}$. Hence, this voltage is $\mathbf{A}_{v13}\mathbf{V}_3$. We represent the input impedance between the base and emitter leads of Q_1 as $\mathbf{Z}_i' = 1/\mathbf{Y}_i'$. $\mathbf{Y}_i$ is the parallel configuration of $\mathbf{Y}_i'$ and $1/R_{B1}$. Then, using the hybrid-pi model for Q_3, we obtain the model shown in Fig. 16-20c, where

$$G_3 = \frac{1}{R_3} = \frac{1}{r_{ce2}} + \frac{1}{R_{C3}} + \frac{1}{R_L} \tag{16-70}$$

Compare the models of Figs. 16-19b and 16-20c. They are the same except for the presence of $\mathbf{Y}_i$ in Fig. 16-20c, so we can use this model for both circuits. If we want to analyze the FET circuit, we simply set $\mathbf{Y}_i = 0$.

Let us now analyze the circuit of Fig. 16-20c. Performing nodal analysis, we have

$$\mathbf{V}_1 G_1 = (G_1 + G_2 + \mathbf{Y}_i + j\omega C_1)\mathbf{V}_3 - G_2\mathbf{V}_2 \tag{16-71a}$$

$$0 = (g_m\mathbf{A}_{v13} - G_2)\mathbf{V}_3 + (G_2 + G_3 + j\omega C_2)\mathbf{V}_2 \tag{16-71b}$$

Solving for $\mathbf{K}_v = \mathbf{V}_2/\mathbf{V}_1$, we obtain

$$\mathbf{K}_v = \frac{-(g_m\mathbf{A}_{v13} - G_2)G_1}{(G_1 + G_2 + \mathbf{Y}_i + j\omega C_1)(G_2 + G_3 + j\omega C_2) + G_2(g_m\mathbf{A}_{v13} - G_2)} \tag{16-72}$$

Manipulation yields

$$\mathbf{K}_v = \frac{-G_1(g_m\mathbf{A}_{v13} - G_2)/(G_1 + G_2 + \mathbf{Y}_i + j\omega C_1)(G_2 + G_3 + j\omega C_2)}{1 + [G_2(g_m\mathbf{A}_{v13} - G_2)/(G_1 + G_2 + \mathbf{Y}_i + j\omega C_1)(G_2 + G_3 + j\omega C_2)]} \tag{16-73}$$

We shall make some approximations here. Consider the terms in the numerator $(g_m\mathbf{A}_{v13} - G_2)$. The component of the gain which is proportional to $g_m\mathbf{A}_{v13}$ is essentially the gain of the amplifier. The component proportional to G_2 represents the direct transmission of the signal through G_2, which is actually a loss rather than a gain. It is very small so this component can be neglected. Hence, over frequencies of interest,

$$|g_m\mathbf{A}_{v13}| \gg G_2 \tag{16-74}$$

Hence, Eq. 16-73 can be written as

$$\mathbf{K}_v = \frac{-G_1 g_m\mathbf{A}_{v13}/(G_1 + G_2 + \mathbf{Y}_i + j\omega C_1)(G_2 + G_3 + j\omega C_2)}{1 + G_2 g_m\mathbf{A}_{v13}/(G_1 + G_2 + \mathbf{Y}_i + j\omega C_1)(G_2 + G_3 + j\omega C_2)} \tag{16-75}$$

If

$$\left|\frac{G_2 g_m\mathbf{A}_{v13}}{(G_1 + G_2 + \mathbf{Y}_i + j\omega C_1)(G_2 + G_3 + j\omega C_2)}\right| \gg 1 \tag{16-76}$$

then Eq. 16-75 becomes

$$\mathbf{K}_v = \frac{-G_1}{G_2} = \frac{-R_2}{R_1} \tag{16-77}$$

Hence, as long as inequality 16-76 is true, the gain is essentially independent of the parameters of the active devices. Of course, as the frequency increases, the gain of each stage will fall off and, at sufficiently high frequencies, inequality 16-76 will no longer be true. Naturally, Eq. 16-77 is not used to compute the effects of feedback on sensitivity and distortion. To do this we use the results of Secs. 16-3 and 16-5 which require a knowledge of the loop gain. Let us determine it. Consider the expression given as the left-hand side of relation 16-76. Let us call this $\mathbf{L}(j\omega)$.

$$\mathbf{L}(j\omega) = \frac{-G_2 g_m \mathbf{A}_{v13}}{(G_1 + G_2 + \mathbf{Y}_i + j\omega C_1)(G_2 + G_3 + j\omega C_2)} \tag{16-78}$$

Let us consider the parts of this expression.

$\mathbf{A}_{v13}$ represents the voltage gain of the first two stages. Now consider

$$\mathbf{L}_1 = -g_m/(G_2 + G_3 + j\omega C_2) \tag{16-79}$$

This represents g_m times the impedance in shunt with the dependent current generator. This is a slight approximation since G_2 is not connected to ground but to $\mathbf{V}_1$. However, $\mathbf{V}_2 \gg \mathbf{V}_1$. Thus, the current through $G_2 \simeq \mathbf{V}_2 G_2$. Thus, for these purposes we can consider that G_2 is connected to ground. Hence, $\mathbf{L}_1$ represents the voltage gain of the third stage.

Now consider

$$\mathbf{L}_2 = G_2/(G_1 + G_2 + \mathbf{Y}_i + j\omega C_1) \tag{16-80}$$

This is a voltage divider ratio where the series arm is G_2 and the shunt arm is the parallel combination of G_1, $\mathbf{Y}_i$, and $j\omega C_1$ in parallel (remember that $\mathbf{Y}_i$ includes R_B). Thus, this represents the loss from $\mathbf{V}_2$ back to the first base through the β network.

Thus, $\mathbf{L}(j\omega) = \mathbf{A}_{v13}\mathbf{L}_1\mathbf{L}_2$ is an approximate expression for the loop gain of the amplifier. Note that we could not use Eq. 16-2 here to compute the gain since $\mathbf{A}$ and $\boldsymbol{\beta}$ could not be identified. However, we obtained a useful result by putting $\mathbf{K}_v$ into the form

$$\mathbf{K}_v = \frac{G}{1 - G\mathbf{B}} \tag{16-81}$$

where $G\mathbf{B}$ was the loop gain, $\mathbf{A}\boldsymbol{\beta}$. In Sec. 16-12 we shall present formal procedures for obtaining the loop gain.

Let us now compute the output impedance of the amplifier. We shall do this by using the relation

$$\mathbf{Z}_o = \frac{\mathbf{V}_{2oc}}{\mathbf{I}_{2sc}} \tag{16-82}$$

To obtain $\mathbf{V}_{2oc}$ we set $G_L = 1/R_L = 0$. We shall call the resulting value of G_3, G_{30} (see Eqs. 16-69 and 16-70). We shall use Eq. 16-75 to compute $\mathbf{V}_{2oc}$.

$$\mathbf{V}_{2oc} = \frac{-G_1 g_m \mathbf{A}_{v13}\mathbf{V}_1/(G_1 + G_2 + \mathbf{Y}_i + j\omega C_1)(G_2 + G_{30} + j\omega C_2)}{1 + G_2 g_m \mathbf{A}_v/(G_1 + G_2 + \mathbf{Y}_i + j\omega C_1)(G_2 + G_{30} + j\omega C_2)} \tag{16-83}$$

To obtain $\mathbf{I}_{2sc}$ we multiply $\mathbf{V}_2$ by G_L and then let $G_L \to \infty$. Note that this also causes G_3 to become infinite. Performing the calculation yields

$$\mathbf{I}_{2sc} = \frac{-G_1 G_L g_m \mathbf{A}_{v13} \mathbf{V}_1}{G_3(G_1 + G_2 + \mathbf{Y}_i + j\omega C_1)} \tag{16-84}$$

As $G_L \to \infty$, $G_L/G_3 \to 1$. Hence,

$$\mathbf{I}_{2sc} = \frac{-G_1 \mathbf{A}_{v13} g_m \mathbf{V}_1}{G_1 + G_2 + \mathbf{Y}_i + j\omega C_1} \tag{16-85}$$

Substituting Eqs. 16-83 and 16-85 into Eq. 16-82 yields

$$\mathbf{Z}_o = \frac{1/(G_2 + G_{30} + j\omega C_2)}{1 + G_2 g_m \mathbf{A}_{v13}/(G_1 + G_2 + \mathbf{Y}_i + j\omega C_1)(G_2 + G_{30} + j\omega C_2)} \tag{16-86}$$

Let us consider this expression. $G_2 g_m \mathbf{A}_{v13}/(G_1 + G_2 + \mathbf{Y}_i + j\omega C_1)(G_2 + G_{30} + j\omega C_2)$ is the loop gain with $G_L = 0$ $(R_L = \infty)$ (see Eq. 16-80), which we shall call $\mathbf{L}_{oc}(j\omega)$. Hence, $\mathbf{Z}_o$ can be written as

$$\mathbf{Z}_o = \frac{1}{1 + \mathbf{L}_{oc}(j\omega)} \frac{1}{G_2 + G_{30} + j\omega C_2} \tag{16-87}$$

Now $G_2 + G_{30} + j\omega C_2$ is (in some approximate sense) the output impedance without feedback. It is the parallel combination of R_2, r_{ce} (or r_d), and R_{C3} (or R_{d3}). Note that, as we discussed earlier, R_2 can be considered to be connected from the output to ground for these purposes. Thus, the output impedance without feedback is reduced by the return difference under open-circuit conditions. This agrees with the results of Sec. 16-6. Note that the results that we have obtained here (see Eq. 16-86) allow us to actually calculate $\mathbf{Z}_o$ as a function of ω.

16-10. OSCILLATION IN FEEDBACK AMPLIFIERS

Whenever a feedback system is designed there is a danger that it may be *unstable*, that is, it may *oscillate*. The howl that results at times in public address systems is an example of oscillation. When an amplifier oscillates, it can no longer function properly as an amplifier. The oscillation, as in the case of the howl, obscures the signal being amplified. Sometimes the oscillation may occur at a frequency far removed from the signal frequencies. For instance, in the case of an audio amplifier, the oscillation might be at an inaudible frequency. Nevertheless, the amplifier still cannot be used since the oscillation will drive it between the extremes of cutoff and saturation so it cannot function properly.

If a feedback amplifier has a loop gain of $+1$ at a frequency ω_0, then a signal of frequency ω_0 will propagate around the feedback loop without any change in amplitude. It may seem as though a loop gain of $+C$ where $C > 1$ would always result in oscillation since it appears as though the amplitude of the signal would increase as it propagates around the loop. However, stability is actually a complex problem and the "obvious solution" is not always the correct one. For instance, if all we know is that at some frequency the loop gain is $+5$, we cannot state with certainty whether or not the amplifier is stable. Remember that the loop gain is measured with the feedback loop open and that conditions will change when it is closed.

A basic technique for determining if a feedback amplifier is stable is to study the Laplace transform of its gain $\mathbf{K}_v(s)$. We are especially interested in the poles of $\mathbf{K}_v(s)$. In Sec. 12-17 we discussed that if the Laplace transform of the gain of an amplifier had poles in the right-half s plane, then the transient response would have terms that *built up* exponentially with time. Suppose that this is the case. Now the response to any signal, or noise, would contain transients that exist indefinitely and build up exponentially. This results in oscillation. Eventually, the nonlinearities of the amplifier (saturation and cutoff) would limit the size of the oscillations, but they would persist indefinitely. On the other hand, if *all* the poles of the amplification $\mathbf{K}_v(s)$ lie in the left-half s plane, then all of the transient terms will be damped and will fall off exponentially with time. Thus, the amplifier will be stable.

Multiple poles that lie on the $j\omega$ axis lead to transient terms, which build up as t^{n-1}, where n is the order of the pole, so multiple poles on the $j\omega$ axis also lead to oscillation. Simple poles on the $j\omega$ axis result in transient terms which neither increase nor decrease (e.g., sinusoids). This is the borderline of oscillation. For our purposes we shall consider this operation to be unstable.

Thus, we state that if *all* the poles of $\mathbf{K}_v$ lie in the left-half s plane, then the amplifier will be stable, while if *any* poles lie either on the $j\omega$ axis or in the right-half s plane, then the amplifier is unstable. A study of the poles of $\mathbf{K}_v$ does not tell the complete story. For instance, suppose that an amplifier consists of a cascade of two amplifiers, one of which has a pole in the right-half plane and the other amplifier has a zero at the same point. For instance, consider

$$\mathbf{K}_v = \mathbf{K}_{v1}\mathbf{K}_{v2} = \frac{1}{(s+1)(s-10)}\,\frac{s-10}{s+2} \tag{16-88}$$

$\mathbf{K}_v$ will have no pole at $s = +10$ since it will be canceled by the zero. Nevertheless, $\mathbf{K}_{v1}$ will be unstable. If both amplifiers were *ideal linear* devices, no oscillation signal would appear at the output and the circuit would function properly. However, when amplifier number 1 oscillates, it will be driven between saturation and cutoff. Hence, it no longer functions properly and cannot be used as an amplifier. In addition, since the circuit is no longer functioning linearly, the oscillation signal will show up at the output. If $\mathbf{K}_v$ has all its poles in the left-half plane, but oscillation of the type discussed occurs, then the oscillation is said to be not *observable*. Of course, inspection of the poles of $\mathbf{K}_v$ will not detect such oscillation.

There is another case where inspection of the poles of $\mathbf{K}_v$ does not tell the complete story about oscillation. In theory, oscillation does not start to build up until a signal initiates it (i.e., oscillation is part of the transient response to a signal). In some cases, the input signal does not cause current to be in some part of a circuit (e.g., the center arm of a balanced bridge). The parameters of this part of the circuit will not affect $\mathbf{K}_v$. This part of the circuit may oscillate. The oscillation will not be initiated by the input signal but by noise. Again, in an ideal linear system, this oscillation would not occur and there would be no right-half plane poles in $\mathbf{K}_v$. However, noise causes the oscillation to build up, and the nonlinearities of the system would cause it to function improperly even if the oscillation does not appear in the output. Such oscillation is said to be *noncontrollable*.

In most feedback amplifiers, nonobservable and noncontrollable oscillations are not problems and, in practice, we can generally use the location of the poles of $\mathbf{K}_v$ as a criterion for stability.

Then, to repeat the basic procedure that we shall use to determine stability, we first study the voltage gain $\mathbf{K}_v$. We replace $j\omega$ with s and factor the denominator. If all the poles lie in the left-half plane, then the amplifier is stable. If any of the poles lie on the $j\omega$ axis, or in the right-half plane, then the amplifier is unstable.

This procedure is very tedious to apply if the denominator of $\mathbf{K}_v(s)$ is of high order, as it usually is, since numerical procedures must be used to obtain the poles. In addition, we would like a procedure that enables us to design feedback amplifiers that are stable, or to stabilize feedback amplifiers that oscillate. Such a procedure will be developed in this chapter.

Note that we do not have to know the locations of the roots exactly. We only need to know if they lie in the right-half plane or on the $j\omega$ axis. We shall see that this allows us to develop procedures that do not require the factoring of the denominator of $\mathbf{K}_v(s)$.

16-11. THE ROUTH–HURWITZ TEST FOR THE LOCATION OF THE ROOTS OF A POLYNOMIAL

We shall now consider two simple tests which determine if a feedback amplifier, whose gain is $\mathbf{K}_v$, is stable. If

$$\mathbf{K}_v(s) = \frac{\mathbf{N}(s)}{\mathbf{D}(s)}$$

where $\mathbf{N}(s)$ and $\mathbf{D}(s)$ are polynomials in s, then, if $\mathbf{D}(s)$ contains roots all of which lie in the left-half plane, the amplifier will be stable. We assume that $\mathbf{N}(s)$ and $\mathbf{D}(s)$ do not have common roots. Note that these tests will not indicate how to remedy the situation if the amplifier is unstable, but they are simple to apply. In the next section we shall discuss procedures that can actually be used in design. A polynomial that has all its roots in the left-half plane is called a *Hurwitz polynomial.* If any of its roots lie on the $j\omega$ axis or in the right-half plane, then it is *not* a Hurwitz polynomial.

Consider that $\mathbf{D}(s)$ is a polynomial that has no roots at $s = 0$.

$$\mathbf{D}(s) = s^k + d_{k-1}s^{k-1} + \cdots + d_1 s + d_0 \tag{16-89}$$

If any of the coefficients are zero or negative, then the polynomial is not a Hurwitz polynomial, and we need test no further. The amplifier is unstable. (Remember that we are considering simple $j\omega$ axis roots as borderline instability.)

We shall now present, without proof, a test called the *Hurwitz test* to determine if a polynomial is a Hurwitz polynomial. Break $\mathbf{D}(s)$ into the sum of two polynomials.

$$\mathbf{D}(s) = \mathbf{m}(s) + \mathbf{n}(s) \tag{16-90}$$

where $\mathbf{m}(s)$ is an even polynomial (i.e., it only contains the even powered terms and the constant), and $\mathbf{n}(s)$ is an odd polynomial (i.e., it contains the odd powered terms). Now we form one of the following fractions.

$$\boldsymbol{\phi} = \frac{\mathbf{m}(s)}{\mathbf{n}(s)} \tag{16-91a}$$

or

$$\boldsymbol{\phi} = \frac{\mathbf{n}(s)}{\mathbf{m}(s)} \tag{16-91b}$$

The fraction formed should have the highest power of the numerator one greater than the highest power of the denominator. Let us assume that Eq. 16-91a is used. We then divide $\mathbf{n}(s)$ into $\mathbf{m}(s)$ *once*.

$$\frac{\mathbf{m}(s)}{\mathbf{n}(s)} = a_1 s + \frac{\mathbf{R}_1(s)}{\mathbf{n}(s)} \tag{16-92}$$

The remainder $\mathbf{R}_1(s)$ will be an even polynomial in s. Its degree will be one less than that of $\mathbf{n}(s)$. We shall demonstrate this in an example subsequently. Next we take the reciprocal of the *remainder* term and divide $\mathbf{R}_1(s)$ into $\mathbf{n}(s)$ once.

$$\frac{\mathbf{n}(s)}{\mathbf{R}_1(s)} = a_2 s + \frac{\mathbf{R}_2(s)}{\mathbf{R}_1(s)} \tag{16-93}$$

We now continue the procedure with the succeeding remainders.

$$\frac{\mathbf{R}_1(s)}{\mathbf{R}_2(s)} = a_3 s + \frac{\mathbf{R}_3(s)}{\mathbf{R}_2(s)} \tag{16-94}$$

$$\vdots$$

The degree of the remainder polynomial decreases with each step and eventually the procedure terminates. Now examine all the $a_1, a_2, a_3, \ldots$. If they are *all positive*, then $\mathbf{D}(s)$ is a Hurwitz polynomial. If *any* of the $a_1, a_2, a_3, \ldots$ is zero or negative, then $\mathbf{D}(s)$ is not a Hurwitz polynomial, and the amplifier is unstable.

Let us consider an example of this procedure.

$$\mathbf{D}(s) = s^4 + 4s^3 + 7s^2 + 8s + 2$$

Then,

$$\mathbf{m}(s) = s^4 + 7s^2 + 2$$

$$\mathbf{n}(s) = 4s^3 + 8s$$

The divisions can be set up in a compact form.

$$\begin{array}{r l}
 & \tfrac{1}{4}s \\
4s^3 + 8s & \overline{)\, s^4 + 7s^2 + 2} \\
 & \underline{s^4 + 2s^2} \qquad \tfrac{4}{5}s \\
 & \qquad 5s^2 + 2\,\overline{)\, 4s^3 + 8s} \\
 & \qquad\qquad \underline{4s^3 + \tfrac{8}{5}s} \quad \tfrac{25}{32}s \\
 & \qquad\qquad\quad \tfrac{32}{5}s\,\overline{)\, 5s^2 + 2} \\
 & \qquad\qquad\qquad \underline{5s^2} \qquad \tfrac{16}{5}s \\
 & \qquad\qquad\qquad\qquad 2\,\overline{)\, \tfrac{32}{5}s} \\
 & \qquad\qquad\qquad\qquad\quad \underline{\tfrac{32}{5}s} \\
 & \qquad\qquad\qquad\qquad\qquad 0
\end{array}$$

The a's are $a_1 = \frac{1}{4}$, $a_2 = \frac{4}{5}$, $a_3 = \frac{25}{32}$, and $a_4 = \frac{16}{5}$. These are all positive and, hence, $\mathbf{D}(s)$ is a Hurwitz polynomial.

Even Polynomial Factors

If $\mathbf{D}(s)$ has a factor that is an even polynomial, then both $\mathbf{m}(s)$ and $\mathbf{n}(s)$ will have this factor. This factor can be canceled if, after we form $\boldsymbol{\phi}$ (see Eqs. 16-91), we recognize that it is present, but it is not usually obvious that such a factor exists. In such cases, the factor will be carried through and will appear as a factor of *each* remainder. Let us illustrate this.

$$\mathbf{D}(s) = (s^2 + 1)(s^2 + 2s + 1) = s^4 + 2s^3 + 2s^2 + 2s + 1$$

We assume that we do not realize that this polynomial can be factored as shown. Then, we form

$$m(s) = s^4 + 2s^2 + 1$$

$$\mathbf{n}(s) = 2s^3 + 2s$$

Note that it is not obvious that these have a common factor. Then, we set up the division

$$
\begin{array}{rlll}
 & \tfrac{1}{2}s & & \\
2s^3 + 2s \,\big) & s^4 + 2s^2 + 1 & & \\
 & s^4 + s^2 & 2s & \\
\hline
 & s^2 + 1 \,\big) & 2s^3 + 2s & \\
 & & 2s^3 + 2s & \\
\hline
 & & 0 + 0 &
\end{array}
$$

Note that the test terminated prematurely since the last divisor was not a constant. Since the even factor is carried through each remainder, we can now state that $(s^2 + 1)$ is a factor of $\mathbf{D}(s)$.

Let us consider the significance of an even polynomial factor. An even polynomial will be of the form

$$\mathbf{E}(s) = s^{2k} + e_{n-1}s^{2k-2} + \cdots + e_2 s^2 + e_0 \tag{16-95}$$

If s_0 is a root of $\mathbf{E}(s)$, then $-s_0$ will also be a root. Thus, if $\mathbf{E}(s)$ has left-half plane roots, it must also have right-half plane roots. The only way that $\mathbf{E}(s)$ will not have right-half plane roots is if all the roots lie on the $j\omega$ axis, which also leads to an unstable condition. Thus, we can state that if the Hurwitz test terminates prematurely, or if any of the a_1, $a_2, \ldots$ are zero or negative, then $\mathbf{D}(s)$ will not be a Hurwitz polynomial. If the Hurwitz test does not terminate prematurely, and all the $a_1, a_2, \ldots$ are positive, then $\mathbf{D}(s)$ is a Hurwitz polynomial.

The Routh Test

The Routh test is essentially the same as the Hurwitz test except that the long division is written in the form of an array, which is convenient and save space. We start as in the Hurwitz test by breaking up $\mathbf{D}(s)$ into its odd and even parts. Now we write this as

$$\mathbf{m}(s) = a_0 s^{2k} + a_1 s^{2k-2} + \cdots + a_k \tag{16-96a}$$

$$\mathbf{n}(s) = b_0 s^{2k-1} + b_1 s^{2k-3} + \cdots + b_{k-1}s \tag{16-96b}$$

The coefficients of $\mathbf{m}(s)$ occupy the first row of the array which we are going to form, while those of $\mathbf{n}(s)$ occupy the second row. We have assumed here that $\mathbf{m}(s)$ is of higher degree than $\mathbf{n}(s)$. [If this were not the case, then the coefficients of $\mathbf{n}(s)$ would occupy the first row of the array and those of $\mathbf{m}(s)$ would occupy the second row.]

We now form an array. The first row consists of the coefficients of $\mathbf{m}(s)$; the second row consists of the coefficients of $\mathbf{n}(s)$. The array is

$$\begin{array}{lllll} a_0 & a_1 & a_2 & \cdots & a_k \\ b_0 & b_1 & b_2 & \cdots & \\ c_0 & c_1 & \cdots & & \\ d_0 & d_1 & \cdots & & \end{array} \tag{16-97}$$

Each row of the array (after the first two) is obtained from the two preceding ones using the following formulas.

$$\begin{aligned} c_0 &= \frac{b_0 a_1 - a_0 b_1}{b_0} \\ c_1 &= \frac{b_0 a_2 - a_0 b_2}{b_0} \\ c_2 &= \frac{b_0 a_3 - a_0 b_3}{b_0} \\ &\vdots \end{aligned} \tag{16-98a}$$

Similarly,

$$\begin{aligned} d_0 &= \frac{c_0 b_1 - b_0 c_1}{c_0} \\ d_1 &= \frac{c_0 b_2 - b_0 c_2}{c_0} \\ &\vdots \end{aligned} \tag{16-98b}$$

If Eqs. 16-98a and 16-98b are studied, it can be seen that the procedures used to set up the array are essentially the same as division.

After the array is set up, the terms in the first column are studied. If they all are positive, then $\mathbf{D}(s)$ is a Hurwitz polynomial. If any of the terms in the first column are zero or negative, then $\mathbf{D}(s)$ is not a Hurwitz polynomial.

Let us consider an example using the same equation as before.

$$\mathbf{D}(s) = s^4 + 4s^3 + 7s^2 + 8s + 2$$

Form the array

$$\begin{array}{lll} 1 & 7 & 2 \\ 4 & 8 & \\ 5 & 2 & \\ \frac{32}{5} & & \\ 2 & & \end{array}$$

Note that a blank space is treated as a zero. All the coefficients in the first column are positive, so $\mathbf{D}(s)$ is a Hurwitz polynomial. (Note that the coefficients in the array are the same as the coefficients of the remainders in the division.) If the Routh test terminates prematurely, then it means that $\mathbf{D}(s)$ had an even polynomial factor. Thus, if $\mathbf{D}(s)$ is to be a Hurwitz polynomial, all the coefficients in the first column of the Routh array must be positive and the test must not terminate prematurely.

16-12. THE NYQUIST CRITERION FOR THE STABILITY OF A FEEDBACK AMPLIFIER

We shall now discuss a test for the stability of feedback amplifiers which will provide a design procedure that leads to stable amplifiers. The test is called the *Nyquist criterion.* We shall restrict ourselves to the basic single loop form of feedback amplifier which we have discussed thus far, and whose signal flow graph is given in Fig. 16-1b. There is only one feedback path and, if the feedback loop is broken at any point, *all* feedback ceases. The gain of such a feedback amplifier can be expressed as

$$\mathbf{K}_v = \frac{\mathbf{A}_v}{1 - \mathbf{A}_v \boldsymbol{\beta}} \tag{16-99}$$

where the loop gain is

$$\mathbf{L} = \mathbf{A}_v \boldsymbol{\beta} \tag{16-100}$$

and the return difference is

$$\mathbf{F} = 1 - \mathbf{L} = 1 - \mathbf{A}_v \boldsymbol{\beta} \tag{16-101}$$

We have seen that, although we cannot use Eq. 16-99 to express the gain, the loop gain and return difference are quantities that can be determined, and the gain can actually be expressed as $\mathbf{G}/\mathbf{F}$.

Now let us express the gain as a function of the Laplace transform variables. Then,

$$\mathbf{K}_v(s) = \frac{\mathbf{A}(s)}{1 - \mathbf{L}(s)} \tag{16-102a}$$

or

$$\mathbf{K}_v(s) = \frac{\mathbf{A}(s)}{\mathbf{F}(s)} \tag{16-102b}$$

If the amplifier is to be stable, then $\mathbf{K}_v(s)$ must have all its poles in the left-half s plane. In general, $\mathbf{A}(s)$ and $\mathbf{F}(s)$ are both the ratios of two polynomials in s. The poles of $\mathbf{K}_v(s)$ are either the poles of $\mathbf{A}(s)$ or the *zeros* of $\mathbf{F}(s)$. Since $\mathbf{A}(s)$ represents the gain of a *non-feedback* amplifier, it will be stable and all its poles will lie in the left-half s plane. Hence, if $\mathbf{K}_v(s)$ is unstable, then $\mathbf{F}(s)$ must have zeros on the $j\omega$ axis or in the right-half plane. Note that it is possible that such zeros could be canceled by zeros of $\mathbf{A}(s)$ and, in this case, the amplifier would be stable even though $\mathbf{F}(s)$ had right-half plane zeros. However, simple amplifier configurations do not have zeros in the right-half s plane or on the $j\omega$ axis and we shall assume that $\mathbf{A}(s)$ does not have such zeros.

Thus, our criterion for stability will be that **F**(s) have no zeros in the right-half plane or on the $j\omega$ axis. There is a theorem in the mathematical topic of the calculus of complex variables which can be used to determine if **F**(s) satisfies these requirements. Although the derivation of this theorem is complex, its application is not. We shall present the procedure here without proof.

In order to determine if **F**(s) has zeros in the right-half s plane, or on the $j\omega$ axis, we must make a polar plot of **F**(s) for all ω. Actually, we can also plot **L**(s) for all ω and obtain the same information since

$$\mathbf{L}(s) = 1 - \mathbf{F}(s) \tag{16-103}$$

Since **L**(s), the loop gain, can be computed directly, we shall state the test in terms of **L**(s).

A polar plot called a *Nyquist plot* or *Nyquist diagram* will be made of **L**($j\omega$). Since this is somewhat different from the usual plot, let us consider it. Choose a value of ω, say ω_0. Compute **L**($j\omega_0$) as a complex number. Plot this on a set of axes, which are Re **L**($j\omega$) and Im **L**($j\omega$). Now repeat this for all ω between 0 and ∞. The resultant plot is the one in question. For instance, suppose that

$$\mathbf{L}(j\omega) = \frac{-5}{[1 + j(\omega/\omega_2)]^3} \tag{16-104}$$

Then, some typical values that we shall plot are

ω/ω_2	$\mathbf{L}(j\omega)$
0	$5.0 \quad \angle 180°$
0.577	$3.25 \quad \angle 90°$
1.732	$0.625 \quad \angle 0°$
∞	0.0

The plot is shown in Fig. 16-21 as the solid curve. Note the dashed curve, which is called the *conjugate curve*. (The conjugate of a complex number consists of a number whose magnitude is the same as the original number's magnitude, but whose angle is the negative of the original number's phase angle.)

The Nyquist criterion states that the amplifier will be stable if the polar plot of **L**($j\omega$) does not encircle the point (1, 0). This point is called the *critical point* and is labeled with an X in Fig. 16-21. The curve of Fig. 16-21 does not encircle the critical point. Thus, the feedback amplifier whose loop gain is given in Fig. 16-21 is stable. Note that we now have a stability criterion that is based upon the magnitude and phase of a frequency response. In the remainder of this chapter we shall see how this can be used in design.

Let us now discuss some practical procedures for obtaining the loop gain. We break the feedback loop at some point and apply a signal $\mathbf{V}_a$ there. We then measure the signal $\mathbf{V}'_a$ returned to the other side of the break. For instance, consider Fig. 16-22a where we show a FET in a feedback amplifier. Typically, it could be one of the FET's of Fig. 16-19a. To measure the loop gain, we could break the feedback loop at the point marked X in

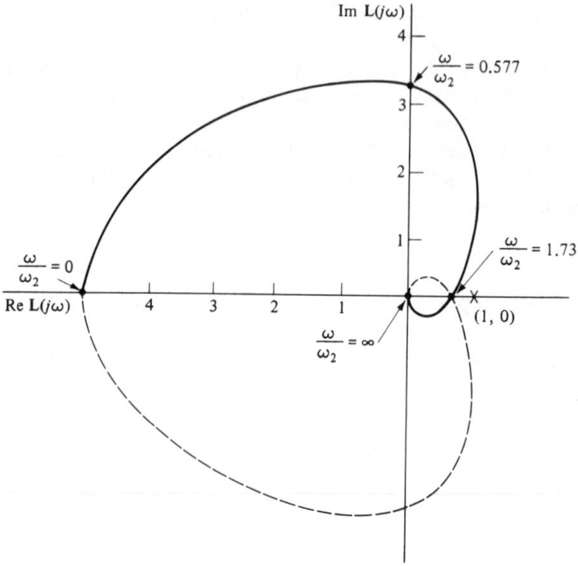

Figure 16-21. A polar plot of $\mathbf{L}(j\omega)$ given in Eq. 16-104.

Fig. 16-22a. The input impedance of the FET is $\mathbf{Y}_i$. The model used to compute the open loop gain is that shown in Fig. 16-22b. Note that, to account for the effect of $\mathbf{Y}_i$, we have "removed" it from the FET and placed it on the other side of the break. This can be done only when computations are performed. If an actual measurement is made, we cannot remove this impedance which is internal to the FET but an admittance equal to $\mathbf{Y}_i$ can be added to the circuit and the measurements can then be made.

The value of $\mathbf{Y}_i$ is affected by C_{gs} (i.e., the Miller effect). Actually, C_{gs} introduces local feedback around each FET, so we no longer have a single loop feedback amplifier

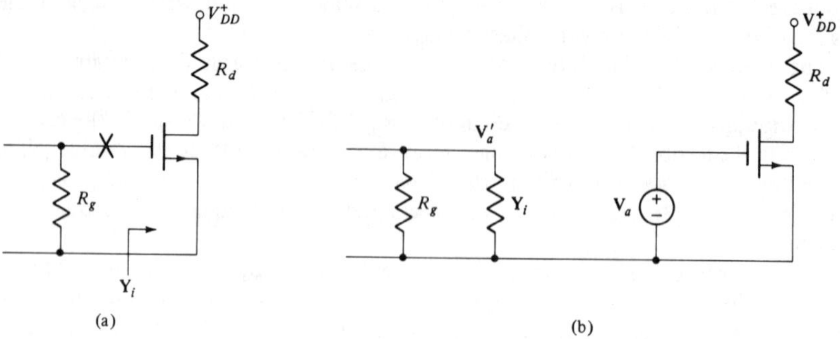

Figure 16-22. (a) A FET in a "single loop" feedback amplifier. (b) The circuit used to compute the loop gain.

and, strictly speaking, the procedures that we have discussed cannot be used. However, we can avoid this difficulty as we did in Sec. 12-3. There we accounted for the effect of C_{gs} on the input and output impedance of the FET but we neglected the other effects of C_{gs}. Thus, the local feedback is removed from the analysis.

There are other forms of local feedback that can be treated in this fashion. For instance, in the model for a transistor, the elements $C_{b'c}$ and $r_{b'c}$ introduce local feedback in a common-emitter transistor amplifier. However, as we discussed in Sec. 12-5, we can, to a high degree of accuracy, redraw the model without these feedback effects. Often this modeling process is satisfactory when we work with feedback amplifiers.

In general, if there is local feedback of the type that we have discussed, or other local types such as an impedance in the source or emitter leads, then, if we consider the effect that the elements have on gain and input impedance, we can often ignore the local feedback when we consider stability. That is, we consider the $\mathbf{A}_v$ circuit to be made up of a cascade of stages. The local feedback is taken into account when the individual stages' gain and input impedances are computed. Of course, each individual stage should be checked to see if it is stable. Ordinarily, this is not a problem unless tuned amplifiers are used.

As a detailed example of the computation of the loop gain, let us obtain $\mathbf{L}(j\omega)$ for the amplifier of Fig. 16-20a. The circuit that we use is shown in Fig. 16-23a. We have broken the feedback loop at the input to the first stage. The input generator is replaced by its internal impedance. (Note that the admittance $\mathbf{Y}_i$ includes R_{B1}.) The model for

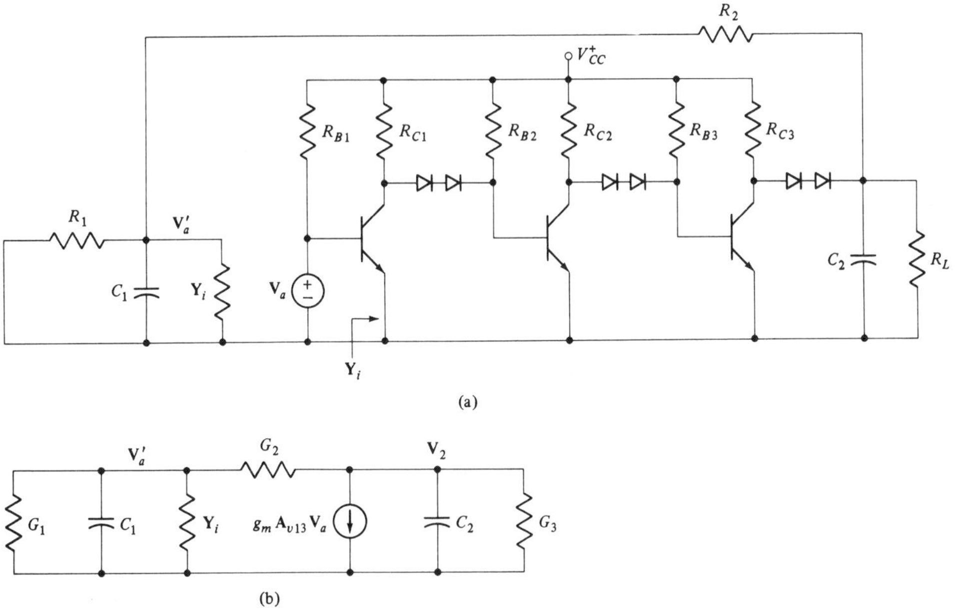

Figure 16-23. (a) The circuit used to compute the loop gain of the amplifier of Fig. 16-20a. (b) Its linear model. Note that $\mathbf{Y}_i$ includes R_{B1}.

this circuit is drawn in Fig. 16-23b. Its construction follows that of Fig. 16-20c. Notice that there is no feedback here since $\mathbf{V}_a$ is an independent variable. Analyzing this model, we obtain

$$0 = (G_1 + G_2 + \mathbf{Y}_i + j\omega C_1)\mathbf{V}'_a - G_2\mathbf{V}_2 \tag{16-105a}$$

$$-g_m\mathbf{A}_{v13}\mathbf{V}_a = -G_2\mathbf{V}'_a + (G_2 + G_3 + j\omega C_2)\mathbf{V}_2 \tag{16-105b}$$

Then, solving for $\mathbf{L}(j\omega) = \mathbf{V}'_a/\mathbf{V}_a$, we obtain

$$\mathbf{L}(j\omega) = \frac{-g_m\mathbf{A}_{v13}G_2}{(G_1 + G_2 + \mathbf{Y}_i + j\omega C_1)(G_2 + G_3 + j\omega C_2) - G_2^2} \tag{16-106}$$

Let us compare this with Eq. 16-78, which is the approximate expression for $\mathbf{L}(j\omega)$ we obtained in Sec. 16-9. We see that the two expressions are identical except for the $-G_2^2$ term in the denominator of Eq. 16-106. Since G_2 is usually considerably smaller than G_1, Eq. 16-106 is accurate. Of course, we now see that it is relatively simple to obtain the exact expression for $\mathbf{L}(j\omega)$, if desired.

16-13. FURTHER DISCUSSION OF STABILITY

The loop gain of Eq. 16-106 is proportional to g_{m3} of the third transistor. Actually, we could also factor out g_{m1} and g_{m2} from the expression for $\mathbf{A}_{v13}$, so that Eq. 16-106 could be rewritten as

$$\mathbf{L}(j\omega) = g_{m1}g_{m2}g_{m3}\mathbf{L}_1(j\omega) \tag{16-107}$$

If g_{m1}, g_{m2}, or g_{m3} is varied, the size of the Nyquist diagram will increase uniformly although its shape will not change otherwise. Thus, by changing the operating point of the active devices, we can change the size of the Nyquist diagram without changing its shape. (Note that changing the operating point will change parameters of the active devices other than g_m so the shape of the Nyquist diagram will change slightly.)

Let us now consider that we can change the magnitude of the loop gain and see how this affects stability. Suppose that we have a Nyquist diagram of the form shown in Fig. 16-24. The length $\overline{OA}$ represents the midband gain. The amplifier will be stable if

$$\overline{OB} < 1 \tag{16-108}$$

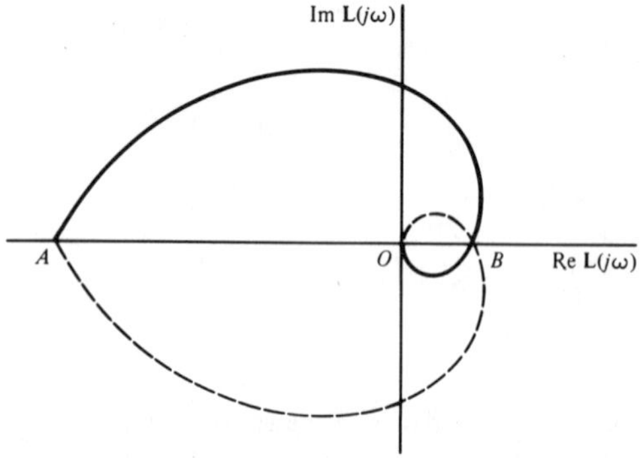

Figure 16-24. A Nyquist diagram which represents a stable amplifier if $\overline{OB} < 1$.

because then the critical point will lie outside of the Nyquist diagram. If $\overline{OB} \geqq 1$ then the amplifier will be unstable. If we vary the size of the diagram, then the ratio $\overline{OA}/\overline{OB}$ remains fixed. Therefore, Eq. 16-108 implies that, if the amplifier is to be stable, the maximum midband value of the loop gain is limited. We shall subsequently illustrate this idea with an example.

Now consider the Nyquist diagram shown in Fig. 16-25. No matter how we increase its size, the critical point (1, 0) will *not* be enclosed so this amplifier is stable for all values of midband loop gain. This type of stability is called *absolute stability.* It may seem as though this is an ideal form of stability. However, in most practical situations, we shall see that it is not possible to have absolute stability.

Finally, let us consider a Nyquist diagram such as that of Fig. 16-26. The amplifier will be stable if

$$\overline{OD} < 1 \tag{16-109a}$$

On the other hand, the amplifier will also be stable if both

$$\overline{OB} < 1$$

and (16-109b)

$$\overline{OC} > 1$$

In a complex case such as this, we must be careful how we define encirclement of the critical point. Consider Fig. 16-26. Imagine that a radius vector is drawn from the critical point to the curve. We have drawn such a radius vector in Fig. 16-26, assuming that the critical point lies between points B and C. Now let the tip of the radius vector move along the curve starting at the point where $\omega = 0$, and proceeding to the point where $\omega = \infty$. Now continue along the conjugate curve from $\omega = \infty$ back to $\omega = 0$. Count the number of *net* rotations the radius vector makes when this path is traversed. (Clockwise rotation is subtracted from counterclockwise rotation.) If the radius vector makes *no* net rotation, then the critical point is not enclosed. If there is *any* net rotation, then the critical point is enclosed and the amplifier is unstable. If we perform this test, then the conditions stated in relations 16-109a and 16-109b are obtained.

Suppose that the amplifier is such that the critical point lies between points B and C. Then the amplifier will be stable. However, it can become unstable if the gain

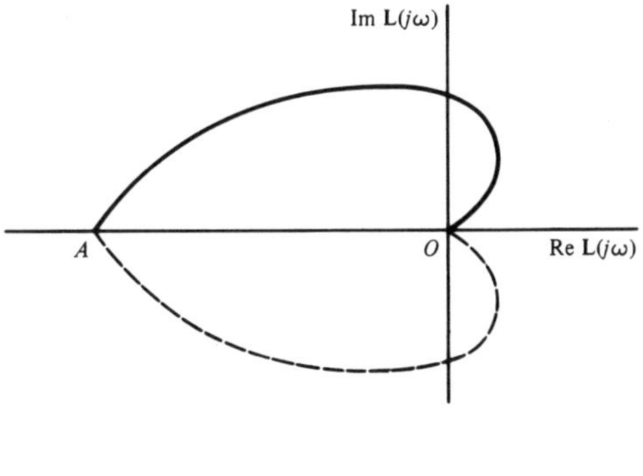

Figure 16-25. A Nyquist diagram for an absolutely stable amplifier.

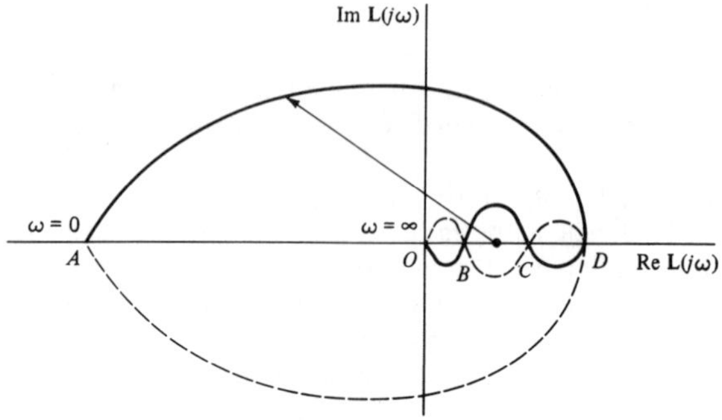

Figure 16-26. A Nyquist diagram for a conditionally stable amplifier. The amplifier will be stable if $\overline{OB} < 1$ and $\overline{OC} > 1$, or if $\overline{OD} < 1$.

increases or if it *decreases.* An amplifier that is stable but will become unstable if the gain decreases is said to be *conditionally stable.*

Usually, when an amplifier is turned on, the power supply voltage takes a short, but nonzero, time to rise to its specified value. Because of this, the gain of the amplifier is initially zero and builds up as the power supply voltage increases. If the amplifier is conditionally stable, then it will start to oscillate when the circuit is initially turned on and the power supply voltage builds up. Once the power supply voltage becomes sufficiently large, the oscillation will usually cease but a problem arises in some cases. If the power supply voltage builds up slowly while the oscillation builds up rapidly, the amplifier can be driven between saturation and cutoff by the oscillation. Saturation and cutoff lower the gain of an amplifier. Thus, the amplifier may remain "trapped" in a low-gain mode and remain oscillating even after the power supply voltage has built up. In such cases, the power supply and amplifier are built with separate switches. The power supply is switched on first and its voltage is allowed to reach its rated value, usually in a fraction of a second, and then the amplifier is switched on. Usually this is not a problem with semiconductor amplifiers and power supplies.

Relatively complex coupling networks are required if conditionally stable amplifiers are to be built. Thus, even though relatively large loop gains can be obtained with conditional stability, such amplifiers are rarely built.

Let us now consider some examples of loop gain and stability. Suppose that we have a single stage negative feedback amplifier. Its loop gain will be of the form

$$\mathbf{L}(j\omega) = \frac{-L_{\text{mid}}}{1 + jf/f_2} \tag{16-110}$$

Let us determine the maximum value L_{mid} can have. The plot of the Nyquist diagram is in Fig. 16-27a. There is absolute stability. Hence, L_{mid} is unlimited in size by stability considerations. Unfortunately, a single-stage amplifier usually cannot provide a great deal of gain so that L_{mid} is limited in practice.

Now let us consider a loop gain with two identical stages. Then,

$$\mathbf{L}(j\omega) = \frac{-L_{\text{mid}}}{(1 + jf/f_2)^2} \tag{16-111}$$

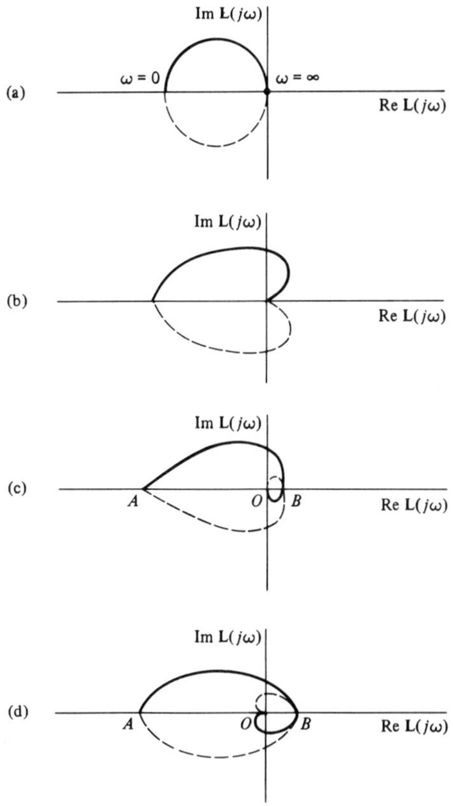

Figure 16-27. Nyquist diagram for the loop gain of: (a) Eq. 16-110. (b) Eq. 16-111. (c) Eq. 16-112. (d) Eq. 16-118.

The Nyquist diagram is shown in Fig. 16-27b. This, too, is unconditionally stable and, hence, L_{mid} is unlimited.

Often, the high-frequency falloff in $\mathbf{L}(j\omega)$ is not merely due to the loss in gain of the amplifier stage. For instance, consider the discussion of Sec. 16-9. The loop gain also fell off because of the capacitive loading of the input circuit. Thus, the loop gain of a two-stage amplifier would have the form of a three "stage" amplifier. Let us now consider such a relation where we have three identical stages.

$$\mathbf{L}(j\omega) = \frac{-L_{\text{mid}}}{(1 + jf/f_2)^3} \tag{16-112}$$

A plot of this loop gain is shown in Fig. 16-27c. If the amplifier is to be stable, then $\overline{OB} < 1$. The length $\overline{OA} = L_{\text{mid}}$. Let us rewrite Eq. 16-112 in polar form.

$$\mathbf{L}(j\omega) = \frac{L_{\text{mid}}}{[(1 + (f/f_2)^2]^{3/2}} \underline{/180^\circ - 3\tan^{-1}(f/f_2)} \tag{16-113}$$

Now let us find f_B that corresponds to point B in Fig. 16-27b. The angle of $\mathbf{L}(j\omega) = 0$ there. Then,

$$180° - 3\tan^{-1}\left(\frac{f_B}{f_2}\right) = 0 \tag{16-114}$$

Solving, we obtain

$$\frac{f_B}{f_2} = \tan 60° = \sqrt{3} \tag{16-115}$$

The magnitude of the gain at $f = f_B$ must be less than unity. Hence,

$$\frac{L_{\text{mid}}}{[1 + (f_B/f_2)^2]^{3/2}} < 1 \tag{16-116}$$

Substituting Eq. 16-115 and manipulating, we have

$$L_{\text{mid}} < 8 \tag{16-117}$$

Thus, the maximum loop gain is 8.

If we connect a cascade of four identical "stages," then

$$\mathbf{L}(j\omega) = \frac{-L_{\text{mid}}}{(1 + jf/f_2)^4} \tag{16-118}$$

The Nyquist diagram is shown in Fig. 16-27d. Proceeding as before, we obtain for stability

$$L_{\text{mid}} < 4 \tag{16-119}$$

If we used additional identical stages, the maximum L_{mid} would fall off further.

Maximum loop gains of 8 and 4 are small. In most situations much more gain is required. The value of L_{mid} is limited because we have required that all the stages be identical. Suppose that we have three nonidentical stages. Then,

$$\mathbf{L}(j\omega) = \frac{-L_{\text{mid}}}{[1 + j(\omega/\omega_{21})][1 + j(\omega/\omega_{22})][1 + j(\omega/\omega_{23})]} \tag{16-120}$$

Assume that

$$\omega_{22} \gg \omega_{21} \tag{16-121a}$$

and

$$\omega_{23} \gg \omega_{21} \tag{16-121b}$$

Then, over much of the range of frequencies, the amplifier would behave as a one-stage amplifier and L_{mid} could be high. At very high frequencies, the effect of the second and third stages would start to be felt. However, at these high frequencies, it is possible that $|\mathbf{L}(j\omega)|$ has become so small (i.e., $|\mathbf{L}(j\omega)| < 1$) so that the second and third stages do not significantly affect the stability. We shall discuss this in detail in Sec. 16-15 where we illustrate and use this idea in the design of feedback amplifiers.

16-14. GAIN AND PHASE MARGIN

The fact that an amplifier does not oscillate is not the only consideration when we study its stability. For instance, suppose that the Nyquist diagram passes very close to the critical point. If the power supply voltage increases, or if any of the parameter values changes, then the gain may increase. Since the Nyquist diagram passes close to unity, this increase in gain can result in the critical point's being enclosed and oscillation results. Thus, some tolerances should be placed on how close the Nyquist diagram comes to the critical point. We shall now do this.

In setting up a criterion we shall assume that the Nyquist diagrams are essentially of the form shown in Fig. 16-27, that is, that the gain falls off monotonically with frequency and the phase shift increases monotonically with frequency. Under these circumstances, if the amplifier is to be stable, then the loop gain must fall off to less than 1 before the phase angle reaches 0°. An alternative criterion is that, when the phase angle reaches 0°, the gain must be less than unity.

Consider Fig. 16-28, which details the part of the Nyquist plot near the critical point. The circle drawn there represents a loop gain whose magnitude is unity, that is, it is the *unit circle*. Beyond point B the Nyquist diagram has crossed the unit circle and, thus, $|\mathbf{L}(j\omega)|$ has become less than unity. The angle $\measuredangle BOA$ is called the *phase margin*. It is an indication of how close the Nyquist diagram comes to the critical point. If the phase margin is large, then the Nyquist diagram probably remains far from the critical point.

Now consider point A. Here the angle of the loop gain is 0°. The length $\overline{OA}$ represents $|\mathbf{L}(j\omega_A)|$ at that frequency ω_A where $\measuredangle\mathbf{L}(j\omega_A) = 0°$. This is also an indication of how close the Nyquist diagram is to the critical point. If $|\mathbf{L}(j\omega_A)|$ is much less than 1, then the Nyquist diagram probably remains far from the critical point. We define the *gain margin* in the following way.

$$GM|_{\text{dB}} = -20 \log_{10} \overline{OA} \tag{16-122}$$

If the gain and phase margins are high, then there will be little danger of the amplifier's oscillating with fluctuations in either power supply voltage or parameter values.

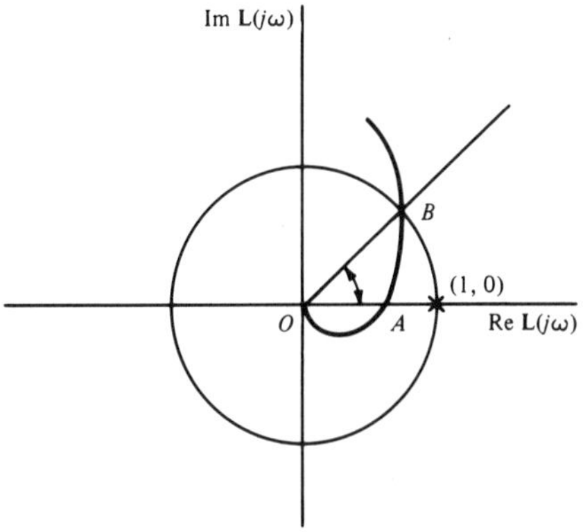

Figure 16-28. Detail of Nyquist diagram near the critical point.

On the other hand, if the gain and phase margins are small, then the danger of such oscillation may indeed be real.

We can study gain and phase margin from a plot of $|\mathbf{L}(j\omega)|$ and $\measuredangle \mathbf{L}(j\omega)$ versus frequency. Such a plot is shown in Fig. 16-29. These curves are drawn so that their frequency axes coincide in position. For convenience, we have drawn the asymptotes. The phase angle where $|\mathbf{L}(j\omega)|_{\mathrm{dB}} = 0$ (i.e., unity gain) is the phase margin. Similarly, the gain margin is the negative of the gain in decibels at the frequency where the phase angle becomes zero degrees.

The reader should note that in using gain and phase margin we attempt to characterize a curve by only two if its points. At times, this can lead to problems. Nevertheless, the specification of adequate gain and phase margins usually leads to stable operation.

If the gain and phase margins are small, then the loop gain is close to $+1$ at some frequencies. Let us consider the consequence of this. From Eq. 16-102a we have

$$\mathbf{K}_v(j\omega) = \frac{\mathbf{A}_v(j\omega)}{1 - \mathbf{L}(j\omega)} \tag{16-123}$$

If

$$|\mathbf{F}(j\omega)| = |1 - \mathbf{L}(j\omega)| < 1 \tag{16-124}$$

then $|\mathbf{K}_v(j\omega)|$ will be greater than $|\mathbf{A}_v(j\omega)|$. If $|\mathbf{F}(j\omega)|$ is very small for some frequencies, then $|\mathbf{K}_v(j\omega)|$ can be very large at those frequencies. The frequency response can then become peaked (see Fig. 16-16). Adequate specifications of gain and phase margins can prevent such peaking from occurring.

Consider Fig. 16-30. We have shown a portion of the Nyquist diagram near the critical point. We have also drawn the phasor $[1 - \mathbf{L}(j\omega)]$ there. Note the circle of radius

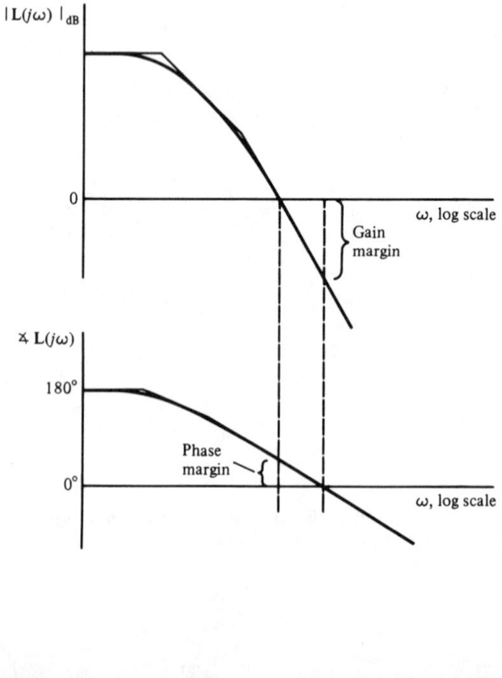

Figure 16-29. Plots of the amplitude and phase of the loop gain illustrating the gain and phase margins.

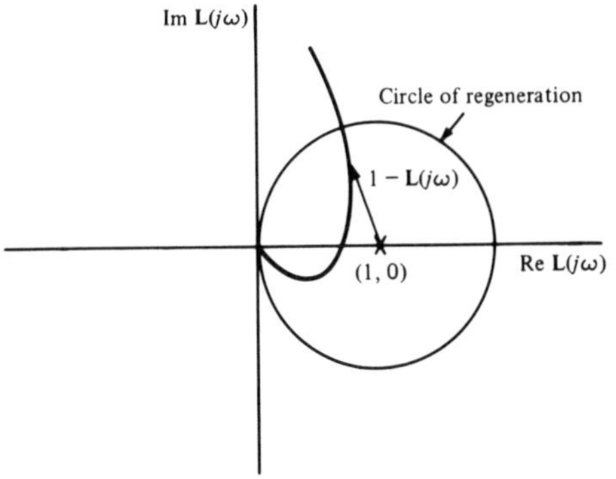

Figure 16-30. Detail of Nyquist diagram near the critical point showing the circle of regeneration.

unity drawn about the critical frequency. This is called the *circle of regeneration.* For all points on the Nyquist diagram within this circle $|1 - \mathbf{L}(j\omega)|$ will be less than 1. Thus, $|\mathbf{K}_v(j\omega)|$ will be greater than $|\mathbf{A}_v(j\omega)|$ for all frequencies of the Nyquist plot which lie within the circle of regeneration. We can consider that negative feedback occurs at all frequencies where the Nyquist diagram lies outside of the circle of regeneration, and that the feedback is positive for those frequencies that lie within the circle of regeneration.

16-15. BASIC DESIGN OF FEEDBACK AMPLIFIERS

In this section we shall discuss fundamental ideas used in the design of feedback amplifiers. In the next section we shall present some additional procedures. The basic ideas were introduced in Sec. 16-13. That is, we shall adjust the frequency response of the loop gain so that the amplifier is stable with the specified phase and/or gain margins.

To illustrate the design we shall assume that we are working with the amplifier of Fig. 16-20a (see Sec. 16-9). Let us repeat some of the pertinent equations. The voltage gain of the circuit is (see Eq. 16-77)

$$\mathbf{K}_v = \frac{-G_1}{G_2} = \frac{-R_2}{R_1} \tag{16-125}$$

We shall use the approximate expression for the loop gain given by Eq. 16-78.

$$\mathbf{L}(j\omega) = \frac{-G_2 g_m \mathbf{A}_{v13}}{(G_1 + G_2 + \mathbf{Y}_i + j\omega C_1)(G_2 + G_3 + j\omega C_2)} \tag{16-126}$$

$\mathbf{A}_{v13}$ represents the gain of the first two stages. We shall write this as

$$\mathbf{A}_{v13} = \frac{(\mathbf{A}_{v1\,\text{mid}})(\mathbf{A}_{v2\,\text{mid}})}{(1 + jf/f_{21})(1 + jf/f_{22})} \tag{16-127}$$

We can also write for the gain of the third stage

$$\frac{-g_m}{G_2 + G_3 + j\omega C_3} = \frac{\mathbf{A}_{v3\,\text{mid}}}{1 + jf/f_{23}} \tag{16-128a}$$

where

$$\mathbf{A}_{v3\,\text{mid}} = \frac{-g_m}{G_2 + G_3} \tag{16-128b}$$

$$f_{23} = \frac{G_2 + G_3}{2\pi(C_2 + C_3)} \tag{16-128c}$$

Similarly,

$$\frac{G_2}{G_1 + G_2 + \mathbf{Y}_i + j\omega C_1} = \frac{A_0}{1 + jf/f_{20}} \tag{16-129a}$$

where we assume that $\mathbf{Y}_i$ can be approximated as $G_i + j\omega C_i$. Then,

$$A_0 = \frac{G_2}{G_1 + G_2 + G_i} \tag{16-129b}$$

$$f_{20} = \frac{G_1 + G_2 + G_i}{2\pi(C_i + C_1)} \tag{16-129c}$$

Hence, the loop gain can be written as

$$\mathbf{L}(j\omega) = \frac{\mathbf{L}_{\text{mid}}}{\left(1 + j\dfrac{f}{f_{21}}\right)\left(1 + j\dfrac{f}{f_{22}}\right)\left(1 + j\dfrac{f}{f_{23}}\right)\left(1 + j\dfrac{f}{f_{20}}\right)} \tag{16-130}$$

$$\mathbf{L}_{\text{mid}} = \mathbf{A}_0\mathbf{A}_{1\,\text{mid}}\mathbf{A}_{2\,\text{mid}}\mathbf{A}_{3\,\text{mid}} \tag{16-131}$$

Note that the forms of the gains and input impedance are only approximately correct. (They are exact for an FET amplifier.) The simplified form usually leads to accurate results. However, after the design is completed, the results can be checked using the relations developed in Chapter 12.

Now let us design an amplifier with the following specifications. The midband voltage gain $\mathbf{K}_v = -50$. The loop gain is to be such that, in the midband region, $\mathbf{L}_{\text{mid}} = -100$. At a frequency of 20,000 Hz $|\mathbf{L}(j\omega)|/\mathbf{L}_{\text{mid}} \geqq 0.9$. There is to be a phase margin of at least 45° and a gain margin of at least 10 dB. (Note that we have not specified the frequency response of $\mathbf{K}_v$ since, in amplifiers such as this, the frequency response of $\mathbf{K}_v$ will be much better than that of the loop gain.)

From the discussion of Sec. 16-13 we have that, if all the half-power frequencies were equal, any $|\mathbf{L}_{\text{mid}}| \geqq 4$ would result in oscillation so we cannot use equal half-power frequencies. Let us assume that three of them are equal to f_a and that one is equal to f_b. At the present time, it does not matter which frequencies we allocate to f_a and which to f_b. We shall consider this subsequently. Then, we can write

$$\mathbf{L}(j\omega) = \frac{-100}{(1 + jf/f_a)^3(1 + jf/f_b)} \tag{16-132}$$

We have used the specified value of 100 for $\mathbf{L}_{\text{mid}}$.

For the time being, let us assume that

$$f_a \gg f_b$$

so that we can approximate $\mathbf{L}(j\omega)$ by $-100/(1 + jf/f_b)$. Now let us determine the frequency where $|\mathbf{L}(j\omega)| = 1$. Let us call this frequency f_c. Then,

$$\frac{100}{\sqrt{1 + (f_c/f_b)^2}} = 1 \tag{16-133}$$

Solving, we have

$$\frac{f_c}{f_b} = 99.995 \simeq 100 \tag{16-134}$$

The angle of $100/(1 + jf_c/f_b) = \tan^{-1} 100 = 89.4°$. If the phase margin is to be 45°, then the component of $\mathbf{L}(j\omega)$ which we have thus far ignored, $[1/(1 + jf/f_a)^3]$, can contribute no more than $180° - 45° - 89.4° = 45.6°$ of phase shift at $f = f_c$. Note that this will actually give us more than 45° of phase margin since $|\mathbf{L}(j\omega_c)|$ will actually be less than 1. This is because, in the computation of Eq. 16-133, we did not take the effect of $1/[1 + (f/f_a)^2]^{3/2}$ into account. Thus, we have

$$3 \tan^{-1}\left(\frac{f_c}{f_a}\right) = 45.6°$$

$$\frac{f_c}{f_a} = \tan 15.2° = 0.272 \tag{16-135}$$

Then, from Eqs. 16-134 and 16-135 we have

$$0.272 f_a = 100 f_b$$

or

$$f_a = 367.6 f_b \tag{16-136}$$

Hence,

$$\mathbf{L}(j\omega) = \frac{-100}{(1 + jf/367.6f_b)^3(1 + jf/f_b)} \tag{16-137}$$

We must now choose f_b. From the specifications $|\mathbf{L}(j\omega)| \geqq 90$ at $f = 20{,}000$ Hz. Thus,

$$90 = \frac{100}{[1 + (20{,}000/367.6f_b)^2]^{3/2}[1 + (20{,}000/f_b)^2]^{1/2}} \tag{16-138}$$

This involves solving a cubic equation. Fortunately, in this case, $f_a \gg f_b$, so that we can approximate the result by

$$0.9 = \frac{1}{\sqrt{1 + (20{,}000/f_b)^2}} \tag{16-139}$$

Solving, we obtain

$$f_b = 41{,}294 \text{ Hz}$$

Let us use

$$f_b = 42{,}000 \text{ Hz}$$

Now let us substitute in Eq. 16-138 to verify if the approximate results are accurate.

$$\frac{100}{[1 + (20{,}000/367.6 \times 42{,}000)^2]^{3/2}[1 + (20{,}000/42{,}000)^2]^{1/2}} = 90.3 > 90$$

Thus, $f_b = 42{,}000$ Hz is a valid value. Then, substituting in Eq. 16-136, we have

$$f_a = 15.4 \times 10^6 \text{ Hz}$$

Let us now check the gain margin. To do this we compute $|\mathbf{L}(j\omega)|$ at that frequency where $\measuredangle \mathbf{L}(j\omega) = 0$. At frequencies above f_c, the phase shift of the stage whose half-power frequency is f_b is essentially 90°. Thus, the $\measuredangle \mathbf{L}(j\omega)$ becomes 0° at $f = f_d$ where the phase shift of each of the other three stages is 30°. Then,

$$\frac{f_d}{f_a} = \frac{f_d}{367.6 f_b} = \tan 30°$$

or $f_d = 212.2 f_b$. The magnitude of $\mathbf{L}(j\omega_d)$ is then

$$|\mathbf{L}(j\omega_d)| = \frac{100}{[1 + (212.2/367.6)^2]^{3/2}[1 + 212.2^2]^{1/2}} = 0.306 \qquad (16\text{-}140)$$

Substituting in Eq. 16-122 we obtain $GM = 10.3$ dB which meets specifications. If this were not the case, we would have to increase the ratio f_a/f_b.

All specifications are met. Thus, of the four half-power frequencies, f_{21}, f_{22}, f_{23}, and f_{24}, three would be 15.4×10^6 Hz while the fourth is 42,000 Hz. Insofar as the stability is concerned, it does not matter how we allocate these frequencies. However, there are practical considerations. Each of the amplifier stages is subject to the type of gain bandwidth limitation discussed in Chapter 12. Thus, it is desirable to allocate the low half-power frequency to one of the amplifier stages. The other three frequencies are then allocated to the other two amplifier stages and to the β network.

Now let us obtain the pertinent element values for the amplifier. From the specifications and Eq. 16-125 we have

$$\frac{R_2}{R_1} = \frac{G_1}{G_2} = 50$$

Now consider Eq. 16-129, $A_0 = G_2/(G_1 + G_2 + G_i)$ represents the "gain" of the β network. Let us assume that $G_i = 0.001$ ($R_i = 1000$ ohms). This must be determined from the parameters of the transistor. Then,

$$A_0 = G_2/(G_1 + G_2 + G_i)$$

In addition we must choose the parameters of the circuit so that $f_{20} = 15.4 \times 10^6$ Hz. Hence (see Eq. 16-129c),

$$G_1 + G_2 + G_i = 2\pi f_{20}(C_i + C_1)$$

The value of C_i depends upon the effective input capacitance of the amplifier which, in turn, depends upon the gain of the first stage. Let us assume that we are using low-capacitance broadband transistors here and that we make the conservative assumption that

$$C_1 + C_i = 150 \text{ pF}$$

This should be verified after the design is performed. If the actual $C_1 + C_i$ is less than 150 pF, then f_{20} will be greater than desired, which will increase the gain and phase margins since the ratio f_a/f_b will be increased. (Of course, the converse occurs if f_{20} is smaller than desired.) The parameters should be adjusted so that the proper f_{20} is obtained. Then

$$A_0 = G_2/(2\pi \times 15.4 \times 10^6 \times 150 \times 10^{-12}) = 68.9G_2$$

Or, equivalently,

$$A_0 = 1.378G_1 = 1.378/R_1$$

If R_1 is made too small, then we may not be able to account for the resistance of the input generator. If R_1 is made too large, then A_0 will become very small and the gain that must be provided by the amplifier portion of the circuit will become excessive. Let us choose

$$R_1 = 200 \text{ ohms}$$

Then,

$$R_2 = 10{,}000 \text{ ohms}$$

and

$$A_0 = 0.00689$$

We require that $|\mathbf{L}_{\text{mid}}| = 100$. Hence,

$$|\mathbf{A}_{v1\,\text{mid}}||\mathbf{A}_{v2\,\text{mid}}||\mathbf{A}_{v3\,\text{mid}}| = \frac{100}{0.00689} = 14{,}514$$

Thus the gain must be divided among three stages, two of which have half-power frequencies of 15.4 MHz and one of which has a half-power frequency of 42,000 Hz. This gain can be achieved. Let us assume that the first stage has a half-power frequency of 42,000 Hz. Then we could have $\mathbf{A}_{v2} = \mathbf{A}_{v3} = 12$ and $\mathbf{A}_{v1} = 100.8$. Note that $|\mathbf{L}_{\text{mid}}|$ must be achieved exactly. It cannot be too large. However, we can increase bandwidth as long as the ratio of $f_a/f_b \geqq 367.6$. In such cases, the bandwidth of the feedback amplifier will be increased.

Note that we require very broad band stages to obtain a feedback amplifier that only works with input frequencies in the range of 0 to 10,000 Hz. If the specified bandwidth were greater, then the bandwidth of the individual stages would have to be proportionally increased. These gain-bandwidth limitations can easily become troublesome. It is these gain-bandwidth limitations which ultimately limit the magnitude of the loop gain which we can obtain. Thus, the techniques discussed in Chapter 12 in regard to broadbanding amplifiers may have to be applied to feedback amplifiers.

Capacitive Compensation

Let us now take a somewhat different viewpoint. Suppose that we have the amplifier of Fig. 16-20a whose loop gain is given by Eq. 16-130 where

$$f_{21} = f_{22} = f_{23} = f_{24} \tag{16-141}$$

If $|\mathbf{L}_{mid}| = 100$, then the amplifier will oscillate. Now suppose that we take a *very* large capacitor and place it from collector to ground in one of the stages. This is called *capacitive compensation*, and it will greatly reduce the half-power frequency of this stage. If the capacitor is made large enough so that the half-power frequency is reduced by a factor of 367.6 (see Eq. 16-136), then the amplifier will become stable with the appropriate gain and phase margins.

Let us contrast this with the previous procedure. It appears similar except that we have added capacitance to reduce the bandwidth, rather than increasing the bandwidth. This reduces the gain-bandwidth product, so by adding capacitance, we have limited bandwidth. Therefore, the procedure of adding capacitance to obtain stability can be a *very poor design procedure* since it may limit bandwidth greatly. However, there are times when it is widely used. For instance, in narrow bandwidth systems, it is acceptable.

Capacitive compensation is widely used with operational amplifiers. In some cases, the large capacitance is fabricated within the amplifier chip. Here it does greatly limit bandwidth. For instance, some operational amplifiers have *upper* half-power frequencies of about 10 Hz. The reader may ask why this is done. The answer is that it ensures that almost any circuit with which the operational amplifier is used will be stable. Operational amplifiers are widely used, often by people who have essentially no understanding of the problems involved in stabilizing feedback amplifiers. If we design an operational amplifier wherein the half-power frequency of one of the stages is 2000 times less than that of the other stages, then that operational amplifier will be stable in almost all configurations. The price paid for this "ease of design" is limited bandwidth. Note (see Sec. 13-2) that $|\mathbf{A}_{v\,mid}|$ for many operational amplifiers is very high, so that $\mathbf{K}_v$ for the operational amplifier circuit may have a reasonable bandwidth. (Not all operational amplifiers have limited bandwidth. Broadband types are available.)

Capacitive compensation of operational amplifiers takes two forms. The compensating capacitor can be an external one, added by the user, which gives the circuit designer some control. Alternatively, the capacitance can be added during manufacture. Let us now consider some circuits that are used.

If the capacitor is to be integrated within the chip, then we want to obtain a large capacitive effect without having to use a large capacitor. In Fig. 16-31 we show a circuit that can be used. The blocks represent three subgroups of stages within an operational amplifier. The second subamplifier has a gain of $-\mathbf{A}_{v2}$. If a capacitor is placed across this stage, then the input capacitance C_i will be

$$C_i = \mathbf{C}(1 - \mathbf{A}_{v2}) \tag{16-142}$$

The capacitance C_i loads the output of the $\mathbf{A}_{v1}$ subamplifier. Since $|\mathbf{A}_{v2}|$ can be very large, C_i can be a very large capacitance without requiring that the actual capacitor C

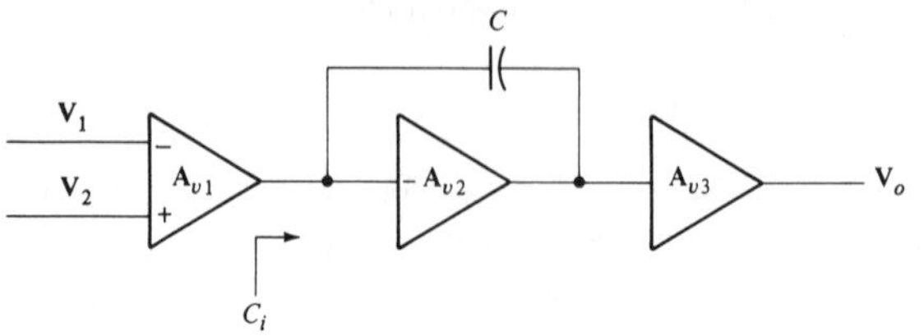

Figure 16-31. A technique of capacitive compensation used in some operational amplifiers.

be large. Thus, we achieve the desired large capacitance without having to fabricate a large capacitance. Note that we have utilized the Miller effect here.

Another compensation technique is shown in Fig. 16-32. Here a capacitor is connected between the two outputs of a differential amplifier. In a differential amplifier

$$\mathbf{V}_{01} = -\mathbf{V}_{02}$$

Hence,

$$\mathbf{I}_C = j\omega\mathbf{C}(\mathbf{V}_{01} - \mathbf{V}_{02}) = 2j\omega\mathbf{C}\mathbf{V}_{01} \tag{16-143}$$

or

$$-\mathbf{I}_C = -2j\omega\mathbf{C}\mathbf{V}_{02}$$

The same currents could be obtained by connecting two capacitors each of capacitance $C_{sh} = 2\mathbf{C}$ from the $\mathbf{V}_{01}$ and $\mathbf{V}_{02}$ outputs to ground. The model of Fig. 14-41b can be used to analyze this circuit if we add the appropriate capacitors. This model is shown in Fig. 16-33. We have only drawn one half of the model here since the other half is the same. In contrast to the procedure of Fig. 16-31, here we only double the effective value of C. However, the capacitance C_i of Eq. 16-142 may vary widely from amplifier to amplifier since $\mathbf{A}_{v2}$ may vary. The procedure of Fig. 16-31 is used to make the half-power frequency of the stage in question very low. However, its actual value is not too important as long as it is low enough (e.g., it may vary from 8 to 12 Hz from one chip to another).

The procedure of Fig. 16-32 is used when a more controlled compensation is used. Here the capacitor **C** is usually an external capacitor whose value is picked by the designer. The specific compensation can then be designed to meet the specifications on the loop gain. As we have discussed, this procedure limits the gain-bandwidth product of the amplifier. In the case of integrated circuit operational amplifiers, the gain of the individual stages cannot be adjusted. Thus, capacitive compensation provides the designer with a simple means of controlling the Nyquist plot when feedback amplifiers are designed using operational amplifiers.

In this section we have considered high-frequency response. If RC or transformer coupling is used, then the low-frequency response must also be considered. If there is

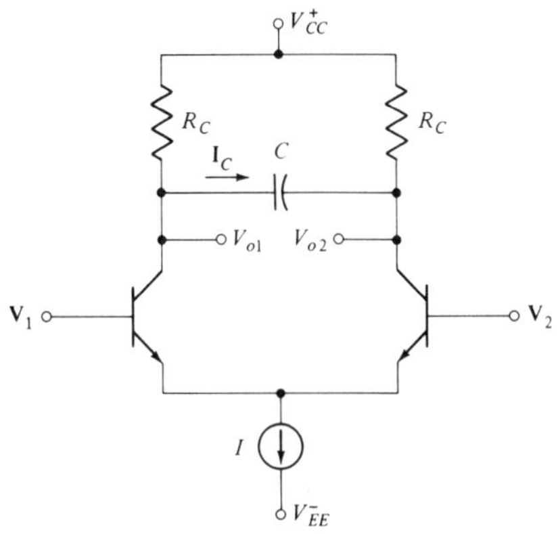

Figure 16-32. A capacitive compensated differential amplifier stage.

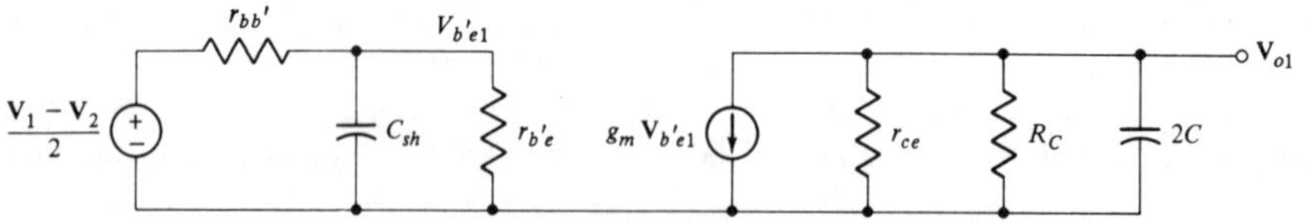

Figure 16-33. One half of the model of Fig. 14-41b which has been modified by the inclusion of the compensating capacitor.

a well-defined midband region, then the low- and high-frequency responses can be considered separately (i.e., two separate Nyquist diagrams can be drawn). The basic ideas used for low-frequency design are the same as those used for high-frequency design except that the phase shifts are the negative of the high-frequency values.

16-16. CORRECTIVE NETWORKS

In the last section we presented a procedure that enabled us to design feedback amplifiers with any reasonable value of midband loop gain. Unfortunately, this required broad bandwidth. This requirement may make it difficult or impossible to construct some amplifiers. In this section we shall discuss a procedure which can reduce but not eliminate this problem.

We can characterize the design procedures by stating that we want to cause the loop gain to fall below unity before the phase shift reaches zero degrees. If we could design a network that would cause the magnitude of $\mathbf{L}(j\omega)$ voltage to fall off with increasing frequency without adding phase shift, it would be ideal, since we could reduce $|\mathbf{L}(j\omega)|$ below unity without causing $\measuredangle\mathbf{L}(j\omega)$ to reach zero degrees. It can be shown that the amplitude and phase are related and that we cannot achieve the desired ideal characteristics. Nevertheless, there are networks that do have some very helpful characteristics. Consider the network of Fig. 16-34 which is called a *phase lag* compensating network. If we let $\mathbf{G} = \mathbf{V}_2/\mathbf{V}_1$ for this network, we have

$$\mathbf{G} = \frac{1 + jf/f_{2a}}{1 + jf/f_{2b}} \tag{16-144}$$

where

$$f_{2a} = \tfrac{1}{2}\pi RC \tag{16-145a}$$

$$f_{2b} = \tfrac{1}{2}\pi(R_1 + R)C \tag{16-145b}$$

A plot of the amplitude and phase of $\mathbf{G}$ is shown in Fig. 16-35. Note that the amplitude falls off monotonically with frequency but the phase angle does *not*. For frequencies

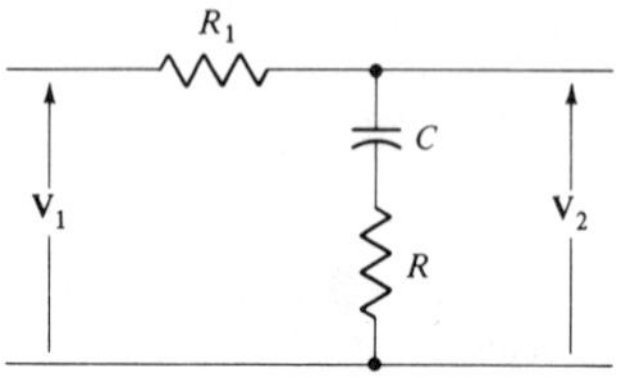

Figure 16-34. A phase lag compensating network.

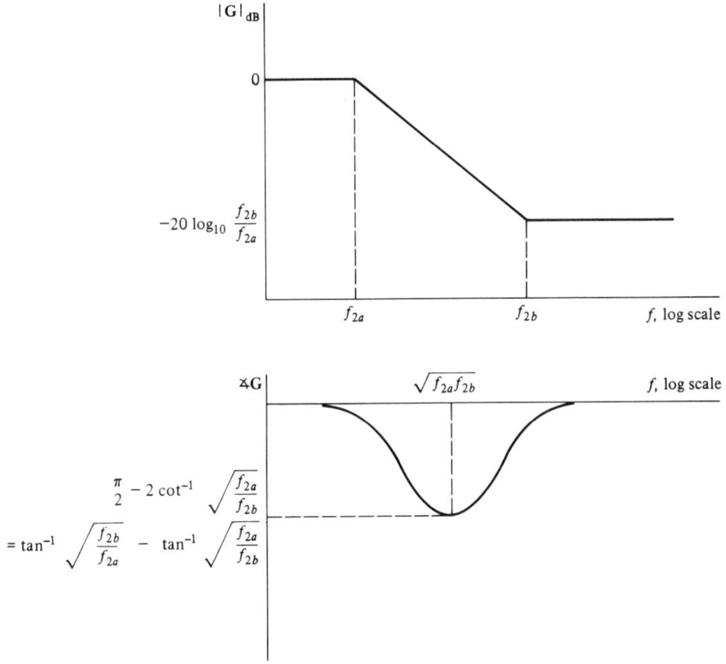

Figure 16-35. The magnitude and phase response for the phase lead network of Fig. 16-34.

above $\sqrt{f_{2a}f_{2b}}$ the phase angle returns toward zero degrees. Thus, this network has some of the desirable features of the ideal network.

Let us now demonstrate how this network can be used. We shall use the plots of the amplitude and phase of $\mathbf{L}(j\omega)$ in this discussion (see Fig. 16-36). The solid curve represents $\mathbf{L}(j\omega)$ before the corrective network has been added. The dashed curve represents the response after the corrective network has been added. In this example, the corrective network adds almost no phase shift at those frequencies where $\measuredangle\mathbf{L}(j\omega)$ is near 180°. Thus, we have achieved a significant increase in gain and phase margins by adding the corrective network. The original amplifier was stable so that all we achieved was an increase in margin. However, the addition of corrective networks can stabilize an oscillating amplifier.

In the example of Fig. 16-36, the phase lag compensating network was almost ideal in that the phase shift of the compensating network did not affect the gain and phase margins. However, this will not always be the case. Suppose that we require more loss in the compensation network. Then f_{2a} would have to be decreased and/or f_{2b} would have to be increased. If f_{2a} is decreased, it can reduce $\mathbf{L}(j\omega)$ in the "midband region." If f_{2b} is increased, then the added phase angle of the phase lag network would now be significant in the region where the angle of the uncompensated $\mathbf{L}(j\omega)$ approaches

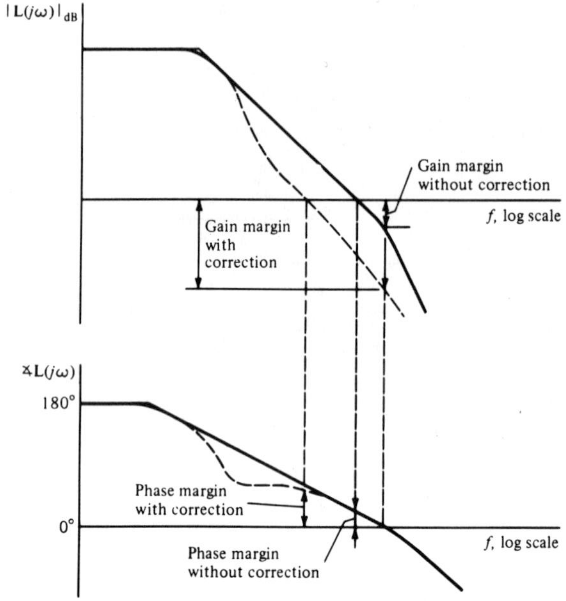

Figure 16-36. An illustration of the use of a phase lag corrective network. The dashed curve represents the response after the corrective networks are added. Only the asymptotes are shown.

zero. This could result in reduced margins or even in oscillation. To offset this, the bandwidth of the amplifier could be increased to provide a greater range of frequencies where f_{2a} and f_{2b} could be placed. Thus, the use of the phase lag network does not remove the requirement for bandwidth, although it does aid in feedback amplifier design.

At times, several corrective networks are used. In this case, the f_{2a} and f_{2b} of the networks should not be equal so that the frequencies of maximum phase shifts of each phase lag network are not equal.

As an example of the use of phase lag networks, let us assume that we add a corrective network to the amplifier designed in the last section and see how it improves the gain and phase margins. Using the data of that section we have sketched the magnitude and phase of the uncompensated $\mathbf{L}(j\omega)$ as the solid curves of Fig. 16-37. Now we have added a phase lag network where $f_{2b} = 200{,}000$ Hz and $f_{2a} = 500{,}000$ Hz. The dashed curves show the modified response. Note that we have sketched the curves as well as the asymptotes here. Observe that the phase margin has increased from 45° to 85.5° and that the gain margin has increased from 10.3 to 18 dB. Actually, we could now redesign the amplifier and reduce the half-power frequencies f_a (see Sec. 16-15). This would reduce the gain and phase margins below specified values. Compensation could then be added to bring them back to specified values. If f_a is reduced then the design is simplified since the half-power frequencies of two of the amplifier stages are now smaller. Thus, some of the gain-bandwidth problems have been reduced.

We have only illustrated one trial of compensation. Actually we should try other values of f_{2a} and f_{2b}. In addition, the design should be attempted using reduced values of f_a. Note that all the specifications should be checked, not only gain and phase margin.

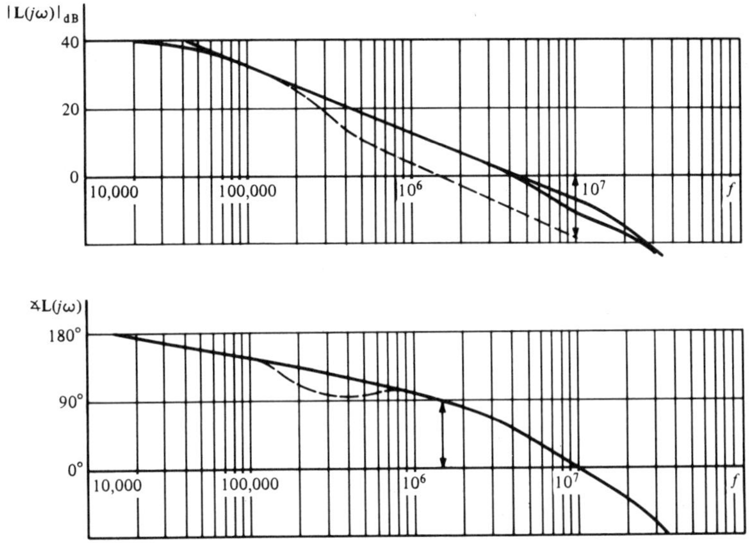

Figure 16-37. The loop gain of the amplifier discussed in Sec. 16-15 after the addition of a phase lag corrective network.

Let us consider the actual implementation of a phase lag network. When common-emitter transistor amplifiers are used, their low-input impedance may load down the phase lag circuit. It may be necessary to use an emitter follower to avoid this problem. Usually, the bandwidth of the emitter follower stage is much greater than that of the other stages so that the response of $\mathbf{L}(j\omega)$ is not adversely affected by the addition of the emitter follower. Indeed, it may actually be improved (see Sec. 12-14). If FET's are used, similar comments apply except that the low-frequency input impedance of the FET is high. Thus, it may not be necessary to use a source follower unless it is necessary to reduce the input capacitance.

A corrective network can also be used for low-frequency compensation. This is called a *phase lead* network. A typical one is shown in Fig. 16-38. The response of this network is given by $\mathbf{G} = \mathbf{V}_2/\mathbf{V}_1$.

$$\mathbf{G} = \frac{f_{1a}}{f_{1b}} \frac{1 + jf/f_{1a}}{1 + jf/f_{1b}} \tag{16-146}$$

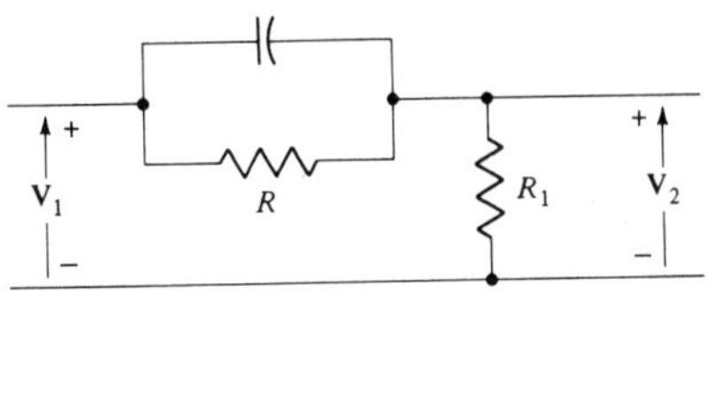

Figure 16-38. A phase lead network.

where

$$f_{1a} = \tfrac{1}{2}RC \tag{16-147a}$$

$$f_{1b} = \frac{R_1 + R}{2\pi R_1 RC} \tag{16-147b}$$

Note that this function is the same as that produced by a bypassed emitter or source impedance (see Sec. 12-7). Thus, these impedances can at times be used to obtain frequency compensation without adding additional networks.

16-17. ANALYSIS AND STABILIZATION OF SERIES-SHUNT FEEDBACK CIRCUITS

Integrated circuit operational amplifiers often use somewhat different feedback circuits than the voltage shunt feedback amplifier that we have been considering. We shall now consider a typical circuit and demonstrate that we can apply the procedures we have developed to other commonly used configurations.

The circuit that we shall study is the series shunt feedback circuit of Fig. 16-39a. A model for the first stage is shown in Fig. 16-39b. Note that Q_3 is an emitter follower stage. We shall assume that its output impedance is low enough so that $\mathbf{V}_2$ is a direct function of $\mathbf{V}_4$ and that the voltage across R_E does not directly affect $\mathbf{V}_2$. (Of course, the voltage across R_E does affect $\mathbf{V}_4$.) The resistance R_{sh} represents the parallel combination of r_{ce} of stage 1, R_{C1}, and the input resistance of stage 2.

Before we analyze the model, let us modify it as shown in Fig. 16-40. Here we have replaced the current generator shunted by r_{ce} and the output voltage generator by their Thévenin equivalents.

Analyzing this circuit, we have

$$\mathbf{V}_1 - \frac{\mathbf{V}_2 R_E}{R_2 + R_E} = (R_1 + r_{bb'} + r_{b'e} + R_T)\mathbf{I}_1 + R_T\mathbf{I}_2 \tag{16-148a}$$

$$-\frac{\mathbf{V}_2 R_E}{R_2 + R_E} = (-g_m r_{b'e} r_{ce} + R_T)\mathbf{I}_1 + (R_{sh} + r_{ce} + R_T)\mathbf{I}_2 \tag{16-148b}$$

Then, solving for I_2

$$\mathbf{I}_2 = \frac{\mathbf{V}_1(g_m r_{b'e} r_{ce} - R_T) - [\mathbf{V}_2 R_E/(R_T + R_E)](g_m r_{b'e} r_{ce} + R_1 + r_{bb'} + r_{b'e})}{g_m r_{b'e} r_{ce} R_T + (R_{sh} + r_{ce})(R_1 + r_{bb'} + r_{b'e} + R_T) + R_T(R_1 + r_{bb'} + r_{b'e})} \tag{16-149}$$

In general,

$$g_m r_{b'e} r_{ce} \gg R_T \tag{16-150a}$$

and

$$g_m r_{b'e} r_{ce} \gg R_1 + r_{bb'} + r_{b'e} \tag{16-150b}$$

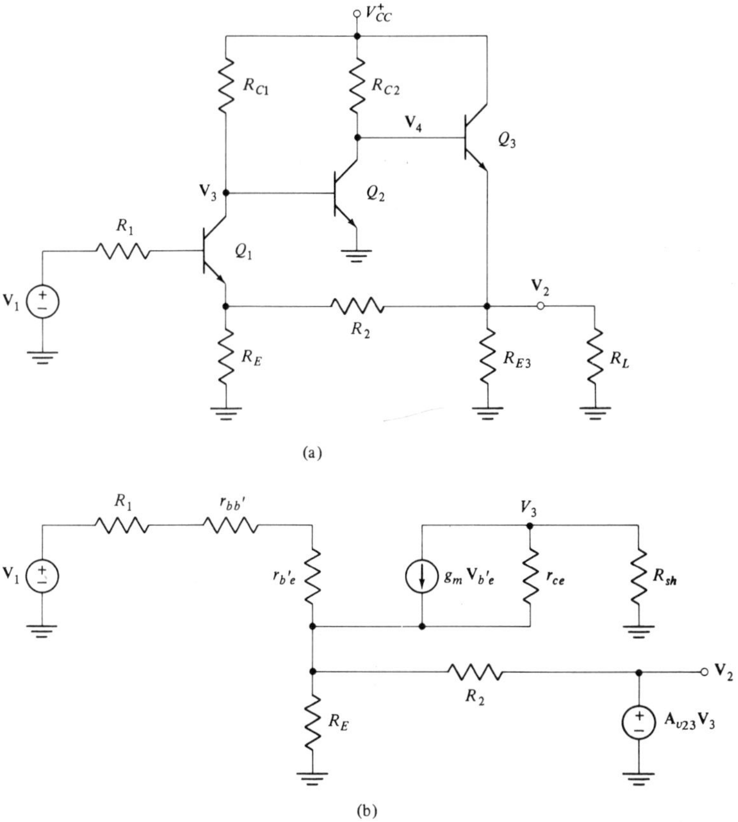

Figure 16-39. (a) A basic series shunt feedback circuit. (b) Its model.

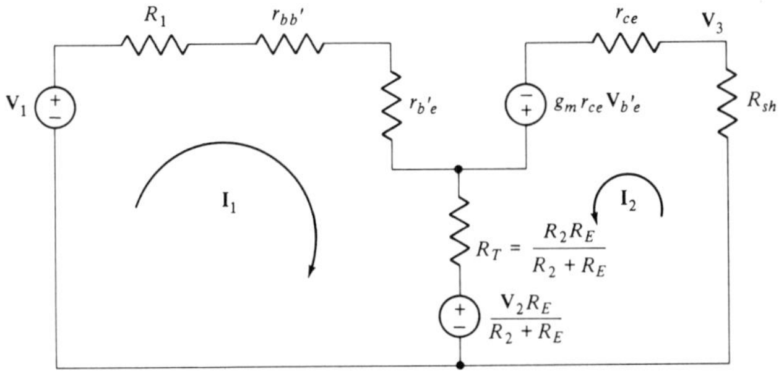

Figure 16-40. A modification of the model of Fig. 16-39b.

In addition,

$$\mathbf{V}_3 = -\mathbf{I}_2 R_{\text{sh}} \tag{16-151}$$

and

$$\mathbf{V}_2 = \mathbf{A}_{v23}\mathbf{V}_3 \tag{16-152}$$

Then, after some simplification using relations 16-50, and manipulating, we have

$$\mathbf{K}_v = \frac{\mathbf{V}_2}{\mathbf{V}_1} = \frac{\mathbf{A}_{v23} R_{\text{sh}} g_m r_{b'e} r_{ce}}{g_m r_{b'e} r_{ce} R_T + (R_{\text{sh}} + r_{ce})(R_1 + r_{bb'} + r_{b'e} + R_T + R_T(R_1 + r_{bb'} + r_{b'e})} \div$$

$$1 - \frac{\mathbf{A}_{v23} R_{\text{sh}} g_m r_{b'e} r_{ce} R_E/(R_T + R_E)}{g_m r_{b'e} r_{ce} R_T + (R_{\text{sh}} + r_{ce})(R_1 + r_{bb'} + r_{b'e} + R_T) + R_T(R_1 + r_{bb'} + r_{b'e})} \tag{16-153}$$

The numerator of Eq. 16-153 is the gain of the amplifier if there were no feedback through R_2. That is, it is the gain if we set the $\mathbf{V}_2 R_E/(R_2 + R_E)$ generator to zero in Fig. 16-40. There is local feedback through R_T but this will not cause the first stage to oscillate. Thus, the numerator represents a stable gain. Equation 16-153 is in the form $\mathbf{A}/1 - \mathbf{A}\boldsymbol{\beta}$. Thus if we desire to study the stability, we can consider that $\mathbf{L}$, given by the following equation, is the loop gain.

$$\mathbf{L} = \frac{\mathbf{A}_{v23} R_{\text{sh}} g_m r_{b'e} r_{ce} R_E/(R_T + R_E)}{g_m r_{b'e} r_{ce} R_T + (R_{\text{sh}} + r_{ce})(R_1 + r_{bb'} + r_{b'e} + R_T) + R_T(R_1 + r_{bb'} + r_{b'e})} \tag{16-154}$$

If we wish to investigate the stability of this amplifier, then $\mathbf{L}(j\omega)$ must be plotted. Of course, the high-frequency response of the amplifier must be included. To do this, Eq. 16-154 can be modified in the following way: Replace $r_{b'e}$ by $r_{b'e}/(1 + j\omega r_{b'e}C)$ (see Fig. 16-20b), and replace R_{sh} by $\mathbf{Z}_{\text{sh}}$ where $\mathbf{Z}_{\text{sh}}$ includes the input capacitance of stage 2. Of course $\mathbf{A}_{v23}$ is the high-frequency gain. We can then apply all the procedures discussed earlier to design the feedback amplifier.

PROBLEMS

16-1. A feedback amplifier is characterized by Eq. 16-2. What is the accuracy of Eq. 16-4 when $\mathbf{A}_v = -100$ and $\boldsymbol{\beta} = 0.1$?

16-2. Repeat Prob. 16-1 but now use $\mathbf{A}_v = -1000$.

16-3. Repeat Prob. 16-1 but now use $\mathbf{A}_v = -10{,}000$.

16-4. Repeat Prob. 16-1 but now use $\mathbf{A}_v = +1000$. Why would this not be done in practice?

16-5. Discuss the difference between negative and positive feedback.

16-6. Discuss the difference between voltage and current feedback.

16-7. Discuss the difference between series and shunt feedback.

16-8. If, for the feedback amplifier of Prob. 16-1, $\mathbf{A}_v$ increases by 10%, what will be the change in $\mathbf{K}_v$?

16-9. Repeat Prob. 16-8 for the amplifier of Prob. 16-2.

16-10. Repeat Prob. 16-8 for the amplifier of Prob. 16-3.

16-11. Compute an expression for the voltage gain of the amplifier of Fig. 16-41. The answer should be in terms of the circuit elements and the parameters of the FET's.

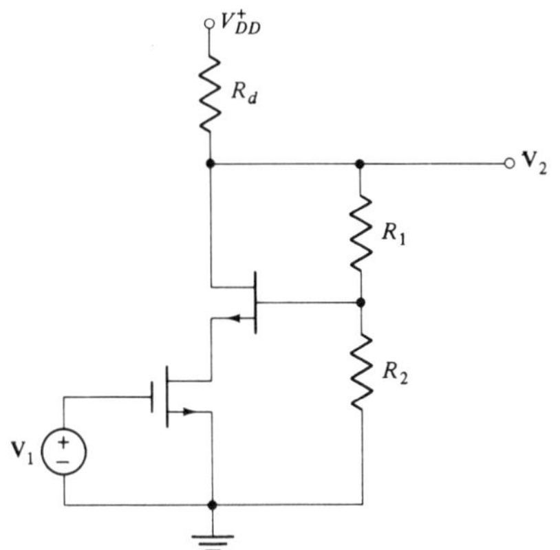

Figure 16-41.

16-12. Compute an exact expression for the voltage gain of the amplifier of Fig. 16-42. The answer should be in terms of the circuit elements and the parameters of the transistors.

16-13. Compute the input impedance $\mathbf{Z}_i$ for the amplifier of Fig. 16-42.

16-14. Compute the output impedance $\mathbf{Z}_o$ for the amplifier of Fig. 16-42.

16-15. Discuss the utility of the expression

$$\mathbf{K}_v = \frac{\mathbf{A}_v}{1 - \mathbf{A}_v \boldsymbol{\beta}}$$

16-16. For the feedback amplifier whose block diagram is given in Fig. 16-43, compute the change $\Delta\mathbf{K}_v$ when $\mathbf{A}_{v1}$ changes by an amount $\Delta\mathbf{A}_{v1}$.

16-17. Repeat Prob. 16-16 but now assume that $\mathbf{A}_{v2}$ changes by an amount $\Delta\mathbf{A}_{v2}$.

16-18. An amplifier is characterized by the block diagram of Fig. 16-1. It is to be such that $\mathbf{K}_v = -50$ and $S_{\mathbf{A}_v}^{\mathbf{K}_v} \leqq 0.01$. Find $\mathbf{A}_v$ and $\boldsymbol{\beta}$.

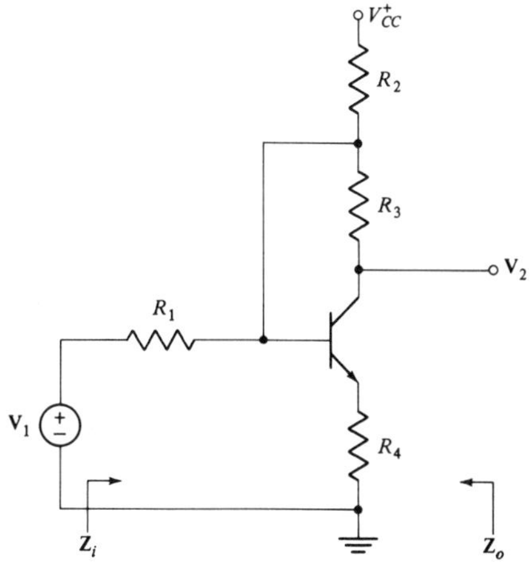

Figure 16-42.

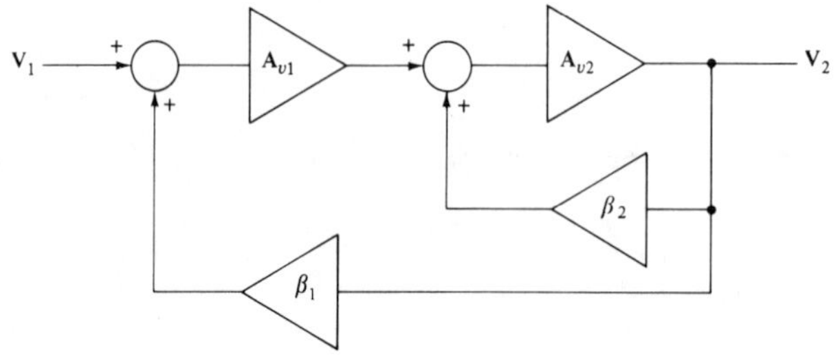

Figure 16-43.

16-19. Repeat Prob. 16-18 but now use $S_{\mathbf{A}_v}^{\mathbf{K}_v} = 0.001$.

16-20. Discuss the importance of the return ratio and return difference.

16-21. A feedback amplifier is characterized by the block diagram of Fig. 16-9. When $\boldsymbol{\beta} = 0$, and the output power is 100 W, there is 5% harmonic distortion. It is desired that the distortion is reduced to 0.1%. When the output power is 100 W, discuss what should be done to accomplish this.

16-22. Compare the ratio $\mathbf{V}_{2d}/\mathbf{V}_{2s}$ for the amplifier whose block diagram is given in Fig. 16-44 for the two cases, $\boldsymbol{\beta}_2 = \boldsymbol{\beta}_1 = 0$ (no feedback) and $\boldsymbol{\beta}_2 = \boldsymbol{\beta}_2$, $\boldsymbol{\beta}_1 = \boldsymbol{\beta}_1$ (i.e., where there is feedback). Assume that $\mathbf{V}_1$ can be varied to keep $\mathbf{V}_{2s}$, the signal component of $\mathbf{V}_2$, constant.

16-23. Repeat Prob. 16-22 but, for the second case, use $\boldsymbol{\beta}_1 = 0$, $\boldsymbol{\beta}_2 = \boldsymbol{\beta}_2$ (i.e., there only is feedback through the $\boldsymbol{\beta}_2$ network).

16-24. Repeat Prob. 16-22 but, for the second case, use $\boldsymbol{\beta}_1 = \boldsymbol{\beta}_1$, $\boldsymbol{\beta}_2 = 0$ (i.e., there only is feedback through the $\boldsymbol{\beta}_1$ network).

16-25. Repeat Prob. 16-22 but now assume that $\mathbf{V}_1$ is fixed.

16-26. Repeat Prob. 16-22 but now assume that $\mathbf{V}_d$ represents a noise signal.

16-27. Repeat Prob. 16-25 but now assume that $\mathbf{V}_d$ represents a noise signal.

16-28. Discuss the effect of feedback on noise.

16-29. Discuss the effect of feedback on impedance levels. Consider all types of feedback in your discussion.

16-30. Discuss the effect of feedback on bandwidth. Why can two identical feedback amplifiers have different usable bandwidths?

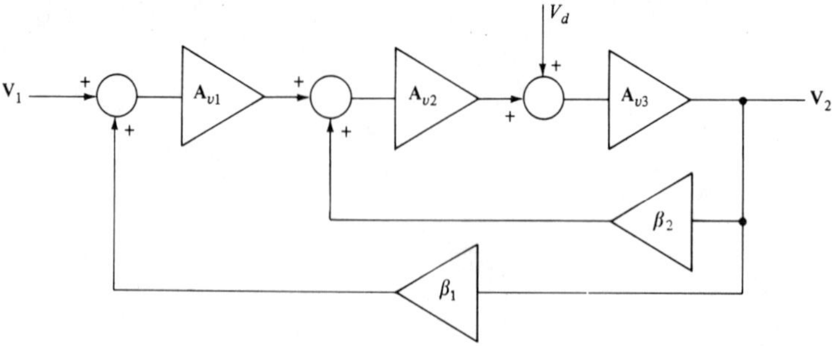

Figure 16-44.

16-31. The gain of a feedback amplifier is given by

$$\mathbf{K}_v = \frac{\mathbf{A}_v}{1 - \mathbf{A}_v \boldsymbol{\beta}}$$

where $\boldsymbol{\beta}$ is a real positive constant. $\mathbf{A}_v$ is given by

$$\mathbf{A}_v = \frac{-\mathbf{A}_{v\,\text{mid}}}{(1 + jf/f_a)(1 + jf/f_b)}$$

If $f_b = 5f_a$, what is the maximum value that $\mathbf{A}_{v\,\text{mid}}$ can have if the poles of $\mathbf{K}_v$ are all to lie on the real axis of the s plane?

16-32. Repeat Prob. 16-31 but now use $f_b = 500f_a$.

16-33. Repeat Prob. 16-31 but now use $f_b = f_a$.

16-34. Compute an exact expression for the voltage gain of the amplifier of Fig. 16-45. Follow the procedure of Sec. 16-9.

16-35. Compute the output impedance $\mathbf{Z}_o$ for the amplifier of Fig. 16-45. Follow the procedure of Sec. 16-9. Relate this result to the discussion of Sec. 16-6.

16-36. Repeat Prob. 16-34 for the amplifier of Fig. 16-15b.

16-37. Repeat Prob. 16-35 for the amplifier of Fig. 16-15b. Relate this result to the discussion of Sec. 16-6.

16-38. Repeat Prob. 16-37 but now compute the input impedance.

16-39. Discuss the basic ideas of stability of feedback amplifiers.

16-40. Discuss the concepts of observability and controllability.

16-41. The gain of a feedback amplifier is given by $\mathbf{K}_s(s) = \mathbf{N}(s)/\mathbf{D}(s)$ where $\mathbf{N}(s)$ and $\mathbf{D}(s)$ are polynomials with no common roots. The denominators are given below. Use the Hurwitz test to determine which of the amplifiers are stable.

(a) $s^4 + 2s^3 + 3s^2 + 2s + 1$
(b) $s^5 + s^4 + s^3 + 2s^2 + 3s + 1$
(c) $s^4 + 2s^3 + 5s^3 + 8s + 1$
(d) $s^4 + 2s^3 + s3 + 1$
(e) $s^5 + 6s^4 + 2s^3 + 2s^2 + s + 1$

16-42. Repeat Prob. 16-41 but now use the Routh test.

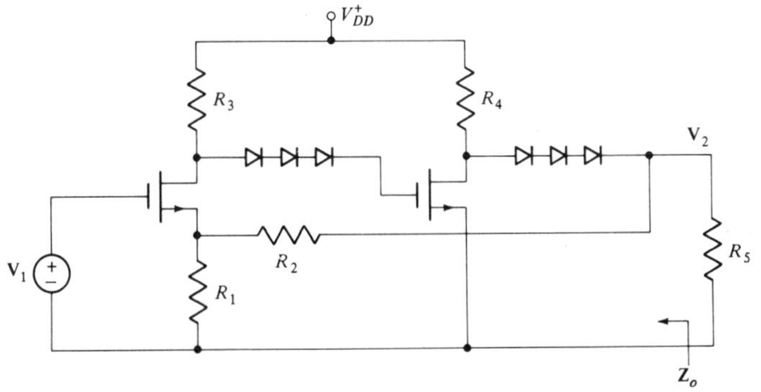

Figure 16-45.

16-43. The loop gain of a feedback amplifier is given by

$$\mathbf{L}(j\omega) = \frac{-100}{1 + jf/5000}$$

Draw the Nyquist diagram. Is the amplifier stable?

16-44. Repeat Prob. 16-43 for

$$\mathbf{L}(j\omega) = \frac{-100}{(1 + jf/109)^3}$$

16-45. Repeat Prob. 16-43 for

$$\mathbf{L}(j\omega) = \frac{-100}{(1 + jf/10^6)^2(1 - j10/f)}$$

16-46. Repeat Prob. 16-43 for

$$\mathbf{L}(j\omega) = \frac{-10}{(1 + jf/10^9)^3}$$

16-47. Repeat Prob. 16-43 for

$$\mathbf{L}(j\omega) = \frac{-20}{(1 + jf/10^8)^2(1 + jf/10^5)}$$

16-48. Obtain an exact expression for the open loop gain of the feedback amplifier of Fig. 16-3a.

16-49. Repeat Prob. 16-48 for the amplifier of Fig. 16-3b.

16-50. Repeat Prob. 16-48 for the amplifier of Fig. 16-43.

16-51. Repeat Prob. 16-48 for the amplifier of Fig. 16-15b.

16-52. Obtain the gain and phase margin for the amplifier whose loop gain is given in Prob. 16-47.

16-53. Repeat Prob. 16-52 for the loop gain of Prob. 16-45. Note that now there are two sets of gain and phase margins, one for the low-frequency response and one for the high-frequency response.

16-54. Repeat the design of Sec. 16-15 but now use a phase margin of 60°.

16-55. Repeat the design of Sec. 16-15 but now use $\mathbf{K}_v = -70$, $\mathbf{L}_{\text{mid}} = 150$ and a phase margin of 60°.

16-56. The low-frequency response of the loop gain of a feedback amplifier is given by

$$\mathbf{L}(j\omega) = \frac{-100}{(1 - jf_{1a}/f)^2(1 - jf_{1b}/f)}$$

It is desired that the amplifier have a 30° phase margin. Determine the relation between f_{1b} and f_{1a} such that this is true. Assume that $f_{1b} \ll f_{1a}$.

16-57. For $\mathbf{L}(j\omega)$ of Prob. 16-56, it is desired that $|\mathbf{L}(j\omega)| \geqq 90$ for all frequencies greater than 10 Hz. Determine the values of f_{1a} and f_{1b} so that the requirements of both this and Prob. 16-56 are met.

16-58. Repeat Prob. 16-56 for

$$\mathbf{L}(j\omega) = \frac{-100}{(1 + jf/f_{2a})^2(1 + jf/f_{2b})}$$

Assume that $f_{2a} \gg f_{2b}$.

16-59. Repeat Prob. 16-58 but now we require that $|\mathbf{L}(j\omega)| \geqq 90$ for all frequencies less than 10^6 Hz. Determine the values of f_{2a} and f_{2b}.

16-60. Repeat Prob. 16-58 for

$$\mathbf{L}(j\omega) = \frac{1}{(1 + jf/f_{2a})^3(1 + jf/f_{2b})}$$

Assume that $f_{2a} \gg f_{2b}$.

16-61. Repeat Prob. 16-54 but now use a corrective network to increase the phase margin to 75°.

16-62. Repeat the design of Prob. 16-55 but now use a corrective network to increase the phase margin to 75°.

16-63. Repeat Prob. 16-54 but now use a corrective network to reduce the bandwidth of the amplifier stages.

16-64. Repeat Prob. 16-63 for the design of Prob. 16-55.

BIBLIOGRAPHY

Bode, H. W. *Network Analysis and Feedback Amplifier Design.* Princeton, N.J.: Van Nostrand, 1945, Chapter 7. (A Classical but difficult graduate level book.)

Chirlian, P. M. *Electronic Circuits: Physical Principles, Analysis and Design.* New York: McGraw-Hill, 1971, Chapter 13.

Gray, P. R. and Mayer, R. G. *Analysis and Design of Analog Integrated Circuits.* New York: Wiley, 1977, Chapters 8 and 9.

Millman, J. *Microelectronics: Digital and Analog Circuits and Systems.* New York: McGraw-Hill, 1979, Chapter 12.

Chapter 17

Bandpass Amplifiers

There are occasions when we want to amplify signals that lie in a certain range, or band, of frequencies. However, we want to reject those signals that lie outside of the specified frequency range. For instance, suppose that we want to receive one radio signal. At any instant of time, there are thousands of radio signals present. We want to reject all of these except the one that we are interested in. An amplifier that meets these specifications by rejecting those signals that occupy different frequencies than the desired one is called a *bandpass amplifier*.

We shall start by discussing basic bandpass amplifier circuits that use inductance and capacitance in order to achieve the desired frequency response. We then shall discuss active filters that do not use inductance and, consequently, the resulting filters are very small and light. These filters lend themselves to integrated circuit fabrication. Active filters are special forms of feedback amplifiers. In this chapter we shall also discuss procedures for obtaining some very useful frequency response characteristics.

17-1. THE IDEAL BANDPASS AMPLIFIER

The ideal bandpass amplifier would have a frequency response like that shown in Fig. 17-1, where we have normalized the response. The response is flat between the frequencies f_{c2} and f_{c1}, which define the *pass band* of the amplifier. $\mathbf{A}_{v0}$ is the response in the "center" of the pass band. (We shall clarify the word "center" in the next section.) Outside of the pass band, the response is zero. In general, if the bandpass amplifier is not to distort the signal, then the response in the pass band must be flat with linear phase shift (see Sec. 12-1). The response of the ideal amplifier is zero outside of the pass band. Hence, any interfering signals that lie outside of the pass band are completely rejected.

The ideal bandpass amplifier cannot be built but its response can be approximated. The design specifications take this into account. In Fig. 17-1b we show some typical

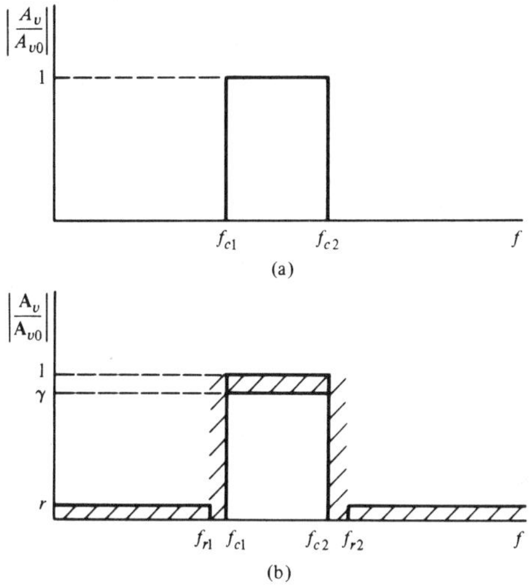

Figure 17-1. (a) The normalized frequency response of an ideal bandpass amplifier. (b) Design requirements for a practical bandpass amplifier. The response must lie in the crosshatched area.

requirements that are imposed upon $|\mathbf{A}_v/\mathbf{A}_{v0}|$. The response in the pass band is constrained to lie between 1 and γ. That is

$$\gamma \leqq \left|\frac{\mathbf{A}_v}{\mathbf{A}_{v0}}\right| \leqq 1, \qquad \text{for } f_{c1} < f < f_{c2} \tag{17-1}$$

In general, γ is a number only slightly less than unity. Hence, the response in the pass band is close to unity.

The *rejection band* or *stop band* are those frequencies where

$$0 \leqq f \leqq f_{r1} \quad \text{and} \quad f_{r2} \leqq f \leqq \infty \tag{17-2}$$

Here the response is to be less than r. In general, r is a small number so that the interfering signals that lie in the stop band are greatly attenuated. The remaining frequencies between f_{r1} and f_{c1} and between f_{c2} and f_{r2} are called the *transition* band. No specifications are placed on $|\mathbf{A}_v/\mathbf{A}_{v0}|$ here, but it is assumed that the response falls from the pass band to the stop band value here. The transition band exists since the response can only change from the pass band value to the stop band value over a nonzero frequency range.

We shall now consider procedures for obtaining bandpass amplifiers that meet specified design criteria. We shall start with simple circuits and then consider more complex ones.

17-2. THE PARALLEL RESONANT CIRCUIT

Before we actually discuss amplifier circuits, we shall study the very simple parallel resonant circuit shown in Fig. 17-2. We shall subsequently demonstrate that the frequency response of the impedance $\mathbf{Z}$ of this network is the same as the response of many bandpass amplifiers.

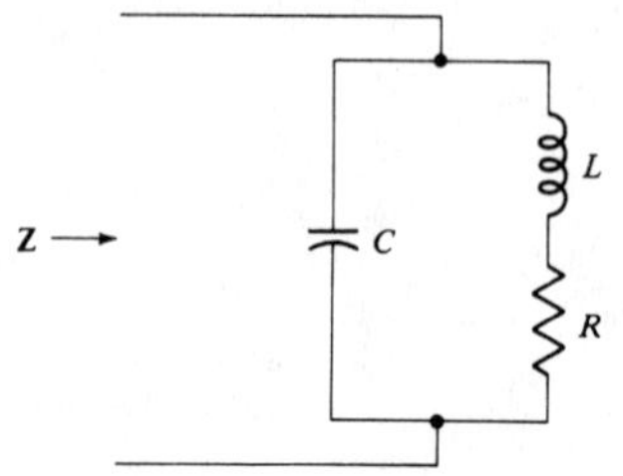

Figure 17-2. A parallel resonant circuit.

The input impedance of this network is given by

$$\mathbf{Z} = \frac{(1/j\omega C)(R + j\omega L)}{R + j(\omega L - 1/\omega C)} \tag{17-3}$$

We shall make the following substitutions.

$$\omega_0 = \frac{1}{\sqrt{LC}} \tag{17-4a}$$

or

$$f_0 = \frac{1}{2\pi\sqrt{LC}} \tag{17-4b}$$

and

$$Q_0 = \frac{\omega_0 L}{R} = \frac{1}{\omega_0 CR} = \frac{1}{R}\sqrt{\frac{L}{C}} \tag{17-5}$$

f_0 is called the *resonant frequency*. Substituting and manipulating, we have

$$\mathbf{Z} = \frac{Q_0^2 R[1 - j(f_0/f)(1/Q_0)]}{1 + jQ_0[(f/f_0) - (f_0/f)]} \tag{17-6}$$

In most bandpass amplifiers, $Q_0 > 10$ and often, $Q_0 > 100$, so that the term $Q_0(f/f_0 - f_0/f)$ is very important. Unless care is taken, inaccurate results will be obtained when this term is evaluated. Usually f is very close to f_0, so that $f/f_0 - f_0/f$ involves the subtraction of two nearly equal numbers. *Large errors can occur when two nearly equal numbers are subtracted unless great accuracy is maintained.* To eliminate the need for extreme accuracy, we shall introduce a new normalized frequency variable δ.

$$\delta = \frac{f - f_0}{f_0} \tag{17-7}$$

The value of δ is known accurately since it is specified by the frequency in question. Substituting in Eq. 17-6, we obtain

$$\mathbf{Z} = \frac{Q_0^2 R\{1 - j[1/(1 + \delta)](1/Q_0)\}}{1 + jQ_0\delta(\delta + 2)/(\delta + 1)} \tag{17-8}$$

The difference between two nearly equal numbers no longer appears and thus we no longer must maintain extreme accuracy.

Usually, $\delta \ll 1$ and $Q_0 \gg 1$. Hence, Eq. 17-8 can be approximated by

$$\mathbf{Z} = \frac{Q_0^2 R}{1 + jQ_0 \delta(\delta + 2)/(\delta + 1)} \tag{17-9}$$

In Eq. 17-9 the maximum value of $\mathbf{Z}$ occurs at $\delta = 0$ ($f = f_0$) and is given by

$$R_0 = Q_0^2 R = Q_0 \omega_0 L = \frac{Q_0}{\omega_0 C} \tag{17-10}$$

Thus, in normalized form, we have

$$\frac{\mathbf{Z}}{R_0} = \frac{1}{1 + jQ_0 \delta(\delta + 2)/(\delta + 1)} \tag{17-11}$$

A plot of $|\mathbf{Z}|/R_0$ is drawn in Fig. 17-3. This is called a *resonance curve*. Note that it becomes sharper as the value of Q_0 increases. The circuit is said to become more *selective* as the width of its resonance curve decreases. We shall see that simple bandpass amplifiers have frequency response curves whose shape is the same as that of Fig. 17-3.

Let us obtain the half-power bandwidth B for the resonance curve.

$$B = f_2 - f_1 \tag{17-12}$$

where

$$f_2 = \text{upper frequency where } \left|\frac{\mathbf{Z}}{R_0}\right| = \frac{1}{2} \tag{17-13a}$$

$$f_1 = \text{lower frequency where } \left|\frac{\mathbf{Z}}{R_0}\right| = \frac{1}{2} \tag{17-13b}$$

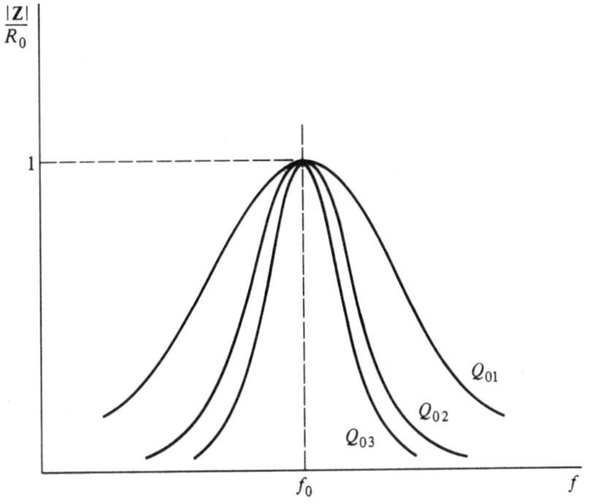

Figure 17-3. The normalized impedance of a parallel resonant circuit $Q_{o3} > Q_{o2} > Q_{o1}$.

Substituting Eq. 17-7 into Eqs. 17-9 and taking the magnitude, we obtain

$$\frac{|\mathbf{Z}|}{R_0} = \frac{1}{\sqrt{1 + Q_0^2(f/f_0 - f_0/f)^2}} \tag{17-14}$$

Then, using f_2 and f_1 given by Eqs. 18-13, we obtain the following two equations.

$$Q_0\left(\frac{f_2}{f_0} - \frac{f_0}{f_2}\right) = 1 \tag{17-15a}$$

$$Q_0\left(\frac{f_1}{f_0} - \frac{f_0}{f_1}\right) = -1 \tag{17-15b}$$

(Note that actually two quadratic equations result and we must be careful to obtain the positive values for f_1 and f_2.) Manipulating, we have

$$f_1 f_2 = f_0^2 \tag{17-16}$$

and

$$B = f_2 - f_1 = \frac{f_0}{Q_0} \tag{17-17}$$

Let us consider the significance of these expressions. The frequencies f_1 and f_2 are spaced with geometric symmetry about f_0. In fact, it can be shown that the entire curve of Eq. 17-14 is geometrically symmetric about f_0. The bandwidth B varies directly with f_0 and inversely with Q_0, so increasing the Q_0 of the circuit decreases its bandwidth. This verifies what we have seen in Fig. 17-3.

Let us obtain the exact expression for f_1 and f_2. Manipulating Eq. 17-15 we obtain

$$f_2^2 - f_2\frac{f_0}{Q_0} - f_0^2 = 0$$

Solving for f_2 and taking the positive root, we have

$$f_2 = \frac{f_0}{2Q_0} + \sqrt{f_0^2\left(1 + \frac{1}{4Q_0^2}\right)} \tag{17-18a}$$

Similarly, we can find

$$f_1 = -\frac{f_0}{2Q_0} + \sqrt{f_0^2\left(1 + \frac{1}{4Q_0^2}\right)} \tag{17-18b}$$

Let us expand the square roots of Eqs. 17-18 in a power series. This yields

$$f_2 = \frac{f_0}{2Q_0} + f_0\left(1 + \frac{1}{8Q_0^2} + \cdots\right) \tag{17-19}$$

In general, $Q_0 \gg 1$. Then

$$1 \gg \frac{1}{8Q_0^2} + \cdots$$

Hence, we have approximately

$$f_2 = f_0\left(1 + \frac{1}{2Q_0}\right) \tag{17-20a}$$

Similarly,

$$f_1 = f_0\left(1 - \frac{1}{2Q_0}\right) \tag{17-20b}$$

Note that even though these two expressions are approximate, they give us the exact expression for $B = f_2 - f_1$. Equations 17-20 demonstrate that, in the high Q_0 case, f_1 and f_2 are arithmetically spaced as well as geometrically spaced about f_0.

17-3. THE SINGLE TUNED CAPACITANCE COUPLED AMPLIFIER

In Fig. 17-4 we show two amplifiers that utilize the parallel resonant circuit. Both are called *single-tuned amplifiers* since there is one tuned circuit (resonant circuit). The tuned circuit replaces the resistance R_C or R_d that we have used before in common-source or common-emitter amplifiers. Since the impedance of a resonant circuit varies with frequency, we should expect the gain of these amplifiers to vary with frequency in a similar way.

Tuned amplifiers are usually cascaded so these amplifiers will often drive similar ones. Before proceeding with their analysis, let us discuss the input and output impedances of the active devices. We can then determine the appropriate models for the complete circuit. In the case of the FET, the input impedance can be represented by the

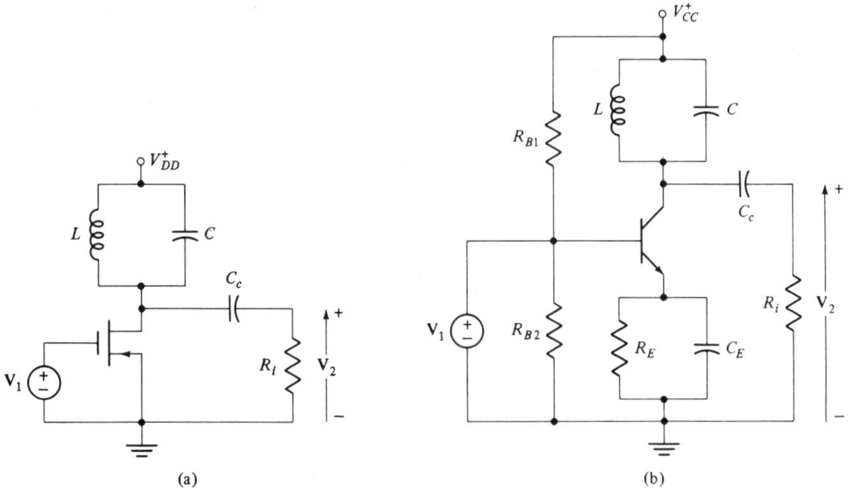

Figure 17-4. Single tuned capacitance coupled amplifiers. (a) Common-source FET amplifier. (b) Common-emitter transistor amplifier.

input capacitance $C_{gs} + C_{gd}(1 - \mathbf{A}_v)$, while the output impedance can be represented by $C_{ds} + C_{gd}$ in parallel with r_d (see Sec. 12-3).

The output impedance of the common-emitter transistor amplifier can be represented by r_{ce} in shunt with $C_{b'c}$. The input impedance can be represented by the circuit of Fig. 17-5a (see Fig. 12-13b). The impedance $\mathbf{Z}_1$ is given by

$$\mathbf{Z}_1 = \frac{r_{b'e}}{1 + j\omega r_{b'e} C_i} \tag{17-21}$$

This can be written as

$$\mathbf{Z}_1 = \frac{r_{b'e} - j\omega r_{b'e}^2 C_i}{1 + \omega^2 r_{b'e}^2 C_i^2} \tag{17-22}$$

Usually, transistors are operated such that

$$r_{b'e} \ll \frac{1}{\omega C_i} \tag{17-23}$$

Hence, $\mathbf{Z} = r_{bb'} + \mathbf{Z}_1$ can be approximated by

$$\mathbf{Z} = r_{bb'} + r_{b'e} - j\omega r_{b'e}^2 C_i$$

The admittance $\mathbf{Y} = 1/\mathbf{Z}$ can be written as

$$\mathbf{Y} = \frac{r_{bb'} + r_{b'e} + j\omega r_{b'e}^2 C_i}{(r_{bb'} + r_{b'e})^2 + \omega^2 r_{b'e}^4 C_i^2}$$

Again, applying inequality 17-23, and noting that $r_{bb'} + r_{b'e} \gg 1$, we have

$$\mathbf{Y} = \frac{1}{r_{bb'} + r_{b'e}} + \frac{j\omega r_{b'e}^2 C_i}{(r_{bb'} + r_{b'e})^2} \tag{17-24}$$

This can be represented by the admittance of Fig. 17-5b. Thus, the input to a transistor can be approximated by a resistance $r_{bb'} + r_{b'e}$ in parallel with a capacitance $r_{b'e}^2 C_i/(r_{bb'} + r_{b'e})^2$. Therefore, the amplifiers of Fig. 17-4 can be represented by the model of Fig. 17-6. The capacitance C represents any actual capacitance placed in the circuit plus the shunt input or output capacitances of the active devices. (In general, C

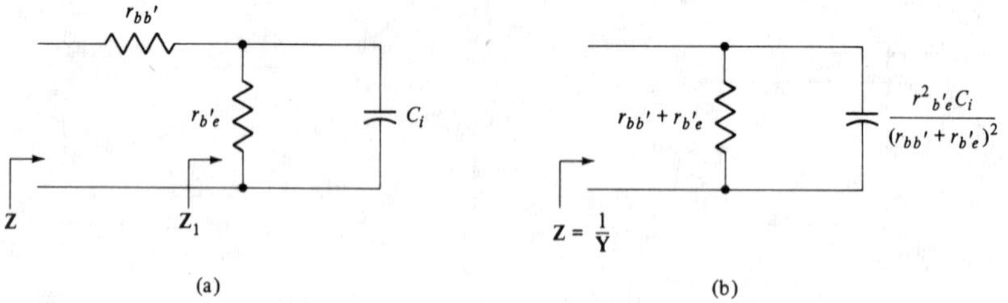

Figure 17-5. (a) A model for the input impedance of a transistor. (b) A modification of the model which is valid if $r_{b'e} \ll 1/\omega C_{b'e}$.

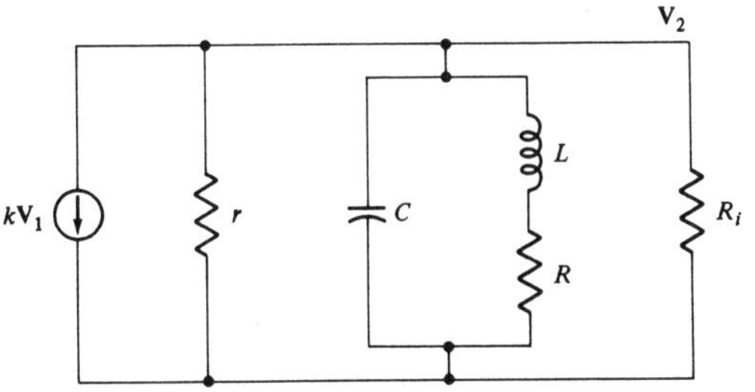

Figure 17-6. A model for the amplifier of Fig. 17-4.

represents the total shunt capacitance.) The resistance r represents the output resistance of the transistor or FET. The resistance R_i represents the load resistance or the parallel combination of the input resistance of the next stage and any shunt resistances such as R_B.

If the active device is a FET, then $k = g_m$, whereas if the active device is a transistor, then $k = g_m r_{b'e}/(r_{bb'} + r_{b'e})$.

Observe the resistance R in Fig. 17-6. This does not appear in the schematic of Fig. 17-4. This resistance is usually not deliberately included in the circuit. It represents the ohmic resistance of the wire used to fabricate the inductance. Ideally, it would be zero but its presence is unavoidable.

We have assumed that the coupling capacitance C_c and the bypass capacitances C_E act as short circuits at the signal frequency. Since these amplifiers are used at relatively high frequencies, this assumption is easy to meet in practice.

Now let us analyze the model. The impedance of the parallel resonant circuit has been analyzed in the last section. Let us call this impedance **Z**. Then,

$$\mathbf{V}_2 = \frac{-k\mathbf{V}_1}{1/r + 1/\mathbf{Z} + 1/R_i} \tag{17-25}$$

Substituting Eq. 17-11, we obtain

$$\mathbf{A}_v = \frac{\mathbf{V}_2}{\mathbf{V}_1} = \frac{-kR_{\text{sh}}}{1 + jQ_{\text{eff}}\delta(\delta + 2)/(\delta + 1)} \tag{17-26}$$

where

$$\frac{1}{R_{\text{sh}}} = \frac{1}{r} + \frac{1}{R_i} + \frac{1}{R_o} \tag{17-27}$$

$$Q_{\text{eff}} = \frac{Q_0 R_{\text{sh}}}{R_o} \tag{17-28}$$

Note that f_o is the resonant frequency of the parallel resonant circuit. $\mathbf{A}_v$ has its maximum value at $f = f_0$, that is, $\delta = 0$. Let us call this $\mathbf{A}_{v0}$

$$\mathbf{A}_{v0} = -kR_{\text{sh}} \tag{17-29}$$

Then, for a FET

$$\mathbf{A}_{v0} = -g_m R_{\text{sh}} \tag{17-30a}$$

while for the transistor amplifier

$$\mathbf{A}_{v0} = \frac{-g_m R_{\text{sh}} r_{bb'}}{(r_{bb'} + r_{b'e})} \tag{17-30b}$$

The normalized voltage gain is given by

$$\frac{\mathbf{A}_v}{\mathbf{A}_{v0}} = \frac{1}{1 + jQ_{\text{eff}}\,\delta(\delta + 2)/(\delta + 1)} \tag{17-31}$$

This curve has exactly the same shape as the resonance curve of Fig. 17-3. Now the Q of the complete circuit is Q_{eff}, which replaces Q_0 in Eq. 17-11. Note that $R_0 \geqq R_{\text{sh}}$, so that $Q_0 \geqq Q_{\text{eff}}$.

The half-power bandwidth of the complete amplifier is (see Eq. 17-17)

$$B = \frac{f_0}{Q_{\text{eff}}} \tag{17-32}$$

At the half-power frequencies the phase shift is $\pm 45°$.

In subsequent sections of this chapter, we shall see that a knowledge of the poles and zeros of the response is useful. Noting that $\delta(\delta + 2)/(\delta + 1) = f/f_0 - f_0/f$, and that $s = j\omega$, we obtain

$$\frac{\mathbf{A}_v(s)}{\mathbf{A}_{v0}} = \frac{\omega_0 s/Q_{\text{eff}}}{s^2 + (\omega_0/Q_{\text{eff}})s + \omega_0^2} \tag{17-33}$$

Thus, there is a zero at $s = 0$ and poles at

$$s_{1,2} = -\frac{\omega_0}{2Q_{\text{eff}}} \pm j\omega_0\sqrt{1 - \frac{1}{4Q_{\text{eff}}^2}} \tag{17-34}$$

where we have assumed that $Q_{\text{eff}} > \frac{1}{2}$. Usually, $Q_{\text{eff}} \gg 1$ and the pole locations can be approximated by

$$s_{1,2} = -\frac{\omega_0}{2Q_{\text{eff}}} \pm j\omega_0 \tag{17-35}$$

Now let us obtain the product of the gain $|\mathbf{A}_{v0}|$ and the half-power bandwidth.

$$|\mathbf{A}_{v0}|B = \frac{kR_{\text{sh}} f_0}{Q_{\text{eff}}} = \frac{k}{2\pi C} \tag{17-36}$$

Thus, for a FET

$$|\mathbf{A}_{v0}|B = \frac{g_m}{2\pi C} \tag{17-37a}$$

whereas for a transistor

$$|\mathbf{A}_{v0}|B = \frac{g_m r_{b'e}/(r_{bb'} + r_{b'e})}{2\pi C} \tag{17-37b}$$

In general (see Sec. 17-1), we specify a certain pass band $f_{c2} - f_{c1}$, and a value of γ which gives us the allowed variation of $|\mathbf{A}_v/\mathbf{A}_{v0}|$ in the pass band. The problem of achieving this design is very similar to that of achieving the design of a broadband amplifier as discussed in Chapter 12. That is, we may have to increase the number of stages to obtain the desired bandwidth and/or gain. The design is also complicated by the stop band requirements. We shall illustrate this with a design later in this section.

In general, if we desire broad bandwidth and high gain it is desirable to have as large a gain bandwidth product as possible. To achieve this, no external capacitance should be added to the circuit. However, if this is done, the inductance L may be too large to be realized practically. In addition, we often want to be able to vary the resonant frequency f_0 so that we can tune our amplifier to different signals. Even if the amplifier is only to be used at a single frequency, there must be some provision to vary f_0 slightly for adjustment purposes. Variable inductances can be constructed. Usually, when this is done, a ferromagnetic core is moved into or out of the coil. If this is done, then no capacitance need be added to the circuit. However, in some frequency ranges, the losses due to the ferromagnetic core can become excessive, causing Q_0 to become very small. In addition, it is easier to construct a variable capacitor than a variable inductor. Several variable capacitors can be easily *ganged* together so that, when a single shaft is turned, all the capacitors are varied simultaneously. Thus, several stages can be tuned simultaneously. For these reasons, external capacitance is often added to the circuit and then C does not consist only of parasitic capacitance. This is especially true when we do not require large bandwidths. Indeed, in narrow bandwidth cases, large variable capacitances are often added to the circuit.

Example

Design a single-tuned RC coupled amplifier of the type shown in Fig. 17-4a. The specifications of the amplifier are.

The pass band is defined by $f_{c2} = 1.005 \times 10^6$ Hz, $f_{c1} = 0.995 \times 10^6$ Hz. Within the pass band $|\mathbf{A}_v/\mathbf{A}_{v0}| \geqq 0.9$.
The stop band is defined by $f_{r2} = 1.01 \times 10^6$ Hz, $f_{r1} = 0.99 \times 10^6$ Hz. At the edges of the stop band, $|\mathbf{A}_v/\mathbf{A}_{v0}| \leqq 0.685$.
The value of $|\mathbf{A}_{v0}| \geqq 250$.
FET's with the following specifications are to be used: $g_m = 1000\ \mu$mho, $r_d = 25{,}000$ ohms

Assume that the total shunt capacitance per stage is 300 pF. We will use a 300-pF variable capacitance. Thus, it can be adjusted to account for the parasitic capacitance of each stage. Let us assume that we can obtain inductors whose $Q_0 = 100$.

We start by considering the pass band requirements.

$$f_0 = \sqrt{f_{c1} f_{c2}} = 0.99999 \times 10^6 \simeq 10^6 \text{ Hz}$$

At f_{c2}, $\delta = 0.005$. Then, $\delta(\delta + 2)/(\delta + 1) = 9.975 \times 10^{-3}$. We start by trying one stage.

$$\left|\frac{\mathbf{A}_v}{\mathbf{A}_{v0}}\right| = \frac{1}{\sqrt{1 + Q_{\text{eff}}^2[\delta^2(\delta + 2)^2/(\delta + 1)^2]}} = 0.9$$

Manipulating, we obtain

$$Q_{\text{eff}} = 48.55$$

Then,

$$R_0 = \frac{Q_0}{2\pi f_0 C} = \frac{100}{2\pi \times 10^6 \times 300 \times 10^{-12}} = 53{,}052$$

and,

$$Q_{\text{eff}} = \frac{Q_0 R_{\text{sh}}}{R_0}$$

$$R_{\text{sh}} = \frac{53{,}052 \times 48.55}{100} = 25{,}757$$

We cannot achieve this value of R_{sh} since r_d is only 25,000 ohms. Next, we try two stages. Now

$$\frac{1}{1 + Q_{\text{eff}}^2 \delta^2(\delta + 2)^2/(\delta + 1)^2} = 0.9$$

$$Q_{\text{eff}} = 33.4$$

and,

$$R_{\text{sh}} = \frac{53{,}052 \times 33.4}{100} = 17{,}719$$

This can be attained. Now let us check the midband gain.

$$\mathbf{A}_0 = (-g_m R_{\text{sh}})^2 = (10^{-3} \times 17{,}719)^2 = 314$$

This is sufficient.

Now let us see if the stop band requirements are met. Note that in our example $f_{r1} f_{r2} = f_0^2$. Thus, we need only check the gain at one of these frequencies. If $f_{r1} f_{r2} > f_0^2$, then we would check the gain at f_{r1}. If $f_{r1} f_{r2} < f_0^2$, then we check the gain at f_{r2}, since these represent the frequencies closest to f_0. At f_{r2}, $\delta = 0.01$ and $\delta(\delta + 2)/(\delta + 1) = 0.0199$. Then,

$$\frac{1}{1 + Q_{\text{eff}}^2 \delta^2(\delta + 2)^2/(\delta + 1)^2} = \frac{1}{1 + 33.4^2(0.0159^2)} = 0.693$$

This is not small enough. Thus, let us try three stages. Then, we start by redesigning to meet the pass band requirements with three stages.

$$\frac{1}{[1 + (9.975 \times 10^{-3} Q_{\text{eff}})^2]^{3/2}} = 0.9$$

$$Q_{\text{eff}} = 27.0$$

At f_{r2} we have

$$\left[\frac{1}{1 + (0.0199 \times 27)^2}\right]^{1.5} = 0.683$$

This meets specifications. $Q_{\text{eff}} = 27.0$. Hence,

$$R_{\text{sh}} = \frac{27 \times 53{,}052}{100} = 14{,}324$$

Then,

$$\mathbf{A}_0 = (-g_m R_{\text{sh}})^3 = -(14{,}324 \times 10^{-3})^3 = 2939$$

This more than meets specifications. In fact, it probably is excessive. The gain *cannot* be reduced by reducing R_{sh} since this would adversely affect the stop band response. The operating point can be shifted to reduce g_m to an acceptable value. For instance, if g_m is halved, then

$$\mathbf{A}_0 = \frac{2939}{8} = 367.3$$

which is acceptable. The value of inductance is

$$L = \frac{1}{(2\pi f_0)^2 C} = \frac{1}{(2\pi \times 10^6)^2 \times 300 \times 10^{-12}} = 84.4\ \mu\text{H}$$

The resistor R_i is found from

$$\frac{1}{R_{\text{sh}}} = \frac{1}{r_d} + \frac{1}{R_o} + \frac{1}{R_i}$$

$$\frac{1}{R_i} = \frac{1}{14{,}324} - \frac{1}{53{,}052} - \frac{1}{25{,}000}$$

$$R_i = 91{,}212 \text{ ohms}$$

The final amplifier is shown in Fig. 17-7. We must adjust the bias to obtain the proper gain. Let us assume that $g_m = 500$ and $r_d = 25{,}000$ ohms when $V_{DS} = 10$ V, $I_D = 1$ mA, and $V_{GS} = -3$ V. Hence, we add a source resistance to attain the required V_{GS}.

$$R_s = \frac{3}{10^{-3}} = 3000 \text{ ohms}$$

We shall use a C_s that is an effective short circuit at $f = 10^6$ Hz. Let us choose $C_s = 0.1\ \mu$F since its reactance is only $-j1.6$ ohms at 1×10^6 Hz. Similarly, we can choose $C_c = 0.01$. Its reactance at 1×10^6 Hz is $-j16$ ohms, which is much less than 91,000 ohms. Because of the high frequencies involved, the choice of coupling and bypass capacitors is a relatively simple task.

Note that (see Fig. 17-7) instead of placing the tuning capacitors across each inductor, we have placed them from the drain to ground since this simplifies the circuit fabrication. Insofar as the signals are concerned, both connections are equivalent. We have shown

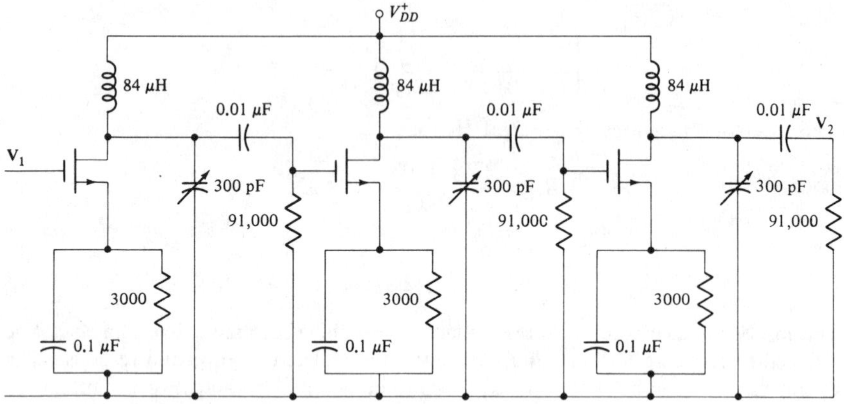

Figure 17-7. The bandpass amplifier. All resistance values are in ohms.

variable capacitors here. After the circuit is constructed, the capacitors should be adjusted to account for stray capacitance. The adjustment process consists of applying a sinusoidal input signal of frequency $f = 10^6$ Hz. Then, each tuning capacitor is adjusted to obtain maximum output voltage.

The amplifier that we have designed here has narrow bandwidth. Thus, we could use the relatively large shunt capacitance (i.e., we did not require large-gain bandwidth product).

This amplifier does not provide very large rejection at the edges of the stop band. However, it is typical for an amplifier of this type. In a subsequent section, we shall consider amplifiers that give much better stop band rejection.

17-4. IMPEDANCE LEVEL CONTROL USING A TAPPED INDUCTANCE

The amplifier designed in the last section required that the resistance $R_i = 91{,}000$ ohms. Suppose that transistors were used rather than FET's. The input resistance of a common-emitter amplifier is typically in the range 1000–2000 ohms. We could not attain $R_i = 91{,}000$ ohms. It is said that the transistors "load down" the tuned circuits too much. There are several procedures that could be used to reduce this loading. Each common-emitter stage could be replaced by an emitter follower, common-emitter pair which would provide the necessary high-input impedance. Note that this "dual stage" could be obtained in a single integrated circuit.

There is another procedure that can be used. Consider the circuit of Fig. 17-8 where we have a *tapped inductance*. Suppose that the contact marked with an arrowhead can be moved along the coil. Let us start by assuming that the contact is at the upper end of the coil. Then R_i is in parallel with the coil as before and it loads down the circuit. If the tap is at the lower end of the coil, then there would be no current in R_i so it will not load down the circuit at all. Of course, $\mathbf{V}_2$ will now be zero. If the tap is close to the bottom of the coil, then there will be a nonzero value of $\mathbf{V}_2$, but the effect of R_i on Q_{eff} will be small.

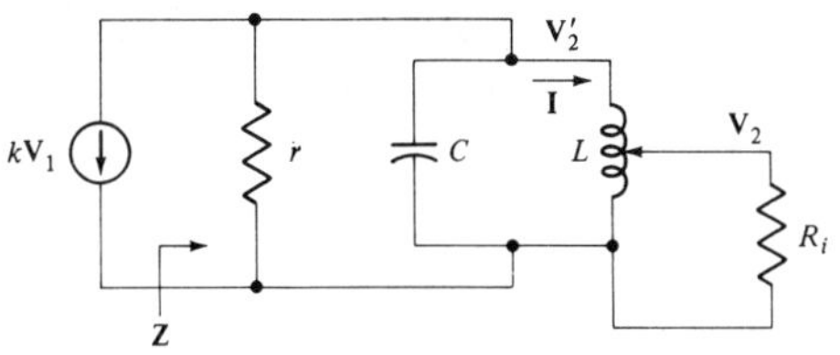

Figure 17-8. A parallel resonant circuit with a tapped inductor.

Let us see how the circuit acts quantitatively. We shall use the circuit of Fig. 17-9 here and compute its input impedance. Writing mesh equations, we have

$$\mathbf{V} = j\omega(L_a + L_b + 2M)\mathbf{I}_a + j\omega(L_b + M)\mathbf{I}_b \tag{17-38a}$$

$$0 = j\omega(L_b + M)\mathbf{I}_a + (j\omega L_b + R_i)\mathbf{I}_b \tag{17-38b}$$

Solving for $\mathbf{Z}_{\text{in}} = \mathbf{V}/\mathbf{I}_a$, we obtain

$$\mathbf{Z}_{\text{in}} = j\omega(L_a + L_b + 2M) + \frac{\omega^2(L_b + M)^2}{R_i + j\omega L_b} \tag{17-39}$$

The inductance of the coil is

$$L = L_a + L_b + 2M \tag{17-40}$$

In most practical applications, L_b is very small so that

$$R_i \gg \omega L_b \tag{17-41}$$

Thus, we can write

$$\mathbf{Z}_{\text{in}} = j\omega L + \frac{\omega^2(L_b + M)^2}{R_i} \tag{17-42}$$

This acts as an inductance L in series with a resistance $\omega^2(L_b + M)/R_i$. The resistance varies with frequency. However, in the range of frequencies which we are interested in, ω varies only slightly about ω_0 so we can approximate the resistance by the constant value $\omega_0^2(L_b + M)^2/R_i$. Hence,

$$\mathbf{Z}_{\text{in}} = j\omega L + \frac{\omega_0^2(L_b + M)^2}{R_i} \tag{17-43}$$

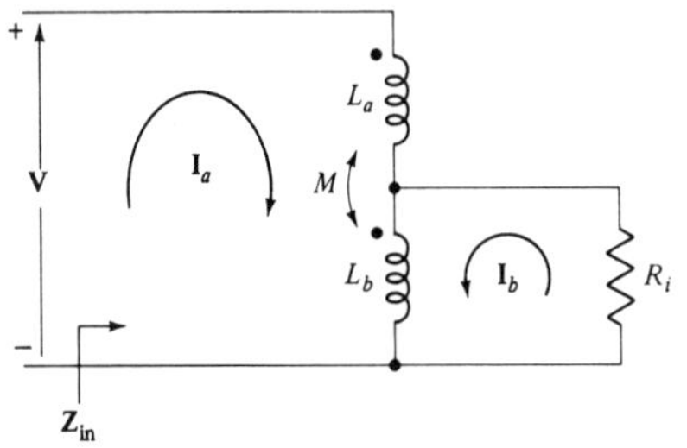

Figure 17-9. A circuit used to calculate the input impedance of the tapped inductance.

Note that we do not approximate the reactive component $j\omega L$ by a constant, since it appears in the difference of two nearly equal quantities (see Eq. 17-3).

Now let us determine the output voltage $\mathbf{V}_2$ for the circuit of Fig. 17-8. Let us assume that the coil has an ohmic resistance R. Then, this resistance is in series with $\omega_0^2(L_b + M)^2/R_i$ so the Q of the coil alone is given by

$$Q_0 = \frac{\omega_0 L}{R + \omega_0^2(L_b + M)^2/R_i} \tag{17-44}$$

Then, proceeding as in the last section

$$\mathbf{Z} = \frac{R_{sh}}{1 + Q_{eff}\,\delta(\delta + 2)/(\delta + 1)} \tag{17-45}$$

where

$$\frac{1}{R_{sh}} = \frac{1}{r} + \frac{1}{R_0} \tag{17-46a}$$

$$R_0 = Q_0 \omega_0 L \tag{17-46b}$$

and

$$Q_{eff} = \frac{Q_0 R_{sh}}{R_0} \tag{17-46c}$$

Then,

$$\mathbf{V}_2' = \frac{-kV_1 R_{sh}}{1 + jQ_{eff}\,\delta(\delta + 2)/(\delta + 1)} \tag{17-47}$$

The current through the coil is given by $\mathbf{V}_2'/[j\omega L + R + \omega_0^2(L_b + M)^2/R_i]$. In general, $\omega L \gg R + \omega_0^2(L_b + M)^2/R_i$. Hence, we have

$$\mathbf{I} = \frac{\mathbf{V}_2'}{j\omega L} \tag{17-48}$$

The power dissipated in the ficticious resistance $\omega_0^2(L_b + M)^2/R_i$ is

$$P = |\mathbf{I}|^2 \frac{\omega_0^2(L_b + M)^2}{R_i} \tag{17-49}$$

This power is actually dissipated in the actual resistance R_i. Hence,

$$P = \frac{|\mathbf{V}_2|^2}{R_i} \tag{17-50}$$

Equating 17-49 and 17-50 and substituting Eq. 17-48, we obtain

$$|\mathbf{V}_2| = |\mathbf{V}_2'| \frac{\omega_0(L_b + M)}{\omega L}$$

As we discussed, ω_0 only varies over a small range and we are not taking the difference between two nearly equal quantities here. Thus, we can replace ω by ω_0 in the above equation. Hence,

$$|\mathbf{V}_2| = |\mathbf{V}_2'|\frac{(L_b + M)}{L} = |\mathbf{V}_2'|\frac{L_b + M}{L_a + L_b + 2M} \tag{17-51}$$

Hence, at resonance,

$$\mathbf{A}_{v0} = -kR_{\text{sh}}\frac{(L_b + M)}{L} \tag{17-52}$$

17-5. MUTUAL INDUCTANCE COUPLED SINGLE-TUNED CIRCUITS

In the last section we discussed the use of a tapped inductance to change the effective loading of a resistance. We can also use mutually inductively coupled coils for this purpose. When such coupling is used, there no longer is any need for coupling capacitors since no direct voltage or current will pass through the coupled coils.

When coupled coils are used, we can tune either the primary side, the secondary side, or both sides. In this section we shall consider the single tuned circuits whose models are shown in Fig. 17-10. The capacitance is placed on the side of the circuit with the higher resistance. For instance, Fig. 17-10a would be used with common-emitter transistor amplifiers since their output impedance is much higher than their input impedance, while Fig. 17-10b would be used with common-source FET amplifiers since their input resistance is extremely high. We shall analyze each of these circuits separately.

Tuned Primary-Untuned Secondary Amplifier

Let us start by computing $\mathbf{Z}_1$, the input impedance of the coupled coil (see Fig. 17-10a). Proceeding as we did in the last section, we obtain

$$\mathbf{Z}_1 = j\omega L_1 + R_1 + \frac{\omega^2 M^2}{R_2 + R_i + j\omega L_2} \tag{17-53}$$

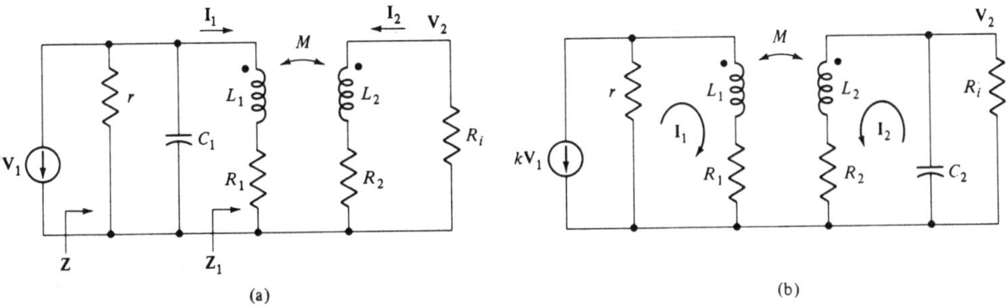

Figure 17-10. Mutual inductance coupled single tuned circuits. (a) Tuned primary. (b) Tuned secondary.

Usually, ωL_2 is such that

$$R_2 + R_i \gg \omega L_2 \tag{17-54}$$

Then, the denominator can be approximated by $R_2 + R_i$. In addition, as we did in the last section, we will approximate the $\omega^2 M^2$ term by $\omega_0^2 M^2$. Hence, the impedance is

$$\mathbf{Z}_1 = j\omega L_1 + R_1 + \frac{\omega_0^2 M^2}{R_2 + R_i} \tag{17-55}$$

where

$$\omega_0 = 1/\sqrt{L_1 C_1} \tag{17-56}$$

Hence, $\mathbf{Z}_1$ acts as an inductance L_1 in series with a resistance $R_1 + \omega_0^2 M^2/(R_2 + R_i)$. Thus, the inductance has a Q of

$$Q_1 = \frac{\omega_0 L_1}{R_1 + \omega_0^2 M^2/(R_2 + R_i)} \tag{17-57}$$

Let us now compute the impedance $\mathbf{Z}$. Proceeding as we did in Secs. 17-2 and 17-3, we have

$$\mathbf{Z} = \frac{R_{\text{sh}}}{1 + j\omega Q_{\text{eff},1}\delta(\delta + 2)/(\delta + 1)} \tag{17-58}$$

where

$$\frac{1}{R_{\text{sh}}} = \frac{1}{Q_1 \omega_0 L_1} + \frac{1}{r} \tag{17-59a}$$

and

$$Q_{\text{eff},1} = \frac{Q_1 R_{\text{sh}}}{Q_1 \omega_0 L_1} = \frac{R_{\text{sh}}}{\omega_0 L_1} \tag{17-59b}$$

Then,

$$\mathbf{I}_1 = \frac{k_1 \mathbf{V}_1 \mathbf{Z}}{j\omega L_1 + R_1 + \omega_0^2 M^2/(R_2 + R_i)}$$

In general,

$$\omega L_1 \gg R_1 + \frac{\omega_0^2 M^2}{R_2 + R_i} \tag{17-60}$$

Hence, we can write

$$\mathbf{I}_1 = \frac{k\mathbf{V}_1 \mathbf{Z}}{j\omega L_1} \tag{17-61}$$

$\mathbf{I}_2$ is given by

$$\mathbf{I}_2 = \frac{j\omega M \mathbf{I}_1}{R_2 + R_i + j\omega L_2} \tag{17-62}$$

Using inequality 17-54 and then substituting Eqs. 17-61 and 17-58 into Eq. 17-62, we have

$$\mathbf{I}_2 = \frac{k\mathbf{V}_1 M}{L_1(R_2 + R_i)} \frac{R_{sh}}{1 + jQ_{eff,1}\delta(\delta + 2)/(\delta + 1)} \tag{17-63}$$

Then,

$$\mathbf{V}_2 = \mathbf{I}_2 R_i$$

Therefore, we can write $\mathbf{A}_v = \mathbf{V}_2/\mathbf{V}_1$. Hence,

$$\frac{\mathbf{A}_v}{\mathbf{A}_{v0}} = \frac{1}{1 + jQ_{eff,1}\delta(\delta + 2)/(\delta + 1)} \tag{17-64}$$

where

$$\mathbf{A}_{v0} = \frac{kMR_{sh}R_i}{L_1(R_2 + R_i)} \tag{17-65}$$

Let us assume that this is a transistor amplifier. Then, (see Eq. 17-30b)

$$\mathbf{A}_{v0} = \frac{g_m r_{bb'} M R_{sh} R_i}{(r_{bb'} + r_{b'e})L_1(R_2 + R_i)} \tag{17-66}$$

This normalized response of Eq. 17-64 has the same form as Eq. 17-31. Hence, this amplifier has the same normalized response as the single tuned amplifier discussed in Sec. 17-3. For instance, the half-power bandwidth is given by

$$B = \frac{f_0}{Q_{eff,1}} \tag{17-67}$$

Note that even if R_i is small, we can reduce M so that R_i does not "load down" $Q_{eff,1}$ too much. Actually, the value of $Q_{eff,1}$ is usually adjusted by varying the mutual inductance. Of course, reducing M will reduce $\mathbf{A}_{v0}$.

Untuned Primary-Tuned Secondary Amplifier

Now let us analyze the circuit of Fig. 17-10b. As discussed, this circuit is frequently used with common-source FET amplifiers. Thus, R_i is very large and can usually be approximated by an open circuit. In addition, let us replace the current generator shunted by r by its Thévenin equivalent. Then, writing mesh equations, we have

$$-k\mathbf{V}_1 r = (r + j\omega L_1 + R_1)\mathbf{I}_1 + j\omega M\mathbf{I}_2 \tag{17-68a}$$

$$0 = j\omega M\mathbf{I}_1 + \left[R_2 + j\left(\omega L_2 - \frac{1}{\omega C_2}\right)\right]\mathbf{I}_2 \tag{17-68b}$$

Then,

$$\mathbf{I}_2 = \frac{k\mathbf{V}_1 r j\omega M}{(r + R_1 + j\omega L_1)\left[R_2 + j\left(\omega L_2 - \dfrac{1}{\omega C_2}\right)\right] + \omega^2 M^2} \tag{17-69}$$

The resistance r represents the output resistance of the active device. Usually this is relatively large so that

$$r + R_1 \gg \omega L_1 \tag{17-70}$$

Hence, $r + R_1 + j\omega L_1$ can be replaced by $r + R_1$ in Eq. 17-69. Doing this, noting that $\mathbf{V}_2 = -\mathbf{I}_2/j\omega C$ and manipulating, we obtain

$$\mathbf{A}_v = \frac{-kMr/C_2 R_2(r + R_1)}{1 + \omega^2 M^2/(r + R_1)R_2 + j\omega(L_2/R_2)(1 - 1/\omega^2 L_2 C_2)} \tag{17-71}$$

As we have done before, we shall replace $\omega^2 M$ by $\omega_0^2 M$. In addition, we shall make the usual substitutions

$$f_0 = 1/2\pi\sqrt{L_2 C_2} \tag{17-72}$$

$$Q_2 = \omega_0 L_2/R_2 \tag{17-73}$$

$$\delta = (f - f_0)/f_0$$

Then, substituting and manipulating, we have

$$\frac{\mathbf{A}_v}{\mathbf{A}_{v0}} = \frac{1}{1 + jQ_{\text{eff},2}\,\delta(\delta + 2)/(\delta + 1)} \tag{17-74}$$

where

$$Q_{\text{eff},2} = \frac{Q_2}{1 + \omega_0^2 M^2/(r + R_1)R_2} \tag{17-75}$$

and

$$\mathbf{A}_{v0} = \frac{-kMr/C_2(r + R_1)R_2}{1 + \omega_0^2 M^2/(r + R_1)R_2} \tag{17-76a}$$

This can be written as

$$\mathbf{A}_{v0} = -\frac{k\omega_0 M Q_2 r/(r + R_1)}{1 + \omega_0^2 M^2/(r + R_1)R_2} = \frac{-k\omega_0 M Q_{\text{eff},2}\, r}{r + R_1} \tag{17-76b}$$

Often, $r \gg R_1$ so that

$$\mathbf{A}_{v0} = -k\omega_0 M Q_{\text{eff},2} \tag{17-77}$$

If the active device is a FET, then

$$\mathbf{A}_{v0} = -g_m \omega_0 M Q_{\text{eff},2} \tag{17-78}$$

Again, the normalized response is the same as that of the amplifier of Sec. 17-3. For instance, the half-power bandwidth is given by

$$B = \frac{f_0}{Q_{\text{eff},2}} \tag{17-79}$$

The design of the single tuned mutually coupled amplifier follows that discussed in Sec. 17-3.

17-6. DOUBLE TUNED AMPLIFIER CIRCUITS

We shall now discuss a circuit that uses a pair of mutually inductively coupled coils where both primary and secondary are tuned. Such a circuit is called a *double tuned amplifier.* We shall see that its response more closely approximates the ideal one.

A model for the double tuned amplifier is shown in Fig. 17-11. To simplify the analysis of this circuit, we shall make some approximations that usually yield accurate results.

We can write the impedance of r in parallel with L_1 as

$$\mathbf{Z} = \frac{j\omega L_1 r}{r + j\omega L_1} = \frac{\omega^2 L_1^2 r + j\omega L_1 r^2}{r^2 + \omega^2 L^2}$$

If $r \gg \omega L$, as is usually the case, then this can be approximated by

$$\mathbf{Z} = \omega_0^2 L_1^2/r + j\omega L_1 \qquad (17\text{-}80)$$

where we have again approximated the frequency dependent resistance $\omega^2 L_1^2/r$ by the constant resistance $\omega_0^2 L_1^2/r$. The frequency f_0 lies within the pass band. We shall specify f_0 subsequently. Hence, the parallel $r - L_1$ circuit can be approximated by a series circuit.

If $R_i \gg \omega L_2$, as it would be in the case of a FET amplifier, then there would be no need to use the tapped inductance L_2. Then, the approximation of Eq. 17-80 can be used for the secondary side also. If R_i is small, as it would be in the case of a transistor amplifier, we would use the tapped inductance as shown in Fig. 17-11a. In this case, we can again represent the circuit as the inductance, L_2 in series with a resistance $\omega_0^2(L_b + M)^2/R_i$ (see Eq. 17-43).

Therefore, the total resistance effectively in series with L_1 is

$$R_p = \frac{\omega_0^2 L_1^2}{r} + R_1 \qquad (17\text{-}81a)$$

The total resistance effectively in series with the L_2 is

$$R_s = \frac{\omega_0^2 (L_b + M)^2}{R_i} + R_2 \qquad (17\text{-}81b)$$

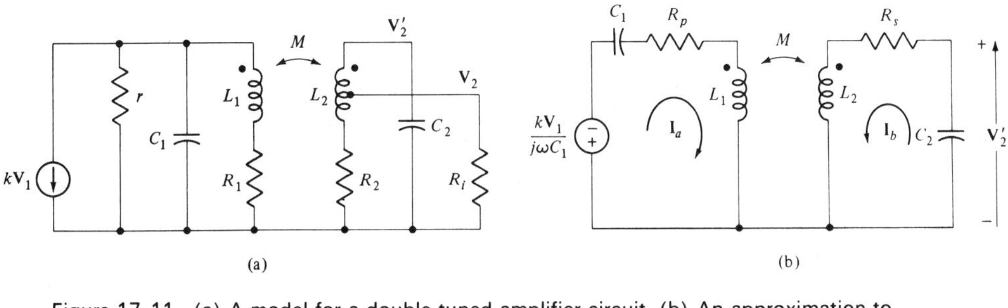

Figure 17-11. (a) A model for a double tuned amplifier circuit. (b) An approximation to this circuit.

If the tap is moved to the top of the coil as it would be if R_i is large, then $L_b + M$ is replaced by L_2.

In Fig. 17-11b we have made the above discussed approximations. In addition we have replaced the current generator shunted by C_1 by its Thévenin equivalent.

Analyzing this circuit we have

$$\frac{-k\mathbf{V}_1}{j\omega C_1} = \mathbf{Z}_p\mathbf{I}_a + j\omega M\mathbf{I}_b \tag{17-82a}$$

$$0 = j\omega M\mathbf{I}_a + \mathbf{Z}_s\mathbf{I}_b \tag{17-82b}$$

where

$$\mathbf{Z}_p = R_p\left[1 + j\frac{\omega L_1}{R_p}\left(1 - \frac{1}{\omega^2 L_1 C_1}\right)\right] \tag{17-83a}$$

and

$$\mathbf{Z}_s = R_s\left[1 + j\frac{\omega L_2}{R_s}\left(1 - \frac{1}{\omega^2 L_2 C_2}\right)\right] \tag{17-83b}$$

Let us assume that the primary and secondary circuits are tuned to the same frequency, as is usually done. That is,

$$L_1 C_1 = L_2 C_2 \tag{17-84}$$

Hence,

$$f_0 = \frac{1}{2\pi\sqrt{L_1 C_1}} = \frac{1}{2\pi\sqrt{L_2 C_2}} \tag{17-85}$$

In addition, we define

$$Q_1 = \frac{\omega_0 L_1}{R_p} \tag{17-86a}$$

and

$$Q_2 = \frac{\omega_0 L_2}{R_s} \tag{17-86b}$$

Then, proceeding as in Sec. 17-2, we have

$$\mathbf{Z}_p = R_p\left[1 + \frac{jQ_1\delta(\delta + 2)}{\delta + 1}\right] \tag{17-87a}$$

$$\mathbf{Z}_s = R_s\left[1 + \frac{jQ_2\delta(\delta + 2)}{\delta + 1}\right] \tag{17-87b}$$

Usually, $\delta = (f - f_0)/f_0 \ll 1$ so that

$$\frac{\delta + 2}{\delta + 1} \simeq 2 \tag{17-88}$$

We shall make this approximation here. Note that we could have done this previously but it was not necessary to do so. We do it now to simplify the resulting expressions. Hence, we shall use

$$\mathbf{Z}_p = R_p(1 + j2Q_1\delta) \tag{17-89a}$$

$$\mathbf{Z}_s = R_s(1 + j2Q_2\delta) \tag{17-89b}$$

Substituting in Eq. 17-82, solving for $\mathbf{I}_b$, and manipulating, we have

$$\mathbf{I}_b = \frac{k\mathbf{V}_1 M/C_1 R_p R_s}{1 - 4\delta^2 Q_1 Q_2 + j2\delta(Q_1 + Q_2) + \omega^2 M^2/R_p R_s}$$

The voltage $\mathbf{V}_2'$ is the actual voltage across the capacitance C_2. In the case of a FET amplifier this would be the actual output voltage. Thus,

$$\mathbf{V}_2' = -\frac{k\mathbf{V}_1 M/j\omega_0 C_1 C_2 R_p R_s}{1 - 4\delta^2 Q_1 Q_2 + j2\delta(Q_1 + Q_2) + \omega_0^2 M^2/R_p R_s} \tag{17-90}$$

We have replaced ω by ω_0 since it does not occur as the difference of two nearly equal terms. Note that $\mathbf{V}_2'$ is a function of M. To study this, and to simplify the relation, let us write

$$b = \frac{\omega_0 M}{\sqrt{R_p R_s}} \tag{17-91}$$

Then, substituting and manipulating, we have

$$\mathbf{A}_v' = \frac{\mathbf{V}_2'}{\mathbf{V}_1} = \frac{-(k/j\omega_0^2 C_1 C_2 \sqrt{R_p R_s})[b/(1 + b^2)]}{1 - [4\delta^2 Q_1 Q_2/(1 + b^2)] + j[2\delta(Q_1 + Q_2)/(1 + b^2)]} \tag{17-92}$$

When $\delta = 0$, $f = f_0$. Then, $\mathbf{A}_v' = \mathbf{A}_{v0}'$.

$$\mathbf{A}_{v0}' = -\frac{k}{j\omega_0^2 C_1 C_2 \sqrt{R_p R_s}} \frac{b}{1 + b^2} \tag{17-93}$$

For a FET, $k = g_m$ and $\mathbf{V}_2'$ is the actual output voltage. Hence,

$$\mathbf{A}_{v0} = -\frac{g_m}{j\omega_0^2 C_1 C_2 \sqrt{R_p R_s}} \frac{b}{1 + b^2} \tag{17-94}$$

For the transistor, the actual output voltage is $\mathbf{V}_2$. Proceeding as in Sec. 17-4, we have

$$\mathbf{A}_{v0} = \frac{-g_m r_{b'e}}{j(r_{bb'} + r_{b'e})\omega_0^2 C_1 C_2 \sqrt{R_p R_s}} \frac{L_b + M}{L_2} \frac{b}{1 + b^2} \tag{17-95}$$

where $L_b + M$ is defined as in Sec. 17-4.

Note that $\mathbf{A}_{v0}$ is a function of b. If we maximize $\mathbf{A}_{v0}$ with respect to b, we obtain

$$b_{\text{opt}} = \pm 1 \tag{17-96a}$$

or, equivalently,

$$M_{\text{opt}} = \frac{\pm\sqrt{R_p R_s}}{\omega_0} \tag{17-96b}$$

Hence,

$$\frac{b_{\text{opt}}}{1 + b_{\text{opt}}^2} = \pm\frac{1}{2} \tag{17-97}$$

It is convenient to normalize the expression of $\mathbf{A}_v$, not with respect to $\mathbf{A}_{v0}$, but with respect to $\mathbf{A}_{v0,\,\text{max}}$ (i.e., when $b = \pm 1$). Doing this for either the transistor or FET, we have

$$\frac{\mathbf{A}_v}{\mathbf{A}_{v0,\,\text{max}}} = \frac{2b/(b^2+1)}{1 - [4\delta^2 Q_1 Q_2/(1+b^2)] + j[2\delta(Q_1+Q_2)/(1+b^2)]} \tag{17-98}$$

In Fig. 17-12 we plot $|\mathbf{A}_v/\mathbf{A}_{v0,\,\text{max}}|$ for the case $Q_1 = Q_2$. If $b \leqq 1$, then the curve resembles the resonance curve that we have obtained for the single tuned amplifier. However, when $b > 1$, the shape changes considerably. The maximum value no longer occurs at $f = f_0$ ($\delta = 0$) and the curve has two peaks. We shall subsequently demonstrate that this type of response is very useful. The selectivity of all three curves in the stop band is much better than the curve for the single tuned circuit of Fig. 17-3. We shall demonstrate this with an example. First let us develop some relations.

Let us determine if and when the double peaked response occurs. Solving

$$\frac{d|\mathbf{A}_v/\mathbf{A}_{v0,\,\text{max}}|}{d\delta} = 0$$

we obtain

$$\delta = 0$$

$$\delta_{p1,\,p2} = \pm\frac{1+b^2}{2Q_1Q_2}\sqrt{\frac{Q_1Q_2}{1+b} - \frac{(Q_1+Q_2)^2}{2(1+b^2)^2}} \tag{17-99}$$

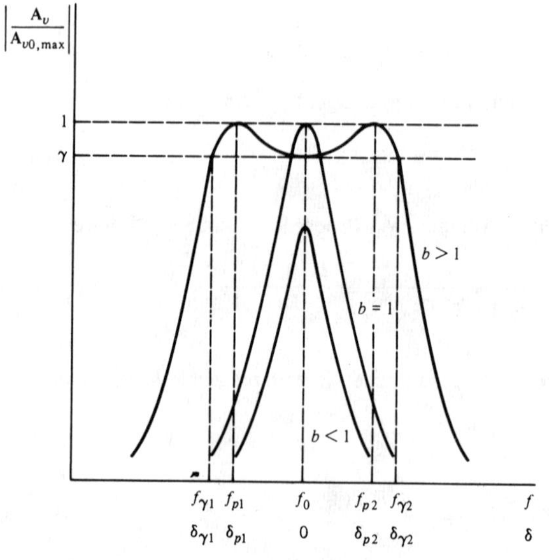

Figure 17-12. The frequency response of the double tuned amplifier for the case $Q_1 = Q_2$.

If

$$\frac{Q_1 Q_2}{1 + b^2} \leqq \frac{(Q_1 + Q_2)^2}{2(1 + b^2)^2}$$

then there will only be one peak at $\delta = 0$. On the other hand, if the inequality is reversed, then $\delta = 0$ will correspond to a minimum and the double peaked curves will result. The critical value of b is

$$b_{\text{crit}} = \frac{1}{\sqrt{2}} \sqrt{\frac{Q_1}{Q_2} + \frac{Q_2}{Q_1}} \tag{17-100}$$

If $b > b_{\text{crit}}$ then the double peaked curve results. To simplify the equations, let us assume that $Q_1 = Q_2 = Q_0$. This can be achieved by adjusting R_i in the case of the FET amplifier or the position of the tap in the case of the transistor amplifier. Then,

$$b_{\text{crit}} = \pm 1 \tag{17-101}$$

In Sec. 17-1 we discussed the design criterion and how, in the pass band, we desired that the normalized pass band response vary between 1 and γ. Hence,

$$\gamma \leqq \left| \frac{\mathbf{A}_v}{\mathbf{A}_{v0,\,\text{max}}} \right| \leqq 1 \tag{17-102}$$

γ is a positive number less than, but usually close to, 1. The double peaked curve allows us to obtain a relatively broad bandwidth. The bandwidth (see Fig. 17-12) lies between $f_{\gamma 1}$ and $f_{\gamma 2}$ or, equivalently, between $\delta_{\gamma 1}$ and $\delta_{\gamma 2}$. Let us now obtain some relations that can be used in design. In order to obtain maximum use of the bandwidth, we shall adjust b so that the response at $\delta = 0$ is γ. Then (see Eq. 17-98)

$$\gamma = \frac{2b}{b^2 + 1} \tag{17-103}$$

Let us solve for b and choose $b > b_{\text{crit}} = 1$. Then,

$$b = \frac{1}{\gamma} + \sqrt{\frac{1}{\gamma^2} - 1} \tag{17-104}$$

Now let us determine the bandwidth. To determine $\delta_{\gamma 1}$ and $\delta_{\gamma 2}$ we set the magnitude of Eq. 17-98 equal to $\gamma = 2b/(b^2 + 1)$, and set $Q_2 = Q_1 = Q_0$, and then solve. Doing this we have

$$\delta_{\gamma 1,\gamma 2} = \pm \frac{1}{\sqrt{2}Q_0} \sqrt{b^2 - 1} \tag{17-105}$$

Noting that $\delta = (f - f_0)/f_0$, we obtain

$$B_\gamma = f_{\gamma 2} - f_{\gamma 1} = \frac{\sqrt{2}}{Q_0} f_0 \sqrt{b^2 - 1} \tag{17-106}$$

The magnitude of b is limited. Let us consider it. The coefficient of coupling, K, of a pair of coupled coils is given by

$$K = \frac{M}{\sqrt{L_1 L_2}} \tag{17-107}$$

It can be shown that the maximum coefficient of coupling is unity. Substituting Eqs. 17-85 into Eq. 17-107 and then substituting the result into Eq. 17-91, we have

$$b = K\sqrt{Q_1 Q_1} \tag{17-108}$$

Thus, the maximum value of b is

$$b_{\text{max}} = \sqrt{Q_1 Q_1} \tag{17-109}$$

Ordinarily, this is a large number which does not limit the value of b in practical situations.

Example

Design a double tuned transistor amplifier which meets the following specifications.

Pass band: for $0.995 \times 10^6 \leqq f \leqq 1.005 \times 10^6$, $0.9 \leqq |\mathbf{A}_v/\mathbf{A}_{v0,\,\text{max}}| \leqq 1$.
Stop band: for $f < 0.95 \times 10^6$ and $f > 1.05 \times 10^6$, $|\mathbf{A}_v/\mathbf{A}_{v0,\,\text{max}}| \leqq 0.0003$.
$|\mathbf{A}_{v0,\,\text{max}}| \geqq 8000$.

We shall use transistors with the following parameter values.

$$r_{bb'} = 100 \text{ ohms}$$

$$r_{b'e} = 900 \text{ ohms}$$

$$r_{ce} = 80{,}000 \text{ ohms}$$

$$C_{b'e} = 30 \text{ pF}$$

$$C_{b'c} = 2 \text{ pF}$$

$$g_m = 75{,}000\ \mu\text{mho}$$

Since a relatively narrow bandwidth is required, we shall add tuning capacitors to the circuit. The capacitances C_1 and C_2 represent the total shunt capacitance of the circuit. We shall use as a first trial

$$C_1 = C_2 = 300 \text{ pF}$$

From Eq. 18-103,

$$b = \frac{1}{0.9} + \sqrt{\frac{1}{0.9^2} - 1} = 1.595$$

Then,

$$B = f_{\gamma 2} - f_{\gamma 1} = 1.005 \times 10^6 - 0.995 \times 10^6 = 10{,}000 \text{ Hz}$$

$$f_0 = \sqrt{1.005 \times 10^6 \times 0.995 \times 10^6} = 0.99999 \times 10^6 \simeq 10^6$$

Then, assuming the equal Q case, we have from Eq. 17-106,

$$Q_0 = \frac{\sqrt{2}\, f_0 \sqrt{b^2 - 1}}{B} = \frac{\sqrt{2} \times 10^6 \sqrt{1.595^2 - 1}}{10^4} = 175.7$$

Let us see if the midband gain can be obtained. For the primary and secondary sides of the coil, we have

$$Q_0 = \frac{2\pi f L_1}{R_p} = \frac{1}{2\pi f_0 C R_p} = \frac{1}{2\pi f_0 C R_s}$$

Therefore,

$$R_p = R_s = \frac{1}{2\pi f_0 C Q_0} = \frac{1}{2\pi \times 10^6 \times 300 \times 10^{-12} \times 175.7}$$

$$R_p = R_s = 3.019 \text{ ohms}$$

Let us assume that each coil has a Q of 200. Hence,

$$\frac{2\pi f_0 L_1}{R_1} = \frac{1}{2\pi f_0 C R_1} = \frac{1}{2\pi f_0 C R_2} = Q = 200$$

$$R_1 = R_2 = 1/(2\pi \times 10^6 \times 300 \times 10^{-12} \times 200) = 2.652$$

Then, (see Eq. 17-81)

$$(\omega_0 L_1)^2/r = 1/(\omega_0 C)^2 r = 3.019 - 2.652 = 0.367$$

$$r = 1/[(2\pi \times 10^6 \times 300 \times 10^{-12})^2 \times 0.367] = 766{,}887 \text{ ohms}$$

This is greater than r_{ce}. Thus, the design cannot be achieved. Let us try two stages. Now

$$\gamma = \sqrt{0.9} = 0.9487$$

$$b = \frac{1}{0.9487} + \sqrt{\frac{1}{0.9487^2} - 1} = 1.387$$

Then,

$$Q_0 = \frac{\sqrt{2} \times 10^6 \sqrt{1.387^2 - 1}}{10^4} = 136$$

Now,

$$R_p = R_s = 1/(2\pi \times 10^6 \times 300 \times 10^{-12} \times 136) = 3.900$$

$$R_p - R_1 = 3.900 - 2.652 = 1.248$$

Now,

$$r = 1/[(2\pi \times 10^6 \times 300 \times 10^{-12})^2 \times 1.248] = 225{,}519 \text{ ohms}$$

This is still greater than r_{ce}. Note that we could tap down on the primary to reduce the effective loading. However, let us attempt a different procedure. Let us increase the value of C. Suppose that $C = 900$ pF. Then,

$$R_1 = R_2 = 2.652/3 = 0.884$$

and for the two-stage case

$$R_p = R_s = 3.900/3 = 1.300 \text{ ohms}$$

$$R_p - R_1 = 1.300 - 0.884 = 0.416$$

Then,

$$r = 1/[(2\pi \times 10^6 \times 900 \times 10^{-12})^2 \times 0.416] = 75{,}173 \text{ ohms}$$

This is less than r_{ce}. Thus, we can achieve the design insofar as r_{ce} is concerned. Now let us consider the secondary.

$$R_s - R_2 = 0.416 = \frac{\omega_0^2(L_b + M)^2}{R_i}$$

$$L_b + M = \frac{\sqrt{0.416} \times \sqrt{1000}}{2\pi \times 10^6} = 3.246 \times 10^{-6} \text{ H}$$

From Eq. 17-85

$$L_1 = L_2 = 1/[(2\pi \times 10^6)^2 \times 900 \times 10^{-12}] = 28.15 \times 10^{-6} \text{ H}$$

Then,

$$\frac{L_b + M}{L_2} = \frac{3.246}{28.15} = 0.115$$

The gain per stage then is (see Eqs. 17-95 and 17-97)

$$|\mathbf{A}_{v0,\,\max}| = \frac{\frac{1}{2} g_m r_{b'e}(L_b + M)/L_2}{(r_{bb'} + r_{b'e})\omega_0^2 C_1 C_2 \sqrt{R_p R_s}}$$

$$|\mathbf{A}_{v0,\,\max}| = \frac{\frac{1}{2} \times 75 \times 10^{-3} \times 900 \times 0.115}{1000 \times (2\pi \times 10^6 \times 900 \times 10^{-12})^2 \times 1.3} = 93.4$$

Then, for two stages, we have

$$|\mathbf{A}_{v0,\,\max}|_T = 93.4^2 = 8723$$

This is sufficient.

Now let us consider the stop band.

$$\sqrt{f_{r1} f_{r2}} = 10^6 \sqrt{0.95 \times 1.05} = 0.9987 \times 10^6$$

Let us check the response at $f_{r2} = 1.05 \times 10^6$. Then, $\delta = +0.05$. Then, from Eq. 17-98 we have for the magnitude of the gain of two stages, at f_{r1}

$$\left|\frac{\mathbf{A}_v}{\mathbf{A}_{v0,\,\max}}\right|_T = \frac{2 \times \dfrac{1.387}{1 + 1.387^2}}{\left[1 - \dfrac{4(0.05)^2 136^2}{1 + 1.387^2}\right]^2 + \left[\dfrac{2(0.05)(136 + 136)}{1 + 1.387^2}\right]^2}$$

$$\left|\frac{\mathbf{A}_v}{\mathbf{A}_{v0,\,\max}}\right|_T = 2.27 \times 10^{-4} = 0.00021 < 0.0003$$

This meets specifications. Thus, the design can be obtained with two stages. If the stop band specifications were not met, we would have to redesign the pass band response for three stages and then determine if the stop band requirements were met. In general, the number of stages is increased, if possible, until the specifications are obtained.

Now let us complete the design. We require $r = 75{,}173$ ohms while $r_{ce} = 80{,}000$ ohms. Hence, a resistance R_3 must be placed in parallel with each coil. Its value is

$$\frac{1}{R_3} = \frac{1}{r} - \frac{1}{r_{ce}} = \frac{1}{75{,}173} - \frac{1}{80{,}000}$$

$$R_3 = 1.25 \times 10^6 \text{ ohms}$$

The mutual inductance is given by Eq. 18-91.

$$M = \frac{b\sqrt{R_p R_s}}{\omega_0} = \frac{1.387 \times 1.3}{2\pi \times 10^6} = 0.287 \times 10^{-6}\ \mu\text{H}$$

The resulting schematic design is shown in Fig. 17-13. Let us assume that the quiescent operating point of the transistor is

$$V_{DSQ} = 10 \text{ V}$$

$$I_{DQ} = 1 \text{ mA}$$

$$I_{BQ} = 15\ \mu\text{A}$$

Then, the power supply voltage is

$$V_{CC} = 10 \text{ V}$$

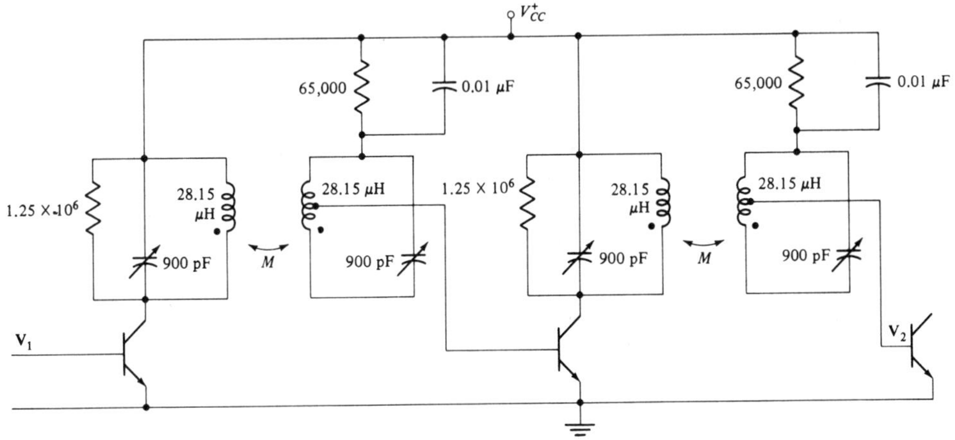

Figure 17-13. The double tuned amplifier. The tap locations are given in the text. All resistance values are in ohms.

The base resistance is

$$R_B = 10/15 \times 10^{-6} = 66{,}667 \text{ ohms}$$

Let us use $R_B = 65{,}000$ ohms. This will only shift the operating point slightly. We shall bypass this resistance by a 0.01-μF capacitance. (Its reactance at 10^6 Hz is $=j16$ ohms.) The design is now complete.

17-7. NEUTRALIZATION

The local feedback through C_{gs} in a common-source FET amplifier or through $C_{b'c}$ in a common-emitter transistor amplifier can, at times, lead to oscillation in tuned amplifier circuits. (The phase shift introduced by the tuned circuit can cause these circuits to be unstable whereas ordinary amplifier circuits are stable.) The criteria discussed in Secs. 16-11 and 16-12 can be used to determine if the circuit will be stable. In addition, simple criteria to be discussed in the next chapter can also be used here.

The amplifier can be made stable by reducing the loop gain. Several procedures can be used to accomplish this. The simplest is to reduce the coupling from output to input This is accomplished by choosing FET's or transistors with small C_{gs} or $C_{b'c}$. The dual gate FET has extremely low coupling between input and output. Tuned amplifiers constructed with such FET's are not prone to oscillation. In addition, there are RF (radio frequency) transistors that have low values of $C_{b'e}$. Thus, circuits using them have less tendency to oscillate.

Other techniques can be used to minimize the coupling between input and output. For instance, the cascode amplifier has extremely low coupling because of the common-base, or common-gate stage (see Sec. 12-15). The cascode consists of two cascaded stages. These can be realized in a single integrated circuit.

There is another procedure used to reduce loop gain. Consider Fig. 17-13. Suppose that the collector of each transistor were connected to a tap on the primary side of the coil. This would reduce the signal component of v_{CE} and, hence, the loop gain would be reduced. Alternatively, the operating point can be adjusted to reduce the gain. Either of these techniques may require that more stages may have to be used to achieve the required overall gain.

We can take a somewhat different approach toward reducing the feedback. Suppose that we cancel the feedback by introducing a current that is equal to, but 180° out-of-phase with, the feedback signal at the input to the active device. The two signals will cancel and the effect of the feedback will be eliminated. This technique is called *neutralization.*

Two neutralizing circuits are shown in Figs. 17-14a and 17-14b. In each case, the coil is center tapped. Since the power supply is equivalent to a ground as far as signals are concerned,

$$\mathbf{V}_a = -\mathbf{V}_b \tag{17-110}$$

Then, in Fig. 17-14a, the feedback current through C_{gd} is given by

$$\mathbf{I}_b = (\mathbf{V}_b - \mathbf{V}_1)j\omega C_{gd}$$

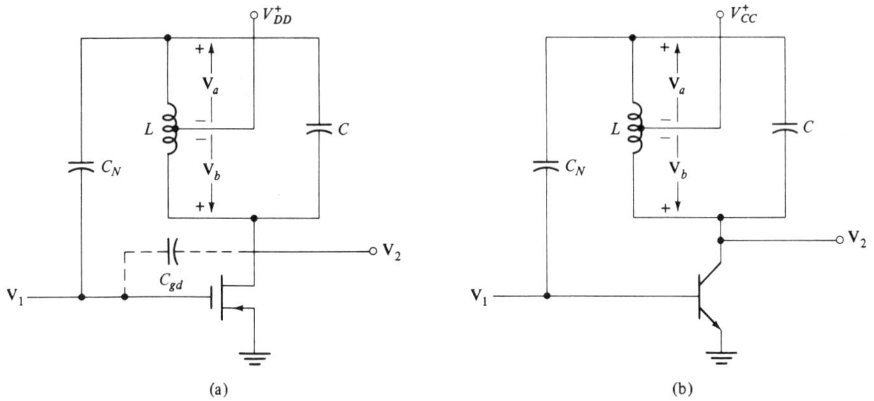

Figure 17-14. Neutralizing circuits. (a) Common-source FET amplifier. (b) Common-emitter transistor amplifier.

Since, in general, $|\mathbf{V}_b| \gg |\mathbf{V}_1|$, we have

$$\mathbf{I}_b = j\omega C_{gd}\mathbf{V}_b \tag{17-111}$$

Now consider the current through the *neutralizing capacitance* C_N.

$$\mathbf{I}_a = j\omega C_N(\mathbf{V}_a - \mathbf{V}_1) \simeq j\omega C_N \mathbf{V}_a \tag{17-112}$$

Thus, if $C_N = C_{gd}$, then $\mathbf{I}_a \simeq -\mathbf{I}_b$. Hence, the effects of the feedback through C_{gd} are neutralized approximately.

In Fig. 17-14b we show a common-emitter transistor amplifier. Again, a neutralizing capacitance has been included. The principles of operation here are the same as in Fig. 17-14a. The feedback circuit within the transistor is more complex and, at times, small series and/or large shunt resistances are included in the neutralizing circuit.

It might seem as though neutralization should always be used since, in addition to preventing oscillation, the Miller effect could be cancelled but this is not the case. In the previous discussion we assumed that the neutralizing circuit was identical to the feedback circuit, but this is not true. For instance, there is series inductance in the leads used to connect C_N into the circuit and there is stray capacitance between C_N and ground. In practice C_N must be adjusted to obtain stability, and the adjustment is only valid over a narrow range of frequencies. Normally, if a component changes slightly due to aging, its circuit will still function. In the case of a neutralizing capacitor, a slight change in C_N can result in oscillation. Then the circuit will not work at all. Thus, in most cases, neutralization is not used except in those circuits where there is a skilled operator who can adjust and possibly readjust the neutralizing capacitance.

17-8. THE SUPERHETRODYNE PRINCIPLE

Very often, a tuned amplifier is such that its "center frequency" f_0 can be varied over a range of frequencies. For instance, a standard radio receiver must tune over a range from

0.55 to 1.8 MHz. If there are many tuned stages, then it is cumbersome to tune all of them simultaneously. We have also seen that double tuned amplifiers have desirable frequency response, but we would then have twice as many circuits whose tuning would have to be varied. In addition, we have seen that bandwidth is proportional to f_0/Q_{eff} so as the amplifier is tuned, the bandwidth is likely to change, which is an undesirable situation.

We shall now consider a circuit called a *superhetrodyne* that eliminates these problems. A block diagram for such a circuit is shown in Fig. 17-15. The first stage of the superhetrodyne circuit is called a *radio frequency* (RF) *amplifier*. It is tuned to f_0, the frequency of the input signal. The next stage is called a *mixer*. Its input is tuned to f_0. (Actually, this is the output tuned circuit of the RF amplifier.) However, the output of the mixer is tuned to a different frequency f_I, called the *intermediate frequency*. This frequency is fixed and is *not* changed even when we change the frequency f_0 (e.g., when we tune to a different radio station). Let us see how this is accomplished. The mixer is operated as an amplifier except that its operating point lies in a nonlinear region of its characteristics so that nonlinear distortion is produced. Two signals are applied to the mixer. They are the input signal and another one which is generated within the receiver in an oscillator, called the *local oscillator*. Such an oscillator produces a sinusoidal signal and its frequency of oscillation is $f_0 + f_I$ which must vary if f_0 varies. (Sinusoidal oscillator circuits will be discussed in the next chapter.)

The output signals of the mixer will be at the same frequencies as its input signals; in addition there will be frequencies that result from the harmonic and intermodulation distortion (see Sec. 5-13). Thus, there are harmonics of the input signal and the oscillator signal, and frequencies that are sum and difference frequencies of the input and oscillator frequencies and their harmonics. The sum and difference frequencies are called *beat frequencies*. Hence, we shall have the following frequencies produced.

$$\begin{aligned} &f_0, 2f_0, 3f_0, \ldots \\ &(f_0 + f_I), 2(f_0 + f_I), 3(f_0 + f_I), \ldots \\ &f_I, 2f_0 + f_I, \ldots \end{aligned} \tag{17-113}$$

Note the frequency f_I, which is the difference between f_0 and $f_0 + f_I$. This will pass through the tuned circuit at the output of the mixer.

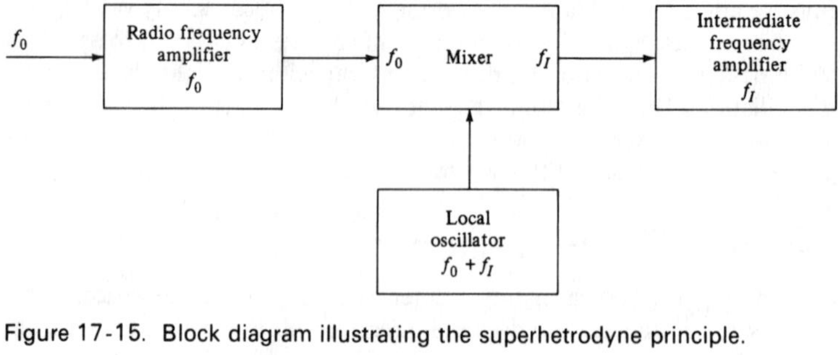

Figure 17-15. Block diagram illustrating the superhetrodyne principle.

The amplifier stages following the mixer are tuned to f_I. Hence, this group of stages is called an *intermediate frequency* (IF) *amplifier*. It usually consists of double tuned stages. The IF amplifier provides most of the selectivity of the circuit as well as most of the gain of the amplifier.

Now let us consider an interfering signal close to f_0 but lying outside of the desired pass band. The RF amplifier is typically a single tuned amplifier and its selectivity is not great. Hence, the interfering signal will at best be slightly rejected by it. The beat frequencies between the interfering signal and the local oscillator frequency $f_0 + f_I$ will lie outside of the pass band of the IF amplifier. This can be a multistage double tuned amplifier and its rejection of the undesirable signal will, in general, be great. Thus, the superhetrodyne circuit functions well and is used in almost all receivers.

There is one interfering signal that will pass through the IF amplifier. Suppose that there is a signal at a frequency $f_0 + 2f_I$. The difference between this frequency and the local oscillator frequency is f_I. Thus, a beat frequency f_I will be produced in the mixer, and the intermediate frequency amplifier will not reject this signal at all. Such an interfering signal is called an *image frequency*. The image frequency is only rejected by the tuned circuits of the RF amplifier and mixer that are tuned to f_0. These are not high selectivity circuits but the image frequency is relatively far from f_0 (the difference is $2f_I$), so extreme selectivity is not required in the RF amplifier and good rejection of the image frequency is usually obtained.

RF amplifiers serve another function besides rejecting the image frequencies. In Sec. 12-18 we discussed the noise produced in amplifiers. The mixer stage will produce, in general, more noise than the RF amplifier because the operating point of the mixer is chosen to obtain the appropriate nonlinearities rather than to obtain optimum amplification. The RF amplifier amplifies the signal before it is amplified by the relatively noisy mixer and this improves the noise figure (see Sec. 12-18) of the circuit. Of course, the RF amplifier does itself produce noise but it is less than that produced by the mixer.

Suppose that we now wish to tune the superhetrodyne circuit to different frequencies. The frequency of the tuned circuits of the RF amplifier and mixer as well as that of the local oscillator must be varied. The frequency of the local oscillator is the frequency $f_0 + f_I$ which is also established by a tuned circuit. There is a problem here. The circuits must be tuned in such a way that the difference between the frequencies to which the RF amplifier and local oscillator are tuned remains fixed at f_I. This causes a problem when the input frequency is varied. Suppose that we have two tuned circuits. We tune one to 1×10^6 Hz and the other to 1.5×10^6 Hz (i.e., $f_I = 0.5 \times 10^6$ Hz). Now if we change both the tuning capacitors by an equal amount, the difference between the resonant frequencies of the two tuned circuits will no longer be 0.5×10^6 Hz. Superhetrodyne receivers usually employ special tuned circuits so that the difference between the local oscillator's frequency and the RF amplifier's resonant frequency remains close to f_I when the circuits are tuned.

17-9. ACTIVE FILTERS—THE THOMAS BIQUAD

The tuned circuits that we have discussed can be used at frequencies of about 50,000 Hz or higher. If we attempt to use them at lower frequencies, the physical size of the inductance usually becomes excessive. In this and the next section we shall consider tuned

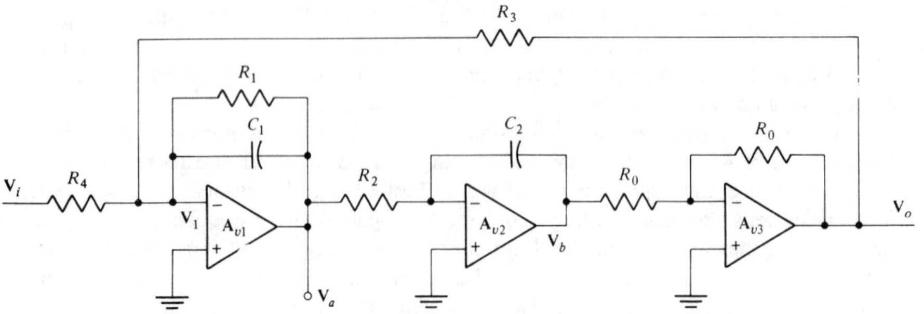

Figure 17-16. The basic Thomas biquad.

amplifiers that do not use inductances. Instead, special feedback amplifier circuits are used to obtain the desired selectivity.

These circuits, called *active filters*, use only resistance, capacitance, and operational amplifiers, but as we shall demonstrate they all have the flexibility of tuned circuits. Indeed, they can be more general than those we have already considered. Active filters are, in general, smaller and lighter than their passive counterparts.

The resistors and capacitors are often fabricated using thin metallic films. These resistors and capacitors can be incorporated on a single insulating substrate with the required operational amplifiers. In such cases, complex filters can be fabricated in a very small volume (e.g., 2 cm × 2 cm × 4 mm). We shall see that active filter circuits require relatively precise adjustment of some of their resistance values. Techniques are presently used which provide adjustment of thin film resistances by "trimming" them with laser beams. Such techniques are very precise. In addition, they can be automated and are fast.

The Thomas Biquad

We shall discuss an active filter called the *Thomas biquad*[1] (see Fig. 17-16). It consists of three operational amplifier circuits in a feedback configuration. The first stage consists of a summer (see Sec. 13-6). Now the feedback element, instead of being a resistance, is a parallel *RC* circuit. Its impedance $R_1/(1 + j\omega R_1 C_1)$ replaces the resistance R_2 in the equation of the summer circuit of Fig. 13-13. If we analyze this circuit as we did in Sec. 13-6, we obtain

$$\mathbf{V}_a = -\mathbf{V}_i \frac{R_1/R_4}{1 + j\omega R_1 C_1} - \mathbf{V}_o \frac{R_1/R_3}{1 + j\omega R_1 C_1} \tag{17-114}$$

We have assumed here that $|\mathbf{A}_{v1}|$ is large enough so that the inequality equivalent to that of Eq. 13-51 is valid.

[1] L. C. Thomas, "The Biquad: Part I, Some Practical Design Considerations; Part II, A Multipurpose Active Filtering System," *IEEE Trans. on Circuit Theory*, CT-18 (1971): 350–357; 358–361.

It is convenient if we write Eq. 17-114 in terms of the Laplace transform variable $s = j\omega$. Thus, we have

$$\mathbf{V}_a = -\frac{\mathbf{V}_i R_1/R_4}{1 + sR_1C_1} - \frac{\mathbf{V}_o R_1/R_3}{1 + sR_1C_1} \tag{17-115}$$

We discussed in Sec. 13-5 that the output impedance of these operational amplifier circuits is very low. Hence, the succeeding stages do not "load them down" and reduce the output.

The second stage is the integrator discussed in Sec. 13-7. Hence, if $|\mathbf{A}_{v2}|$ is such that relation 13-59 is satisfied, then the output is given by

$$\mathbf{V}_b = \frac{-1}{sR_2C_2}\mathbf{V}_a \tag{17-116}$$

The last stage is simply a unity gain amplifier. Its purpose is only to multiply the signal by -1 so that the feedback from $\mathbf{V}_o$ to $\mathbf{V}_1$ is negative. Hence, if $|\mathbf{A}_{v3}|$ is large enough

$$\mathbf{V}_o = -\mathbf{V}_b \tag{17-117}$$

Combining Eq. 17-114, 17-115, and 17-116, we obtain

$$\mathbf{K}_v = \frac{\mathbf{V}_o}{\mathbf{V}_i} = \frac{-1/R_4R_2C_1C_2}{s^2 + (1/R_1C_1)s + (1/R_3R_2C_1C_2)} \tag{17-118}$$

We can also use $\mathbf{V}_a$ as an output using Eqs. 17-116, 17-117, and 17-118. We obtain

$$\mathbf{K}_{va} = \frac{\mathbf{V}_a}{\mathbf{V}_1} = \frac{s/R_4C_1}{s^2 + (1/R_1C_1)s + 1/R_3R_2C_1C_2} \tag{17-119}$$

We want to compare this with the response of the single tuned RC amplifier whose gain is given by Eq. 17-33. Let us set

$$R_2C_2 = R_3C_1 \tag{17-120}$$

Then, comparing Eq. 17-119 and 17-33 we have

$$\omega_0 = \frac{1}{R_3C_1} = \frac{1}{R_2C_2} \tag{17-121a}$$

$$\frac{\omega_0}{Q_{\text{eff}}} = \frac{1}{R_1C_1} \tag{17-121b}$$

$$\mathbf{K}_{v0} = \frac{Q_{\text{eff}}}{\omega_0}\frac{1}{R_4C_1} \tag{17-121c}$$

Then, Eq. 17-119 can be written as

$$\mathbf{K}_{va} = \frac{-s/R_4C_1}{s^2 + (\omega_0/Q_{\text{eff}})s + \omega_0^2} \tag{17-122}$$

Thus, the response of the Thomas biquad is the same as the single tuned amplifier. Hence, we can replace single tuned amplifiers by the inductorless Thomas biquad circuit.

We can rewrite Eq. 17-119 as

$$\mathbf{K}_{va} = \frac{-\mathbf{K}_s}{s^2 + (\omega_0/Q_{\text{eff}})s + \omega_0^2} \tag{17-123}$$

where

$$\omega_0 = \frac{1}{R_3 C_1} = \frac{1}{R_2 C_2} \tag{17-124a}$$

$$Q_{\text{eff}} = \frac{R_1}{R_3} \tag{17-124b}$$

$$\mathbf{K} = \frac{1}{R_4 C_1} \tag{17-124c}$$

Similarly, we can write

$$\mathbf{K}_v = \frac{-\mathbf{K}_1}{s^2 + (\omega_0/Q_{\text{eff}})s + \omega_0^2} \tag{17-125}$$

where

$$\mathbf{K}_1 = \frac{1}{R_4 R_2 C_1 C_2} \tag{17-126}$$

We can obtain more general results from the Thomas biquad if we add an additional summer (see Fig. 17-17). Hence,

$$\mathbf{V}_c = -\frac{R}{R_7}\mathbf{V}_i - \frac{R}{R_5}\mathbf{V}_a - \frac{R}{R_6}\mathbf{V}_o \tag{17-127}$$

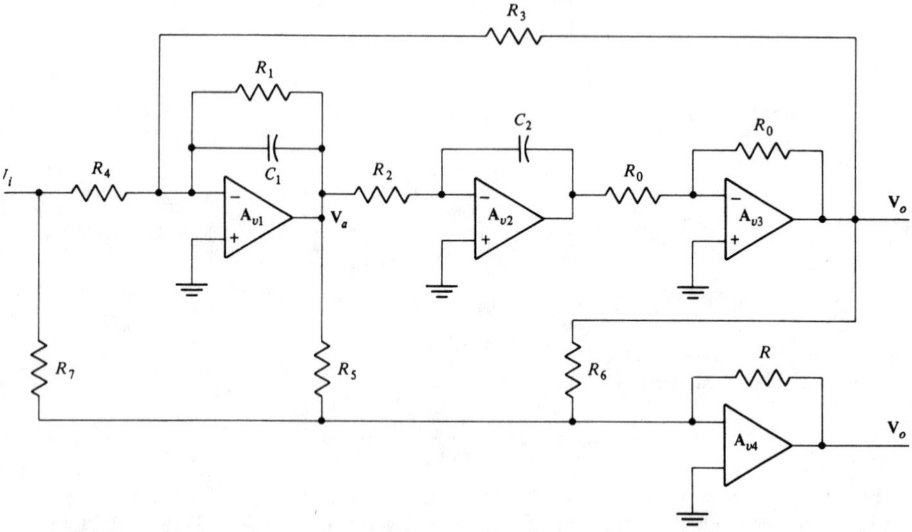

Figure 17-17. A more general form of Thomas biquad.

Substituting Eqs. 17-123 and 17-125 and manipulating we obtain

$$\mathbf{K}_{vc} = \frac{\mathbf{V}_c}{\mathbf{V}_i} = \frac{-\mathbf{K}_c(s^2 + (\omega_z/Q_z)s + \omega_z^2)}{s^2 + (\omega_0/Q_{\text{eff}})s + \omega_0^2} \tag{17-128}$$

where

$$\omega_z^2 = \omega_0^2\left(1 - \frac{R_7}{R_6}\frac{R_3}{R_4}\right) \tag{17-129a}$$

$$Q_z = \frac{Q_{\text{eff}}\,\omega_z}{\omega_0}\,\frac{1}{1 - (R_7/R_5)(R_1/R_4)} \tag{17-129b}$$

and

$$\mathbf{K}_c = \frac{R}{R_7} \tag{17-129c}$$

Thus we can realize zeros as well as poles. A_{vc} is the ratio of two quadratic equations. This accounts for the name biquad.

Example

Obtain an amplifier whose voltage gain is given by

$$\frac{-10s}{s^2 + 100s + 10^8}$$

This is the type of response that we obtain from a single tuned amplifier. Here we shall use the Thomas biquad. Comparing the specified gain with Eq. 17-123 we see that

$$\mathbf{K}_{va} = \frac{-\mathbf{K}s}{s^2 + (\omega_0/Q_{\text{eff}})s + \omega_0^2}$$

Here,

$$\omega_0 = 10^4$$

$$Q_{\text{eff}} = 100$$

$$K = 10$$

Thus,

$$\omega_0 = 10^4 = \frac{1}{R_3 C_1} = \frac{1}{R_2 C_2}$$

Let us use

$$C_1 = C_2 = 0.1\ \mu\text{F}$$

Then,

$$R_2 = R_3 = 1000 \text{ ohms}$$

$$Q_{\text{eff}} = \frac{R_1}{R_3}$$

$$R_1 = 100 \times 1000 = 100{,}000 \text{ ohms}$$

$$\mathbf{K} = \frac{1}{R_4 C_1}$$

$$R_4 = \frac{1}{10 \times 0.1 \times 10^{-6}} = 10^6 \text{ ohms}$$

The value of R_0 can be chosen almost arbitrarily although it should not be too large or too small. A typical value is

$$R_0 = 10{,}000 \text{ ohms}$$

Thus, the realization is shown in Fig. 17-16 using the values of resistance and capacitance that we have obtained here.

Note that this design proceeded smoothly. By first realizing ω_0 and next realizing Q_{eff}, and finally obtaining **Z**, we always had an unspecified resistance value to adjust.

Sensitivity to Changes in $\mathbf{A}_v$

In Sec. 13-2 we studied the sensitivity of the gain of an operational amplifier circuit to changes in $\mathbf{A}_v$. It is extremely important to study such sensitivity when active filters are designed. For instance, suppose that changes in $\mathbf{A}_{v1}$, $\mathbf{A}_{v2}$, or $\mathbf{A}_{v3}$ caused ω_0 or Q_{eff} to change substantially. Then, this circuit would probably be unsuitable. Note that in a tuned amplifier such parameters do change with L and C but the change in the passive element values will, in general, be small, while the change in an operational amplifier's gain can be large. In fact, many active synthesis procedures that appeared attractive at first glance, actually were never used because the sensitivity of ω_0 and Q_{eff} (as well as other parameters) to changes in $\mathbf{A}_v$ was large. The sensitivity of any active filter should be investigated before it is used. The sensitivity of the Thomas biquad is small enough for most purposes.

In order to compute the sensitivity of the Thomas biquad, we would have to compute exact expressions for the gains of Eqs. 17-118 and 17-119. These would include the values of $\mathbf{A}_{v1}$, $\mathbf{A}_{v2}$, and $\mathbf{A}_{v3}$. We would then proceed as in Sec. 13-2 and assume that $\mathbf{A}_{v1}$ changes by an amount $\Delta\mathbf{A}_{v1}$. Then, $\Delta\omega_0$, the change in ω_0, would be computed. We define the sensitivity as (see Sec. 17-3)

$$S_{\mathbf{A}_{v1}}^{\omega_0} = \frac{\Delta\omega_0/\omega_0}{\Delta\mathbf{A}_{v1}/\mathbf{A}_{v1}} \tag{17-130}$$

Actually, the calculation of this quantity is very tedious and it is conventional in active filters to use derivatives rather than finite differences. In this case, the definition for sensitivity becomes

$$S_{\mathbf{A}_{v1}}^{\omega_0} = \frac{\mathbf{A}_{v1}}{\omega_0} \frac{d\omega_0}{d\mathbf{A}_{v1}} \tag{17-131}$$

If we perform all the tedious calculations of gain and take the derivatives (and make some approximations) we have

$$S_{\mathbf{A}_{v1}}^{\omega_0} \simeq \frac{1}{2} \frac{1}{1 + |\mathbf{A}_{v1}|/|\mathbf{A}_{v2}| + |\mathbf{A}_{v1}|} \tag{17-132}$$

Since the magnitude of the gains are high, this approaches

$$A_{\mathbf{A}_{v1}}^{\omega_0} \simeq \frac{1}{2|\mathbf{A}_{v1}|} \tag{17-133}$$

We obtain similar expressions for the sensitivity of ω_0 with respect to $\mathbf{A}_{v2}$ and $\mathbf{A}_{v3}$.

Since the gains of the operational amplifiers are very high, the sensitivity will be very low.

If the power supply voltage or ambient temperature change, then the gains of all three operational amplifiers will change simultaneously. Let us consider that this occurs. We shall now assume that the three operational amplifiers have equal gains $\mathbf{A}_v$. Then, the sensitivity is

$$S_{|\mathbf{A}_{vT}|}^{\omega_0} \approx \frac{3}{2|\mathbf{A}_v|} \tag{17-134}$$

Note that $|\mathbf{A}_v|$ is the gain of a *single* operational amplifier. This is larger than the value given by Eq. 17-133 but it is still small. Let us now consider the sensitivity of Q_{eff}. We shall assume that all three amplifiers change simultaneously. Then,

$$S_{|\mathbf{A}_{vT}|}^{Q_{\text{eff}}} \approx \frac{2Q_{\text{eff}}}{|\mathbf{A}_v|} \tag{17-135}$$

The sensitivity will be higher than that of ω_0 because of the Q_{eff} term in the numerator, but since $|\mathbf{A}_v|$ can be very large, the sensitivity can still be low. (Again note that $\mathbf{A}_v$ is the gain of a single operational amplifier.)

We have ignored the operational amplifier frequency response. Suppose that each operational amplifier has a gain $-\mathbf{A}_{v\,\text{mid}}/(1 + j\omega/\omega_\alpha)$ where ω_α is very small. In such cases, the sensitivity becomes[2]

$$S_{|\mathbf{A}_{vT}|}^{\omega_0} = \frac{3}{2} \frac{\omega_0}{|\mathbf{A}_{v\,\text{mid}}|\omega_\alpha} \tag{17-136}$$

and

$$S_{|\mathbf{A}_{vT}|}^{Q_{\text{eff}}} = -4Q_{\text{eff}} \frac{\omega_0}{|\mathbf{A}_{v\,\text{mid}}|\omega_\alpha} \tag{17-137}$$

[2] G. Daryanani, *Principles of Active Network Synthesis and Design* (New York: Wiley, 1976), Chapter 10.

The sensitivities can be degraded considerably if $\omega_\alpha < \omega_0$. The parameter values can change substantially from the calculated values. In fact, in some cases, instability can result and oscillation occurs.

The Thomas biquad uses three or four operational amplifiers, which seems to be a large number but remember that four operational amplifiers can be obtained on a single integrated circuit chip. In the next section we shall consider a procedure that uses only one operational amplifier.

17-10. THE DELYIANNIS ACTIVE FILTER

We shall now consider another active filter which uses only one operational amplifier (see Fig. 17-18). This is called the Delyiannis filter.[3] Analyzing the circuit, we have

$$\mathbf{V}_i - \mathbf{V}_o = \mathbf{I}_a\left(R_1 + \frac{1}{sC_2}\right) + \frac{1}{sC_2}\mathbf{I}_b \tag{17-138a}$$

$$0 = \frac{1}{sC_2}\mathbf{I}_a + \left(R_2 + \frac{1}{sC_1} + \frac{1}{sC_2}\right)\mathbf{I}_b \tag{17-138b}$$

$$\mathbf{V}_o = \mathbf{A}_v(\mathbf{V}_2 - \mathbf{V}_1) \tag{17-138c}$$

$$\mathbf{V}_1 = \mathbf{V}_i - \mathbf{I}_a R_1 + \frac{\mathbf{I}_b}{sC_1} \tag{17-138d}$$

$$\mathbf{V}_2 = \frac{R_A}{R_A + R_B}\mathbf{V}_o \tag{17-138e}$$

Manipulating these equations and assuming that $|\mathbf{A}_v|$ is very large, we obtain

$$\mathbf{K}_v = \frac{\mathbf{V}_o}{\mathbf{V}_i} = -\frac{\mathbf{K}s}{s^2 + \omega_0/Q_{\text{eff}} + \omega_0^2} \tag{17-139}$$

where

$$\omega_0 = \frac{1}{\sqrt{R_1R_2C_1C_2}} \tag{17-140a}$$

$$Q_{\text{eff}} = \frac{\sqrt{R_2/R_1}}{\sqrt{C_2/C_1} + \sqrt{C_1/C_2} - (R_AR_2/R_BR_1)\sqrt{C_1/C_2}} \tag{17-140b}$$

$$\mathbf{K} = \frac{R_A + R_B}{R_1C_2R_B} \tag{17-140c}$$

There are more variable circuit elements than circuit parameters so that we have some freedom here. It is often convenient to fabricate the capacitors such that

$$C_1 = C_2 = C \tag{17-141}$$

[3] T. Delyiannis, "High Q Factor Circuits with Reduced Sensitivity," *Electronics Letter*, 4 December, 1968, p. 577.

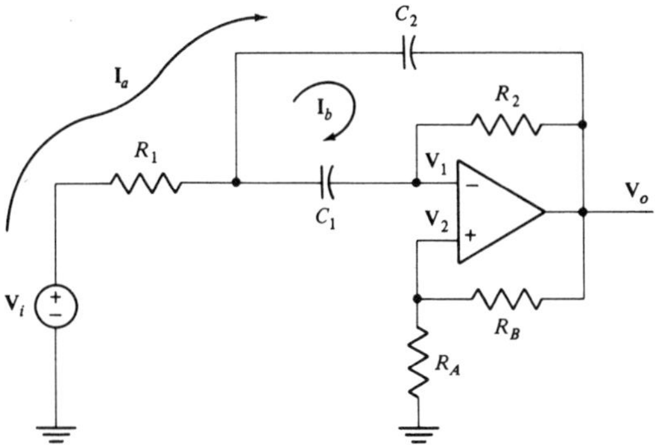

Figure 17-18. The Delyiannis active filter.

Let us also define

$$b = \frac{R_2}{R_1} \tag{17-142}$$

Then, we have

$$\omega_0 = \frac{1}{R_1 C\sqrt{b}} \tag{17-143a}$$

$$Q_{\text{eff}} = \frac{\sqrt{b}}{2 - bR_A/R_B} \tag{17-143b}$$

and

$$\mathbf{K} = \frac{1 + R_A/R_B}{R_1 C} = \omega_0\sqrt{b}\left(1 + \frac{R_A}{R_B}\right) \tag{17-143c}$$

If we do not desire a zero at the origin then a modification of this circuit called the Friend filter[4] can be used (see Fig. 17-19). Proceeding as before, we find that the gain of this circuit is

$$\mathbf{K}_v = \frac{\mathbf{K}_1}{s^2 + (\omega_0(Q_{\text{eff}})s + \omega_0^2} \tag{17-144}$$

where

$$\omega_0 = \sqrt{\frac{1 - (R_2/R_1)(R_A/R_B)}{R_2 R_3 C_1 C_2}} \tag{17-145a}$$

$$Q_{\text{eff}} = \frac{C_1 C_2 \omega_0}{C_2(1/R_1 + 1/R_2 + 1/R_3) - C_1(R_B/R_A)(1/R_3)} \tag{17-145b}$$

$$\mathbf{K}_1 = \frac{1 + R_A/R_B}{C_1 C_2 R_1 R_3} \tag{17-145c}$$

[4] J. J. Friend, C. A. Harris, and D. Hilberman, "STAR: An Active Biquadiate Filter Section," *IEEE Trans. on Circuits and Systems* CAS-22 (1975): 115–121.

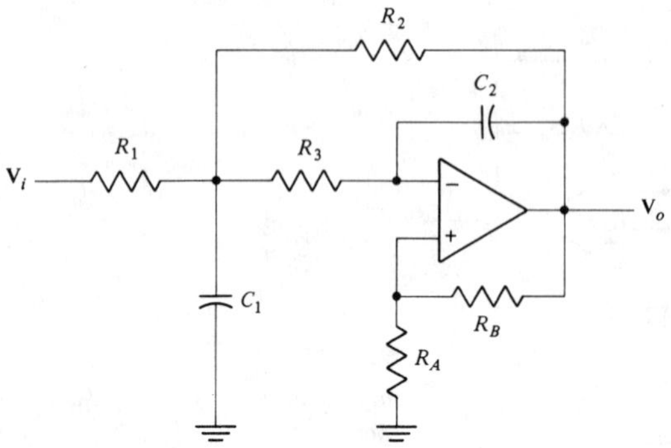

Figure 17-19. The Friend active filter.

If we set

$$C_1 = C_2 = C$$

and define b as in Eq. 17-142, we have

$$\omega_0 = \frac{1}{C}\sqrt{\frac{1 - bR_A/R_B}{R_2R_3}} \tag{17-146a}$$

$$Q_{\text{eff}} = \frac{CR_1\omega_0}{(1 + 1/b + R_1/R_3) - (R_B/R_A)(R_1/R_3)} \tag{17-146b}$$

$$\mathbf{K}_1 = \frac{1 + R_A/R_B}{C^2R_1R_3} \tag{17-146c}$$

These networks have been widely fabricated as thin film devices.[4]

Example

Obtain an amplifier whose voltage gain is

$$\mathbf{K}_V = -\frac{\mathbf{K}_0 s}{s^2 + 0.1s + 100}$$

where $\mathbf{K}_0 \geqq 10$. Hence,

$$\omega_0 = 10$$

$$Q_{\text{eff}} = 100$$

We shall use the Delyiannis filter. $\mathbf{K} \geqq 10$. Then, from Eq. 17-143 we have

$$R_1 = \frac{1}{\omega_0 C\sqrt{b}} = \frac{1}{10C\sqrt{b}} \tag{17-147a}$$

$$\frac{R_B}{R_A} = \frac{Q_{\text{eff}}\, b}{2Q_{\text{eff}} - \sqrt{b}} = \frac{100b}{200 - \sqrt{b}} \tag{17-147b}$$

$$\mathbf{K} = 10\sqrt{b}\left(1 + \frac{R_A}{R_B}\right) \tag{17-147c}$$

To ensure that we have sufficient gain, let us choose $b = 1$. Then, from Eq. 17-147b,

$$\frac{R_B}{R_A} = \frac{100}{199} = 0.5025$$

$$\mathbf{K} = 10\left(1 + \frac{1}{0.5025}\right) = 29.9$$

Let us choose $C = 0.1\ \mu\text{F}$. Then,

$$R_1 = 10^6 \text{ ohms}$$

and

$$R_2 = 10^6 \text{ ohms}$$

Let us choose $R_A = 10{,}000$ ohms. Then,

$$R_B = 5025 \text{ ohms}$$

Thus, the design has been completed.

Note that the design using the Thomas biquad is simpler since there is always an independent resistance that can be varied to obtain the desired parameter. This is not only a computational advantage. After the filter is built, the values of the parameters such as Q_{eff} and ω_0 must be adjusted. This is usually done by adjusting the resistances. In the Thomas biquad, if this is done in the proper order with the proper resistance, each parameter can be adjusted without changing the values that have already been adjusted. On the other hand, with the filter discussed in this section, there will be some interaction between Q_{eff} and $\mathbf{K}$. However, this may not be serious and the filter discussed here uses far fewer elements and operational amplifiers.

Sensitivity with Respect to Operational Amplifier Gain

If the exact expression for the gain of the Delyiannis circuit is computed, we can obtain

$$S_{|\mathbf{A}_v|}^{\omega_0} \simeq S_{|\mathbf{A}_v|}^{Q_{\text{eff}}} \simeq \frac{1}{2} \frac{\omega_0}{\mathbf{A}_{\text{mid}}\,\omega_\alpha} \frac{(1 + R_B/R_A)^2}{(R_B/R_A)^2} \sqrt{\frac{R_2 C_1}{R_1 C_2}} \tag{17-148}$$

where we have assumed that the gain of the operational amplifier is $\mathbf{A}_{\text{mid}}/(1 + j\omega/\omega_\alpha)$, where ω_α is very small (see Sec. 17-9). Again, we see that the sensitivity will be small if $\mathbf{A}_{v\,\text{mid}}$ is large. Note that, as in Sec. 17-9, if $\omega_0 \gg \omega_\alpha$ the sensitivity can become large.

If $C_1 = C_2 = C$, then Eq. 17-148 becomes

$$S_{|\mathbf{A}_v|}^{\omega_0} \simeq S_{|\mathbf{A}_v|}^{Q_{\text{eff}}} \simeq \frac{1}{2} \frac{\omega_0}{\mathbf{A}_{v\,\text{mid}}\,\omega_\alpha} \frac{(1 + R_B/R_A)^2}{(R_B/R_A)^2} \sqrt{b} \tag{17-149}$$

Proper choice of $\sqrt{b}$ and R_B/R_A can minimize these sensitivities.

17-11. BUTTERWORTH FILTER CHARACTERISTICS

We shall now discuss procedures for obtaining bandpass filter characteristics. We have thus far considered bandpass circuits wherein all the stages were tuned to the same frequency. This is called *synchronous tuning*. Although this is simple, it does not always lead to the simplest filters, since the number of stages used may be excessive. In the next three sections we shall consider procedures for obtaining bandpass amplifiers wherein the resonant frequencies of the tuned circuits are not all the same. This is called *stagger tuning*. Simpler filters often result when this procedure is used.

Actually, in this and the next section we shall consider low-pass amplifiers, or low-pass filters, rather than bandpass filters. We shall see in Sec. 17-13 that once a low-pass filter is obtained, it is a relatively simple matter to convert it to a bandpass filter.

The design specifications for low-pass filters which correspond to Fig. 17-1b are shown in Fig. 17-20. Note that the pass band, stop band, and transition band correspond to those in the bandpass filter. Now the pass band lies in the range of frequency from $f = 0$ to $f = f_c$. The stop band is those frequencies for which $f \geqq f_r$.

Butterworth Polynomials

We shall now consider a set of polynomials which provide us with the desired filter functions. (In the next section we shall consider another set.) The *Butterworth polynomials* are polynomials of order n whose magnitude is given by

$$\left|B_n\left(\frac{\omega}{\omega_a}\right)\right| = \sqrt{1 + \left(\frac{\omega}{\omega_a}\right)^{2n}} \tag{17-150}$$

We form low-pass filters by taking the reciprocal of these polynomials.

$$\left|\frac{\mathbf{A}_v}{\mathbf{A}_{v0}}\right| = \frac{1}{\sqrt{1 + (\omega/\omega_a)^{2n}}} \tag{17-151}$$

A plot of this function is shown in Fig. 17-21. Equation 17-151 is said to define a *Butterworth polynomial filter*. As n increases, $|\mathbf{A}_v/\mathbf{A}_{v0}|$ becomes closer to 1 for $\omega < \omega_a$, and $|\mathbf{A}_v/\mathbf{A}_{v0}|$ falls off more sharply for $\omega > \omega_a$. When $\omega = \omega_a$, $|\mathbf{A}_v/\mathbf{A}_{v0}| = 1/\sqrt{2}$ regardless of n.

Equation 17-150 gives the magnitude of the Butterworth polynomial. In Table 17-1 we list the actual polynomials. We have replaced $j\omega$ by the Laplace transform variable s here.

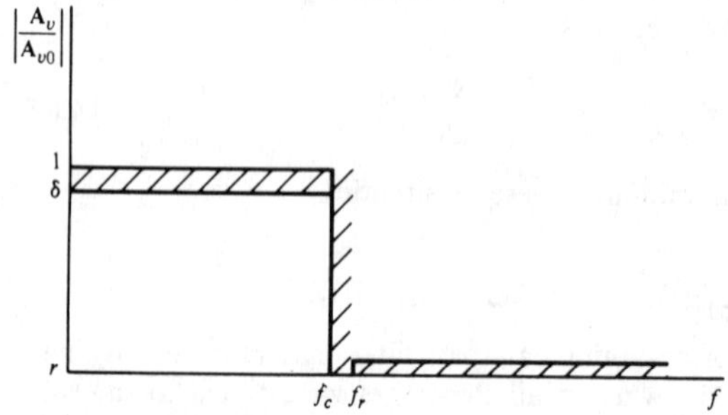

Figure 17-20. The design specifications for a low-pass filter.

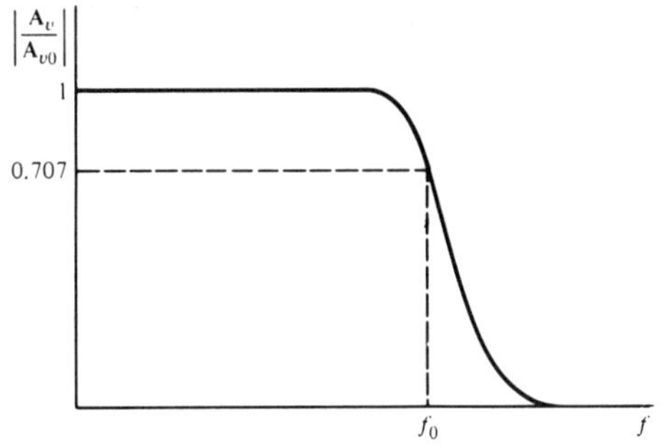

Figure 17-21. Plot of a typical Butterworth polynomial filter.

Let us consider how we can design a low-pass filter using Butterworth polynomials. In order to actually realize this filter we could factor the denominator and determine the pole locations. Then, either procedure of the last two sections could be used to realize the filter. (We shall illustrate this later in this section.) Note that a single filter section of the type shown in Figs 17-16 and 17-19 will realize a pair of complex conjugate poles. Thus, we require three filter sections. If n were odd, then there would be a pole that lies

Table 17-1 BUTTERWORTH POLYNOMIALS

Order	Polynomial
1	$\frac{s}{\omega_a} + 1$
2	$1 + 1.414\frac{s}{\omega_a} + \left(\frac{s}{\omega_a}\right)^2$
3	$1 + 2\frac{s}{\omega_a} + 2\left(\frac{s}{\omega_a}\right)^2 + \left(\frac{s}{\omega_a}\right)^3$
4	$1 + 2.613\frac{s}{\omega_a} + 3.414\left(\frac{s}{\omega_a}\right)^2 + 2.613\left(\frac{s}{\omega_a}\right)^3 + \left(\frac{s}{\omega_a}\right)^4$
5	$1 + 3.236\left(\frac{s}{\omega_a}\right) + 5.236\left(\frac{s}{\omega_a}\right)^2 + 5.236\left(\frac{s}{\omega_a}\right)^3 s + 3.236\left(\frac{s}{\omega_a}\right)^4 + \left(\frac{s}{\omega_a}\right)^5$
6	$1 + 3.864\left(\frac{s}{\omega_a}\right) + 7.464\left(\frac{s}{\omega_a}\right)^2 + 9.141\left(\frac{s}{\omega_a}\right)^3 + 7.464\left(\frac{s}{\omega_a}\right)^4 + 3.864\left(\frac{s}{\omega_a}\right)^5 + \left(\frac{s}{\omega_a}\right)^6$
7	$1 + 4.494\left(\frac{s}{\omega_a}\right) + 10.098\left(\frac{s}{\omega_a}\right)^2 + 14.592\left(\frac{s}{\omega_a}\right)^3 + 14.592\left(\frac{s}{\omega_a}\right)^4 + 10.098\left(\frac{s}{\omega_a}\right)^5 + 4.494\left(\frac{s}{\omega_a}\right)^6 + \left(\frac{s}{\omega_a}\right)^7$
8	$1 + 5.153\left(\frac{s}{\omega_a}\right) + 13.137\left(\frac{s}{\omega_a}\right)^2 + 21.846\left(\frac{s}{\omega_a}\right)^3 + 25.688\left(\frac{s}{\omega_a}\right)^4 + 21.846\left(\frac{s}{\omega_a}\right)^5 + 13.137\left(\frac{s}{\omega_a}\right)^6 + 5.153\left(\frac{s}{\omega_a}\right)^7 + \left(\frac{s}{\omega_a}\right)^8$

on the negative σ axis. This could be realized by a special filter section that only produces a single pole. Alternatively, we can always increase the degree of the filter by one. This will not be a problem when we consider bandpass filters.

Poles of Butterworth Filters

It appears as though factoring the Butterworth polynomial to obtain the poles is a tedious procedure but this is not the case. The roots of a Butterworth polynomial can be found easily. We write a Butterworth polynomial in factored form as

$$B_n\left(\frac{s}{\omega_a}\right)(s - s_1)(s - s_2)\cdots(s - s_n) \qquad (17\text{-}152)$$

Then, the roots are given by

$$s_k = \sigma_k \pm j\omega k$$

where

$$\sigma_k = \omega_a \cos\left[\frac{\pi}{2} + \frac{2k+1}{n}\frac{\pi}{2}\right] \qquad k = 0, 1, \ldots, n-1 \qquad (17\text{-}153a)$$

$$\omega_k = \omega_a \sin\left[\frac{\pi}{2} + \frac{2k+1}{n}\frac{\pi}{2}\right] \qquad k = 0, 1, \ldots, n-1 \qquad (17\text{-}153b)$$

The roots all lie on a circle of radius ω_a. Each root is separated from its neighbor by an angle of π/n rad. The pole locations are shown in Fig. 17-22. Thus the poles can easily be obtained.

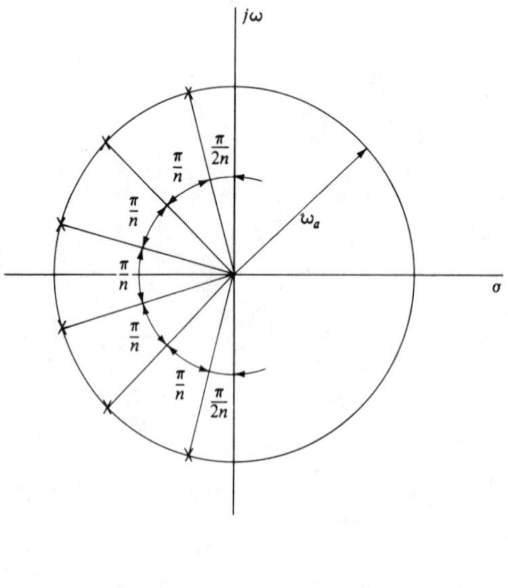

Figure 17-22. An illustration of Butterworth filter pole locations.

Example

Let us obtain the pole locations for the poles of the previous example of this section.

$$\sigma_k = \omega_a \cos\left(\frac{\pi}{2} + \frac{2k+1}{6}\frac{\pi}{2}\right) \quad k = 0, 1, 2$$

$$\omega_k = \pm\omega_a \sin\left(\frac{\pi}{2} + \frac{2k+1}{n}\frac{\pi}{2}\right)$$

Substituting we obtain

$$s_{1,4} = \omega_a(-0.259 \pm j0.966)$$

$$s_{2,5} = \omega_a(-0.707 \pm j0.707)$$

$$s_{3,6} = \omega_a(-0.966 \pm j0.259)$$

Note that $\omega_a = 2\pi fa$. Hence, $\omega_a = 71{,}911$ rad/s.

We have specified the amplifier gain in terms of ω_0 and Q_{eff}. Each pair of complex conjugate poles will be realized by a single amplifier stage. We will now relate Q_{eff} and ω_0 for that stage to the location of a pair of complex conjugate poles. Let us assume that we are to obtain an amplifier with the poles

$$s_{k1,k2} = \sigma_k \pm j\omega_k \tag{17-154}$$

The gain of the amplifier stage will be

$$\mathbf{A}_{vk} = \frac{\mathbf{K}_k}{s^2 + (\omega_{0k}/Q_{\text{eff},k})s + \omega_{0k}^2} \tag{17-155}$$

Then, (see Eq. 17-34) the poles of this amplifier are

$$s_{k1,k2} = -\frac{\omega_{0k}}{2Q_{\text{eff},k}} \pm j\omega_{0k}\sqrt{1 - \frac{1}{4Q_{\text{eff},k}^2}}$$

Hence,

$$\sigma_k = \frac{-\omega_{0k}}{2Q_{\text{eff},k}} \tag{17-156a}$$

and

$$\omega_k = \omega_{0k}\sqrt{1 - \frac{1}{4Q_{\text{eff},k}^2}} \tag{17-156b}$$

Solving this pair of equations, we have

$$\omega_{0k} = \sqrt{\omega_k^2 + \sigma_k^2} \tag{17-157a}$$

$$Q_{\text{eff},k} = -\frac{\sqrt{\omega_k^2 + \sigma_k^2}}{2\sigma_k} = -\frac{\omega_{0k}}{2\sigma_k} \tag{17-157b}$$

Example

Determine the values of Q_{eff} and ω_0 for each pair of pole locations determined in the previous example of this section.

Substituting the pole locations in Eq. 17-157, we have

$$\omega_{01} = \omega_a$$

$$Q_{\text{eff},1} = 1.93$$

$$\omega_{02} = \omega_a$$

$$Q_{\text{eff},2} = 0.707$$

$$\omega_{03} = \omega_a$$

$$Q_{\text{eff},3} = 0.517$$

Remember that $\omega_a = 71.911$ rad/s.

We now can realize the low-pass amplifier using the circuits of Fig. 17-16 or 17-19. Hence, we can cascade three Thomas biquads or three Friend filters to obtain the desired amplifier.

17-12. THE CHEBYSHEV FILTER CHARACTERISTIC

There is another filter characteristic, the *Chebyshev filter*, which, in general, will use far fewer amplifier stages than the Butterworth filters. The response of the Chebyshev in the pass band is not as smooth as that of the Butterworth filter. The phase shift of the Butterworth filter is also somewhat more linear than that of the Chebyshev filter.

The Chebyshev filter utilizes a set of polynomials called *Chebyshev polynomials.* Some of these are listed in Table 17-2. The Chebyshev polynomials $T_n(\omega/\omega_a)$ have the following property. For

$$-1 \leqq \frac{\omega}{\omega_a} \leqq 1$$

they "ripple" between -1 and 1. That is,

$$-1 \leqq T_n\left(\frac{\omega}{\omega_a}\right) \leqq 1$$

For $(\omega/\omega_a) > 1$, $|T_n(\omega/\omega_a)| > 1$ and increases monotonically as $|\omega/\omega_a|$ increases. Two Chebyshev polynomials are plotted in Fig. 17-23.

The form of the Chebyshev filter function is

$$\left|\frac{\mathbf{A}_v}{\mathbf{A}_{v0}}\right| = \frac{1}{\sqrt{1 + \varepsilon^2 T_n^2(f/f_c)}} \tag{17-158}$$

Table 17-2 CHEBYSHEV POLYNOMIALS

Order	Polynomial
0	1
1	$\dfrac{\omega}{\omega_a}$
2	$2\left(\dfrac{\omega}{\omega_a}\right)^2 - 1$
3	$4\left(\dfrac{\omega}{\omega_a}\right)^3 - 3\left(\dfrac{\omega}{\omega_a}\right)$
4	$8\left(\dfrac{\omega}{\omega_a}\right)^4 - 8\left(\dfrac{\omega}{\omega_a}\right)^2 + 1$
5	$16\left(\dfrac{\omega}{\omega_a}\right)^5 - 20\left(\dfrac{\omega}{\omega_a}\right)^3 + 5\left(\dfrac{\omega}{\omega_a}\right)$
6	$32\left(\dfrac{\omega}{\omega_a}\right)^6 - 48\left(\dfrac{\omega}{\omega_a}\right)^4 + 18\left(\dfrac{\omega}{\omega_a}\right)^2 - 1$
7	$64\left(\dfrac{\omega}{\omega_a}\right)^7 - 112\left(\dfrac{\omega}{\omega_a}\right)^5 + 56\left(\dfrac{\omega}{\omega_a}\right)^3 - 7\left(\dfrac{\omega}{\omega_a}\right)$
8	$128\left(\dfrac{\omega}{\omega_a}\right)^8 - 256\left(\dfrac{\omega}{\omega_a}\right)^6 + 160\left(\dfrac{\omega}{\omega_a}\right)^4 - 32\left(\dfrac{\omega}{\omega_a}\right)^2 + 1$

Note that we set $f_a = f_c$. This response has the form shown in Fig. 17-24. This is called an *equiripple* response. Let us relate Eq. 17-158 to the filter characteristic. For $0 \leqq f \leqq f_c$, $-1 \leqq T_n(f/f_c) \leqq 1$. Therefore,

$$\frac{1}{\sqrt{1+\varepsilon^2}} \leqq \left|\frac{\mathbf{A}_v}{\mathbf{A}_{v0}}\right| \leqq 1 \tag{17-159}$$

Hence,

$$\gamma = \frac{1}{\sqrt{1+\varepsilon^2}} \tag{17-160a}$$

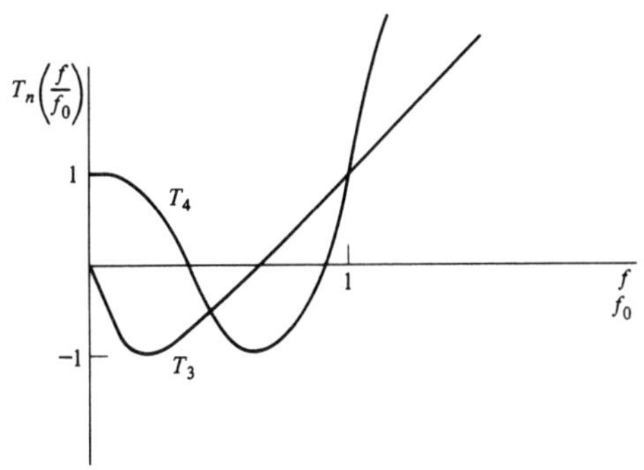

Figure 17-23. Plots of two Chebychev polynomials.

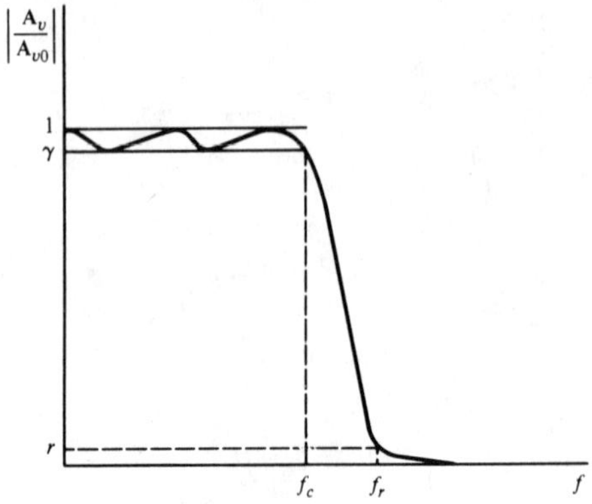

Figure 17-24. A typical Chebyshev filter characteristic.

or, equivalently,

$$\varepsilon = \sqrt{\frac{1}{\gamma^2} - 1} \tag{17-160b}$$

Outside of the pass band (i.e., for $f > f_c$), the Chebyshev polynomial increases very rapidly so $|\mathbf{A}_v/\mathbf{A}_{v0}|$ falls off at a very rapid rate. As the degree of the polynomial increases, this rate of falloff increases. The degree of the Chebyshev polynomial which is required depends upon r and the ratio f_r/f_c. A study of the Chebyshev polynomial indicates that

$$r = \frac{1}{\sqrt{1 + \varepsilon^2 \cosh^2[n \cosh^{-1}(f_r/f_c)]}} \tag{17-161}$$

Manipulating this equation we have

$$n = \frac{\cosh^{-1}[\sqrt{(1/r^2 - 1)}/\varepsilon]}{\cosh^{-1}(f_r/f_c)} \tag{17-162}$$

Example

Obtain a low-pass filter with a Chebyshev polynomial which meets the following specifications.

$$0.9 \leq \left|\frac{\mathbf{A}_v}{\mathbf{A}_{v0}}\right| \leq 1 \qquad \text{for} \quad 0 \leq f \leq 10{,}000 \text{ Hz}$$

$$\left|\frac{\mathbf{A}_v}{\mathbf{A}_{v0}}\right| \leq 0.05 \quad \text{for} \quad f > 20{,}000 \text{ Hz}$$

Then, from Eq. 17-160

$$\varepsilon = \frac{1}{0.9^2} - 1 = 0.234$$

and from Eq. 18-162,

$$n = \frac{\cosh^{-1}[\sqrt{(1/0.05)^2 - 1}/0.234]}{\cosh^{-1}(2)} = \frac{\cosh^{-1} 85.4}{\cosh^{-1} 2} = \frac{5.14}{1.32} = 3.89$$

Thus, we use $n = 4$. The amplifier gain is then given by

$$\left|\frac{\mathbf{A}_v}{\mathbf{A}_{v0}}\right|^2 = \frac{1}{1 + 0.234^2[8(f/10{,}000)^4 - 8(f/10{,}000)^2 + 1]^2}$$

The Chebyshev filter we designed in this section is of fourth order. In the last section we realized the same filter requirements using a Butterworth filter but a sixth order filter was required. Hence, the Butterworth realization required three sections to realize it, whereas the Chebyshev realization only required two. In general, fewer stages will be required with the Chebyshev filter. At times, the savings in the number of stages is considerably greater when the Chebyshev filter is used.

Poles of the Chebyshev Filter

A detailed study of the poles of the Chebyshev filter indicates that the following are its pole locations.

$$\sigma_k = \omega_c \cos\left[\frac{\pi}{2} + \frac{2k+1}{n}\frac{\pi}{2}\right]\sinh\left[\frac{1}{n}\sinh^{-1}\frac{1}{\varepsilon}\right] \qquad k = 0, 1, \ldots, n-1 \qquad (17\text{-}163a)$$

$$\omega_k = \omega_c \sin\left[\frac{\pi}{2} + \frac{2k+1}{n}\frac{\pi}{2}\right]\cosh\left[\frac{1}{n}\sinh^{-1}\frac{1}{\varepsilon}\right] \qquad k = 0, 1, \ldots, n-1 \qquad (17\text{-}163b)$$

where

$$\omega_c = 2\pi f_c \qquad (17\text{-}163c)$$

Typical pole locations are plotted in Fig. 17-25. The poles lie on an ellipse whose major axis is $2\omega_c \cosh(1/n)\sinh^{-1}(1/\varepsilon)$ and whose minor axis is $2\omega_c \sinh(1/n)\sinh^{-1}(1/\varepsilon)$.

Example

Obtain the pole locations for the Chebyshev filter of the previous example. Then, for the fourth order Chebyshev filter, we have

$$s_{1,3} = \omega_c(-0.217 \pm j1.062)$$

$$s_{2,4} = \omega_c(-0.523 \pm j0.440)$$

where $\omega_c = 2\pi \times 10{,}000 = 62{,}800$ rad/s.

The realization of $Q_{\mathrm{eff},k}$ and ω_0 for each amplifier section are determined using the procedure discussed in the last section. Thus, this filter can be realized by a cascade of two stages of the type shown in Figs. 17-16 or 17-19.

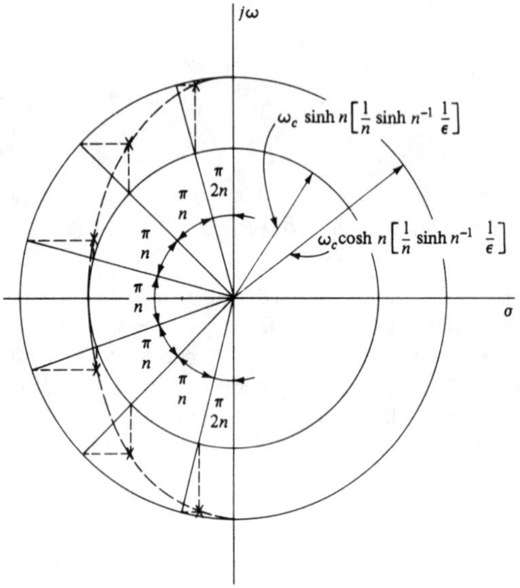

Figure 17-25. Chebyshev filter pole locations.

17-13. THE LOW-PASS–BANDPASS TRANSFORMATION

We have developed procedures for obtaining low-pass filters. In this section we shall develop a procedure called a *low-pass–bandpass transformation* which will enable us to easily obtain bandpass filters from low-pass filters. Suppose that we want to obtain a bandpass filter whose specifications are the type shown in Fig. 17-1b. That is,

$$\delta < \left|\frac{\mathbf{A}_v}{\mathbf{V}_{v0}}\right| \leqq 1 \qquad f_{c1} \leqq f \leqq f_{c2} \tag{17-164a}$$

$$\left|\frac{\mathbf{A}_v}{\mathbf{A}_{v0}}\right| \leqq r \qquad f_{r1} > f \quad \text{and} \quad f > f_{r2} \tag{17-164b}$$

where

$$f_{c1} f_{c2} = f_{r1} f_{r2} = f_b^2 \tag{17-165}$$

Note that we have used f_b rather than f_0 here since f_0 has also been used as the "resonant frequency" of a specific amplifier.

To obtain the desired bandpass characteristic we shall first obtain a suitable low-pass characteristic called the *low-pass prototype* and then convert it to a bandpass characteristic. Let us see how this can be done.

Suppose that we realize a low-pass characteristic (e.g., Butterworth or Chebyshev) which meets the following specifications.

$$\delta \leqq |F(j\omega)| \leqq 1 \qquad f \leqq f_{CL} \tag{17-166a}$$

$$|F(j\omega)| \leqq r \qquad f > f_{RL} \tag{17-166b}$$

where

$$f_{CL} = f_{c2} - f_{c1} \tag{17-167a}$$

$$f_{RL} = f_{r2} - f_{r1} \tag{17-167b}$$

Now suppose that, in the low-pass filter function $F(j\omega)$, we replace $j\omega$ by $j\omega + (\omega_b^2/j\omega)$. This will give us the desired bandpass characteristic. Let us demonstrate this. Consider the function

$$F\left[j\left(\omega - \frac{\omega_b^2}{\omega}\right)\right]$$

When $\omega = \omega_b$, $\omega - (\omega_b^2/\omega) = 0$. Thus, $\omega = 0$ in the original function corresponds to $\omega = \omega_b$ in the new function. Hence, $\omega = \omega_b$ will lie in the pass band of the new function.

Let us define the edges of the pass band. This occurs at those values of ω which satisfy

$$\omega - \frac{\omega_b^2}{\omega} = \pm\omega_{CL} \tag{17-168a}$$

or, equivalently at those values of f which satisfy

$$f - \frac{f_b^2}{f} = \pm f_{CL} \tag{17-168b}$$

Note the $\pm$ sign. The plus sign is used when $f > f_b$ and the minus sign is used when $f < f_b$. Note that $|F|$ is an even function of ω. Then, Eq. 17-168b represents the two equations

$$f^2 \mp f_{CL}f - f_b^2 = 0 \tag{17-169}$$

Solving these equations and taking the positive roots, we have

$$f_{c2} = \frac{f_{CL} + \sqrt{f_{CL}^2 + 4f_b^2}}{2} \tag{17-170a}$$

$$f_{c1} = \frac{-f_{CL} + \sqrt{f_{CL}^2 + 4f_b^2}}{2} \tag{17-170b}$$

Then

$$B_\gamma = f_{c2} - f_{c1} = f_{CL} \tag{17-171}$$

Also,

$$f_{c1} f_{c2} = f_b^2 \tag{17-172}$$

Thus, the pass band will be placed with geometric symmetry about f_b. The bandwidth is the same as that of the low-pass prototype.

In a similar way if we determine the frequency that corresponds to the rejection band of the low-pass prototype, we have

$$f - \frac{f_b^2}{f} = \pm f_{RL} \tag{17-173}$$

Manipulating, we obtain

$$f_{r2} - f_{r1} = f_{RL} \tag{17-174}$$

$$f_{r2} f_{r1} = f_b^2 \tag{17-175}$$

Thus, if we have a low-pass prototype of the type defined in Eqs. 17-166 and we replace $j\omega$ by $j\omega + (\omega_b^2/j\omega)$, we shall obtain a bandpass filter. The bandwidth B_γ will equal f_{CL} and the response in the pass band will lie between 1 and γ just as in the low-pass prototype. The stop band is as defined in Eq. 17-175 and will correspond to the low-pass prototype.

We use the poles of the filter function to realize each amplifier stage. Let us see how the low-pass–bandpass transformation changes the pole location.

Suppose that the low-pass prototype has a filter function

$$\mathbf{F}(s) = 1/[(s - s_1)(s - s_2)\cdots(s - s_n)] \tag{17-176}$$

In terms of the Laplace transform variables, the low-pass–bandpass transformation becomes

$$j\omega + \omega_b^2/j\omega \rightarrow s + \omega_b^2/s \tag{17-177}$$

Now let us see what happens to each pole.

$$\frac{1}{s - s_k} \rightarrow \frac{1}{(s + \omega_b^2/s - s_k)} = \frac{s}{s^2 - s_k s + \omega_b^2} \tag{17-178}$$

The roots of $s^2 - s_k s + \omega_b^2$ are

$$s_{k1,k2} = \frac{s_k}{2} \pm j\sqrt{\omega_b^2 - \frac{s_k^2}{4}} \tag{17-179}$$

Hence, for each pole the low-pass–bandpass transformation results in

$$\frac{1}{s - s_k} \rightarrow \frac{s}{(s - s_{k1})(s - s_{k2})} \tag{17-180}$$

Thus, each pole in the prototype low-pass filter becomes a pair of poles in the bandpass filter. In addition for each pole in the prototype low-pass filter, there is a zero at $s = 0$ in the bandpass filter.

Often,

$$\omega_b \gg s_k \tag{17-181}$$

Then, Eq. 17-179 becomes

$$s_{k1,k2} = \frac{s_k}{2} \pm j\omega_b \tag{17-182}$$

Thus, the poles at s_k are divided by 2 and then translated by $\pm j\omega_b$. (Note that s_k will, in general, be a complex number.) In Fig. 17-26 we illustrate this procedure. Figure 17-26a illustrates the pole locations of a sixth order Butterworth low-pass prototype filter. In Fig. 17-26b the pole-zero diagram of the resulting bandpass filter is shown. Each pole of Fig. 17-26a results in two poles and a zero in Fig. 17-26b. Thus, the bandpass filter has 6 zeros at the origin and 12 poles (6 complex conjugate pairs).

(a)

(b)

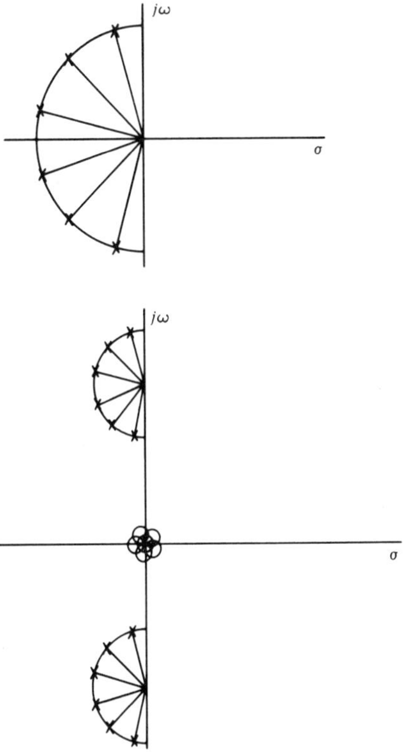

Figure 17-26. An illustration of low-pass bandpass transformation. (a) Low-pass prototype. (b) Bandpass filter.

Example

Obtain the pole zero locations for a bandpass Chebyshev filter with the following characteristics.

Pass band:

$$0.9 \leqq \left|\frac{\mathbf{A}_v}{\mathbf{A}_{v0}}\right| \leqq 1 \qquad \text{for} \quad 0.995 \leqq f \leqq 1.005 \times 10^6$$

$$\left|\frac{\mathbf{A}_v}{\mathbf{A}_{v0}}\right| \leqq 0.05 \qquad \text{for} \quad f \leqq 0.99 \times 10^6 \quad \text{and} \quad f \geqq 1.01 \times 10^6$$

The first step is to obtain a low-pass prototype. Its characteristics are Bandwidth:

$$B_\gamma = 1.005 \times 10^6 - 0.995 \times 10^6 = 10{,}000 \text{ Hz}$$

Similarly,

$$0.99 \times 10^6 - 1.01 \times 10^6 = 20{,}000 \text{ Hz}$$

Thus, we start by obtaining a low-pass prototype with the characteristics

$$0.9 \leqq \left|\frac{\mathbf{A}_{vP}}{\mathbf{A}_{v0P}}\right| \leqq 1 \qquad 0 \leqq f \leqq 10{,}000 \text{ Hz}$$

$$|\mathbf{A}_{vP}| \leqq 0.05 \qquad \text{for} \quad f > 20{,}000 \text{ Hz}$$

The pole locations for this prototype were obtained in Sec. 18-12. Hence, the prototype pole locations are

$$s_{P1,P3} = 62{,}800(-0.217 \pm j1.062) = -13.627 \pm j66{,}693$$

$$s_{P2,P4} = 62{,}800(-0.523 \pm j0.440) = -32{,}844 \pm j27{,}632$$

Now let us obtain the bandpass filter.

$$f_b = 10^6\sqrt{0.995 \times 1.005} = 10^6 \text{ Hz} \quad \text{and} \quad \omega_b = 6.28 \times 10^6$$

In general,

$$\omega_b \gg |s_{Pk}|$$

Hence, the approximation of Eq. 17-182 can be used. Thus, the pole locations are

$$s_1 = \frac{-13{,}627 + j63{,}693}{2} + j6.28 \times 10^6 = -6813 + j6.312 \times 10^6$$

$$s_8 = -6813 - j6.312 \times 10^6$$

$$s_2 = \frac{-13{,}627 - j63{,}693}{2} + j6.28 \times 10^6 = -6813 + j6.248 \times 10^6$$

$$s_7 = -6813 - j6.248 \times 10^6$$

$$s_3 = \frac{32{,}844 + j27{,}632}{2} + j6.28 \times 10^6 = 16{,}422 + j6.294 \times 10^6$$

$$s_6 = -16{,}422 - j6.294 \times 10^6$$

$$s_4 = \frac{-32{,}844 - j27{,}632}{2} + j6.28 \times 10^6 = -16{,}422 + 6.266 \times 10^6$$

$$s_5 = -16{,}422 - j6.266 \times 10^6$$

Then, the filter function is

$$\frac{\mathbf{A}_v}{\mathbf{A}_{v0}} = \frac{s^4}{(s - s_1)(s - s_1^*)(s - s_2)(s - s_2^*)(s - s_3)(s - s_3^*)(s - s_4)(s - s_4^*)}$$

The superscript asterisk (*) indicates complex conjugate. We can write the filter function of the previous example as

$$\frac{A_v}{\mathbf{A}_{v0}} = \left[\frac{s}{(s - s_1)(s - s_1^*)}\right]\left[\frac{s}{(s - s_2)(s - s_2^*)}\right]\left[\frac{s}{(s - s_3)(s - s_3^*)}\right]\left[\frac{s}{(s - s_4)(s - s_4^*)}\right] \tag{17-183}$$

Each bracketed term can be realized using a single conventional tuned amplifier such as that of Fig. 17-4. Thus there are four amplifiers in the cascade. Note that each amplifier is tuned to a different frequency and has a different Q_{eff}. The value of ω_{0k} and $Q_{eff,k}$ are found from the pole locations using the procedure at the end of Sec. 17-11. Thus, we can realize the bandpass amplifier of Eq. 17-183 using four stages of the type shown in Fig. 17-4. On the other hand, if we want to use active filters, we can cascade four stages of the type shown in Fig. 17-16 or Fig. 17-18.

PROBLEMS

17-1. Discuss the ideal bandpass characteristic of Fig. 17-1a. Relate this to the practical specifications of Fig. 17-1b.

17-2. The circuit of Fig. 17-2 has the following parameter values.

$$L = 50\ \mu\text{H}$$
$$C = 500\ \text{pF}$$
$$R = 20\ \text{ohms}$$

Determine **Z**, the input impedance and sketch it as a function of frequency.

17-3. Repeat Prob. 17-2 but now use

$$R = 0.2\ \text{ohms}$$

Compare the result with that of Prob. 17-2.

17-4. Repeat Prob. 17-3 but now use

$$R = 0.1\ \text{ohm}$$

17-5. Repeat Prob. 17-2 but now use

$$L = 100\ \mu\text{H}$$

Compare the result with that of Prob. 17-2.

17-6. Repeat Prob. 17-2 but now use

$$C = 1000\ \text{pF}$$

17-7. Why is substitution of Eq. 17-7 used with resonant circuits?

17-8. Find the half-power bandwidth for the circuit of Prob. 17-2.

17-9. Repeat Prob. 17-8 when $R = 0.2$ ohms.

17-10. Repeat Prob. 17-8 for $L = 100\ \mu$H.

17-11. Repeat Prob. 17-8 for $C = 1000$ pF.

17-12. The parameters of the amplifier of Fig. 17-4a are

$$L = 50\ \mu\text{H}$$
$$C = 500\ \text{pF}$$

The coil is such that

$$Q_0 = 200$$
$$R_i = 10{,}000\ \text{ohms}$$

The parameters of the FET are

$$g_m = 5000\ \mu\text{mho}$$
$$r_d = 50{,}000\ \text{ohms}$$

Compute the voltage gain $\mathbf{A}_v$ for the circuit and sketch it as a function of frequency.

17-13. Repeat Prob. 17-12 for the amplifier of Fig. 17-4b. The parameters of the transistor are

$$g_m = 75{,}000\ \mu\text{mho}$$
$$r_{bb'} = 100 \text{ ohms}$$
$$r_{b'e} = 900 \text{ ohms}$$
$$r_{ce} = 50{,}000 \text{ ohms}$$
$$C_{b'e} = 50 \text{ pF}$$
$$C_{b'c} = 2 \text{ pF}$$

17-14. Design a FET *RC*-coupled single-tuned bandpass amplifier that meets the following specifications.

$$\mathbf{A}_{v0} = 200$$

$$0.92 \leqq \left|\frac{\mathbf{A}_v}{\mathbf{A}_{v0}}\right| \leqq 1 \qquad \text{for} \quad 1.99 \times 10^6 \leqq f \leqq 2.01 \times 10^6$$

$$\left|\frac{\mathbf{A}_v}{\mathbf{A}_{v0}}\right| \leqq 0.4 \qquad \text{for} \quad f > 2.3 \times 10^6 \quad \text{and} \quad f_c < 1.7 \times 10^6$$

Use one or more FET's with the following parameters.

$$g_m = 10{,}000\ \mu\text{mho}$$
$$r_d = 50{,}000 \text{ ohms}$$
$$C_{gs} = 2 \text{ pF}$$
$$C_{gd} = 0.2 \text{ pF}$$
$$C_{ds} = 0.5 \text{ pF}$$

Assume that the load impedance is a similar FET amplifier and that $Q_0 = 100$.

17-15. Design a transistor *RC*-coupled single-tuned amplifier that meets the following specifications

$$\mathbf{A}_{v0} = 200$$

$$0.92 \leqq \left|\frac{\mathbf{A}_v}{\mathbf{A}_{v0}}\right| \leqq 1 \qquad \text{for} \quad 1.99 \times 10^6 \leqq f \leqq 2.01 \times 10^6$$

$$\left|\frac{\mathbf{A}_v}{\mathbf{A}_{v0}}\right| \leqq 0.4 \qquad \text{for} \quad f > 2.3 \times 10^6 \quad \text{and} \quad f < 1.7 \times 10^6$$

Use one or more transistors with the following parameters.

$$g_m = 75{,}000\ \mu\text{mho}$$
$$r_{bb'} = 100 \text{ ohms}$$
$$r_{b'e} = 900 \text{ ohms}$$
$$r_{ce} = 75{,}000 \text{ ohms}$$
$$C_{b'e} = 50 \text{ pF}$$
$$C_{b'c} = 2 \text{ pF}$$

Note that a tapped inductance may have to be used here. Assume that the load impedance is a similar transistor amplifier and that $Q_0 = 100$.

17-16. Repeat the design of Prob. 17-14 but now change the specifications in the following way.

$$\left|\frac{\mathbf{A}_v}{\mathbf{A}_{v0}}\right| \leqq 0.01 \quad \text{in the stop band}$$

17-17. Repeat the design of Prob. 17-15 but now change the specifications in the following way

$$\left|\frac{\mathbf{A}_v}{\mathbf{A}_{v0}}\right| \leqq 0.01 \quad \text{in the stop band}$$

17-18. Discuss the advantages and disadvantages of adding shunt capacitance to a tuned amplifier.

17-19. Repeat the design of Prob. 17-14 but now use the mutual inductance coupled circuit of Fig. 17-10b.

17-20. Repeat the design of Prob. 17-15 but now use the mutual inductance coupled circuit of Fig. 17-10a.

17-21. Repeat the design of Prob. 17-19 but now change the specifications in the following way

$$\left|\frac{\mathbf{A}_v}{\mathbf{A}_{v0}}\right| \leqq 0.01 \quad \text{in the stop band}$$

17-22. Repeat the design of Prob. 17-20 but now change the specifications in the following way

$$\left|\frac{\mathbf{A}_v}{\mathbf{A}_{v0}}\right| \leqq 0.01 \quad \text{in the stop band}$$

17-23. Compare the three resonance curves shown in Fig. 17-12. What are the advantages of the curves plotted for $b > 1$?

17-24. The parameters of the circuit of Fig. 17-11a are

$$L_1 = L_2 = 50\ \mu\text{H}$$
$$C_1 = C_1 = 500\ \text{pF}$$
$$r = R_i = 50{,}000\ \text{ohms}$$
$$R_1 = R_2 = 5\ \text{ohms}$$

The tap is at the "top" of L_2. Compute the response of the circuit as a function of frequency for

$$b = 0.8$$
$$b = 1.0$$
$$b = 1.2$$

17-25. Why is the approximation of Eq. 17-88 used with the double-tuned circuit and not with the single-tuned circuits?

17-26. Design a double-tuned transistor amplifier that meets the following specifications.

$$|\mathbf{A}_{v0}| = 6000$$

$$0.95 \leqq \left|\frac{\mathbf{A}_v}{\mathbf{A}_{v0}}\right| \leqq 1 \qquad \text{for} \quad 0.995 \times 10^6 \leqq f \leqq 1.005 \times 10^6$$

$$\left|\frac{\mathbf{A}_v}{\mathbf{A}_{v0}}\right| \leqq 0.0005 \qquad \text{for} \quad f < 0.95 \times 10^6 \quad \text{and} \quad f > 1.05 \times 10^6$$

Use transistors with the following parameter values.

$$g_m = 75{,}000\ \mu\text{mho}$$
$$r_{bb'} = 100\ \text{ohms}$$
$$r_{b'e} = 900\ \text{ohms}$$
$$r_{ce} = 80{,}000\ \text{ohms}$$
$$C_{b'e} = 30\ \text{pF}$$
$$C_{b'c} = 2\ \text{pF}$$

Assume that the load is a similar transistor input and that the a of each coil is equal to 200.

17-27. Repeat Prob. 17-26 but now change the specifications in the following way.

$$\left|\frac{\mathbf{A}_v}{\mathbf{A}_{v0}}\right| \leqq 0.00001 \quad \text{in the stop band}$$

17-28. Design a double-tuned FET amplifier that meets the following specifications.

$$0.95 \leqq \left|\frac{\mathbf{A}_v}{\mathbf{A}_{v0}}\right| \leqq 1 \qquad \text{for} \quad 0.995 \times 10^6 \leqq f \leqq 1.005 \times 10^6$$

$$\left|\frac{\mathbf{A}_v}{\mathbf{A}_{v0}}\right| \leqq 0.0005 \qquad \text{for} \quad f < 0.95 \times 10^6 \quad \text{and} \quad f > 1.05 \times 10^6$$

Use FET's with the following parameter values.

$$g_m = 10{,}000\ \mu\text{mho}$$
$$r_d = 10{,}000\ \text{ohms}$$
$$C_{gs} = 2\ \text{pF}$$
$$C_{ds} = 0.5\ \text{pF}$$
$$C_{gd} = 0.5\ \text{pF}$$

Assume that the load is a similar FET stage.

17-29. Repeat Prob. 17-28 but now change the specifications in the following way.

$$\left|\frac{\mathbf{A}_v}{\mathbf{A}_{v0}}\right| \leqq 0.00001 \qquad \text{in the stop band}$$

17-30. Discuss why tuned amplifier circuits may have to be neutralized.

17-31. Discuss the operation of the circuits of Fig. 17-14.

17-32. Discuss the superhetrodyne principle.

17-33. What is meant by an image frequency? What is done to reduce interference by the image frequency?

17-34. What circuit produces most of the selectivity in a superhetrodyne receiver?

17-35. Use the Thomas biquad to realize the following amplifier.

$$\mathbf{A}_v = \frac{K}{s^2 + 0.4s + 400}$$

where $K \geqq 10$.

17-36. Repeat Prob. 17-35 but now realize

$$\mathbf{A}_v = \frac{K}{s^2 + 0.1s + 1000}$$

17-37. Repeat Prob. 17-36 but now realize

$$\mathbf{A}_v = \frac{Ks}{s^2 + 0.4s + 400}$$

17-38. Repeat Prob. 17-36 but now realize

$$\mathbf{A}_v = \frac{K_s}{s^2 + 0.1s + 1000}$$

17-39. If we desire $S^{Q_{eff}}_{|\mathbf{A}_{vT}|} \leqq 0.001$ for the amplifier of Prob. 17-35, what is the minimum value that $|\mathbf{A}_v|$ can have? Assume that all three operational amplifiers have identical gains and that they all vary simultaneously. Also assume that the operational amplifiers have very broad bandwidth.

17-40. Discuss how the operational amplifier's frequency response affects the result of Prob. 17-39.

17-41. Repeat Prob. 17-35 but now use the Friend filter.

17-42. Repeat Prob. 17-36 but now use the Friend filter.

17-43. Repeat Prob. 17-37 but now use the Delyiannis filter.

17-44. Repeat Prob. 17-38 but now use the Delyiannis filter.

17-45. Repeat Prob. 17-39 for the amplifier of Prob. 17-43.

17-46. Repeat Prob. 17-40 for the amplifier of Prob. 17-43.

17-47. Obtain the poles for the following low-pass filter characteristic.

$$0.9 \leqq \left|\frac{\mathbf{A}_v}{\mathbf{A}_{v0}}\right| \leqq 1 \qquad \text{for} \quad 0 \leqq f \leqq 15{,}000$$

$$\left|\frac{\mathbf{A}_v}{\mathbf{A}_{v0}}\right| \leqq 0.05 \qquad \text{for} \quad f > 40{,}000$$

Obtain the characteristic using a Butterworth filter

17-48. Modify the design of Prob. 17-47 so that

$$\left|\frac{\mathbf{A}_v}{\mathbf{A}_{v0}}\right| \leqq 0.001 \qquad \text{in the stop band.}$$

17-49. Realize the filter of Prob. 17-48 using Thomas biquads.

17-50. Realize the filter of Prob. 17-48 using Friend filters.

17-51. Repeat Prob. 17-47 but now use a Chebyshev filter characteristic.

17-52. Repeat Prob. 17-48 but now use a Chebyshev filter characteristic.

17-53. Realize the filter of Prob. 17-51 using Thomas biquads.

17-54. Realize the filter of Prob. 17-51 but now use Friend filters.

17-55. Obtain the poles and zeros of the bandpass amplifier whose specifications are given in Prob. 17-26. A Butterworth characteristic should be used.

17-56. Repeat Prob. 17-55 for the specifications of Prob. 17-27.

17-57. Repeat Prob. 17-55 but now use a Chebyshev characteristic.

17-58. Repeat Prob. 17-56 but now use a Chebyshev characteristic.

17-59. Design a *RC*-coupled transistor amplifier to realize the filter of Prob. 17-55. The parameters of the transistor are given in Prob. 17-26. The midband gain is to be equal to or greater than 1000.

17-60. Repeat Prob. 17-59 for the amplifier of Prob. 17-57.

17-61. Design a *RC*-coupled FET amplifier to meet the specifications of Prob. 17-55. The parameters of the FET are given in Prob. 17-28.

17-62. Repeat Prob. 17-61 for the amplifier of Prob. 17-57.

17-63. Repeat Prob. 17-55 but now divide all frequency specifications by 200. Then realize the network using Thomas biquads.

17-64. Repeat Prob. 17-63 but now use Delyiannis filters.

17-65. Repeat Prob. 17-57 but now divide all frequency specifications by 200. Then realize the network using Thomas biquads.

17-66. Repeat Prob. 17-65 but now use Delyiannis filters.

BIBLIOGRAPHY

Comer, D. J. *Modern Electronic Circuit Design*. Reading, Mass: Addison-Wesley, 1976, Chapter 12.

Daryanani, G. *Principles of Active Network Synthesis and Design*. New York: Wiley, 1976, Chapters 9 and 10.

Millman, J. *Microelectronics: Digital and Analog Circuits and Systems*. New York: McGraw-Hill, 1979, Chapter 16.

Chapter 18

Oscillators

There may be occasions when we want to produce a sinusoidal signal. One such case is the local oscillator in a superhetrodyne receiver. Test equipment and radio transmitters also require the generation of sinusoidal signals. The circuit that produces these signals is called a *sinusoidal oscillator*.

We do not always wish to generate a sinusoid. For instance, the clock in a digital circuit is an oscillator that produces rectangular pulses.

In this chapter we shall discuss oscillator circuits that produce various waveforms. Some techniques for shaping waveforms will also be discussed.

18-1. RF OSCILLATORS—CRITERIA FOR OSCILLATION

In this section we shall discuss some sinusoidal radio frequency (RF) oscillator circuits. Oscillators of this type are used in the approximate frequency range from 50 KH_z to 100 MHz (50,000–100 × 10^6 Hz).

We shall also develop a criterion for oscillation. Actually, we have already done this in Chapter 16. That is, the Nyquist or Routh–Hurwitz criteria can always be used. However, we can simplify these tests. The Nyquist plots of circuits, which are designed to be oscillators, are typically simple. The magnitude of the loop gain falls off monotonically as we depart from some frequency ω_0. The phase shift also varies monotonically about this point. Hence, if at some frequency ω_0, the loop gain $L(j\omega_0)$ is real and greater than 1, the amplifier will oscillate. That is, for these simple circuits, we can state that the circuit will oscillate if there is an ω_0 such that the loop gain

$$L(j\omega_o) = M \tag{18-1a}$$

where M is real and

$$M > 1 \tag{18-1b}$$

This is called the *Barkhausen criterion.* Actually, it states that the loop gain must exactly equal unity. However, M is usually made greater than 1 to ensure that the circuit will oscillate. We shall consider this in greater detail in Sec. 18-4.

In this section we shall develop another criterion that is also easy to apply. It actually is equivalent to Eq. 18-1. Note that our philosophy is the converse of that of Chapter 16. There we desired to design a feedback amplifier that did not oscillate. Here we want to ensure that the circuits we design do oscillate.

In Fig. 18-1 we show some types of RF oscillators. Basically, they consist of tuned amplifiers wherein we have included a feedback circuit. The feedback is positive since we desire that the circuits oscillate. In these diagrams, the capacitors C_A, C_B, and C_E are bypass capacitors and they will be considered to be short circuits at the signal frequency. The resistors R_B and R_C should be large. At times, the resistors are replaced by inductances which provide low-impedance paths for direct current, but they act as open circuits at the signal frequency. Such inductances are called *radio frequency chokes* (RFC). The tuned circuits consist of the inductances L_1 and L_2 or L, and C_1 and C_2 or C. We shall see that the frequency of oscillation is essentially determined by the resonant frequency of these circuits.

Let us now determine the criterion for oscillation. We could break the feedback loop, solve for the loop gain, and set it equal to unity but we shall consider an alternative, equivalent procedure.

Let us illustrate the procedure with two examples. We shall start with the circuit of Fig. 18-1a. Its model is given in Fig. 18-2. Note that R_1 and R_2 represent the coil resistances which are not shown in the schematic. We have used the low-frequency model here to simplify the equations. In the next example we shall use the high-frequency model. The mesh equations for this circuit are

$$\mu \mathbf{V}_{gs} = (r_d + R_1 + j\omega L_1)\mathbf{I}_1 + j\omega M \mathbf{I}_2 \tag{18-2a}$$

$$0 = j\omega M \mathbf{I}_1 + \left[R_2 + j\left(\omega L_2 - \frac{1}{\omega C}\right)\right]\mathbf{I}_2 \tag{18-2b}$$

$$\mathbf{V}_{gs} = -\frac{1}{j\omega C}\mathbf{I}_2 \tag{18-2c}$$

Manipulating, we have

$$0 = (r_d + R_1 + j\omega L_1)\mathbf{I}_1 + \left(\frac{\mu}{j\omega C} + j\omega M\right)\mathbf{I}_2 \tag{18-3a}$$

$$0 = +j\omega M \mathbf{I}_1 + \left[R_2 + j\left(\omega L_2 - \frac{1}{\omega C}\right)\right]\mathbf{I}_2 \tag{18-3b}$$

Now let us solve these equations in determinant form for I_2.

$$\mathbf{I}_2 = \frac{\begin{vmatrix} r_d + R_1 + j\omega L_1 & 0 \\ j\omega M & 0 \end{vmatrix}}{\begin{vmatrix} r_d + R_1 + j\omega L_1 & \dfrac{\mu}{j\omega C} + j\omega M \\ + j\omega M & R_2 + j\left(\omega L_2 - \dfrac{1}{\omega C}\right) \end{vmatrix}} \tag{18-4}$$

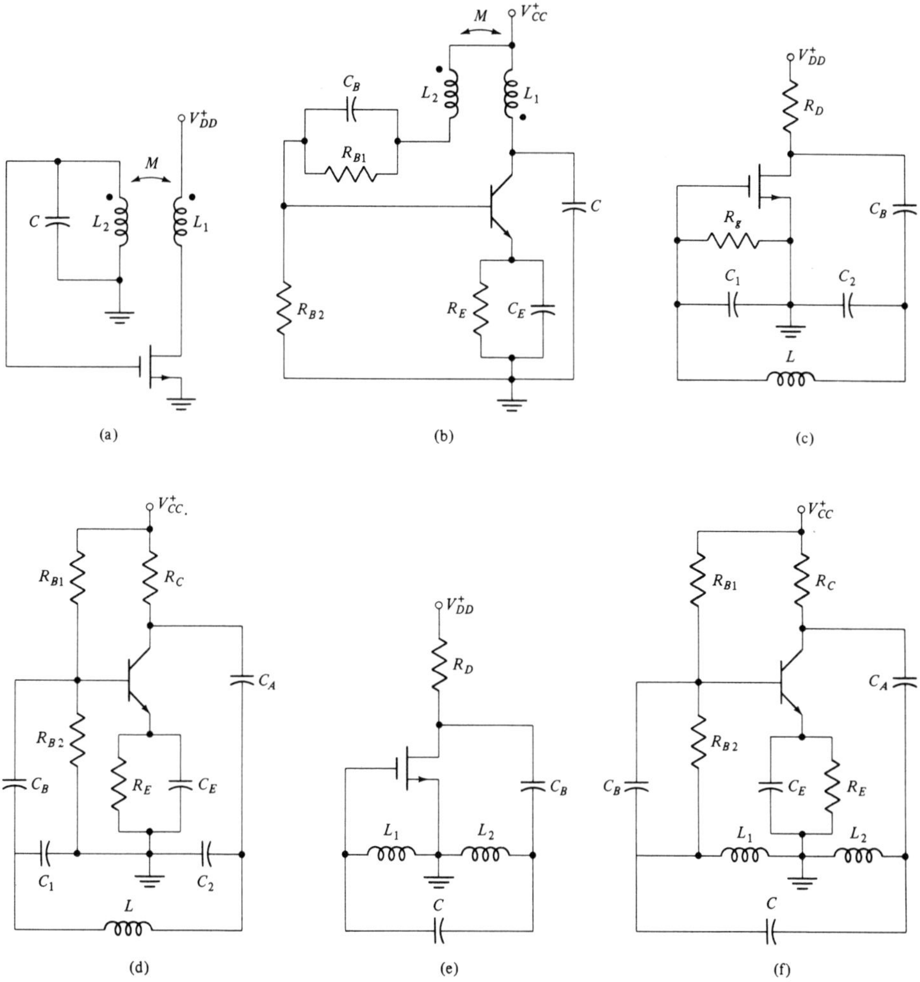

Figure 18-1. Radio frequency oscillator circuits. (a) Tuned input. (b) Tuned output. (c) and (d) Colpitts. (e) and (f) Hartley.

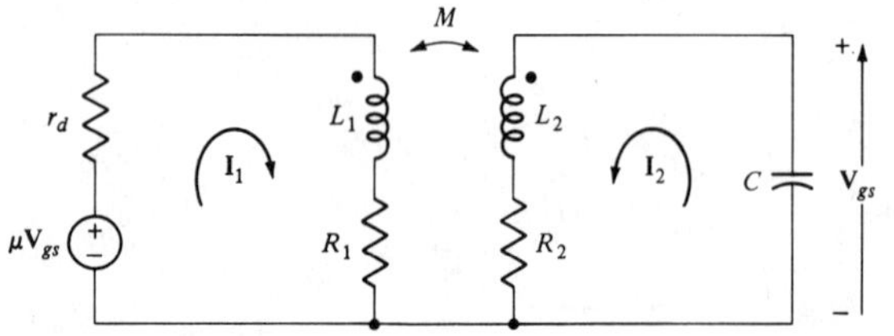

Figure 18-2. A model for the oscillator of Fig. 18-1a.

The numerator determinant will be zero. This is to be expected since the circuit is essentially an amplifier *without an input*. If there is to be an output, then the denominator determinant (i.e., the *characteristic determinant* or the *circuit determinant*) must be zero. Note that oscillation can be considered to be the production of an output when the input is zero. Hence, the condition for oscillation is

$$(r_d + R_1 + j\omega L_1)\left[R_2 + j\left(\omega L_2 - \frac{1}{\omega C}\right)\right] - j\omega M\left[\frac{\mu}{j\omega C} + j\omega M\right] = 0 \qquad (18\text{-}5)$$

Manipulating, we have

$$(r_d + R_1)R_2 - \omega L_1\left(\omega L_2 - \frac{1}{\omega C}\right) - \frac{\mu M}{C} + \omega^2 M^2 + j\left[\omega L_1 R_2 + (r_d + R_1)\left(\omega L_2 - \frac{1}{\omega C}\right)\right] = 0 \qquad (18\text{-}6)$$

This single (complete) equation actually represents two (real) equations. That is, if we have

$$A + jB = 0 \qquad (18\text{-}7a)$$

then

$$A = 0 \qquad (18\text{-}7b)$$

and

$$B = 0 \qquad (18\text{-}7c)$$

Hence, we can write

$$(r_d + R_1)R_2 - \omega L_1\left(\omega L_2 - \frac{1}{\omega C}\right) - \frac{\mu M}{C} + \omega^2 M = 0 \qquad (18\text{-}8a)$$

and

$$\omega L_1 R_2 + (r_d + R_1)\left(\omega L_2 - \frac{1}{\omega C}\right) = 0 \qquad (18\text{-}8b)$$

If these equations are satisfied, then there can be an output when there is no input. Hence, these are the criteria for oscillation. Manipulating Eq. 18-8b, and solving for ω we have

$$\omega_0 = \frac{1}{\sqrt{C[L_2 + L_1R_2/(r_d + R_1)]}} \tag{18-9}$$

where we have called the solution ω_0. This will be the frequency of oscillation. In a typical circuit

$$r_d \gg R_1 \tag{18-10a}$$

$$r_d \gg R_2 \tag{18-10b}$$

and

$$L_2 > L_1 \tag{18-11}$$

Hence,

$$\omega_0 \simeq \frac{1}{\sqrt{L_2 C}} \tag{18-12}$$

Now solve Eq. 18-8 for μ. This yields

$$\mu = \left[(r_d + R_1)R_2 - \omega_0 L_1\left(\omega_0 L_2 - \frac{1}{\omega_0 C}\right) + \omega_0^2 M^2\right]\frac{C}{M} \tag{18-13}$$

Equations 18-9 and 18-13 are the conditions for oscillation. Equation 18-9 gives the frequency of oscillation $f_0 = \omega_0/2\pi$, while Eq. 18-13 gives the value of μ needed for oscillation. Actually, if these equations are just met, it can be shown that the Nyquist diagram will just pass through the critical point. Thus, if the assumptions concerning the shape of the Nyquist diagram made earlier in this section are true, any μ equal to or greater than that given in Eq. 18-13 will result in oscillation. Usually a value of μ somewhat larger than necessary is used to ensure that the circuit will oscillate if the power supply voltage drops or the temperature changes, and so forth. Often we wish to express this condition for oscillation in terms of g_m. Then, dividing both sides of Eq. 18-13 by r_d and replacing the equals sign by an inequality, we have

$$g_m \geqq \left[\left(1 + \frac{R_1}{r_d}\right)R_2 - \frac{\omega_0 L_1}{r_d}\left(\omega_0 L_2 - \frac{1}{\omega_0 C}\right) + \frac{\omega_0^2 M^2}{r_d}\right]\frac{C}{M} \tag{18-14}$$

In general,

$$\omega_0 L_2 \simeq \frac{1}{\omega_0 C}$$

Then,

$$g_m \geqq \left[\left(1 + \frac{R_1}{r_d}\right)R_2 + \frac{\omega_0^2 M^2}{r_d}\right]\frac{C}{M} \tag{18-15}$$

Hence, Eq. 18-12 and 18-15 give approximate conditions for oscillation. Note that the frequency of oscillation is essentially determined by the tuned circuit.

Let us now consider another example and obtain the conditions for oscillation for the Colpitts oscillator of Fig. 18-1d. Now we shall consider the high-frequency model for the transistors (see Fig. 18-3). Note that $1/R_B = 1/R_{B1} + 1/R_{B2}$. We have also included R, the resistance of the inductance, which is not shown in the schematic. Noting that $\mathbf{V}_2 = \mathbf{V}_{b'e}$, we have for the nodal equations

$$0 = \left[\frac{1}{R_B} + \frac{1}{r_{bb'}} + j\omega C_1 + \frac{1}{j\omega L + R}\right]\mathbf{V}_1 - \frac{1}{r_{bb'}}\mathbf{V}_2 - \frac{1}{j\omega L + R}\mathbf{V}_3 \tag{18-16a}$$

$$0 = -\frac{1}{r_{bb'}}\mathbf{V}_1 + \left[\frac{1}{r_{bb'}} + \frac{1}{r_{b'e}} + j\omega(C_{b'e} + C_{b'c})\right]\mathbf{V}_2 - j\omega C_{b'c}\mathbf{V}_3 \tag{18-16b}$$

$$0 = -\frac{1}{j\omega L + R}\mathbf{V}_1 + (g_m - j\omega C_{b'c})\mathbf{V}_2 + \left[\frac{1}{r_{ce}} + \frac{1}{R_C} + j\omega(C_2 + C_{b'c}) + \frac{1}{j\omega L + R}\right]\mathbf{V}_3 \tag{18-16c}$$

Note that R represents the resistance of the coil. Thus, the condition for oscillation is

$$\begin{vmatrix} \frac{1}{R_B} + \frac{1}{r_{bb'}} + j\omega C_1 - \frac{1}{j\omega L_1 + R} & -\frac{1}{r_{bb'}} & -\frac{1}{j\omega L + R} \\ -\frac{1}{r_{bb'}} & \frac{1}{r_{bb'}} + \frac{1}{r_{b'e}} + j\omega(C_{b'e} + C_{b'c}) & -j\omega C_{b'c} \\ -\frac{1}{j\omega L + R} & g_m - j\omega C_{b'c} & \frac{1}{r_{ce}} + \frac{1}{R_C} + j\omega(C_2 + C_{b'c}) + \frac{1}{j\omega L + R} \end{vmatrix} = 0 \tag{18-17}$$

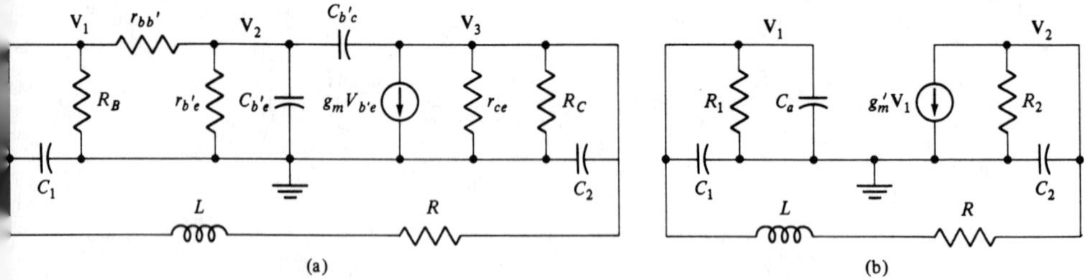

Figure 18-3. (a) Model for the oscillator of Fig. 18-1d. (b) Approximate model. $1/R_1 = (1/R_B) + [1/(r_{bb'} + r_{b'e})]$, $C_a = r_{b'e}^2 C_i/(r_{bb'} + r_{b'e})^2$, $1/R_2 = (1/r_{ce}) + (1/R_C)$ and $g'_m = g_m r_{b'e}/(r_{bb'} + r_{b'e})$

Solving this determinant yields two equations that give the exact expression for the frequency of oscillation and the conditions on g_m for oscillation. In order to obtain some more readily interpreted results, we shall approximate the input to the transistor as shown in Fig. 17-5 and also ignore the feedback through $C_{b'e}$. The model is then shown in Fig. 18-3b. If we were plotting a Nyquist diagram that had to be valid over a wide range of frequencies, we could not make this approximation, but the calculations that we are making here need only be valid over a narrow range of frequencies and thus, the model of Fig. 18-3b can be used here.

The nodal equations for this approximate model are

$$0 = \left(G_1 + j\omega C_1' + \frac{1}{R + j\omega L}\right)\mathbf{V}_1 - \frac{1}{R + j\omega L}\mathbf{V}_2 \tag{18-18a}$$

$$0 = \left(g_m' - \frac{1}{R + j\omega L}\right)\mathbf{V}_1 + \left(G_2 + j\omega C_2 + \frac{1}{R + j\omega L}\right)\mathbf{V}_2 \tag{18-18b}$$

where

$$G_1 = \frac{1}{R_2} \tag{18-19a}$$

$$G_2 = \frac{1}{R_2} \tag{18-19b}$$

$$C_1' = C_1 + C_a \tag{18-19c}$$

Multiplying both equations by $R + j\omega L$ we find the criterion for oscillation to be

$$[1 + G_1R - \omega^2LC_1' + j\omega(LG_1 + C_1'R)][1 + G_2R - \omega^2LC_2 + j\omega(LG_2 + C_2R)] + g_m'(R + j\omega L) - 1 = 0 \tag{18-20}$$

If we equate the real part of this equation to zero, we obtain

$$\omega^4L^2C_1'C_2 - \omega^2[L(C_1' + C_2) + LR(C_2G_1 + C_1G_2) + (LG_1 + C_1'R)(LG_2 + C_2R)] + R(G_1 + G_2) + G_1G_2R^2 + g_m'R = 0 \tag{18-21}$$

The positive root of this quadratic yields ω^2. Let

$$a = L^2C_1'C_2 \tag{18-22a}$$

$$b = L(C_1' + C_2) + LR(C_2G_1 + C_1G_2) + (LG_1 + C_1'R)(LG_2 + C_2R) \tag{18-22b}$$

$$d = R(G_1 + G_2) + G_1G_2R^2 + g_mR \tag{18-22c}$$

Then,

$$\omega_0 = \sqrt{\frac{b + \sqrt{b^2 - 4ad}}{2a}} \tag{18-23}$$

Then, from the imaginary part of Eq. 18-20, we have

$$g_m' \geqq [(\omega_0^2LC_1' - 1 - G_1R)(LG_2 + C_2R) + (\omega_0^2LC_2 - 1 - G_2R)(LG_1 + C_1'R)]/L \tag{18-24}$$

Note that Eqs. 18-23 and 18-24 interact in that ω_0 is a function of g_m. In practice, this is usually not the case since G_1, G_2, and R are small, so that $b^2 \gg |4ad|$, and in addition, $b = L(C_1' + C_2)$. Then, the value of ω_0 is approximately given by

$$\omega_0 = \sqrt{\frac{C_1' + C_2}{LC_1'C_2}} \tag{18-25}$$

Typically, ω_0 will be close to this value even if b^2 is only somewhat greater than $|4ad|$. This will be illustrated in an example. Now suppose that $C_1' = C_2 = C$. Then,

$$\omega_0 = \sqrt{\frac{2}{LC}}$$

and

$$\omega_0^2 LC_1' = \omega_0^2 LC_2 = 2 \tag{18-26}$$

Then, Eq. 19-24 becomes, after replacing g_m' by $g_m r_{b'e}|(r_{bb'} + r_{b'e})$

$$g_m \geqq \left[\frac{(1 - G_1R)(LG_2 + CR) + (1 - G_2R)(LG_1 + CR)}{L}\right]\frac{r_{b'e} + r_{be'}}{r_{b'e}} \tag{18-27}$$

In general,

$$1 \gg G_1R$$

Hence, Eq. 18-27 becomes

$$g_m \geqq \left[G_1 + G_2 + \frac{2CR}{L}\right]\frac{r_{b'e} + r_{bb'}}{r_{b'e}} \tag{18-28}$$

Manipulating and substituting, we have

$$g_m \geqq [G_1 + G_2 + R\omega_0^2 C^2]\frac{r_{bb'} + r_{b'e}}{r_{b'e}} \tag{18-29}$$

In general, ω_0 will be specified. Thus, the smallest requirements will be imposed upon g_m when we minimize the value of C^2. We shall subsequently see that it is *not* always desirable to do this.

Example

Design a Colpitts oscillator whose frequency of oscillation is 10^6 Hz.

We shall assume that coils with $Q_0 = 50$ are available, which is conservative. Coils with higher Q are usually available.

The circuit of Fig. 18-1d will be used. Let us attempt to use a transistor with the following parameter values.

$$g_m = 75{,}000\ \mu\text{mho}$$
$$r_{bb'} = 100\ \text{ohms}$$
$$r_{b'e} = 900\ \text{ohms}$$
$$r_{ce} = 50{,}000\ \text{ohms}$$
$$C_{b'e} = 50\ \text{pF}$$
$$C_{b'c} = 3\ \text{pF}$$

The quiescent operating point is

$$I_{CQ} = 1.0 \text{ mA}$$

$$I_{BQ} = 10 \ \mu\text{A}$$

$$V_{CE} = 10 \text{ V}$$

Assume that the maximum supply voltage is 21 V. Let us assume that $R_E = 1000$ ohms. Then

$$R_C = \frac{21 - 1 - 10}{1.0 \times 10^{-3}} = 10{,}000 \text{ ohms}$$

For the transistor, $R_i = 1000$ ohms. This will be much less than R_B. Hence,

$$G_2 = \frac{1}{50{,}000} + \frac{1}{10{,}000} = 0.00012$$

$$G_1 = \frac{1}{1000} = 0.001$$

Let us try $C_1' = C_2 = 1000$ pF. Then, using the approximation of Eq. 18-25, we have

$$L = \frac{C_1' + C_2}{\omega_0^2 C_1' C_2} = \frac{1}{(2\pi \times 10^6)^2 \times 500 \times 10^{-12}} = 50.7 \ \mu\text{H}$$

$$R = \frac{\omega_0 L}{Q_0} = \frac{2\pi \times 10^6 \times 50.7 \times 10^{-6}}{50} = 6.37 \text{ ohms}$$

Then, substituting in Eq. 18-29, we obtain

$$g_m \geqq [0.00012 + 0.001 + 6.37(2\pi \times 10^6)^2(1000 \times 10^{-12})^2]\frac{1000}{900}$$

$$g_m \geqq 1524 \ \mu\text{mho}$$

Since $g_m = 75{,}000$ μmho, the design can easily be achieved.

Let us now verify that $b^2 \gg 4ad$ (see Eq. 18-22).

$$\begin{aligned} b = {} & 50.7 \times 10^{-6}(2000 \times 10^{-12}) + 50.7 \times 10^{-6} \\ & \times 6.37(1000 \times 10^{-12} \times 0.001 + 1000 \times 10^{-12} \times 0.00012) \\ & + (50.7 \times 10^{-6} \times 0.001 + 1000 \times 10^{-12} \times 6.37) \\ & \times (50.7 \times 10^{-6} \times 0.00012 + 1000 \times 10^{-12} \times 6.37) \end{aligned}$$

$$b = 1.024 \times 10^{-13}$$

$$b^2 = 1.050 \times 10^{-26}$$

$$\begin{aligned} 4ad = {} & 4(50.6 \times 10^{-6})^2(1000 \times 10^{-12})^2[6.36(0.00112) \\ & + 0.001 \times 0.00012 \times 6.36^2 + 75 \times 10^{-3} \times 6.36] \end{aligned}$$

$$4ad = 4.99 \times 10^{-27}$$

It does not appear as though b^2 is too much greater than $4ad$. However, if we substitute in Eq. 18-23 we obtain

$$f_0 = 1.005 \times 10^6 \text{ Hz}$$

Thus, the approximation is valid. Note that Eq. 18-25 was very accurate even though b^2 was only about twice as large as $|4ad|$. In any event some provision must be made to vary either L or C to adjust f_0.

In the example, the g_m of the transistor was much larger than needed. Often, a g_m three to five times larger than needed is used to ensure that the circuit will oscillate. In this case the g_m is much more than this. The capacitor sizes could then be increased. In Sec. 18-5 we shall discuss that this is often an advantage.

18-2. THE *RC* PHASE SHIFT OSCILLATOR

The frequency of oscillation of all the RF oscillators shown in Fig. 18-1 is very close to the resonant frequency of their tuned circuits. At low frequencies (e.g. audio frequencies) the size of the inductance becomes excessive. We shall now consider the oscillators of Fig. 18-4 which use only resistors and capacitors. These are all called *RC phase shift oscillators.* We discussed in Sec. 16-13 that a negative feedback amplifier with three identical stages, would oscillate if the midband loop gain were greater than 8. In Fig. 18-4 we utilize that idea. Instead of using three stages we have only one stage of amplification but three stages of *RC* coupling. The results will be somewhat different than with three stages of amplification since now there will be interaction between the *RC* networks.

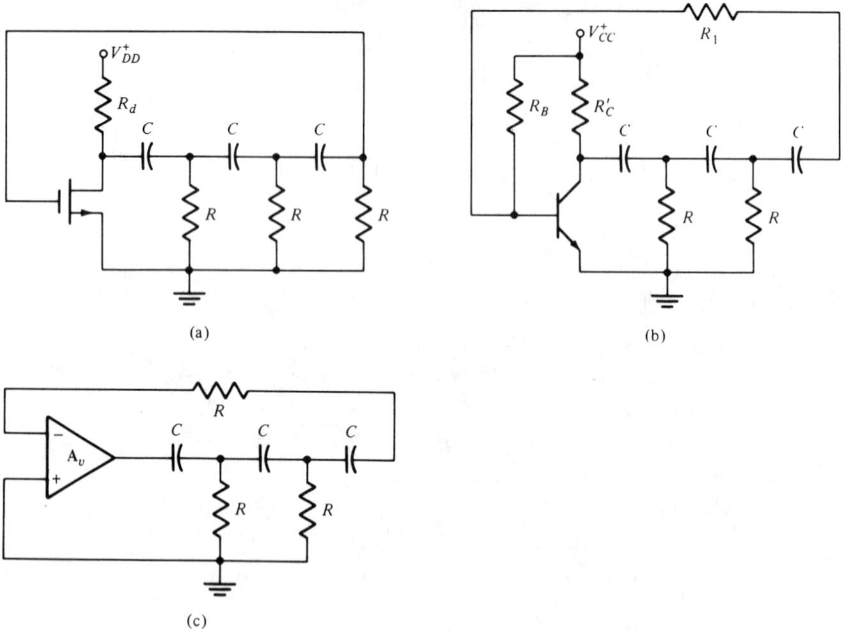

Figure 18-4. RC phase shift oscillators. (a) FET. (b) Transistor. (c) Operational amplifier.

In this section we shall determine the criterion for oscillation by setting the loop gain equal to unity. Let us start by considering the FET oscillator of Fig. 18-4a. Note that since this is a low-frequency oscillator, we can use the low-frequency models for the FET. In this circuit we have again assumed that

$$R \gg R_d$$

Then, proceeding as in Sec. 16-12 we obtain, for the loop gain

$$\mathbf{L}(j\omega) = \frac{\mathbf{A}_{v\,\mathrm{mid}}}{1 - 5(f_1/f)^2 - j[6(f_1/f) - (f_1/f)^3]} \tag{18-30}$$

where

$$f_1 = \frac{1}{2\pi RC} \tag{18-31a}$$

and

$$\mathbf{A}_{v\,\mathrm{mid}} = -g_m R_{\mathrm{sh}} \tag{18-31b}$$

$$\frac{1}{R_{\mathrm{sh}}} = \frac{1}{r_d} + \frac{1}{R_L} \tag{18-31c}$$

Then, setting $\mathbf{L}(j\omega) = 1$, we have

$$1 - 5\left(\frac{f_1}{f}\right)^2 - j\left[6\left(\frac{f_1}{f}\right) - \left(\frac{f_1}{f}\right)^3\right] - \mathbf{A}_{v\,\mathrm{mid}} = 0 \tag{18-32}$$

Equating the imaginary part to zero, we have

$$6\left(\frac{f_1}{f}\right) - \left(\frac{f_1}{f}\right)^3 = 0$$

The nonzero root of this equation is

$$f_0 = \frac{f_1}{\sqrt{6}} \tag{18-33}$$

Substituting this value into Eq. 18-32, we obtain

$$\mathbf{A}_{v\,\mathrm{mid}} = -g_m R_{\mathrm{sh}} = -29 \tag{18-34}$$

Thus, this circuit will oscillate when $|\mathbf{A}_{v\,\mathrm{mid}}| > 29$.

Now let us consider the transistor circuit. The model for this circuit is shown in Fig. 18-5. We have assumed here that $R_B \gg r_{bb'} + r_{b'e}$ so that R_B can be omitted from the model. In addition, we have used the notation

$$\frac{1}{R_C} = \frac{1}{r_{ce}} + \frac{1}{R'_C} \tag{18-35}$$

In general, the input resistance of the transistor $r_{bb'} + r_{b'e}$ is much less than R. The resistor R_1 is chosen so that the right-hand resistance of Fig. 18-5 is equal to R. That is,

$$R = R_1 + r_{bb'} + r_{b'e} \tag{18-36}$$

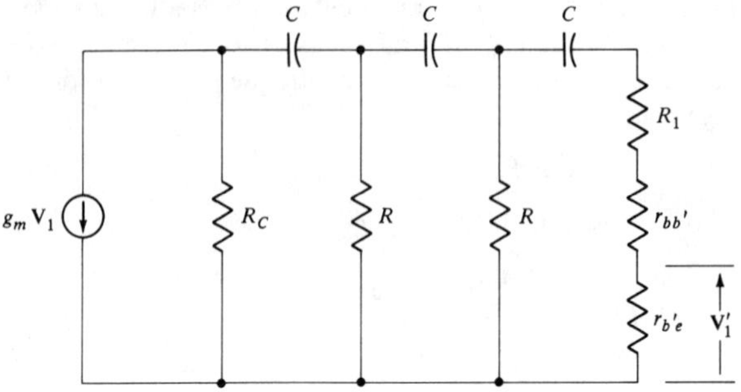

Figure 18-5. A model for the circuit of Fig. 18-4b.

The loop gain is $\mathbf{L}(j\omega) = \mathbf{V}_1'/\mathbf{V}_1$. Then,

$$\mathbf{L}(j\omega) = \frac{-g_m r_{b'e}}{3 - (f_1/f)^2 - j4(f_1/f) + (R/R_C)[1 - 5(f_1/f)^2 - j(6f_1/f - f_1^3/f^3)]} \tag{18-37}$$

where f_1 is defined in Eq. 18-31a. Setting the imaginary part of Eq. 18-37 equal to zero, we have

$$4\frac{f_1}{f} + \frac{R}{R_C}\left[6\frac{f_1}{f} - \left(\frac{f_1}{f}\right)^3\right] = 0$$

Solving this for $f = f_0$, we have

$$f_0 = \frac{f_1}{\sqrt{6 + 4(R_C/R)}} \tag{18-38}$$

Substituting back into Eq. 18-37, and setting the resulting equation equal to unity, we have

$$g_m \geqq \frac{1}{r_{b'e}}\left(23 + 4\frac{R_C}{R} + \frac{29R}{R_C}\right) \tag{18-39}$$

We often wish to minimize the value of g_m which is required for oscillation. Let us choose the optimum value of R_C/R which accomplishes this. Differentiating the right-hand side of relation 18-39 with respect to R_C/R and setting the denominator equal to zero, we obtain

$$\frac{R_C}{R} = \sqrt{\frac{29}{4}} \tag{18-40}$$

Substituting back into Eq. 18-39, we have

$$g_m \geqq \frac{44.54}{r_{b'e}} \tag{18-41}$$

Operational Amplifier *RC* Phase Shift Amplifier

In Fig. 18-4c we have a *RC* phase shift oscillator where the active device is an operational amplifier. Proceeding as before, the loop gain for this circuit is

$$\mathbf{L}(j\omega) = \frac{-\mathbf{A}_v R/R_0}{3 - (f_1/f)^2 - j4(f_1/f) + (R/R_0)[1 - 5(f_1/f)^2 - j6(f_1/f - f_1^3/f^3)]} \tag{18-42}$$

where R_0 is the output resistance of the operational amplifier. We have again assumed that $R \gg R_0$. Comparing this with Eq. 18-37 we see that the frequency of oscillation is

$$f_0 = \frac{f_1}{\sqrt{6 + 4R_0/R}} \tag{18-43}$$

The criterion for oscillation is

$$\mathbf{A}_v \geqq 23\frac{R_0}{R} + 4\left(\frac{R_0}{R}\right)^2 + 29 \tag{18-44}$$

This achieves its minimum value when R_0/R is zero, so it is desirable for R_0/R to be as small as possible. In general, $R \gg R_0$ and Eq. 18-44 becomes

$$\mathbf{A}_v \geqq 29$$

If this analysis is to be valid, then the response of the operational amplifier must be essentially flat well beyond f_0.

18-3. THE WEIN BRIDGE OSCILLATOR

Another form of *RC* oscillator, called a *Wein bridge oscillator*, is shown in Fig. 18-6. We have shown an operational amplifier as the active device, but the gain can also be provided by a single transistor of FET. We shall again assume that the frequency response of the amplifier is flat well beyond the frequency of oscillation. Hence, we have

$$\mathbf{V}_1 = \frac{R_1}{R_1 + R_2}\mathbf{V}_0 \tag{18-45a}$$

$$\mathbf{V}_2 = \frac{j\omega CR\mathbf{V}_0}{1 - \omega^2R^2C^2 + 3j\omega RC} \tag{18-45b}$$

and

$$\mathbf{V}_0 = \mathbf{A}_v(\mathbf{V}_2 - \mathbf{V}_1) \tag{18-45c}$$

Manipulating, we obtain

$$\mathbf{V}_0\left[1 + \frac{R_1\mathbf{A}_v}{R_1 + R_2} - \frac{j\omega RC\mathbf{A}_v}{1 + \omega^2R^2C^2 + 3j\omega RC}\right] = 0$$

Hence, for oscillation,

$$1 + \frac{R_1\mathbf{A}_v}{R_1 + R_2} - \frac{j\omega RC\mathbf{A}_v}{1 - \omega^2R^2C^2 + 3j\omega RC} = 0 \tag{18-46}$$

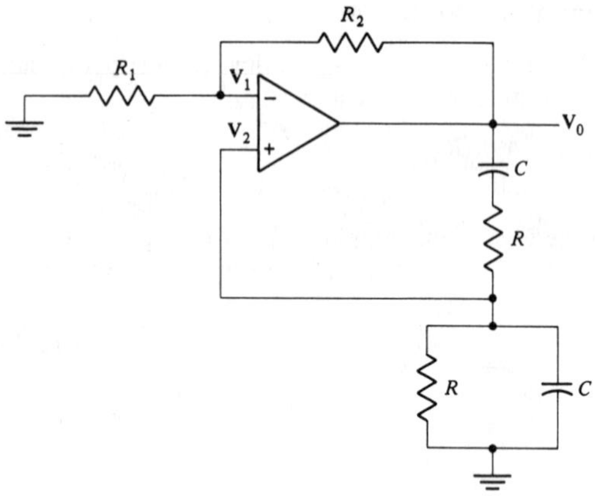

Figure 18-6. A Wein bridge oscillator.

Equating the imaginary part of this equation to zero, we have

$$f_0 = \frac{1}{2\pi RC} \tag{18-47}$$

Substituting this value into Eq. 18-46, we obtain

$$1 + \mathbf{A}_v\left[\frac{R_1}{R_1 + R_2} - \frac{1}{3}\right] = 0 \tag{18-48}$$

Therefore,

$$\mathbf{A}_v \geqq \frac{1}{\frac{1}{3} - [R_1/(R_1 + R_2)]} = \frac{3(1 + R_1/R_2)}{1 - 2(R_1/R_2)} \tag{18-49}$$

Note that if

$$\frac{R_2}{R_1} = 2$$

then we require infinite gain.

The circuit of Fig. 18-6 is called a bridge because the resistances R_1 and R_2 and the RC circuits form a bridge. The "output" of the bridge is connected to the $\mathbf{V}_1$ and $\mathbf{V}_2$ terminals of the amplifier. The input is between $\mathbf{V}_0$ and ground.

18-4. LINEAR AND NONLINEAR OPERATION OF SINUSOIDAL OSCILLATORS

When an oscillator is turned on, the signal builds up exponentially until the nonlinearities of the circuit limit its value. If the active devices are driven between saturation and cutoff, then the signal will not be sinusoidal. That is, a great deal of distortion will be produced. In a tuned oscillator the tuned circuit will tend to reject the harmonics so that the output will be reasonably close to a sinusoid, but when an RC oscillator is used, there will be no rejection of the harmonics so the output may be very distorted.

To obtain low distortion, the amplitude of oscillation must be limited. We shall discuss several procedures that can be used. Consider the Wein bridge oscillator of Fig. 18-6. The criterion for oscillation is (see Eq. 18-49)

$$\mathbf{A}_v \geqq \frac{3(1 + R_1/R_2)}{1 - 2R_1/R_2} \tag{18-50}$$

As $2R_1/R_2$ approaches 1, the required gain approaches infinity. Suppose that we have $2R_1/R_2 < 1$ but cause R_2 to be a nonlinear resistance such that, as the amplitude of oscillation builds up, R_2 decreases in such a way that $2R_1/R_2$ approaches 1. This will then limit the size of the oscillation since the circuit will not oscillate if $2R_1/R_2 = 1$. But R_1/R_2 will be small enough so that oscillation occurs if the amplitude of the oscillation is small.

A circuit that accomplishes this is shown in Fig. 18-7. The Zener diode pair is such that when the voltage across it exceeds the breakdown voltage, it conducts. Then, when the diode pair is cut off

$$R_2 = R_{2a}$$

When the diode pair conducts

$$\frac{1}{R_2} = \frac{1}{R_{2a}} + \frac{1}{R_{2b}}$$

The values of R_{2a} and R_{2b} are chosen so that

$$\frac{1}{R_{2a}} + \frac{1}{R_{2b}} = \frac{1}{2R_1} \tag{18-51}$$

Thus, the gain of the oscillator is limited since, when the diodes conduct, the circuit will not oscillate since infinite gain is required. However, the diode pair acts as an open circuit unless the voltage across it is large enough and then R_2 is such that Eq. 18-50 is

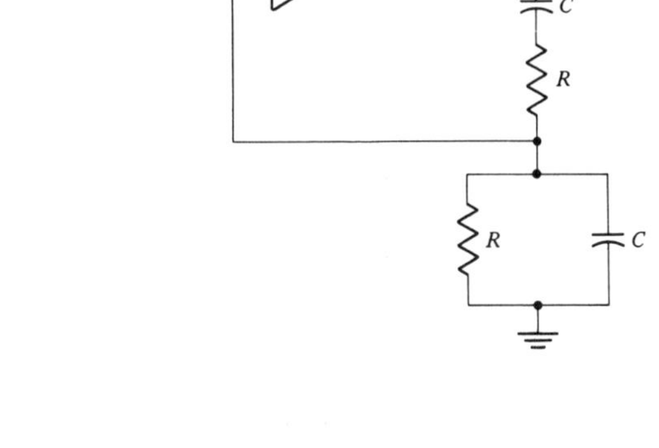

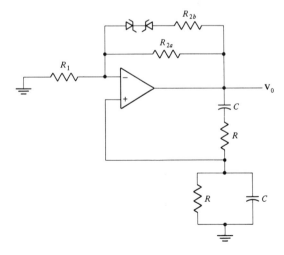

Figure 18-7. An amplitude stabilized Wein bridge oscillator.

satisfied. Thus, the circuit will oscillate but at a limited amplitude. If only a small amplitude of oscillation is required then ordinary diodes can replace the Zener diodes.

Other procedures for producing nonlinear resistance are also used. For instance, a tungsten lamp can be used as a part of R_1 since its resistance increases as the current through it increases.

The use of nonlinear resistance tends to distort the signal somewhat. If a very precise sinusoid is required, then the circuit of Fig. 18-8 is used. We have used a FET *RC* phase shift oscillator here. The resistor R_1 is chosen

$$R_1 \ll R \tag{18-52}$$

so that the R_1C_1 circuit does not affect the oscillator circuit. In general, the g_m of the *n*-channel FET decreases as V_{GSQ} becomes more negative. The operational amplifier amplifies the output signal; then the diode rectifies it. The *RC* filter removes the alternating component of the output. Thus, C_1 is usually very large. Hence, the voltage $\mathbf{V}_a$ will be a negative direct voltage proportional to the output signal of the oscillator. Therefore, as the amplitude of the oscillation builds up, the direct voltage $\mathbf{V}_a$ builds up negatively. This voltage biases the FET so that as the magnitude of $\mathbf{V}_a$ increases, g_m decreases. Hence, the amplitude of the oscillation is limited. If the gain of the amplifier circuit is high, the level of oscillation can be low and, therefore, the operation will be linear.

The input impedance of the operational amplifier circuit is $2R$. Hence, the rightmost resistor of the *RC* phase shift circuit is also $2R$ ohms. Hence, the two resistances in parallel act as a R ohm resistance.

Care should be taken with circuits of the type of Fig. 18-8. There are two feedback loops, one within the *RC* phase shift oscillator and the other through the amplitude stabilizing circuit. This feedback loop can also cause oscillation which manifests itself as the amplitude of the oscillation changing periodically. A Nyquist diagram for this circuit can be obtained by breaking the feedback loop at the point marked with an X. (An additional R_1 and C_1 are then added to the left of the diode). A signal is then applied

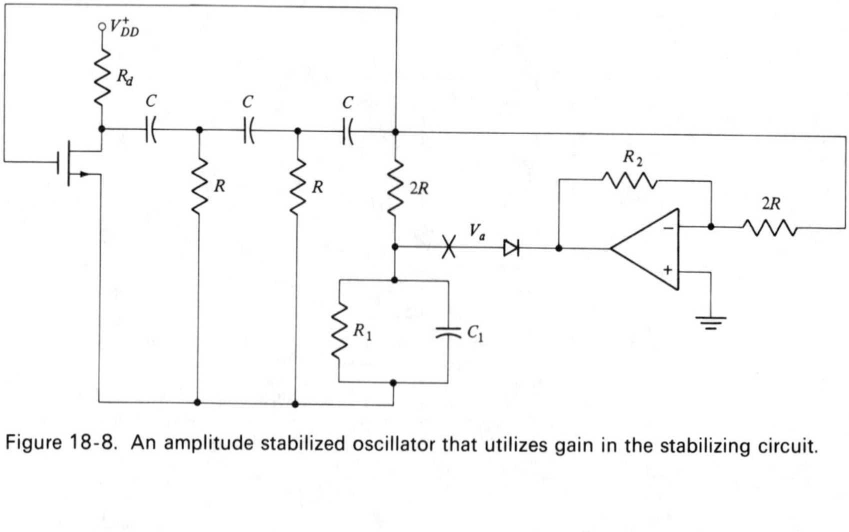

Figure 18-8. An amplitude stabilized oscillator that utilizes gain in the stabilizing circuit.

between the lower end of the $2R$ ohm resistance and ground. The signal consists of a direct voltage (which is the normal operating bias) and a much smaller sinusoidal component. The ratio of the sinusoidal signal and the sinusoidal signal returned to the $\mathbf{V}_a$ point gives the loop gain. Note that the frequency of this signal is varied from zero (i.e., direct voltage) up to a frequency where the gain essentially becomes zero. Since C_1 is made very large, the maximum frequency used to compute the Nyquist diagram is usually well below the oscillation frequency. Stabilization of this type of circuit is usually accomplished by increasing the bandwidth of the amplifier circuit or increasing the size of C_1.

18-5. FREQUENCY STABILITY

The frequency of an oscillator circuit will not remain constant but will slowly drift. For some applications, the frequency need only remain within a few percentage points of the nominal frequency f_0. On the other hand, there are applications where the stability of the frequency of oscillation is measured in terms of parts per million or less. Let us see how oscillators with very stable frequency of oscillation can be built.

In general, the frequency of oscillation is determined both by passive elements of the circuit and by the parameters of the active device. For instance, consider Eqs. 18-9 or 18-23. The parameters of the active device tend to change with power supply voltage and with temperature. Thus, it is desirable for the frequency of oscillation to be as independent of the active device's parameters as possible. From Eqs. 18-9 and 18-23 we see that this occurs if the losses of the circuit are low. That is, if we can reduce the power consumption of the elements external to the active device, the frequency of oscillation tends to become independent of the active device. For instance, in Fig. 18-2, if R_1 and R_2 can be reduced, the loss of the circuit is reduced and f_0 becomes more independent of the parameters of the active device. Similarly, in Fig. 18-3, if R_1 and R_2 are made very large (G_1 and C_2 are made small) and R is made small, the frequency becomes independent of the transistor's parameters. Note that these statements apply to parameters such as $g_m, r_d, r_{bb'}, r_{b'e}$, and so forth. They do not apply to the capacitances of the active device.

We shall now discuss frequency stabilization in terms of the Colpitts oscillator of Fig. 18-1d. We shall assume that the losses are kept low so that the frequency of oscillation is given by Eq. 18-25.

$$\omega_0 = \sqrt{\frac{C_1' + C_2}{C_1' C_2 L}} \tag{18-53}$$

Note that C_1' is not only a passive capacitance, $C_1' = C_1 + C_a$, where C_a is the effective input capacitance of the transistor. Similarly, C_2 would also contain any shunt output capacitance of the transistor.

We shall now consider the effect of a variation in capacitance. To simplify the analysis let us combine the capacitances into a single one.

$$\frac{1}{C} = \frac{C_1' + C_2}{C_1 C_2} \tag{18-54}$$

Then, the frequency of oscillation is given by

$$\omega_0^2 = \frac{1}{LC} \tag{18-55}$$

We shall work with ω_0^2 to eliminate the square roots from the analysis. Now suppose that C changes by ΔC. That is, C becomes $C + \Delta C$. Then, manipulating Eq. 18-55, we obtain

$$\Delta\omega_0^2 = -\frac{L\Delta C}{LC(LC + L\Delta C)} \tag{18-56}$$

In general, $C \gg \Delta C$ so that we can write Eq. 18-56 as

$$\frac{\Delta\omega_0^2}{\omega_0^2} = -\frac{\Delta C}{C} \tag{18-57}$$

Suppose that ΔC is due only to a change in the capacitance of the active device. Then, if we increase the size of the external capacitance $\Delta C/C$ will be reduced. However, the size of the external capacitance is limited by two factors. Consider Eq. 18-29. As C is increased, the required value of g_m is also increased. Thus, the maximum value of C is limited by the g_m of the transistor.

There is another factor that often limits C. From Eq. 18-55 we see that, as C is increased, L must be reduced. There is a minimum L that can practically be used. This minimum L often limits the maximum C that can be used.

There is a modification of the Colpitts oscillator called a *Clapp oscillator* or a *series tuned oscillator* that avoids this difficulty and also improves the frequency stability. The inductance in the Colpitts circuit is replaced by a series LC circuit. The tuned circuit of the Clapp oscillator is shown in Fig. 18-9. The resonant frequency of this circuit is given by

$$\omega_0 = \frac{1}{\sqrt{LC_{\text{eff}}}} \tag{18-58}$$

where

$$C_{\text{eff}} = \frac{CC_3}{C + C_3} \tag{18-59}$$

Note that if C is very large, $C_{\text{eff}} = C_3$. Hence, L need not be made very small even if C is very large. Now, proceeding as before, we have

$$\frac{\Delta\omega_0^2}{\omega_0^2} = -\frac{\Delta C_{\text{eff}}}{C_{\text{eff}}} \tag{18-60}$$

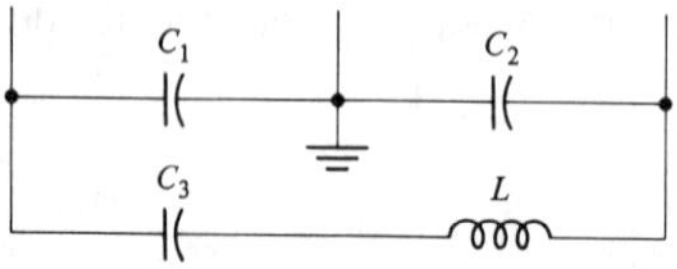

Figure 18-9. The tuned circuit of a Clapp oscillator.

Again, let us assume that the change in C_{eff} is due to the active devices. Then, C will change but C_3 will not. Then, proceeding as in the derivation of Eq. 18-57, we obtain

$$\frac{\Delta C_{\text{eff}}}{C_{\text{eff}}} \simeq \frac{\Delta C}{C} \frac{C_{\text{eff}}}{C} \tag{18-61}$$

When the Clapp circuit is used, C can be made larger than in the Colpitts circuit. Thus, $\Delta C/C$ will be reduced. In addition, we often have

$$C_{\text{eff}}/C \ll 1 \tag{18-62}$$

Thus, the frequency stability of the Clapp oscillator can be considerably better than that of the Colpitts or other common oscillator circuits insofar as changes in the active devices capacitance is concerned. In general, when the Clapp oscillator is used, the capacitances C_1 and C_2 are made as large as practical although they are limited by a relation such as Eq. 18-29. Remember that there must be a safety factor so that g_m must be larger than the value determined by Eq. 18-29.

We have thus far ignored the variation in the passive circuit elements. The values of the L and C elements will change primarily because of temperature variations. In very high stability oscillator circuits, the critical elements, such as C_3 and L in Fig. 18-9, are kept in a temperature controlled oven. The mechanical stability of the elements is also made high.

The measures that we have discussed are used for special high stability circuits. For most applications, the oscillator circuits of Figs. 18-1, 18-4, or 18-6 are used.

In this section we have discussed oscillators whose frequency can be varied by varying the circuit elements. In the next section we shall consider a high-stability oscillator that is used when the frequency is fixed.

18-6. CRYSTAL OSCILLATORS

Often, we want to build an oscillator that is only to operate at a single fixed frequency. The frequency of oscillation is to be maintained with very high stability. An oscillator can be built with exception frequency stability using *piezoelectric crystals*. These crystals, which are usually made of quartz, will deform if a voltage is placed across their parallel faces. Similarly, if the crystal is mechanically deformed, a voltage will appear across its opposite faces.

The piezoelectric crystal has a mechanical resonant frequency. Its electrical impedance is similar to a very high Q electrical circuit. The symbol for a piezoelectric crystal and its linear model are shown in Fig. 18-10. It acts as a very high Q series resonant

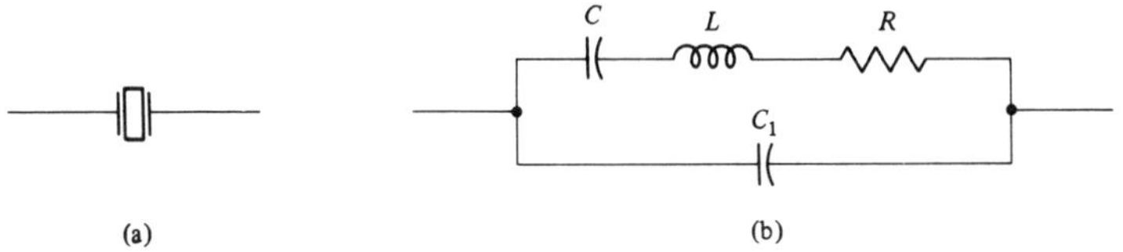

Figure 18-10. The piezoelectric crystal. (a) Its symbol. (b) Its linear model.

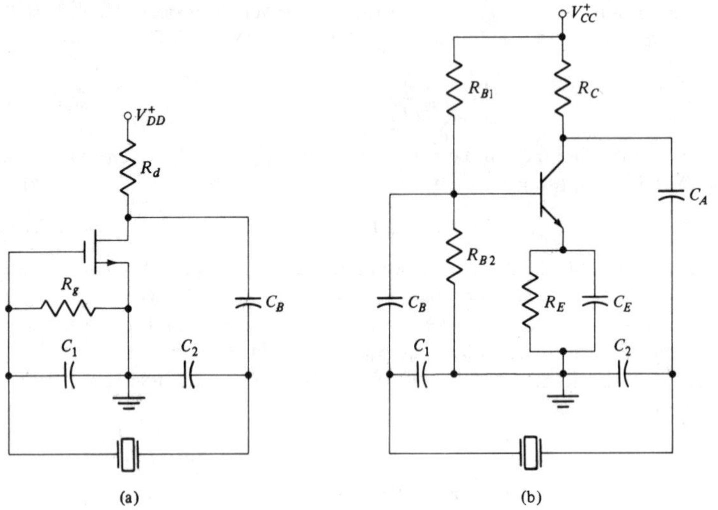

Figure 18-11. Pierce crystal oscillator circuits. (a) FET. (b) Transistor.

circuit shunted by a small capacitance C_1. Thus, the piezoelectric crystal can be used to replace the C_3 and L circuit in the Clapp oscillator. Since R is small, C_1 and C_2 can be made very large which improves the frequency stability. In addition, the frequency stability of the crystal itself is very high so that crystals usually do not have to be stabilized by placing them in a controlled temperature environment. If extreme stability is required, then the crystal is placed in a temperature controlled oven.

Two typical crystal oscillators are shown in Fig. 18-11. They are both called Pierce oscillators. Note that they are Clapp oscillators with the series resonant circuit replaced by a piezoelectric crystal.

Piezoelectric crystals are used in a variety of oscillator circuits. We have presented two of them in this section.

The output of this or other tuned oscillators can be taken across the elements of the resonant circuit. However, changes in the load impedance will change the frequency of oscillation. To prevent this, an isolating or *buffer* amplifier can be placed between the oscillator and the load.

18-7. THE TRANSISTOR ASTABLE MULTIVIBRATOR

Let us now consider a circuit that can be used to produce a square wave. This circuit is one of a class called *free running multivibrators* or *astable multivibrators*, or *astable flip-flops*. The flip-flops discussed in Chapter 10 are actually called bistable flip-flops or bistable multivibrators. Usually, the word flip-flop without any modifier refers to a bistable flip-flop.

The circuit that we shall discuss is shown in Fig. 18-12. Consider that both Q_1 and Q_2 are operating in their active region and are conducting equally. Suppose that a

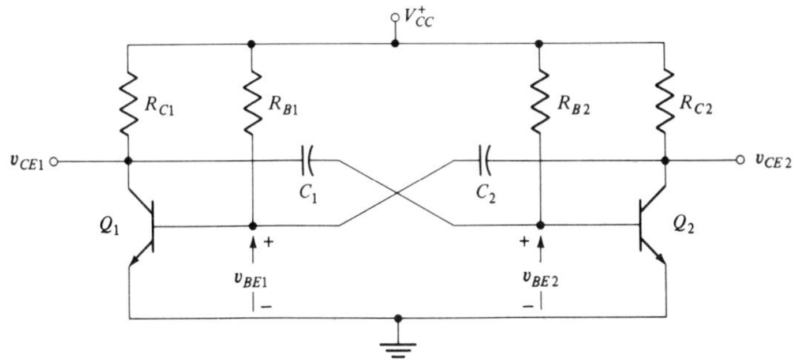

Figure 18-12. A free running multivibrator.

random fluctuation increases i_{C1}, which then decreases v_{CE1}. Since the voltage across the capacitors cannot change instantaneously. v_{BE2} will decrease. This will decrease i_{C2} and cause v_{CE2} to increase. This in turn will increase v_{BE1} which will further increase i_{C1} which further decreases v_{CE1}. This process keeps repeating just as in the case of the Schmitt trigger until Q_1 is saturated and Q_2 is cut off. Now v_{CE1} is a very small value (0.3 V). Because of the capacitors, the circuit will not remain in this state. (If the voltages remain constant the capacitors would eventually act as open circuits and each transistor would have to conduct equally.) Capacitor C_1 will be charged through R_{B2}. This will cause v_{BE2} to increase. Eventually, v_{BE2} will rise above the cut in voltage $V_{BE\gamma}$ and Q_2 will start to conduct. This will cause v_{CE2} to drop which, in turn, will drop v_{BE1}. The process will then continue until Q_2 is saturated and Q_1 is cut off. This process will continue to repeat. The waveforms of this circuit are shown in Fig. 18-13. The solid curve assumes ideal transistors while the dashed curve shows actual response. We have shown the waveform for transistor Q_1. Those for Q_2 differ from these by one half-cycle.

Let us assume that Q_1 is cut off. Then v_{BE1} rises. When v_{BE1} reaches $V_{BE\gamma}$, the operation flips (i.e., Q_1 will saturate and Q_2 will cut off). Note that this tends to drive v_{BE1} positive. However, the base-emitter diode limits the maximum positive value of v_{BE}. Once v_{BE1} exceeds V_γ, switching takes place as fast as the transistor can respond. Ideally this is instantaneous, but actually it is limited by the switching speed of the transistor (see dashed curve).

Let us determine the period of the oscillation. Suppose that Q_1 is saturated and G_2 is cut off. At the instant of switching the voltage across C_2 is $V_{CC} - V_{BES}$. This voltage cannot change instantaneously. Hence, when Q_2 saturates, v_{BE1} will become $-V_{CC} + V_{BES} + V_{CES}$. Q_1 will then be cut off and remain in that state until v_{BE1} rises to $V_{BE\gamma}$. Then, a half-period $T/2$ is the time required for v_{BE} to change from $-V_{CC} + V_{BES} + V_{CES}$ to $V_{BE\gamma}$. The time constant of the circuit is $R_{B1}C_2$. If we assume that, during the period, v_{CE2} remains at V_{CES}, then we can write for the time that Q_1 is cut off

$$v_{BE1} = V_{CC} - (2V_{CC} - V_{CES} - V_{BES})e^{-t/R_{B1}C_2} \tag{18-63}$$

where we have assumed that the action has been initiated at $t = 0$. Then, the cycle flips when v_{BE1} rises to V_γ, the cut-in voltage. Hence,

$$V_{BE\gamma} = V_{CC} - (2V_{CC} - V_{CES} - V_{BES})e^{-T/2R_{B1}C_2} \tag{18-64}$$

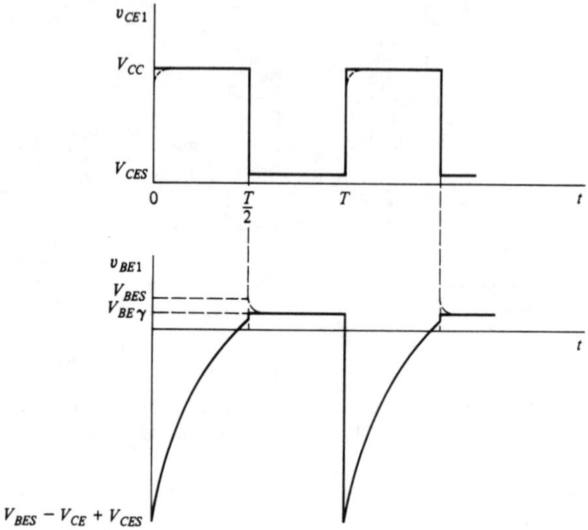

Figure 18-13. Waveform in a free running multivibrator. (a) Collector-emitter voltage. (b) Base-emitter voltage.

Manipulating, we obtain

$$\frac{T}{2} = -R_{B1}C_2 \ln \frac{V_{CC} - V_{BE\gamma}}{2V_{CC} - V_{CES} - V_{BES}} \tag{18-65}$$

In general, $V_{CC} \gg V_{BE\gamma}$ and $V_{CC} \gg V_{CES} + V_{BES}$ so that Eq. 18-65 becomes

$$\frac{T}{2} = R_{B1}C_2 \ln 2$$

Then, the period is

$$T = 2R_B C \ln 2 \tag{18-66}$$

We have assumed here that $R_{B1} = R_{B2} = R_B$ and $C_1 = C_2 = C$. If this is not the case, then the two halves of the square waves will have different periods. Proceeding as before, for each half-period, we have

$$T_1 = R_{B1}C_2 \ln 2 \tag{18-67a}$$

$$T_2 = R_{B2}C_1 \ln 2 \tag{18-67b}$$

The total period is

$$T = T_1 + T_2 \tag{18-68}$$

Note that, if both Q_1 and Q_2 are initially saturated, the circuit will remain in this state and oscillation will not start. Usually it can be initiated by turning the power supply off and on.

At times, we want to *synchronize* the oscillator with an external signal, so that they both operate at exactly the same frequency. Suppose that a signal is applied to the base of the cutoff transistor which drives it into the active region. The flipping action will be initiated. Assume that the frequency of the free running multivibrator is adjusted to be slightly less than that of the periodic input signal. The input signal will then initiate the cycle for every period and thus, the multivibrator will oscillate at the same frequency as the input signal. Actually the procedure is more general than we have indicated. Suppose that the multivibrator frequency is approximately twice that of the signal. The external signal will synchronize it on alternate cycles. Note that we assume that the external signal is small enough so that it will not drive the cutoff transistor into the active region unless its base-emitter voltage is close to V_{BE}. Hence, there will only be synchronization on alternate cycles. Thus, the free running multivibrator now oscillates at a frequency that is exactly twice that of the input signal. By properly adjusting the frequency of the free running multivibrator, it can be made to oscillate at an exact harmonic or subharmonic of the input signal.

18-8. THE COMPARATOR ASTABLE MULTIVIBRATOR

We shall now consider an alternate form of astable multivibrator that generates both square and triangular waveforms. These circuits use comparators and operational amplifiers. The circuit is shown in Fig. 18-14. Note that the operational amplifier and R_2 and R_1 form a basic Schmitt trigger configuration although here we do not have to set $R_1 \ll R_2$ (see Sec. 13-12).

The waveforms in this circuit are shown in Fig. 18-15. We assume that the output voltage of the operational amplifier can vary between V_A and $-V_A$. To simplify the analysis we shall assume that $\mathbf{A}_v$ is very large so that $v_o = V_A$ if $v_2 - v_1 > 0$ and $v_o = -V_A$ if $v_2 - v_1 < 0$. Hence,

$$v_2 = \frac{V_A R_1}{R_1 + R_2} \quad \text{if} \quad v_1 < v_2 \tag{18-69a}$$

$$v_2 = -\frac{V_A R_1}{R_1 + R_2} \quad \text{if} \quad v_1 > v_2 \tag{18-69b}$$

Now suppose that we set up an initial voltage across the capacitor equal to

$$v_1 = -\frac{V_A R_1}{R_1 + R_2} \tag{18-70}$$

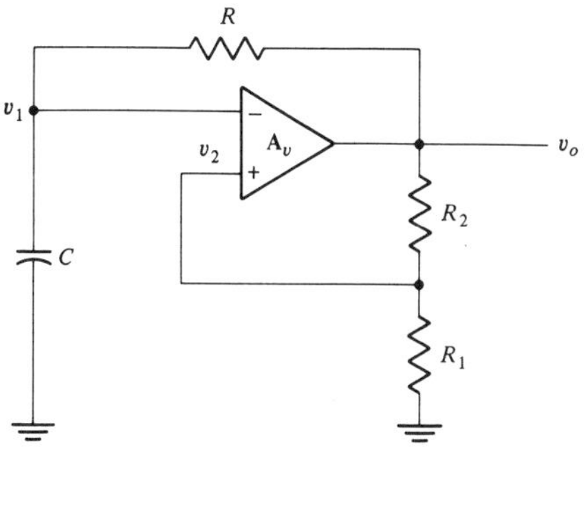

Figure 18-14. An astable multivibrator square wave generator that uses a comparator.

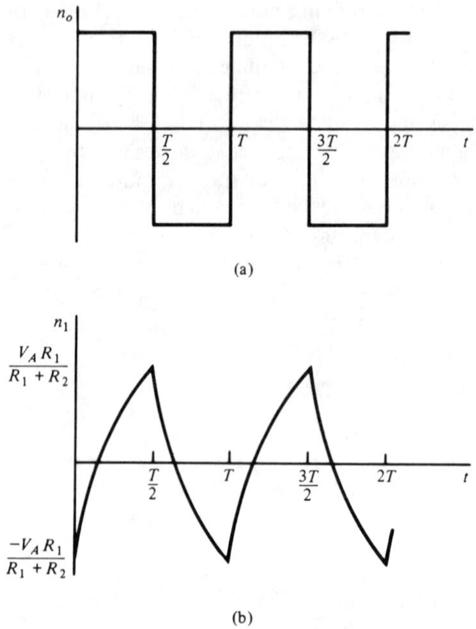

Figure 18-15. Waveform in the square wave generator of Fig. 18-14. (a) v_o. (b) v_i.

Then, v_2 will be given by Eq. 18-69a and v_1 will rise exponentially toward V_A, that is, v_o acts as a power supply equal to V_A volts. When $v_1 = V_A R_1/(R_1 + R_2)$, then $v_1 - v_2 = 0$. If v_2 rises any higher, then $v_1 - v_2$ becomes positive and v_o switches to $-V_A$. The "power supply" voltage has now changed polarity. Now v_1 falls exponentially toward $-V_A$. Similarly, when v_1 becomes equal to $-V_A R_1/(R_1 + R_2)$, the circuit switches again. (Note that when v_o changes polarity, v_2 will also change polarity.)

The time for a half-period can be found in the following way. Suppose that v_1 equals $-V_A R_1/(R_1 + R_2)$, at $t = 0$, and is increasing toward the "power supply" voltage V_A. Then

$$v_1 = V_A\left[1 - \left(1 + \frac{R_1}{R_1 + R_2}\right)e^{-t/RC}\right] \qquad 0 \leqq t \leqq \frac{T}{2} \tag{18-71}$$

When $v_1 = V_A R_1/(R_1 + R_2)$, then $t = T/2$. Manipulating, we obtain

$$T = 2RC \ln\left(1 + \frac{2R_1}{R_2}\right) \tag{18-72a}$$

The frequency of oscillation is given by $1/T$. Therefore,

$$f = \frac{1}{2RC \ln(1 + 2R_1/R_2)} \tag{18-72b}$$

Triangular Waveform Generator

At times, we want to generate a triangular waveform. The voltage v_1 of Fig. 18-14 approximates a triangular waveform, but it is actually composed of segments of exponentials. The RC circuit functions as an approximate integrator (see Sec. 13-7). An ideal integrator would have as its output a triangular rather than an exponential waveform. We can improve the performance of the simple RC integrator if we replace it by an operational amplifier integrator. Such a circuit is shown in Fig. 18-16a. The operational amplifier integrator introduces a 180° phase shift. To eliminate this, an amplifier whose gain is minus one is included in the circuit.

If we assume an ideal integrator, then Eq. 18-71 becomes

$$v_1 = -\frac{V_A R_1}{R_1 + R_2} + \frac{1}{RC}\int_0^t V_A\,dt \qquad 0 \leqq t \leqq \frac{T}{2} \tag{18-73}$$

Now v_1 increases linearly with time. Thus,

$$v_1 = -\frac{V_A R_1}{R_1 + R_2} + \frac{V_A t}{RC} \qquad 0 \leqq t \leqq \frac{T}{2} \tag{18-74}$$

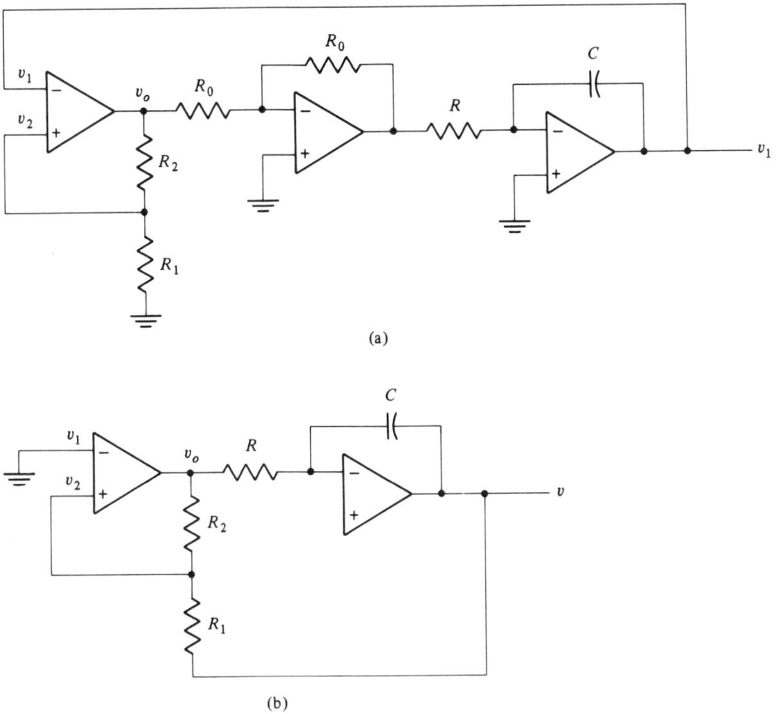

Figure 18-16. (a) A triangular waveform generator based on the circuit of Fig. 18-14. (b) A modification of this circuit which uses one less operational amplifier.

When $t = T/2$, then $v_1 = V_A R_1/(R_1 + R_2)$. Hence

$$T = \frac{4RCR_1}{R_1 + R_2} \tag{18-75a}$$

Or, equivalently, the frequency is

$$f = \frac{1 + R_1/R_2}{4RC} \tag{18-75b}$$

The circuit of Fig. 18-16a uses one operational amplifier to reverse the phase of the output of the integrator. This phase reversal circuit can be eliminated if the output of the integrator is returned to the positive input of the operational amplifier (see Fig. 18-16b). Now

$$v_2 = \frac{v_0 R_1}{R_1 + R_2} + \frac{vR_2}{R_1 + R_2}$$

Now the output switches when $v_2 = 0$. Or, equivalently

$$v = \pm \frac{V_A R_1}{R_2}$$

The output of the integrator is then

$$v = -\frac{V_A R_1}{R_2} + \frac{1}{RC}\int_0^t V_A\,dt \qquad 0 \leqq t \leqq \frac{T}{2}$$

When $t = T/2$ then $v = V_A R_1/R_2$. Hence

$$T = \frac{4RCR_1}{R_2}$$

Or, equivalently

$$f = \frac{R_2/R_1}{4RC}$$

Note that we have considered ideal operational amplifiers here. In particular, the maximum rate at which an amplifier can switch is limited. Hence, the output will not be the ideal waveform that we have sketched.

Just as in the case of Fig. 18-14, the outputs labeled v_o in Figs. 18-16a and 18-16b will be square waves. Hence these circuits produce both square and triangular waves.

Example

Obtain a square wave generator that has a frequency of 100 Hz. The circuit of Fig. 18-14 will be used. Hence, Eq. 18-72 applies here.

$$0.01 = 2RC \ln\left(1 + \frac{2R_1}{R_2}\right)$$

Let us set $R = 0.1R_2$. Then,

$$RC = \frac{0.01}{2}\frac{1}{\ln 1.2} = 0.0274$$

If we choose

$$C = 0.1\ \mu\text{F}$$

then,

$$R = 274{,}000 \text{ ohms}$$

R would probably be a variable resistance so that the frequency could be accurately adjusted.

18-9. A VOLTAGE CONTROLLED OSCILLATOR

We have discussed oscillators whose frequency can be varied by changing the value of the circuit components (i.e., the capacitors, resistors, or inductors). It would be convenient if we could change the frequency of oscillation simply by varying an applied voltage. A Varactor diode (see Sec. 1-8) can be used to accomplish this. The capacitance of these diodes varies in accordance with Eq. 1-37. Hence, if they are used as part of the tuned circuit of an oscillator, then the frequency of oscillation can be varied by varying the voltage across the reverse biased Varactor diode. Such circuits can be used for small frequency variations but there are applications where we want to vary the frequency of oscillation over a wide range. In addition, we desire that this frequency vary linearly with the controlling voltage.

The circuit of Fig. 18-17 accomplishes this. It is basically the same as that of the triangular generator of Fig. 18-16, but the voltage at the input to the integrator is not equal to $\pm V_A$ (see Sec. 18-8). The comparator output v_o drives the electronic switch

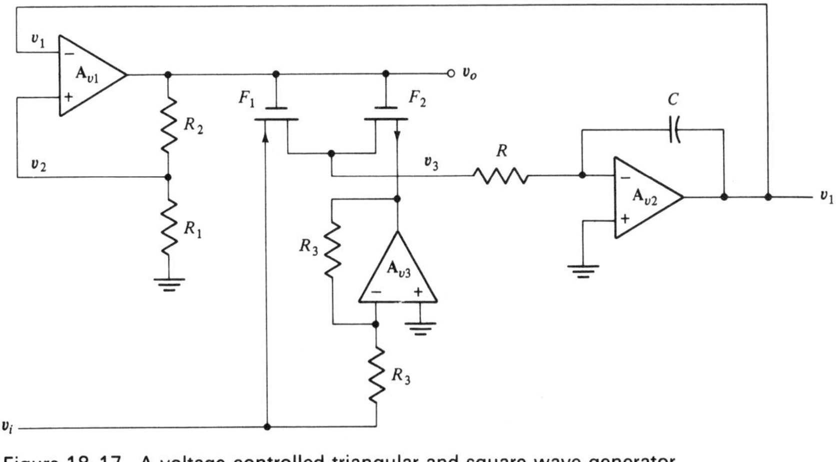

Figure 18-17. A voltage controlled triangular and square wave generator.

consisting of the n-channel and p-channel FET's, F_1 and F_2. When v_o is negative, F_1 conducts and F_2 is cut off and then $v_3 = v_i$. When v_o is positive, then F_1 is cut off and F_2 conducts now $v_3 = -v_i$. Note that the purpose of the $\mathbf{A}_{v3}$ circuit is simply to multiply v_i by -1. We assume that $v_i \geqq 0$ in this discussion. The phase reversal circuit of Fig. 18-16a can be omitted here since the electronic switch reverses the polarity of v_o.

To determine the frequency of oscillation of the circuit we can use Eq. 18-73 except that the voltage that is integrated is v_i, not V_A. That is,

$$v_1 = -\frac{V_A R_1}{R_1 + R_2} + \frac{v_i}{RC}\int_0^t dt \qquad 0 \leqq t \leqq \frac{T}{2} \tag{18-76}$$

This equation assumes that v_i is constant. The circuit will "flip" when $v_1 = V_A R_1/(R_1 + R_2)$. Hence,

$$V_A \frac{R_1}{R_1 + R_2} = -\frac{V_A R_1}{R_1 + R_2} + \frac{v_i}{RC}\int_0^{T/2} dt$$

Therefore,

$$T = 4\frac{V_A}{v_i}\frac{RCR_1}{R_1 + R_2} \tag{18-77a}$$

or, equivalently,

$$f = \frac{v_i}{V_A}\frac{1 + R_2/R_1}{4RC} \tag{18-77b}$$

Thus, the frequency varies linearly with v_i. Note that if v_i is made too large the operational amplifier $\mathbf{A}_{v3}$ will saturate and the circuit will not function properly. Actually, the frequency does not vary linearly with v_i over very wide frequency ranges.

18-10. THE ONE-SHOT OR MONOSTABLE MULTIVIBRATOR

In many applications a short pulse occurs whose purpose is to initiate an action or a sequence of actions. For instance, in a computer circuit, the pulse could serve as a clock pulse which activates a counter or other circuitry. However, the pulse may be too short for some of the circuits to react to it. In these cases we need a circuit that will convert each short pulse into a single longer pulse of predetermined duration. This length of time should be independent of the time duration of the input pulse. For instance, pulses of 10–100 ns duration (1 ns $= 10^{-9}$ s) could initiate or trigger a pulse of 10 μs (1 μs $= 10^{-6}$ s). A circuit that accomplishes this is called a *one-shot multivibrator* or a *monostable multivibrator*. Another application of the one-shot multivibrator circuit is to create a time delay. For instance, in Sec. 10-10 we discussed circuits that were triggered on the trailing edges of pulses. If the one-shot multivibrator produces a single pulse of time duration T, then the trailing edge of the output pulse will occur T s after the input (triggering) pulse, thus producing the desired time delay. (That is, no action occurs until the trailing edge of the multivibrator pulse.)

A circuit for a monostable multivibrator is shown in Fig. 18-18. For the time being, ignore the circuit consisting of R_1 and C_1. The remaining circuit is essentially the same as

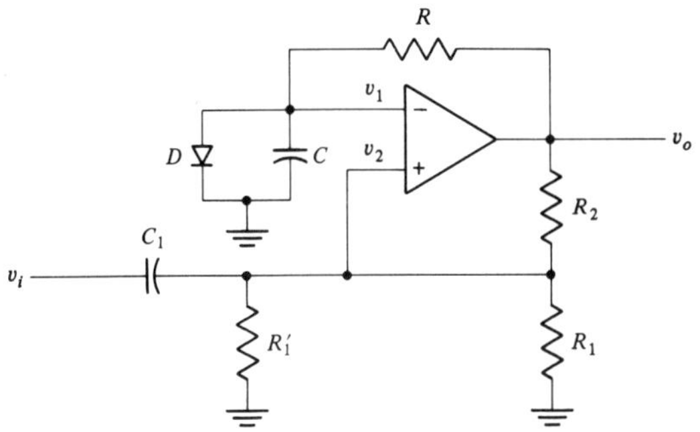

Figure 18-18. A monostable multivibrator rectangular pulse generator.

that of the free running multivibrator of Fig. 18-14 except that a diode is placed across the capacitor C. This diode prevents v_1 from becoming positive. Actually, v_1 can become slightly positive but the magnitude of the positive voltage is limited.

Suppose that $v_o = V_A$ (see Sec. 18-8). Then, $v_2 = V_A R_1/(R_1 + R_2)$ and v_1 will remain fixed at a very small positive value. Hence, this will be a stable condition and v_o will not change.

Now suppose that we momentarily apply a negative input voltage at the v_2 terminal. If it is sufficiently large, v_0 will now switch to $-V_A$. Even if the input voltage becomes zero v_2 will still be negative since $v_2 = v_o R_1/(R_1 + R_2)$ (we assume that the impedance of the input generator is much greater than R_2). The negative $v_o = -V_A$ will now charge the capacitor since the diode now acts as an open circuit. When v_1 reaches $-V_A R_1/(R_1 + R_2)$, v_o will switch and become $+V_A$ (see Sec. 18-8). Then, when v_o is negative, the circuit functions just as did the free running multivibrator but once v_o becomes positive, then the output remains constant until another negative input signal drives v_2 negative.

The waveforms in the monostable multivibrator are shown in Fig. 18-19. The input waveform is shown in Fig. 18-19a. This drives v_2 negative, so that v_o switches as shown. Then, v_2 becomes $-V_A R_1/(R_1 + R_2)$. Now capacitor C starts to charge (negatively). The relation for its charging is

$$v_1 = -V_A + (V_A + V_{DS})e^{-t/RC} \qquad 0 \leqq t \leqq T \tag{18-78}$$

where V_{DS} is the voltage across the conducting diode. The output remains constant at $-V_A$ until v_1 becomes $-V_A R_1/(R_1 + R_2)$. At that time, the output switches back to $+V_A$ and remains stable. Let us determine the time duration T. Substituting in Eq. 18-78 and manipulating, we have

$$T = RC \ln\left[\left(1 + \frac{V_{DS}}{V_A}\right)\left(1 + \frac{R_1}{R_2}\right)\right] \tag{18-79}$$

After time T the output becomes $+V_A$. Thus, the voltage across the capacitor increases (decreases in magnitude). See Fig. 18-19b. Its value is given by

$$v_1 = V_A - \left(V_A + \frac{V_A R_1}{R_1 + R_2}\right)e^{-(t-T)/RC} \qquad T_1 > t > T \tag{18-80}$$

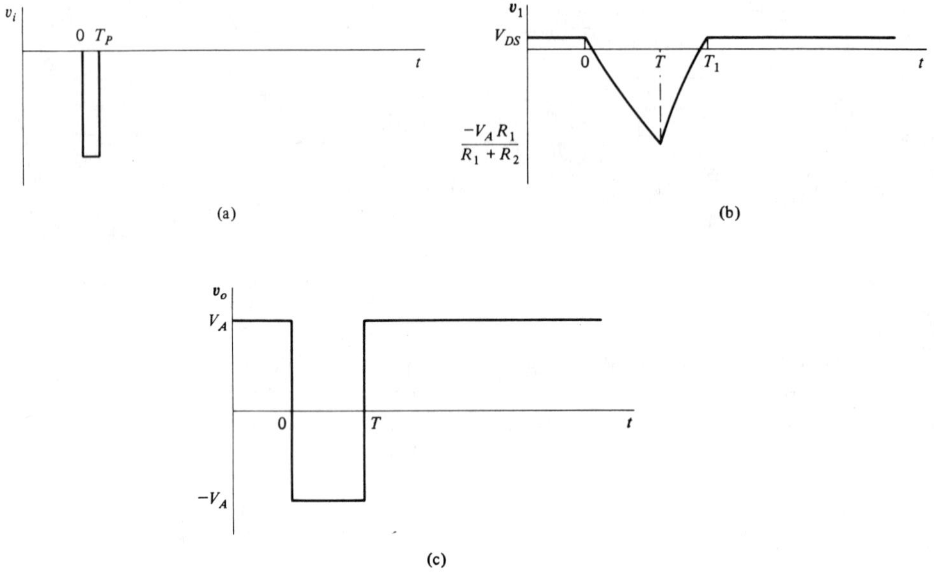

Figure 18-19. Waveform in the monostable multivibrator. (a) Input waveform. (b) v_1. (c) v_o.

At time T_1, $v_1 = V_{DS}$. Hence,

$$T_1 - T = RC \ln\left[\frac{1 + 2R_1/R_2}{(1 - V_{DS}/V_A)(1 + R_1/R_2)}\right] \tag{18-81}$$

Note that between time T and time T_1, the output is constant at V_A although v_1 is still changing. During this time, a negative pulse applied to v_2 may not activate the circuit since v_1 is also negative. The time $T_1 - T$ is called the *recovery time*. If every input pulse is to produce an output pulse, then the time between input pulses should be at least T_1 s. That is, the time duration between pulses must be at least equal to the recovery time plus the pulse time T.

We have thus far ignored R_1' and C_1. Indeed, the circuit functions without them. R_1 and C_1 form a simple differentiating circuit (see Sec. 13-9). A negative pulse at v_2 activates the circuit. The output of the simple differentiator will be a negative signal whenever the input signal changes negatively. Thus, the circuit will be triggered on the negative going edge of a pulse. The R_1C_1 circuit also blocks direct voltage. For instance, a negative direct voltage applied to this circuit will trigger it only once, at its initial application, and it will then not further affect the circuit. If v_i varies slowly, then the output of the differentiating circuit will be small and thus, it will probably not trigger the circuit. Thus, the inclusion of R_1' and C_1 tends to ensure that only pulses or rapidly changing signals can trigger the circuit. (Note that the parallel combination of R_1 and R_1' should replace R_1 in the previous discussion.)

18-11. INTEGRATED CIRCUIT WAVEFORM GENERATORS—TIMERS

In Secs. 18-7 to 18-10 we discussed circuits that produce a variety of waveforms. These circuits are often fabricated as integrated circuit chips which contain all of the elements except for the frequency determining resistors and capacitors. These are externally connected by the user. Such chips are called *timers*. The principles discussed in this chapter are often the basis of their circuitry.

18-12. CLIPPING AND CLAMPING CIRCUITS

We shall now discuss several circuits that are not oscillator circuits, but they can be used to shape waveforms.

Clipping Circuits

The *clipping circuit* prevents an applied signal from exceeding a predetermined value. A simple clipping circuit is shown in Fig. 18-20a. Let us assume that the diodes are ideal, that is, that they act as short circuits when they are forward biased and as open circuits when they are reverse biased. Suppose that v_i is zero and increases positively. Then, D_2 will be cut off. Diode D_1 will also be cut off until v_i becomes more positive than V_1 V. Now, D_1 conducts. Since it now is a short circuit, the output voltage will not rise above V_1 V. A similar discussion can be made for negative voltage and V_2. Hence, the input-output characteristics for the clipping circuit are as shown in Fig. 18-19b. The clipping circuit is also called a limiting circuit since the value of the signal is limited by it.

Let us consider one application for a clipping circuit. Suppose that $V_1 = V_2$ and $v_i = V_{max} \sin \omega t$, where $V_{max} \gg V_1$. Most of the sine wave will be clipped. Thus, the output will closely resemble a square wave. Therefore, the clipping circuit can be used to produce approximate square waves.

An actual clipping circuit will not have the ideal characteristics of Fig. 18-20b. The forward (conducting) resistance of the diode, although low, is not zero, and the diodes do not start to conduct until the cut-in voltage is reached.

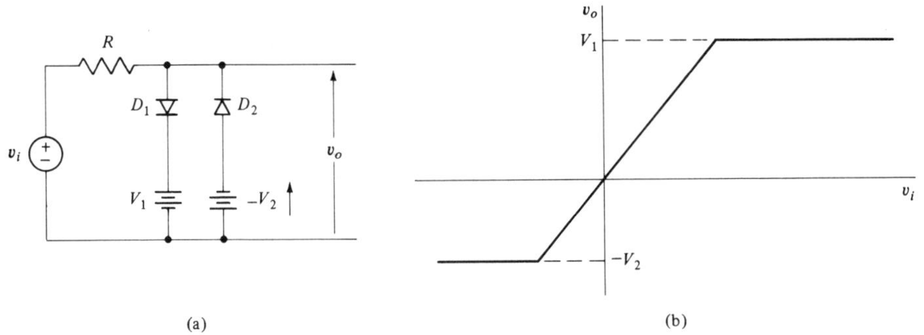

Figure 18-20. (a) A simple diode clipping circuit. (b) Its idealized characteristic.

We can use operational amplifier circuits to establish circuits that function as almost ideal limiters. In Fig. 13-3 we illustrated the characteristics of an operational amplifier. They are essentially the same as those of the ideal limiter. We cannot arbitrarily vary the levels of V_1 and V_2 (see Fig. 18-20b) of an operational amplifier limiter, but these levels can be varied over relatively wide ranges by changing the positive and negative power supply voltages.

Clamping Circuits

At times we have a signal that swings positive and negative and we want to add a direct component to it so that the waveform never becomes negative (or positive). The waveform is not to be changed in any other way. In addition, we want the minimum value to be zero. For instance, suppose that we have a waveform such as that of Fig. 18-21a and we want to shift it, without distortion, to the form of Fig. 18-21b. If V_1 were a constant, then we could accomplish this shift by adding a direct voltage power supply equal to V_1 to the circuit. However, in general, V_1 is a variable (i.e., the signal shape and level will change with time) and thus, we cannot use a fixed power supply to shift the level. The circuit of Fig. 18-21c produces the desired results. When v_i is negative, the diode will conduct and the voltage across the capacitor will become V_1 V, with the polarity shown. Note that when D conducts, the resistance in the circuit is very small. Thus, the voltage across C reaches its maximum value when v_i is at its most negative value. As v_i rises above $-V_1$, the voltage $V_1 + v_i$ will reverse bias the diode and cut it off. We assume that

$$RC \gg T \tag{18-82}$$

where T is the period of the input signal. Thus, the voltage across the capacitor will remain essentially constant at V_1 because the RC time constant is much longer than the period of the signal. Then, we can write

$$v_o = V_1 + v_i \tag{18-83}$$

Hence, we have shifted the waveform by the desired amount and the output waveform will be as shown in Fig. 18-20b. Note that the capacitor charges at a much faster rate than it discharges since the forward resistance of the diode is very low (ideally zero).

Now suppose that V_1 decreases. Let us call the new value of V_1, V'_1. The capacitor voltage will gradually fall to the new value of V'_1, and again the waveform will be as in

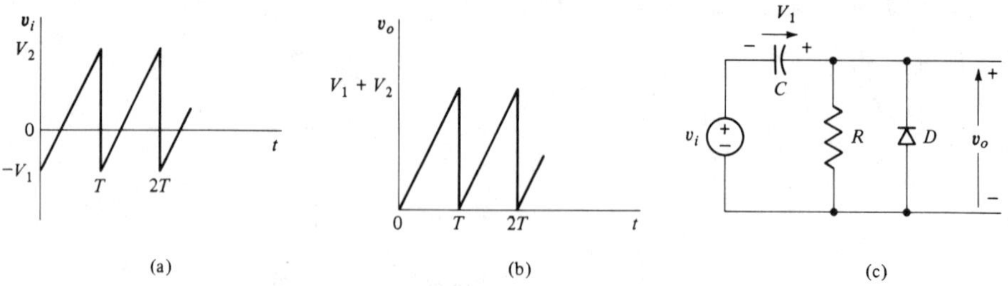

Figure 18-21. (a) The input to a clamping circuit. (b) Its output. (c) The clamping circuit.

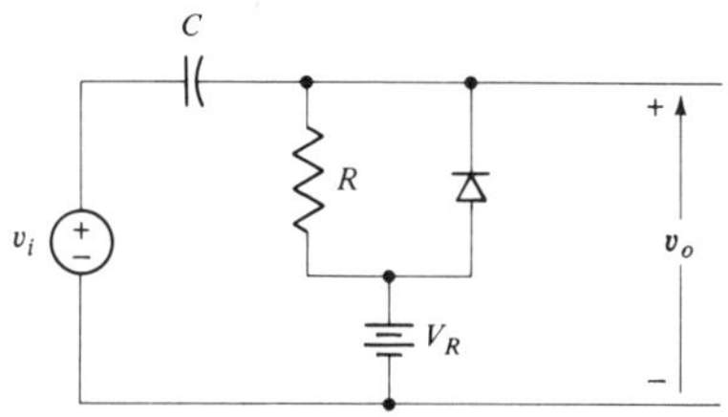

Figure 18-22. A clamping circuit that shifts the voltage to a level V_R.

Fig. 18-21c. The rate of the capacitor discharge depends upon the *RC* time constant. Thus, it may take many cycles before the circuit readjusts itself. However, this is usually just a short time and the circuit usually functions in a satisfactory manner.

In an actual circuit there will be some slight distortion of the signal and some small negative voltage. This is because the diode is not ideal and does not conduct until its cut-in voltage is exceeded and also because its forward resistance is not zero.

At times, we want to shift the signal level so that its minimum value is not zero but some predetermined value. This can be accomplished using the circuit of Fig. 18-22. This circuit functions in essentially the same way as the circuit of Fig. 18-21c except now the signal is shifted to the level v_R. This is

$$v_o = v_i + V_R + V_1 \tag{18-84}$$

These circuits are called *clamping circuits* since the minimum voltage is "clamped" to a specific value.

The clamping circuits that we have discussed essentially preserve the waveform. At times, we are only concerned with its peak value or its value when it exceeds V_R. In such cases, the operational amplifier circuit of Fig. 18-23a can be used. Let us consider it. If $v_1 < v_R$ then v_o' will be positive and the diode *D* will conduct. Hence, the circuit functions as a voltage follower (see Sec. 13-3) and if $v_i < v_R$, then $v_o = V_R$.

If $v_i > v_R$, then v_o will be negative and the diode will be cut off. Then,

$$v_o = \frac{v_i R_3}{R_1 + R_3} \tag{18-85}$$

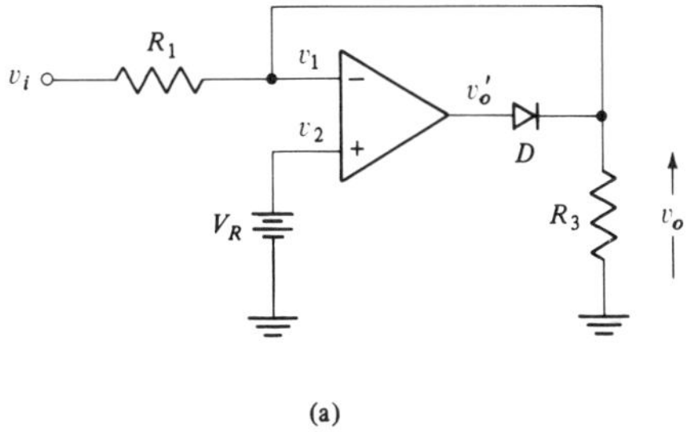

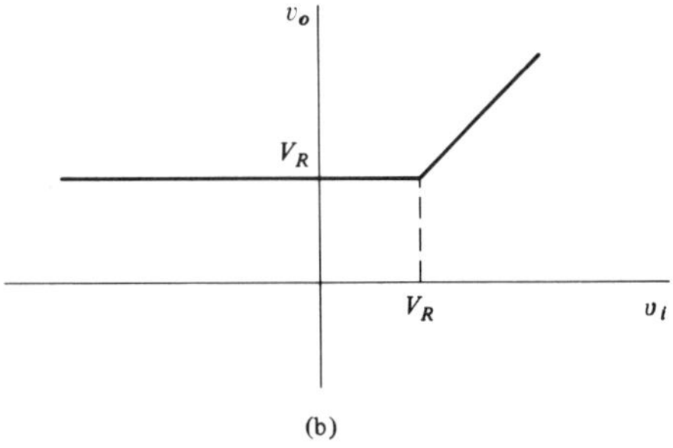

Figure 18-23. (a) An operational amplifier clamping circuit. (b) Its input-output characteristic.

If we make $R_3 \gg R_1$, then

$$v_o = v_i \tag{18-86}$$

Thus, the clamping circuit will have the input-output characteristic shown in Fig. 18-23b.

The effect of the diodes' cut-in voltage is greatly diminished in this circuit. For instance, ideally, the diode should start to conduct when $v_i = V_R$. However, now $v_o' = 0$. The diode will not conduct until $v_o' = V_\gamma$, the cut-in voltage. Let us see how much we must increase v_i to account for this. Let us call this increase $V_{i\gamma}$. Its value is given by

$$V_{i\gamma} = \frac{V_\gamma}{|\mathbf{A}_v|} \tag{18-87}$$

Since $|\mathbf{A}_v|$ is usually very large, $V_{i\gamma}$ can be considered to be essentially zero.

The effect of the diodes' series resistance is also greatly reduced because of the feedback around it (see Sec. 13-5). Thus, in this circuit, the diode acts as though it were essentially ideal.

PROBLEMS

18-1. Discuss why the criteria for oscillation that we used for oscillators are simpler than those used for feedback amplifiers.

18-2. Determine the criteria for oscillation for the Colpitts oscillator circuit of Fig. 18-1c. Use the low-frequency model for the FET.

18-3. Repeat Prob. 18-2 for the Hartley circuit of Fig. 18-1e.

18-4. Determine the criteria for oscillation for the Colpitts oscillator circuit of Fig. 18-1b. Use the high-frequency hybrid-pi model for the transistor.

18-5. Repeat Prob. 18-4 but now use the approximate model for the transistor of Fig. 18-3b.

18-6. Repeat Prob. 18-4 for the Hartley oscillator of Fig. 18-1f.

18-7. Repeat Prob. 18-6 but now use the approximate model of Fig. 18-3b.

18-8. Design a FET Colpitts oscillator that oscillates at a frequency $f_0 = 2 \times 10^6$ Hz. Use a FET with the following parameter values

$$g_m = 10{,}000\ \mu\text{mho}$$
$$r_d = 10^5\ \text{ohms}$$
$$C_{gs} = 1.0\ \text{pF}$$
$$C_{gd} = 0.5\ \text{pF}$$
$$C_{ds} = 0.1\ \text{pF}$$

The operating point is

$$V_{DS} = 10\ \text{V}$$
$$I_D = 1\ \text{mA}$$
$$V_{GS} = 0\ \text{V}$$

Assume that $V_{DD,\text{max}} = 25$ V and that the G of the coil is 100.

18-9. Repeat Prob. 18-8 but now use the oscillator circuit of Fig. 18-1a.

18-10. Repeat Prob. 18-8 but now use the oscillator circuit of Fig. 18-1e.

18-11. Design a transistor Colpitts oscillator that oscillates at a frequency of $f_0 = 2 \times 10^6$ Hz. The parameters of the transistor are

$$g_m = 75{,}000\ \mu\text{mho}$$
$$r_{bb'} = 100 \text{ ohms}$$
$$r_{b'e} = 1500 \text{ ohms}$$
$$r_{ce} = 100{,}000 \text{ ohms}$$
$$C_{b'e} = 30 \text{ pF}$$
$$C_{b'c} = 2 \text{ pF}$$

The operating point is

$$V_{CE} = 10 \text{ V}$$
$$I_C = 1 \text{ mA}$$
$$I_B = 10\ \mu\text{A}$$

Assume that $V_{DD,\max} = 25$ V and that the G of the coil is 100.

18-12. Repeat Prob. 18-11 but now use the oscillator circuit of Fig. 18-1b.

18-13. Repeat Prob. 18-11 but now use the Hartley oscillator circuit of Fig. 18-1f.

18-14. Derive the conditions for oscillation (Eqs. 18-31, 18-33, and 18-34 for the RC phase shift oscillator of Fig. 18-4a.

18-15. Derive the conditions of oscillation (Eqs. 18-38, 18-39) for the RC phase shift oscillator of Fig. 18-4b.

18-16. Design a FET RC phase shift oscillator that oscillates at $f_0 = 200$ Hz. The parameters of the FET are given in Prob. 18-8.

18-17. Repeat Prob. 18-16 for a transistor RC phase shift oscillator. The parameters of the transistor are given in Prob. 18-11.

18-18. Repeat Prob. 18-16 for an operational amplifier RC phase shift oscillator. Specify the minimum gain that the operational amplifier can have. Assume that $R_0 = 100$ ohms.

18-19. Design an operational amplifier Wein bridge oscillator that oscillates at $f_0 = 200$ Hz.

18-20. Obtain the conditions for oscillation for a Wein bridge oscillator that uses FET's as the active devices. Deduce the circuit from Fig. 18-6.

18-21. Repeat Prob. 18-20 for a Wein bridge oscillator that uses transistors as the active elements.

18-22. Discuss the procedures used to stabilize the amplitude of the output of an oscillator.

18-23. Modify the design of the oscillator of Prob. 18-19 so that the amplitude of oscillation is limited to about 0.6 V. (This is the cut in voltage of an ordinary diode.)

18-24. The parameters of the FET used in the circuit of Fig. 18-8 are given in Prob. 18-8. In addition, assume that g_m falls off linearly to 25 when $V_{GS} = -5$ V. Design an amplitude stabilized RC phase shift oscillator whose frequency of oscillation is 200 Hz and whose amplitude of oscillation is to be about 0.1 V.

18-25. Discuss the procedures for obtaining an oscillator with very high frequency stability.

18-26. Repeat the design of Prob. 18-8 but now use a Clapp oscillator. Make the capacitors C_1 and C_2 as large as possible. (There should be a "safety factor" of 2 when C_1 and C_2 are picked.)

18-27. Why does the frequency stability of a Clapp oscillator increase as g_m increases?

18-28. Compare the frequency stability of the Colpitts and Clapp oscillator circuits.

18-29. Discuss the reasons for the stability of crystal oscillators.

18-30. Design a multivibrator of the type shown in Fig. 18-12 that meets the following specifications.

$$T = 0.001 \text{ s}$$

or

$$f = 1000 \text{ Hz}$$

The parameters of the transistor are given in Prob. 18-11.

18-31. Repeat Prob. 18-30 but now make the two halves of the period asymmetric such that

$$T_1 = 0.0005 \text{ s}$$

$$T_2 = 0.001 \text{ s}$$

18-32. Design a multivibrator square wave generator of the type shown in Fig. 18-14 that meets the following specifications

$$f_0 = 1000 \text{ Hz}$$

18-33. Repeat Prob. 18-32 but now use

$$f_0 = 10{,}000 \text{ Hz}$$

18-34. Will the circuit of Fig. 18-14 oscillate for all values of $|\mathbf{A}_v|$? If it does not oscillate for all $|\mathbf{A}_v|$ then determine the minimum $|\mathbf{A}_v|$ that can be used to obtain oscillation.

18-35. Design a triangular wave generator that oscillates at a frequency of 1000 Hz. Assume that the operational amplifier is such that $V_A = 15$ V.

18-36. Discuss the use of varactor diodes in voltage controlled oscillators.

18-37. Discuss the operation of the voltage controlled oscillator of Fig. 18-17.

18-38. Design an oscillator whose frequency of oscillation is given by

$$f_0 = 1000 v_i$$

where v_i is an input voltage. Assume that operational amplifiers with $V_A = 15$ V are used and that $0 \leqq V_i \leqq 5$ V.

18-39. Design a one-shot multivibrator that produces pulses 10^{-3} s long when a negative going pulse is applied to its input. Assume that the operational amplifier is such that $V_A = 15$ V.

18-40. What is the recovery time of the circuit of Prob. 18-39?

18-41. Repeat Prob. 18-39 but now increase the pulse length to 0.1 s.

18-42. Repeat Prob. 18-40 for the circuit of Prob. 18-41.

18-43. Discuss the operation of the clipping circuit of Fig. 18-20a.

18-44. The clamping circuit of Fig. 18-21c is to work with signals whose minimum frequency is 10^6 Hz. If the level of the signal changes, the circuit is to recover in 10^{-2} s. Design the circuit that will accomplish this.

18-45. Discuss the operation of the circuit of Fig. 18-22.

18-46. Discuss the operation of the circuit of Fig. 18-23a.

BIBLIOGRAPHY

Chirlian, P. M. *Electronic Circuits: Physical Principles, Analysis and Design.* New York: McGraw-Hill, 1971, Chapters 14 and 15.

Holt, C. A. *Electronic Circuits, Digital and Analog.* New York: Wiley, 1978, Chapter 22.

Millman, J. *Microelectronics: Digital and Analog Circuits and Systems.* New York: McGraw-Hill, 1979, Chapter 17.

Chapter 19

Modulation and Demodulation

A communications system transmits information from one point to another. When there is radio transmission, the frequency of transmission is of great importance. For instance, at frequencies below 100 KHz, the size of the transmitting and receiving antennas becomes very large, while at frequencies above 30 MHz, the transmission essentially is line of sight. Thus circumstances often dictate the frequency of transmission. In this chapter we shall discuss procedures that allow us to select the frequency at which information is transmitted.

A sinusoid that is constantly on does not convey any information. In order to provide information, the sinusoid must be made to vary in accordance with the information. There are various schemes for varying a sinusoid. The amplitude of the sinusoid can be made to vary in accordance with the information. Similarly, the frequency and/or phase can be made to vary. The process by which a function (e.g., a sinusoid) is made to vary in accordance with some information is called *modulation*. The inverse process wherein the information is recovered from the modulated signal is called *demodulation* or *detection*.

19-1. AMPLITUDE MODULATION

One widely used procedure for modulating a sinusoid is called *amplitude modulation* (AM). Here the amplitude, or maximum value of the sinusoid is made to vary in accordance with some signal. Let us assume that we have a voltage

$$v(t) = V \cos \omega_c t \tag{19-1}$$

If V is a constant, then this is just a simple unmodulated sinusoid. It is called the *carrier*. Now suppose that we have some information $v_m(t)$. For instance, $v_m(t)$ could be an audio signal that we want to transmit by radio. In amplitude modulation we cause V to vary in accordance with the signal in the following way.

$$v(t) = [V_c + kv_m(t)]\cos \omega_c t \tag{19-2}$$

where k is a constant. An example of amplitude modulation is shown in Fig. 19-1. Note how the peak value of the modulated signal varies in accordance with the information, which is also called the modulating signal.

There are many questions one can ask about a modulated signal. One important one is how much bandwidth does it occupy. A casual glance at Eq. 19-2 might seem to indicate that $v(t)$ only occupies a single frequency, ω_c but we shall see that this assumption is incorrect. Another important question concerns the power of the modulated signal.

In order to study amplitude modulation, we shall assume for the time being that the modulating signal (i.e., the information) is also a sinusoid.

$$v_m = V_m \cos \omega_m t \tag{19-3}$$

Hence,

$$v(t) = V_c\left[1 + \frac{kV_m}{V_c}\cos \omega_m t\right]\cos \omega_c t \tag{19-4}$$

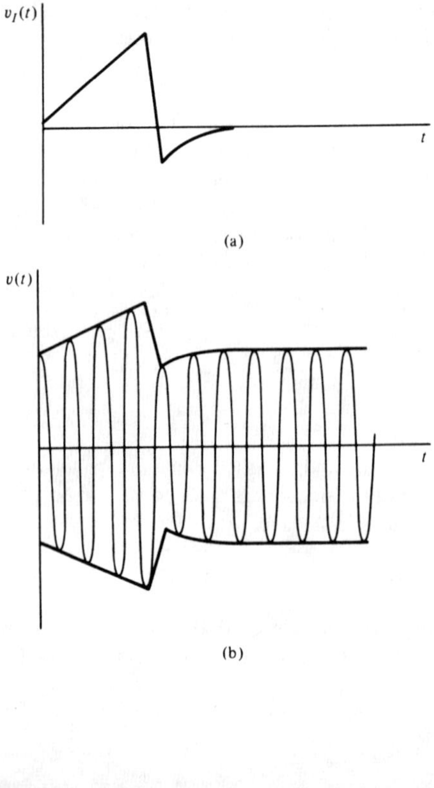

Figure 19-1. An example of amplitude modulation. (a) The modulating signal. (b) The modulated signal.

Let us define

$$m = \frac{kV_m}{V_c} \tag{19-5}$$

m is called the *index of modulation.* If we multiply m by 100, the resulting number is called the *percent modulation.* Then

$$v(t) = V_c[1 + m \cos \omega_m t]\cos \omega_c t \tag{19-6}$$

A curve of this function is plotted in Fig. 19-2. The cosinusoid varies between two curves called the *envelope of modulation.*

As a practical matter, in most amplitude modulation systems, we restrict m such that

$$0 \leqq m \leqq 1 \tag{19-7}$$

Mathematically, values of m greater than one are acceptable. This means that the lower envelope of modulation becomes positive for some values of time, and that the upper envelope of modulation becomes negative for those values of time. However, most electronic devices do not respond in this way. If $m > 1$, they usually cut off, resulting in distortion. Even if this distortion did not occur, we shall see that most detection circuits would produce a greatly distorted signal since the envelope no longer has the same shape as the information.

Now let us determine the frequency components of Eq. 19-4. Using the trigonometric relations for the product of cosines, we have

$$v(t) = V_c \cos \omega_c t + \frac{mV_c}{2}\cos(\omega_c + \omega_m)t + \frac{mV_c}{2}\cos(\omega_c - \omega_m)t \tag{19-8}$$

Two additional frequencies called *sidebands* have been produced by the modulation process. Note that the carrier has been *unchanged.* In general, the carrier will be unchanged by amplitude modulation.

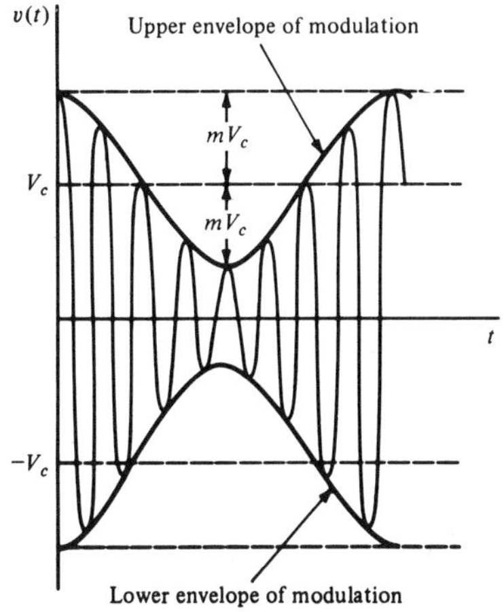

Figure 19-2. Amplitude modulation by a cosinusoid.

Now let us consider the bandwidth of the signal of Eq. 19-8. Signals lie in the range from $\omega_c - \omega_m$ to $\omega_c + \omega_m$. Hence the bandwidth is

$$B = \frac{2\omega_m}{2\pi} = 2f_m \tag{19-9}$$

Plots of the relative amplitude, called *frequency spectra*, are often made to illustrate the various frequency components. In Fig. 19-3 we have such a plot for Eq. 19-8.

Now let us assume that the modulating signal is not a sinusoid but is an arbitrary periodic signal so that it can be expressed in a Fourier series. Such a typical frequency spectrum is shown in Fig. 19-4a. When this signal is used to amplitude modulate a carrier, each sinusoidal component will produce a pair of sidebands. Hence, the frequency spectrum of the resulting amplitude modulated signal will be as shown in Fig. 19-4b. The bandwidth required by the signal is twice the highest frequency contained in the modulating signal. The relative amplitudes of the sidebands are the same as the relative amplitudes of the frequency components of the modulating signal.

In Chapter 17 we considered bandpass amplifiers and discussed how a flat response was required in the pass band if distortion was not to result. We can now see why this is so. Suppose that the signal of Fig. 19-4b was amplified by a bandpass amplifier. If all the sidebands were not amplified equally, this would have the same effect as if the modulating signal were passed through a low-pass amplifier that did not amplify all its frequency components equally.

Let us now consider the power contained in the carrier and sidebands. Power is proportional to voltage squared. Therefore, from Eq. 19-8, we have for the carrier power

$$P_c = KV_c^2/2 \tag{19-10a}$$

while the sideband power is

$$P_{sb} = Km^2V_c^2/4 \tag{19-10b}$$

Hence,

$$\frac{P_{sb}}{P_c} = \frac{m^2}{2} \tag{19-11}$$

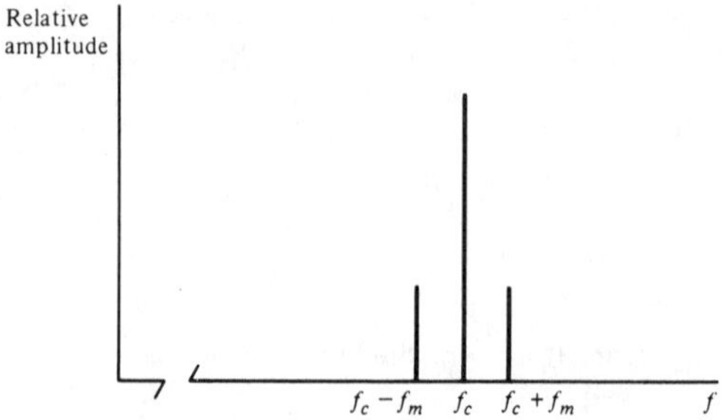

Figure 19-3. Frequency spectrum of an amplitude modulated waveform when the modulating signal is a sinusoid.

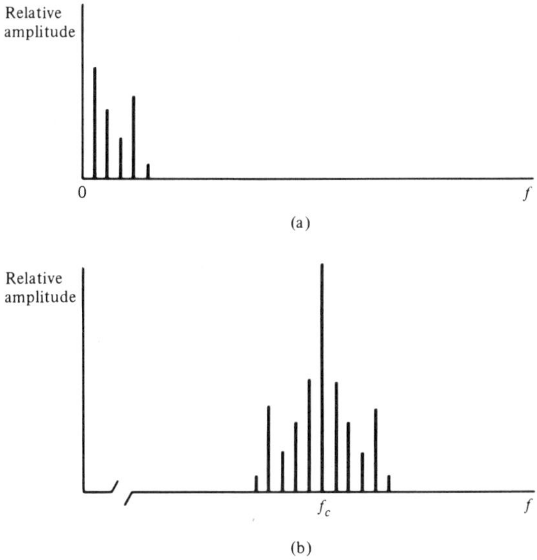

Figure 19-4. (a) Frequency spectrum of a nonsinusoidal modulating signal. (b) The frequency spectrum of the resulting amplitude modulated signal. Note the break in the frequency axis of Fig. 19-4b.

Hence, even if there is 100% modulation, the sideband power will only be one half that of the carrier. Equation 19-11 is only valid for modulation by a sinusoid and the ratio P_{sb}/P_c will be different for other waveforms. For instance, suppose that the carrier is 100% modulated by a square wave. Then, the maximum signal will be $2V_c$ for half the period and 0 for the other half. The total power (carrier plus sidebands) is then

$$P_c + P_{sb} = K\frac{1}{2}\left(\frac{4V_c^2}{2}\right) = KV_c^2$$

The carrier power is unchanged by modulation. Therefore, it is given by Eq. 19-10a. Hence, for 100% modulation by a square wave

$$\frac{P_{sb}}{P_c} = 1 \tag{19-12}$$

Since the carrier is unchanged by modulation, it provides no information. Then, we can state that the information is contained in the sidebands. The process of amplitude modulation is inefficient since much of the power is contained in the carrier. Efficient transmission schemes have been devised wherein the carrier is suppressed. The receiver then has an oscillator which generates a signal which replaces the carrier, but this leads to problems since, if the frequency of the oscillator does not exactly coincide with that of the suppressed carrier, excessive distortion can result. Thus, the frequency oscillation must be precisely controlled. In ordinary conventional AM broadcasting, the carrier is not suppressed in order to keep the receivers simple.

There are other procedures used to reduce power and bandwidth. Commercial television requires a 4.5-MHz bandwidth for the video information. This is transmitted using AM. The carrier and one sideband are partially suppressed to reduce bandwidth and power requirements. This is called *vestigial sideband* transmission. In this case a carrier is present. Some distortion results due to this procedure but its effect upon the television picture is not great. In other procedures, only a *single sideband* is transmitted. This reduces both power and bandwidth requirements. Since there is no carrier, the above discussed problems result.

19-2. METHODS OF AMPLITUDE MODULATION

Let us now consider the procedures that are used to generate amplitude modulated signals. When high-power radio frequency signals are transmitted, efficiency is often an important consideration. Hence, such amplifiers are often operated class C (or class B if the power level is not too high). The harmonic distortion produced by these amplifiers is, in large part, removed by the tuned circuits associated with the amplifier. Class C amplifiers are nonlinear in that the output signal is not a linear function of the input signal. Hence, if an amplitude modulated signal is the input to a class C amplifier, the output will be greatly distorted. Thus, when class C amplifiers are used, the modulation must be introduced in the class C (output) stage.

Collector Circuit Modulation

It can be shown that if a class C transistor amplifier is operated so that when the collector current is at maximum and the transistor is saturated, then the peak value of the RF signal will be almost proportional to the power supply voltage.

A class C modulated RF amplifier is shown in Fig. 19-5. If we ignore the audio input and the associated audio transformer, then this is just a tuned class C amplifier. (It is assumed that the bias voltages are appropriate for class C operation.) Now consider the audio voltage v_m which appears across the secondary of the audio transformer. This is in series with V_{CC}. Thus, the effective power supply voltage v_{CC} is the sum of the direct voltage V_{CC} and the audio voltage v_m. Hence,

$$v_{CC} = V_{CC} + v_m \tag{19-13}$$

Suppose that

$$v_m = V_m \cos \omega_m t \tag{19-14}$$

Then,

$$v_{CC} = V_{CC} + V_m \cos \omega_m t \tag{19-15}$$

The RF input will be at the carrier frequency. Then, if the output voltage is proportional to the power supply voltage, we have

$$v_o = kV_{CC}\left(1 + \frac{2V_m}{V_{CC}} \cos \omega_m t\right)\cos \omega_c t \tag{19-16}$$

and we have achieved amplitude modulation. Note that the bypass capacitor C_A should act essentially as a short circuit at ω_c but it should act as an open circuit at audio frequencies. This can easily be achieved since, in general, $\omega_c \gg \omega_m$.

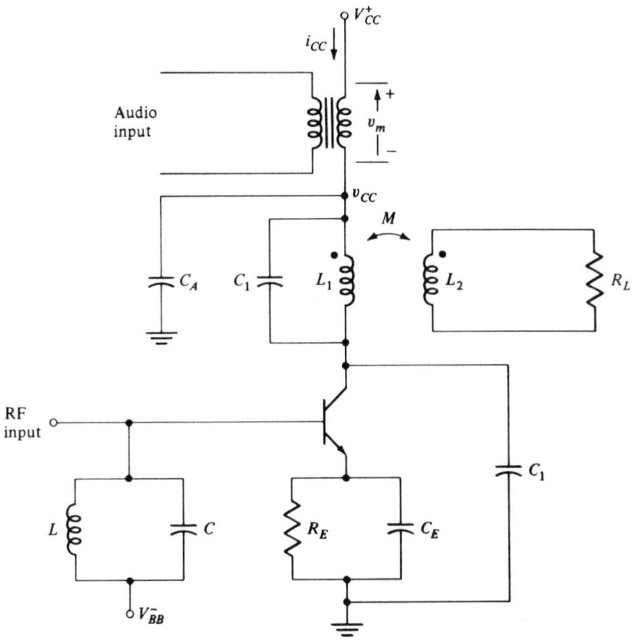

Figure 19-5. A collector modulator.

Let us now consider the power that is supplied by the V_{CC} power supply and the audio circuit. Since C_A acts as a short circuit for RF frequencies, the current i_{CC} will have only direct and audio components.

$$i_{CC} = I_{OA} + 2(I_{m1} \cos \omega_m t + I_{m2} \cos 2\omega_m t + \cdots) \tag{19-17}$$

Then, the power supplied by the power supply is

$$P_{OO} = V_{CC} I_{OA} \tag{19-18}$$

Thus, using Eq. 19-14, we have for the power supplied by the audio circuit

$$P_m = V_m I_{m1}/2 \tag{19-19}$$

If there is low distortion, then I_{OA} will be essentially independent of the modulating signal. Hence, P_{OO} will be unchanged by the modulation. Let us assume that the efficiency of the circuit is η. Then, if there is no modulation

$$P_c = P_{OO}\eta \tag{19-20}$$

In general, the efficiency does not vary substantially with the modulation. Since the efficiency, P_c, and P_c are essentially independent of modulation, we can then state that the sideband power must be supplied by the audio circuit. Thus,

$$P_c + P_{sb} = (P_{OO} + P_m)\eta \tag{19-21}$$

Hence,

$$P_m = \frac{P_{sb}}{\eta} \tag{19-22}$$

Note that the power supplied by the audio circuit may be substantial. In such cases, the audio signal must be supplied by a high-power audio amplifier. This is called a *modulator*.

Example

A class C RF amplifier operates at 90% efficiency. The carrier power is 50,000 W. What is the maximum power that will be supplied by the modulator?

From Eq. 19-22 we have

$$P_m = \frac{P_{sb}}{0.9}$$

If we assume sinusoidal modulation then, from Eq. 19-11, we have

$$P_{sb,\,\max} = \frac{P_c}{2} = 25{,}000 \text{ W}$$

Hence,

$$P_m = 27{,}778 \text{ W}$$

On the other hand, if we assume that a square wave is the input, then (see Eq. 19-12)

$$P_{sb} = 50{,}000 \text{ W}$$

and

$$P_m = 55{,}556 \text{ W}$$

The results of the previous example seem to indicate that the power which the modulator can supply should be equal to P_c/η. This is certainly true if 100% square waves are to be transmitted. However, for most audio applications, such signals are rarely encountered and the modulators are usually designed to be able to provide $P_c/2\eta$.

The input power that is not supplied as carrier or sidebands is dissipated within the transistor (we are ignoring any dissipation in the external elements here). Hence,

$$P_{OD} = (P_c + P_{sb})\left(\frac{1}{\eta} - 1\right) \tag{19-23}$$

Note that the dissipation will increase with modulation and the design must take this into account.

We have called the modulation that we have discussed *collector modulation*. If an FET is used as the active device then it is called *drain modulation*.

Base Current Modulation

We can also obtain amplitude modulation by varying the input current bias. For instance, in Fig. 19-5, the audio transformer could be put in series with V_{BB}. This has the advantage of substantially reducing the power requirements on the modulator. On the other hand, it has several disadvantages. There is more distortion produced by this circuit and its efficiency is lower than that of the collector modulated circuit. For these reasons, the collector modulated circuit is often used when the power levels are high.

In this discussion we have assumed that the modulating signal was in the audio frequency range but this need not be the case. For instance, these circuits can be used with video information. In such cases, the coupling between the modulator and the class C amplifier might not be a transformer. RC coupling could be used. Note that no matter what type of coupling is used, it must be able to withstand the power supply voltage.

Nonlinear Modulation

We shall now discuss a type of modulation that is not related to class C amplifiers. Now we shall obtain modulation by inputting the carrier and the information to a nonlinear amplifier. Let us see how this is accomplished. Suppose that we have a nonlinear amplifier whose input-output characteristic is given by

$$v_o = a_0 + a_1 v_i + a_2 v_i^2 \tag{19-24}$$

If the input signal is given by

$$v_i = V_c \cos \omega_c t + V_m \cos \omega_m t \tag{19-25}$$

(again assuming that the modulating signal is a sinusoid) then, substituting in Eq. 19-24 and manipulating, we obtain

$$\begin{aligned} v_o = a_0 &+ \frac{a_2}{2}(V_c^2 + V_m^2) + a_1(V_c \cos \omega_c t + V_m \cos \omega_m t) \\ &+ \frac{a_2}{2}(V_c^2 \cos 2\omega_c t + V_m^2 \cos 2\omega_m t) + a_2 V_c V_m \\ &[\cos(\omega_c + \omega_m)t + \cos(\omega_c - \omega_m)t] \end{aligned} \tag{19-26}$$

Now let us assume that $\omega_c \gg \omega_m$ and that the signal is passed through a bandpass amplifier which only passes those signals that are close to ω_c. The resulting output would be

$$v_o = a_1 V_c \left\{ \cos \omega_c t + \frac{a_2 V_m}{a_1} [\cos(\omega_c + \omega_m) + \cos(\omega_c - \omega_m)t] \right\} \tag{19-27}$$

Hence, we have achieved amplitude modulation. This is called *square law modulation* because the sidebands are produced by the v_i^2 terms of Eq. 19-24. In order to achieve square law modulation, a class A amplifier is operated in the nonlinear region of its characteristic. Thus, the circuit will be very inefficient. In addition, an actual amplifier's Taylor series (see Eq. 19-24) will contain cubic and higher ordered terms which will result in nonlinear distortion. Because of this, the use of nonlinear modulation is limited.

19-3. DETECTION OF AMPLITUDE MODULATED SIGNALS

We shall now discuss procedures for retrieving the information from an amplitude modulated wave. Such a circuit is called a *demodulator* or *detector*.

Linear Detection

A commonly used amplitude modulation detector called the *linear diode detector* is shown in Fig. 19-6. The name linear is somewhat misleading since the diode is, of course, a nonlinear device (i.e., it has a low forward resistance and a high reverse resistance). Actually, detection is a nonlinear process and cannot be accomplished by a truly linear circuit.

Let us consider the operation of the circuit. To simplify the discussion, we shall consider that the diode is ideal. We assume that

$$RC \gg \frac{2\pi}{\omega_c} \tag{19-28}$$

That is, the time constant of the *RC* circuit is very much larger than the period of the carrier. We shall see that this is necessary for proper operation.

Now consider the input waveform shown by the dashed curve of Fig. 19-7. At the first positive peak, the capacitor will charge to the peak voltage. Because of inequality 19-28, the diode will cease to conduct at a time slightly past the peak of v_i. Now $v_o > v_i$ and the diode is cut off. The capacitor discharges through R so v_o falls off exponentially as shown in Fig. 19-7. This discharge continues until the next cycle when v_i becomes equal to v_o. Now the diode conducts so that $v_o = v_i$ and v_o increases. This cycle repeats itself so that the output waveform has the form shown in Fig. 19-7. The jagged appearance is greatly exaggerated. We have drawn the figure showing ω_c about 10 times ω_m. Typically, ω_c is 100 or more times ω_m. Thus, the output curve is usually much smoother than we have indicated. The jagged components are also removed by the resulting audio amplifier since they represent high (ω_c and its harmonics) frequency components.

Let us now determine the choice of the *RC* product. If the *RC* product is too small, then the capacitor will discharge too much between successive cycles of the carrier. If relation 19-28 is satisfied, this problem will be eliminated.

If we make the *RC* product too large, then the output voltage will not be able to fall off when the modulating voltage falls off. For instance, if we replace R by an open circuit, then the capacitor will charge up to the peak value and remain there. In this case, the output will be a direct voltage. Thus, if v_o is to be able to follow the fall of the envelope,

$$RC \ll \frac{2\pi}{\omega_{m,\max}} \tag{19-29}$$

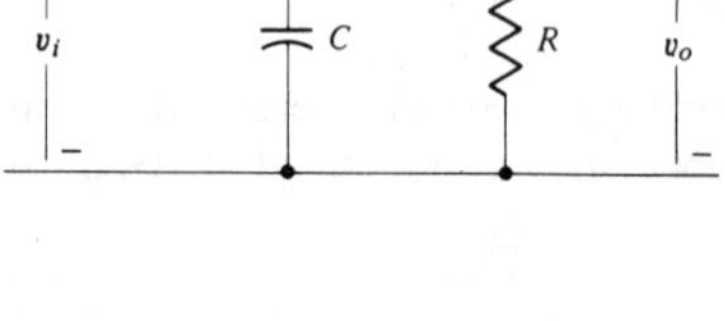

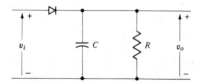

Figure 19-6. A linear diode detector.

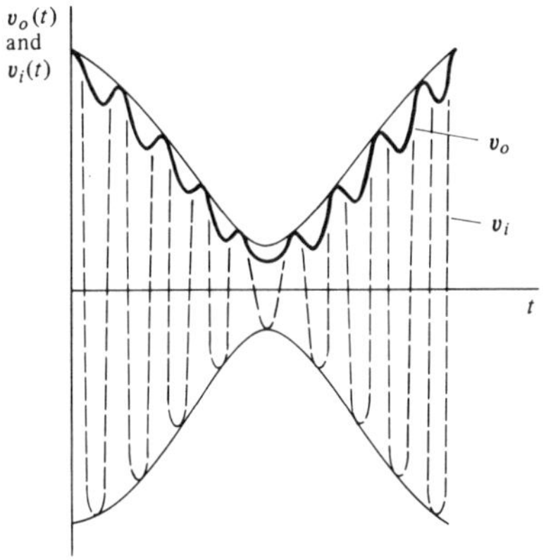

Figure 19-7. Waveforms of the linear diode detector.

where $\omega_{m,\,\max} = 2\pi f_{m,\,\max}$ and $f_{m,\,\max}$ is the highest frequency component of the modulating frequency. Relations 19-28 and 19-29 can usually both be satisfied since

$$\omega_c \gg \omega_m \tag{19-30}$$

The output voltage of the detector of Fig. 19-6 has a direct component that may be undesirable. To eliminate it, the circuit of Fig. 19-8 can be used. The coupling capacitor has been included to "block" the direct component. It is assumed that C_c is an effective short circuit at all signal (modulating) frequencies.

Care must be taken with this circuit because distortion can result if the resistances are not chosen properly. Let us consider this. Comparing Figs. 19-2 and 19-7, we have

$$v_o = V_c + mV_c \cos \omega_c t \tag{19-31}$$

Now let us determine the current i_i (see Fig. 19-8). The load for direct voltage is R, while that for the signal is R_{ac} where

$$\frac{1}{R_{\text{ac}}} = \frac{1}{R} + \frac{1}{R_L} \tag{19-32}$$

Hence,

$$i_i = \frac{V_c}{R} + \frac{mV_c}{R_{\text{ac}}} \cos \omega_c t \tag{19-33}$$

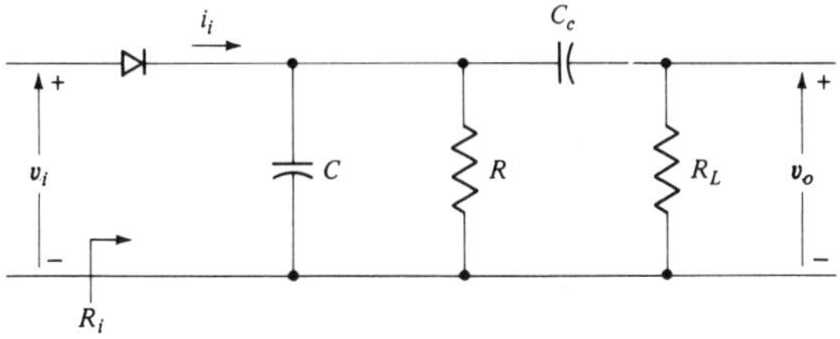

Figure 19-8. A diode detector with RC coupling.

R_{ac} will be smaller than R so it is possible for mV_c/R_{ac} to be larger than V_c/R. If this occurs, then, for some values of t, i_i as calculated by Eq. 19-33 will become negative. However, the diode will not allow this to occur. As a result, the signal will be clipped and distortion will result. To prevent this, we must have

$$\frac{1}{R} \geqq \frac{m}{R_{ac}} \tag{19-34}$$

Thus, if distortion is not to result, the maximum index of modulation that we can use is

$$m_{max} = \frac{R_{ac}}{R} \tag{19-35}$$

In general, we would like to be able to detect signals of up to essentially 100% modulation without distortion. This requires that $R_{ac} \simeq R$, or equivalently,

$$R_L \gg R \tag{19-36}$$

Let us now compute the input impedance of the circuit of Fig. 19-8. We shall again assume that the diode is ideal and that relation 19-36 is satisfied. Let us also assume that the input voltage is just an unmodulated carrier.

$$v_i = V_c \cos \omega_c t \tag{19-37}$$

Then, the voltage across the capacitor and resistor R will be a direct voltage equal to V_c. Hence, the power dissipated in R will be

$$P_2 = \frac{V_c^2}{R} \tag{19-38a}$$

The input power is given by

$$P_1 = \frac{V_c^2}{2R_i} \tag{19-38b}$$

Since the diode is ideal, $P_1 = P_2$. Hence,

$$R_i = \frac{R}{2} \tag{19-39}$$

When the input signal is modulated, the input resistance will remain unchanged provided that $R_L \gg R$ so that $R_{ac} = R$.

Nonlinear Detection

If an amplitude modulated signal such as that of Eq. 19-6 is applied to a square law circuit such as the one characterized by Eq. 19-24, detection will take place. This is called *nonlinear detection.* Assume that the output of the square law circuit, whose input is given by Eq. 19-6, is amplified by a low-pass amplifier which rejects all frequencies close to or greater than ω_c (e.g., it only passes audio components). The output of this amplifier will be

$$v_o(t) = a_2 V_c^2 m\left(\cos \omega_m t + \frac{m}{4} \cos 2\omega_m t\right) \tag{19-40}$$

The signal has been demodulated. However, $25m\%$ harmonic distortion has resulted. If the Taylor's series of Eq. 19-24 contains higher ordered terms, then additional distortion terms will be obtained. Thus, square law detectors are not widely used.

One place that nonlinear detection is used is in the mixer of a superheterodyne receiver (see Sec. 17-8). Remember that we described the mixer as an amplifier operated in its nonlinear region. Thus, it is just a nonlinear detector (or a nonlinear modulator).

Automatic Gain Control

If, in the detector of Fig. 19-6, we make the RC product very large, so that

$$RC \gg \frac{2\pi}{\omega_{m,\min}} \tag{19-41}$$

where $\omega_{m,\min}$ is the *lowest* modulating frequency, then the output will not be able to follow the variations of the envelope. In this case, v_o will be a direct voltage which is proportional to the amplitude of the carrier. Thus, we can obtain a direct voltage that will vary if the amplitude of the carrier varies. Note that this variation is assumed to be very slow so that relation 19-41 does not apply to it.

This voltage can be used to control the gain of a radio receiver automatically. Such circuits are called *automatic gain controls* (AGC) and are included on almost all receivers. For instance, suppose that you are listening to a radio in a moving automobile. The signal strength will vary continuously. If it were not for the AGC circuit, it would be necessary to constantly adjust the volume. Similarly, when we tune to different stations, the signal strengths may differ greatly but the volume remains relatively constant because of the AGC circuit.

A block diagram of an amplitude modulated receiver with AGC is shown in Fig. 19-9. The AGC detector produces a direct voltage proportional to the strength of the input carrier. This voltage is used to bias the preceding amplifier stages. The polarity of the bias voltage is such that the gain decreases as its magnitude increases so the gain will decrease if the input signal strength increases and we have achieved the desired effect.

At times, the AGC bias is not applied to the first stage. This stage is operated at maximum gain to improve the noise figure.

An implementation of an AGC circuit is shown in Fig. 19-10. The detector consisting of D_2, C_1, and R_1 produces a negative voltage proportional to the signal strength.

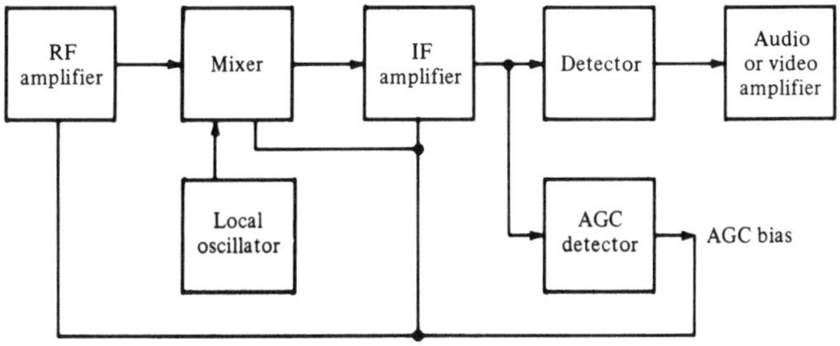

Figure 19-9. Block diagram of a superhetrodyne receiver with an AGC circuit.

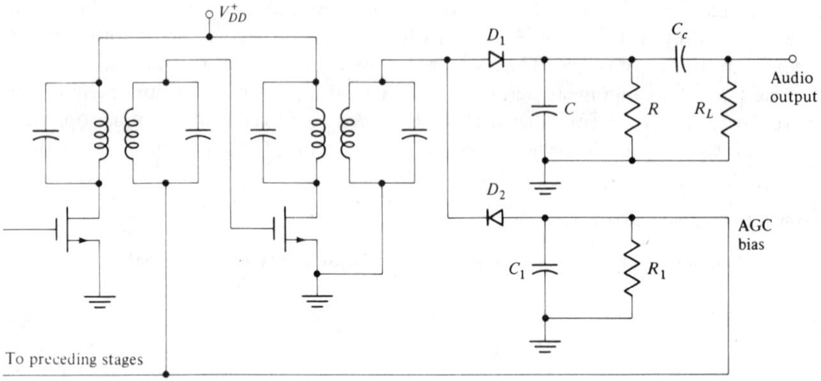

Figure 19-10. A portion of an AGC circuit.

This voltage becomes the direct gate to source bias of the preceding amplifier stages. As V_{GS} becomes more negative, the g_m of the FET's decreases as desired.

If $R_1 C_1$ is not made large enough, then the AGC bias will follow the low-frequency components of the envelope and tend to reduce these "changes in signal strength." Then, the low-frequency response of the detected signal will be reduced. Thus, care should be taken to ensure that R_1C_1 is large enough. Of course, if the time constant is made too large, then it will take too long for the AGC circuit to respond to changes in signal strength. Thus, some compromise is necessary.

The AGC circuit is a feedback circuit and, under certain conditions, it can oscillate. The ideas used in the stabilization of this circuit are similar to those discussed in conjunction with the amplitude stabilized oscillator (see Sec. 18-4).

19-4. FREQUENCY AND PHASE MODULATION

We shall now discuss frequency modulation and phase modulation where the frequency or phase of the carrier is varied in accordance with the information. Before actually considering the modulation, let us define frequency precisely. Suppose that we have a sinusoid

$$v(t) = V \cos[\omega_c t + \phi(t)] \tag{19-42}$$

where V is a constant. We can write

$$\Theta(t) = \omega_c t + \phi(t) \tag{19-43}$$

where $\Theta(t)$ is the instantaneous phase angle of the cosinusoid. Frequency is mathematically defined as the rate of change of phase angle. That is, the instantaneous angular frequency is given by

$$\omega_i = \frac{d\Theta(t)}{dt} \tag{19-44}$$

For instance, suppose that $\phi(t)$ equals a constant. Then, substituting Eq. 19-43 into Eq. 19-44, we have

$$\omega_i = \omega_c \tag{19-45}$$

which agrees with the usual definition.

If the instantaneous frequency varies in accordance with the modulating signal, then we have *frequency modulation* (FM). In this case,

$$\omega_i = \omega_c + k_2 v_m(t) \tag{19-46}$$

where $v_m(t)$ is the modulating signal. Substituting in Eq. 19-44 and solving for Θ we obtain

$$\Theta = \omega_c t + k_2 \int v_m(t)dt \tag{19-47}$$

Then, the waveform of a frequency modulated signal is

$$v(t) = V \cos\left[\omega_c t + k_2 \int v_m(t)dt\right] \tag{19-48}$$

There is another form of modulation called *phase modulation* (PM) that is closely related to frequency modulation. Here the phase angle $\phi(t)$ is made to vary in accordance with the information

$$\phi(t) = k_3 v_m(t) \tag{19-49}$$

Hence, the phase modulated waveform is of the form

$$v(t) = V \cos[\omega_c t + k_3 v_m(t)] \tag{19-50}$$

Although Eqs. 19-48 and 19-50 appear to be different, frequency and phase modulation are closely related. For instance, suppose that we have a circuit that produces phase modulation. If we pass the modulating signal through an integrator (see Sec. 13-7) before we apply it to the phase modulator, then the output is frequency modulated. Similarly, a frequency modulating circuit can be converted to a phase modulating circuit by differentiating the modulating signal before it is supplied to the modulator.

Let us now consider the analysis of Eqs. 19-48 and 19-50 to determine the bandwidth occupied by the modulated signals. For the analysis of the FM circuit, let us assume that

$$v_m(t) = V_m \cos \omega_m t \tag{19-51}$$

Substituting in Eq. 19-48, we have

$$v(t) = V\cos\left(\omega_c t + \frac{k_2 V_m}{\omega_m} \sin \omega_m t\right) \tag{19-52}$$

(We have assumed that the constant of integration is zero. In any event, it merely represents an arbitrary fixed phase angle.) Let us define the *index of frequency modulation* as

$$m_f = \frac{k_2 V_m}{\omega_m} \tag{19-53}$$

Then, Eq.19-52 can be written as

$$v(t) = V\cos(\omega_c t + m_f \sin\omega_m t) \tag{19-54}$$

Before proceeding further, let us consider phase modulation. In this case we shall assume that the modulating signal is

$$v_m(t) = V_m \sin\omega_m t \tag{19-55}$$

Substituting in Eq. 19-50, we have

$$v(t) = V\cos(\omega_c t + k_3 V_m \sin\omega_m t) \tag{19-56}$$

Now let us define the *index of phase modulation*, m_p, as

$$m_p = k_3 V_m \tag{19-57}$$

Thus, we can write Eq. 19-56 as

$$v(t) = V\cos(\omega_c t + m_p \sin\omega_m t) \tag{19-58}$$

If we compare Eqs. 19-54 and 19-58, we see that they are essentially the same. Let us define

$$m_F = m_f \qquad \text{for} \quad FM \tag{19-59a}$$

and

$$m_F = m_p \qquad \text{for} \quad PM \tag{19-59b}$$

Hence we can write both Eqs.19-54 and 19-58 as

$$v(t) = V\cos(\omega_v t + m_F \sin\omega_m t) \tag{19-60}$$

and analyze frequency and phase modulation simultaneously.

We can express Eq. 19-60 as

$$v(t) = V[\cos\omega_c t\cos(m_F \sin\omega_m t) - \sin\omega_c t\sin(m_F \sin\omega_m t)] \tag{19-61}$$

There are trigonometric identities that allow us to express the cosine and sine of $m_F \sin\omega_m t$. They are

$$\cos(m_F \sin\omega_m t) = J_0(m_F) + 2J_2(m_F)\cos 2\omega_m t + 2J_4(m_F)\cos 4\omega_m t + \cdot \tag{19-62a}$$

$$\sin(m_F \sin\omega_m t) = 2J_1(m_F)\sin\omega_m t + 2J_3(m_F)\sin 3\omega_m t + \cdots \tag{19-62b}$$

The $J_0(m_F), J_1(m_F), \ldots$ are Bessel's functions of the first kind of order k. They are obtained from power series. The first six Bessel's functions are plotted in Fig. 19-11 as a function of m_F. Note that for a fixed m_F, the $J_k(m_F)$ are constants. Substituting Eqs. 19-62 into Eq. 19-61 and manipulating, we have

$$\begin{aligned} v(t) = V\{&J_0(m_F)\cos\omega_c t \\ &+ J_1(m_F)[\cos(\omega_c + \omega_m)t - \cos(\omega_c - \omega_m)t] \\ &+ J_2(m_F)[\cos(\omega_c + 2\omega_m)t + \cos(\omega_c - \omega_m)t] + \cdots\} \end{aligned} \tag{19-63}$$

Thus, a carrier and an *infinite* set of sidebands result. Then, frequency and phase modulation, in theory, require infinite bandwidth. In practice, the higher ordered sidebands are

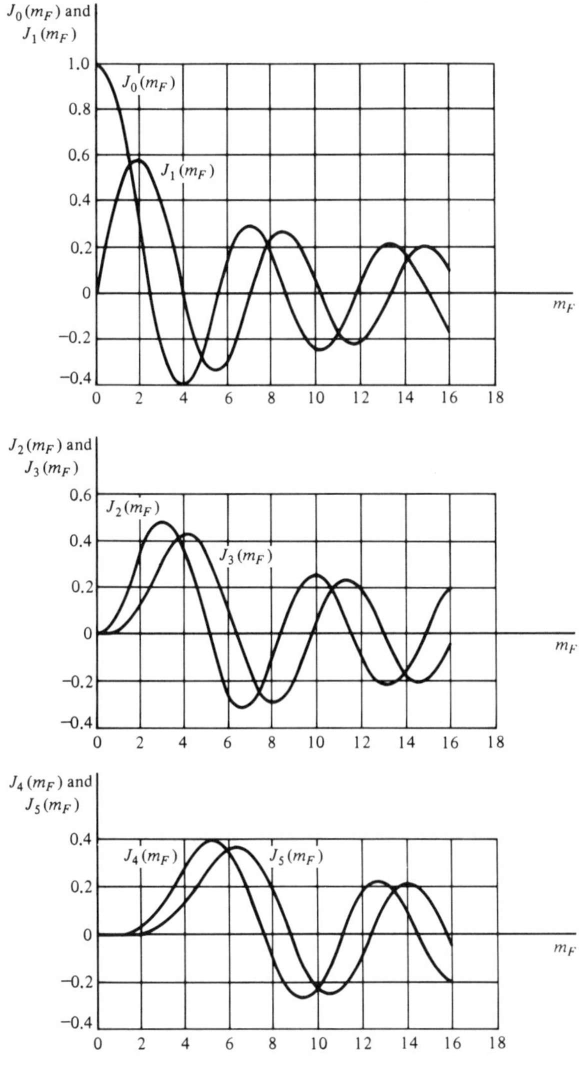

Figure 19-11. Plots of Bessels function of the first kind (from F. E. Terman, *Radio Engineer's Handbook*, copyright 1943, McGraw-Hill Book Co., used by permission).

often very small and can be neglected. Thus, frequency and phase modulated signals *can* be transmitted within a finite bandwidth.

Example

Compute the relative amplitude of the carrier and first five sidebands for an FM or PM system modulated by a sinusoid for the three cases where $m_F = 0.1, 1, 10$.

We shall use Fig. 19-11 (supplemented by a table of Bessel's functions) to obtain the values of the Bessel's functions. For $m_F = 0.1$, we have

$$J_0(0.1) = 0.99$$
$$J_1(0.1) = 0.05$$
$$J_2(0.1) = 0.002$$
$$J_3(0.1) = 0.00004$$
$$J_4(0.1) = 5 \times 10^{-7}$$
$$J_5(0.1) = 5.2 \times 10^{-9}$$

For $m_F = 1$

$$J_0(1) = 0.76$$
$$J_1(1) = 0.44$$
$$J_2(1) = 0.12$$
$$J_3(1) = 0.02$$
$$J_4(1) = 0.003$$
$$J_5(1) = 0.0003$$

For $m_F = 10$

$$J_0(10) = -0.25$$
$$J_1(10) = 0.04$$
$$J_2(10) = 0.25$$
$$J_3(10) = 0.06$$
$$J_4(10) = -0.22$$
$$J_5(10) = -0.23$$

The minus signs just indicate a phase reversal.

From the example and the curves of Fig. 19-11, we see that if m_F is small ($m_F \ll 1$), only the carrier and one pair of sidebands are important. On the other hand, if m_F is large, then greater bandwidth is required. For instance, if $m_F = 1$, then there are two significant pairs of sidebands. If $m_F = 10$, then there are more than five significant pairs of sidebands. Actually, if we had additional curves, we would see that there are 11 significant pairs of sidebands in this case. It is empirically found that if $m_F > 1$, then $m_F + 1$ pairs of sidebands are necessary. Thus, the bandwidth required is

$$B = 2(m_F + 1)f_{m,\,\max}$$

where $f_{m,\,\max}$ is the highest modulating frequency. Note that in frequency and phase modulation, the *amplitude of the carrier does vary.*

The bandwidth requirements of a frequency or phase modulated system will actually be equal to or greater than the bandwidth requirements of the corresponding amplitude modulated system. This disadvantage can sometimes be used to advantage when there are interfering signals. The interfering signal will result in a detected (e.g., audio) signal which is interference. Consider an AM system with an interfering signal. We want to improve the ratio of the detected signal to the detected interference. To do this, either the transmitter power or the index of modulation can be increased. In an AM system, the index of modulation is limited by the peak value of the modulating signal and the fact that $0 < m < 1$. Thus, increasing the power is often the only practical alternative to increasing the ratio of the detected signal to the interference. Increasing the power is not always a feasible alternative. In frequency and phase modulation systems, m_F can be increased without producing distortion so the detected signal can be increased without increasing the power. Of course, greater bandwidth is required. Indeed, if the bandwidth is not greater than that of the corresponding AM system, no improvement is obtained. Broadband RM and PM systems are commercially used because such systems are much freer from interference than the corresponding AM systems. There are low-interference broadband AM systems. However, they require much more complex receiving equipment than the corresponding FM and PM systems. For this reason, FM is used for low-interference commercial broadcasting.

19-5. FREQUENCY AND PHASE MODULATING CIRCUITS

In this section we shall discuss circuits that can be used to produce frequency and phase modulated signals. As we discussed in the last section, it is a relatively simple matter to convert a frequency modulator into a phase modulator, and vice versa.

Variable Reactance Circuits

In Chapter 18 we determined that the frequency of oscillation of RF oscillators was essentially determined by the resonant frequency ω_0 of a LC circuit. If we could cause the value of the inductance or capacitance to vary in accordance with the modulating signal, then frequency or phase modulation would result.

There are various procedures for obtaining a reactance whose value is a function of voltage. A simple one is to use a reverse (varactor) diode (see Sec. 1-8), whose capacitance is given by

$$C = kv^{-n} \tag{19-64}$$

where k and n are constants that depend upon the geometry and doping, and v is the reverse bias voltage. In general, $0 < n < 1$. If the reverse biased diode is placed in parallel with an inductor, we have a tuned circuit that can be used to produce phase modulation. Such a circuit and its linear model are shown in Fig. 19-12. The resistance R represents the parallel combination of R_1 and the reverse resistance of the diode. We assume here that C_c acts as a short circuit frequency.

The resonant frequency of this tuned circuit is given by

$$f_0 = \frac{1}{2\pi\sqrt{LC}}$$

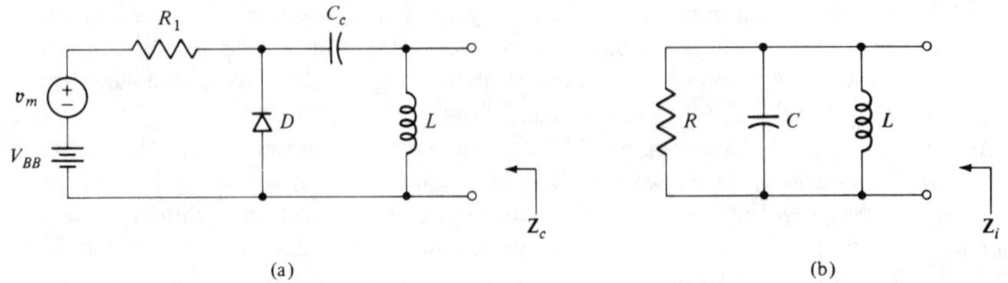

Figure 19-12. (a) A diode reactance modulator. (b) Its linear model.

The voltage across the capacitor is

$$v = V_{BB} + v_m \tag{19-65}$$

Substituting Eqs. 19-64 and 19-65 into the expression for f_0, we obtain

$$f_0 = \frac{1}{2\pi\sqrt{Lk}} V_{BB}^{n/2}\left(1 + \frac{v_m}{V_{BB}}\right)^{n/2} \tag{19-66}$$

We want f_0 to vary linearly with v_m. Let us see how this can be achieved. We assume that

$$\left|\frac{v_m}{V_{BB}}\right| < 1$$

Thus, Eq. 19-66 can be expanded in a Taylor's series. Doing this we obtain

$$f_0 = \frac{V_{BB}^{n/2}}{2\pi\sqrt{kL}}\left[1 + \frac{nv_m}{2V_{BB}} + \frac{n}{4}\left(\frac{n}{2} - 1\right)\left(\frac{v_m}{V_{BB}}\right)^2 + \cdots\right] \tag{19-67}$$

If we make

$$\left|\frac{v_m}{V_{BB}}\right| \ll 1 \tag{19-68}$$

then Eq. 19-68 can be approximated by

$$f_0 = \frac{V_{BB}^{n/2}}{2\pi\sqrt{kL}}\left(1 + \frac{nv_m}{2V_{BB}}\right) \tag{19-69}$$

and the desired linear response has been obtained.

If

$$v_m = V_m \sin \omega_m t$$

then the instantaneous frequency is given by

$$f_i = \frac{V_{BB}^{n/2}}{2\pi\sqrt{kL}}\left(1 + \frac{nV_m}{2V_{BB}} \sin \omega_m t\right) \tag{19-70}$$

Hence (see Eqs. 19-55 and 19-56) phase modulation results. The index of modulation is given by

$$m_p = \frac{nV_m}{2V_{BB}} \tag{19-71}$$

If frequency modulation is desired, then the input (modulating) signal need only be integrated.

Inequality 19-68 requires that the deviation of f_0 and, hence, m_p be kept small. Thus, it appears as though the circuit cannot be used with wide deviation PM or FM. However, a procedure can be used to increase the frequency deviation. If a tuned amplifier is operated in its nonlinear region and the output tuned circuit is tuned to an integral multiple K of the input frequency, then the output frequency will be K times the input frequency. Such a circuit is called a *frequency multiplier*.

Suppose that a frequency or phase modulated signal is applied to a frequency multiplier that multiplies the frequency K times. Then the frequency deviation will be multiplied by K. The frequency can also be translated using a heterodyne technique. Thus, a circuit such as that of Fig. 19-11a can be used to obtain linear frequency modulation even if relatively large values of m_p or m_f are required.

VCO Frequency Modulation

A very linear frequency modulator can be obtained from a voltage controlled oscillator such as that of Fig. 18-17. For this circuit, the frequency of oscillation varies linearly with applied voltages over very wide frequency ranges. Thus, circuits of this type can be used to produce linear frequency modulation. The output of the circuit of Fig. 18-17 is either a triangular or square wave so wave shaping or filtering can be used to convert it into a sinusoid. Heterodyne techniques can be used to shift the center frequency about some desired carrier frequency. Frequency multiplication can also be used with this circuit to increase the frequency deviation.

Variable Phase Shift Amplifier

We shall now consider a circuit that does not vary the frequency of an oscillator. This circuit is an amplifier in which the phase shift of its gain is made to vary in accordance with a modulating signal. The input to the amplifier is a simple sinusoid whose frequency is fixed at the carrier frequency, ω_c. This signal can be generated by a crystal oscillator so a very stable value of ω_c is obtained. The modulating signal varies the phase shift of the amplifier and produces the desired modulation.

The circuit that we shall use is shown in Fig. 19-13. The input signal V_1 is an unmodulated sinusoid whose frequency is the carrier frequency ω_c. The generator v_m and the power supply V_{GG} establish the bias for the FET. The tuned circuits act as high impedances for those frequencies close to ω_c but as low impedance otherwise so that no components of v_m appear in the output.

The model for the amplifier is shown in Fig. 19-13b. We have assumed that the tuned circuits are open circuits at the signal frequency and that the coupling capacitor acts as a short circuit.

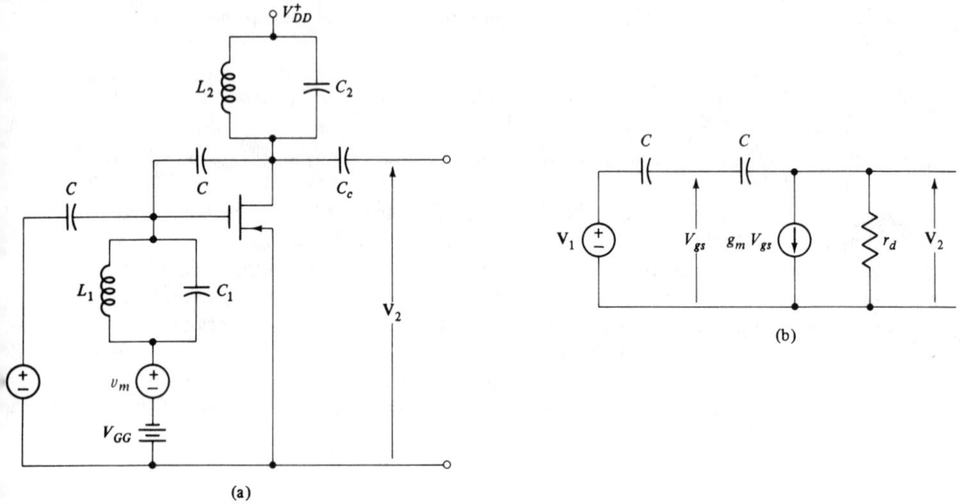

Figure 19-13. (a) A phase modulator. (b) Its linear model.

If we analyze the model of Fig. 19-13b, and assume that

$$\frac{1}{wC} \ll r_d$$

we obtain

$$\mathbf{A}_v = \frac{\omega C + jg_m}{\omega C - jg_m} = 1\angle 2\tan^{-1} g_m/\omega C \qquad (19\text{-}72)$$

Thus, the gain of the circuit is unity and its phase shift is a function of g_m. Then, as v_m varies, the gate to source bias will vary. Hence, g_m will vary and phase modulation will be obtained. The phase shift of the amplifier is

$$\phi = 2\tan^{-1}\frac{g_m}{\omega C} \qquad (19\text{-}73)$$

This is not a linear function of g_m and g_m is also not a linear function of v_{GS}. However, we can write

$$v_{GS} = V_{GG}\left(1 + \frac{v_m}{V_{GG}}\right) \qquad (19\text{-}74)$$

Then, if we make v_m/V_{GG} small enough, the phase shift will become a linear function of v_m. This follows arguments similar to those of the discussion of Eqs. 19-65 to 19-69. If the fact that $|v_m/V_{GG}| \ll 1$ limits the phase shift too much, then frequency multiplication can be used here just as it was in the previously discussed case of frequency modulation.

19-6. FREQUENCY AND PHASE MODULATION DETECTORS THAT USE REACTIVE COMPONENTS

In this section we shall discuss the detection of frequency and phase modulated signals using tuned circuits. Again, the relation between frequency and phase modulation can be utilized to convert a detector of one type to another. For instance, a frequency modulation detector can be converted to a phase modulation detector by integrating the output.

Slope Detectors

A basic procedure for detecting frequency modulated signals is to pass them through a tuned circuit whose gain varies linearly with frequency. Thus, the amplitude of the resulting signal will vary linearly with its instantaneous frequency. That is, an amplitude modulated signal will be produced from a frequency modulated signal. If this signal is then detected by an amplitude modulation detector of the type shown in Fig. 19-6, the output will be the demodulated FM signal.

A simple way of obtaining a circuit whose frequency response approximates the desired one is to use a simple tuned amplifier. However, the center frequency ω_0 is not adjusted to the carrier frequency. This is illustrated in Fig. 19-14. The resonant circuit is adjusted so that ω_c lies as shown. Now if the frequency decreases, the output voltage will increase, while if the frequency increases, the output voltage will decrease. This is called *slope detection* since the slope of the resonance characteristic is utilized.

The amplifier of Fig. 19-10 can be used to detect frequency modulation in this way. The rightmost double tuned circuit is adjusted so that $k < 1$ (see Sec. 17-6) and so that $\omega_c > \omega_0$. The circuit then functions as a slope detector.

Slope detector circuits are simple but they are not very linear. In order to obtain more linearity, a more complex resonant circuit is used. We shall now consider it.

The Discriminator

The detection scheme that we shall now consider utilizes the same ideas as does slope detection except that a more complex tuned circuit is used to obtain greater linearity. The circuit, called a *phase shift discriminator*, is shown in Fig. 19-15. The coil labeled *RFC* is an inductance which is large enough so that it can be considered to be an open circuit at all frequencies of interest.

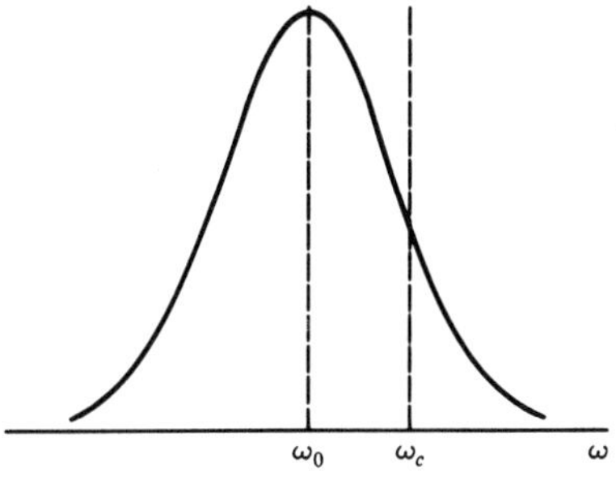

Figure 19-14. The response of a single tuned amplifier used to illustrate slope detection

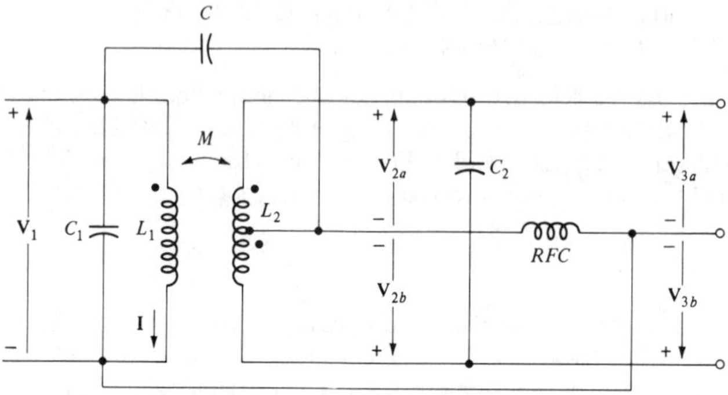

Figure 19-15. A phase shift discriminator.

Let us now analyze this circuit. We shall assume that ωL_1 is much greater than the series resistance of L_1 plus any impedance that is mutually coupled into L_1 and that C acts as a short circuit at signal frequencies. Then

$$\mathbf{I} = \frac{\mathbf{V}_1}{j\omega L_1} \tag{19-75}$$

Then, the secondary voltages are

$$\mathbf{V}_{2a} = \frac{j\omega M L_2 \mathbf{V}_1}{2L_1\left[R + j\left(\omega L_2 - \dfrac{1}{\omega C_2}\right)\right]} \tag{19-76a}$$

$$\mathbf{V}_{2b} = \frac{-j\omega M L_2 \mathbf{V}_1}{2L_1\left[R + j\left(\omega L_2 - \dfrac{1}{\omega C_2}\right)\right]} \tag{19-76b}$$

where R is the total resistance of the secondary coil. Then,

$$\mathbf{V}_{3a} = \mathbf{V}_1 + \mathbf{V}_{2a} \tag{19-77a}$$

$$\mathbf{V}_{3b} = \mathbf{V}_1 + \mathbf{V}_{2b} \tag{19-77b}$$

A phase diagram for this is shown in Fig. 19-16a. Note that, at resonance, $\mathbf{V}_{2a}$ and $\mathbf{V}_{2b}$ are 180° out-of-phase and $|\mathbf{V}_{3a}| = |\mathbf{V}_{3b}|$. Now suppose that the frequency is increased above resonance. The Q's of the circuit are kept low so that the magnitudes of the voltages only change slightly. The change of phase with frequency is more sensitive than the change of amplitude and the phasor diagram then looks like Fig. 19-16b. Now $|\mathbf{V}_{3b}| > |\mathbf{V}_{3a}|$. When the frequency decreases below ω_0, $|\mathbf{V}_{3b}| < |\mathbf{V}_{3a}|$. Then, the magnitude of the voltages vary with frequency so that this circuit is a potential FM detector.

The actual circuit that we shall use is shown in Fig. 19-17. It is called a *Foster–Seeley discriminator*. There are two amplitude modulation detectors whose output voltages are the peak values of v_{3a} and v_{3b}. Hence,

$$v_o = |V_{3a,\,\max}| - |V_{3b,\,\max}|$$

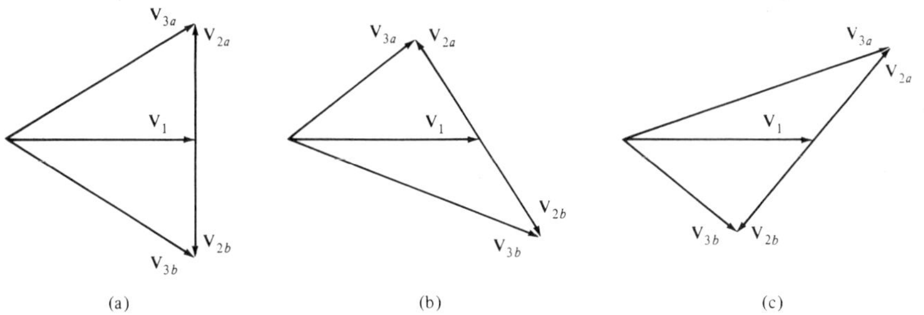

Figure 19-16. Phasor diagrams for the phase shift discriminator of Fig. 19-14. (a) $\omega = \omega_0$. (b) $\omega > \omega_0$. (c) $\omega < \omega_0$.

It is found that the output voltage varies very linearly with frequency as shown in Fig. 19-18. The falloff in amplitude at frequencies far removed from ω_0 occurs because of the response of the tuned circuits.

If the magnitude of the input signal varies, then the output voltage v_o will also vary so the Foster–Seeley discriminator is sensitive to amplitude modulation. In Sec. 19-4 we discussed that wide band FM signals were relatively insensitive to interference. However, the interference will produce significant amplitude modulation of the signals. If the detector is sensitive to AM as well as to FM, then interference will be present in the output even if the original interference did not frequency modulate the signal. Thus, the amplitude fluctuations must be removed from the signal. This can be accomplished by putting the signal through a clipper of the type discussed in Sec. 18-11. Actually, in FM receivers, this effect is accomplished by having a very high gain IF amplifier. The amplification is so great that some of the stages are driven between saturation and cutoff. This removes the amplitude modulation and reduces the AM interference. Of course, the input signal must be large enough for saturation and cutoff to occur. An IF amplifier operated in this way is called a *limiter*.

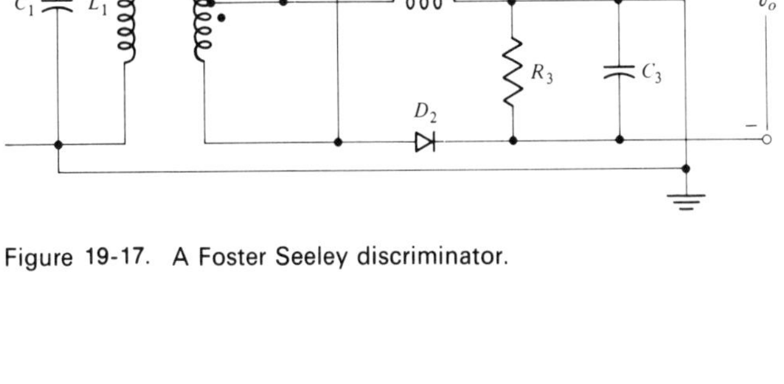

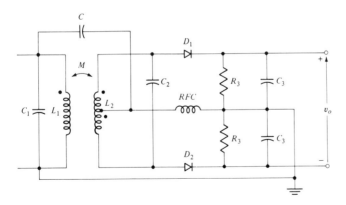

Figure 19-17. A Foster Seeley discriminator.

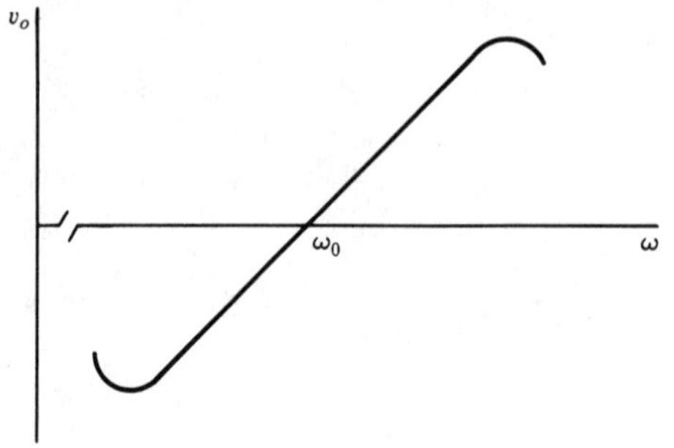

Figure 19-18. A plot of output voltage versus frequency for a Foster Seeley discriminator.

A typical limiter IF amplifier that utilizes integrated circuits is shown in Fig. 19-19. Very high-gain broadband operational amplifiers are used. The filtering action is obtained from passive filters. Note that phase distortion in the IF amplifier is equivalent to nonlinear distortion of a phase or frequency modulated signal. Thus, it is desirable for the filter to have linear phase characteristics. Because of the very high gain of the amplifiers, very good limiting is obtained with this circuit.

The Ratio Detector

If the Foster–Seeley circuit is slightly modified, an FM detector that is relatively insensitive to amplitude modulation is obtained. Such a circuit is shown in Fig. 19-20. One of the diodes has been reversed so that

$$v_5 = |V_{3a,\max}| + |V_{3b,\max}| \tag{19-78}$$

where $\mathbf{V}_{3a}$ and $\mathbf{V}_{3b}$ are defined in Fig. 19-15. For the moment let us ignore the capacitance C_4. Then

$$v_o = v_{4a} - \frac{v_5}{2} \tag{19-79}$$

Hence,

$$v_0 = (|V_{3a,\max}| - |V_{3b,\max}|)/2 \tag{19-80}$$

The voltage v_5 does not change substantially as f_i, the frequency of the input signal changes. This is due to the fact that as f_i varies, an increase in $\mathbf{V}_{3a}$ is accompanied by a decrease in $\mathbf{V}_{3b}$, and vice versa (see Fig. 19-16).

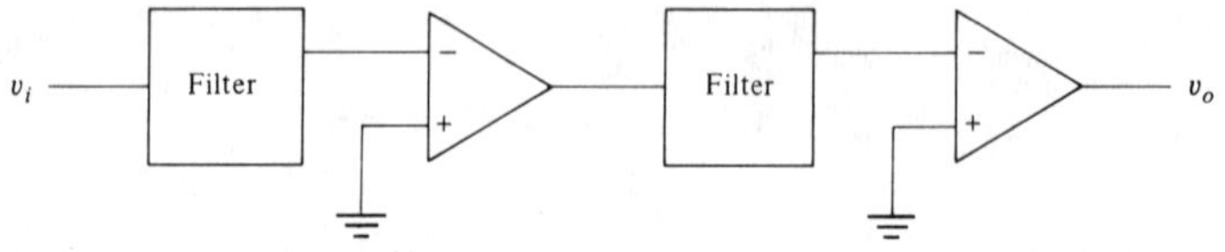

Figure 19-19. A limiting IF amplifier that uses integrated circuits.

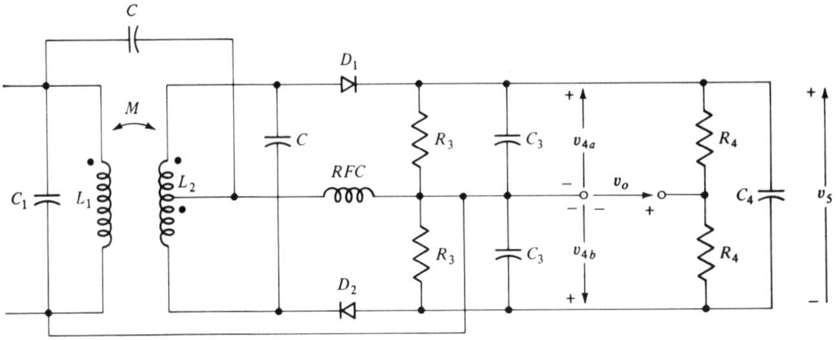

Figure 19-20. A ratio detector.

Now let us consider C_4. It is made very large so that the time constant RC_4 is much larger than the period of any audio signal, for instance, 0.3 s. (R represents twice the resistance of R_3 and R_4 in parallel.) Since f_i varies at an audio rate, v_5 will tend to remain fixed as the frequency of the input signal varies. (Remember that v_5 does not vary substantially in any event.) Hence, the sum $|\mathbf{V}_{3a,\max}| + |\mathbf{V}_{3b,\max}|$ will not change as the frequency of the input signal varies. However, the *ratio* $|V_{3a,\max}|/|V_{3b,\max}|$ will vary. The values of $|V_{3a}|$ and $|V_{3b}|$ are changed somewhat by the constraint on their sum. This reduces the linearity of the circuit slightly. If the *amplitude* of the input signal changes, $|V_{3a,\max}| + |V_{3b,\max}|$ will change slowly since the rate of this change is limited by the RC_4 time constant.

Now let us consider the rejection of amplitude modulation by this circuit. Suppose that noise amplitude modulates the signal at an audio rate. When the amplitude of the signal increases, both $|V_{3a}|$ and $|V_{3b}|$ will tend to increase but their sum is (ideally) constant because of the presence of C_4. The ratio of $|V_{3a}|$ to $|V_{3b}|$ is a function of the instantaneous frequency so (ideally) v_o will not respond to amplitude modulation of the signal. In practice, v_0 does vary somewhat with changes in the amplitude of the signal since the RC_4 time constant is not infinite. Note that v_o will respond to slow changes in the magnitude of the signal, but if they are below the audio rate, this is often acceptable.

A good FM receiver will always have a limiter since it is far more effective than the ratio detector in eliminating the effects of amplitude modulation. The ratio detector will increase the rejection of AM.

The discriminator tends to be slightly more linear and, hence, produces somewhat less nonlinear distortion than the ratio detector. The discriminator's output signal is twice as large. The output of the ratio detector is single ended (one output line is grounded), while the discriminator has a balanced output and, thus, should drive a balanced amplifier.

19-7. THE PHASE LOCKED LOOP

There is another form of detector called the *phase locked loop* that can provide very low-distortion detection of FM or PM signals. In addition, this circuit does not require the use of inductances so that it can be fabricated on a single integrated circuit chip. There may be some external resistors and capacitors required. Another advantage of the phase locked loop is that it provides its own filtering action.

The block diagram for a phase locked loop is shown in Fig. 19-21. Let us consider its operation. The input signal is given by

$$v_i(t) = V \sin[\omega_c t + \phi_i(t)] \tag{19-81}$$

Note that $\phi_i(t)$ is used to represent change in frequency. For instance, if the frequency is constant and equal to ω_d (not ω_c), then $\phi_i(t) = (\omega_d - \omega_c)t$.

There is a voltage controlled oscillator (VCO) whose output is

$$v_2(t) = V_2 \cos[\omega_c t + \phi_2(t)]$$

The signal from the VCO and the input signal are put into a circuit that multiplies them. Its output is v_a where

$$v_a = VV_2 \sin[\omega_c t + \phi_i(t)]\cos[\omega_c t + \phi_2(t)] \tag{19-82}$$

Manipulating, we have

$$v_a = \frac{VV_2}{2}\{\sin[2\omega_c t + \phi_i(t) + \phi_2(t)] + \sin[\phi_i(t) - \phi_2(t)]\} \tag{19-83}$$

The low-pass filter will reject the high-frequency components of the signal. Hence,

$$v_o = \frac{AVV_2}{2}\sin[\phi_i(t) - \phi_2(t)] \tag{19-84}$$

Not only is this the output voltage, it is also the controlling voltage for the VCO. Let us assume that the VCO is constructed so that its instantaneous frequency is given by

$$\omega_2 = \omega_c + Kv_o \tag{19-85}$$

Then, if v_o is positive, ω_2 will be greater than ω_c, while if v_o is negative, ω_2 will be less than ω_c.

Suppose that both the input frequency and the oscillator frequency are ω_c, and then the input frequency increases to $\omega_c + \Delta\omega_i$. The phase angle $\phi_i(t)$ will increase and $\phi_i(t) - \phi_2(t)$ will become positive. Thus, v_o will become a positive voltage and increase the oscillator frequency. If the circuit is functioning properly, the frequency of the

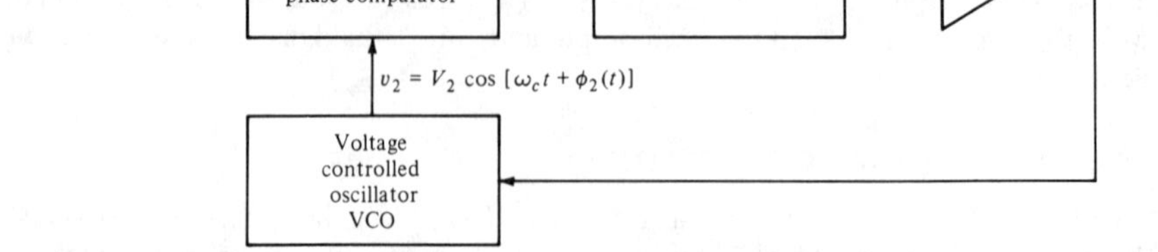

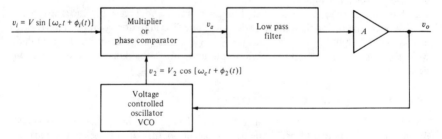

Figure 19-21. The block diagram of a phase locked loop.

oscillator will then *lock on* to the input frequency. That is, the two frequencies will become identical. In this case,

$$\phi_i(t) - \phi_o(t) = K_1 \tag{19-86}$$

where K_1 is a constant whose value is such that $\frac{1}{2}AV_1V_2 \sin K_1$ causes ω_2, the frequency of the VCO, to equal $\omega_c + \Delta\omega_i$. Note that this circuit is self-regulating. If the VCO frequency is greater than the input frequency, then $\sin(\phi_i - \phi_2)$ will become negative and reduce the VCO frequency. When the VCO frequency locks onto the input frequency, *capture* or *lock* is said to occur.

Let us assume that the VCO locks on to the input frequency ω_i. If ω_i is constant, then v_o will be a direct voltage proportional to

$$\Delta\omega_i = \omega_c - \omega_i \tag{19-87}$$

From Eq. 19-85, we have

$$v_o = \frac{\Delta\omega_i}{K} \tag{19-88}$$

Thus, the output is proportional to the deviation of the frequency from the carrier frequency so we have obtained a frequency modulation detector. Since VCO's (see Sec. 18-9) can be constructed with very linear voltage versus frequency characteristics, the phase locked loop can be a very low-distortion FM detector.

We have assumed that the VCO locks on to the input frequency. Let us see under what conditions this occurs. We shall assume that the instantaneous input frequency is

$$\omega_i = \omega_c + \Delta\omega_i \tag{19-89}$$

We shall determine the maximum value that $|\Delta\omega_i|$ can have if lock is to occur. From Eq. 19-88, we have

$$\Delta\omega_i = Kv_o \tag{19-90}$$

The maximum value that $\sin[\phi_i(t) - \phi_2(t)]$ can have is 1. Hence (see Eq. 19-84)

$$|v_o|_{\max} = \frac{AVV_2}{2}$$

Substituting in Eq. 19-90, we have

$$|\Delta\omega_i|_{\max} = \frac{KAVV_2}{2} \tag{19-91}$$

This value of $|\Delta\omega_i|_{\max}$ is called $\Delta\omega_L$, the *lock range*. If $|\Delta\omega_i|$ is greater than the lock range, then capture cannot occur. Thus, if we wish proper detection to occur, the maximum frequency deviation must lie within the lock range.

If the frequency of the input signal lies outside of the lock range, then the difference between the input frequency and the VCO frequency will be large. This beat frequency will appear in the voltage v_a. If this frequency is rejected by the low-pass filter, then v_o will be zero. Thus, frequencies that lie outside of the lock range will produce no output so the phase locked loop acts as a filter. For instance, suppose that there are two FM signals, one with a carrier frequency ω_c and an interfering signal outside of the lock range. The VCO will lock on the desired signal and detect it but no lock can occur with the interfering signal, so filtering has been achieved.

The phase lock loop is not an ideal filter in that, even though lock does not occur with an interfering signal, beat frequencies between the VCO and it will occur. This will result in "jittering" of the VCO frequency. It is the function of the low-pass filter to eliminate these undesired signals. Note that we can use a simple low-pass filter to replace the function of a bandpass filter.

If a signal lies outside of the lock range, then lock will not occur, but if a signal lies within the lock range there is no guarantee that it will be captured. We have thus far ignored the low-pass filter. Before lock occurs, v_o will vary. The low-pass filter will reduce the signal so the signal controlling the VCO is reduced. For this reason, the value of $|\Delta\omega_i|_{\max}$ for lock will be less than the value predicted by Eq. 19-91. An exact analysis of this is tedious and difficult. We shall make some approximations that greatly simplify the analysis while still yielding reasonably accurate results.

Suppose that we break the feedback loop at the input to the VCO. Since we are not supplying any control voltage, the VCO frequency is ω_c. Now suppose that the input voltage is at a frequency $\omega_c + \Delta\omega_{\text{cap}}$. Then, the low-frequency component of the output of the multiplier will be

$$v_a = \frac{VV_2}{2} \sin \Delta\omega_{\text{cap}} t \tag{19-92}$$

Let us assume that the low-pass filter has a characteristic $\mathbf{H}(\omega)$. For instance, for the circuit of Fig. 19-22

$$\mathbf{H}(\omega) = \frac{1}{1 + j\omega RC} = \frac{1}{1 + jf/f_2} \tag{19-93a}$$

where

$$f_2 = \frac{1}{2\pi RC} \tag{19-93b}$$

This will tend to reduce v_o. For instance, if

$$v_o = |V_o| \sin \Delta\omega_{\text{cap}} t \tag{19-94}$$

then

$$|V_o| = A\frac{VV_2}{2}|\mathbf{H}(\Delta\omega_{\text{cap}})| \tag{19-95}$$

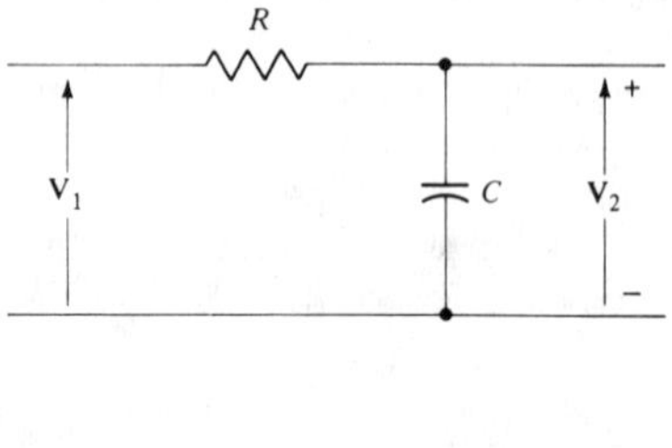

Figure 19-22. A simple low-pass filter.

The maximum value that v_o can have is reduced by $|\mathbf{H}(\Delta\omega_{cap})|$. Thus, if lock is to occur (see Eq. 19-88),

$$\Delta\omega_{cap} = (AVV_2K/2)|\mathbf{H}(\Delta\omega_{cap})| \tag{19-96}$$

Substituting Eq. 19-91, we have

$$\Delta\omega_{cap} = \Delta\omega_L|\mathbf{H}(\Delta\omega_{cap})| \tag{19-97}$$

The solution of the equation is called the *capture range* $\Delta\omega_{cap}$.

In general, we can state the following: If $\Delta\omega$ lies outside of the lock range, then lock *will not* occur. If $\Delta\omega$ lies within the capture range, then lock *will* occur.

Example

For the phase locked loop shown in Fig. 19-21, the input voltage has a peak voltage of 0.5 V and the oscillator has a peak voltage of 1 V. The amplifier gain is 1000. The frequency-voltage characteristic of the VCO is $\omega = \omega_c + 200v_i$. The low-pass filter is of the form shown in Fig. 19-22 where $f_2 = 10{,}000$ Hz. Determine the lock range and the capture range.

The lock range is given by Eq. 19-91. Thus,

$$\Delta\omega_L = (200 \times 1000 \times 0.5 \times 1.0)/2 = 50{,}000 \text{ rad/s}$$

or

$$\Delta f_L = \frac{\Delta\omega_c}{2\pi} = 7957 \text{ Hz}$$

Now let us determine the capture range. From Eq. 19-97, we have

$$\Delta\omega_{cap} = 50{,}000\left|\frac{1}{1 + j[\Delta\omega_{cap}/(2\pi \times f_2)]}\right|$$

Let

$$\Delta\omega_{cap} = x$$

$$x = 50{,}000\frac{1}{\sqrt{1 + x^2/(62{,}832)^2}}$$

Solving, we have

$$\Delta\omega_{cap} = 41{,}669$$

or

$$\Delta f_{cap} = 6632 \text{ Hz}$$

Note that the capture range is somewhat less than the lock range.

Note that v_o is proportional to V, the magnitude of the input signal. Hence, the phase locked loop is sensitive to amplitude modulation. Hence, as in the case of the discriminator, the signals should be limited before they are input to the phase locked loop. A limiting IF amplifier such as that of Fig. 19-19 can precede the phase locked loop. However, since it provides its own filter in some applications, a simple limiting amplifier or AGC amplifier is used to eliminate the AM and no additional filter is needed.

Note that the phase locked loop can be used as an amplitude modulation detector. In this case, the VCO locks on the carrier. The output is then proportional to the peak signal. Very linear AM detectors can be obtained in this way.

Phase Comparator

We have assumed that the voltage v_a is obtained as the output of a multiplier (see Fig. 19-21). Actually, it can also be obtained easily from a circuit called a *phase comparator*.

Let us see now how this can be implemented. Consider the circuit of Fig. 19-23. The FET acts as a switch. Let us assume that it is closed when the VCO voltage is positive and open when the VCO voltage is negative. Thus, $v_a = V \sin[\omega_c t + \phi_i(t)]$ when the switch is closed and it is 0 when the switch is open. Now let us assume that there is lock. The frequency of the input signal and the VCO will each be ω_i (this need not be ω_c). Then the input voltage will be

$$v_i = V \sin(\omega_i t + \Phi_i) \tag{19-98}$$

and the output of the VCO will be

$$v_2 = V_2 \cos(\omega_i t + \Phi_2) \tag{19-99}$$

Note that we have not written the phase angles in terms of ω_c here so that Φ_i and Φ_2 do not vary with time (i.e., they are constants). The low-frequency output of the phase comparator should be proportional to $\sin(\Phi_i - \Phi_2)$. This is a direct component since there is lock. Now let us determine its value. Suppose that, during one period, $v_2 \geqq 0$ for $T_2 \leqq t \leqq T_1$. Then,

$$v_a = \frac{\omega_i}{2\pi} \int_{T_1}^{T_2} V \sin[\omega_i t + \Phi_1]\, dt \tag{19-100}$$

(We have ignored the high-frequency components of v_a which shall be rejected by the low-pass filter.) Let us determine T_1 and T_2 for one period. v_2 will be positive when

$$-\frac{\pi}{2} \leqq \omega_i t + \Phi_2 \leqq \frac{\pi}{2} \tag{19-101a}$$

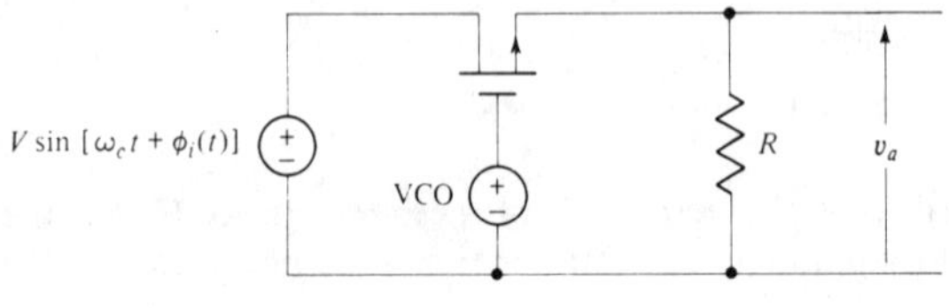

Figure 19-23. A phase comparator.

or equivalently, when

$$-\frac{1}{\omega_i}\left(\frac{\pi}{2}+\Phi_2\right) \leqq t \leqq \frac{1}{\omega_i}\left(\frac{\pi}{2}-\Phi_2\right) \tag{19-101b}$$

Then,

$$v_a = \frac{\omega_i}{2\pi}\int_{-(1/\omega_i)(\pi/2+\Phi_2)}^{(1/\omega_i)(\pi/2-\Phi_2)} V\sin(\omega_i t + \Phi_i)\,dt \tag{19-102}$$

Integrating, we obtain

$$v_a = \frac{V}{\pi}\sin(\Phi_i - \Phi_2) \tag{19-103}$$

The result is proportional to the $\sin(\Phi_i - \Phi_2)$ as it should be. If we compare this with the output of the multiplier given by Eq. 19-83, we see that instead of having a coefficient of $VV_2/2$, we now have V/π. If we proceed as before, the lock range will be given by

$$\Delta\omega_L = |KAV|/\pi \tag{19-104}$$

Equation 19-97 can still be used for the capture range. Of course, the value of $\Delta\omega_L$ given by Eq. 19-104 should be used here.

The function of the VCO is to turn the FET switch on or off. The operation would be improved if the output of the VCO was a square wave rather than a sinusoid. Actually, this is a great help since we can now use the VCO circuit of Sec. 18-9. In addition to producing square waves, the frequency of this VCO varies very linearly with voltage. Hence, it is ideal for this purpose.

19-8. PULSE MODULATION

In Secs. 13-13 to 13-16 we discussed how an analog signal could be sampled and then be digitally encoded using an A/D converter. This encoded information could then be transmitted. At the receiving end, a D/A converter restores the information to its original form. This is one example of a *pulse modulation* system. If the transmission is to take place over a radio link, then the pulses are used to amplitude, frequency, or phase modulate a carrier.

The system that we have just discussed is called pulse code modulation (PCM). Many of its details have been discussed in Chapter 13, and we shall not repeat them here.

When PCM is used, the signals are either 0's or 1's. One advantage of transmitting information in this way is that the nonlinearities of the system do not introduce distortion.

Pulse code modulation provides a relatively simple procedure for transmitting signals in the presence of noise. In such a system, noise can perturb a 0 so that it appears as a 1 or vice versa but, no matter how great the noise, the probability that the correct signal is received is always (at least slightly) greater than the probability that an incorrect signal is received. Note that if we simply guess at whether a signal should be a 0 or a 1, we will be right (on the average) half of the time.

We can use redundancy to reduce the effect of noise. Suppose that each bit is transmitted three times and we use a majority rule to determine if the group of three represents a 1. Ideally, if a 1 is transmitted, the sequence 1, 1, 1 would be received. Similarly, each 0 would be represented by the sequence 0, 0, 0. There must be at least two errors in the received signal before a mistake is made (i.e., 101, 110, 011 will all be interpreted as a 1). Thus, the probability of error has been reduced. By increasing the redundancy (i.e., the number of times that a bit is repeated) the effect of noise can be reduced to arbitrarily small values. Note that if more pulses are transmitted, it will take longer to transmit the message so that there is a tradeoff between the reduction in the effect of the noise and speed of transmission.

There are other pulse modulation schemes that do not involve encoding the signal into binary bits. One of these is called pulse amplitude modulation (PAM). Here, pulses are transmitted whose amplitude is equal to the amplitude of the analog signal. Such a system is illustrated in Fig. 19-24. The advantage of this system over a PCM system is that relatively simple equipment can be used to code and decode the signals. However, since the amplitude of the signals conveys the information, nonlinear distortion is a problem, which is a major advantage to PCM.

A modulator for PAM is shown in Fig. 19-25. The signal is sampled and held and then passed through the transistor switch. The signal levels are such that the transistor is cut off when the clock pulses are present. When the clock signal is absent, the circuit functions as an emitter follower "amplifier," whose output is proportional to the output of the sample and hold circuit. Often, the sample and hold circuit is omitted and the signal is applied directly to the left side of R_1. This is because the duration of the clock pulse is short and the signal changes very little during the time that the clock is on.

The PAM signal can be recovered by putting the signal through an AM detector If the pulses are close enough together, this does a reasonable job of reinstating the signal. There are more sophisticated schemes that do a better job, however.

We often want to simultaneously transmit several different signals through one communications channel (e.g., a telephone system coaxial cable). When pulse modulation of the types discussed are used, there is a simple procedure for accomplishing this. Consider Fig. 19-26 which shows clock pulses. Suppose that an information pulse is transmitted whenever CP_1 is positive. Most of the time (i.e., between pulses) nothing will be transmitted. Now suppose that we have a second set of clock pulses CP_2 and they

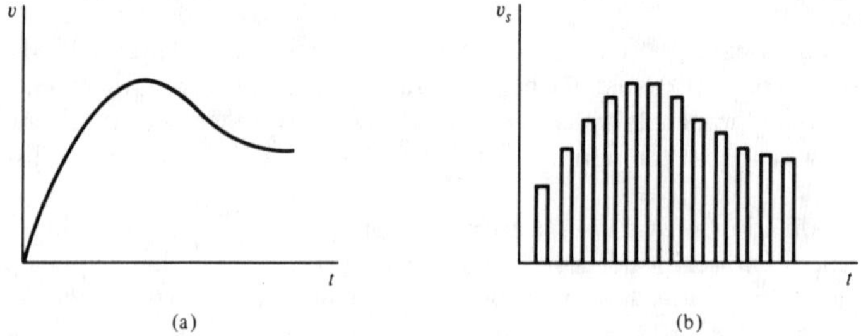

Figure 19-24. An example of pulse amplitude modulation. (a) The analog signal. (b) The PAM representation.

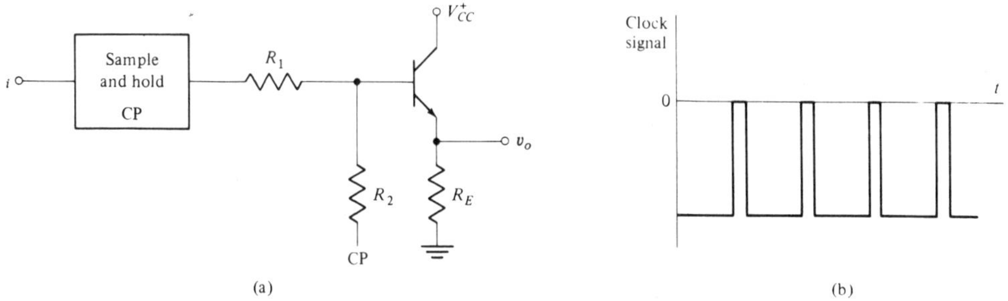

Figure 19-25. (a) A pulse amplitude modulator. (b) The clock pulses used with this circuit.

are used to control the transmission of the second set of pulses. Transmission occurs in the "spaces between the first set of pulses." The first set of pulses could represent the information in one telephone conversation and the second set the information in a second conversation. Now we can simultaneously transmit both conversations over the same channel. At the receiving end, similar sets of clock pulses are used to separate the two conversations. In practice, many conversations can be sent in this way over a single channel. Information to synchronize the clock pulses is also sent over the channel.

The procedure where many signals are transmitted along a single channel is called *time multiplexing*. There is also *frequency multiplexing* where signals are separated in frequency rather than in time. For instance, commercial radio signals are frequency multiplexed. That is, each station transmits over a different frequency band, and bandpass amplifiers are used to select the desired signal. Note that bandwidth limits the number of signals which can be sent over the same channel when either type of multiplexing is used.

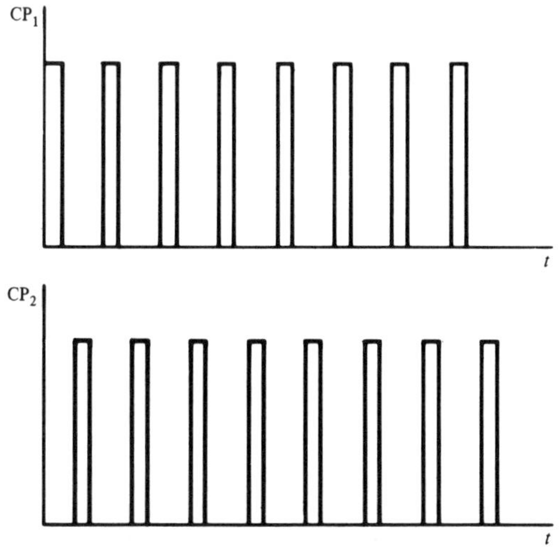

Figure 19-26. Clock pulses used in a time multiplex system.

For instance, when frequency multiplexing is used, the bandwidth of the channel is equal to the sum of the bandwidths of the individual signals. Bandwidth also limits the number of signals that can be transmitted using time multiplexing. For instance, consider the pulses of Fig. 19-24. Perfect rectangular pulses can only be transmitted by a channel of infinite bandwidth. If the pulses are perfect rectangles, then they can be spaced arbitrarily close together. If the bandwidth is finite, the pulses would be rounded with finite rise and fall times. Now the pulses could not be too close together since they would interfere with each other. In general, no matter what scheme is used, the rate at which information can be transmitted through a channel is limited by its bandwidth.

There is another pulse modulation scheme called *pulse width modulation* (PWM) or *pulse duration modulation.* Here the signal is sampled and a pulse is transmitted. The width or duration of the pulse is then proportional to the amplitude of the signal at the sampling time. This is illustrated in Fig. 19-27. Note that we have distorted the time scale here for illustrative purposes. The sampling period should be short enough so that the signal does not change significantly between pulses.

Let us consider how these pulses could be generated. Suppose that we have an astable (one shot) multivibrator (see Sec. 18-10) whose pulse length is voltage controlled. Such a circuit can be obtained by combining the circuits of Figs. 18-17 and 18-18. For instance, if we add a diode between the v_1 terminal and ground in Fig. 18-17, as we did in Fig. 18-18, then this circuit becomes an astable multivibrator whose pulse length is controlled by v_i. (It will be proportional to $1/v_i$.) The circuit will be triggered by an input at the v_2 terminal.

A pulse modulator is shown in Fig. 19-28. The voltage controlled astable multivibrator is triggered by the clock which also triggers the sample and hold circuit. (We assume here that the pulse length is proportional to v_i.) This sampled input signal is applied to the voltage control, so the output pulse duration will be proportional to the input signal. Note that the sample and hold circuit must have a delay incorporated into it so that its output does not change until the pulse is completed.

The signal can be reconstructed simply by passing the pulse through a low-pass circuit whose cutoff is considerably below the clock frequency. (An analysis of the PWM

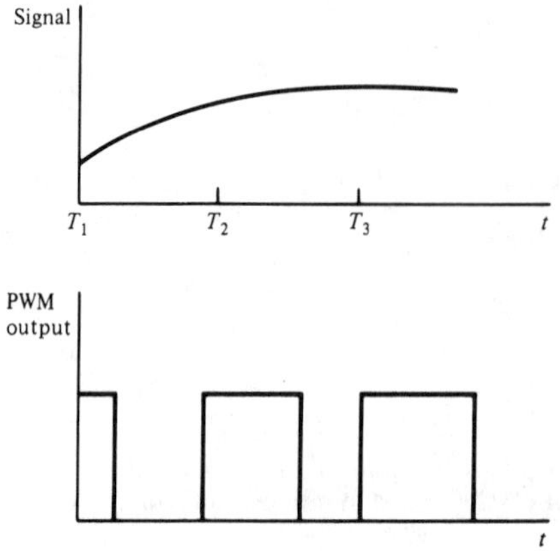

Figure 19-27. An illustration of pulse width modulation. (a) The input signal. (b) The PWM signal.

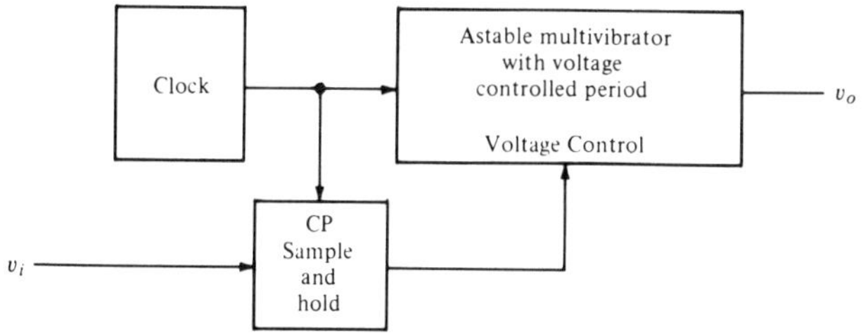

Figure 19-28. A pulse width modulator.

signal shows that it contains a low-frequency component equal to the original signal plus high-frequency components.) At times, PWM is used to obtain high-efficiency audio amplifiers. The pulses can be amplified by a power amplifier which is driven between saturation and cutoff so it is very efficient. (Such a circuit is sometimes called class D amplifier.) A simple passive low-pass filter is then used to remove the high-frequency components and high-efficiency audio power amplification has been achieved. For audio applications, both positive and negative signals are required. Two circuits of the type shown in Fig. 19-28 can be used to obtain positive and negative pulses corresponding to positive and negative values of the signal.

There is another form of pulse modulation used called *pulse position modulation* (PPM). In this system, if no signal is present, a pulse is transmitted at the time of each clock pulse. When a signal is present, the pulse position no longer coincides with the clock pulse time, but is displaced from it. The displacement is proportional to the input signal.

19-9. DELTA MODULATION

In the last section we discussed the encoding of signals as a digital code (PCM). In this section we shall consider another digital encoding scheme called *delta modulation* (DM). It is found that, for voice transmission, delta modulation can often be used with fewer samples per second than with conventional PCM.

Let us consider a simple system to illustrate the ideas of delta modulation. A device is constructed, called a *processor*, that is used to estimate the input signal. A simple delta modulation system is shown in Fig. 19-29. Here the processor consists of an UP/DOWN counter and a D/A converter. Hence, v_e, the output of the processor, is a voltage that is proportional to the count of the counter. (We shall assume that all signals are positive.) The input voltage v_i and the estimated voltage v_e are applied to the comparator as shown. The comparator output is kept constant between clock pulses by the sample and hold circuit. The comparator output is such that if v_e is less than v_i, the counter will count up and v_e will increase, while if v_e is greater than v_i, then the counter will count down and v_e will decrease. Assume that the counter is such that if v_o is a 1, it will count up, whereas if v_o is a 0, then it will count down. Note that v_e will increase and decrease in constant (equal) steps.

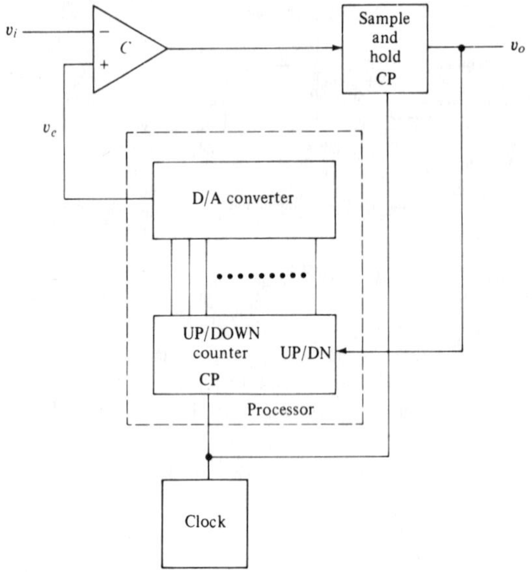

Figure 19-29. A simple delta modulator.

Now consider the waveforms shown in Fig. 19-30. The initial count is 0 so initially, $v_e = 0$. Thus, $v_e < v_i$. Therefore v_o becomes a 1 and the counter counts up by 1. Then v_e increases as shown. At the second clock pulse, we still have $v_e < v_o$ so the output remains 1 and the counter counts up so that v_e increases by one step. Similarly, at the third pulse, $v_e < v_i$, and v_o remains a 1 and v_e increases. At the fourth pulse, $v_e > v_i$. Then v_o becomes a 0 and the counter counts down and v_e decreases. Proceeding in this way we have the waveform of Fig. 19-30. If the clock period is shortened, the estimate is improved.

Now let us consider how the signal $v_o(t)$ can be used to reconstruct the input signal. Suppose that v_o is applied as the input voltage to a processor which is identical to the one that was used in Fig. 19-29. The output will be exactly the same as v_e. Let us consider this. In the modulator, the input of v_o to the processor results in the output of v_e. Thus, if v_o is applied to an identical processor, the output will be v_e. Hence, we can simply demodulate the signal.

Actually, we can use a simpler demodulation scheme. Suppose that the recovered signal is shifted by a voltage equal to one-half the voltage level of a 1. Then a 1 will be equivalent to a voltage $+V_o$ and a 0 is equivalent to a voltage $-V_o$. If this waveform is applied to an integrator circuit, then a reasonable estimate of the input is obtained. In Fig. 19-30b, the dashed curve represents the integral of the shifted $v_o(t)$. If the clock period is made small enough, then the difference between the integrated output and v_i can be made arbitrarily small. Actually, an integrator can also be used as the processor. Now the comparator must be such that its output is positive if $v_i > v_e$ and the comparator output is negative if $v_i < v_e$.

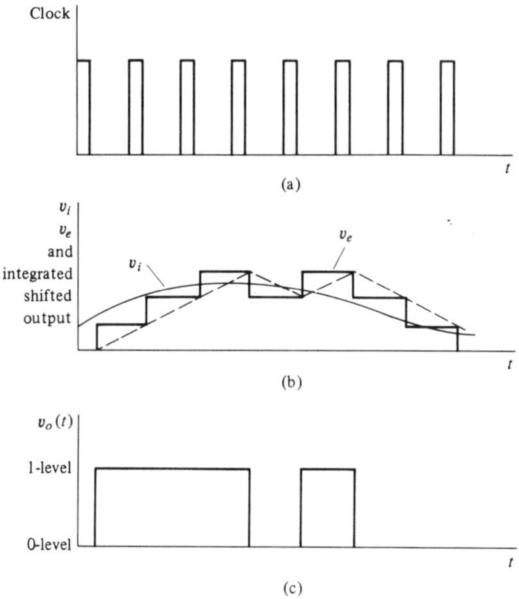

Figure 19-30. Signals in a delta modulation system. (a) Clock. (b) Input and estimate. Integrated and shifted output is shown dashed. (c) delta modulated output.

The delta modulation scheme that we have discussed is called linear delta modulation. Each step is the same size. Large errors can result if v_i increases for a long time at a rate that is greater than the step size. In this case, the error will increase with each sample period. There are delta modulation schemes called *nonlinear*, or *adoptive*, delta modulation. Here the step size is made to be a function of the past history. For instance, if there is a sequence of 1's (two or more) in the output, then the step size is increased. Thus, as the number of 1's in a sequence increases, the step size increases further. Thus, v_e will tend to "catch up" to rapidly increasing initial signals. Now there can be large and small steps in v_e.

PROBLEMS

19-1. A sinusoid of frequency ω_c is amplitude modulated by a sinusoid of frequency ω_m, where $\omega_c \gg \omega_m$. The index of modulation is 0.4. Plot the resulting waveform and frequency spectrum. Obtain the relative power in the sidebands and carrier.

19-2. Repeat Prob. 19-1 but now assume that $m = 2.5$. Assume that the envelopes do not change sign. For instance, for those times that the upper index of modulation is mathematically negative, it actually is zero. To find the spectrum, obtain a Fourier series of the envelope.

19-3. Repeat Prob. 19-1 but now assume that the modulating signal is a square wave.

19-4. Discuss the operation of the amplitude modulator of Fig. 19-5.

19-5. Assume that the circuit of Fig. 19-5 has an efficiency of 85%. The carrier output power is to be 20,000 W. If the carrier is to be 100% modulated by a sinusoid, what are the power requirements on the power supply and on the modulator? What is the power dissipated within the transistor?

19-6. Repeat Prob. 19-5 but now assume that the maximum percent modulation is 80%.

19-7. Repeat Prob. 19-5 but now assume that the modulating signal is a square wave.

19-8. Repeat Prob. 19-6 but now assume that the modulating signal is a square wave.

19-9. A nonlinear modulator has the characteristic

$$v_o = 1.0v_i + 1.0v_i^2$$

If the input signal is

$$v_i = 10 \sin \omega_c t + 0.5 \sin \omega_m t$$

where

$$\omega_c \gg \omega_m$$

what will be the value of v_o? Now assume that v_o is amplified by a bandpass amplifier that only passes frequencies close to ω_c. What is the amplitude modulated output voltage of this circuit? Is the amplitude modulated signal distorted? Explain.

19-10. Repeat Prob. 19-9 but now assume that the nonlinear characteristic is given by

$$v_o = 1.0v_i + 1.0v_i^2 + 1.0v_i^3$$

Is the amplitude modulated signal distorted? Explain.

19-11. Discuss the operation of the linear diode detector of Fig. 19-6.

19-12. The detector of Fig. 19-8 is to be used to detect AM signals whose maximum index of modulation is 99% if $R = 10{,}000$ ohms. What is the minimum value of R_L that could be used if there is to be no distortion?

19-13. Repeat Prob. 19-12 but now use 99.8% modulation.

19-14. An amplitude modulating signal is given by

$$v = V[\cos \omega_c t + 0.3 \cos(\omega_c + 1900)t + 0.3(\omega_c - 1900)t + 0.4 \cos(\omega_i + 2600)t + 0.4 \cos(\omega_c - 2600)t]$$

It is supplied to a nonlinear detector whose characteristic is

$$v_o = 1.0v_i + 1.0v_i^2$$

and then put through a low-pass filter. What is the output voltage? Identify the distortion term(s).

19-15. Repeat Prob. 19-14 but now assume that the nonlinear characteristic is

$$v_o = 1.0v_i + 1.0v_i^2 + 0.5v_i^3$$

19-16. Describe the AGC block diagram of Fig. 19-9.

19-17. Describe the operation of the AGC circuit of Fig. 19-10. Why must relation (19-41) be satisfied?

19-18. Discuss oscillation in AGC circuits.

19-19. Sketch the waveform of $v(t)$ given by Eq. 19-54 if $\omega_c = 10^8$, $m_f = 5$, and $\omega_m = 10^3$.

19-20. Relate frequency and phase modulation. How can one system be converted into the other? Discuss both modulation and detection.

19-21. Compute the relative magnitudes of the carrier and first five sidebands for an FM or PM system modulated by a sinusoid, if the index of modulation is $m_F = 0.2$. Use a table of Bessel's functions if available.

19-22. Repeat Prob. 19-21 for $m_F = 2$.

19-23. Repeat Prob. 19-21 for $m_F = 20$.

19-24. There is a bandwidth of 100,000 Hz available to transmit a sinusoid of 1000 Hz, using frequency or phase modulation. What is the maximum value of m_F that can be used?

19-25. Discuss how FM or PM can be modified so that the effect of an interfering signal can be reduced without increasing signal power.

19-26. The frequency of the variable reactance tuned circuit of Fig. 19-12 is given as

$$f_o = K\left[1 + 0.5\left(\frac{v_m}{V_{BB}}\right) + 0.2\left(\frac{v_m}{V_{BB}}\right)^2\right]$$

where $v_m = V_m \sin \omega_m t$. The third term must be less than 0.1 times the second. What is the maximum value of m_p that can be obtained from this circuit?

19-27. How can the frequency deviation of a FM signal be increased?

19-28. What is a frequency multiplier? How does it work?

19-29. Compute the gain of the phase modulating amplifier of Fig. 19-13a. Do not assume that r_d is infinite.

19-30. Discuss the ideas of slope detection.

19-31. Discuss the design of a slope detection circuit.

19-32. What are the advantages of the discriminator over a slope detector circuit?

19-33. Compute exact expressions for $\mathbf{V}_{3a}$ and $\mathbf{V}_{3b}$ given by Eqs. 19-77. Then use these to obtain an expression for the output of a Foster–Seeley discriminator.

19-34. What is a limiter used with a FM receiver?

19-35. Draw a circuit for a typical limiter.

19-36. Repeat Prob. 19-33 for the ratio detector.

19-37. Discuss the operation of the phase locked loop of Fig. 19-21.

19-38. The phase locked loop of Fig. 19-21 has the following parameter values: $V = 2.0$ V, $V_2 = 2.5$ V, $A = 500$. The VCO has the characteristics

$$\omega_2 = \omega_c + 25v_o$$

The low-pass filter has the characteristic

$$H(\omega) = \frac{1}{1 + j\omega/\omega_2}$$

where $\omega_2 = 30{,}000$ rad/s. Compute the lock range and the capture range.

19-39. Repeat Prob. 19-38 for $\omega_2 = 20{,}000$ rad/s.

19-40. Repeat Prob. 19-38 for $\omega_2 = 50{,}000$ rad/s.

19-41. Design a phase locked loop whose capture range is 10,000 Hz and whose lock range is 9000 Hz.

19-42. Repeat Prob. 19-41 for a capture range of 100,000 Hz, and a lock range of 80,000 Hz.

19-43. Repeat Prob. 19-38 but now use a phase locked loop that uses a phase comparator rather than a multiplier.

19-44. Repeat Prob. 19-43 for $\omega_2 = 20{,}000$ rad/s.

19-45. Repeat Prob. 19-43 for $\omega_2 = 50{,}000$ rad/s.

19-46. Repeat the design of Prob. 19-41 but now use a phase locked loop that uses a phase comparator rather than a multiplier.

19-47. Repeat the design of Prob. 19-42 but now use a phase lock loop that uses a phase comparator rather than a multiplier.

19-48. Discuss pulse code modulation.

19-49. Discuss how redundancy can reduce interference in a pulse code modulation system.

19-50. Discuss and compare time and frequency multiplexing.

19-51. Discuss how a high-efficiency audio amplifier can be built using pulse width modulation.

19-52. Design an astable multivibrator whose period is voltage controlled. The period of the output pulse is to be given by $0.001v_i$.

19-53. Discuss the basic ideas of delta modulation.

19-54. What are the problems associated with linear delta modulation?

19-55. Design a delta modulator that uses an integrator as a processor.

BIBLIOGRAPHY

Clarke, K. K. and Hess, D. *Communication Circuit Analysis and Design.* Reading, Mass.: Addison-Wesley, 1971, Chapters, 8, 10, 11, and 12.

Comer, D. J. *Modern Electronic Circuit Design.* Reading, Mass.: Addison-Wesley, 1976.

Moyschytz, G. S. Miniaturized *RC* Filtering Using Phase-Locked Loops. *Bell System Technical Journal* XLIV: 823–870, 1965.

Taub, H. and Schilling, D. J. *Principles of Communication Systems.* New York: McGraw-Hill, 1971.

Taub, H. and Schilling, D. J. *Digital Integrated Electronics.* New York: McGraw-Hill, 1977, Chapter 14.

Chapter 20

Power Supplies

All the electronic devices that we have considered require direct voltage power supplies. The voltage supplied by electric utilities is alternating. That is, it (ideally) is sinusoidal in waveform. Typically, the frequency is 60 (or 50) Hz. In this chapter we shall consider circuits that convert the alternating voltage to direct voltage. We shall start by considering *rectification*, wherein alternating voltages are converted to pulsating direct voltage, that is, voltage that does not change polarity but does change in amplitude. We shall next consider *power supply filters* that smooth the pulsating voltage so that it is essentially constant. Voltage regulators that can be used to keep the power supply voltages essentially independent of line voltage fluctuations or changes in load will also be discussed. We shall conclude with a discussion of special circuits that are used to control alternating current power circuits.

20-1. RECTIFIERS

Most electric equipment receives power from the commercial power lines. These (ideally) supply sinusoidal voltages whose rms values range from 110 to 440 V at a frequency of 60 (or 50) Hz. In this section we shall discuss diode *rectifier* circuits that can be used to convert this to a unidirectional voltage (i.e., one that does not change polarity).

The Half-Wave Rectifier

A basic rectifier is shown in Fig. 20-1. The diode only allows current in one direction so the output waveform is as shown in Fig. 20-1b. This circuit is called a *half-wave rectifier* since half of the waveform is lost.

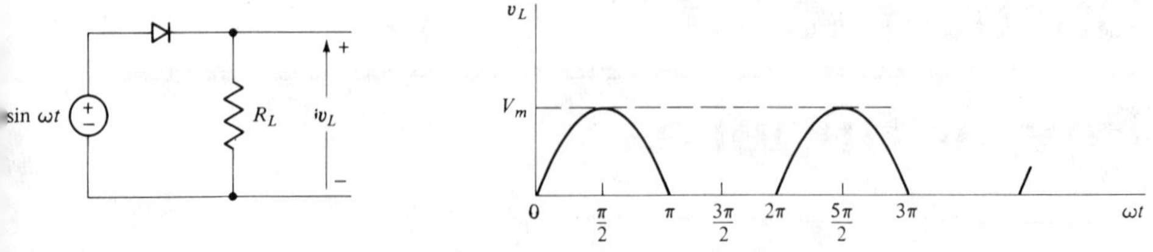

(a) (b)

Figure 20-1. (a) A basic half-wave rectifier. (b) The output of this rectifier when the diode is ideal.

To simplify the analysis let us make the usual assumption that the voltage drop across the conducting diode is V_d. We shall also assume that this is equal to the cut-in voltage. Then, the output voltage is (for the first period)

$$\begin{aligned} v_L &= V_m \sin \omega t - V_d \qquad \sin^{-1}\frac{V_d}{V_m} \leqq \omega t \leqq \pi - \sin^{-1}\frac{V_d}{V_m} \\ &= 0 \qquad 0 \leqq \omega t \leqq \sin^{-1}\frac{V_d}{V_m} \quad \text{and} \quad \pi - \sin^{-1}\frac{V_d}{V_m} \leqq \omega t \leqq 2\pi \end{aligned} \tag{20-1}$$

That is, the diode does not conduct until V_d becomes positive. If

$$V_m \gg V_d \tag{20-2}$$

then Eq. 20-1 can be approximated by

$$\begin{aligned} v_L &= (V_m - V_d) \sin \omega t \qquad 0 \leqq \omega t \leqq \pi \\ &= 0 \qquad \pi \leqq \omega t \leqq 2\pi \end{aligned} \tag{20-3}$$

The direct component of voltage is then

$$V_{\text{Ldc}} = \frac{1}{2\pi} \int_0^{2\pi} v_L \, d\omega t \tag{20-4}$$

Substituting Eq. 20-3 we obtain

$$V_{\text{Ldc}} = \frac{V_m - V_d}{\pi} \tag{20-5}$$

If inequality 20-2 is true then

$$V_{\text{Ldc}} = \frac{V_m}{\pi} \tag{20-6}$$

In the next section we shall see that the use of nonlinear filtering can greatly increase the direct component of v_L.

A figure of merit that is used in power supplies is the *ripple factor*, γ, which is defined as

$$\gamma = \frac{\text{rms value of alternating components of } V_L}{V_{\text{Ldc}}} = \frac{V_{\text{Lac}}}{V_{\text{Ldc}}} \tag{20-7}$$

Ideally, the ripple factor should be zero so that there are no alternating components present. In this case it is easier to calculate $V_{L,\text{eff}}$, the rms value of v_L than it is to calculate $V_{L\text{ac}}$. Then,

$$V_{L\text{ac}}^2 = V_{L,\text{eff}}^2 - V_{L\text{dc}}^2 \tag{20-8}$$

Hence,

$$\gamma = \sqrt{\frac{V_{L,\text{eff}}^2}{V_{L\text{dc}}^2} - 1}$$

For the half-wave rectifier

$$V_{L,\text{eff}} = \frac{V_m}{2} \tag{20-9}$$

(We assume that Eq. 20-6 is valid here.) Therefore,

$$\gamma = \sqrt{\frac{\pi^2}{4} - 1} = 1.21 \tag{20-10}$$

This is an extremely large ripple factor. For instance, if the circuit of Fig. 20-1a were used here with an audio amplifier, a very loud hum would result. Thus, filters must be used.

The Full-Wave Rectifier

A circuit that has better performance than that of the half-wave rectifier is shown in Fig. 20-2a. It basically consists of two half-wave rectifiers that conduct on alternate half-cycles. Thus, the output waveform of Fig. 20-2b results. This is called a *full-wave rectifier* since conduction takes place for a full cycle.

Proceeding as in the case of the half-wave rectifier, we have

$$\begin{aligned} v_L &= V_m \sin \omega t - V_d \qquad \sin^{-1}\frac{V_d}{V_m} \leqq \omega t \leqq \pi - \sin^{-1}\frac{V_d}{V_m} \\ &= 0 \qquad 0 \leqq \omega t \leqq \sin^{-1}\frac{V_d}{V_m} \quad \text{and} \quad \pi - \sin^{-1}\frac{V_d}{V_m} \leqq \omega t \leqq \pi \end{aligned} \tag{20-11}$$

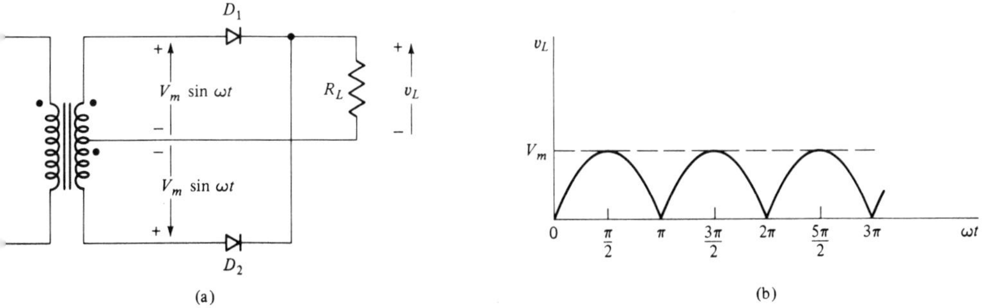

Figure 20-2. (a) A full-wave rectifier. (b) The output of this rectifier when the diodes are ideal.

This repeats periodically. If relation 20-2 is satisfied we can approximate Eq. 20-11 by

$$v_L = (V_m - V_d) \sin \omega t \qquad 0 \leqq \omega t \leqq \pi \tag{20-12}$$

This repeats periodically. Substituting in Eq. 20-4 we have

$$V_{L\text{dc}} = 2(V_m - V_d)/\pi \tag{20-13}$$

Since $V_m \gg V_d$, we can write

$$V_{L\text{dc}} = \frac{2V_m}{\pi} \tag{20-14}$$

The rms value of v_L is $V_m/\sqrt{2}$. Hence, the ripple factor is given by

$$\gamma = \sqrt{\frac{\pi^2}{8} - 1} = 0.483 \tag{20-15}$$

Thus, the full-wave rectifier produces double the direct voltage with a significantly lower ripple factor than the half-wave rectifier. The ripple factor is still much too high to be used with most electronic devices, however.

Note that the full-wave rectifier circuit of Fig. 20-2a requires the use of a center tapped transformer which provides two input signals that are 180° out-of-phase. Transformers are often required to step the voltages up or down and to provide isolation from the power line. When a transformer is used with a full-wave rectifier, the direct component of current through each half of the transformer sets up flux in the core. These two components cancel each other. This reduces the saturation of the core so that a smaller core can be used. This cancellation of the direct component of flux does not occur with the half-wave rectifier.

The Bridge Rectifier

We can obtain full-wave rectification without using a transformer, or, if one is used, it need not be center tapped. Such a rectifier, called a *bridge rectifier*, is shown in Fig. 20-3. When $V_m \sin \omega t$ is positive, diodes D_2 and D_4 conduct, while when $V_m \sin \omega t$ is negative, diodes D_1 and D_3 conduct. Thus, the current will have the form shown in Fig. 20-2b. Equations 20-1 through 20-15 are valid here also, except that now the voltage V_d must be replaced by $2V_d$ since there are always two diodes in series which are conducting.

Diode Ratings

The diodes used in power supplies must, of course, be operated within their ratings. The power dissipation rating should not be exceeded. Very high power diodes may require

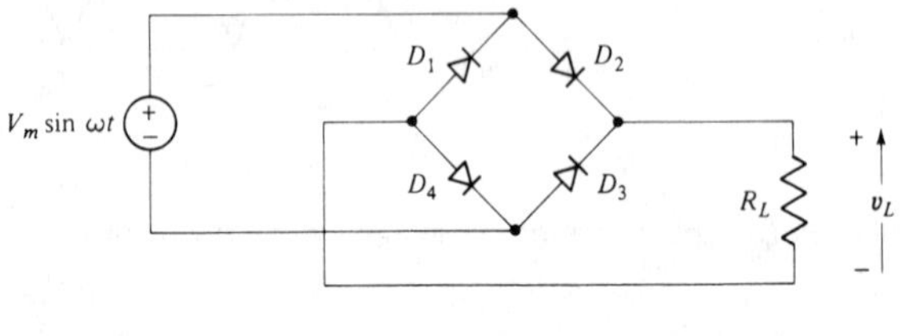

Figure 20-3. A full-wave bridge rectifier.

heat sinks (see Sec. 15-9). A maximum direct current rating is also specified and the peak current through the diode will also be limited.

The diodes in rectifier circuits are subjected to rather large reverse voltages. If the reverse breakdown voltage is exceeded, the rectifier will not function properly since the diode will conduct in the reverse direction. Thus, the reverse breakdown voltage should not be exceeded. The maximum reverse voltage across a diode is called the *peak inverse voltage*.

In the circuit of Fig. 20-1a, the peak inverse voltage is V_m. However, in the circuit of Fig. 20-2a, the peak inverse voltage is $2V_m$. For instance, when D_1 conducts, the full transformer secondary voltage is across the reverse biased diode D_2. The peak value of this voltage is $2V_m$.

In the bridge circuit, the peak voltage of V_m appears across each diode when it is reverse biased. In general, the rectifier circuit should be considered carefully to determine the value of the peak inverse voltage.

20-2. THE CAPACITOR FILTER

The power supplies of electronic devices must have ripple factors that are much less than those produced by the rectifiers discussed in Sec. 20-1. In this section we shall discuss a simple, widely used filter called the *capacitor filter*, which reduces the ripple factor to usable values. The circuit is shown in Fig. 20-4 with a half-wave rectifier. The output voltage v_L is plotted in Fig. 20-5a. To simplify the analysis, we shall assume that the diode is ideal. The operation of this circuit is very similar to that of the diode detector (see Sec. 19-3). At the first cycle, the capacitor voltage v_L becomes V_m. Because of the diode, the capacitor can only discharge through R_L. We assume that

$$R_L C \gg \frac{2\pi}{\omega} \tag{20-16}$$

Hence, shortly after $\omega t = \pi$, that is, at $\omega t = \Theta_2$, the diode will cease to conduct and v_L will exponentially fall off as shown. After the next cycle, $V_m \sin \omega t$ will eventually become greater than v_L (i.e., at $t = 2\pi + \Theta_1$). The diode will conduct so that $V_L = V_m \sin \omega t$. Thus we can state

$$v_L = V_m \sin \omega t \qquad \Theta_1 \leqq \omega t \leqq \Theta_2 \tag{20-17a}$$

$$v_L = V_m \sin \Theta_2 e^{-t/R_L C} \qquad \Theta_2 \leqq \omega t \leqq 2\pi + \Theta_1 \tag{20-17b}$$

This waveform is repeated periodically. In order to determine v_L we must determine Θ_1 and Θ_2. This involves solving a transcendental equation. This is an extremely tedious procedure which will not yield design equations. To obtain these we shall use an approximate analysis that yields reasonably accurate results when the ripple factor is small.

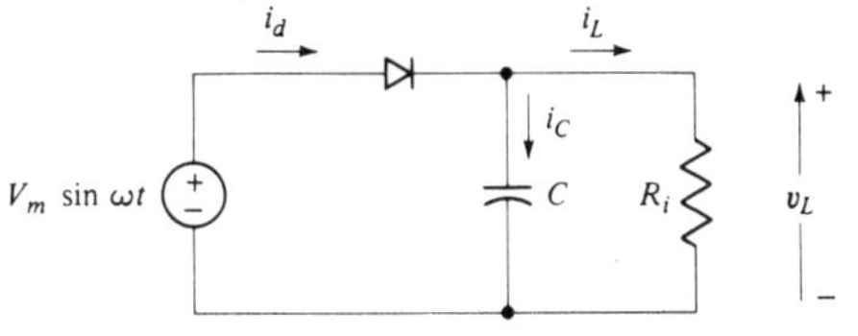

Figure 20-4. A half-wave rectifier with a capacitor filter.

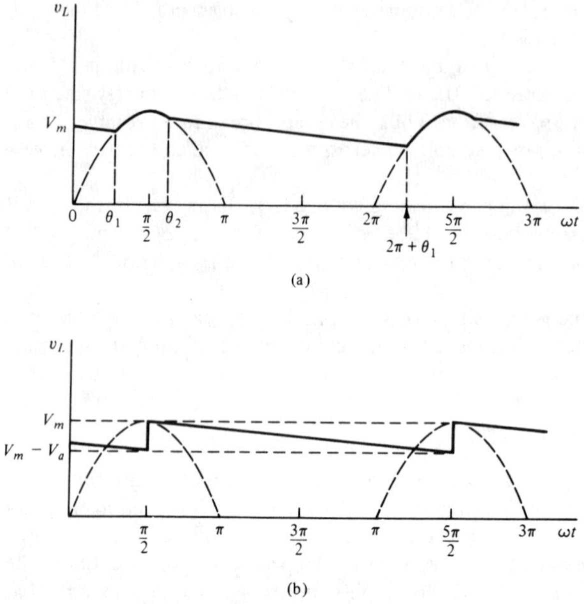

Figure 20-5. (a) The output voltage of a capacitor filter used with a half-wave rectifier. (b) An approximation to this curve.

In this approximation the waveform will be approximated by the confluent straight line segments shown in Fig. 20-5b. The value of V_a is an unknown which we must obtain. If we average the waveform of Fig. 20-5b, we have

$$V_{L\text{dc}} = V_m - \frac{V_a}{2} \tag{20-18}$$

Now consider Fig. 20-4. V_a represents the change in the voltage across the capacitor and so it can be expressed in terms of the change in the stored charge. Thus,

$$V_a = \frac{\Delta Q}{C} \tag{20-19}$$

Since the voltage across the capacitor is assumed to decrease linearly, the current from it must be constant. During discharge, the diode is cut off so that the capacitor current must be the load current. Hence,

$$I_{L\text{dc}} = \frac{\Delta Q}{T} = \Delta Q f \tag{20-20}$$

where $\omega = 2\pi f$.

Note that there is an apparent paradox here. We assume that the current through R_L is constant while we simultaneously assume that the voltage v_L across it falls off linearly with time. (Hence, $i_L \neq v_L/R_L$.) This paradox occurs because we assume that voltage falls off linearly whereas it really falls off exponentially. Nevertheless, the results that we shall obtain are accurate. Substituting Eqs. 20-19 and 20-20 into Eq. 20-18, we obtain

$$V_{Ldc} = V_m - \frac{I_{Ldc}}{2fC} \tag{20-21}$$

Using the relation

$$V_{Ldc} = I_{Ldc} R_L \tag{20-22}$$

We can express Eq. 20-21 as

$$V_{Ldc} = \frac{V_m}{1 + 1/2fR_L C} \tag{20-23}$$

Now let us compute the ripple factor. The alternating component of v_L is a triangular wave that varies from $V_a/2$ to $-V_a/2$. Its effective value is

$$V_{ac,\,eff} = \frac{V_a}{2\sqrt{3}} \tag{20-24}$$

Substituting Eqs. 20-24, 20-20, and 20-19 into Eq. 20-7, we have

$$\gamma = 1/(2\sqrt{3}f R_L C) \tag{20-25}$$

Let us now determine the peak diode current. During the time that the diode conducts, the current through the capacitor is given by

$$i_c = V_m \omega C \cos \omega t \qquad \Theta_1 \leqq \omega t \leqq \Theta_2 \tag{20-26}$$

and the current through the load is

$$i_L = \frac{V_m}{R_L} \sin \omega t \qquad \Theta_1 \leqq \omega t \leqq \Theta_2 \tag{20-27}$$

The diode current is

$$i_d = i_c + i_L \tag{20-28}$$

In general,

$$\omega C \gg R_L \tag{20-29}$$

so that we can approximate i_d by i_c. Now the maximum value of i_c occurs when $\omega t = \Theta_1$. Hence,

$$i_{d,\,max} = V_m \omega C \cos \Theta_1 \tag{20-30}$$

We must now determine Θ_1. We can approximate its value by assuming that conduction starts when $V_m \sin \omega t = V_a$. Then,

$$V_m \sin \Theta_1 = V_m - V_a \tag{20-31}$$

Substituting Eqs. (20-19, 20-20, 20-22, and 20-23, we obtain

$$\Theta_1 = \sin^{-1} \frac{2fR_LC - 1}{2fR_LC + 1} \tag{20-32}$$

Hence, the peak diode current can be obtained.

Now let us determine the peak inverse voltage. In general, the ripple is very small (i.e., the variation in v_L shown in Fig. 20-5 is greatly exaggerated). Therefore, the load voltage will remain constant at approximately V_m. Thus, the peak inverse voltage will be $2V_m$.

Now let us consider that the capacitor filter is used with a full-wave rectifier. The approximate waveform will be as shown in Fig. 20-6. This is essentially the same as the approximate curve of Fig. 20-5b except that the period is halved. Thus, the relations for the full-wave rectifier can be obtained from those for the half-wave rectifier by replacing f by $2f$. Then,

$$V_{Ldc} = V_m - \frac{I_{Ldc}}{4fC} \tag{20-33}$$

$$V_{Ldc} = \frac{V_m}{1 + 1/4fR_LC} \tag{20-34}$$

$$\gamma = \frac{1}{4\sqrt{3}fR_LC} \tag{20-35}$$

$$\Theta_1 = \sin^{-1} \frac{4fR_LC - 1}{4fR_LC + 1} \tag{20-36}$$

When these expressions are compared with those for a half-wave rectifier, it can be seen that the full-wave rectifier requires only one half as large a capacitance as does the half-wave rectifier for the same V_{Ldc} and γ.

When a power supply is designed, the quantities specified are V_{Ldc}, $I_{Ldc, max}$, ripple factor γ, and the amount that V_{Ldc} can change when I_L changes from 0 to its maximum

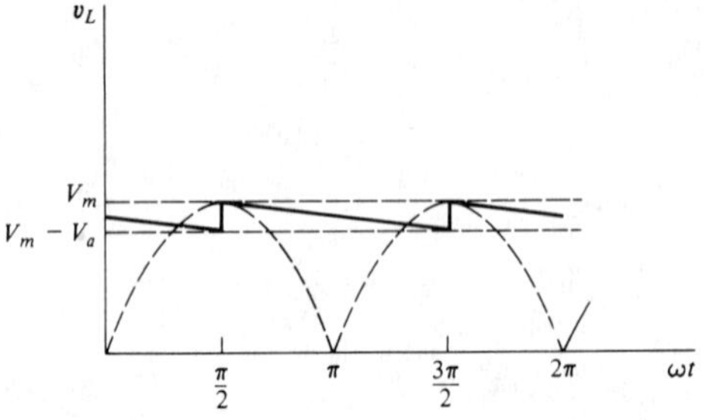

Figure 20-6. The approximate output voltage of a capacitor filter used with a full-wave rectifier.

value. We can manipulate the previously developed equations to obtain some relations that are useful in design. Let us do this for the case of the full-wave rectifier.

$$C \geqq \frac{1}{4\sqrt{3} f R_L \gamma} \tag{20-37}$$

$$C \geqq \frac{I_{Ldc,\,max}}{4f(V_{Ldc} - V_{Ldc,\,min})} \tag{20-38}$$

$$V_m = V_{Ldc}(1 + \sqrt{3}\gamma) \tag{20-39}$$

The change in load voltage with load current is termed the *regulation*. It is defined by

$$\%\ \text{regulation} = \frac{V_{Ldc,\,max} - V_{Ldc,\,min}}{V_{Ldc,\,max}} \times 100\,\% \tag{20-40}$$

where $V_{Ldc,\,max}$ is the load voltage when the load current is zero.

We have neglected the voltage drop V_d across the conducting diode. Since that voltage is essentially constant, we can increase V_m by V_d to account for it.

Example

Design a power supply with the following specifications.

$$V_{Ldc} = 20 \text{ V}$$

$$I_{Ldc,\,max} = 100 \text{ mA}$$

$$\gamma \leqq 0.01$$

The maximum change in voltage as the load current varies from 0 to I_{max} is to be 0.5 V, that is, the regulation = (0.5/20) × 100 = 2.5%. The power line frequency is 60 Hz.

Then,

$$R_L = \frac{V_{Ldc}}{I_{L,\,max}} = \frac{20}{0.1} = 200 \text{ ohms}$$

Substituting in Eqs. 20-37 to 20-39, we have

$$C \geqq \frac{1}{4\sqrt{3} f R_L \gamma} = \frac{1}{4\sqrt{3} \times 60 \times 200 \times 0.01} = 1203\ \mu\text{F}$$

$$C \geqq \frac{0.1}{4 \times 60(0.5)} = 833\ \mu\text{F}$$

$$V_m = 20(1 + \sqrt{3} \times 0.01) = 20.4 \text{ V}$$

The value of Θ_1 is given by Eq. 20-36.

$$\Theta_1 = \sin^{-1} \frac{4 \times 60 \times 200 \times 1203 \times 10^{-6} - 1}{4 \times 60 \times 200 \times 1203 \times 10^{-6} + 1} = 75^\circ$$

Then, the peak diode current is given by Eq. 20-30,

$$i_{d,\max} = 20.4 \times 2\pi \times 60 \times 1203 \times 10^{-6} \times \cos 75^\circ = 2.39 \text{ A}$$

Thus, we use a full-wave rectifier with $V_m = 20.4$ V and a $1203 \simeq \mu 1200$ F capacitor. The diode must be capable of passing an average current of 100 mA and a peak current of 2.39 A. The peak inverse voltage is 40.8 V.

Relatively large capacitors are used in capacitor filters. Electrolytic capacitors are usually used in power supplies. In the example, the regulation is $0.5/20 \times 100 = 2.5\%$ and the ripple factor is 0.01. Often, better performance is required. It appears as though extremely large capacitors would be required but this is not the case. Electronic regulator circuits can be used to reduce both the regulation and the ripple factor by very substantial amounts. We shall consider this in Sec. 20-5. There are other filter circuits that can be used to improve the regulation and the ripple factor. We shall discuss them next.

20-3. OTHER FILTER CIRCUITS

We shall now consider some additional power supply filter circuits that use inductances as well as capacitances. These filters can be used to improve the regulation and ripple factor without using excessively large capacitances. At one time, these filters were widely used but they have now been replaced, in large part, by filters that use simple capacitor filters and electronic regulators. Nevertheless, filters using inductors are still used with high-efficiency power supplies and regulators.

A full-wave rectifier with an *inductance input filter* is shown in Fig. 20-7. The inductance will tend to keep the current from becoming zero at any time. If we assume that i is always positive, then either D_1 or D_2 will always be conducting. The rectifier now acts as a power supply that produces the waveform shown in Fig. 20-2b. We can now apply linear analysis to this circuit. (Note that we could not do this to the capacitor filter discussed in the last section because the diode did not conduct for part of the cycle. Hence, the rectifier could not be considered to be a linear power supply since its output impedance varied depending upon whether or not the diode was conducting.) In the case of Fig. 21-7 we can express v_I in terms of its Fourier series and apply linear analysis. The Fourier series for a full-wave rectifier output voltage is

$$v_I = V_m\left(\frac{2}{\pi} - \frac{4}{3\pi}\cos 2\omega t - \frac{4}{15\pi}\cos 4\omega t - \cdots\right) \tag{20-41}$$

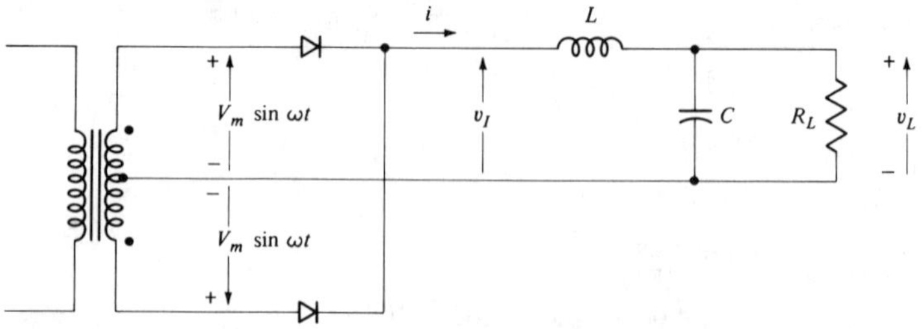

Figure 20-7. A full-wave rectifier with an inductor input filter.

Then, the direct component of the output voltage is

$$V_{L\mathrm{dc}} = \frac{2V_m}{\pi} \tag{20-42}$$

Note that this is independent of load current so that, ideally, this circuit has perfect regulation. In practice, the inductor always has some series resistance so that

$$V_{L\mathrm{dc}} = \frac{2V_m}{\pi} - RI_{L\mathrm{dc}} \tag{20-43}$$

Now let us consider the alternating component across the output. In general, at the frequency ω and its harmonics

$$\frac{1}{\omega C} \ll R_L \tag{20-44}$$

Hence, the resistor can be neglected when we compute the alternating components of the output voltage. Then, using conventional circuit analysis, for the component at frequency 2ω, we obtain

$$v_{L2} = -\frac{4V_m}{3\pi(1 - 4\omega^2 LC)} \cos 2\omega t \tag{20-45}$$

The effective value of the voltage is

$$V_{L2,\mathrm{eff}} = \left| \frac{2\sqrt{2}V_m}{3\pi(1 - 4\omega^2 LC)} \right| \tag{20-46}$$

In general,

$$\omega L \gg \frac{1}{\omega C} \tag{20-47}$$

Hence, we have

$$V_{L2,\mathrm{eff}} = V_m/(3\sqrt{2}\pi\omega^2 LC) \tag{20-48}$$

Similarly, for the component at frequency 4ω, we have

$$V_{L4,\mathrm{eff}} = V_m/(60\pi\sqrt{2}\omega^2 LC) \tag{20-49}$$

Note that $V_{L4,\mathrm{eff}}$ is only $\frac{1}{20}$ of $V_{L2,\mathrm{eff}}$. The higher ordered components are even smaller. We can then approximate $V_{\mathrm{ac,eff}}$ by $V_{L2,\mathrm{eff}}$. Hence, the ripple factor is given by

$$\gamma = 1/(6\sqrt{2}\omega^2 LC) \tag{20-50}$$

In this analysis we assumed that i_L was never zero. If R_L is made large enough, then i_L will become zero. For instance, if R_L becomes an open circuit, the capacitor will eventually charge so that $V_{L\mathrm{dc}}$ becomes V_m. In this case, neither diode will ever conduct and the previous analysis becomes invalid. Note that $V_{L\mathrm{dc}}$ is larger than predicted by Eq. 20-42. The curve of $V_{L\mathrm{dc}}$ versus $I_{L\mathrm{dc}}$ will be as shown in Fig. 20-8. Note that if $I_{L\mathrm{dc}}$ becomes too small, we no longer have ideal regulation. Let us now solve for i and determine

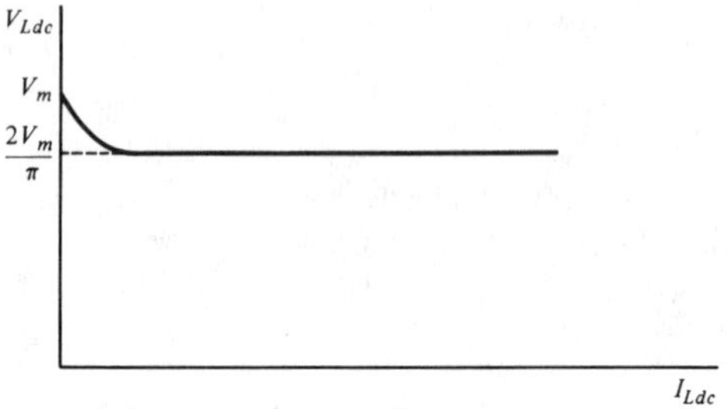

Figure 20-8. V_{Ldc} versus I_{Ldc} for an inductor input filter.

the conditions imposed upon it so that it does not become zero. We shall again assume that relations 20-44 and 20-47 are valid. We can then approximate v_I by its direct component plus the component at frequency 2ω.

$$i = \frac{2V_m}{\pi R_L} - \frac{2V_m}{3\pi\omega L}\cos\left(2\omega t - \frac{\pi}{2}\right) \tag{20-51}$$

(Note that $\omega L \gg 1/\omega C$. Hence, the inductance determines the component of current at 2ω.) Although Eq. 20-51 can become negative, the actual current *cannot* become negative since the diodes will prevent it. If neither diode is conducting, the linear analysis is no longer valid. Thus, if the circuit is to function as predicted,

$$\frac{2V_m}{\pi R_L} \geqq \frac{2V_m}{3\pi\omega L}$$

Manipulating, we have

$$L \geqq \frac{R_L}{3\omega} \tag{20-52}$$

The value $L = R_L/3\omega$ is called the *critical inductance*. If good regulation is desired, then the value of the inductance should always be greater than the critical inductance. It is possible that R_L may vary from an open circuit to some minimum value. In such cases, Eq. 20-52 cannot be satisfied since an infinite inductance would be required. In such cases, a resistance is placed in parallel with the load. This then limits the maximum value of the effective load resistance. Such a resistance is called a *bleeder resistance*. It also serves another function. In high-voltage power supplies, high-quality capacitors are often used. If the load resistance becomes disconnected, these capacitors can store their charge for relatively long times. *Thus, a high-voltage power supply can present a serious shock hazard even if it is turned off.* The bleeder resistance provides a discharge path for the capacitor. For reasons of safety such bleeder resistors should be connected directly across the capacitor. Carbon resistors, rather than wire wound resistors should be used here since they are less likely to open circuit.

An inductor input filter can achieve better regulation than the simple capacitor filter. In addition, smaller values of ripple factor can be achieved with smaller capacitors. However, the inductors used in such filters are iron cored and are large, heavy, and expensive so power supply filters using inductors have usually been replaced by simple capacitor filters are voltage regulators of the type that will be discussed in Sec. 20-5.

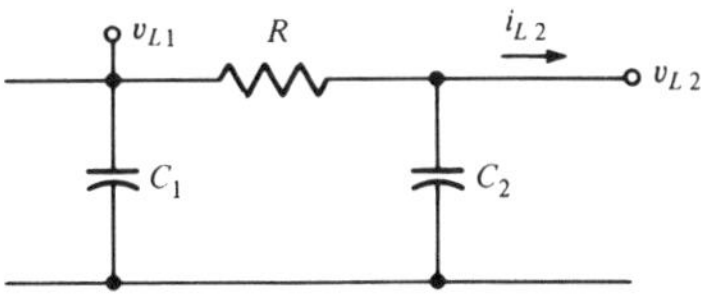

Figure 20-9. A resistor-capacitor power supply filter.

Inductor filters are still used in power supplies where the voltage levels become high enough to preclude the use of the semiconductor voltage regulators. Inductors are also used in high-efficiency voltage regulators which will be discussed in Sec. 20-6.

Multiple Section Filters

If extremely small ripple factors are desired, additional filter sections of series inductors and shunt capacitors can be added to the power supply filter. Very small ripple factors can be attained in this way without using very large values of inductors or capacitors.

Resistor-Capacitor Filters

The filter of Fig. 20-9 sometimes proves useful when there are two different power supply voltages needed. There will be a direct voltage drop across R so that

$$V_{L2\text{dc}} = V_{L1\text{dc}} - I_{L2\text{dc}}R \tag{20-53}$$

The resistor R and the capacitor C_2 also further reduce the ripple factor for the output v_{L2}. If

$$\frac{1}{\omega C_2} \ll R_{L2}$$

where R_{L2} is the load resistance connected to output 2 ($R_{L2} = V_{L2\text{dc}}/I_{L2\text{dc}}$). Then, the RC circuit will reduce the ripple factor at output 2 from that at output 1 by the factor

$$\gamma' = 1/(2\pi f RC_2) \tag{20-54}$$

where, for a full-wave rectifier, f is twice the power line frequency.

20-4. OUTPUT IMPEDANCE OF POWER SUPPLIES

An ideal power supply would have zero output impedance. For instance, when we analyzed amplifiers using linear models, we always replaced the power supplies by short circuits. If the power supply impedance is not low, then it causes more problems than simply changing the gain of an amplifier stage. Feedback can be introduced by a nonzero power supply impedance, since signal voltage can appear across the power supply. For instance, if all the stages of an amplifier share a common power supply, then signals from the output stage can be fed back into the input stage. Such feedback often results in oscillation. If the power supply impedance is very low, then any components of signal voltage which appear across the power supply will be very small so the loop gain will be reduced and oscillation will not occur.

At high frequencies, the output impedance of the power supply can be kept low because the output element is always a shunt capacitance. At low frequencies, the output impedance is determined by the regulation. For instance, for the full-wave rectifier, with capacitor filter, we determined that the output voltage was (see Eq. 20-33),

$$V_{Ldc} = V_m - \frac{I_{Ldc}}{4fC}$$

Hence, this circuit acts as though it had a series resistance

$$R_{dc} = \frac{1}{4fC} \tag{20-55}$$

where f is the power line frequency, *not* the signal frequency. If we want to reduce the effective value of R_{dc}, we must increase C. This can result in excessively large values of C.

Example

The low-frequency resistance of a power supply that consists of a full-wave rectifier with a capacitor filter is to be less than 0.1 ohms. What is the minimum value of C which can be used? The power line frequency is 60 Hz.

From Eq. 20-55, we have

$$C = 1/4fR_{dc} = 1/(4 \times 60 \times 0.1) = 41{,}667\ \mu\text{F}$$

The value of capacitance calculated in this example is excessive. However, a value of $R_{dc} \leqq 0.1$ ohms is *not* an unreasonable requirement. In the next section we shall discuss electronic voltage regulators that can reduce the effective output resistance of a power supply to very small values. Note that if the power supply voltage is

$$V_{Ldc} = V_m - KI_{Ldc} \tag{20-56}$$

then the effective output resistance is K. Hence, if the regulation is good, the output resistance will be very low.

20-5. VOLTAGE REGULATORS

It is desirable for the output voltage of a power supply to remain constant independent of load current and the supply line fluctuations. In this section we shall discuss voltage regulators that accomplish this. Note that in the unregulated supplies discussed earlier in this chapter, the output voltage fluctuations were the same as those of the supply line voltages.

Zener Diode Regulators

The simplest regulator consists of the Zener diode (see Sec. 1-6) circuit shown in Fig. 20-10. The battery V represents a filtered but unregulated power supply. Let us analyze the circuit. The characteristics for a Zener diode are given in Fig. 20-11. The breakdown region is shown. Note that the voltage drop across the diode is almost independent of the current through it. To analyze the circuit, we replace the circuit consisting of V, R, and R_L by its Thévenin equivalent. The load line shown can then be drawn.

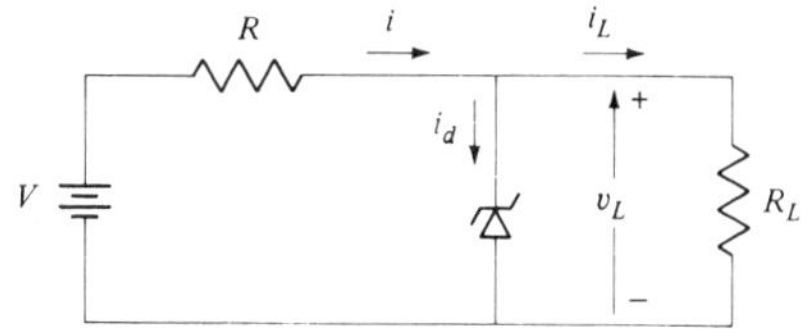

Figure 20-10. A Zener diode voltage regulator circuit.

Now suppose that the supply voltage V changes. The load line will shift parallel to itself. Note that when this happens, the value of V_{Ldc} hardly changes at all even though V may change significantly. (Of course very large changes in V will cause V_{Ldc} to vary.)

Suppose that the load resistance changes. Then the slope of the line will change. However, again we see that there can be significant changes in slope, but V_{Ldc} will remain essentially constant.

The actual change in V_{Ldc} depends upon the actual characteristics of the Zener diode and must be determined from the specific graphic characteristics. However, in general, the voltage regulation obtained with Zener diodes is excellent.

Regulator circuits of the type shown in Fig. 20-10 are inefficient. The voltage regulation occurs because the voltage drop across R varies to offset changes in V_L. If V_L tends to rise, then i_d increases greatly. This increases i so that the drop across R almost completely compensates for the increase in voltage. If this type of action is to occur, then i_d must be an appreciable fraction of the current i. Hence, the power dissipated in the Zener diode will be a large fraction of the power dissipated by the load. There must also be appreciable power dissipated by R. Hence, the efficiency will usually be well under 50%. For this reason, Zener diode regulator circuits are only used in low-power circuits. Of course, the power dissipation is one factor that must be taken into account when Zener diodes are chosen. We shall next consider considerably more efficient voltage regulators.

Series Voltage Regulator

Consider the circuit of Fig. 20-12. It is called a *series voltage regulator*. The voltage drop across transistor Q_1, which is in series with the load, is adjusted to keep v_L constant. Let

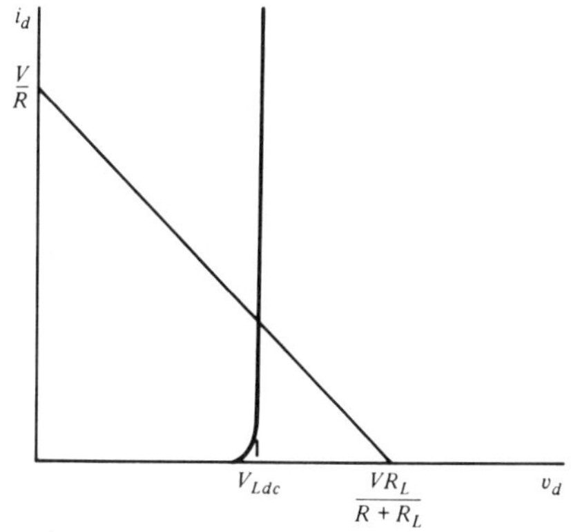

Figure 20-11. The voltage current characteristics for a Zener diode. Note that the breakdown region (reverse bias) is plotted.

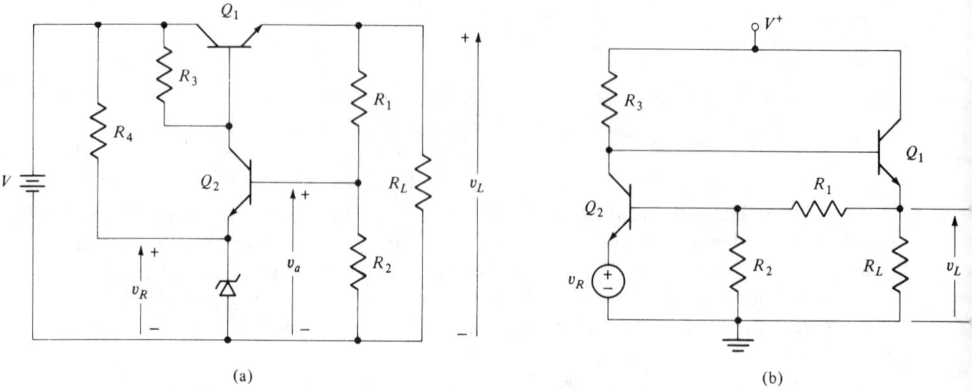

Figure 20-12. (a) A series voltage regulator. (b) The circuit redrawn.

us consider the operation of this circuit. The voltage V represents a filtered, but unregulated power supply. V must be at least 3–5 V greater than V_L. Suppose that V decreases. Then V_a will decrease. The voltage v_R is kept essentially constant by the Zener diode so v_{BE2} will decrease. (The numerical subscript indicates that v_{BE2} is the base-emitter voltage of Q_2.) This will decrease i_{C2}, the collector current of Q_2 so v_{CE2} will increase. This will increase v_{BE3} and, hence, reduce the voltage drop v_{CE1}. This tends to offset the decrease in V and, hence, regulation is obtained. Note that $v_a + v_{CE2} > v_i$. If V increases, the converse operation will occur (i.e., v_{CE1} increases).

In a similar way, if R_L increases, which tends to increase v_L, then V_a will increase, which will then reduce v_{CE2}. Hence, v_{BE1} will become smaller. Thus, v_{CE1} will become larger again regulating the voltage.

To gain some additional insight, let us redraw the regulator circuit as in Fig. 20-12b. We can now see that it is a negative feedback amplifier. The output stage is an emitter follower. Thus, its output impedance is low. The voltage negative feedback then reduces the already low output impedance to extremely low values (see Sec. 16-6). The input signal is the constant voltage v_R. Therefore, the regulator can be thought of as a negative voltage feedback amplifier whose power supply voltage fluctuates. If the gain is independent of power supply fluctuations, then the output voltage will remain independent of the power supply voltage. In Sec. 16-3 we saw that the sensitivity of the overall gain to fluctuations in the parameters of the circuit was inversely proportional to the return difference. Hence, if the loop gain is high, the output voltage can be made very independent of power supply fluctuations. Also, the output impedance is inversely proportional to the return difference. Thus, the regulating ability of the circuit is related to the loop gain of the amplifier.

Note that the loop gain of the amplifier cannot be arbitrarily increased. This is a feedback circuit and can oscillate. The procedures of Secs. 16-10 to 16-16 should be used to ensure that the amplifier is stable.

Integrated circuit voltage regulators are built. In this case, the regulators are much more elaborate than those shown in Fig. 20-12. For instance, more amplifier stages can be used to obtain greater loop gain. In Fig. 20-13, we illustrate such a regulator. The entire regulator could be fabricated on a single chip. The amplifier A is an operational amplifier which replaces transistor Q_2 in Fig. 20-12. Note that this amplifier is powered from the input power supply. We specifically indicate this here since, if V fluctuates, A will change, as will the gain of Q_1. The changes in the *closed loop gain* and, hence, v_L, are reduced by the return difference (see Sec. 16-3). We have included an optional external capacitance C to reduce the output impedance at high frequencies. This is usually not necessary.

The circuit consisting of transistors Q_3 and R_5 prevents the output current from becoming excessive. Normally, the drop across R_5 is so small that Q_3 is cut off and the circuit functions as though there were no current limiter. On the other hand if i_L tends to become excessive, the voltage drop across R_5 becomes large enough to turn Q_3 on. This reduces the base current of Q_1 and limits the output current. This circuit functions in essentially the same way as the current limiter of Sec. 14-8.

Integrated circuit voltage regulators are supplied in several ways. Some have fixed voltage and current limits. For instance, they will maintain the output voltage at 5 V and limit the current to 1.0 A. Such circuits have only three leads. Other regulators have provision for external resistors that can be used to adjust the regulated voltage and current limiting values. Of course, in all cases, the input voltage V must remain within specified limits.

When high-current regulators are used, the series transistor Q_1 is usually mounted external to the remainder of the regulator. Since transistor Q_1 is operated in the active region, the power dissipated in it will be large and, in general, it must be heat sinked (see Sec. 15-9).

Ripple in the power supply voltage V can be thought of as power supply fluctuation. These regulators respond rapidly enough so that they substantially reduce the ripple factor, often by a factor of 10,000 or more. In Sec. 20-2, we discussed that when a capacitor filter was used, very large values of C were required to obtain small ripple factors and good regulation. However, the use of a voltage regulator can provide low ripple factor and relatively poor regulation. Thus, high-quality supplies can be obtained

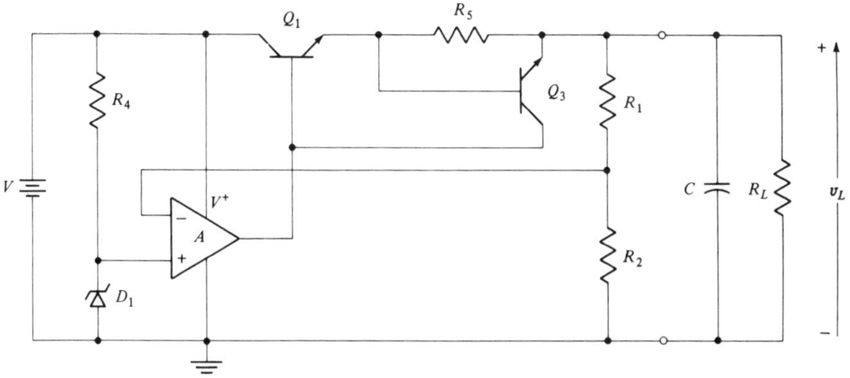

Figure 20-13. A more elaborate series regulator with current limiting.

using relatively small single capacitor filters with a voltage regulator. Such power supplies can be relatively small and light.

20-6. SWITCHING REGULATORS

The series regulators discussed in the last section provide excellent regulation and reduction of ripple factor and so are widely used. However, they are relatively inefficient in that the transistor Q_1 is operated in the active region and must pass the full current taken by the load. Hence, the power dissipation of Q_1 is relatively high. There are some applications where efficiency is of great importance. In such cases, the *switching regulator* we shall now discuss is used. However, this regulator is by no means as free from ripple as is the series regulator.

A switching regulator was briefly considered in Sec. 13-11. We shall now consider it in detail. The basic switching regulator circuit is shown in Fig. 20-14. The part of the circuit consisting of A_v, R_1, and R_2 is a Schmitt trigger (see Sec. 13-12). R_3 and D_1 are a Zener diode reference circuit. L and C serve as a power supply filter. (We shall discuss D_2 subsequently.) Now consider the operation. For the moment, let us ignore hysteresis in the Schmitt trigger and assume that it switches when $v_L = V_R$ V. The transistor Q is either cut off or saturated. When v_L falls below V_R, the output of the operational amplifier increases and causes Q to saturate. The voltage V is considerably greater than v_L and, hence, v_L increases. When v_L increases above v_R, the Schmitt trigger switches and cuts off Q. The voltage v_L now begins to fall. Thus, Q will be continuously switched on and off and, in this way, v_L will be regulated. Since Q is either cut off or saturated, the efficiency is high. In a practical Schmitt trigger, hysteresis is present and the level of v_L which causes Q to switch on will be less than the level of v_L which causes it to switch off. This will result in some ripple being present in the output. We shall see in our analysis that the magnitude of the ripple is considerably greater than the width of the hysteresis.

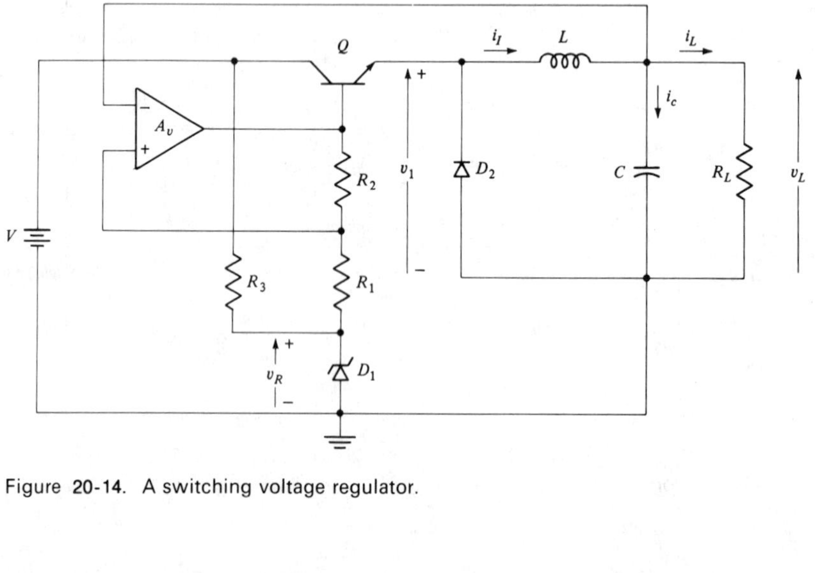

Figure 20-14. A switching voltage regulator.

Actually, hysteresis is not a complete disadvantage. Hysteresis ensures that Q will remain saturated or cut off for a finite time. Hence, it will not operate in the active region for any substantial time.

The diode D_2 provides a path for the inductor current i_I when Q is cut off, preventing the formation of excessive voltage. The presence of D_2 also makes the analysis simpler. The impedance of the "power supply" driving the impedance remains low, even if Q is cut off. Thus, the power supply can be considered to be linear.

Let us now analyze the circuit. In Fig. 20-15 we show some pertinent waveforms. The voltage v_1 is either equal to V_I or to 0. The value of V_I is given by

$$V_I = V - V_{CE,\,\mathrm{sat}} \tag{20-57}$$

(Note that $V_{CE,\,\mathrm{sat}} \simeq 0.3$ V.) Thus, we can perform a linear analysis assuming that the power supply voltage is as shown in Fig. 20-15a. Hence, the direct component of v_i, which is also the direct component of v_L, is

$$V_{L\mathrm{dc}} = V_{I\mathrm{dc}} = V_{\mathrm{dc}} = V_I T_1/T \tag{20-58}$$

The value of v_L will fluctuate only slightly about V_{dc} (i.e., the ripple will be small). Hence, v_L will be close to V_{dc}. (Note that $T_{\max}$ occurs after T_1 since $i_I(T_1) > I_{\mathrm{dc}}$.)

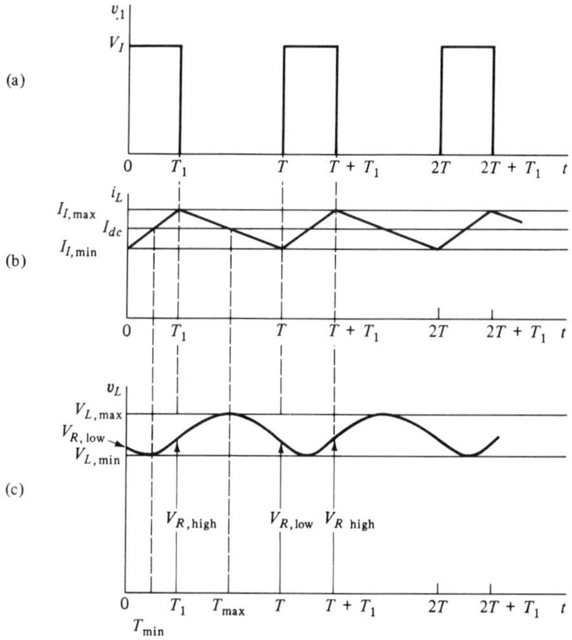

Figure 20-15. Waveforms in the switching regulator. (a) The filter input voltage. (b) The inductor current. (c) The load voltage.

Now let us consider the current i_I in the inductance L. When Q_1 is on, the voltage across the inductance is approximately $V_I - V_{dc}$. Hence,

$$L\frac{di_I}{dt} = V_I - V_{dc} \qquad 0 \leqq t \leqq T_1 \tag{20-59a}$$

Similarly, when Q is cut off, the voltage across the inductance is $-V_{dc}$ (if we neglect the voltage drop across the diode). Hence,

$$L\frac{di_I}{dt} = -V_{dc} \qquad T_1 \leqq t \leqq T \tag{20-59b}$$

Thus, the current increases and decreases linearly as shown. Its average value is I_{dc}.

$$I_{dc} = (I_{I,\max} + I_{I,\min})/2 \tag{20-60}$$

Let us define

$$\Delta I = I_{I,\max} - I_{I,\min} \tag{20-61a}$$

From Eq. 20-59a, we have

$$\Delta I = [(V_I - V_{dc})/L]T_1 \tag{20-61b}$$

Then, we can write

$$i_I = I_{I,\min} + \frac{\Delta I}{T_1}t \qquad 0 \leqq t \leqq T_1 \tag{20-62a}$$

and

$$i_I = I_{I,\min} + \Delta I - \frac{\Delta I}{T - T_1}(t - T_1) \qquad T_1 \leqq t \leqq T \tag{20-62b}$$

The actual load voltage will fluctuate as shown in Fig. 20-15c. Let us determine the voltage levels at which the Schmitt trigger switches. At $t = 0$, transistor Q is turned on. Hence, $v_L(0)$ is the low switching voltage

$$V_{R,\text{low}} = v_L(0) \tag{20-63a}$$

Similarly,

$$V_{R,\text{high}} = v_L(T_1) \tag{20-63b}$$

(The subscript R stands for reference.) Note that at this point many of these values are unknowns. We shall now perform some circuit analysis that relates the various quantities of the circuit. We can obtain the output voltage by assuming that the current i_I of Fig. 20-15b drives the RC circuit consisting of the capacitor C and the load (see Fig. 20-16).

We must consider the analysis both when Q is on and when it is off. Let us start when Q is on. Hence, $0 \leqq t \leqq T_1$. Then, i_I is given by Eq. 20-62a. This is applied to the circuit

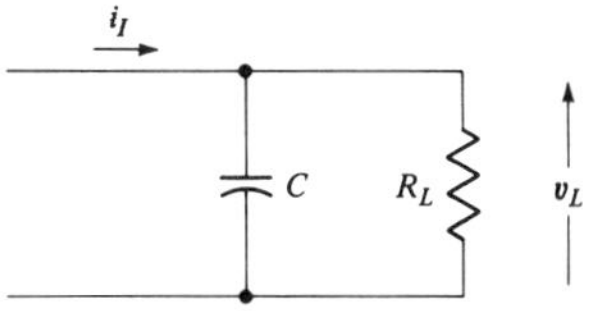

Figure 20-16. Circuit used to determine v_L.

of Fig. 20-16. The initial voltage across the capacitor is $V_{R,\,\text{low}}$ (see Fig. 20-15c). Then, a transient analysis of Fig. 20-16 yields

$$v_L(t) = V_{R,\,\text{low}}e^{-t/RC} + R\left(I_{I,\,\text{min}} - \frac{RC\,\Delta I}{T_1}\right)(1 - e^{-t/RC}) + \frac{R\,\Delta I}{T_1}t \qquad 0 \leqq t \leqq T_1 \tag{20-64}$$

We want to determine the ripple so we must find the voltage $V_{L,\,\text{min}}$ (see Fig. 20-15). At this point $dv_L(t)/dt = 0$. Then, differentiating Eq. 20-64 and setting the derivative equal to zero we have

$$T_{\text{min}} = RC\,\ln\left[1 + \frac{T_1}{RC\,\Delta I}\left(\frac{V_{R,\,\text{low}}}{R} - I_{I,\,\text{min}}\right)\right] \tag{20-65}$$

Let us consider the operation when Q is cut off. Now i_I of Fig. 20-16 is given by Eq. 20-62b and the initial voltage across the capacitor is $V_{R,\,\text{high}}$. Then, analyzing this circuit, we obtain

$$v_L(t) = V_{R,\,\text{high}}e^{-(t-T_1)/RC} + R\left(I_{I,\,\text{min}} + \Delta I + \frac{RC\,\Delta I}{T - T_1}\right)(1 - e^{-(t-T_1)/RC}) - \frac{R\,\Delta I}{T - T_1}(t - T_1) \qquad T_1 \leqq t \leqq T \tag{20-66}$$

The time of occurrence of the maximum value of v_L can be found by differentiating Eq. 20-66 and setting the derivative equal to zero. Doing this we have

$$T_{\text{max}} = RC\,\ln\left[1 - \frac{T - T_1}{RC\,\Delta I}\left(\frac{V_{R,\,\text{high}}}{R} - I_{I,\,\text{min}} - \Delta I\right)\right] + T_1 \tag{20-67}$$

Equations 20-64 and 20-66 are both valid at $t = T_1$ so the values of $v_L(T_1)$ that they yield must be equal. Then, substituting $t = T_1$ into both equations and equating, we have

$$V_{R,\,\text{high}} = V_{R,\,\text{low}}e^{-T_1/RC} + R\left(I_{I,\,\text{min}} - \frac{RC\,\Delta I}{T_1}\right)(1 - e^{-T_1/RC}) + R\,\Delta I \tag{20-68}$$

The voltage $v_L(t)$ is periodic so the value of v_L obtained from Eq. 20-66 at $t = T$ must be the same as that obtained from Eq. 20-64 at $t = 0$. Then, equating these values, yields

$$V_{R,\,\text{low}} = V_{R,\,\text{high}}e^{-(T-T_1)/RC} + R\left(I_{I,\,\text{min}} + \Delta I + \frac{RC\,\Delta I}{T - T_1}\right)(1 - r^{-(T-T_1)/RC}) - R\,\Delta I \tag{20-69}$$

Equations 20-68 and 20-69 can be solved for $V_{R,\text{low}}$ and $V_{R,\text{high}}$. Doing this we obtain for the triggering levels of the Schmitt trigger,

$$V_{R,\text{low}} = RI_{I,\min} + \frac{R^2C\,\Delta I}{T - T_1}\left[1 - \frac{T}{T_1}\frac{(1 - e^{T_1/RC})}{(1 - e^{T/RC})}\right] \tag{20-70}$$

$$V_{R,\text{high}} = R(I_{I,\min} + \Delta I) + \frac{R^2C\,\Delta I}{T - T_1}\left[1 + \frac{T}{T_1}\frac{(e^{T/RC} - e^{(T-T_1)/RC})}{1 - e^{T/RC}}\right] \tag{20-71}$$

The hysteresis is then

$$V_H = V_{R,\text{high}} - V_{R,\text{low}}$$

$$= R\,\Delta I + \frac{R^2C\,\Delta I}{T - T_1}\left(\frac{T}{T_1}\right)\frac{[1 + e^{T/RC} - e^{T_1/RC} - e^{(T-T_1)/RC}]}{1 - e^{T/RC}} \tag{20-72}$$

The equations that we have obtained are complicated and cannot be easily manipulated to give design relations. Thus, some cutting and trying is necessary. Often, the following quantities are specified: V_{Ldc}, the output voltage, I_{Ldc}, the load current or R_L, the load resistance, V, the input unregulated supply, the ripple factor γ, and the frequency at which the circuit switches. Note that

$$f = \frac{1}{T} \tag{20-73}$$

This is often of importance since the resulting signal can generate interference.

The value of V specifies V_I (see Eq. 20-57). The ratio of V_{Ldc}/V_I determines T_1/T (see Eq. 20-58). The value of L then determines I (see Eq. 20-61b). A value of C should then be picked. It is found that the first ripple for the value of C should be such that the resonant frequency is about $\frac{1}{15}$ of the switching frequency at full load. If C is too large, the hysteresis can become so small that it is difficult to design the Schmitt trigger. If C is too small then the ripple will be large. Then, the other parameters are uniquely specified. The ripple factor should be calculated. The peak to peak ripple is found using Eqs. 20-64 to 20-67. Ripple is usually specified in this way for these regulators. If the ripple is too large, then L or C should be increased. Let us illustrate the design with an example.

Example

Design a switching regulator that meets the following specifications: $V_{dc} = 5$ V, $I_{dc} =$ 1 A, switch frequency at full load 25,000 Hz, maximum peak to peak ripple ≤ 0.08 V. The unregulated supply is 25 V.

As a first trial let us choose

$$L = 2 \text{ mH}$$

Then we choose C such that

$$1/2\pi\sqrt{LC} = 25{,}000/15 = 1666$$

Solving, we have

$$C = 4.56\ \mu\text{F}$$

Let us use

$$C = 5\ \mu\text{F}$$

These are much smaller than those for the filter capacitor which we have previously considered. This is because the frequency of 25,000 Hz is much greater than the power line frequency of 60 Hz, and also because an inductance is present. Now,

$$R = \frac{V_{dc}}{I_{dc}} = 5 \text{ ohms}$$

From Eq. 20-57 we have

$$V_I = 25 - 0.3 = 24.7 \text{ V}$$

Then, from Eq. 20-58

$$\frac{T_1}{T} = \frac{V_{dc}}{V_I} = \frac{5}{24.7} = 0.20243$$

$$T = \frac{1}{f} = \frac{1}{25{,}000} = 4 \times 10^{-5}$$

Hence,

$$T_1 = 0.8097 \times 10^{-5}$$

Then, from Eq. 20-61b

$$\Delta I = \left(\frac{24.7 - 5}{2 \times 10^{-3}}\right) 0.8097 \times 10^{-5} = 0.079755$$

The dc load current is given by

$$I_{dc} = I_{I,\min} + \frac{\Delta I}{2}$$

Hence,

$$I_{I,\min} = 1 - 0.07975/2 = 0.960125 \text{ A}$$

Then, substituting in Eqs. 20-70 and 20-71, we have

$$V_{R,\text{high}} = 4.9675$$

$$V_{R,\text{low}} = 4.9637$$

The hysteresis is $V_H = 0.013$ V

Substituting in Eqs. 20-65 and 20-67, we have

$$T_{\max} = 2.1546 \times 10^{-5} \text{ s}$$

$$T_{\min} = 3.1104 \times 10^{-6} \text{ s}$$

Corresponding to these times, we have

$$V_{L,\max} = 5.0313 \text{ V}$$

$$V_{L,\min} = 4.9538 \text{ V}$$

The peak to peak ripple is then

$$V_{\text{ripple}} = 0.0775 \text{ V}$$

The hysteresis value of 0.013 V is easily obtainable. From Eq. 13-95 we have, for the hysteresis H of a Schmitt trigger (we are ignoring V_α here),

$$V_H = \frac{2V_A R_1}{R_1 + R_2}$$

Suppose that $V_A = 15$ V. Then,

$$\frac{R_1}{R_1 + R_2} = \frac{0.013}{30} = 4.333 \times 10^{-4} \tag{20-74}$$

We require that

$$\frac{A_v R_1}{R_1 + R_2} > 1$$

Hence, only a moderately high-gain operational amplifier is required here. From Eq. 13-92, we have

$$V_{R,\text{low}} = \frac{V_R R_2}{R_1 + R_2} - \frac{V_A R_1}{R_1 + R_2} = 4.9637$$

Substitution yields

$$\frac{V_R}{1 + R_1/R_2} = 4.9637 - \frac{V_H}{2} = 4.9572$$

Then, from Eq. 20-74, we obtain

$$\frac{R_2}{R_1} = 2307$$

Hence,

$$V_R = 4.9572(1 + 1/2307) = 4.9593 \text{ V}$$

If we choose

$$R_1 = 100 \text{ ohms}$$

then

$$R_2 = 230{,}000 \text{ ohms}$$

The design is now complete.

If, in the previous example, the ripple was excessive, then the design could be repeated with a larger L or C. If the hysteresis of the Schmitt trigger was too small, a smaller value of C should be used. Thus, there is some compromise that may be required here.

The switching regulator and the series regulator are used for different purposes. The switching regulator is used when high efficiency is important. In general, it uses more expensive components than the series regulator and its ripple is higher.

20-7. SCR's, DIACS AND TRIACS

There are many applications where we desire to vary the power taken by an alternating current device. Motor speed control and incandescent lamp dimmers are two such applications. This control could be obtained by placing a resistance in the circuit but this would be inefficient and the resulting heat dissipation would be troublesome.

A more efficient procedure is to place a controlled switch in the circuit. If this opened and closed so that it only allowed the passage of current for a fraction of each cycle, then control would be obtained. Such a switch would dissipate no power resulting in efficient operation. We shall consider two types of switching devices in this section, one that rectifies the voltage and one that does not.

Controlled Rectifiers

Suppose we have a rectifier that functions as an ordinary rectifier except that it only conducts for a fraction of a cycle as shown in Fig. 20-17. This would be the current through a diode which does not conduct until Θ rad past the start of each positive cycle. The load current is given by

$$\begin{aligned} i &= i_{\max} \sin \omega t \qquad \Theta \leqq \omega t \leqq \pi \\ &= 0 \qquad 0 \leqq \omega t \leqq \Theta, \qquad \pi \leqq \omega t \leqq 2\pi \end{aligned} \tag{20-75}$$

and repeats periodically. The direct component of i is given by

$$I_{dc} = \frac{1}{2\pi} I_{\max}(1 + \cos \Theta) \tag{20-76a}$$

The effective value is given by

$$I_{eff} = \frac{I_{\max}}{2\sqrt{\pi}} \sqrt{\pi - \Theta + \tfrac{1}{2} \sin 2\Theta} \tag{20-76b}$$

As Θ varies from 0 to π rad, both I_{dc} and I_{eff} vary from their maximum values to zero. Thus, if we could build a rectifier that allowed the angle Θ to be varied, we would achieve the desired control.

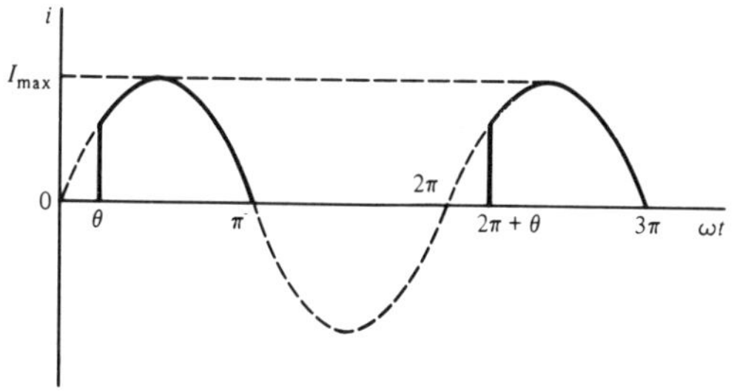

Figure 20-17. Current in a controlled rectifier.

The SCR: The *p-n-p-n* Controlled Rectifier

We shall now discuss a device called a *silicon controlled rectifier* (SCR). It is the *p-n-p-n* structure shown in Fig. 20-18a. It has three leads called the *anode, cathode*, and the *gate.* In order to understand the operation of the SCR, consider Fig. 20-18b. We have redrawn the structure but broken it into two transistors, a *n-p-n* transistor and a *p-n-p* transistor. In Fig. 20-18c, we have placed the two transistor structure in a simple circuit. Let us consider its operation. The generator v represents the main supply (alternating) voltage and R_L is the load. Suppose that $V_{g1} = 0$. Then both transistors will be cut off and $i_L = 0$. Thus the SCR acts as an open switch. Now suppose that we increase the gate current i_g. This will cause i_{B1} (the base current of Q_1) to increase. Now Q_1 will enter its active region. Thus, i_{B2} will become nonzero. Hence, Q_2 will no longer be cut off; $i_L = i_{E2}$ will increase. In general, R_g is relatively large so that

$$i_{E2} \simeq i_{B1} \tag{20-77}$$

Thus, i_{B1} will increase i_{B2} and the process will repeat so that both Q_1 and Q_2 will become saturated. Thus, the SCR approximates an ideal switch. Note that the gate can initiate conduction. Now suppose that v_g becomes zero. The base current i_{B1} will still be supplied by Q_2 so the device will remain saturated. Thus, once conduction is started, the gate loses control. Note that if $R_g = 0$, then making v_g zero would cause transistor Q_1 to be cut off. In practical circuits, R_g is made large enough so that this does not happen.

For the type of control shown in Fig. 20-17, there must be control for each cycle so the gate must regain control of the circuit in every cycle. Let us see how this can be accomplished. Suppose that v is an alternating voltage

$$v = V_{max} \sin \omega t \tag{20-78}$$

When v becomes zero or negative, the transistors will no longer conduct current and i_L will fall to zero. Once this happens, $i_{B1} = 0$ and the gate regains control. On the next positive cycle, current cannot be initiated until v_g causes i_g to increase. A symbol for the SCR is shown in Fig. 20-19.

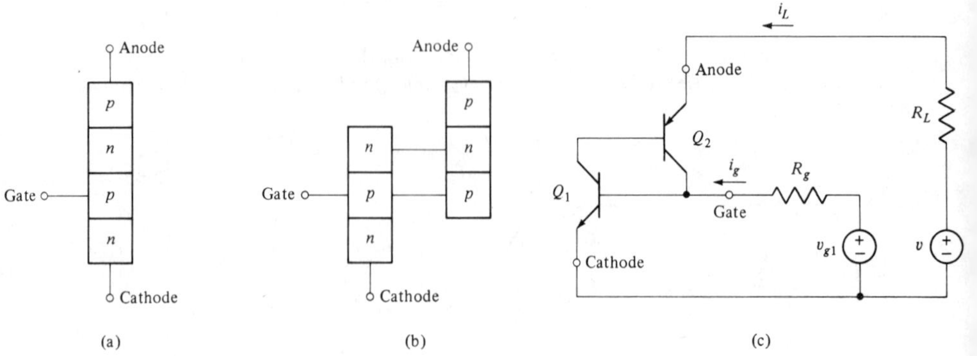

Figure 20-18. (a) The basic structure of a SCR. (b) A two-transistor representation of this circuit. (c) A two-transistor representation of a SCR connected into a simple circuit.

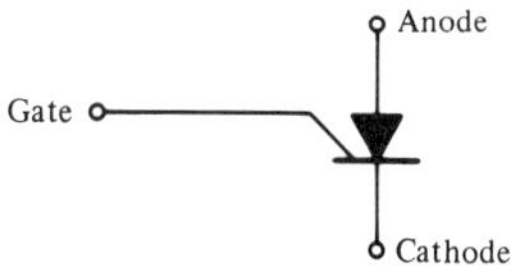

Figure 20-19. The symbol for the SCR.

Now let us see how we can construct a circuit that gives us the waveform of Fig. 20-17. Consider the circuit of Fig. 20-20a. There are two sinusoidal generators. One lags behind the other by Θ_1 degrees. Their waveforms are shown in Fig. 20-20b. Now suppose that the SCR is turned on when the gate voltage v_g exceeds the small value V_C shown by the dashed line. The SCR will start to conduct at the angle Θ. Note that if

$$V_m \gg V_C \tag{20-79}$$

then, $\Theta = \Theta_1$. We must find a circuit that gives us the desired phase shifted voltage. Before doing this, let us consider another device.

The Diac

The *diac* is a *p-n-p* device with two terminals (see Fig. 20-21a). It basically consists of two diodes connected in series such that one of the diodes is always reverse biased. Thus, the diac acts as an open circuit. However, when the breakdown voltage of the reverse biased diode is exceeded, it then acts as a low impedance.

Diacs are often used in SCR circuits. Let us illustrate this with the circuit of Fig. 20-22. The diac ensures that the SCR will not be triggered until the control voltage reaches a value that can break down the diac. The voltage that triggers the SCR diac combination is designated as V_C in Fig. 20-22b. Now consider the phase shift circuit. There is a resistance with an adjustable tap and the diac is connected to this tap. Let us consider how v_d varied as the tap is changed. In general $R_L \ll R$. Hence, before the SCR conducts, $v_a = V_M \sin \omega t$. Consider the waveforms of Fig. 20-22b. When the tap on the variable resistance is on the upper end, $v_d = v_a$, and the SCR will conduct when $\omega t = \Theta_{min}$ as shown in Fig. 20-22b. Hence, there will be conduction for almost the full cycle. When the tap is at the low end of the resistance, then $v_d = v_b$ and conduction will not start until

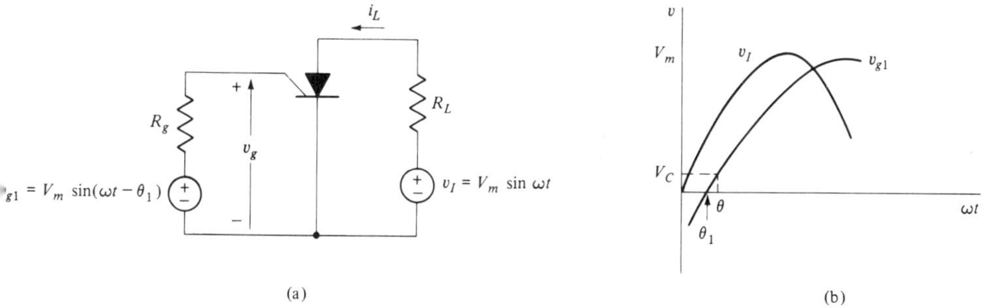

Figure 20-20. (a) A simple SCR circuit. (b) Waveforms in this circuit.

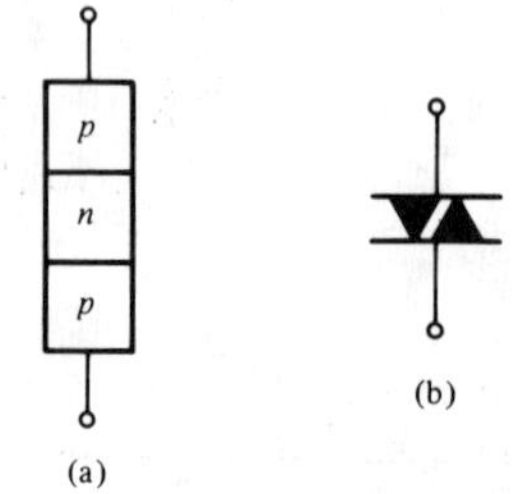

Figure 20-21. (a) The diac. (b) Its symbol.

$\Theta = \Theta_{max}$. Thus, the current will be much less than maximum. Then Θ can be varied from Θ_{min} to Θ_{max} and this circuit provides the type of control we desire.

The phase angle of the circuit cannot be varied to 180° which would allow the continuous reduction of the current from a maximum value to zero, but the current can be reduced to relatively low values. There are more elaborate phase shifting circuits that allow 180° phase shifts to be obtained. However, the circuit of Fig. 20-22a is used for many applications.

The Triac

The SCR functions as a rectifier so in the circuit that we have considered, current is zero for half a cycle. Often, this is undesirable. For instance, in Fig. 20-22, if R_L consists of an incandescent lamp, then full brightness could not be achieved since current would always be zero for the half-cycle that $V_m \sin \omega t$ was negative. One procedure to eliminate this problem is to use a bridge rectifier to convert the sinusoidal power line voltage into a signal of the type shown in Fig. 20-22b. Now the SCR will conduct for each half-cycle (rather than on alternate half-cycles).

There is another device called a triac that can be used. It can be considered to be two SCR's connected "back to back" in parallel (see Fig. 20-23a). For instance, suppose that the pair was used in the circuit of Fig. 20-22a in place of the SCR. Now one SCR would conduct during the positive half-cycle and the other SCR would conduct during the

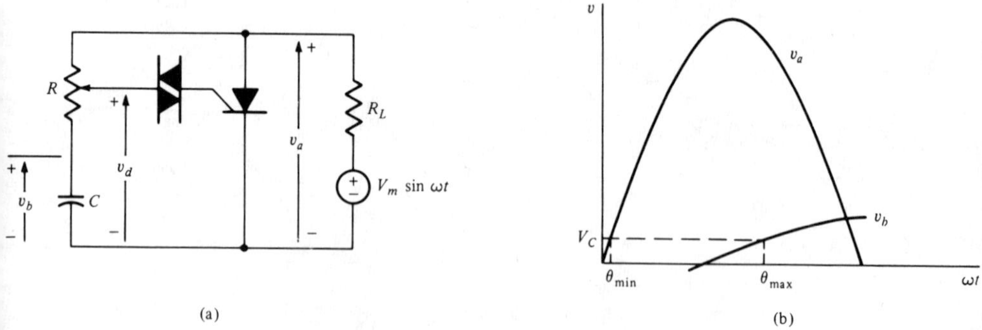

Figure 20-22. (a) A SCR-diac circuit. (b) Some waveforms of this circuit. These are drawn assuming that the SCR is cut off.

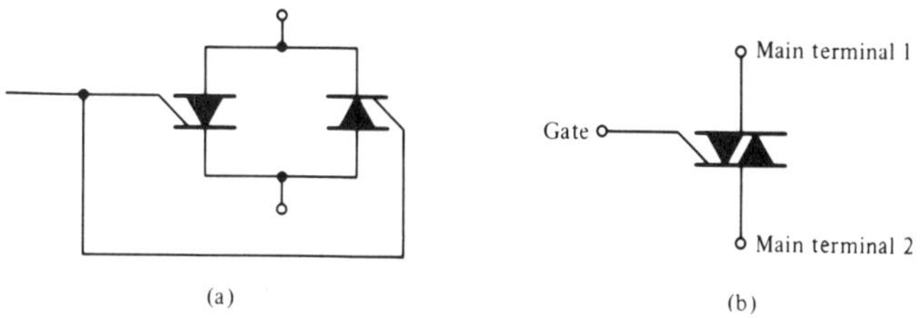

Figure 20-23. The triac: (a) A representation using two SCR's (b) The schematic representation.

negative cycle. Hence, we would have a controlled device whose current waveform would be as shown in Fig. 20-24. Thus, we have achieved the control we have desired.

The schematic representation for a triac is shown in Fig. 20-23b. Note that its leads are called *main terminal* 1, *main terminal* 2, and *gate*. A typical triac circuit can be obtained from Fig. 20-22a by replacing the SCR with a triac.

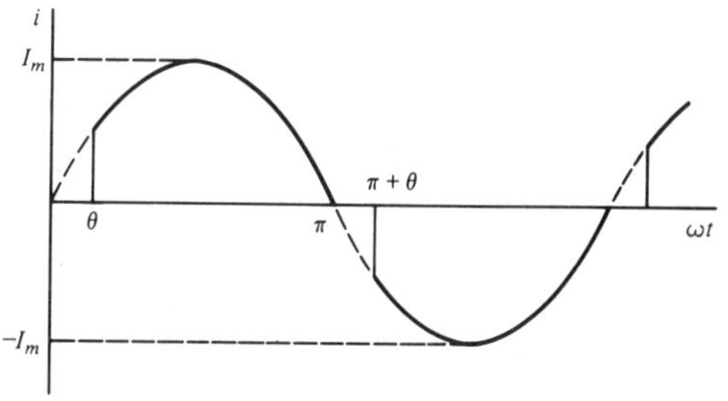

Figure 20-24. Waveform in a triac controlled circuit.

PROBLEMS

In all the following problems that require numerical solutions, assume that the power line frequency is 60 Hz.

20-1. The half-wave rectifier of Fig. 20-1a is such that $V_m = 150$ V and $R_L = 100$ ohms. Assume that the voltage drop across the conducting diode is 0.8 V. Compare the approximate expression of Eq. 20-3 with that of Eq. 20-1.

20-2. Repeat Prob. 20-1 but now assume that $V_m = 20$ V.

20-3. Compute V_{Ldc} for the rectifier of Prob. 20-1.

20-4. Repeat Prob. 20-3 for the rectifier of Prob. 20-2.

20-5. Compute the power dissipated in the diode for the circuit of Prob. 20-1.

20-6. Repeat Prob. 20-5 for the circuit of Prob. 20-2.

20-7. The full-wave rectifier of Fig. 20-2a is such that $V_m = 150$ V and $R_L = 100$ ohms. Assume that the voltage drop across each conducting diode is 0.8 V. Compare the accuracy of the approximate expression 20-12 with that of Eq. 20-11.

20-8. Repeat Prob. 20-7 but now assume that $V_m = 20$ V.

20-9. Compute V_{Ldc} for the rectifier of Prob. 20-7.

20-10. Compute V_{Ldc} for the rectifier of Prob. 20-8.

20-11. Compute the power dissipated in each diode for the circuit of Prob. 20-7.

20-12. Repeat Prob. 20-11 for the circuit of Prob. 20-8.

20-13. Repeat Prob. 20-11 but now use a bridge rectifier.

20-14. Repeat Prob. 20-12 but now use a bridge rectifier.

20-15. Compute the peak inverse voltage across the diode in the circuit of Prob. 20-1.

20-16. Compute the peak inverse voltage across each of the diodes in the circuit of Prob. 20-7.

20-17. Compute the peak inverse voltage across each of the diodes of Prob. 20-13.

20-18. Design a capacitor filter that meets the following specifications: $V_{Ldc} = 50$ V, $I_{Ldc} = 100$ mA, $\gamma = 0.01$, % regulation = 1%. Use a full-wave rectifier.

20-19. Repeat Prob. 20-18 but now use a ripple factor of 0.003 and 0.5% regulation.

20-20. Repeat Prob. 20-18 but now use a half-wave rectifier.

20-21. Repeat Prob. 20-19 but now use a half-wave rectifier.

20-22. Repeat Prob. 20-18 but now use an inductor input filter. The regulation should be 0%. The minimum $I_{Ldc} = 10$ mA.

20-23. Repeat Prob. 20-19 but now use an inductor input filter. The regulation should be 0%. The minimum $I_{Ldc} = 10$ mA.

20-24. What problem might arise if an inductor input filter were used with a half-wave rectifier?

20-25. What is the purpose of a bleeder resistance?

20-26. A power supply produces a voltage of 25 V with a ripple factor of 0.01. Add a *RC* filter to this which reduces the ripple factor to 0.001 and the voltage to 15 V when the load current is 1.0 mA.

20-27. Why is it desirable for a power supply to have a low-output impedance?

20-28. A power supply with a full-wave rectifier and a capacitor filter is to have an output resistance that is equal to or less than 0.01 ohms. What is the minimum value of C that can be used? In this a practical value?

20-29. The circuit of Fig. 20-10 is such that V can vary from 20 to 26 V. R_L may vary from 1000 to 2000 ohms. The load voltage is to be kept substantially constant at 14 V. Determine the value of R such that the design is achieved. The characteristics of the Zener diode are given in Fig. 20-25.

20-30. What is the maximum power dissipation of the Zener diode of Prob. 20-29?

20-31. Describe the operation of the series regulator of Fig. 20-12a?

20-32. What is the output impedance of the series regulator of Fig. 20-12a?

20-33. Repeat Prob. 20-31 for the circuit of Fig. 20-13.

20-34. Repeat Prob. 20-32 for the circuit of Fig. 20-13.

20-35. The series regulator of Fig. 20-12 produces a regulated output voltage of 5 V, $V = 15$ V, and the load current is 150 mA. Compute the power dissipated in Q_1.

20-36. Design a switching regulator of the type shown in Fig. 20-14. The design parameters are

$$V_{dc} = 5 \text{ V}$$
$$I_{DC} = 1.5 \text{ A}$$
$$V = 30 \text{ V}$$
$$f = 20{,}000 \text{ Hz}$$

peak to peak ripple $\leqq 0.08$ V

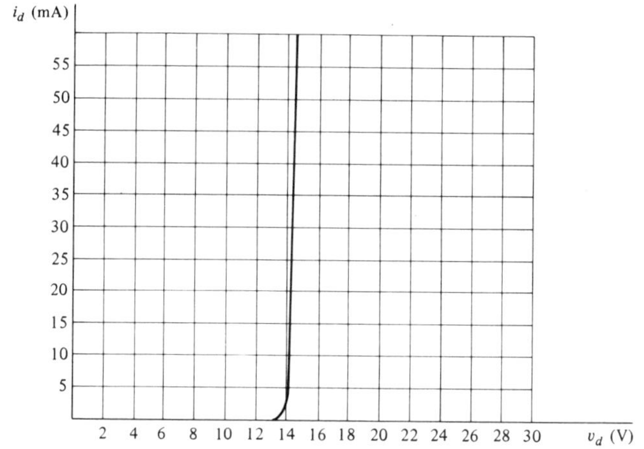

Figure 20-25.

20-37. Repeat Prob. 20-36 but now use

$$f = 30{,}000 \text{ Hz}$$

20-38. Repeat Prob. 20-36 but now use

$$\text{peak to peak ripple} < 0.04 \text{ V}$$

20-39. Repeat Prob. 20-36 but now use

$$V = 50 \text{ V}$$

20-40. Compare the series regulator and the switching voltage regulator.

20-41. The SCR-diac circuit of Fig. 20-22 is to be such that the conduction angle can be varied from almost 0° to 120°. Assume that the SCR diac combination is such that the SCR will conduct if v_a exceeds 10 V. $V_m = 150$ V. Determine values of R and C such that the design is achieved.

20-42. Compute the power dissipated in R_L for the circuit of Prob. 20-41 when Θ varies from its maximum to its minimum value. Use $R_L = 20$ ohms. Neglect the voltage drop across the conducting SCR.

20-43. How would the circuit of Prob. 20-41 be modified if we desire conduction on each successive half-cycle?

20-44. Repeat Prob. 20-42 but now replace the SCR with a triac. The conduction angle is to be varied in each half-cycle.

BIBLIOGRAPHY

Chirlian, P. M. *Electronic Circuits: Physical Principles, Analysis and Design*. New York: McGraw-Hill, 1971, Chapter 17.

Comer, D. J. *Modern Electronic Circuit Design*. Reading, Mass.: Addison-Wesley, 1976, Chapter 15.

Holt, C. A. *Electronic Circuits, Digital and Analog*. New York: Wiley, 1978, Chapter 24.

RCA Designers Handbook, "Solid State Circuits," RCA Corp., 1971. pp. 194–242.

Index

This index covers all three volumes of the book. The figure printed in **bold type** before each entry, or group of entries, indicates the volume in which that page number, or numbers, will be found. **1.App.**, followed by a Roman numeral, indicates that the material is to be found in the Appendix to Volume 1.